# Integrating Educational Technology into Teaching

**Second Edition**

M. D. Roblyer
*The State University of West Georgia*

Jack Edwards
*The Webster School*

Merrill
an imprint of Prentice Hall
*Upper Saddle River, New Jersey    Columbus, Ohio*

**Library of Congress Cataloging-in-Publication Data**
Roblyer, M. D.
    Integrating educational technology into teaching / M. D.
Roblyer, Jack Edwards.
      p. cm.
    Includes bibliographical references and index.
    ISBN 0-13-974387-1
    1. Educational technology—United States.   2. Computer-assisted
instruction—United States.   3. Curriculum planning—United States.
  I. Edwards, Jack  II. Title.
    LB1028.3 .R595 2000
    371.33—dc21

                    99-33275
                      CIP

Editor: Debra A. Stollenwerk
Developmental Editor: Gianna M. Marsella
Editorial Assistant: Penny S. Burleson
Production Editor: Mary Harlan
Photo Coordinator: Anthony Magnacca
Design Coordinator: Diane C. Lorenzo
Production Supervision and Text Design: Elm Street Publishing Services, Inc.
Cover Designer: Ceri Fitzgerald
Cover Art: ©SuperStock
Production Manager: Pamela D. Bennett
Director of Marketing: Kevin Flanagan
Marketing Manager: Meghan Shepherd
Marketing Coordinator: Krista Groshong

This book was set in Times Roman by Elm Street Publishing Services, Inc. and was
printed and bound by Banta Company. The cover was printed by Banta Company.

Chapter Opener Photo Credits: Courtesy of Bill Wiencke and Carrollton Elementary School, p. 4;
Courtesy of Bill Wiencke, p. 28; Scott Cunningham/Merrill, pp. 48, 268, and 279; C. Will Hart, 1996,
p. 80; Anthony Magnacca/Merrill, pp. 112, 191, 207, 241, 254, and 292; M. D. Roblyer, p. 164;
Georgia Tech Communications, p. 228; and Tom Watson/Merrill, p. 307.

Printed in the United States of America

10 9 8 7 6 5 4 3 2 1

ISBN: 0-13-974387-1

Prentice-Hall International (UK) Limited, *London*
Prentice-Hall of Australia Pty. Limited, *Sydney*
Prentice-Hall of Canada, Inc., *Toronto*
Prentice-Hall Hispanoamericana, S. A., *Mexico*
Prentice-Hall of India Private Limited, *New Delhi*
Prentice-Hall of Japan, Inc., *Tokyo*
Prentice-Hall (Singapore) Pte. Ltd., *Singapore*
Editora Prentice-Hall do Brasil, Ltda., *Rio de Janeiro*

*To Bill and Paige Wiencke,*
*two of my best and most patient teachers*

—M.D.R.


*To Robert W. Edwards, in memory of Mary E. Edwards,*
*and to Jordan M. Burke*

—J.E.

# Preface

*"Come to the edge," he said.*
*They said, "We are afraid."*
*"Come to the edge," he said.*
*They came.*
*He pushed them.*

*And they flew.*

Apollinaire, as quoted by Elliot W. Eisner in *Educational Researcher* (August–September, 1997)

As we stand at the edge of this new millennium, gazing out into its uncharted expanse, some of us feel as if we are stepping out onto a launching pad; others feel at the brink of an abyss. Some see the challenges and the marvels to come and are exhilarated; some see only the certainty of change and its uncertain outcomes and are apprehensive. How amazing it is that the influence of technology is a primary force shaping both perspectives. All of us recognize the vital role computers and other electronic tools have played in bringing us to the place where we stand now. But our views on what technology means to us as a society and what our responses to it should be differ primarily because of the way we define technology, our views on who controls how technology is used in education, and our knowledge about teaching.

- **The way we define technology.** Rather than seeing technology as some foreign invader that has come to confuse and complicate the simple life of the past, educators must recognize that our technology is very much *our own response* to overcoming obstacles that stand in the way of a better, more productive way of life. As Walt Kelly's "profound 'possum" Pogo said, "We has met the enemy, and he is us." *Technology is us*—our tools, our methods, and our own creative attempts to solve problems in our environment. We are the culprit responsible for the turmoil we experience as we go through periods of transition, adapting to the new environment we ourselves have created.

- **Our views on who controls how technology is used in education.** As a follow-up to our recognition that "technology is us," we must recognize the truth of Peter Drucker's statement: "The best way to predict the future is to create it." Both individual teachers and teaching organizations must see themselves as shapers of our future. Each teacher must take a position on what the future of education should look like; each should acquire skills to help work toward realizing that vision.

- **Our knowledge about teaching.** No matter how much we know about how to use technology tools, educational practice never will improve unless we have clear goals for what teaching and learning should accomplish and we see the path we want to take to achieve them. Technology-using teachers never can be a force for improved education unless they are first and foremost informed, knowledgeable shapers of their craft. Before integrating technology into their teaching, educators must know a great deal, for example, about why there are different views on appropriate teaching strategies, how societal factors and learning theories have shaped these views, and how each strategy can address differing needs.

The purpose of this book is to show that whether we fall or fly into the future of educational technology rests to a great degree on us: how we view technology, how we respond to the challenge it presents, and how we see it helping us accomplish our own informed vision of what teaching and learning should be. Our approach to accomplishing this purpose rests on the following three premises.

• **Integration methods should be based both in learning theory and teaching practice.** There is no shortage of innovative ideas in the field of instructional technology—new and interesting methods come forward about as often as new and improved gadgets. Those who would build on the knowledge of the past should know why they do what they do as well as how to do it. Thus, we have linked various technology-based integration strategies to well-researched theories of learning, and we have illustrated them with examples of successful practices based on these theories.

• **Integration should match specific teaching and learning needs.** Technology has the power to improve teaching and learning, but it can also make a teacher's life more complicated. Therefore, each resource should be examined for its unique qualities and its potential benefits for teachers and students. Teachers should not use a tool simply because it is new and available—each integration strategy should be matched to a recognized need. We do not oppose experimentation, but we do advocate informed use.

• **Old integration strategies are not necessarily bad; new strategies are not necessarily good.** As technology products change and evolve at lightning speed, there is a decided tendency toward throwing out older teaching methods with the older machines. Sometimes this is a good idea; sometimes it would be a shame. Each of the integration strategies recommended in this book is based on methods with proven usefulness to teachers and students. Some of the strategies are based on directed methods that have been used for some time; other strategies are based on the newer, constructivist learning models. Each is recommended on the basis of its usefulness rather than its age.

This edition differs in some structural ways from the first, but its goal remains the same: *to help teachers see their role in shaping the future of technology in education.* This book can help them perceive that stepping out from the edge where we stand requires some faith in ourselves, a belief that we can fly with wings of our own making.

## Who Will Find This Book Helpful

This book is designed to help teach both theoretical and practical characteristics of technology integration strategies. It should be useful in several different types of education settings:

• **As primary instructional material.** It should benefit instructional technology courses for preservice teachers and workshops and graduate courses for inservice teachers.

• **As supplemental instructional material.** It should support research and content-area methods courses.

• **As a reference.** It should provide topical information in K–12 school libraries/media centers and university college of education libraries and media centers.

## New to This Edition

This edition has added new information and reorganized some information from the first edition to help make sense of both new and emerging concepts. Readers will note the following changes and improvements:

• **More emphasis on integration rationales and strategies.** Chapter 2 has more detailed information on integration steps, and Chapter 3 has additional discussion on learning theory (e.g., Howard Gardner's Theory of Multiple Intelligences) and integration procedures based on them. Much of the background information on computers and technical information on microcomputers

has been de-emphasized to better focus on integration. For example, sections on hardware and software were moved to the Appendix.

- **Better, more in-depth treatment of emerging technologies.** This edition has expanded coverage of new and emerging technologies and how they will help shape the future of education.

- **Expanded coverage of distance learning.** In light of the growing importance of distance learning in education and training, this edition has two chapters in this area: one on distance learning options and the other focusing on the Internet.

- **Addition of integration strategies for health and physical education.** In response to many reviewers' requests, a new Chapter 14 addresses integration strategies for these important content areas.

- **Links to integration lesson plans on a CD-ROM database.** This textbook is packaged with a CD-ROM containing 250 example technology integration lesson plans. Spanning a variety of content areas and grade levels, these teacher-tested lessons are keyed to national standards. Users can modify existing lesson plans or add new ones. Look for the CD-ROM icon throughout the text. A User's Guide to the CD-ROM starts on page 347.

- **Companion Web site.** A Web site with additional support materials for students and instructors is available at http://www.prenhall.com/roblyer. The Web site includes chapter objectives, online quizzes with immediate feedback, links to related Web sites, a message board, an online syllabus manager, and other exciting tools. Look for the companion Web site icon at the end of each chapter.

## Organization of the Text

This text is organized into four sections—one of background and three of resources and applications.

**Part I: Introduction and Background on Integrating Technology in Education.** Einstein is said to have observed that "Everything should be made as simple as possible, but not more so." Using technology as a force for change becomes simpler when one understands the foundations upon which integration strategies are based—but that is no small task in itself. This section provides a "big picture" background on technology's role in education, reviews a variety of planning issues to be addressed prior to and during integration, and describes learning theories and teaching/learning models related to technology integration.

**Part II: Using Software and Media Tutors and Tools: Principles and Strategies.** To paraphrase a popular jingle, "Software—it ain't just CAI anymore." This section describes more than 40 types of instructional software products ranging from drill and practice to integrated learning systems, from word processing to groupware. Multimedia and hypermedia are now in this section, since they fit so well under the rubric of tools. Each software and media product description covers unique qualities, potential benefits, and sample integration strategies.

**Part III: Linking to Learn—Principles and Strategies.** This section represents the most significant revision from the first edition. In light of the growing importance of connecting people and resources for a technology-permeated future, two chapters are devoted to the types and uses of distance technologies. As with Part II, example lesson plans or activities are given for each recommended integration strategy. Chapter 9 provides a "link to the future," courtesy of William R. Wiencke, in describing technologies that are changing the way members of our society live, work, and communicate.

**Part IV: Integrating Technology into the Curriculum.** These six chapters describe and give examples of technology resources and integration strategies for several different content areas. In addition to a new chapter on health and physical education, content areas covered in the first edition have been updated: language arts and foreign languages, math and science, social sciences, the arts, and special education. Although these chapters separate the areas into topics, the chapters themselves recognize and incorporate the current trends toward thematic, interdisciplinary instruction. Many of the examples cross discipline boundaries and serve to illustrate how the concepts of several content areas can be merged into a single lesson or learning activity—and how technology can support the process.

## Special Features

Each chapter has the following features to help both the instructor and the student.

- **A list of descriptive topics and objectives.** This list appears at the beginning of each chapter.
- **Illustrative screens.** Figures show screen displays from software, media, and networks whenever possible.
- **Summary tables of important information.** These aid recall and analysis.
- **Sample, teacher-designed lesson plans.** All from published sources, these materials match integration strategies. Links also are given to information on a companion Web site and on the lesson plan CD-ROM, *Integrating Technology Across the Curriculum.*
- **Exercises.** Improved end-of-chapter questions, many of them linked to the companion Web site and CD-ROM, call for students to analyze and apply what they have read to problems in education and in applying technology.
- **A list of sample resources.** References for further reading end each chapter.

Instructors also have access to two additional resources:

- **A comprehensive Instructor's Manual.** The manual contains content overviews, teaching strategies and activities, and additional resources (including a list of Web sites).
- **A computerized Test Bank.** Available for either Windows or Macintosh, the Test Bank includes a variety of question formats, such as true-false, multiple choice, short answer, and essay.

## Acknowledgments

The first thing we would like to acknowledge is that this second edition was not—as we had been promised—easier to write than the first. If anything, it was more difficult! Educational technology not only is changing rapidly, it's expanding quickly. It is an even more challenging task to capture and communicate its scope and essence than it was in 1996. However, several people helped us meet this challenge.

The following reviewers provided insightful and practical critiques and advice, all of which helped us clarify our prose and sharpen our focus: Diane F. Cauble, Catawba College; Michelle Churma, Ashland University; Farah Fisher, California State University, Dominguez Hills; Sarah Huyvaert, Eastern Michigan University; Kathleen P. King, Widener University/Pennsylvania Institute of Technology; and Decker Walker, Stanford University.

Colleagues like Anita Best of ISTE; Donna Baumbach and Mary Bird at the University of Central Florida; Richard A. Smith of the Houston Independent School District; Melinda Crowley of the Florida Department of Education; and Ronnie Akers, Diane Boothe, Judy Butler, Letty Ekhaml, Elizabeth Kirby, Karen Lee, Angela Lumpkin, Lisa Marcotte, Barbara McKenzie, Mary Ann Myers, Elaine Roberts, and Joanne Schick from the State University of West Georgia responded graciously and quickly to our requests for articles, sources, and advice. Thanks also to Nicole Stewart, Meg Cooper, Tiffani Hines, Richard Logan, and Lisa Marcotte for their last-minute help with our photo shoots. As before, we must acknowledge the wisdom of a saying in special education that "people don't care how much you know until they know how much you care." The field of educational technology—indeed, education itself—is fortunate to have such knowledgeable and caring professionals.

We would like to acknowledge the assistance of many people whom we have never met but who took time from busy schedules to send a photo or give permission to use a diagram. Among them are Sandra Powell of Texas Instruments, Yvonne Ruwe of the American Education Company, and Dawn Torre of Vernier Software.

As usual, the enormous professional and personal support given by the Merrill editorial staff is impossible to measure. The firm vision and competent direction of editor Debbie Stollenwerk helped us conceptualize and carry out the work on this edition. With skill and professionalism, the support, editorial, and production team members (Gianna Marsella, Penny Burleson, Mary Harlan, and Carol Sykes from Prentice Hall; and Phyllis Crittenden from Elm Street Publishing Services) made our ideas and words both attractive as well as useful.

As before, we would like to thank our families for taking second place for so many weekends and holidays while we dedicated the time and work required to accomplish this "little revision." M. D. Roblyer would like to recognize the enduring love and patience of her family, Bill and Paige Wiencke and Tom and Becky Kelley; the tenacious loyalty of old friends like Barbara Hansen and Sherry Alter; and the support offered by new friends and colleagues like Cher Chester, Elizabeth Kirby, Letty Ekhaml, Barbara McKenzie, Mary Ann Myers, Priscilla Bennett, and Laurie Tennant at the State University of West Georgia. Jack Edwards would like to recognize the special support given by colleagues Mary Lou Beverly and Scarlet Harriss; his father, Robert W. Edwards; and his son, Jordan M. Burke. Also, we would like to continue to remember and acknowledge the enduring contributions of those who are with us now only in memory: S. L. Roblyer, Raymond and Marjorie Wiencke, and Mary E. Edwards.

And, as always, we must recognize the contributions of all the educators who have worked so long and so hard to make it possible for us to wing our way into the next century with a renewed sense of purpose, direction, and courage.

M. D. Roblyer
Carrollton, Georgia

Jack Edwards
St. Augustine, Florida

# Discover the Companion Web Site Accompanying This Book

## The Prentice Hall Companion Web Site: A Virtual Learning Environment

Technology is a constantly growing and changing aspect of our field that is creating a need for content and resources. To address this emerging need, Prentice Hall has developed an online learning environment for students and professors alike—Companion Web Sites—to support our textbooks.

In creating a Companion Web Site, our goal is to build on and enhance what the textbook already offers. For this reason, the content for each user-friendly Web site is organized by chapter and provides the professor and student with a variety of meaningful resources. Common features of a Companion Web Site include:

### For the Professor—

Every Companion Web Site integrates **Syllabus Manager™**, an online syllabus creation and management utility.

- **Syllabus Manager™** provides you, the instructor, with an easy, step-by-step process to create and revise syllabuses, with direct links into Companion Web Sites and other online content without having to learn HTML.

- Students may logon to your syllabus during any study session. All they need to know is the Web address for the Companion Web Site and the password you've assigned to your syllabus.

- After you have created a syllabus using **Syllabus Manager™**, students may enter the syllabus for their course section at any point in the Companion Web Site.

- Class dates are highlighted in white and assignment due dates appear in blue. Clicking on a date, the student is shown the list of activities for the assignment. The activities for each assignment are linked directly to actual content, saving time for students.

- Adding assignments consists of clicking on the desired due date, then filling in the details of the assignment—name of the assignment, instructions, and whether or not it is a one-time or repeating assignment.

- In addition, links to other activities can be created easily. If the activity is online, a URL can be entered in the space provided, and it will be linked automatically in the final syllabus.

- Your completed syllabus is hosted on our servers, allowing convenient updates from any computer on the Internet. Changes you make to your syllabus are immediately available to your students at their next logon.

### For the Student—

- **Chapter Objectives**—outline key concepts from the text
- **Interactive Self-quizzes**—complete with hints and automatic grading that provides immediate feedback for students

After students submit their answers for the interactive self-quizzes, the Companion Web Site **Results Reporter** computes a percentage grade, provides a graphic representation of how many questions were answered correctly and incorrectly, and gives a question-by-question analysis of the quiz. Students are given the option to send their quizzes to up to four e-mail addresses (professor, teaching assistant, study partner, etc.).

- **Message Board**—serves as a virtual bulletin board to post—or respond to—questions or comments to/from a national audience
- **Net Searches**—offer links by key terms from each chapter to related Internet content
- **Web Destinations**—links to www sites that relate to chapter content

To take advantage of these and other resources, please visit the *Integrating Educational Technology into Teaching* Companion Web Site at http://www.prenhall.com/roblyer.

# About the Authors

**M. D. Roblyer** has been a technology-using teacher and a contributor to the field of educational technology for over 25 years. She began her exploration of technology's benefits for teaching in 1971 as a graduate student at one of the country's first successful instructional computer training sites, Pennsylvania State University, where she helped author tutorial literacy lessons in Coursewriter II on an IBM 1500 dedicated instructional mainframe. While obtaining a Ph.D. in Instructional Systems at Florida State University, she worked on several major courseware development and training projects with Control Data Corporation's PLATO system. After working as Instructional Technology Coordinator for the Florida Educational Computing Project (the predecessor of what is now the state's Bureau of Educational Technology), she became a private consultant, working for companies such as Random House and the Apple Computer Company. In 1981–82, she designed one of the early microcomputer software series, *Grammar Problems for Practice,* in conjunction with the Milliken Publishing Company.

She has written extensively and served as contributing editor for educational technology publications such *Educational Technology* and *Learning and Leading with Technology.* Her book with Castine and King, *Assessing the Impact of Computer-based Instruction: A Review of Research* (Haworth, 1988), is widely considered the most comprehensive review and meta-analysis ever written on the effects of computer technology on learning.

Currently, she is Professor of Educational Technology at the University of West Georgia's College of Education in Carrollton, Georgia, where she teaches graduate courses in technology, instructional design, and diffusion of innovation. She is married to William R. Wiencke and is the mother of a daughter, Paige.

**Jack Edwards** has been using instructional technology in his classroom since 1988 when he was hired to teach gifted students at the Webster School in St. Augustine, Florida. In that same year, the Webster School was selected to be one of the Florida Department of Education's five Model Technology Schools. In 1990, he was one of 28 teachers from Florida selected to spend the summer at the Florida Institute of Technology participating in the Florida Science Videodisc Project.

Edwards has trained thousands of Florida teachers over the past 10 years. His training experience includes spending three years as a teacher-on-special-assignment with the University of Central Florida's Instructional Technology Resource Center. During that time he traveled throughout Florida consulting with school districts and teachers on strategies for technology integration.

Edwards also served as the lead faculty member for instructional technology with the University of North Florida's First Coast Urban Academy from 1993 to 1995. This academy served as a catalyst for initiating systemic change in seven inner-city schools. He is former president of the Florida Association for Computers in Education (FACE), a state affiliate of the International Society for Technology in Education (ISTE).

In addition to teaching fifth grade gifted students, Edwards is also an instructor at St. Johns River Community College in St. Augustine. He resides in St. Augustine with his son, Jordan, and his boxer, Kozmo.

# Brief Contents

# Contents

# Part I

## Introduction and Background on Integrating Technology in Education

### The chapters in this part will help teachers learn:

1. How technology in education has evolved from its beginnings to its present day resources and applications and where it might be going in the future

2. Issues and concerns that become important when implementing technology resources in schools and classrooms

3. How learning theories influence the development of technology integration strategies

### Introduction: We Want to Be Ready

About 20 years ago, when microcomputers were beginning to appear somewhat regularly in K-12 classrooms, one of the authors visited two teachers at a middle school to see how they were using some recent purchases: two Apple II computers and instructional software, primarily simple mathematics games and drills. As the teachers demonstrated the programs and their classroom applications, they coped with a variety of technical problems.

Some of the software was designed for an earlier version of the Apple operating system, and each disk required a format adjustment every time it was used. Other programs would stall when students entered something the programmers had not anticipated; users either would have to adjust the code or restart the programs. In addition, the computers needed a small device to allow text to appear in both upper- and lower-case on the screen, but this worked with only some programs. In spite of these and other problems, the teachers were excited about their computer resources and spoke with enthusiasm about their hopes, plans, and expectations.

"You guys are obviously doing a great job with your computers," the visitor said, "and I don't mean to seem negative about them. But this sure seems like an awful lot of trouble for what you get out of it. What motivates you to keep investing all the time you do?" The teachers' answer was both instructive and prophetic: "We know the time is coming when computers will be in all classrooms. Software will be better and equipment will be easier to use. When this time comes, we want to be among those prepared to use computers in teaching. We want to be ready."

As we look today at what technology is doing—and what it promises to do—in classrooms across the country, we see that those middle school teachers were right: What is happening now is worth the preparation. Computers and other technology resources have improved in capabilities and user-friendliness to educators. Some of the most innovative and promising practices in education today involve technology, and the promise of even more exciting capabilities foreshadow even greater benefits for teachers.

This book presents some of the most powerful and capable educational technology resources available today. It also demonstrates how teachers can take advantage of this power and capability. Despite advances, "being ready" still requires an investment of time. This introductory section discusses the knowledge and skills teachers need to prepare themselves to apply technology, especially computer technology, effectively in classrooms.

## What Do Teachers Need to Be Ready for Technology?

In a field with a wide range of powerful and complex tools, experts cannot help but disagree about what teachers need to know and where they should begin. Not long ago, many experts believed that teachers who wanted to become "computer literate" must learn to write programs in computer languages such as FORTRAN and BASIC. Few people today believe that teachers need this level of technical skill; however, textbooks continue to provide a wide variety of information for beginning technology users. The background information in this section is based on the following steps that beginning technology users need to take:

### Develop a Philosophy

Teachers must observe where current resources and types of applications fit in the history and current scope of the field. Then they must begin developing personal perspectives on the current and future role of technology in education and in their own classrooms.

### Purchase Products

Teachers must become informed, knowledgeable consumers of computer products and select wisely among available alternatives.

### Identify and Solve Problems

To discriminate between problems they can correct and those that will require outside help, teachers must be able to troubleshoot computer systems they use.

### Speak the Language

Sufficient understanding of the terms and concepts related to technology allows users to exchange information with other teachers and experts and to ask and answer questions to expand their knowledge.

### See Where Technology Fits in Education

Perhaps the most important—and the most difficult—challenge is for teachers to identify specific teaching and learning problems technology can help address or how it can create important educational opportunities that did not exist without it. As part of this process, teachers decide what they need to make these changes occur. This process of determining where and how technology fits is known among users of educational technology as *integration*.

## Required Background for Teachers

In Part I, three chapters provide the information and skills that will help teachers accomplish their goals.

## Chapter 1: Educational Technology in Context: The Big Picture

Computer technology has nearly a 50-year history in education; other kinds of technology have been in use for much longer. Classroom technology resources have changed dramatically over time, but a broad perspective of the field helps illuminate many of today's concepts, terms, and activities. Chapter 1 describes the history of computer resources and related applications of educational technology in order to show how they have evolved—and are still evolving—into the tools described later in this book. The chapter also provides a general overview of technology resources in education today and where computer technology fits into this picture.

## Chapter 2: Planning and Implementation for Effective Technology Integration

Educators must resolve many complex issues to apply technology solutions to educational problems. They must address many concerns before and during implementation to ensure that technology has the desired effects on students and schools. These concerns range from funding to selection and placement of technology resources. Chapter 2 acts as a planning guide at three different levels, with planning done by the education community, the school, and the teacher. The chapter discusses each of the issues involved and recommends useful and practical steps educators may take to deal with each level of preparation.

## Chapter 3: Learning Theories and Integration Models

The last chapter in Part I provides an important link between learning and technology. It emphasizes the need to reach beyond the "nuts and bolts" of how technology resources work. Successful integration requires a connection between how people learn and how teachers employ technology to assist and enhance this learning. Chapter 3 begins with an overview of learning theories and related research findings and introduces two different perspectives on how to integrate technology into teaching and learning activities. These two perspectives are known as *directed models* and *constructivist models*. Finally, Chapter 3 develops some specific integration strategies based on each of these models.

# Chapter 1

## Educational Technology in Context: The Big Picture

Science is a process, not an edifice, and sheds old concepts as it grows.

Timothy Ferris in *Coming of Age in the Milky Way* (1988)

The more we know of our heritage, the more we earn the right to lead the field forward in our own time.

Don Ely in Paul Saettler's *The Evolution of American Educational Technology* (1990)

**This chapter covers the following topics:**

* Various definitions of key educational technology terms and how they originated

* A brief history of computer technology in education and what we have learned from it

* Justification for technology purchases by relating them to potential improvements in teaching and learning

* An overview of current technology systems and applications in education and the major issues and concerns that guide their uses

* Issues that shape technology's current and future role in restructuring education

## Objectives

1. Given an evolving definition of the term educational technology, give four different aspects of that definition and identify professional associations and events that represent each view.

2. Identify periods in the history of educational computing and describe what we have learned from past applications and decisions.

3. Identify reasons that would and would not be appropriate to help justify a school or district purchase and use of technology.

4. Identify the general categories of educational technology hardware resources: standalone computer, network, centralized processor, and related device/system.

5. Identify the general categories of educational technology software resources: instructional software, software tool, multimedia, distance learning, or a virtual reality environment.

6. Explain the impact of each of the following societal issues on current uses of technology in education: cultural diversity, educational equity, ethical practices, and the increasing role of technology in modern life.

When a classroom teacher browses the Internet for new teaching materials or has students look up a definition in an on-disc word atlas, that teacher is using some of the latest and best of what is commonly called *technology in education* or *educational technology*. But educational technology is not new at all, and it is by no means limited to the use of equipment, let alone electronic equipment. Modern tools and techniques are simply the latest developments in a field that some believe is as old as education itself.

In his excellent, comprehensive historical description, *The Evolution of American Educational Technology* (1990), Paul Saettler begins by pointing out that "Educational technology … can be traced back to the time when tribal priests systematized bodies of knowledge, and early cultures invented pictographs or sign writing to record and transmit information.… It is clear that educational technology is essentially the product of a great historical stream consisting of trial and error, long practice and imitation, and sporadic manifestations of unusual individual creativity and persuasion" (p. 4).

This chapter explores the link between the early applications of educational technology and those of today and tomorrow. This exploration includes some historical and technical background. Many readers will grow impatient when they encounter these paragraphs of description and explanation. This impatience is understandable in a field

where the real excitement for teachers and students lies in hands-on exploration of the newest gadgets and techniques. We encourage you to read for three reasons:

- **Looking back before going ahead.** This information shows where the field is headed by demonstrating where it began. It points out the current status in the evolution of the technology of education along with changes in goals and methods over time. It provides a foundation on which to build more successful and useful structures to respond to the challenges of modern education.

- **Learning from past mistakes.** This background also helps those just embarking on their first applications of educational technology to make the best use of their learning time by avoiding mistakes that others have made and by choosing directions that experience has shown to be promising.

- **Developing a "big picture."** Finally, this background helps new learners to develop mental pictures of the field, what Ausubel (1968) might call *cognitive frameworks* through which to view all applications—past, present, and future.

## What Is "Educational Technology"?

### Origins and Definitions of Key Terms

Teachers will see references to the terms *educational technology* and *instructional technology* in many professional journals. Perhaps no other topics are the focus of so much new development in so many content areas, yet no single, acceptable definition for these terms dominates the field. Paul Saettler, a recognized authority on the history of instructional and educational technology, notes uncertainty even about the origins of the terms. The earliest reference he can confirm for the term educational technology was in an interview with W. W. Charters in 1948; the earliest known reference he finds for the term instructional technology was in a 1963 foreword by James Finn for a technology development project sponsored by the National Education Association.

For many educators, any mention of technology in education immediately brings to mind the use of some device or a set of equipment, particularly computer equipment. Muffoletto (1994) says that "Technology is commonly thought of in terms of gadgets, instruments, machines, and devices … most (educators) will defer to technology as computers" (p. 25). Only about 15 years ago, a history of technology in education since 1920 placed the emphasis on radio and television, with computers as an afterthought (Cuban, 1986). If such a description were written now, the Internet might be a central focus. Twenty years from now the focus might be Intelligent Computer Assisted Instruction (ICAI) or Virtual Reality (VR) or whatever they are called then.

In one sense, all these views are correct, since definitions of state-of-the-art instruction usually mention the most recently developed tools. But Saettler (1990) urges those seeking precision to remember that "the historical function of educational technology is a *process* rather than a product. No matter how sophisticated the media of instruction may become, a distinction must always be made between the process of developing a technology of education and the use of certain products or media within a particular technology of instruction" (p. 4). Therefore, in the view of most writers, researchers, and practitioners in the field, useful definitions of educational technology must focus on the process of applying tools for educational purposes as well as the tools and materials used. As Muffoletto (1994) puts it, "Technology … is not a collection of machines and devices, but a way of acting" (p. 25). Based on this background, the authors assign educational technology the following "evolving" definition:

> Educational technology is a combination of the processes and tools involved in addressing educational needs and problems, with an emphasis on applying the most current tools: computers and their related technologies.

### Four Perspectives on Educational Technology: Media, Instructional Systems, Vocational Training, and Computers

If educational technology is viewed as both processes and tools, it is important to begin by examining four different historical perspectives on these processes and tools, all of which have helped shape current practices in the field. These influences come to us from four groups whose origins and views are summarized in Figure 1.1.

**Technology in education as media and audiovisual communications.** The earliest view of educational technology and one that continues today emphasizes technology as media. This view grew out of what Saettler (1990) calls the *audiovisual movement*: ways of delivering information used as alternatives to lectures and books. Beginning in the 1930s, some higher education instructors proposed that media such as slides and films delivered information in more concrete, and therefore more effective, ways. This perspective later developed into *audiovisual communications,* the "branch of educational theory and practice concerned primarily with the design and use of messages which control the learning process" (Saettler, 1990, p. 9). However, the view of technology as media continued to

dominate areas of education and the communications industry. Saettler reports that as late as 1986, the National Task Force on Educational Technology used a definition that equated educational technology with media, treating computers simply as another medium.

The Association for Educational Communications and Technology (AECT) tends to represent this view of technology as media and communications systems. Originally a department of the National Education Association (NEA) that focused on audiovisual instruction, the AECT was until very recently concerned primarily with devices that carry messages and the applications of these devices in instructional situations. After a reorganization in 1988, it broadened its mission to include other concerns such as instructional uses of telecommunications and computer/information systems. Several of its divisions, however, still focus on the concerns of media educators and many of its state affiliates still refer to themselves as media associations.

**Technology in education as instructional systems.** The instructional design or instructional systems movement took shape in the 1960s and 1970s, adding another dimension to the media-and-communications view of technology in education. Systems approaches to solving educational problems originated in military and industrial training but later emerged in university research and development projects. K-12 school practices began to reflect systems approaches when university personnel began advocating them in their work with schools. These approaches were based on the belief that both human *and* nonhuman resources (teachers and media) could be parts of a system for addressing an instructional need. From this viewpoint, educational technology was seen not just as a medium for communicating instructional information, but as a systematic approach to designing, developing, and delivering instruction matched to carefully identified needs (Heinich, Molenda, Russell, & Smaldino, 1997). Resources for delivering instruction were identified only after detailed analysis of learning tasks and objectives and the kinds of instructional strategies required to teach them.

From the 1960s through the 1980s, applications of systems approaches to instruction were influenced and shaped by learning theories from educational psychology. Behaviorist theories held sway initially and cognitive theories gained influence later. Views of instructional systems

**Figure 1.1    Four Perspectives That Shaped Educational Technology**

| Four Historical Perspectives | Origins | Current Organization |
|---|---|---|
| Media and AV communications | Higher education instructors, 1930s | AECT |
| Instructional systems | Military/industrial trainers; later, university R&D, 1960s–1970s | ISPI |
| Vocational training (technology education) | Industry trainers, vocational educators, 1980s | ITEA |
| Computer systems (educational computing) | Programmers, systems analysts; later, university R&D, 1960s | ISTE |

in the 1990s also were influenced by popular learning theories; however, these theories criticized systems approaches as too rigid to foster some kinds of learning, particularly higher-order ones. Thus, the current view of educational technology as instructional systems seems to be changing once again. (See Chapter 3 for more information on two approaches to educational technology as instructional systems and how each influences methods of integration.)

Just as the AECT had its origins in the media systems view of educational technology, the International Society for Performance Improvement (ISPI) grew out of the view of educational technology as a systems approach to instruction. Originally named the National Society for Programmed Instruction, the ISPI is still concerned primarily with creating and validating instructional systems.

**Technology in education as vocational training tools.** Another popular view of technology in education has developed from the perspective of technology as tools used in business and industry. Generally referred to as *technology education,* this view originated with industry trainers and vocational educators in the 1980s and reflects their need for technology to enhance training in specific job skills. This perspective is based on two premises. First, it holds that one important function of school learning is to prepare students for the world of work. Therefore, students need to learn about and use technology that they will encounter after graduation. For example, technology educators believe that every student should learn word processing to help them to perform in many jobs or professions. Second, technology educators believe that vocational training can be a practical means of teaching all content areas such as math, science, and language. Technology education also includes other topics such as robotics, manufacturing systems, and computer-assisted design (CAD) systems.

The organization that espouses this view is the International Technology Education Association (ITEA), formerly the American Industrial Arts Association. The ITEA has helped shape a major paradigm shift in vocational training in K-12 schools. Most schools currently are changing from industrial arts curricula centered in wood shops to technology education courses taught in labs equipped with high-technology resources such as CAD stations and robotics systems.

**Technology in education as computers and computer-based systems.** Another view of educational technology originated with the advent of computers in the 1950s. Business, industry, and military trainers, as well as educators in K-12 and higher education recognized the potential of computers as instructional tools. Many of these trainers and educators predicted that computer technology quickly would transform education and become the most important component of educational technology. Although instructional applications of computers did not produce the anticipated overnight success, they inspired the development of another branch of educational technology. From the time that computers came into classrooms in the 1960s until about 1990, this perspective was known as *educational computing* and encompassed both instructional and support applications of computers.

Educational computing applications originally were influenced by technical personnel such as programmers and systems analysts. By the 1970s, however, many of the same educators involved with media, audiovisual communications, and instructional systems were directing the course of research and development in educational computing. By the 1990s, these educators began to see computers as part of a combination of technology resources, including media, instructional systems, and computer-based support systems. At that point, educational computing became known as *educational technology.*

The organization that represents this view of technology in education is the International Society for Technology in Education (ISTE), the product of a merger between two computer-oriented groups: the International Council for Computers in Education (ICCE) and the International Association for Computers in Education (IACE). IACE was known for most of its existence from 1960 until 1986 as the Association for Educational Data Systems (AEDS). A major ISTE publication, *The Computing Teacher,* reflected the original computer orientation of the organization. In 1995, it was renamed *Learning and Leading with Technology.*

## This Textbook's Emphasis on Technology in Education

Each of these perspectives on technology in education has made significant contributions to the current body of knowledge about processes and tools to address educational needs. But, as Saettler points out, no single paradigm that attempts to describe educational technology can characterize satisfactorily what is happening with technology in education today and what will happen in the future. Furthermore, all of the organizations described here seem engaged in a struggle to claim the high-profile term *educational technology.* Each seems determined to assign a definition based on the perspective and concerns of its members; each wants to be identified with and help shape the future of educational technology. However, these often-conflicting views of the role of technology in education confuse newcomers to the field and make it difficult for them to learn the role of technology; the resources and issues differ depending on whose descriptions teachers hear and which publications they read. This textbook attempts to address the disparate views on this topic in the following ways:

- **Processes.** For the processes, or instructional procedures for applying tools, we look to two different areas. First, we look at learning theories based on the sciences of human behavior. Some of these theories are systems-oriented; others are based on various views of how best to foster learning. Second, this textbook acknowledges that many of the applications of

**Figure 1.2    Various Approaches to Technology in Education**

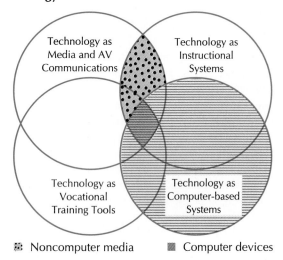

Noncomputer media        Computer devices

**Figure 1.3    Milestones and Trends in Educational Computing Technology**

**The Era Before Microcomputers**

| | |
|---|---|
| 1950 | First instructional computer use: Computerized flight simulator used to train pilots at MIT |
| 1959 | First computer use in schools: IBM 650 |
| 1966 | IBM offers the 1500 system: Dedicated instructional mainframe |
| 1967 | CCC offers first minicomputer-based instructional system (DEC PDP/1); Mitre Corporation offers TICCIT system |
| 1970s | CDC offers the PLATO instructional delivery system |

**The Microcomputer Era and Beyond**

| | |
|---|---|
| 1977 | First microcomputers enter schools |
| 1980 | Seymour Papert writes *Mindstorms*: The Logo movement begins |
| 1980s | MECC offers microcomputer software; educational materials publishers begin courseware development and marketing |
| | The courseware evaluation is emphasized: MicroSIFT, EPIE, others |
| | The computer literacy movement begins, then wanes after 1988 |
| 1990s | Use of ILS and other networked systems increases; multimedia use and development increases |

**The Internet Era**

| | |
|---|---|
| 1994 | Widespread use of the Internet begins |
| 2000 | Virtual reality systems and other virtual environments are emphasized |

technology focus on preparing students for future jobs by helping them acquire skills in using current tools as well as skills in "learning to learn" for tools of the future that are not yet invented—or even imagined.

- **Tools.** Although this textbook looks at technology tools as an overlapping combination of media, instructional systems, and computer-based support systems (see Figure 1.2), it emphasizes a subset of all these resources, focusing primarily on computers and their roles in instructional systems. There are three reasons for this focus:

1. Computers as media are more complex and more capable than other media such as films or overheads and require more technical knowledge to operate.

2. Computer systems are currently moving toward subsuming all other media within their own resources. For example, CD-ROMs and videodiscs now store images that once were shown on filmstrips and slides. Presentation software can generate overhead transparencies.

3. The complexity of computer-based systems traditionally has made it more complicated for educators to integrate various forms of software and computer-driven media into other classroom activities. Educators can see much more easily—some would say even intuitively—how to integrate less technical media such as films or overheads.

Thus, "integrating educational technology" refers to the process of determining which *electronic tools* and which methods for implementing them are appropriate for given classroom situations and problems.

## Looking Back: How Has the Past Influenced Today's Educational Technology?

In no small part, developments in computer technology have shaped the history of educational technology. Since

we have learned much from our past experience that can and should help any future work in this area, this section will describe some of this history and what we have learned from it.

### A Brief History of Educational Computing Activities and Resources

Since integrated circuits made computers both smaller and more accessible to teachers and students, microcomputers became a major turning point in the history of the field. This history is told in two periods: before and after the introduction of microcomputers (Niemiec & Walberg, 1989; Roblyer, 1992). (See Figure 1.3.)

**The pre-microcomputer era.** Many of today's technology-oriented teachers have been using computer systems only since microcomputers came into common use, but a thriving educational computing culture predated that development by 20 years. The first documented instructional use of a computer was in 1950 with a computer-driven flight simulator used to train pilots at MIT. The first use with school children was in 1959 when an IBM 650 computer helped to teach binary arithmetic to New York City elementary school students. The intense development and research with mainframe-based computer systems in schools, colleges, and universities peaked in the early and mid-1970s with federal government funds supporting many large-scale projects. During this time, there was growing excitement and interest in computer-based instruction, also known as *computer-assisted instruction* or *CAI*. Although they used earlier technologies, each of these activities had an impact on current computer uses in education.

***Mainframe and minicomputer systems by IBM, CCC, and CDC.*** From about 1972 to 1980, the development and marketing efforts of IBM, the Computer Curriculum Corporation (CCC), and the Control Data Corporation (CDC) dominated the educational computing field. Stanford University used the **IBM 1500 system**, the first computer system dedicated solely to instruction and research on learning, and a high-level language called *Coursewriter.* The resulting lessons were called *courseware,* or *instructional software.* This system also was the first multimedia learning station; it had a cathode ray tube (CRT) screen, earphones, a microphone, an audiotape player, and a slide projector. Until 1975, when IBM discontinued support, some 25 universities and school districts had these systems and were following Stanford's model. Stanford also developed CAI for one of the first minicomputers: **Digital Equipment Corporation's PDP-1**. Professor Patrick Suppes, the first CCC president, led an extensive research and development effort that earned him the honorary title "Grandfather of Computer-assisted Instruction." Dr. Don Bitzer, working at the University of Illinois in conjunction with CDC, initiated yet a third line of development: an instructional system called **Programmed Logic for Automatic Teaching Operations (PLATO)**. The PLATO system had a terminal with a plasma screen (argon/neon gas contained between two glass plates with wire grids running through them), a specially designed keyboard, and an authoring system similar to Coursewriter called *Tutor,* which it used to develop tutorial lessons and complete courses rather than just drill and practice lessons. CDC's president, Dr. William Norris, had an almost messianic belief that PLATO would revolutionize classroom practice (Norris, 1977); he channeled significant funding and personnel into development of PLATO between 1965 and 1980.

***Other major products: TICCIT, PLAN, and IPI.*** Parallel lines of development took place at Brigham Young University (BYU) and the University of Pittsburgh. At BYU, Dr. Victor Bunderson and Dr. Dexter Fletcher added color television to a computer learning station and developed Time-shared Interactive Computer-Controlled Information Television (TICCIT). Other products, such as the Program for Learning in Accordance with Needs (PLAN) developed at the American Institutes for Research,

and the Individually Prescribed Instruction (IPI) system at the University of Pittsburgh, focused on using computer systems to support mastery learning models with computer-managed instruction (CMI) systems.

***University time-sharing systems.*** During the 1960s and 1970s, as CAI and CMI development was taking place, a thriving computer culture developed at 22 universities around the country where faculty and students used mainframe systems to teach programming, develop programs and utilities, and share them among members of the academic community. The first meeting of these groups in Iowa City in 1979 was the National Education Computing Conference (NECC), now the largest educational technology conference in the country.

***Administrative computing systems.*** While interest in instructional applications grew, educational organizations worked to computerize more and more of their administrative activities (e.g., student and staff records, attendance, report cards). Since mainframe computer systems were both expensive and technically complex, school district offices, rather than with schools or individual teachers, controlled both instructional and administrative computer hardware and applications. Data-processing specialists administered most of these systems. This lack of local control was not always popular with teachers, who neither understood the computer systems that delivered the instruction nor had much say in the curriculum developed for them. By the late 1970s, interest in CAI seemed to decline as it became clear that computers could not revolutionize classrooms in the same way that they were changing business offices in post–World War II America; this kind of revolution was neither feasible nor desirable in education.

***The microcomputer revolution in education.*** The first microcomputers came into schools in 1977 and the focus rapidly shifted from mainframes to desktop microcomputer systems. The introduction of these locally controlled resources also transformed the computer's role in education. Computer resources and their instructional applications were no longer managed by large companies or school district offices. Classroom teachers could decide what they wanted to do with computers. Even some administrative applications began to migrate to school-based computers, much to the dismay of personnel in district data-processing centers. Microcomputers made school-based management even more feasible.

***The software publishing/courseware evaluation movement.*** Before microcomputers, courseware came primarily from hardware manufacturers such as IBM and CDC, software systems companies like CCC, and university development projects. As microcomputers gained popularity, a new software market for education driven primarily by teachers emerged. The nonprofit Minnesota Educational Computing Consortium (MECC), with funding from the National Science Foundation, developed much of its original instructional software on mainframes but later transferred these programs to microcomputers and, for a time, became the largest single provider of courseware. Other major software publishing companies quickly jumped into the courseware development market, and a plethora of small companies, many of them cottage industries, were also organized. As the dominance of mainframes ended, teachers learned that having lessons on microcomputers did not guarantee quality or usefulness. Activities like the Northwest Regional Educational Laboratory's *MicroSIFT* project and the Educational Products Information Exchange (EPIE) as well as those by professional organizations, magazines, and journals sprang up to evaluate courseware. So many reviews were produced, *other* organizations began to compile and summarize reviews. Most of these groups eventually went out of business as courseware evaluation became less essential and school districts developed committees to select courseware.

*Courseware authoring activities.* As teachers began to clamor for more input into the design of courseware, some companies saw another potential market for tools to let educators develop their own courseware. These *authoring systems* were the predecessors of modern tools such as HyperCard and Linkway. Some authoring systems were more like high-level languages (PILOT and SuperPILOT), while others prompted systems that allowed developers to choose from menus of options (GENIS, PASS). For a time, teacher-developed software became popular, but interest faded as teachers realized how much time, expertise, and work had to be invested to develop courseware that would prove more useful than what they could buy.

*The computer literacy movement.* From the beginning, teachers wanted students to learn *about* (as well as with) computers, an activity that came to be called *computer literacy.* The term is thought to have been coined by educational computing pioneer Dr. Arthur Luehrmann (Roblyer, 1992), who originally believed that computer literacy was defined as programming skills and use of tools such as word processing. Later, it became associated with a variety of skills. A popular fear in the 1980s was that students who were not "computer literate" would be left behind academically, further widening the gap between the advantaged and disadvantaged (Molnar, 1978). By 1985, computer literacy skills began to appear in required curricula around the country; but by around 1990, they were dropped as educators began to feel that computer literacy could not be linked to any specific set of skills. However, the late 1990s saw renewed interest in this topic as districts began requiring "technology literacy" skills (North Carolina, 1999).

*Logo and the problem-solving movement.* From 1980 until about 1987, Logo had a profound influence on instructional computing; Logo-based products, activities, and research dominated the field. Logo was developed and promoted as a programming language for young children by Seymour Papert, an MIT mathematics professor (Cuban, 1986).

Through Papert's prolific writings and speeches, Logo also became a challenge to traditional instructional methods and to the computer uses that had supported them (drill and practice, tutorial uses). Papert based his philosophy of computer use on his interpretation of the work of his mentor, developmental theorist Jean Piaget (see Chapter 3). In his popular book *Mindstorms,* Papert proposed that child-directed exploration was better than teacher-directed instruction and that Logo-based projects could be the basis for such exploration. Versions of the Logo language were developed, derivative products were marketed (Logowriter, LegoLogo), and Logo assumed the characteristics of a craze: Logo clubs, user groups, and T-shirts filled the schools. Although research showed that the applications Papert proposed could be useful in some contexts, by 1985 educators said that "Logo promised more than it has delivered" (Papert, 1986, p. 46) and interest waned. Logo is still in use, but Logo's main contribution may have been its example of how technology could be used to revise and restructure educational methods.

*Integrated learning systems (ILSs) and other networked systems.* ILSs were a mirror image of the types of systems first developed and marketed in the 1970s, some even using curricula derived from those developed by Stanford's Pat Suppes. ILSs came about because both school districts and software companies realized that one of the most common applications of microcomputers—and one with strong validation by research—was instruction and practice in basic skills. They saw that microcomputers networked to a central server could provide this instruction more cost-effectively than a system using disks on standalone microcomputers. ILSs also could track and report data on student progress and allow quick access to various courseware types in one location. In 1991, when curriculum trends moved toward less structured and teacher-directed methods, companies began to market other networked systems sometimes called *"multimedia learning systems," "integrated technology systems,"* or *"open learning systems"* (Hill, 1993, p. 29). But, since there was no universally accepted alternative name for these less-structured systems, any networked instructional delivery system usually is called an ILS. By any name, all systems networked with a central server mark a significant movement away from single computer systems under the control of individual teachers and back toward more centralized control of instructional computing resources.

*The birth of the World Wide Web.* As exciting and challenging as they were, the first 30 years of educational computing technology seem mundane compared to what occurred about five years before the new millennium. The emergence of the Internet has been likened to "fire ... more important than the invention of movable type" (Remnick, 1997, p. 214). A text-based version of the Internet was used by university educators since the 1980s to exchange information (see Chapter 8). In 1994, the program Mosaic made it possible to see information as a combination of pictures and text; and popular interest was sparked in a way no one had predicted. Teachers joined the ranks of people in all areas of society in recognizing the power of the Internet: ready access to people and information, the ability to send and receive multimedia displays, and an increasingly realistic simulation of "being there." Educators who had never before been interested in technology began to envision the possibilities. The *Information Superhighway* became an expressway for education.

## What Have We Learned from the Past?

A history of educational technology is interesting, but useless unless we apply the information to future decisions and actions. What have we learned from some 50 years of applying technology to educational problems that can improve our strategies now? Educators are encouraged to draw their own conclusions from these and other descriptions they might read. However, the following points also are important:

- **No technology is a panacea for education.** Educators and parents tend to look to technology for answers to education's most difficult problems, but great expectations for products like Logo and ILSs have taught us that even the most current, capable technology resources offer no quick, easy, or universal solutions. Computer-based materials and strategies are usually tools in a larger system and must be integrated carefully with other resources and with teacher activities. If we begin with more realistic expectations in mind, we have more potential for success and impact on teaching and learning. Planning must always begin with the question: What specific needs do my students and I have that (any given) resources can help meet?

- **Computer literacy/technological literacy is a moving target.** Experience has shown that there is no concise, agreed-upon definition for *"computer literacy"* or *"technological literacy."* The skills that define these terms vary according to student needs and age levels as well as the focus of the groups defining them. Further, we know now that, as technology evolves, the skills students will require for the future tend to change, often dramatically and quickly. As they did for a period of time in the 1980s, school districts and state departments again are beginning to add technology skills to their required curriculum, along with reading, writing, and mathematics. But the skills they are adding are far different now in scope and purpose from those of just 10 years ago, and this trend of technology skills as a moving target seems likely to continue indefinitely.

- **Computer literacy/technological literacy offers a limited integration rationale.** Many parents and educators want technology tools in the classroom primarily because they feel technical skills will give students the *technological literacy* to prepare them for the workplace. But an employability rationale provides limited guidelines for how and where to integrate technology. The capabilities of technology resources and methods must be matched to content area skills that display obvious need for improvement in our current system of education, for example, reading, writing, and mathematics skills; research and information-gathering; and problem solving and analysis.

- **Standalone computers and networked computers have benefits and limitations.** The pendulum of emphasis in education has swung from networked systems to standalone systems, then back to networked systems. Yet no single delivery system or configuration has proven ideal for all situations. Networks make it more feasible to standardize materials across classrooms, schools, or districts; allow easier tracking of student usage and progress; and facilitate collaboration among teachers and students. Standalone computers offer more individual and/or local control and are more flexible to schedule and access. Each type of system will continue to be needed.

- **Teachers usually do not develop technology materials or curriculum.** Teaching is one of the most time-and-labor intensive jobs in our society. With so many demands on their time, most teachers cannot be expected to develop software or create most integration strategies. In the past, publishers, school or district developers, or personnel in funded projects have provided this assistance, and this seems unlikely to change in the future.

- **Technically possible does not equal desirable, feasible, or inevitable.** A popular saying is that today's technology is yesterday's science fiction. But science fiction also shows us that technology brings undesirable—as well as desirable—changes. For example, distance technologies have allowed people to attend professional conferences online, rather than by traveling to another location; however, people continue to want to travel and meet face-to-face. As we write this book, procedures for human cloning are within reach and genetic engineering is increasingly feasible. In education, we can simulate face-to-face communication to an increasingly realistic degree. All these new technological horizons make it evident that it is time to analyze carefully the implications of each implementation decision. Better technology demands that we become critical consumers of its power and capability. We are responsible for deciding just which science fiction becomes reality.

- **Things change faster than teachers can keep up.** History in this field has shown that resources and accepted methods of applying them will change, sometimes quickly and dramatically. This places a special burden on already overworked teachers to continue learning new resources and changing their teaching methods. Gone are the days, if, indeed, they ever existed, when a teacher could rely on the same handouts, homework, or lecture notes from year to year. Educators may not be able to predict the future of educational technology, but they know that it will be different from the present, that is, they must anticipate and accept the inevitability of change and the need for a continual investment of their time.

- **Older technologies can be useful.** Technology in education is an area especially prone to what Roblyer (1990) called the "glitz factor." With so little emphasis on finding out what actually works, any "technological guru" who gives a glib rationale for new methods can lead a new movement in education. When dramatic improvements fail to appear, educators move on to the next fad. This approach fails to solve real problems and it draws attention away from the effort to find legitimate solutions. Worse, teachers sometimes throw out methods that had potential if only they had realistic expectations. The past has shown that teachers must be careful, analytical consumers of technological innovation, looking to what has worked in the past to guide their decisions and measure their expectations. Educational practice tends to move in cycles, and "new" methods often are old methods in new dressing. In short, teachers must be as informed and analytical as they want their students to become.

• **Teachers always will be important.** With each new technological development that appears on the horizon, the old question seems to resurface: Will computers replace teachers? The developers of the first instructional computer systems in the 1960s foresaw them replacing many teacher positions; some advocates of today's distance learning methods envision a similar impact on future education. Yet the answer to the old question is the same and is likely to remain so: Good teachers are more essential than ever. One reason for this was described in *MegaTrends,* "... whenever new technology is introduced into society, there must be a counterbalancing human response ... the more high tech (it is), the more high touch (is needed)" (Naisbitt, 1984, p. 35). Also, we need more teachers who understand the role technology plays in society and in education, who are prepared to take advantage of its power, and who recognize its limitations. In an increasingly technological society, we need more teachers who are both "technology-savvy" and child-centered.

## Why Use Technology? Developing a Sound Rationale

The history of educational technology also teaches us the importance of the "why?" question. Many educators, parents, and students believe the reasons for using technology seem so obvious that everyone should recognize them. Their common sense rationale is based on two major beliefs: (1) technology is everywhere and therefore, should be in education and (2) research has shown how and where computer-based methods are effective. Both of these commonly held beliefs have some validity and both provide rationales for using technology—at least as far as they go. But we also need answers to some practical questions:

1.  Should technology take over most or all of a teacher's role? If not, how should it fit in with what teachers already do?

2.  Should schools rely on computers at all levels, for all students, or for all topics? If not, which levels, students, or topics suit computer-based methods?

3.  Does some reliable information suggest specific benefits of using technology in certain ways?

To justify the expensive and time-consuming task of integrating technology into education, teachers must identify specific contributions that technology can and should make to an improved education system. Funding agencies, for example, can reasonably ask why a school should choose a technology-based resource or method over another path to reach its desired goals. As Soloman (1995) said, "It's the vision thing ... we first have to ask 'What do we need technology for?' We must create our vision, define technology's role in our schools, then plan for its use" (p. 66). The rationale we choose for using technology will

guide our goals and help identify the skills and resources needed to accomplish these goals.

**Problems with research-based justifications for educational technology.** Many educators look to educational research for evidence of technology's present and potential benefits. Although technology (especially computers) has been in use in education since the 1950s, research results have not made a strong case for its impact on teaching and learning. In general, the number and quality of studies on educational impact have been disappointing (Roblyer, Castine, & King, 1988). But researchers such as Clark (1983, 1985, 1991, 1994) have openly criticized "computer-based effectiveness" research such as meta-analyses to summarize results across studies comparing computer-based and traditional methods. After considerable research in this area, Clark concluded that most such studies suffered from confounding variables. The studies attempted to show a greater impact on achievement of one method over the other without controlling for other factors such as instructional methods, curriculum contents, or novelty. These differences could either increase or decrease achievement. Clark (1985) exhorted educators to "avoid rationalizing computer purchases by referencing the achievement gains" (p. 259) in such studies. Kozma (1991, 1994) responded to these challenges by proposing that research should look at technology not as a medium to deliver information but in the context of "the learner actively collaborating with the medium to construct knowledge" (p. 179). In light of the lack of consensus, however, it seems best to follow Clark's advice to refrain from using past reviews of research to justify investments in technology. However, several promising lines of research and several aspects of technology use (shown in Figure 1.4) offer elements of a rationale for continuing or expanding the use of technology in education.

**Justifying technology use: The case for motivation.** Motivating students to learn, to enjoy learning, and to want to learn more has assumed greater importance in recent years as we recognize strong correlations between dropping out of school and undesirable outcomes such as criminal activity. The drive to keep students in school is an urgent national priority. Technology has an important role to play in achieving this goal. Kozma and Croninger (1992) described several ways in which technology might help to address the cognitive, motivational, and social needs of at-risk students; Bialo and Sivin (1989) listed several software packages that were either designed or adapted to appeal to these kinds of students. Technology-based methods have successfully promoted several kinds of motivational strategies that may be used individually or in combination:

*Gaining learner attention.* Renowned learning theorist Robert Gagné proposed that gaining the learner's attention is a critical first event in providing optimal conditions for

## Figure 1.4  Elements of a Rationale for Using Technology in Education

1. **Motivation**
   - Gaining learner attention
   - Engaging the learner through production work
   - Increasing perceptions of control

2. **Unique instructional capabilities**
   - Linking learners to information sources
   - Helping learners visualize problems and solutions
   - Tracking learner progress
   - Linking learners to learning tools

3. **Support for new instructional approaches**
   - Cooperative learning
   - Shared intelligence
   - Problem solving and higher-level skills

4. **Increased teacher productivity**
   - Freeing time to work with students by helping with production and recordkeeping tasks
   - Providing more accurate information more quickly
   - Allowing teachers to produce better-looking, more "student-friendly" materials more quickly

5. **Required skills for an information age**
   - Technology literacy
   - Information literacy
   - Visual literacy

instruction. Although other aspects of instruction must direct this attention toward meaningful learning, the visual and interactive features of many technology resources seem to help focus students' attention and encourage them to spend more time on learning tasks (Pask-McCartney, 1989; Summers, 1990–1991). Substantial empirical evidence indicates that teachers frequently capitalize on the novelty and television-like attraction of computers and multimedia to achieve the essential instructional goal of capturing and holding students' attention.

***Engaging the learner through production work.*** To make learning more meaningful to students, teachers often try to engage them in creating their own technology-based products. This strategy has been used effectively with word processing (Tibbs, 1989; Franklin, 1991), hypermedia (Volker, 1992; LaRoue, 1990), computer-generated art (Buchholz, 1991), and telecommunications (Taylor, 1989; Marcus, 1995). Students seem to like the activities because they promote creativity, self-expression, and feelings of self-efficacy and result in professional-looking products they can view with pride.

***Increasing perceptions of control.*** Many students are motivated by feeling they are in control of their own learning

(Arnone & Grabowski, 1991; Relan, 1992). Learner control seems to have special implications for at-risk students and others who have experienced academic failure. When students perceive themselves as in control of their learning, the result has been called *intrinsic motivation,* or being motivated by the awareness that they are learning. This finding, reported from the earliest uses of computer-based materials, continues to be one of the most potentially powerful reasons for using technology resources as motivational aids. However, when learning paths become complex (with hypertext environments and interactive videodisc applications), students with weak learning skills seem to profit most when teachers supply structure to the activities (Kozma, 1991, 1994; McNeil & Nelson, 1991).

**Justifying technology use: Unique instructional capabilities.** Another powerful case for using technology resources is that some technological media can facilitate unique learning environments or contribute unique features to make traditional learning environments more powerful and effective.

***Linking learners to information sources.*** In hypertext systems, as seen on many Internet Web pages, students can select a keyword from a screen and get pointers from several other sources with information on the same topic. These lead to other related sources and topics, forming an endless chain of information. Kozma (1991, 1994) reports that, while little research has focused on hypertext to date, preliminary findings suggest that a hypertext learning environment "both calls on and develops skills in addition to those used with standard text" (1991, p. 203) and "helps the reader build links among texts … and construct meaning based on these relationships" (1991, p. 204). Computers handle the logistics of this complex activity and, though it remains a complicated process, they make it more feasible for classroom activities.

***Helping learners visualize problems and solutions.*** Kozma (1991) also reports that interactive visual media (videodisc applications) seem to have unique instructional capabilities for topics that involve social situations or problem solving. He notes that these media provide powerful visual means of "representing social situations and tasks such as interpersonal problem solving, foreign language learning, or moral decision making" (p. 200). The growing number of videodisc and CD-ROM products designed for these kinds of topics (the *AIDS* videodisc from ABC News, Computer Curriculum Corporation's *SuccessMaker*) confirms that designers and educators are recognizing and exploiting these unique and powerful qualities.

***Tracking learner progress.*** Integrated learning systems (ILSs) and subsequent products based on them have capitalized on the computer's unique ability to capture, analyze, and present data on students' performances during learning (*Electronic Learning,* 1990, 1992; *Educational Technology,* 1992). A teacher attempting to demonstrate a set of skills to a large group of students needs accurate, up-to-date, easy-to-analyze information on what each student is and is not learning. A well-designed computer-based system for data collection (sometimes called a *computer managed instruction* or *CMI* system; see Chapter 6) can most effectively provide this essential information. Small, palm-top computers allow teachers and researchers to keep moment-to-moment records of their observations of students; we anticipate affordable expert systems that can provide instruction, analyze students' errors and learning styles, and provide feedback tailored to unique learning needs (McArthur & Stasz, 1990).

***Linking learners to learning tools.*** The ability to link learners at distant sites with each other and with widely varied online resources long has been recognized for its unique potential to support instruction and enhance learning (*U.S. News and World Report,* 1993; Marcus, 1995). These capabilities include getting access to information not available through local sources, developing research and study skills that will benefit students in all future learning, and providing multicultural activities without leaving the classroom. Some unique affective benefits have also been observed, including increased multicultural awareness as students of different cultures interact online (Roblyer, 1991) and enhanced communication skills when students correspond with each other (Cohen & Riel, 1989).

**Justifying technology use: Support for new instructional approaches.** The educational system is struggling to revamp its instructional goals and methods in preparation for the complex demands of life in the technology-driven 21st century (SCANS Report, 1992). Educators are beginning to look at technology resources to help make these new directions at once feasible and motivational to students. Several new instructional initiatives can benefit from applications of technology:

- **Cooperative learning.** As the traditional American cultural emphasis on individualism is seen as insufficient for the complex problem solving that lies ahead, there is increased emphasis on small-group instruction that involves cooperative learning. Many technology-based activities lend themselves to cooperative, small-group work: development of hypermedia products and special-purpose databases and research projects using online and offline databases and videodiscs and multimedia.

- **Shared intelligence.** An emerging definition for intelligence is termed *shared intelligence* or *distributed intelligence.* According to some theorists, the capabilities afforded by new technologies make the concept of intelligence as something that resides in each person's head too restrictive. "Intellectual partnership with computers suggests the possibility that resources enable and shape activity and do not reside in one or another agent but are genuinely distributed between persons, situations, and tools" (Polin, 1992, p. 7). Therefore, some educators hypothesize that the most important role for technology might be to change the goals of education as well as the measures of educational success.

- **Problem solving and higher-order skills.** Basic communications and mathematics skills remain essential, but so is the need to solve problems and think critically about complex issues. In addition, curriculum is beginning to reflect the belief that students need not master basic skills before going on to higher-level skills. The engaging qualities of technology resources such as multimedia and the Internet allow teachers to set complex, long-term goals that call for basic skills, thus motivating students to learn lower-level skills they need at the same time they acquire higher-level ones.

**Justifying technology use: Increased teacher productivity.** An important but often overlooked reason for using technology resources is to help teachers cope with their growing paperwork load. Teachers and organizations have recognized that if they spend less time on recordkeeping and preparation they can spend more time analyzing student needs and having direct contact with students. Teachers can become more productive through training in technology-based methods and quick access to accurate information that may help them meet individual needs. Many technology resources can help teachers increase their productivity: word processing, spreadsheet, database, gradebook, graphics, desktop publishing, instructional management, and test generator programs along with online communications between teachers (e-mail) and other online services.

**Justifying technology use: Required skills for an Information Age.** A final and most compelling reason for integrating technology into teaching and learning is the need for students to learn skills that will prepare them to become lifelong learners in an information society. Since the emergence of the Internet, many processes involved in locating and communicating information now involve some form of technology. Three kinds of competencies are becoming widely recognized as basic skills for citizens of an Information Age (Moursund, 1995).

***Technology literacy.*** Soloman (1995) says that "Technology for students is about economic competitiveness" (p. 67). The International Society for Technology in Education (ISTE), the group that recently collaborated with the National Council for the Accreditation of Teacher Education (NCATE) to develop educational technology standards for preservice programs, also developed the National Educational Technology (NET) Standards (ISTE, 1998) for K-12 students. Standards for all students are shown in Figure 1.5; standards specific to each grade level also are available. Both sets of standards are recognition that technology skills are becoming required job skills. Several states (e.g., North Carolina) are also establishing their own required technology skills for K-12 students. This trend makes it essential that teachers both model and teach the use of technology-based methods to their students.

***Information literacy.*** Although information literacy skills may be simply a subset of the technology literacy skills

**Figure 1.5    ISTE National K-12 Educational Technology Standards**

1. Basic operations and concepts. Students:

   demonstrate a sound understanding of the nature and operation of technology systems

   are proficient in the use of technology

2. Social, ethical, and human issues. Students:

   understand the ethical, cultural, and societal issues related to technology

   practice responsible use of technology systems, information, and software

   develop positive attitudes toward technology uses that support lifelong learning, collaboration, personal pursuits, and productivity

3. Technology productivity tools. Students:

   use technology tools to enhance learning, increase productivity, and promote creativity

   use productivity tools to collaborate in constructing technology-enhanced models, preparing publications, and producing other creative works

4. Technology communications tools. Students:

   use telecommunications to collaborate, publish, and interact with peers, experts, and other audiences

   use a variety of media and formats to communicate information and ideas effectively to multiple audiences

5. Technology research tools. Students:

   use technology to locate, evaluate, and collect information from a variety of sources

   use technology tools to process data and report results

   evaluate and select new information resources and technological innovations based on the appropriateness to specific tasks

6. Technology problem-solving and decision-making tools. Students:

   use technology resources for solving problems and making informed decisions

   employ technology in the development of strategies for solving problems in the real world

Source: Reprinted by permission of the International Society for Technology in Education.

described previously, some educators think they are so important they should receive special emphasis (Truett, 1996; Roblyer, 1998). Johnson and Eisenberg (1996) call them the "Big Six" skills: task definition, information-seeking strategies, location and access, use of information, synthesis, and evaluation. Although they pre-date the World Wide Web, the information explosion fostered by the Internet has made the Big Six skills more important to learning and more involved with technology. However, Roblyer (1998) notes that students seem to find the first three skills—the ones requiring use of technology procedures—more enjoyable and easier to do. It is the application and analysis tasks that present the most difficulty. However, all these skills appear likely to be essential ones.

*Visual literacy.* Like information literacy, visual literacy may be thought of as a subset of technology literacy. However, as our society relies more heavily on images and visual communication strategies, educators are beginning to emphasize the special need for better visual literacy skills (Christopherson, 1997; Roblyer, 1998). Christopherson says that a visually literate person can interpret, understand, and appreciate the meaning of visual messages; communicate more effectively through applying the basic principles and concepts of visual design; produce visual messages using the computer and other technology; and use visual thinking to conceptualize solutions to problems (p. 173).

Roblyer (1998) reports on research that correlates visual literacy skills to higher scores on intelligence tests and to later success in more technical vocational areas such as engineering. Christopherson observes that "students with visual communication skills are more marketable" (p. 174) but that these skills soon will be required rather than merely desirable. These reports create a powerful reason for teachers to integrate technology at early levels into students' communication methods.

## Looking Around, Looking Ahead: What Factors Shape the Current and Future Climate for Technology in Education?

As we have seen from our historical overview, educational technology is defined by the resources available at a given time and the ways educators apply them to solve educational problems. We have also seen that educational technology is set in a larger context of societal influences that shape its use and determine, to a large extent, the impact it will have. As the history of educational technology demonstrates, the field is most often driven by a combination of educational trends and priorities, economic factors, and the marketing efforts of individuals and companies. This section gives an

**Figure 1.6    The Educational Technology Tree of Knowledge**

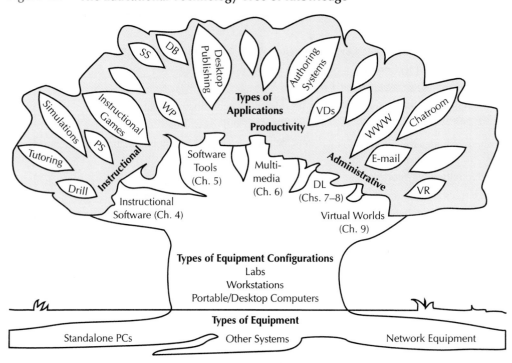

overview of current technology resources, how they are used, and societal factors and issues that shape their impact.

## Current Educational Technology Systems and Their Applications

To some extent, education's integration of technology-based methods reflects currently available equipment and materials and how they are used in other areas of society. However, as recent federal reports emphasize (President's Committee, 1997; U.S. Congress, 1995), many available devices and technology materials are in limited use in schools; they may be too expensive, schools may lack the infrastructure to support them, or teachers may be unfamiliar with and untrained in their use. Yet it is essential that educators know the potential—as well as the current reality—of technology in education. Technology resources most commonly used in education are shown in Figure 1.6.

**Equipment types.** The basic equipment types are standalone microcomputers, networks, and computer-related devices and systems such as Virtual Reality and I/O devices. (A basic overview of computer systems components such as hardware and software parts of a computer system, input/output devices, and memory concepts and how they work together is provided in the Appendix: Fundamentals of Microcomputer Systems.)

**Equipment configurations.** The various types of equipment may be configured as single units, workstations (a classroom learning station consisting of 2–3 microcomputers with a scanner and printer), labs, and movable media-

type carts. The benefits of each configuration are discussed in more detail in Chapter 2. (See Figure 1.7a for more details on equipment and equipment configurations common to education.)

**Software and materials.** These are discussed in more detail later in this text: instructional software (Chapter 4), tool software (Chapter 5), multimedia/hypermedia (Chapter 6), distance (linking to learn) applications (Chapters 7–8), and emerging resources (Chapter 9).

**Types of applications.** Computer applications in education may be categorized as:

- **Instructional.** Students use them to learn information or skills through demonstrations, examples, explanation, or problem solving.

- **Productivity.** Both teachers and students use them to support planning, materials development, and recordkeeping.

- **Administrative.** Administrators at school, state, and district levels use these to support recordkeeping and exchanges of information among various agencies.

**A special word about networks.** Networks are assuming an increasingly prominent role in education; thus, it is important to know something about their components and options. Networks can be extremely complex to select, use, and maintain. Most educators may consider them too technically complicated to master, but they at least should be aware of the primary components and the terminology used by networking experts. Most of these experts handle the complexity of network architecture by thinking and talking

**Figure 1.7a  Current Equipment and Equipment Configurations Used in Education**

| Equipment Categories | Types of Equipment | Examples | TYPICAL CONFIGURATIONS | | | | Typical Uses |
|---|---|---|---|---|---|---|---|
| | | | Single Units | Workstations | Labs | Carts | |
| Standalone microcomputers | Portable units | | | | | | |
| | Laptop computers | Macintosh Powerbook, IBM Thinkpad | X | X | X | | Instruction, productivity |
| | Handheld palmtop computers | Palm III | X | | | | Productivity |
| | Desktop microcomputers | IBM Pentium II, Macintosh G3 | X | X | X | X | Instruction, productivity, multimedia development |
| Networks | Local area networks (LANs) | Jostens Learning or CCC ILSs, or computers networked in a school | | | X | | Integrated Learning Systems (ILSs), multimedia development, Internet access, and administrative tasks |
| | Metropolitan area networks (MANs) | A city-wide network of connected computers | | | | | Connections among school computers in schools throughout a city |
| | Wide area networks (WANs) | Interconnected LANs or MANs | | | | | Connections among computers and networks for information exchange, e-mail, distance learning management, and delivery |
| Related devices and systems | Videodisc players: Primarily Levels I and III | Pioneer Laserdisc | X | | | X | Instruction, multimedia development |
| | Virtual reality systems | NASA training systems | X | | | | Instruction, R&D projects; simulated activities (flight simulators) |
| | Graphing calculators | TI graphing calculator | X | | X | | |
| | Input devices | Scanners, barcode readers, etc. | | | | | Used with various computer systems |
| | Output devices | Printers, plotters, projection panels, etc. | | | | | Used with various computer systems |

Figure 1.7b   **An Overview of Networks Used in Education**

| Types of Components | Description |
|---|---|
| Topologies | The physical layout of a network (how the parts relate to each other) |
| Star |  |
| Bus | 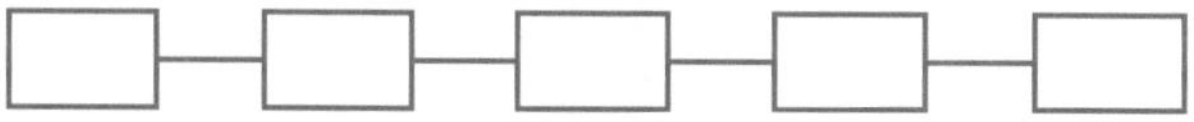 |
| Ring | 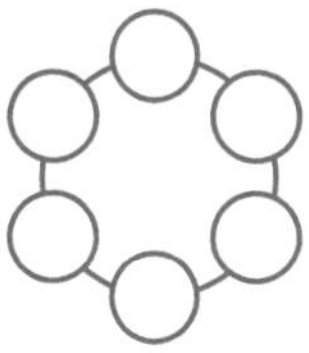 |
| Hybrids | 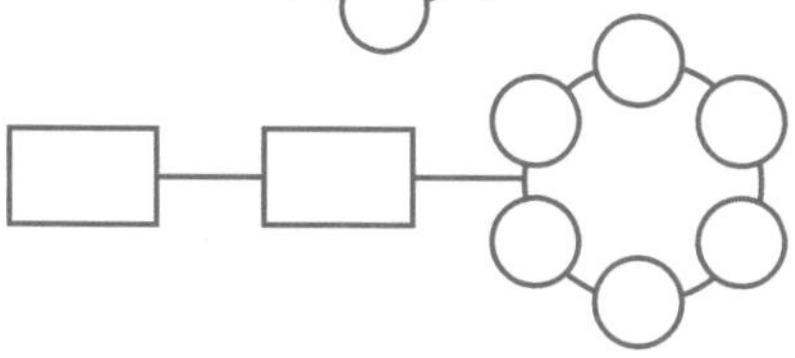 |
| Network architectures | The various designs for how networks transmit information |
| Token Ring | An older architecture used for smaller networks with fewer users |
| ARCnet | Older but "persistent" architecture; has had some updates to maintain compatibility with newer technology |
| Ethernet | Currently in most common use; constantly being updated for compatibility with newer technology |
| Asynchronous Transfer Mode (ATM) | A newer network architecture, but allows fast transmitting of data; may be the "architecture of the future" |
| Types of connecting devices | Network components that connect parts of a network or handle traffic among components |
| Repeaters, concentrators, and hubs | Devices placed at various central points to connect computers in different parts of the same network |
| Routers and bridges | Devices used to organize the traffic among users on a network |
| Types of connecting methods/media | Various types of "roads" to allow transmitting data among network users |
| Wireless | Computers in a network send data as transmitted signals rather than those carried by cable |
| Cabling | Physical wiring used to connected parts of a network |
| Coaxial | Used primarily in cable TV and certain types of networks; can transfer signals with minimal interference |
| Twisted pair | Telephone lines; often used to transfer signals between modems on microcomputers |
| Fiber optic | Glass strands with plastic coating, plus plastic covering; allows sending large amounts of data at high speeds |
| Communication lines | Allow faster, more versatile communication compared to ordinary telephone lines |
| ISDN (Integrated Services Digital Network) | Fast: sends voice, TV, computer signals on same line at 128 kilobits per second (128 kbps) |
| T1 | Faster: Same as ISDN but at 1.5 megabits per second (1.5 Mbps) |
| Cable modem and fiber optic cabling | Fastest: Organizes and sends signals among computers via fiber optics at 10 megabytes per second (10 Mbps) |

about them in terms of the seven-layer Open System Interconnection (OSI) Model (Kee, 1994), designed by an international standards committee and approved in 1980 by the Institute of Electrical and Electronic Engineers (IEEE). This model helps engineers communicate with each other, but educators will probably find Nance's (1997) introduction to networking easier to understand and more helpful. (See Figure 1.7b for a description of network components.)

## Today's Big Issues in Education and Technology: Societal, Cultural/Equity, Educational, and Technical

One of the things that makes teaching so challenging is that it goes on in an environment that mirrors—and sometimes magnifies—some of society's most profound and problematic issues. Adding computers to this mix makes the situation even more complex. Yet to integrate technology successfully into their teaching, educators must recognize and be prepared to work in this environment with all of its subtleties and complexities. Some of today's important issues and their implications for technological trends in education are described here and summarized in Figure 1.8. (Chapter 2 gives recommendations for addressing these issues in ways that help assure technology integration will have the maximum positive impact on teaching and learning.)

**Societal issues.** Economic, political, and social trends have a great impact on whether or not innovations take hold, or have limited acceptance, or are ignored completely. At this time, these trends are generating strong pro- and anti-technology views:

- **Pro-technology movements in society.** Increasing costs of education (especially teacher salaries) and dissatisfaction with current education systems have made us look closely at what technology may do to make teaching and learning more cost-effective. Many decision makers and funding agencies see distance learning as a means of decreasing the costs of delivering a quality education. Educational institutions tend to see it as an opportunity for increasing their share of the student market (Sherritt, 1996). Thus, distance learning as a delivery system has become much more popular than, say, computer software used on standalone computers or even networked systems. Also, many institutions feel that computers play such an important part in learning that they should be required student purchases, a trend that is being analyzed regarding its implications for lower-income students who may have trouble affording their purchase and upkeep. But it is evident that technology, both as a tool and an instructional delivery system, is enjoying unprecedented widespread support at all levels of education. This support especially is evident in the increased federal funding earmarked for technology in current and anticipated budgets.

- **Anti-technology movements in society.** The growing popularity of technology is paralleled by a view that some costs of technology outweigh its benefits. Critics point out that ordinary activities like washing clothes and enjoying music are complicated by the pervasive presence of computers

because more and more devices are computer-driven and thus susceptible to computer error. Increased communications made possible by e-mail, cellular phones, and fax machines mean a person can never be alone or out of the reach of authority—a situation many feel runs counter to the freedom and independence that symbolize the American lifestyle. Some feel that increased technology fuels a trend toward moral decay and see "cyberspace as an electronic red-light district" (Young, 1998)—an environment that nurtures cyber-porn and cyberpunk. A Luddite-like backlash against the onslaught of technology in society has been documented (Quittner, 1995), and a parallel backlash exists in education. Berube (1998) cautions that educators who are "teaching 10,000 students ... over the Internet" (p. B5) cannot give the personal, individual contact that is the most valuable part of an education. Some like Oppenheimer (1997) believe that school districts are cutting programs—music, art, physical education—that enrich children's lives to make room for this dubious nostrum (p. 45). How much counter-technology views will influence support for technology in education is unknown at this time, but educators must be aware that they exist and that they can exert a powerful influence on the level of local support that technology integration could receive.

**Cultural and equity issues.** Four kinds of factors that reflect the complex racial and cultural fabric of our society continue to have a great impact on technology use. As Molnar pointed out in his landmark 1978 article "The Next Great Crisis in American Education: Computer Literacy," the power of technology is a two-edged sword, especially for education. While it presents obvious potential for changing education and empowering teachers and students, technology also may further divide members of our society along socioeconomic, ethnic, and cultural lines and widen the gender gap. Teachers will lead the struggle to make sure technology use promotes, rather than conflicts with, the goals of a democratic society. Factors that must be considered include economic bias, multicultural issues, gender bias, and accommodations for students' special needs.

*Economic and ethnic inequity.* Some evidence supports Molnar's prediction that students with initial educational advantages will get more access to technology resources than those who could use the extra help. Demographic studies by Becker (1985, 1986a, and 1986b) confirmed the predictable correlation between school districts' socioeconomic levels and their levels of microcomputer resources. As Lockard, Abrams, and Many (1994) pointed out, this discrepancy is to be expected since "Computers only call further attention to the fact that schools in the U.S. are anything but equal. Inequities affect everything from basic supplies such as paper and pencils to library resources and even the quality of teachers" (p. 411). They observe that students from wealthier families are also far more likely to have computers and other technology resources at home than those from poorer families. All of these conditions are well-documented (Sanders & Stone, 1986; Neuman, 1991).

Evidence of the educational and/or economic crises that Molnar predicted has been more difficult to obtain.

**Figure 1.8    Current Trends and Issues Shaping the Use of Technology in Education**

| Types of Issues Having Impact on Technology in Education | Topics Under Each Issue | Current Issues Having Impact on Technology in Education | Implications for Technology in Education |
| --- | --- | --- | --- |
| Societal | Economic trends | Higher education costs | Distance learning emphasis to make education more cost-effective |
| | Political trends | Politicians call for lower-cost, more effective education | More reliance on DL and other technologies to increase consistency of quality, stretch scarce resources |
| | Social trends | Recognition of need for technology literacy | Computers becoming a required student purchase |
| | | Increased communications results in less privacy | Possible suspicion of technology-delivered education |
| | | Growing popular distrust of technology | Possible suspicion of technology-delivered education |
| Cultural/Equity | Economic/ Ethnic | Lower income schools equals less access to computers | Low-income students must have equal access to technology |
| | | More minority students in lower income schools | Minority students must have equal access to technology |
| | Multicultural | "Computer culture" is pervasive in society | Students must use computers regardless of cultural bias |
| | Gender | Technology remains a male-dominated area | Females' use of computers in education must increase |
| | Special needs | Special devices and methods can allow special needs students equal access to technology but are expensive to obtain and implement | Disabled students must receive equal access to technology regardless of high costs to educational system |
| Educational | Directed versus constructivist views | Directed uses of technology (drill, tutorial) are proven effective but often considered passé | Demonstrated effective technology uses may be discarded |
| | | Constructivist uses are emphasized but little evidence exists on their effectiveness | More research needed on newer technology uses |
| | Single-subject versus interdisciplinary | Past emphasis on teaching subjects in isolation | Continued emphasis on use of single skill software |
| | | Current trend toward integrated curriculum or merging several subjects into one activity | Increasing use of multimedia and other technologies that support more complex, interdisciplinary activities |
| Technical | Rapid change | Technology changes too quickly for teachers to keep up | The latest technologies are in limited use in education |
| | | Educators cannot afford most current technology | Schools usually have out-of-date equipment, materials |
| | Complexity | Teacher training is not keeping up with technology developments | Majority of teachers have insufficient training in technology materials and uses |
| | | Schools lack the infrastructure to keep up with new technologies | Schools cannot take advantage of newest, most powerful technological developments |

Widespread recognition of the need for computer literacy as conceived in 1982 never really emerged; indeed, no definition of computer literacy ever was established. However, it seems logical that students who have more access to computers also will have better, more efficient learning tools at their disposal; this access seems likely to become increasingly important as technological learning tools increase in power. Use of technology tools may also logically correlate to students' ability to enter mathematics, science, and technical areas such as engineering. Despite the lack of concrete evidence of an economic impact, the possibility seems certain that poorer students could be hampered in their learning (and therefore earning) potential due to their unequal access to technology tools.

The same problems with differences in technology access between economic subgroups also may apply to ethnic groups. Engler reported that the number of course prerequisites for computer programming studies (usually in mathematics classes) often increase as the percentage of minority enrollment increases. Although this may be an unintended inequity, minority students clearly do not have the same access to these courses as their white peers have. Trotter (1997) said that the results of a study by the Educational Testing Services show that "The most needy students are getting the least access to technology" (p. 1). According to a study reported by Miller, in 1998, the technology gap may be narrowing for Hispanic students, but remains wide between whites and African-Americans. Another study by Hoffman and Novak (1998) confirms that African-Americans are less likely than whites to have a computer at home (44 percent versus 29 percent), although more likely to have access to one at work.

Data show clearly that minorities continue to be underrepresented in the fields of mathematics, science, and engineering. Though less access to technology in K-12 schools may not have caused this problem, it clearly has the potential to make it worse and prolong its effects.

*Multicultural inequity.* Roblyer, Dozier-Henry, and Burnette (1996) describe several current uses of technology related to multicultural education, including telecommunications activities to promote communications among people of different cultures; applications that address the special language, visual, and experience needs of ESL and ESOL students; and multimedia applications with examples that enhance understanding of cultures. But they also describe several culture-related problems related to technology use. For example, "the Western idea of progress is the more technology, the better! However, … the reverence with which technology is held in the U. S. may be in direct contradiction to the perceptions of cultures that are heavily relationship oriented" (Roblyer, Dozier-Henry, & Burnette, 1996, p. 9). These authors also acknowledge the existence of a growing counter-computer culture in the United States that is based on social, psychological, and even religious grounds.

They also observe an over-reliance on technology to achieve the goals of multicultural education. They find that while technology can be helpful (making students aware of cultures other than their own, creating an interest in interacting with people of other cultures, and teaching about common attributes of all cultures despite their many differences), the next steps are more difficult because they require accepting, learning from, and appreciating people of other cultures. Schools must build upon the relatively superficial activities of tele-pals and learning about various foods and holidays in other cultures. Technology may

have a limited role in this deeper and more meaningful study.

Recent findings by Hoffman and Novak (1998) raise the issue of whether cultural factors help determine desire or willingness to use computers. Their studies found that even adjusting for income, whites were far more likely to have computers at home than African-Americans. Also, white students without computers at home were far more likely to have used the Web in other locations than were African-American students. As Hoffman and Novak said, these findings are in urgent need of further explication.

*Gender inequity.* Research has documented thoroughly the fact that girls tend to use computers less than boys (Bohlin, 1993; Sanders, 1993; Warren-Sims, 1997). This unequal proportion extends to vocational areas where computers are more frequently used: mathematics, science, and technical areas such as engineering and computer science (Sanders & Stone, 1986; Fredman, 1990; Holmes, 1991; Nelson & Watson, 1991; Engler, 1992; Fear-Fenn & Kapostacy, 1992; Stumpf & Stanley, 1997). A variety of reasons have been proposed for this disparity. Children may be reacting to stereotypes on television and in publications where men appear as primary users of computers. Depictions of women using computers tend to involve clerical tasks. The association of technology with machines, mathematics, and science—all stereotypically male areas—makes girls think of computers as masculine.

Gender bias may spring up in software that features competitive activities preferred more by males than females and an emphasis on violent video games that appeal more to boys. Finally, many blame subtle and overt classroom practices for making girls think that computers are not intended for them. These range from a lack of female teacher role models to teachers' assumptions that girls are simply not as interested in computer work. Whatever combination of factors is involved, females clearly are being excluded in large numbers from using the power of technology and jobs that require technology skills.

*Equity for special-needs students.* Neuman (1991) warns that technology and equity are not "inevitable partners." She lists factors that can inhibit equitable access to technology for rural, handicapped, and differently-abled students. (The special problems of rural schools in supplying their students with adequate technology resources are discussed in Chapter 2.) Thurston (1990) and Holland (1995) observe that rural schools have more severe equity problems of all types (economic, gender, and ethnic equity) than their urban counterparts.

A variety of adaptive devices have been designed to allow handicapped students to take advantage of the power of technology and to enhance personal freedom. Fredman (1991) says that "using the computer unlocks their potential. It is an enabling tool—allowing them to function as other students function without the barriers that their handicaps impose" (p. 47). However, Neuman (1991) and Engler (1992) report potential inequities in funding for these devices, and computer resources often are housed in locations that are not wheelchair accessible.

A more subtle kind of technology inequity has been observed with handicapped, lower-ability, and learning-disabled students (Fredman, 1991; Engler, 1992). Frequently, these students' uses of computers have been limited to low-level ones such as remedial drill and practice applications. The more powerful, higher-level applications such as hypermedia and Logo production work often are directed toward higher-ability students. This finding is especially disconcerting since many of these subgroups are also at-risk students who might profit from the motivation stimulated by higher-level uses.

**Educational issues.** Trends in the educational system are intertwined with trends in technology and society. Two kinds of issues currently of great interest to educators have special implications for the ways technology will be used in teaching and learning.

*The directed versus constructivist debate.* Chapter 3 describes two different ways of viewing teaching and learning and the implications of this dichotomy for technology applications. Roblyer (1996) refers to these contrasting views as the directed versus constructivist debate. Directed methods are more traditional, teacher-delivered ones, and technology uses matched to them have a longer, more established tradition of addressing certain kinds of educational problems. However, educators who promote constructivist teaching and learning strategies are critical of directed methods, calling them outmoded and unsuccessful in addressing education's most pressing problems. Proponents of directed methods feel that constructivist methods are unscientific and impractical. This debate is unfortunate, since the authors of this text feel strongly that each kind of strategy—and the technology uses matched to them—can be useful. Educators who take a position in favor of one strategy only may ignore many potentially useful applications.

*Interdisciplinary versus single-subject instruction.* The debate over interdisciplinary studies versus single-subject emphasis is not new in education. Plato thought that interdisciplinary instruction would allow a student to gain a broad understanding of complex ideas. Aristotle believed that pure knowledge of a discipline is necessary to gain true understanding. The debate over breadth versus depth continues today. The traditional structure of the curriculum usually has divided it into discrete subject areas, teaching each in isolation. Curriculum designers saw this as the most efficient way to assure instruction is given in specific skills for a variety of content areas. To a great extent, the integration of technology into the curriculum has followed a similar pattern. Software companies and developers have geared their products to traditional subject areas; this method of integrating technology persists widely today.

In recent years, however, curriculum development has reflected a tendency to link several disciplines in the context of a single unit or lesson. This trend toward interdisci-

plinary instruction may, in fact, reflect a much larger societal trend as people recognize that systems work much better when there are connections between components. Teachers who become more comfortable with technology in their classrooms seem to take more flexible, even experimental, approaches to teaching (Sheingold & Hadley, 1990). This trend, coupled with a concerted effort by many software companies to offer products that model subject-area integration, portends an integrated environment for technology in curriculum.

**Technical issues.** As Chapter 9 documents, technology changes so quickly that many businesses and industries whose survival depends on anticipating technological change employ whole teams of people to keep up-to-date on various changes, anticipated changes, and the implications of these changes for their product or service (Remnick, 1997). The "business of education" also will be affected by changing technology, but educational organizations are much less equipped to anticipate and cope with change. Teachers have little time for training in new applications or methods for integrating them—even if they could afford them. In addition, schools currently lack the infrastructure to allow access to new applications (President's Committee, 1997). In addition, technology use in recent years has increased in technical complexity; a prime example is the increasing dependence on networks. Networks are becoming recognized as a way of connecting people with each other and with resources and as a means of increasing the power and usefulness of standalone machines. Although a powerful solution, networks are so technically complex that most educators find it difficult to comprehend enough about them to make good decisions on their many options and uses.

The answer seems to lie in adopting two strategies. First, all technology-using educators should understand network basics such as the types of networks available, their most common uses, and the most common components and connection methods. (See Figure 1.7b.) Second, those tasked with maintaining an existing network either must assign or become a network administrator, or an expert in the functions of that particular system.

### New Challenges and the Skills to Deal with Them

Clearly, 21st century educators will have to deal with issues that their predecessors could not even have imagined and must have skills and knowledge not previously recognized. Some of these are:

**Technology skills for all teachers.** The National Council for Accreditation (NCATE), the agency responsible for accrediting colleges of education, has joined with ISTE in not only establishing standards for teaching about technology in education (see Figure 1.9), but saying that schools of education should increase their emphasis on the use of technology in teacher training (NCATE, 1997).

**Figure 1.9    ISTE/NCATE Required Technology Competencies for Educational Technology Leaders**

| Required Technology Competencies for All Teachers | Chapter Covered |
|---|---|
| Operate a computer system to use software successfully. | Appendix |
| Evaluate and use computers and other technologies to support instruction. | 4, 7 |
| Explore, evaluate, and use technology-based applications for communications, presentations, and decision making. | 5–6 |
| Apply current instructional principles and research and appropriate assessment practices to the use of computers and related technologies. | 3, 10–15 |
| Demonstrate knowledge of uses of computers for problem solving, data collection, information management, communications, presentations, and decision making. | 5–7 |
| Develop student learning activities that integrate computers and technology for a variety of student grouping strategies and for diverse student populations. | 2–3, 10–15 |
| Evaluate, select, and integrate computer/technology-based instruction in the curriculum in a subject area and/or grade level. | 10–15 |
| Demonstrate knowledge of uses of multimedia, hypermedia, and telecommunications tools to support instruction. | 7–8 |
| Demonstrate skills in using productivity tools for professional and personal use, including word processing, database management, spreadsheet software, and print/graphic utilities. | 5–6 |
| Demonstrate knowledge of equity, ethical, legal, and human issues of computing and technology use as they relate to society, and model appropriate behavior. | 1–2 |
| Identify resources to keep current in applications of computing and related technologies in education. | 1–2 |
| Use technology to access information to enhance personal and professional productivity. | 5–8 |
| Apply computers and related technologies to facilitate emerging roles of learners and educators. | 7–9 |

Source: Reprinted by permission of the International Society for Technology in Education.

**Staying abreast of local and societal attitudes.** Educators must stay in tune with pro- and anti-technology sentiments by reading the local indicators (newspaper letters, columns, and stories; remarks by local leaders) that signal the support (or lack of support) for technology integration. Then they must help foster support for their planned integration strategies by establishing contacts with local forums and influential leaders and seeking their assistance with the plans.

**Using strategies to ensure equity.** Every teacher must acknowledge a personal responsibility to ensure equitable use of technology for everyone, including economically disadvantaged, minority, female, and differently-abled students. Pro-active educators who want to be agents for change and progress will identify inequities that present the greatest problems for their particular school or district and make these issues the focus of special activities.

**Matching integration strategies with needs.** Technology-using teachers must recognize that integration strategies differ according to which instructional model is followed. Effective strategies are the result of analyzing which kind of instructional approach is needed (directed, constructivist, single-subject, interdisciplinary) for each learning situation and using appropriate technology resources and integration strategies that help carry out the approach.

In addition to these issues, skills and attitudes that are necessary for teachers to stay current on future technology developments are described in Chapter 9.

# Exercises

## Record and Apply What You Have Learned

**Activity 1.1: Chapter 1 Self-Test** To review terms and concepts in this chapter, take the Chapter 1 self-test. Select Chapter 1 from the front page of the companion Web site (located at http://www.prenhall.com/roblyer), then choose the *Multiple Choice* module.

**Activity 1.2: Portfolio Activities** The following activities will help you add to your professional portfolio. To complete these activities online and save or submit the materials electronically, select Chapter 1 from the front page of the companion Web site (http://www.prenhall.com/roblyer), then choose the *Portfolio* module.

***Overview of the Field***  Demonstrate your knowledge about the various kinds of equipment, software, and media used in educational technology and understand how these relate to each other by preparing your own overview of the field like the one shown in Figure 1.6. Instead of a "tree metaphor," select your own way of showing the resources (chart, concept map, or picture of an educational technology building).

***Professional Skills***  Using word processing or other software, prepare your own checklist of the ISTE competencies given in this chapter. As you acquire each competency throughout this course and other experiences, indicate on your checklist where and how you learned this skill.

**Activity 1.3: Questions for Thought and Discussion** These questions may be used for small group or class discussion or may be subjects for individual or group activities. To take part in these discussions online, select Chapter 1 from the front page of the companion Web site (http://www.prenhall.com/roblyer), then choose the *Message Board* module.

- In his book *Silicon Snake Oil,* Clifford Stoll says that cyberspace is … a nonexistent universe … a soluble tissue of nothing (Quittner, 1995, p. 56) and that life in the real world is far more interesting, far more important, far richer than anything you'll ever find on a computer screen (p. 57). What information from Chapter 1 might help you respond to this statement?

- Saettler (1990) said that "Computer information systems are not just objective recording devices. They also reflect concepts, hopes, beliefs, attitudes" (p. 539). What concepts, hopes, beliefs, and attitudes do our past and current uses of technology reflect?

- Richard Clark's now-famous comment about the impact of computers on learning was that the best current evidence is that media are mere vehicles that deliver instruction but do not influence student achievement any more than the truck that delivers our groceries causes changes in our nutrition (Clark, 1983, p. 445). Why do you think this statement has had such a dramatic impact on the field of educational technology?

**Activity 1.4: Collaborative Activities**  The following projects are designed for small groups.

***Educational Technology Defined***  Prepare an overview of the four areas of emphasis in educational technology: media, systems, vocational training, and computers. For each emphasis, explain what the emphasis is, why it is an important aspect, what people and groups are involved, and what impact it has on how education uses technology.

***History of Computers in Education: People and Projects*** Prepare a report on one of the following topics:

- Five People Who Changed Education with Technology (choose your own top 5)

- Five Things We Learned from the Mainframe Era of Educational Technology

- Five Ways Microcomputers Changed the Face of Education

- Five Important Lessons We (Should Have) Learned from Past Uses of Technology in Education

***Technology in Education: Issues and Concerns***  Prepare and carry out a debate for the class on one of the following topics:

- Do Schools Need More Computers or More Teachers?

- Is Technology Further Widening the Gap Between Rich and Poor?

- Should Technology Resources Be Focused on Basic Skills or Higher-Level Thinking?

**Activity 1.5: Integrating Technology Across the Curriculum Activities**  Use the *Integrating Technology Across the Curriculum* CD-ROM packaged with this textbook to complete the following exercise:

Which of the "branches" (e.g., instructional software, software tools, multimedia) of the "educational technology tree" have the most applications in education? You can get an idea of the answer to this by searching for lessons using the Technologies descriptors. Go to *Find Lesson Plan* and click on *Find by Criteria.* Under the *Technologies* descriptor, select ones such as "tutorial," "spreadsheet," or "multimedia" and click *Search.* Count the numbers of lessons listed under each one.

# References

## Technology Effectiveness Research

Bialo, E. & Sivin, J. (1989). Computers and at-risk youth: Software and hardware that can help. *Classroom Computer Learning, 9*(5), 48–55.

Clark, R. (1983). Reconsidering research on learning from media. *Review of Educational Research, 53*(4), 445–459.

Clark, R. (1985). Evidence for confounding in computer-based instruction studies: Analyzing the meta-analyses. *Educational Communications and Technology Journal, 33*(4), 249–262.

Clark, R. (1991). When researchers swim upstream: Reflections on an unpopular argument about learning from media. *Educational Technology, 31*(2), 34–40.

Clark, R. E. (1994). Media will never influence learning. *Educational Technology Research and Development, 42*(2), 21–29.

Kozma, R. (1991). Learning with media. *Review of Educational Research, 61*(2), 179–211.

Kozma, R. (1994). Will media influence learning? Reframing the debate. *Educational Technology Research and Development, 42*(2), 5–17.

Kozma, R. & Croninger, R. (1992). Technology and the fate of at-risk students. *Education and Urban Society, 24*(4), 440–453.

Roblyer, M., Castine, W. & King, F. J. (1988). *Assessing the impact of computer-based instruction: A review of recent research.* New York: Haworth Press.

Roblyer, M. (1992). Computers in education. In G. Bitter (Ed.), *Macmillan encyclopedia of computers.* New York: Macmillan.

## Rationales for Using Technology

Arnone, M. & Grabowski, B. (1991). Effects of variations in learner control on children's curiosity and learning from interactive video. Proceedings of Selected Research Presentations at the Annual Convention of the AECT (ERIC Document Reproduction No. ED 334 972).

Buchholz, W. (1991). A learning activity for at-risk ninth through twelfth grade students in creating a computer-generated children's storybook design. Master's thesis, New York Institute of Technology (ERIC Document Reproduction No. ED 345 695).

Christopherson, J. (1997). The growing need for visual literacy at the university. Proceedings of the International Visual Literacy Association 1996 Annual Meeting, Cheyenne, WY (ERIC Document Reproduction No. 408 963)

Cohen, M. & Riel, M. (1989). The effect of distant audiences on children's writing. *American Educational Research Journal, 26*(2), 143–159.

*Educational Technology* (1992), *32,* 9.

*Electronic Learning* (1990), *10,* 1.

*Electronic Learning* (1990), *11,* 1.

Franklin, S. (1991). Breathing life into reluctant writers: The Seattle Public Schools laptop project. *Writing Notebook, 8*(4), 40–42.

Gagné, R. (1965). *The conditions of learning.* New York: Holt, Rinehart & Winston.

International Society for Technology in Education. (1998). *National educational technology standards for students.* Eugene, OR: ISTE.

Kozma, R. (1991). Learning with media. *Review of Educational Research, 61*(2), 179–211.

Kozma, R. (1994). Will media influence learning? Reframing the debate. *Educational Technology Research and Development, 42*(2), 5–17.

Kozma, R. & Croninger, R. (1992). Technology and the fate of at-risk students. *Education and Urban Society, 24*(4), 440–453.

Kurshan, B. (1990). Educational telecommunications connections for the classroom. Part I. *The Computing Teacher, 17*(6), 30–35.

LaRoue, A. (1990). The M.A.P. shop: Integrating computers into the curriculum for at-risk students. *Florida Educational Computing Quarterly, 2*(4), 9–21.

Marcus, S. (1995). E-meliorating student writing. *Electronic Learning, 14*(4), 18–19.

McArthur, D. & Stasz, C. (1990). An intelligent tutor for basic algebra. (ERIC Document Reproduction No. ED 334 069)

McNeil, B. & Wilson, K. (1991). Meta-analysis of interactive video instruction: A 10-year review of achievement effects. *Journal of Computer-Based Instruction, 18*(1), 1–6.

Minnesota State Department of Education. (1989). Computer tools for teachers: A report (ERIC Document Reproduction No. ED 337 130).

Moursund, D. (1995). The basics do change. *Learning and Leading with Technology, 23*(1), 6–7.

Pask-McCartney, C. (1989). A discussion about motivation. Proceedings of Selected Research Presentations at the Annual Convention of the AECT (ERIC Document Reproduction No. ED 308 816).

Polin, L. (1992). Looking for love in all the wrong places? *The Computing Teacher, 20*(2), 6–7.

Relan, A. (1992). Motivational strategies in computer-based instruction: Some lessons from theories and models of motivation. Proceedings of Selected Research Presentations at the Annual Convention of the AECT (ERIC Document Reproduction No. ED 348 017).

Roblyer, M. (1991). Electronic hands across the ocean: The Florida-England connection. *The Computing Teacher, 19*(5), 16–19.

Roblyer, M. D. (1998). The other half of knowledge: Information literacy skills. *Learning and Leading with Technology, 25*(6), 54-55.

Roblyer, M. D. (1998). Visual literacy: Views on a new rationale for teaching with technology. *Learning and Leading with Technology, 26*(2), 51–54.

SCANS (Secretary's Commission on Achieving Necessary Skills) Report (1992). Washington, DC: U.S. Department of Labor.

Schank, R. (1997). *Virtual learning: A revolutionary approach to building a highly skilled workforce.* New York: McGraw-Hill.

Soloman, G. (1995). Planning for technology. *Learning and Leading with Technology, 23*(1), 66–67.

Summers, J. (1990–1991). Effect of interactivity upon student achievement, completion intervals, and affective perceptions. *Journal of Educational Technology Systems, 19*(1), 53–57.

Taylor, D. (1989). Communications technology for literacy work with isolated learners. *Journal of Reading, 32*(7), 634–639.

Tibbs, P. (1989). Video creation for junior high language arts. *Journal of Reading, 32*(6), 558–559.

Truett, C. (1996). Information literacy: When computers aren't enough. *Learning and Leading with Technology, 23*(5), 65–67.

Volker, R. (1992). Applications of constructivist theory to the use of hypermedia. Proceedings of Selected Research Presentations at the Annual Convention of the AECT (ERIC Document Reproduction No. ED 348 037).

## Today's Big Issues in Education and Technology

Becker, H. (1985). The second national survey of instructional uses of school computers: A preliminary report (ERIC Document Reproduction Service No. ED 274 307).

Becker, H. (1986a). Instructional uses of school computers. Reports from the 1985 National Survey. Issue No. 1 (ERIC Document Reproduction Service No. ED 274 319).

Becker, H. (1986b). Instructional uses of school computers. Reports from the 1985 National Survey. Issue No. 3 (ERIC Document Reproduction Service No. ED 279 303).

Berube, M. (1998, March 27). Why inefficiency is good for universities. *Chronicle of Higher Education, 44*(29), B4–B5.

Bohlin, R. (1993). Computers and gender difference: Achieving equity. *Computers in the Schools, 9*(2–3), 155–166.

Dozier-Henry, O. (1995). Technology and cultural diversity: The "uneasy alliance." *Florida Technology in Education Quarterly, 7*(2), 11–16.

Engler, P. (1992). Equity issues and computers. In G. Bitter (Ed.), *Macmillan encyclopedia of computers.* New York: Macmillan.

Fear-Fenn, M. & Kapostacy, K. (1992). Math + science + technology = Vocational preparation for girls: A difficult equation to balance. Columbus, OH: Ohio State University, Center for Sex Equity (ERIC Document Reproduction No. 341 863).

Fredman, A. (1990). *Yes, I can. Action projects to resolve equity issues in educational computing.* Eugene, OR: International Society for Technology in Education.

Holland, H. (1995). Needles in a haystack. *Electronic Learning, 14*(7), 26–28.

Holmes, N. (1991). The road less traveled by girls. *School Administrator, 48*(10, 11, 14), 16–20.

Johnson, D. & Eisenberg, M. (1996). Computer literacy and information literacy: A natural combination. *Emergency Librarian, 23*(5), 12–16.

Lockard, J., Abrams, P., & Many, W. (1994). *Microcomputers for 21st century educators.* New York: HarperCollins.

Miller, L. (1998, April 30). Hispanic "tech-gap" less gaping. *USA Today.*

Miller-Lachman, L. (1994). Bytes and bias: Eliminating cultural stereotypes from educational software. *School Library Journal, 40*(11), 26–30.

Molnar, A. (1978). The next great crisis in American education: Computer literacy. *AEDS Journal, 12*(1), 11–20.

Naisbitt, J. (1984). *MegaTrends.* New York: Warner Books.

Nelson, C. & Watson, J. (1991). The computer gender gap: Children's attitudes, performance, and socialization. *The Journal of Educational Technology Systems, 19*(4), 345–353.

Neuman, D. (1991). Beyond the chip: A model for fostering equity. *School Library Media Quarterly, 18*(3),158–164.

North Carolina Public Schools. (1997). Long-Range State Technology Plan. [Available at: http://www.ncdpi.org/Tech.Plan/Long-Range.Tech.Plan.html]

Polin, L. (1992). Looking for love in all the wrong places? *The Computing Teacher. 20*(2), 6–7.

Roblyer, M., Dozier-Henry, O., & Burnette, A. (1996). Technology and multicultural education: The "uneasy alliance." *Educational Technology 35*(3), 5–12.

Sanders, J. (1993). Closing the gender gap. *Executive Educator, 15*(9), 32–33.

Sanders, J. & Stone A. (1986). The neuter computer. Computers for girls and boys. New York: Neal Schuman Publishers.

Stumpf, H. & Stanley, J. (1997). The gender gap in advanced placement computer science. *College Board Review, 181,* 22–27.

Thurston, L. (1990). Girls, computers, and amber waves of grain: Computer equity programming for rural teachers. Paper presented at the Annual Conference of the National Women's Studies Association (ERIC Document Reproduction Service No. ED 319 660).

Young, J. (1998, March 23). "Techno-realists" hope to enrich debate over policy issues in cyberspace. *Chronicle of Higher Education* [online].

**Other References**

Ausubel, D. (1968). *Educational psychology: A cognitive view.* New York: Holt, Rinehart & Winston.

Carlitz, R. & Lenz, M. (1995). Standards for school networking. *T.H.E. Journal, 22*(9), 71–74.

Collis, B. (1988). *Computers, curriculum, and whole-class instruction: Issues and ideas.* Belmont, CA: Wadsworth.

Cuban, L. (1986). *Teachers and machines: The classroom use of technology since the 1920s.* New York: Teachers College Press.

Esquivel, E. (1998). Infrastructure requirements for schools. *T.H.E. Journal, 25*(11), 14A–16A.

Hazari, S. (1995). Multi-protocol LAN design and implementation: A case study. *T.H.E. Journal, 22*(9), 80–86.

Heinich, R., Molenda, M., Russell, J., & Smaldino, S. (1997). *Instructional media and technologies for learning.* Englewood Cliffs, NJ: Merrill, an imprint of Prentice Hall.

Hill, M. (1993). Chapter 1 revisited: Technology's second chance. *Electronic Learning, 12*(1), 27–32.

Hoffman, D. & Novak, T. (1998, April 17). Bridging the racial divide on the Internet. *Science,* online version.

Kee, E. (1994). *Networking illustrated.* Indianapolis, IN: Que Corporation.

Lidke, D. (1992). History of computers. In G. Bitter (Ed.), *Macmillan encyclopedia of computers.* New York: Macmillan.

Molnar, A. (1978). The next great crisis in American education: Computer literacy. *T.H.E. Journal, 5*(4), 35–38.

Muffoletto, R. (1994).Technology and restructuring education: Constructing a context. *Educational Technology, 34*(2), 24–28.

Nance, B. (1997). *Introduction to networking.* Indianapolis, IN: Que Education and Training.

National Council for Accreditation of Teacher Education. (1997). *Technology and the new professional teacher. Preparing for the 21st century classroom.* Washington, DC: NCATE.

National Education Association Communications Survey. (1993). *Report of the findings.* Princeton, NJ: Princeton Survey Research Associates.

Niemiec, R. & Walberg, R. (1989). From teaching machines to microcomputers: Some milestones in the history of computer-based instruction. *Journal of Research on Computing in Education, 21*(3), 263–276.

Norris, W. (1977). Via technology to a new era in education. *Phi Delta Kappan, 58*(6), 451–459.

Oppenheimer, T. (1996, July). The computer delusion. *The Atlantic Monthly,* 45–62.

Papert, S. (1980). *Mindstorms: Children, computers, and powerful ideas.* New York: Basic Books.

Papert, S. (1986). Different visions of Logo. *Classroom Computer Learning, 7,* 46–49.

Petrusco, S. & Humes, V. (1994). Hybrid fiber/copper LAN meets school's 25-year networking requirements. *T.H.E. Journal, 21*(10), 86–90.

President's Committee of Advisors on Science and Technology. (1997, March). *Report to the President on the use of technology to strengthen K-12 education.* Washington, DC: Executive Office of the President of the United States.

Quittner, J. (1995). Back to the real World. *TIME, 145*(16), 56–57.

Remnick, D. (1997, October 20 and 27). The next magic kingdom: Future perfect. *The New Yorker,* 210–224.

Roblyer, M. (1990). The glitz factor. *Educational Technology, 30*(10), 34–36.

Roblyer, M. (1992). Computers in education. In G. Bitter (Ed.), *Macmillan encyclopedia of computers.* New York: Macmillan.

Roblyer, M. D. (1996). The constructivist/objectivist debate: Implications for instructional technology research. *Learning and Leading with Technology, 24*(2), 12–17.

Saettler, P. (1990). *The evolution of American educational technology.* Englewood, CO: Libraries Unlimited.

Sherritt, C. (1996). A fundamental problem with distance programs in higher education (ERIC Document Reproduction No. 389 906).

Trotter, A. (1997, May 21). Inequities in access to technology documented. *Education Week,* online version.

U.S. Congress, Office of Technology Assessment (1995). *Teachers and technology: Making the Connection.* OTA-EHR-616. Washington, DC: U.S. Government Printing Office.

# Chapter 2

## Planning and Implementation for Effective Technology Integration

"Let the ideas speak for themselves," more than one scientist told me, "and never mind the people involved." Alas, it isn't quite that simple.

Paula McCorduck, from *Machines Who Think* (1979)

### This chapter covers the following topics:

- How to develop long- and short-range plans required at three different levels for effective technology integration: education community, school, and teacher

- Issues and recommendations related to funding for technology purchases and uses

- Issues and concerns related to teacher training for technology

- How to address ongoing equity, ethical, and legal issues related to technology at school and district levels

- How to prepare a school environment for effective technology use

- Effective procedures for maintenance, security, and virus protection

- How to prepare a classroom environment for effective technology use

- Procedures teachers can use to design effective technology integration strategies

# Objectives

1. Identify personnel, issues, and concerns involved at each of three levels of planning and preparation for technology integration.

2. Be able to develop a sample district or school technology plan that addresses all elements required for effective technology implementation.

3. Recommend one or more effective strategies for obtaining funds to support technology purchases and uses.

4. Recommend an appropriate strategy for a teacher to deal with situations involving each of the following:

   - Making the most of scarce technology resources
   - Choosing hardware and/or software resources
   - Setting up physical spaces for and configuring computer resources
   - Maintaining facilities and equipment
   - Setting up appropriate security measures, including protection against viruses

5. Identify classroom preparation activities required for designing effective technology integration strategies.

The literature on educational technology is full of glowing promises of dramatic and meaningful improvements to classroom activities and outcomes. But the mere presence of technology is not an automatic guarantee for improved education. Despite its potential power, educational technology has had some well-documented, high-profile failures (Ferrell, 1986; Morehouse, Hoaglund, & Schmidt, 1987; The revolution that fizzled, 1991). Success with any technology is rarely serendipitous. Certain factors profoundly affect whether or not technology helps education take a leap forward or a pratfall. Furthermore, technology has its high-profile critics (Baines, 1997; Oppenheimer, 1997) and justifying the high costs of technology in education is becoming increasingly important.

This chapter describes three levels of planning that should be done to increase the likelihood that technology will have the desired impact on teaching and learning. There is, of course, overlap among these checklists, depending on the size of the schools and districts involved. But typically, the first level of planning is done by the education community, the second level of planning is done by each school, and the last level is done by individual teachers or teachers working in teams. Tasks involved in all three levels are shown in checklist form in Figure 2.1.

**Figure 2.1   A Checklist of Technology Planning and Preparation Tasks**

**Education Community Level Tasks**

___ 1. Identify and appoint members of a committee to develop a technology plan.

___ 2. Develop a technology plan that includes:

   - A vision for how technology will improve and restructure the system
   - A well-documented rationale for using technology resources
   - Description of the current status of technology
   - List of goals that describes a guiding framework for using technology
   - Description of activities to accomplish goals, including teacher training
   - Identify effective measures to address equitable access and use; ethical behavior of all staff, educators, and students
   - An evaluation plan for measuring progress toward goals
   - A budget that specifies annual amounts for technology

___ 3. Identify funding sources, including state and local sources and grants.

___ 4. Develop and publicize district/school position statements on ethical and legal use of technology resources.

**School Level Tasks**

___ 1. Put measures into place to optimize available resources.

___ 2. Select and place hardware and software to meet identified needs.

___ 3. Set up and publicize procedures for using computers in classrooms and labs.

___ 4. Set up procedures for maintaining and repairing equipment.

___ 5. Set up procedures to keep equipment and materials secure from vandalism and theft.

___ 6. Set up measures to prevent spread of viruses.

**Teacher Level Tasks**

___ 1. Match curriculum needs with technology resources.

___ 2. Plan activities that integrate technology into learning activities using available resources.

___ 3. Prepare an optimal classroom environment to support technology use.

___ 4. Prepare and test out equipment and technology materials prior to use by students.

___ 5. Prepare students to use technology.

___ 6. Try out and revise activities.

## Technology Planning and Preparation by the Education Community

Some decisions about the selection and use of technology resources are more cost-effective if made at the upper levels of an education system, such as by state resource coordinators or school district administrators. This maximizes the usefulness of activities such as obtaining equipment and software bids; hiring experts and consultants with specialized expertise; and documenting a plan for how schools will use technology, obtain funding for technology, and train teachers.

### Who Should Be Involved in Planning?

Before planning can begin, the planners must be identified. Most reports of first-hand experience with planning for technology (Apple Computer Company, 1991; Association for Media and Technology, 1991; See, 1992; Bruder, 1993; Dyrli & Kinnaman, 1994a; Wall, 1994; Brody, 1995; Bailey, 1997) recommend assigning the task to a technology planning committee made up of both educators and technology experts as well as representatives from all groups in the school or district. Dyrli and Kinnaman (1994a) and Brody (1995) point out that such committees are most effective when appointed by top-level administrators who give them authority to implement what they recommend. Kwajewski (1997) adds one more concern: educational leaders must view technology as a "core value" if it is to work effectively in the school system.

### Developing District and School Technology Plans

Setting appropriate goals and developing sound plans for reaching them are such common-sense prerequisites for success in any endeavor that it could be assumed that any technology project would follow a well-conceived plan. Sadly, this is not always the case. Surveys indicate that schools and districts often purchase technology resources without first adopting technology usage plans (Dyrli & Kinnaman, 1994a). Technology experts and technology-oriented educators generally agree that developing and maintaining a school-level and/or a district-level plan increases significantly the likelihood of receiving the full benefits of technology's potential for improving teaching, learning, and productivity. A technology plan helps a school or district ensure that its investment in technology pays expected dividends.

**Planning saves time and money.** A technology plan helps prevent purchases and activities that do not move the organization toward its goals and avoids wasteful duplication of efforts.

**Planning helps achieve goals.** Without a clear idea of what a technology initiative should accomplish, it is diffi-

cult to know if technology is achieving its goals and, if not, how to make changes. Technology plans require educators to set goals, periodically evaluate their progress toward achieving them, and revise them based on concrete evidence.

**Planning builds in support.** Planning for technology forces participation by key people from each group in the organization. They become acquainted with the potential benefits and are more likely to become advocates for technology, working to convince other members of their groups to use resources that become available.

**Planning strategies and steps.** Several good sources document the steps that a planning committee should follow to develop a sound technology plan. An excellent multimedia planning guide is IDE's *Technology Infusion Toolkit.* (See Figure 2.2 for sample.) Dyrli and Kinnaman (1994a) also describe a good sequence of planning steps, and Brody (1995) gives a well-prepared summary of planning steps and guidelines. A recommended sequence common to these and other sources includes the six steps show in Figure 2.3.

**Figure 2.2    Four Sample Screens from IDE's Technology Infusion Toolkit**

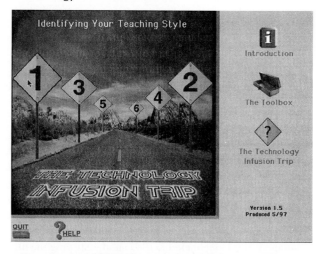

**Figure 2.2   *Continued***

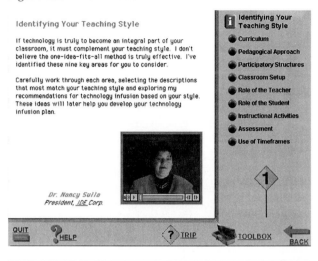

Source: Courtesy of IDE Corp. www.idecorp.com.

**Figure 2.3   A Checklist of Planning Steps**

___  **1.  Create a "merged vision"**

Envision potential applications of technology

Identify a clear statement of organization mission and philosophy

Focus on activities that will promote and reflect organization priorities

Research technology resources and activities that merge organization vision and technology benefits

___  **2.  Assess the current status**

Review organization's current uses of technology (with surveys, visits)

Present summary data in visual ways (charts and graphs)

___  **3.  Set goals**

Address instructional, administrative, and teacher productivity uses

Review previously developed plans

Review/reflect on potential goals, revise, and develop final goals

___  **4.  Develop activities**

Outline specific activities to take the organization from current to desired status (purchases, training, time frame for each)

Develop a presentation package to communicate the plan

___  **5.  Implement the plan**

Obtain approval and endorsement of key decision makers (school board, principal, and/or PTO)

Have someone (technology coordinator) carry out activities

___  **6.  Evaluate and revise the plan**

Do continuous monitoring of activities

Revise as necessary to keep compliant with organization goals

**Characteristics of good planning.** Apple (1991), See (1992), Dyrli and Kinnaman (1994a), Wall (1994), and Bailey (1997) offer good advice to assure effective completion of all phases of technology planning. Some important points to consider are summarized here.

- **Planning should continue at both district and school levels.** Some decisions are best made at the district level and some are best left for each school to consider; but plans at each level should coordinate with other plans. Dyrli and Kinnaman (1994a) recommend that each school designate a technology liaison/coordinator to act as the school's representative in a districtwide planning committee.

- **Involve teachers and other personnel at all levels.** To obtain widespread support for a plan, the planning team should include parents, community leaders, school and district administrators, and teachers. Involving teachers is especially important. Any technology plan must show where and how technology resources will fit into instructional plans for all grade levels and content areas. Just as curriculum plans require input from teachers, technology plans depend on direct guidance from those who will implement them.

- **Budget yearly amounts for technology purchases.** Technology changes too rapidly for schools to expect one-

time purchases of equipment or software to suffice. A technology plan should allow for yearly upgrades and additions to keep resources current and useful.

- **Make funding incremental.** Few schools' yearly budgets allow the purchase of all needed resources or teacher training. A plan should identify a specific amount to spend each year and a priority list of activities to fund over the life of the plan.

- **Emphasize teacher training.** Knowledgeable people are as important to a technology plan as up-to-date technology resources. Successful technology programs hinge on well-trained, motivated teachers. A technology plan should acknowledge and address this need with appropriate training activities. See (1992) recommends close coordination between technology training plans and staff development plans.

- **Apply technology to needs and integrate curriculum.** Effective planning focuses on the correct questions. For example, planners should ask: What are our current unmet needs and how can technology address them? Too many planners skip this question and jump to: How can we use this equipment and software? It is difficult to identify needs since the emergence of new technology has a way of changing them. Many educators did not realize they needed faster communications until the fax machine, e-mail, and cellular telephones became available. Curriculum integration should also focus on unmet needs. Technology should become an integral part of new methods to make education more efficient, exciting, and successful. Planners should ask: "What are we teaching now that we can teach better with technology?" and "What can we teach with technology that we could not teach before but that should be taught?"

- **Keep current and build in flexibility.** Both technology and users' opinions about how to implement technology change daily. Leading-edge technology solutions can become out-of-date soon after their development as more capable resources emerge and new research and information clarify what works best. To keep up with these changes, educators must constantly read and attend conferences, workshops, and meetings. Each school's and district's technology plan should address how it will obtain and use technology resources over a 3- to 5-year period (Mageau, 1990; Orlando, 1993). But any technology plan should be designed to incorporate new information and changing priorities through yearly reviews and revisions (See, 1992).

- **Avoid common pitfalls.** Wall (1994), Dyrli and Kinnaman (1994a), and Bailey (1997) note some common pitfalls to avoid:

  - Failing to link the organization's education goals to its technology planning goals

  - No clear focus for technology use

  - Preoccupation with overly detailed recordkeeping or surveys that obscure or overlook the big picture of technology use

  - Making plans too general (stating goals too vaguely) or too specific (requiring purchases of hardware that will become obsolete over time)

  - Making massive investments in untried, first-generation technology

  - Ill-defined processes to acquire hardware and software

  - Failure to provide necessary support systems such as procedures for storing and cataloging electronic software and media

Van Dam (1994) gives a down-to-earth description of one school's experience in renovating its facility to accommodate and promote the use of new technologies. Palazzo (1995) describes five great technology plans that won a planning contest sponsored by a magazine.

## Funding for Technology Resources

In a field known for its lack of consensus, it is remarkable that general agreement exists that adequate funding can determine the success or failure of even the best technology plans (November & Huntley, 1988; Bullough & Beatty,

1991). Funding issues may be defined by three critical questions:

1. What do schools need to address their current problems?
2. What kind of investments will it take?
3. Where and how will schools get the funds?

Several problems make it complicated to respond to these questions.

**The high price of keeping up with technology.** There is both a high initial cost and the cost of keeping current with technology. Educators often are surprised at how quickly their equipment becomes out-of-date, its lack of incompatibility with newer models, and how quickly the perspective on "best applications" changes.

**The lack of hard evidence on effectiveness.** As Chapter 1 indicated, advocates of technology often have trouble isolating clear evidence about technology's impact on any of these criteria. It is difficult to propose expensive technology programs or resources with hypothetical, rather than proven benefits.

**Special problems for rural schools.** The usual problems with funding for technology seem magnified for schools in rural communities (Clauss & Witwer, 1989; Clark, 1990; Inman-Freitas, 1991; Freitas, 1992; Holland, 1995). State funding formulas tend to favor larger, more urban districts which often results in less state funding for areas that need it most (Clark, 1990). Since nearly a quarter of funding for educational technology comes from state revenues (Mernit, 1993), this is a significant problem for a large segment of the country's educational community.

**Recommended funding strategies.** More positive trends seem likely, however, because most people are becoming aware of the increasingly pervasive influence of technology throughout society. Investments in technology are at an all-time high in education because educators and parents recognize its critical role in current and planned efforts to make a foundering educational system more efficient and more responsive to the needs of today's students (Branson, 1988; Dede, 1992). Current uses of technology based on past experience help to define and shape this future role. This accompanies a growing awareness among legislators and funding agencies that technology in education will require major investments—both initially and continually (Clark, 1990; Rose, 1992). Several tactics can help educators who need funding for technology resources to identify the most promising technology-based activities and maximize their chances for finding financial support for their plans. These include forming partnerships with business and industry and responding to requests for proposals from funding agencies that support technology.

Smith (1997a, 1997b) gives comprehensive and useful advice on how to write successful proposals for technology funding. He says successful proposals follow guidelines of the funding source; are written clearly and succinctly; have an attractive, professional look; use existing resources where possible and do not propose to reinvent the wheel; and establish the successful track record of the proposers. Also, they include required components: an introduction, statement of need, goals and objectives, plan of operation, evaluation plan, and an appendix with supporting letters and resumés.

## Training Teachers

Properly trained teachers make the difference between success or failure of an integration effort (Sheingold, 1991; Munday, Windham, & Stamper, 1991; Dyrli & Kinnaman, 1994b; Siegel, 1995). Recent studies have settled on the kinds of areas in which teachers should be trained; and the National Council for Accreditation (NCATE), the agency responsible for accrediting colleges of education, has established standards for teaching about technology in education (see Chapter 1). Atkins and Vasu (1998) give a summary designed by North Carolina to help schools and districts assess the kinds of training they need to do. This is shown in Figure 2.4.

Despite general agreement on the necessity of technology skills that should be required of teachers, Sheingold (1991) pinpoints a fundamental stumbling block that will complicate teacher training for some time to come: "Teachers will have to confront squarely the difficult problem of creating a school environment that is fundamentally different from the one they themselves experienced" (p. 23). Using technology does not stop with computer-based grades or assigning students to use word processing to produce traditional book reports. Instead, technology confronts teachers with both new possibilities and imperatives for radical changes in teaching behaviors. Collins (1991) describes how these new teaching/learning environments differ from those of the past by citing eight trends identified from observations of schools that have begun using technology. He notes the following shifts in classroom behaviors from:

- Whole-class to small-group instruction
- Lecture and recitation to coaching
- Working with better students to working with weaker ones
- From passive to more engaged students
- Test-based assessment to that based on products, progress, and effort
- Competitive to cooperative social structures
- All students learning the same things to students learning different things
- Primarily verbal learning to an integration of visual and verbal thinking

Roblyer and Erlanger (1998) summarize findings from the literature on what makes teacher training programs most effective:

- **Hands-on, integration emphasis.** Technology integration skills cannot be learned sitting passively in a classroom, listening to an instructor, or watching demonstrations. Participants must have an opportunity to navigate through a program and complete a set of steps to create a new product. The focus must be on how to use the technology resources in classrooms, rather than just technical skills.

- **Training over time.** Many schools are discovering that traditional models of staff development, particularly "one-shot" inservice training for the entire faculty, are ineffective for teaching skills and for helping teachers develop methods to use computers as instructional tools (Benson, 1997). Technology inservice training must be ongoing.

- **Modeling, mentoring, and coaching.** Instructors who model the use of technology in their own teaching long have been acknowledged as the most effective teacher trainers (Handler, 1992; Wetzel, 1993). Research also indicates that one-to-one mentoring and coaching programs are effective for new teachers (Benson, 1997). Linking teachers to each other and to staff developers have also been shown to be effective (OTA, 1995; Ringstaff & Yocam, 1995). Most teachers seem to learn computer skills through colleague interaction and information sharing (Oliver, 1994).

- **Post-training access.** Teachers not only need adequate access to technology to accomplish training, they also need access *after* training to practice and use what they have learned (Standish, 1996).

## Addressing Equity Issues

The power of technology is a two-edged sword, especially for education. Although it presents obvious potential for changing education and empowering teachers and students, technology also has potential for further dividing society along socioeconomic, ethnic, and cultural lines and for widening the gender gap. Teachers will lead the struggle to make sure technology uses promote, rather than conflict with, the goals of a democratic society. Planning at top levels of educational communities must confront and put in place long-term solutions to the equity issues described in detail in Chapter 1: economic, cultural/ethnic, and gender inequity and equity for the disabled.

**Recommendations to address all equity issues.** Engler (1992) and Warren-Sams (1997) recommend strategies that can help state and district leaders and policy makers assure more equitable access to technology for all students. Warren-Sams' booklet, *Closing the Equity Gap in Technology Access and Use,* describes three major areas in which inequities can arise: access, types of use, and curriculum. She suggests dozens of solutions to put into place at administrative, district, and school levels. Engler's practical recommendations include:

**Figure 2.4   The North Carolina Teaching with Technology Instrument**

## TEACHING WITH TECHNOLOGY INSTRUMENT

**Instructions.** The purpose of these questions is to examine the current status of your beliefs, understanding, and use of technology in your classroom. Please read each statement and indicate whether you possess that skill by placing a check mark in either the yes or the no box to the left.

Yes No

1. Use a word processor to enter text, edit, change the format of a document, save and retrieve documents, check spelling, print documents, and use graphics tools.

2. Use desktop-publishing software to import text, format text and layout, and import graphics by producing a class newsletter.

3. Demonstrate how word processing enhances the writing process.

4. Compose and send e-mail to support classroom projects.

5. Understand the social, legal, and ethical issues related to telecommunication use.

6. Use writing/communication technology in the discipline/subject for learning.

7. Understand how writing/communication technology can be used to meet the learning styles of students.

8. Plan writing/communication activities for computer labs and/or classrooms with one or multiple computer resources.

9. Demonstrate a knowledge of installation of writing and telecommunication hardware/software and appropriate troubleshooting techniques.

10. Explore how higher order thinking skills and problem solving can be enhanced by writing/communication technology.

11. Apply understanding of physical settings, organizational and classroom management strategies that support active student involvement, inquiry, and collaboration.

12. Apply understanding of the goals of the North Carolina Computer Skills Curriculum as related to writing and communication.

13. For the title of a document, I can vary the typeface and size (e.g., I can use 18 point Times rather than 10 point Helvetica).

14. Explain how to insert a forced page break into a document.

15. Use a spreadsheet by accessing an existing spreadsheet and creating a new spreadsheet to manage and interpret information.

16. Create a bar graph on the computer that is linked to a spreadsheet.

17. Enter a function in a spreadsheet cell.

18. Use a database by sorting an existing database and creating a new database to manage and interpret information.

19. Use telecommunications by accessing bulletin boards, online services, and the Internet.

20. Access resources for planning instruction available through telecommunications (e.g., experts, lesson plans, authentic data, and curriculum materials).

21. Understand differences between public domain, freeware, shareware, and commercial sources of software.

22. Understand the role of media in effective communication.

23. Understand social, legal, and ethical issues related to information access and management.

24. Demonstrate the use of information access and management in the discipline/subject for learning and as a medium for communication.

25. Understand the characteristics, strengths, and weaknesses of media-communication tools and techniques.

Yes No

26. Demonstrate effective and appropriate use of computers and other technologies to communicate information in a variety of formats on student learning to colleagues, parents, and others.

27. Understand how information access and management can be used to meet the various learning styles of students.

28. Plan information access/management activities for computer labs and classrooms with one or multiple computer resources.

29. Demonstrate a knowledge of installation of hardware/software and appropriate troubleshooting techniques as related to information access and management.

30. Explore how information access/management technology can enhance higher order thinking skills and problem solving.

31. Explain what WWW and Veronica mean within the telecommunications context.

32. Demonstrate or explain to another person how to access an e-mail account.

33. Understand how to set up and manage a telecommunications project between schools in different geographical areas.

34. Effectively use distance learning, online conferences relevant to professional information needs, desktop teleconferencing, and tele-teaching technologies.

35. Demonstrate development of performance tasks that require students to locate and analyze information as well as draw conclusions and use a variety of media to communicate results clearly.

36. Apply understanding of the goals of the North Carolina Computer Skills Curriculum as related to information access and management.

37. Demonstrate a knowledge of installation of hardware/software and troubleshooting techniques (i.e., CD-ROMs, laserdisc players, LCD panels, television monitors, video equipment, scanners, digital cameras, and teleconferencing equipment).

38. Understand differences between public domain, freeware, shareware, and commercial sources of software and review copyright laws to ensure compliance with copyright law, fair-use guidelines, security, and child protection.

39. Understand social, legal, and ethical issues related to multimedia production.

40. Use and understand the differences between linear multimedia presentation and a nonlinear multimedia presentation. Understand terms such as media, multimedia, hypermedia, and clip media.

41. Demonstrate multimedia use in the discipline/subject for learning and as a medium for communication.

42. Understand how multimedia production can be used to meet the various learning styles of students.

43. Plan multimedia activities for computer labs and/or classrooms with one or multiple computer resources.

44. Plan a lesson incorporating appropriate technology that includes use of productivity software, online resources, or both.

45. Explore how multimedia production can enhance higher order thinking skills and problem solving.

46. Apply understanding of the goals of the North Carolina Computer Skills curriculum as related to multimedia production.

*An ISTE Copy-Me Page*

- **Accountability measures.** Monitor and document disproportionate participation to increase awareness of the problem.
- **Incentives and priority funding.** Tie state grant funds and entitlements to districts' efforts to address the needs of underrepresented students.
- **Innovative programs.** Develop and support new initiatives aimed at improving student access to technology.
- **Enrichment programs.** Supply funding for computer contests, summer camps with technology themes, and similar activities directed at offering special opportunities to disadvantaged students.
- **Recognition.** State-level and district-level awards and publications could feature successful equity-related technology programs.
- **Business and community partnerships.** Place business-sponsored magnet schools and other programs in neighborhoods where students have usually had lower access to technology resources.
- **Staff development.** Educate teachers, parents, and school personnel to increase their expectations and support of girls, minorities, and other groups.
- **Student recruitment.** Set entrance requirements for special and gifted programs to include alternatives to test scores (e.g., portfolios) to encompass a wider variety of student groups and actively seek participation of these students.

**Recommendations specific to gender equity issues.** Engler (1992), Fredman (1990), and Sanders and Stone (1986) recommend classroom-level strategies by which teachers can encourage greater participation by girls, minorities, and disadvantaged students. Rosenthal and Demetrulias (1988) supply helpful guidelines to help detect gender bias as teachers select software for classroom use (e.g., software that has male names only).

**Recommendations specific to equity for disabled students.** Access is the key issue for handicapped and learning disabled students. Physically handicapped students must get the technological devices they need to achieve learning opportunities more equal to those of their non-disabled counterparts. Planning must include measures to increase awareness at two levels.

- Students and their families must learn about assistive devices and the funding sources they can use to purchase them.
- Decision makers must recognize the obstacles to technology access for physically disabled students; understand how to bring about access; and keep students, families, and administrators apprised of these important issues.

**Recommendations to address cultural issues.** A major strategy recommended by Engler (1992), Salehi (1990), and others is networking with others to identify resources, either through statewide systems or local projects. Communicating electronically can allow minority students and teachers to exchange information with others of similar or different

ethnic backgrounds in the United States and other countries. This opportunity can create a powerful motivation to learn about and use higher-level technology skills while building multicultural awareness. As one of their more difficult challenges, teachers who want to use technology must remain sensitive to cultural differences among their students. Miller-Lachman (1994) provides a checklist of criteria for selecting software free of built-in cultural biases:

1. What is the purpose of presenting other cultures? (p. 26) (Is it integral to the program or an irrelevant add-on?)
2. Do people of color and their cultures receive as much attention as people of European descent? (p. 27)
3. How accurate is the presentation of various nationalities? (p. 27) (For example, portraying ancient Egyptians as having pink-colored skin would not be accurate.)
4. Are the language and terms appropriate? (p. 27) (For example, referring to people from any culture as savages is pejorative.)
5. Do the illustrations or sounds distort or ridicule members of other cultures? (p. 28)
6. Does the program present a true picture of the culture's diversity and complexity? (p. 28)
7. Who are the characters and what roles do they play? (p. 28) (Are the "good guys" always white, but the villains always include persons of color?)
8. From whose perspective is the story presented? (p. 29) Is the viewpoint of the software always the settlers and never the Native Americans?
9. Does the documentation allow the instructors to go beyond the program itself? (p. 29)
10. Should some simulations not be played? What kinds of actions are the players asked to undertake so that they may succeed? For example, should students engage in treachery and theft in order to capture an Aztec treasure? (p. 29)

### Addressing Ethical and Legal Issues

In many ways, technology users represent the society in a microcosm. The culture, language, and problems of the larger society also emerge among technology users and their activities reflect many of the rules of conduct and values of society in general. Top-level state, district, and school planning should be prepared for the problems that will arise when people try to work outside those values and rules. Carpenter (1996) gives an excellent summary of these ethical issues. Planning should address three major kinds of ethical and legal issues: copyright infringement, illegal access, and online ethics.

**Recognizing and preventing copyright infringement.** Software packages are much like books: companies put up development money to produce them and then sell copies in the hope of recouping their initial investments and earning profits. Like book publishers, software companies protect their products against illegal copying under U.S. copyright law. When microcomputer software became an industry, the problem of illegal copying of disks, called *software piracy,* became widespread. Illegal copying has also become common among individuals, especially in education where teachers usually need multiple copies but cannot afford per-copy prices. Many school personnel either are not aware of laws protecting software copyrights, do not feel it is important enough to observe these laws, or have not understood clearly when copying is illegal. Even when teachers clearly grasp these issues, their students may make illegal copies; both schools and districts and their personnel can be held legally responsible unless they have developed and publicized policies against software piracy and taken measures to enforce them (Becker, 1992; Simpson, 1997).

Simpson (1997) gives an excellent summary of the laws related to software copying, recommendations on publicizing software policies, and example copyright statements that schools and districts can use. The Software Publishers Association (SPA) has also developed summary guidelines for software copying and media communication which are available on request. (See more information on their Web site: http://www.spa.org). Simpson emphasizes that software companies are serious about enforcing software copyright laws and will prosecute offenders. Administrative organizations must protect themselves against copyright infringement suits by stating and publicizing a policy regarding software copying, by requiring teacher and staff training on the topic, and by requiring hard drive and network programs that discourage users from making illegal copies. Districts and schools should also consider options for providing adequate numbers of copies for their users (e.g., by purchasing site licenses, lab packs, or networkable versions).

**Recognizing and preventing illegal access.** When computer users gain illegal access to private information, the problem is known either as *computer crime* or *hacking.* Individuals gain illegal access to computerized records for illicit purposes such as transferring bank funds into their own accounts or gathering confidential information from which they can profit. Computer crime also includes software piracy and acts of mischief such as viruses and destruction of information.

Hackers are people who are so captivated by the power and intricacies of computer systems that they adopt computer activities as a hobby. Hacking is not illegal but becomes a crime when it turns toward exploring ways to invade privately held information. It is a serious problem in education, since students just learning about the computer can easily cross the line between harmless exploration and illegal access. Schools and districts that maintain computer files on students and staff must take steps to restrict illegal access. Teachers of programming and computer applications should guard against giving future white-collar criminals the tools they need. Teachers should be sure to cover the topics of computer crime and ethical behavior and help students to understand the implications of illegal access.

**Dealing with online ethics issues.** The latest ethical issue to confront educators is the easy availability of dangerous or inappropriate information on the Internet. There have been many demonstrations of just how easy it is to inadvertently run across Web sites containing shocking images or solicitations. Some states or districts take the initiative with this problem by placing "firewall" software on their networks. This software prevents access to specific Web sites or any Web sites that contain certain keywords or phrases. Other districts or schools choose to use commercially available filtering software such as the 10 packages reviewed by Munro (1998, March 24).

## School Planning and Preparation for Technology Use

Even though state agencies and school districts may make many planning and preparation decisions that affect the schools, the current trend is for each school to develop and maintain its own technology. Jankowski (1996) gives planning guidelines specific to school-level technology plans, and the Southern Technology Council (1997) gives many good examples of planning at this level. Some of the issues particularly important for school-level technology planning and implementation include methods of optimizing resources, choosing software and hardware, and setting up and maintaining facilities.

### Optimizing School Level Technology Resources

Strategies for optimizing resources include (Jordan, 1996; Education Council, 1998):

- Requiring competitive bids for large items or frequently used supplies
- Upgrading current software whenever possible
- Recycling whenever possible
- Using older equipment to meet lower-profile, noninstructional needs
- Using donated equipment (California's Education Council for Technology in Learning, 1998)
- Sharing resources among groups whenever feasible
- Assembling systems from the working parts of each broken computer
- Using parent volunteers to locate funds for new equipment (Ohlrich, 1996)
- Holding fund-raising events

### Choosing the Right Software and Hardware for Your Needs

The first question that technology planners must answer is: What do you want technology to help you do? Software and hardware selections depend on the answer to this ques-

**Figure 2.5    Factors to Consider in Software and Hardware Selection**

---

**Software Factors**

1. **Quality.** Use software reviews and recommendations, pilot test the software before buying it, review support documentation on program operation.

2. **Number (and type) of copies.** Use companies' flexible pricing structures: "lab packs" or price discounts for buying multiple copies, site licenses, or networked versions.

3. **Source of best prices.** Use dealers who have lower prices than the publisher (Educational Resources, the Educational Software Institute).

4. **Match with curriculum and students.** Choose wisely between two packages that seem to do the same thing (match software carefully to the student levels and curriculum specific needs).

**Hardware Factors**

1. **Type of hardware platforms.** Consider software compatibility; when considering Macintosh or MS-DOS machines, consider ease of use for target population; pricing for comparable features; who will support equipment; and intended use.

2. **How many computers?**

   Number of computers to buy based on how equipment will be configured and used (classroom computers or workstations versus centralized learning lab or media center)

   Number of computers per lab depends on how many people to serve and how often

3. **Individual computer characteristics.** Consider size of random access memory or RAM; size of the hard drive, number, speed, and kind of peripherals (CD-ROMs, DVDs, modems); and computer processor speed.

4. **Other kinds of equipment**

   Modems

   Videodisc players

   CD-ROM players

   Large-screen projection devices

   Printers (inkjet and laser printers, speed of each)

---

tion. Educators should consider the several factors shown in Figure 2.5

**The problem of hardware incompatibility.** Incompatibility problems add to the expense of technology investments. Educators must guard against two kinds of incapability: differences among brands and those between older and the upgraded versions of a single brand. Both can pose obstacles to educators with limited funds. As computer companies become more sensitive to the needs of their customers, they are attempting to maintain some degree of compatibility when they upgrade their products.

Some larger school districts and schools minimize compatibility problems by simultaneously purchasing and upgrading most or all of their technology resources. These larger entities frequently use their purchasing power to get computer and software companies to help them find solutions to incompatibilities between versions and brands. This preferred strategy requires a great deal of top-down management authority, careful planning, and arduous negotiations with computer companies.

However, most schools either cannot or do not operate this way. They always encounter incompatibility problems because they never have the funds they need to replace older equipment and software with up-to-date versions. The most common school technology inventory consists of a variety of resources acquired at different times for different purposes. Such a school should try to make the most effective possible use of the resources it has while allocating a part of its yearly budget for upgrades and new technology. Several strategies help educators to make the best use of available resources while dealing with incompatible brands and versions: group similar resources, use older equipment for simpler purposes, upgrade or sell older equipment (Jordahl, 1995).

In all of these strategies, schools do not attempt to make different brands compatible or older equipment compatible with newer acquisitions. They simply isolate incompatible systems from each other by having each perform different functions. It is essential that educators recognize that a state-of-the-art microcomputer does not exist. Technical developments are happening so rapidly that microcomputer buyers should follow practices similar to those for car purchases. Look for the features you need and those that will probably stay around a while, and be aware that a computer is out-of-date when you "drive it off the lot."

**Setting Up Physical Facilities**

Schools have developed several common arrangements for technology equipment. Figure 2.6 details the benefits and limitations of each. These choices are influenced by the kinds of instruction that a school needs and wants to

**Figure 2.6    Types of Technology Facilities and Their Uses**

|  | Benefits/Possibilities | Limitations/Problems | Common Uses |
|---|---|---|---|
| **Laboratories** | Centralized resources are easier to maintain and keep secure; software can be networked and shared. | Need permanent staff to supervise and maintain resources. Students must leave their classrooms | See below |
| Special-purpose labs | Permanent setups group resources specific to the needs of certain content areas or types of students. | Usually exclude other groups. Isolate resources | Programming courses; word processing classes of students in mathematics, science, etc.; teacher work labs; vocational courses (CAD, robotics); Chapter I students; multimedia production courses and activities |
| General-use computer labs open to all school groups | Accommodate varied uses by different groups | Difficult to schedule specific uses. Usually available to only one class at a time | Student productivity tasks (preparation of reports, assignments); class demonstrations; followup work |
| Library/media center labs | Same as general-use labs, but permanent staff are already present. Ready access to all materials to promote integration of computer and noncomputer resources | Same as general-use labs Staff will need special training. Classes cannot do production or group work that may bother other users of the library/media center | Same as general-use labs |
| **Mobile workstations** | Stretch resources by sharing them among many users | Moving equipment increases breakage and other maintenance problems. Sometimes difficult to get through doors or up stairs | Demonstrations |
| **Mobile PCs (laptops, PDAs)** | On-demand access | Portability increases security problems | Individual student or teacher production tasks; teachers' assessment tasks |
| **Classroom workstations** | Easily accessible to teachers and students | No immediate assistance available to teachers. Only a few students can use at one time | Tutoring and drills; demonstrations; production tasks for cooperative learning groups; e-mail between other teachers |
| **Standalone classroom computers** | Easily accessible to teachers and students | Same as classroom workstations | Tutoring and drills; whole-class demonstrations; pairs/small workgroups |

emphasize (Milone, 1989). Labs, for example, are usually considered more useful for providing group instruction and are more common at secondary levels; individual workstations seem better suited to small-group, classroom work, and they appear more often in lower grades.

Ideally, a school would use what Fraundorf (1997) describes as a "distributed approach," that is, a combination of labs and classroom computers. Each classroom should have a workstation capable of performing the full gamut of technology-based instructional and productivity activities from word processing to multimedia applications. This station should act as a learning area to support either individual or small-group work. In addition to classroom resources, every school with an enrollment of 1,000 students or more should also have at least one general-purpose lab with at least 15 to 20 stations to serve the productivity needs of students and teachers. Generally, larger schools have more special-purpose labs.

**Designing technology resources for the classroom.** Although every school may not be able to attain these ideal conditions immediately, each school should identify the facilities it wants in its technology plan and set up a priority list that will help it work toward achieving them.

**Designing a microcomputer lab.** Bunson (1988) gives a rather complete list of concerns to address when setting up a microcomputer lab in a media center. These include **environmental factors** (equipment and traffic flow; furniture; power outlets, uninterrupted power sources and backup power; antistatic mats and sprays; and proper temperature, lighting, and acoustics) and **administration** (copyright enforcement; equipment distribution, control, and access; staff responsibilities and training; budgeting for hardware, software, personnel, supplies, and maintenance).

Manczuk (1994) addresses other concerns such as equity and access issues to assure that special populations (e.g., physically handicapped users) can benefit from the center; automated systems to maintain and locate resources easily; security measures and safety features; and "scaled down" workstations for smaller students (Wilson, 1991).

**Redesigning school facilities.** Van Dam (1994) is among a growing number of educators who urge schools to provide facilities that allow teachers "access to information via voice, video, and computer data, anytime, anyplace" (p. 56). For many schools, this requires complete redesign—sometimes referred to as *retrofit*—of their facilities, including new wiring and power supplies. Van Dam describes how her school went about this effort. Such dramatic change is an expensive undertaking, but some organizations consider it so important to the future of technology integration that they have decided to allocate special funds to support these redesign or retrofit activities (Macon, 1992).

## Maintaining Physical Facilities: Lab Rules, Maintenance, Security, and Virus Protection

Despite all their power and capabilities, computers and related technologies are simply machines. They are subject to the same mundane and frustrating problems as any equipment; that is, they can break down, malfunction, or become damaged or stolen. As microcomputers came into schools in greater numbers in the 1980s, these problems became increasingly important—and expensive. Schools found that the initial cost of equipment was only a fraction of the funds required to keep it available and useful to teachers. They have found no easy answers to maintenance and security issues, and these subjects represent an important aspect of planning for technology use. This section describes some ongoing maintenance and security concerns that will continue to powerfully affect teachers' ability to integrate technology.

**Lab rules.** Most labs adopt rules intended to extend the lives of the resources they buy and to ensure that the labs fulfill the purposes for which they were designed. Teachers will find that most of these same rules should apply to classroom workstations. Lab rules and regulations should be posted prominently and should apply to everyone who uses the lab, from the principal to the teacher aides:

- No eating, drinking, or smoking should be allowed near equipment.
- Lab resources should be reserved for instructional purposes only.
- Only authorized lab personnel should check out lab resources.
- Group work should be encouraged, but lab users should show respect for others by maintaining appropriate noise levels.
- Schedules for use should be strictly observed.
- Problems with equipment should be reported promptly to designated personnel.

**Maintenance needs and options.** Each teacher who uses technology needs training in simple troubleshooting procedures such as making sure a printer is plugged in and online, or what to do if a computer says a disk is "unreadable." Educators should not be expected to address more complicated diagnostic and maintenance problems, though. Nothing is more frustrating than depending on a piece of equipment to complete an important student project only to discover it is broken or malfunctioning. A technology plan must make some prior provision to expediently replace and repair equipment designated for classroom use.

Schools can minimize technology repair problems if users follow good usage rules and conduct preventive maintenance procedures. Even under the best circumstances, however, computers and other equipment will break or suffer damage. A school with more resources can expect to need a larger repair budget.

Schools and districts have tried to deal with these problems in many ways. Whole businesses have sprung up to provide maintenance for microcomputers. Educational organizations usually choose one of the following maintenance options: maintenance contracts with outside suppliers; in-house maintenance office, built-in maintenance with each equipment purchase; and a repair and maintenance budget. Each of these methods has its problems and limitations and debate continues over which method or combination of methods is most cost-effective depending on an organization's size and its number of computers and peripherals.

**Security requirements.** Microcomputers and peripherals such as disk drives and printers can be very portable. Security is a separate, but equally important, equipment maintenance issue. Loss of equipment from vandalism and theft is a common problem in schools. Again, several options are available to deal with this problem: **monitoring and alarm systems**, **security cabinets**, and **lock-down systems**. As with maintenance strategies, each method of protecting equipment from loss is less than perfect and each involves considerable expense. Everyone should start with the assumption that unprotected equipment *will* be stolen. Although security can be a significant technology-related expense, it is usually cheaper than replacing stolen or vandalized equipment.

**Viruses: Causes, prevention, and cures.** Computer viruses are programs written specifically to cause damage or do mischief to other programs or information (Hansen & Koltes, 1992). Like real viruses, these programs can pass to other programs they contact but are passed only by connecting one computer to another via telecommunications or by inserting a disk containing the virus into a computer. Some viruses are carried into a computer system on "Trojan horses," or attractive programs ostensibly designed for another purpose but which also carry instructions that get around protection codes (Lee, 1992). Some viruses are "worms," or programs designed specifically to run simultaneously with other programs; others are "logic bombs" that carry out destructive activities at certain dates or times. Many different strains of viruses plague computer systems and more are being generated all the time. Hansen and Koltes (1992) hypothesize that most viruses are written out of curiosity or as intellectual challenges. Less often, they seem to have been produced as destructive forms of political or personal protest or revenge. However, Mungo and Clough (1992) warn that this latter kind of activity may be increasing.

The impact of a virus can take many forms. Some viruses eat through data stored in a computer. Others replicate copies of themselves in computer memory and destroy files. Still others print mischievous messages or cause unusual screen displays. No matter what their purposes, viruses have the general effect of tying up computer resources, frustrating users, and wasting valuable time. Even after a virus has been detected and removed from hard drives, it can return if users do not diligently examine their floppy disks as they insert them into the cleaned computer.

Randall (1998) warns that viruses via the Internet are becoming commonplace. Since computer viruses are currently as widespread and as communicable as the common cold and they often can interfere with planned activities, teachers and schools must take precautions against contracting these electronic diseases. Dormady (1991) recommends a four-point program to minimize the impact of viruses: establish good practices (scan systems and disks regularly, back up important data or files); enforce safety policies (no unauthorized programs); use virus management programs and "cookie managers" (Randall, 1998); and educate users on how to prevent, detect, and remove viruses.

## Teacher Planning and Preparation for Technology Use

The third level of planning and preparation for technology integration must be done by individual teachers or teachers working in teams. Even if the educational community and/or school has done its best to plan for and support technology implementation, most schools around the country do not have the funds to provide an adequate level of equipment, materials, or technical support for teachers as they integrate technology. Despite this, each teacher or teaching team is responsible for creating an environment in which technology can effectively enhance learning. Teachers who do this well address five kinds of tasks: matching needs and materials, designing appropriate curriculum integration strategies, preparing the classroom environment, training students, and evaluating and revising integration strategies.

### Step 1: Needs Assessment—Matching Needs and Technology Resources

Perhaps one of the reasons technology isn't working as well or as efficiently as many had hoped by now is that too frequently technology is chosen for insufficient reasons: because the school has it on hand; the teacher next door is using it; the principal likes it; or it is part of the school culture. None of these reasons is necessarily a bad motivation; but if technology is to improve, teachers must recognize the difference between a technology solution that makes a difference and one that is an inessential add-on.

After teachers are well-acquainted with current technology resources and know how each can enhance teaching and learning, they begin to spot places in their curriculum where it does, indeed, make sense to integrate technology. Chapter 3 discusses more specific types of technology integration strategies and lesson activities/examples are given throughout Chapters 4–15. The following describe other information to help guide this planning:

**Assessing needs.** How does a teacher know when a technology resource is the answer? This decision may come about in several ways, but always begins with a problem to solve. For example:

- A high school writing teacher finds that his students will not rewrite their compositions by hand because it is too laborious and time-consuming. (Word processing can help.)

- A middle school teacher has great difficulty motivating her students to do math problem-solving activities. (Video-based problem scenarios can help.)

- A science teacher wants to give her students practice in performing experiments using a scientific inquiry method, but has few consumables required for such activities. (Software simulations can help.)

- A special education teacher is having trouble keeping up with the IEP generation and tracking for his students. (A computer-based management system can help.)

It takes time and experience to develop skill in recognizing situations where technology may be used with maximum benefits, but the most difficult part is identifying activities in which the benefits justify the time and expense involved.

The checklist shown in Figure 2.7 (Step 1) can help teachers decide if technology is the solution to their problem.

### Step 2: Planning Instruction—Designing Appropriate Integration Strategies

An entire topic rarely revolves around the technology resource; it fits into the activities a teacher uses to help students learn. The teacher must make several decisions at this point (see Step 2 of Figure 2.7).

### Step 3: Logistics—Preparing the Classroom Environment

Schools rarely have enough equipment to seat every student at a standalone computer or technology station. Therefore, teachers must determine the factors shown in Step 3 of Figure 2.7. Consider the following:

**One-computer classrooms.** Although not an optimal situation, one-computer classrooms are commonplace and a great deal has been written on how to make best use of this limited resource. Collis (1988) wrote the definitive book on planning and activities for one-computer classrooms. More recently, Dillon (1996), Kahn (1996–1997), and Tan (1998) offer suggestions for one-computer activities, including demonstrations, posing problems that cooperative groups work on later, and letting students watch the collection and analysis of scientific data. These activities work better if the teacher has a projection system or large monitor attached to the computer so everyone in the class can see the screen display clearly. Some software packages are designed to promote problem solving and cooperative work in a one-computer classroom.

**Other configurations.** If more than one computer is available but resources still are limited, teachers may choose from several strategies. Again, they may choose a learning station approach with computers used as reference stations (with CD-ROM encyclopedias or Internet connections). Or the teacher may decide to take groups or an entire class to a nearby lab or media center for product development work.

### Figure 2.7 Technology Integration Checklists for Teachers

**Step 1: Needs assessment—Deciding instructional problems that have technology solutions**

—— Topics that seem especially difficult for students to learn because concepts involved are abstract or foreign to students' experience; students have trouble visualizing meaning and relevance.

—— Activities involved in learning present logistical hurdles for students (handwriting, calculations, data collection) which interfere with acquiring higher level skills.

—— Learning requires extensive individual, teacher-corrected practice; leaving limited time for individual help.

—— Students find topics uninteresting/tedious; motivation and transfer are constant problems.

—— Teacher-led activities are needed, but teacher and/or materials are not available.

—— Students resist preparing and making paper-based reports and presentations of their work.

—— Students resist working collaboratively on a research and/or development project, and a teacher wants a format that will motivate them to work and present products together.

—— To do a research project, students need information and expertise not available locally.

—— Students need practice in skills that will make them technologically competitive as students and workers: technology literacy, information literacy, and visual literacy.

**Step 2: Planning instruction—Designing appropriate integration strategies**

—— Will the instruction be single-subject or interdisciplinary?

—— Should activities be individual, paired, small group, large group, whole class, or a combination of these?

—— What instructional activities need to come before the introduction of the technology resource?

—— What instructional activities need to follow the introduction of the technology resource?

—— How will you assess students' learning progress and products: criteria checklists, rubrics.

**Step 3: Logistics—Preparing the classroom environment—Arranging resources**

—— How many computers will be needed? Will the teacher need to schedule time in a lab or media center? Or will the classroom computers be adequate?

—— If demonstrations and learning stations can be used, will projection devices or large screen monitors be needed?

—— What other equipment, software, media, and other resources will be needed (printers, printer paper, software/probeware, videodiscs/CDs)?

—— Over what time period and for how long will technology resources be needed?

*Continued*

Figure 2.7    *Continued*

---

**Step 4: Preparing yourself and students to use resources**

____ Become familiar with troubleshooting procedures specific to the piece of hardware or software package being used (equipment and software manuals often list such procedures).

____ Test run an equipment setup before students arrive. (Even if the setup was working the day before, check it once again before class.)

____ Backup your own files and train students to backup theirs.

____ Have the original program disks/discs handy to re-install them, if necessary.

____ Allow students time to get used to materials before beginning a graded activity.

____ Demonstrate the skills students will need to use both the equipment and the specific software for the lesson.

____ Encourage students to use the help sections in the software manuals.

**Step 5: Try it! Evaluating and revising integration strategies**

____ Consider alternative ways to set up equipment to make things easier.

____ Solicit feedback from students about how to improve activities.

*How do you know when you've integrated technology well? (based on Milone's (1998) points)*

____ An outside observer sees the technology activity as a seamless part of the lesson.

____ The reason for using the technology is obvious to you, the students, and others.

____ The students are focusing on learning, not on the technology.

____ You can describe how technology is helping a particular student.

____ You would have difficulty accomplishing lesson objectives if the technology weren't there.

____ You can explain easily and concisely what the technology is supposed to contribute.

____ All students are participating with the technology and benefiting from it.

*How do you know when you haven't integrated technology well? (based on Milone's (1998) points)*

____ You consistently see the technology as more trouble than it's worth.

____ You have trouble justifying cost and preparation time in terms of benefits to your students.

____ Students spend more time trying to make the technology work than learning the topic.

____ The problem you were trying to address is still there.

---

### Step 4: Preparing You and Your Students to Use Resources

Teachers also face the major challenge of structuring class time so students use technology effectively and efficiently. Some of these challenges involve equipment logistics; some are preparing students. Some students tend to play and experiment with a program without moving on to become proficient. Others become totally dependent on the teacher and ask for help with every problem. The teacher must balance the role of providing answers against the role of encouraging students to learn independently (see Step 4 of Figure 2.7.)

### Step 5: Try It! Evaluating and Revising Integration Strategies

Trying something new when things may not work out as expected is a great opportunity to model risk-taking as is spending time reflecting on classroom success and how to improve it. The checklists shown in Step 5 of Figure 2.7 can help teachers evaluate their progress.

## Exercises

### Record and Apply What You Have Learned

**Activity 2.1: Chapter 2 Self-Test**  To review terms and concepts in this chapter, take the Chapter 2 self-test.

Select Chapter 2 from the front page of the companion Web site (located at http://www.prenhall.com/roblyer), then choose the *Multiple Choice* module.

**Activity 2.2: Portfolio Activities**  The following activities will help you add to your professional portfolio. To complete these activities online and save or submit the materials electronically, select Chapter 2 from the front page of the companion Web site (http://www.prenhall.com/roblyer), then choose the *Portfolio* module.

**Technology Plan** Choose the level or type of school in which you currently work or think you may be working someday. Describe how the school should go about developing a technology implementation plan for the school and outline the elements of the plan. Tell:

- Who should serve on the planning committee? (Be sure to represent all necessary groups.)

- What steps should the committee follow to develop the plan?

- What issues and guidelines in your plan probably will be decided at the school district level and handed down to you?

- What will the plan look like in outline form? (List all concerns to be addressed; you may do a text outline or a graphic outline, chart, or diagram on the computer.)

**Integration Strategy** Assume you are a classroom teacher at a level and type of school of your choice. You have an idea for using a computer resource in your one-computer classroom. Describe your idea and the steps necessary to make the activity a successful one. Be sure to tell:

- Where does the activity fit into the curriculum unit or lesson you have in mind?

- What unique benefits does this resource have for the curriculum or lesson?

- Will your students be working individually, in small groups, or as a whole class?

- What hardware and software will you need?

- How many computers and copies of the software or media will you need to carry out this activity?

- Will the activity be held in your classroom or in another location such as a lab?

- How much time will it take your students to complete the activity? Will they use computers only once or several times?

- What activities will be done before students use computer materials? after?

**Activity 2.3: Questions for Thought and Discussion** These questions may be used for small group or class discussion or may be subjects for individual or group activities. To take part in these discussions online, select Chapter 2 from the front page of the companion Web site (http://www.prenhall.com/roblyer), then choose the *Message Board* module.

• Sheingold (1991) said that teachers will have to confront squarely the difficult problem of creating a school environment that is fundamentally different from the one they themselves experienced (p. 23). In what ways is the K-12 environment for which you are planning now different from the one you experienced? What are some strategies teachers can use to overcome this obstacle?

• NCATE's document *Technology and the New Professional Teacher* (1997) said that, in addition to technology skills, teachers need an attitude that is fearless in the use of technology, encourages them to take risks, and inspires them to be life-long learners (p. 4). What current factors and activities can help teachers develop such an attitude? What factors make it difficult for them to acquire it?

**Activity 2.4: Collaborative Activities** The following sets of problems and products may be done in small group work. Each group should present the findings to the class in a format they know how to use (word processed report, presentation software, multimedia product). Completed group products may be copied and shared with the entire class and/or included in each person's Personal Portfolio.

**Set 1—Each group chooses one** Each group chooses or is assigned one of the following scenarios. Each group should develop an appropriate response, describe it for the class, and tell why their answer is appropriate.

**Problem 1** You are a sixth-grade teacher in an inner-city school. You would like to do some multimedia production work with your low-motivated, lower-achieving students. However, the Chapter I teacher in your school says that these students should use computers strictly for drill and practice in remedial skills because it is important that low-achieving students get a good grounding in basic skills before attempting any activities that require higher-order thinking and problem solving. What do you say?

**Problem 2** In addition to your teaching duties, you have been placed in charge of the school's one general-use computer lab. One of the teachers in your school has just purchased an expensive science software package for use in the 15-computer lab. When you ask how she is going to get the software on all the machines, she replies that she will simply place the software on the hard drives of each computer. When her students are finished using it, she will erase it from the hard drives. What do you say?

**Problem 3** As new principal of a rural high school, you realize that all students in the school's Advanced Placement (AP) Computer Science courses and its "Komputer Klub for Kids" are white males. The teacher for the courses (also the club's sponsor) says it has always been that way and won't change. He says girls and others do not like these activities, aren't good at them, and can't be forced to do them. What do you say?

**Problem 4**  You are one of several teachers who worked on a successful grant to get multimedia equipment, software, videodiscs, and an Internet connection for your students. The school has suffered break-ins before, and you are concerned about the security of these new resources. You talk to the principal about your concerns, but she says the school probably cannot afford any security measures.

**Problem 5**  You are a teacher of grade 11–12 social studies. You are excited because your school has just received six multimedia computers, some printers, and a videodisc player. You have plans to begin using these resources with your classes. The principal says that space is tight in the school and is considering placing these resources in a hallway outside the library/media center. He says that way they would both be accessible and highly visible to everyone.

**Set 2—All groups**  Develop an idea for a technology-based activity that would require your school to purchase resources such as multimedia hardware and software or more computers with Internet access. Develop a brief proposal to a principal, district, or funding agency that outlines the costs of these resources and gives a convincing justification for the purchases by explaining the unique benefits you expect from the activity.

**Activity 2.5: Integrating Technology Across the Curriculum Activities**  Use the *Integrating Technology Across the Curriculum* CD-ROM packaged with this textbook to complete the following exercise:

One question teachers frequently address during planning for integration is: How many computers are available to carry out the lesson? Several lessons are designed for a one-computer classroom. Others let students work in pairs or small groups to optimize available resources. Find some lesson integration examples for each grouping strategy by searching for lessons under each of the Grouping Strategies. Go to *Find Lesson Plan* and click on *Find by Criteria*. Under the *Grouping Strategies* descriptor, select Individual, Pairs, and other strategies; click *Search*. Review the types of lessons designed for each strategy.

# References

### Introduction to Technology Integration

Baines, L. (1997). Future schlock: Using fabricated data and politically correct platitudes in the name of education reform. *Phi Delta Kappan, 78*(7), 492–498.

Ferrell, B. (1986). Evaluating the impact of CAI on mathematics learning: Computer immersion project. *Journal of Educational Computing Research, 2*(3), 327–336.

Morehouse, D., Hoaglund, M., & Schmidt, R. (1987). *Technology demonstration project final report.* Menomonie, WI: Quality Evaluation & Development.

Oppenheimer, T. (1997). The computer delusion. *The Atlantic Monthly, 280*(1), 45–62.

The revolution that fizzled. (1991, May 20). *Time*, 48.

### Planning for Technology

Apple Computer Company (1995). *Teaching, learning, and technology: A planning guide* (Multimedia package). Cupertino, CA: Author.

Association for Media and Technology in Education (1991). K–12 educational technology planning: The state of the art. A selected bibliography. Hot topic No. 1 (ERIC Document Reproduction No. 346 819).

Atkins, N. & Vasu, E. (1998). The teaching with technology instrument. *Learning and Leading with Technology, 25*(8), 35–39.

Brody, P. (1995). *Technology planning and management handbook.* Englewood, NJ: Educational Technology.

Bruder, I. (1993). Technology in the USA: An educational perspective. *Electronic Learning, 13*(2), 20–28.

Dyrli, O. & Kinnaman, D. (1994a). District wide technology planning: The key to long-term success. *Technology and Learning, 14*(7), 50–54.

Jankowski, L. (1996). Guidelines for school technology development plans. *Learning and Leading with Technology, 23*(5), 38–40.

Kwajewski, K. (1997). Technology as a core value. *Learning and Leading with Technology, 24*(5), 54–56.

Mageau, T. (1990). ILS: Its new role in schools. *Electronic Learning, 10*(1), 22–24, 31–32.

Palazzo, A. (1995). Great technology plans. *Electronic Learning, 14*(7), 31–39.

Roblyer, M. (1993). Why use technology in teaching: Making a case beyond research results. *The Florida Technology in Education Quarterly, 5*(4), 7–13.

See, J. (1992). Ten criteria for effective technology plans. *The Computing Teacher, 19*(8), 34–35.

Southern Technology Council. (1997). *Making technology happen.* Research Triangle Park, NC: Author.

Van Dam, J. (1994). Redesigning schools for 21st century technologies. *Technology and Learning, 14*(4), 54–58, 60–61.

Wall, T. (1994). A technology planning primer. *The American School Board Journal, 81*(3), 45–47.

### Funding

Bailey, T. (1990). The superintendent's perception of the benefit of instructional technology in Virginia school divisions. Virginia State Department of Education, Richmond, VA (ERIC Document Reproduction Service No. ED 329 233).

Branson, R. (1988). Why the schools can't improve: The upper limit hypothesis. *Journal of Instructional Development, 10*(4), 15–26.

Bullough, R. & Beatty, L. (1991). *Classroom applications of microcomputers.* New York: Merrill/Macmillan.

Clark, C. (1990). Linking educational finance reform and educational technology in Texas. Paper presented at the Annual Meeting of the American Education Finance Association, Las Vegas (ERIC Document Reproduction Service No. ED 324 751).

Clauss, W. & Witwer, F. (1989). Establishing legislative support for the funding of technology in rural schools. *Rural Special Education Quarterly, 9*(4), 25–28.

Dede, C. (1992). The future of multimedia: Bridging to virtual worlds. *Educational Technology, 32*(5), 54–60.

*Electronic Learning* (1993). *12,* 5.

Freitas, D. (1992). Managing smallness: Promising fiscal practices for rural school district administrators. ERIC Clearinghouse on Rural Education and Small Schools, Charleston, WV (ERIC Document Reproduction Service No. ED 348 205).

Holland, H. (1995). Needles in a haystack. *Electronic Learning, 14*(7), 26–28.

Inman-Freitas, D. (1991). Efficient financial management in rural schools: Common problems and solutions from the field. ERIC Clearinghouse on Rural Education and Small Schools, Charleston, WV (ERIC Document Reproduction Service No. ED 335 206).

Mahmood, M. & Hirt, S. (1992). Evaluating a technology integration causal model for the K-12 public school curriculum: A LISREL analysis (ERIC Document Reproduction Service No. ED 346 847).

November, A. (1990). Big dreams, no money. *Classroom Computer Learning, 10*(5), 14, 18–19.

November, A. & Huntley, M. (1988). Kids and computers '88: How one state's CUE organization changed the way politicians think about technology. *Classroom Computer Learning, 9*(2), 5–12.

Rose, A. (1992). Financing technology. *American School Board Journal, 178*(7), 17–19.

Smith, R. (1992). Teaching with technology: The classroom manager. Cost-conscious computing. *Instructor, 10*(6), 60–61.

Smith, R. A. (1997a). Proposal writing for technology money (Part I). *Technology Connection, 4*(2), 17–19.

Smith, R. A. (1997b). Proposal writing for technology money (Part II). *Technology Connection, 4*(3), 18–19.

*Technology and Learning* (1992). *12*(4), 36–47.

Webb, D. Everything I needed to know about fund raising for technology was learned the hard way. *ISTE Update, 6*(1), 6–7.

## Optimizing Resources

Education Council for Technology in Learning. (1998). Donated computers in K-12 education. *Learning and Leading with Technology, 25*(5), 52–56.

Finkel, L. (1993). Planning for obsolescence: Upgrading and replacing old computers. *Electronic Learning, 12*(7), 18–19.

Jordan, A. (1996). Back from the dead: Rescuing computers from the morgue. *Learning and Leading with Technology, 24*(2), 61–62.

Ohlrich, K. (1996). Parent volunteers: An asset to your technology plan. *Learning and Leading with Technology, 24*(2), 51–52.

## Selecting Hardware, Software, and Facilities

Apple Computer Company (1991). *Apple technology in support of learning: Creating and managing an academic computer lab.* Sunnyvale, CA: Apple Computer Co.

Bunson, S. (1988). Design and management of an IMC micro center. *Educational Technology, 28*(8), 29–36.

Dyrli, O. & Kinnaman, D. (1994b). Gaining access to technology: The first step in making a difference for your students. *Technology and Learning, 14*(4), 16–20, 48–50.

Finkel, L. (1993). Planning for obsolescence: Upgrading and replacing old computers. *Electronic Learning, 12*(7), 18–19.

Fraundorf, M. (1997). Distributed computers and labs: The best of both worlds. *Learning and Leading with Technology, 24*(7), 50–53.

Freitas, D. (1992). Managing smallness: Promising fiscal practices for rural school district administrators. ERIC Clearinghouse on Rural Education and Small Schools (ERIC Document Reproduction No. ED 348 205).

Holland, H. (1995). Needles in a haystack. *Electronic Learning, 14*(7), 26–28.

Macon, C. (1992). The retrofit for technology project: A Florida initiative. *Florida Technology in Education Quarterly, 4*(4), 65–76.

Manckzuk, S. (1994). Planning for technology: A newcomer's guide. *Journal of Youth Services in Libraries, 7*(2), 199–206.

Milone, M. (1989). Classroom or lab: How to decide which is best. *Classroom Computer Learning, 10*(1), 34–43.

Muffoletto, R. (1994). Technology and restructuring education: Constructing a context. *Educational Technology, 34*(2), 24–28.

Neuman, D. (1991). Technology and equity. *ERIC Digest* (ERIC Document Reproduction No. ED 339 400).

Van Dam, J. (1994). Redesigning schools for 21st century technologies. *Technology and Learning, 14*(4), 54–58, 60–61.

Wilson, J. (1991). Computer laboratory workstation dimensions: Scaling down for elementary school children. *Computers in the Schools, 8*(4), 41–48.

## Support Personnel and Teacher Training

Benson, D. (1997). Technology training: Meeting teacher's changing needs. *Principal, 76*(3), 17–19.

Brooks, D. & Kopp, T. (1989). Technology in teacher education. *Journal of Teacher Education, 40*(4), 2–8.

Collins, A. (1991). The role of computer technology in restructuring schools. *Phi Delta Kappan, 73*(1), 28–36.

Dyrli, O. & Kinnaman, D. (1994b). Gaining access to technology: The first step in making a difference for your students. *Technology and Learning, 14*(4), 16–20, 48–50.

Handler, M. (1992). Preparing new teachers to use technology: Perceptions and suggestions for teacher educators. *Computers in Education, 20*(2), 147–156.

International Society for Technology in Education (ISTE). (1992). *Curriculum guidelines for accreditation of educational computing and technology programs.* Eugene, OR: ISTE.

Marker, G. & Ehman, L. (1989). Linking teachers to the world of technology. *Educational Technology, 29*(3), 26–30.

Marshall, G. (1993). Four issues confronting the design and delivery of staff development programs. *Journal of Computing in Teacher Education, 10*(1), 4–10.

Munday, R., Windham, R., & Stamper, J. (1991). Technology for learning: Are teachers being prepared? *Educational Technology, 31*(3), 29–32.

Oliver, H. (1994). Book review. Education and informatics worldwide: The state of the art and beyond. *Journal of Research on Computing in Education, 26*(2), 285–290.

OTA (1995). *Teachers and technology: Making the connection.* (OTA-EHR-616). Washington, DC: U.S. Government Printing Office.

Ringstaff, C. & Yocam, K. (1995). *Creating an alternative context for teacher development: The ACOT teacher development centers. ACOT Report, H #18.* Cupertino, CA: Apple Computer, Inc.

Roblyer, M. D. (1994). Creating technology-using teachers: A model for preservice technology training. Final report of the model preservice technology integration project. Tallahassee, FL: Florida A&M University.

Sheingold, K. (1991). Restructuring for learning with technology: The potential for synergy. *Phi Delta Kappan, 73*(1), 17–27.

Siegel, J. (1995). The state of teacher training. *Electronic Learning, 14*(8), 43–53.

Standish, D. (1996). Ignite technology: Making the difference with staff development. *Educational Media and Technology Yearbook, 21,* 126–135.

Todd, N. (1993). A curriculum model for integrating technology in teacher education courses. *Journal of Computing in Teacher Education, 9*(3), 5–11.

Warren-Sams, B. (1997, June). *Closing the equity gap in technology access and use.* Portland, OR: Northwest Regional Educational Laboratory.

Wetzel, K. (1993). Teacher educators use of computers in teaching. *Journal of Technology and Teacher Education, 1*(4), 335–352.

## Security and Maintenance

Brody, P. (1995). *Technology planning and management handbook.* Englewood, NJ: Educational Technology.

Randall, N. (1998, March 24). Defend against invaders. *PC Magazine,* 177–182.

White, L. (1992) Beyond the educational structure: A conceptual framework for computer security. *Florida Technology in Education Quarterly, 4*(4), 77–83.

## Equity Issues

Becker, H. (1985). The second national survey of instructional uses of school computers: A preliminary report (ERIC Document Reproduction Service No. ED 274 307).

Becker, H. (1986a). Instructional uses of school computers. Reports from the 1985 National Survey. Issue No. 1 (ERIC Document Reproduction Service No. ED 274 319).

Becker, H. (1986b). Instructional uses of school computers. Reports from the 1985 National Survey. Issue No. 3 (ERIC Document Reproduction Service No. ED 279 303).

Bohlin, R. (1993). Computers and gender difference: Achieving equity. *Computers in the Schools, 9*(2–3), 155–166.

Engler, P. (1992). Equity issues and computers. In G. Bitter (Ed.), *Macmillan encyclopedia of computers.* New York: Macmillan.

Fear-Fenn, M. & Kapostacy, K. (1992). Math + science + technology = Vocational preparation for girls: A difficult equation to balance. Columbus, OH: Ohio State University, Center for Sex Equity (ERIC Document Reproduction No. 341 863).

Fredman, A. (1990). *Yes, I can. Action projects to resolve equity issues in educational computing.* Eugene, OR: International Society for Technology in Education.

Holmes, N. (1991). The road less traveled by girls. *School Administrator, 48*(10, 11, 14), 16–20.

Lockard, J., Abrams, P., & Many, W. (1994). *Microcomputers for 21st century educators.* New York: HarperCollins.

McAdoo, M. (1994). Equity: Has technology bridged the gap? *Electronic Learning, 13*(7), 24–34.

Merrill, D., Hammons, K., Tolman, M., Christensen, L., Vincent, B., & Reynolds, P. (1992). *Computers in education.* Boston, MA: Allyn & Bacon.

Miller-Lachman, L. (1994). Bytes and bias: Eliminating cultural stereotypes from educational software. *School Library Journal, 40*(11), 26–30.

Molnar, A. (1978). The next great crisis in American education: Computer literacy. *AEDS Journal, 12*(1), 11–20.

Nelson, C. & Watson, J. (1991). The computer gender gap: Children's attitudes, performance, and socialization. *The Journal of Educational Technology Systems, 19*(4), 345–353.

Neuman, D. (1991). Beyond the chip: A model for fostering equity. *School Library Media Quarterly, 18*(3), 158–164.

Polin, L. (1992). Looking for love in all the wrong places? *The Computing Teacher, 20*(2), 6–7.

Roblyer, M., Dozier-Henry, O., & Burnette, A. (1996). Technology and multicultural education: The "uneasy alliance." *Educational Technology, 35*(3), 5–12.

Rosenthal, N. & Demetrulias, D. (1988). Assessing gender bias in computer software. *Computers in the Schools, 5*(1–2), 153–163.

Salehi, S. (1990). *Promoting equity through educational technology networks.* Baltimore, MD: Maryland State Department of Education (ERIC Document Reproduction Service No. ED 322 897).

Sanders, J. & Stone A. (1986). The neuter computer. Computers for girls and boys. New York: Neal Schuman Publishers.

Sanders, J. (1993). Closing the gender gap. *Executive Educator, 15*(9), 32–33.

Thurston, L. (1990). Girls, computers, and amber waves of grain: Computer equity programming for rural teachers. Paper presented at the Annual Conference of the National Women's Studies Association (ERIC Document Reproduction Service No. ED 319 660).

## Ethical and Legal Issues

Becker, G. (1992). *Copyright: A guide to information and resources.* Lake Mary, FL: Gary H. Becker Consultants.

Carpenter, C. (1996). Online ethics: What's a teacher to do? *Learning and Leading with Technology, 23*(6), 40–41, 60.

Dormady, D. (1991). Computer viruses: Suggestions on detection and prevention. *Florida Technology in Education Quarterly, 3*(4), 93–98.

Forester, T. (1990, March). Software theft and the problem of intellectual property rights. *Computers and Society,* 2–11.

Hansen, B. & Koltes, S. (1992). Viruses. In G. Bitter (Ed.), *Macmillan encyclopedia of computers.* New York: Macmillan.

Lee, J. (1992). Hacking. In G. Bitter (Ed.), *Macmillan encyclopedia of computers.* New York: Macmillan.

Mungo, P. & Clough, B. (1992). *Approaching zero: The incredible underworld of hackers, phreakers, virus writers, and keyboard criminals.* New York: Random House.

Munro, K. (1998, March 24). Monitor a child's access. *PC Magazine,* 185–194.

Simpson, C. M. (1997). *Copyright for schools: A practical guide (2nd ed.).* Worthington, OH: Linworth Publishing, Inc.

Software Publishers Association. (1994). Is it okay to copy my colleague's software? Washington, DC: SPA.

### Teacher Level Curriculum Planning and Implementation

Collis, B. (1988). *Computers, curriculum, and whole-class instruction.* Belmont, CA: Wadsworth Publishing Co.

Dillon, R. (1996). Team problem solving activities. *Learning and Leading with Technology, 24*(1), 21.

Kahn, J. (1996–97). Help I only have one computer! *Learning and Leading with Technology, 24*(4), 16.

Milone, M. (1998). Technology integration master class. *Technology and Learning, 19*(1), 6–10.

Tan, S. B. (1998). Making one-computer teaching fun. *Learning and Leading with Technology, 25*(5), 6–10.

# Chapter 3

## Learning Theories and Integration Models

Our major concern is to find a reasonable answer to the question: What is learning?

Robert M. Gagné, from *The Conditions of Learning*

Anyone who makes a responsible and systematic study of the human animal eventually feels the awe that moved Shakespeare to write "What a piece of work is a man!"

George B. Leonard, from *Education and Ecstasy*

This chapter covers the following topics:

- Background on behavioral and cognitive learning theories

- How these learning theories contributed to current models of instruction

- Technology integration strategies based on each model of instruction

- An example of how these approaches are combined in a curriculum unit

# Objectives

1. Describe concepts associated with behaviorist, information processing, and other cognitive learning theories.

2. Identify teaching/learning problems that directed and constructivist models were designed to address.

3. Identify teaching practices associated with directed and constructivist approaches.

4. Identify technology integration strategies associated with directed and constructivist approaches.

5. Design a lesson that integrates technology using a combination of directed and constructivist approaches.

# Introduction

Debate swirls around the question of what is the most appropriate instructional role for technology, particularly computer technology. Prior to about 1980, the answer would have been easy. According to respected writers of the time (Taylor, 1980), the issue divided people into three groups: those who advocated using computers primarily as tools (for word processing and numerical calculations), those who viewed them mainly as teaching aids or tutors (for drills, tutorials, and simulations), and those who believed the most powerful use was programming (the tutee use). But these groups generally would have agreed that each of these approaches had its place, and there were popular classroom strategies for each use. These were simpler times, both for educational technology and for education itself, although few would have believed it then.

## Changes Brought about by Technology

In subsequent years, two trends have affected profoundly the course of educational technology: (1) an increase in the number and types of technology resources available and (2) dramatic shifts in beliefs about the fundamental goals and strategies of education itself. These two trends have not developed in isolation; their roots are intertwined in the larger social and economic conditions that define and shape our modern world. In the past, educational goals reflected society's emphasis on the need for basic skills—such as reading, writing, and arithmetic—and an agreed-upon body of information considered essential for everyone. Students were deemed educated if they could read at a certain comprehension level; apply grammar, usage, and punctuation rules in written work; solve arithmetic problems that required addition, subtraction, multiplication, and division; and state certain series of historical facts.

As technology becomes more capable and pervades more aspects of society, everyday life also has become more complex and demanding. When students in the class of 2015 graduate, many of them will take jobs that did not exist when they entered school and will use technologies not yet invented. More information is deemed important to learn than ever before and the base of essential information grows constantly. Many educators now believe that the world is changing too quickly to define education in terms of specific information or skills; they believe education should focus on more general capabilities such as "learning to learn" skills that will help future citizens cope with inevitable technological change. Educators believe that knowing what questions to ask and how to ask them will be as important as, or more important than, giving the "right answers." In sum, technology seems to have both increased the number of decisions that people must make and forced them to become more skilled decision makers.

## Current Educational Goals and Methods: Two Views

As education changes to reflect new social and educational needs, teaching strategies also change; consequently, strategies change for integrating technology into teaching and learning. Today, educators' definition of the appropriate role of technology depends on their perceptions of the goals of education itself and appropriate instructional methods to help students attain those goals.

Most educators seem to agree that changes are needed in education. But learning theorists disagree on which strategies will best achieve today's educational goals. This controversy has served as a catalyst for two different views on teaching and learning. One view, which we will call *directed instruction,* is grounded primarily in behaviorist learning theory and the information-processing branch of the cognitive learning theories. The other view, which we will refer to as *constructivist,* evolved from other branches of thinking in cognitive learning theory. A few technology applications such as drill and practice and tutorials are associated only with directed instruction; most others (problem solving, multimedia production, Web-based learning) can enhance either directed instruction or constructivist learning, depending on how they are used.

The authors of this book see meaningful roles for both directed instruction and constructivist strategies and the technology applications associated with them; both can help schools meet the many and varied requirements of learning. That belief guides the purposes of this chapter.

# An Overview of Directed and Constructivist Instructional Methods

## A Comparison of Terminologies and Models

**Differences in terminologies.** People with radically different views on an issue frequently use different terms to describe essentially the same things. Sfard (1998) says that

**Figure 3.1    Differences in Terminology among Objectivists and Constructivists**

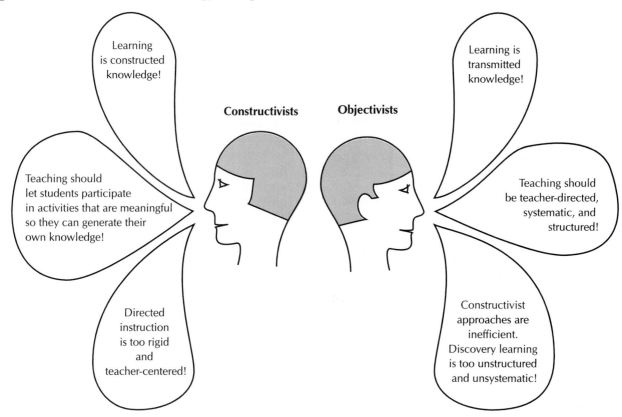

differences in the language used to describe learning spring from two different metaphors used for learning: the acquisition metaphor and the participation metaphor. She notes that "… the acquisition metaphor is likely to be more prominent in older writings, (and) more recent studies are often dominated by the participation metaphor" (p. 5). In any case, these differences in language signal fundamental differences in thinking about how learning takes place and how we can foster it. Figure 3.1 introduces these differences.

How did these differences come about? It is important to recognize that both directed instruction and constructivist approaches attempt to identify what Gagné (1985) called the *conditions of learning* or the "sets of circumstances that obtain when learning occurs" (p. 2). Both approaches are based on the work of respected learning theorists and psychologists who have studied both the behavior of human beings as learning organisms and the behavior of students in schools and classrooms. The two approaches diverge when they define *learning* and describe the conditions required to make learning happen and the kinds of problems that interfere most with learning. They disagree because they attend to different philosophies and learning theories, and they take different perspectives on improving current educational practice. Yet many believe that both kinds of strategies may prove useful to teachers in address-

ing commonly recognized instructional and educational problems.

**Differences in philosophical foundations.** The differences begin with underlying epistemologies: beliefs about the origins, nature, and limits of human knowledge. Constructivists and objectivists come from separate and different epistemological "planets," although both nurture many different tribes or cultures (Molenda, 1991; Phillips, 1995). On the objectivist side, philosophers believe that knowledge has a separate, real existence of its own outside the human mind; advocates of directed instruction believe that learning happens when this knowledge is transmitted to and acquired by learners. Constructivists believe that humans construct all knowledge in their minds by participating in certain experiences; learning happens when one constructs both mechanisms for learning and his or her own unique version of the knowledge, colored by background, experiences, and aptitudes (Willis, 1995; Sfard, 1998). Two issues of *Educational Technology* (May 1991 and September 1991) do a good job of explaining these philosophical differences and the instructional approaches that sprang from them.

**Merging the two approaches.** As Molenda (1991) observed, an *either-or* stance seems to gain us little. Rather, both sides need to find a way to merge the two approaches in a way that will benefit learners and teachers. A link between the two planets must be forged so that students may travel freely from one to the other, depending on the characteristics of the topics at hand and individual learning needs. Sfard (1998) agrees that "one metaphor is not enough" to explain how all learning takes place or to address all problems inherent in learning (p. 10).

Bereiter (1990) initially supported directed instruction methods and later shifted toward constructivist principles. He suggests that much of what educators want students to achieve is sufficiently complex that none of the existing learning theories can account for how it is actually learned, let alone the conditions that should be arranged to facilitate learning. He points out the futility of theory and research that attempts to (1) identify relevant social, environmental, or individual influences on learning such as prior experiences, types of reinforcement, and learning styles and (2) quantify their comparative contribution to what he calls difficult learning, that is, higher-order thinking and problem solving.

Bereiter also observes that each of these contributing factors tends to interact with the others, thus changing their relative importance. He quotes Cronbach's vivid metaphor: "Once we attend to interactions [between these relevant factors], we enter a hall of mirrors that extends to infinity" (Bereiter, 1990, p. 606). Practicing teachers could encounter endless variations of explanations about how people learn or fail to learn. Escaping from this hall of mirrors will require, Bereiter maintains, a more all-inclusive learning theory than those currently available. In light of Bereiter's observations, the debate between directed and constructivist proponents seems likely to inspire different methods primarily because they focus on different kinds of problems (or different aspects of the same problems) confronting teachers and students in today's schools. Like the blind men trying to describe the elephant, each focuses on a different part of the problem, and each is correct in limited observations. Needs addressed primarily by each model are described here and summarized in Figure 3.2.

## Instructional Needs and Problems Addressed by Directed Instruction Strategies

Although they are based primarily on early theories of learning, directed instruction methods target some very real problems that originated many years ago but are still with us.

America emerged from World War II with an intense awareness of the importance of education. More students were staying in school than ever before, and schools faced ever-increasing numbers of students with widely varying capabilities. More students than ever before aspired to college studies, which they viewed as a key to realizing "the American dream." Despite this dramatic increase in the numbers of students and the pressure it placed on school resources, schools still had to certify that students had

**Figure 3.2  Needs/Problems Addressed by Each Teaching/Learning Model**

**Needs Addressed by Directed Instruction**

1. Individual pacing and remediation, especially when teacher time is limited

2. Making learning paths more efficient, especially for instruction in skills that are prerequisite to higher-level skills

3. Performing time-consuming and labor-intensive tasks (e.g., skill practice), freeing teaching time for other, more complex student needs

4. Supplying self-instructional sequences, especially when teachers are not available, teacher time for structured review is limited, and/or students are already highly motivated to learn skills

**Needs Addressed by Constructivism**

1. Making skills more relevant to students' backgrounds and experiences by anchoring learning tasks in meaningful, authentic, highly visual situations

2. Addressing motivation problems through interactive activities in which students must play active rather than passive roles

3. Teaching students how to work together to solve problems through group-based, cooperative learning activities

4. Emphasizing engaging, motivational activities that require higher-level skills and prerequisite lower-lever skills at the same time.

earned high school diplomas and were ready for entrance into higher education. At the same time, teachers had to meet the individual pacing and remedial needs of each student while assuring that all students were learning required skills. Individualization became both the goal and the terror of teachers in the 1960s.

By the 1970s, *systems approaches* were widely proposed as a way for teachers and others to design self-instructional packages for students to separate directed instruction from the need for the teacher to deliver it. Self-instruction was more efficient than trying to serve the pacing and content needs of each student. It also assured that instruction was replicable, that is, quality was uniform from presentation to presentation. However, systems approaches also were seen as a way to design more effective teacher-delivered presentations.

In the 1970s and 1980s, many educators recognized how technology resources such as computer software could help them overcome some of the logistical obstacles to individualized instruction. Some courseware helped students get needed practice; other courseware guided their learning of difficult concepts through step-by-step, self-paced teaching sequences; still other courseware let students change the variables in given situations (population growth, stock market purchases) and see the effects of their decisions. All of these activities allowed teachers time to work with students who needed personal help. Teachers were encouraged to design more systematic instruction and to insert computer-based materials as needed to carry out the sequences they designed.

In the 1990s and for the foreseeable future, teachers still face the problems of having too many students, too many required skills to teach, and not enough time to deal with individual learning differences. Systematically designed, self-instructional materials often have been used to teach many important skills. They have proven especially useful for students who need a structured learning environment. Depending on other important factors, various kinds of drills, tutorials, and other older kinds of packages have effectively supplemented and, more rarely, replaced teacher-led directed instruction. Studies comparing teacher-led versus computer-based instruction in certain skill areas and with certain kinds of students have frequently found that students can learn faster via computer-based learning systems. Of course, this is not always the case; the key requirements seem to include students' motivation to learn, a well-designed overall instruction routine, and an integral role for the technology resource in the plan.

### Instructional Needs and Problems Addressed by Constructivist Strategies

In the late 1970s and 1980s, criticism of the educational system accelerated and a critical perspective of curriculum gained prominence. Many educators began to echo critics from years before that education pursued inappropriate, outdated goals; they felt that education should go beyond programs to learn isolated skills and memorize facts. They called for more emphasis on the abilities to solve problems, find information, and think critically about information. In other words, critics called for more emphasis on learning *how* to learn instead of learning specific content.

They also decried the large number of required skills and traditional learning activities that seemed abstract and unrelated to any practical skills. Students could see little relevance between skills they learned in school and those they used in their daily lives. Individualized learning drew criticism because students did not develop the ability to work well together in groups, an important workplace competency for the 1990s and beyond. These were not new criticisms, but the increase in the school dropout rate and poor national performance compared to other countries' gave the issues the status of a national crisis. The United States was "a nation at risk" (National Commission on Excellence in Education, 1983), and some changes had to be made.

New ideas from cognitive science propose the importance of *anchoring instruction* in activities that students find meaningful and authentic in the context of their own experiences. Proponents of these theories say that students who learn skills in isolation from such real-life problem solving will not remember to apply this prerequisite information when

required. They also believe that passive learners, students who view learning as something that happens *to* them rather than something they generate, are more likely to be poorly motivated to learn. To answer all these needs, constructivists propose arranging instruction around problems that students find compelling and that require them to acquire and use skills and knowledge to formulate solutions. Constructivists call for more emphasis on engaging students in the process of learning than on finding a single correct answer.

Many newer technology applications such as multimedia development and Web-based learning seem to provide ideal conditions for nurturing constructivist curriculum goals. They provide vivid visual support which helps students develop better mental models of problems to be solved. These visual media help make up for student deficiencies in such prerequisites as reading skills; they help to involve and motivate students by using graphics and other devices students find interesting and attractive. Visual media also let students work together in cooperative groups to construct products. In short, they meet all of the requirements for fulfilling the constructivist prescription for improving learning environments and refocusing curriculum.

### How Learning Theories Shape Teaching Practices and Technology Uses

Clearly, the instructional problems identified by objectivists and constructivists are common to most schools or classrooms, regardless of level or type of students or content. Teachers will always use some directed instruction as the most efficient means of teaching students required skills; teachers will always need motivating, cooperative learning activities to ensure that students want to learn and that they can transfer what they learn to problems they encounter. Tinker (1998) warns that "It is a fallacy to think that technology will make traditional content outdated … The corollary to this thinking that traditional content is less important than learning to learn … is a dangerous doctrine" (p. 2). Proficient technology-oriented teachers must learn to combine directed instruction and constructivist approaches. To implement each of these strategies, teachers select technology resources and integration methods that are best suited to carry them out.

Together, the two ostensibly different views of reality may merge to form a new and powerful approach to solving some of the major problems of the educational system, each contributing an essential element of the new instructional formula. Some practitioners believe that constructivism will eventually dominate overall educational goals and objectives such as learning to apply scientific methods, while systematic approaches will assure specific prerequisite skills. Tennyson (1990) has suggested, for example, that about 30 percent of learning time be spent on what he terms *acquiring knowledge*—verbal information and procedural knowledge. The remaining 70 percent should be spent on the *employment of knowledge* (contextual skills, cognitive strategies, and creative processes).

**Figure 3.3  Summary of Characteristics of Two Teaching/Learning Models**

> **Directed Instructional Models Tend to:**
>
> 1. Focus on teaching sequences of skills that begin with lower-level skills and build to higher-level skills
> 2. Clearly state skill objectives with test items matched to them
> 3. Stress more individualized work than group work
> 4. Emphasize traditional teaching and assessment methods: lectures, skill worksheets, activities and tests with specific expected responses
>
> **Constructivist Learning Models Tend to:**
>
> 1. Focus on learning through posing problems, exploring possible answers, and developing products and presentations
> 2. Pursue global goals that specify general abilities such as problem solving and research skills
> 3. Stress more group work than individualized work
> 4. Emphasize alternative learning and assessment methods: exploration of open-ended questions and scenarios, doing research and developing products; assessment by student portfolios, performance checklists, and tests with open-ended questions; and descriptive narratives written by teachers

Over the next decade, teachers will test Tennyson's and others' proposals for merging systematic and constructivist methods in classrooms across the country; educators will confront the task of identifying the best mix of approaches for each content area. The decade will also bring challenges to traditional views on curriculum organization such as interdisciplinary courses versus single subject ones as well as how schools can best help students to learn (direct teaching or transmission of knowledge versus providing resources and guiding learning). As they prepare to meet this challenge, teachers need to know how these methods came about, how each addresses classroom needs, and how each suggests that they integrate technology resources. Subsequent sections of this chapter will give more specific information on the origins and uses of each of the two approaches described here. Figure 3.3 gives characteristic features of directed instruction and constructivist models.

## Theoretical Foundations of Directed Instruction

### Learning Theories Associated with Directed Instruction

Two different theories of learning contributed to the development of directed instruction:

- **Behavioral theories.** Behavioral theorists concentrated on immediately observable, thus, behavioral, changes in performance (tests) as indicators of learning.

- **Information-processing theories.** These theories developed from a branch of cognitive psychology that focused on the memory and storage processes that make learning possible. They viewed the process of learning in human beings as similar to the way a computer processes information. Theorists in this area explored how a person receives information and stores it in memory, the structure of memory that allows learning something new to relate to and build on something learned previously, and how a learner retrieves information from short- and long-term memory and applies it to new situations.

The early work of giants in behavioral psychology such as B. F. Skinner and Edward Thorndike preceded work by information-processing theorists such as Richard Atkinson and David Ausubel. Robert Gagné was a leader in building upon both of these behavioral and cognitive theories to recommend approaches to instruction. Gagné also played a key role in an area of development referred to as *instructional systems design* or the systematic design of instruction. Others associated with research and development underlying these systems approaches include Leslie Briggs, Robert Glaser, Lee Cronbach, David Merrill, Charles Reigeluth, Michael Scriven, and Robert Tennyson.

### The Contributions of Behavioral Theories

Considered the grandfather of behaviorism, B. F. Skinner generated much of the experimental data that serves as the basis of behavioral learning theory. (See InSight 3.1.) Skinner and others viewed the teacher's job as modifying the behavior of students by setting up situations to reinforce students when they exhibit desired responses, teaching them to exhibit the same response in all such situations. These behavioral principles underlie two well-known trends in education: behavior modification techniques in classroom management and programmed instruction. Although current use of programmed instruction is limited, its principles form much of the basis of effective drill and practice and tutorial courseware.

### The Contributions of Information-Processing Theories

Many educational psychologists found the emphasis on observable outcomes of learning unsatisfying. They did not agree with behaviorists' views that stimulus-response learning alone could form the basis for building higher-level skills. As they focused on capabilities such as rule learning and problem solving, they became more concerned with the internal processes that went on during learning. With this knowledge, they hoped to arrange appropriate instructional conditions to promote learning of these kinds of skills. (See InSight 3.2).

## InSight 3.1

# Skinner's Behaviorist Theories of Learning: Building on the S-R Connection

Before B. F. Skinner, theories of learning were dominated by *classical conditioning* concepts proposed by Russian physiologist Ivan Pavlov, who said that behavior is largely controlled by involuntary physical responses to outside stimuli (e.g., dogs salivating at the sight of a can of dog food). Skinner's *operant conditioning* theory said that people can have mental control over their responses (e.g., a child reasons he will get praise if he behaves well in school). Eggen and Kauchak (1999) said that Skinner believed "behavior is more controlled by the *consequences of actions* than by events *preceding the actions.* A consequence is an outcome (stimulus) after the behavior (that can) influence future behaviors" (p. 201). Skinner's work made him "the most influential psychologist of the 20th century" (Eggen & Kauchak, 1999, p. 201).

Skinner reasoned that the internal processes (those inside the mind) involved in learning could not be seen directly. (Scientific work had not advanced sufficiently at that time to observe brain activity.) Therefore, he concentrated on cause-and-effect relationships that could be established by observation. He found that human behavior could be shaped by "contingencies of reinforcement" or situations in which *reinforcement* for a learner is made contingent upon a desired response. He identified three kinds of situations that can shape behavior:

- **Positive reinforcement.** A situation is set up so that an *increase* in a desired behavior will result from a stimulus, for example, to earn praise or good grades (positive reinforcement), a learner studies hard for a test (desired behavior).
- **Negative reinforcement.** A situation is set up so that an *increase* in a desired behavior will result from avoiding or removing a stimulus. For example, to avoid going to detention (negative reinforcement), a student is quiet in class (desired behavior).
- **Punishment.** A situation is set up so that a *decrease* in a desired behavior will result from undesirable consequences, such as when a student knows she will get grounded at home (punishment) if she misbehaves in school (undesirable behavior).

**Implications for education.** Skinner's influential book, *The Technology of Learning* (1968), gave a detailed theory of how classroom instruction should reflect these behaviorist principles, and many of his classroom management and instructional techniques still are widely used today. To Skinner, teaching was a process of arranging contingencies of reinforcement effectively to bring about learning. He believed that even such high-level capabilities as critical thinking and creativity could be taught in this way; it was simply a matter of establishing chains of behavior through principles of reinforcement. Skinner felt that programmed instruction was the most efficient means available for learning skills. Educational psychologists such as Benjamin Bloom also used Skinnerian principles to develop methods that became known as *mastery learning.*

**Implications for technology integration.** Most original drill and practice software was based on Skinner's reinforcement principles, for example, when students knew they would get praise or an entertaining graphic if they gave correct answers. Tutorial software usually is based on the idea of programmed instruction. Since the idea behind drill software is to increase the frequency of correct answering in response to stimuli, these packages often are used to help students memorize important basic information, while tutorial software gives students an efficient path through concepts they want to learn.

Sources: Gagné, R. (1985). *The conditions of learning* (4th ed.). New York: Holt, Rinehart and Winston; Skinner, B. F. (1938). *The behavior of organisms.* New York: Appleton; Skinner, B. F. (1968). *The technology of teaching.* New York: Appleton; and Eggen, P. & Kauchak, D. (1999). *Educational psychology: Windows on classrooms.* Upper Saddle River, NJ: Merrill/Prentice Hall. Photo from Corbis-Bettman.

## InSight 3.2

# The Information-Processing Theorists: The Mind as Computer

Behaviorists like Skinner focused only on external, directly observable indicators of human learning. Many people found this explanation insufficient to guide instruction. During the 1950s and 1960s, a group of researchers known as the cognitive-learning theorists began to hypothesize a model that would help people "describe and visualize what is impossible to observe directly" (Eggen & Kauchak, 1997, p. 239). Though some constructivists disassociate themselves with them, the information-

***Continued***

processing theorists were among the first and most influential of the cognitive-learning theorists. They hypothesized processes inside the brain that allow human beings to learn and remember.

Although no single, cohesive information-processing theory of learning summarizes the field, the work of the information-processing theorists is based on a model of memory and storage originally proposed by Atkinson and Shiffrin (1968). According to them, the brain contains certain structures that process information much like a computer. This model of the mind as computer hypothesizes that the human brain has three kinds of memory or "stores" (see model from Ormrod, 2000, p. 225):

- **Sensory registers.** The part of memory that receives all the information a person senses
- **Short-term memory (STM).** Also known as working memory, the part of memory where new information is held temporarily until it is either lost or placed into long-term memory
- **Long-term memory (LTM).** The part of memory which has an unlimited capacity and can hold information indefinitely

According to this model, learning occurs in the following way. First, information is sensed through receptors: eyes, ears, nose, mouth, and/or hands. This information is held in the sensory registers for a very short time (perhaps a second), after which it either enters STM or is lost. Many information-processing theorists believe that information can be sensed but lost before it gets to STM if the person is not paying attention to it. Anything people pay attention to goes into working memory, where it can stay for about 5 to 20 seconds (Ormrod, 2000). After this time, if information is not processed or practiced in a way that causes it to transfer to LTM, then it, too, is lost. Information-processing theorists believe that for new information to be transferred to LTM, it

must be linked in some way to prior knowledge already in LTM. Once information does enter LTM, it is there essentially permanently, although some psychologists believe that even information stored in LTM can be lost if not used regularly (Ormrod, 2000).

**Implications for education.** Information-processing views of learning have become the basis for many common classroom practices. For example, teachers ask interesting questions and display eye-catching materials to increase the likelihood that students will pay attention to a new topic. While presenting information, they give instructions that point out important points and characteristics in the new material and suggest methods of "encoding" or remembering them by linking them to information students already know. Teachers also give students practice exercises to help assure the transfer of information from short- to long-term memory.

Educational psychologists such as Gagné (see InSight 3.3) and Ausubel provided many instructional guidelines designed to enhance the processes of attention, encoding, and storage. Gagné proposed that teachers use a hierarchical "bottom-up approach," making sure that students learn lower-order skills first and build on them. Ausubel, by contrast, recommended a "top-down" approach; he proposed that teachers provide "advance organizers" or overviews of the way information will be presented to help students develop mental frameworks on which to "hang" new information (Gage & Berliner, 1988).

**Implications for technology integration.** Information-processing theories have also guided the development of artificial intelligence (AI) applications, an attempt to develop computer software that can simulate the thinking and learning behaviors of humans. Much of the drill and practice software available is designed to help students encode and store newly-learned information into long-term memory.

## A model of the human memory system

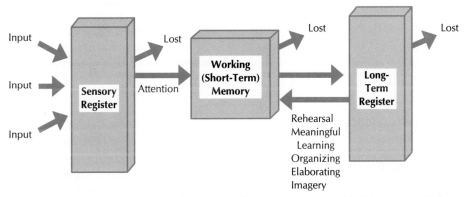

Source: From *Educational Psychology: Developing Learners* by Ormrod, p. 225, copyright © 2000 Prentice-Hall, Upper Saddle River, NJ.

Sources: Atkinson, R. & Shiffrin, R. (1968). Human memory: A proposed system and its control processes. In K. Spence & J. Spence (Eds.). *The psychology of learning and motivation: Vol. 2.* New York: Academic Press; Eggen, P. & Kauchak, D. (1999). *Educational psychology: Windows on classrooms.* Upper Saddle River, NJ: Merrill/Prentice-Hall; Gage, N. & Berliner, D. (1988) *Educational psychology* (4th ed.). Boston: Houghton Mifflin; Gagné, R. (1985). *The conditions of learning* (4th ed.). New York: Holt, Rinehart and Winston; Klatzky, R. (1980). *Human memory: Structures and processes* (2nd ed.). San Francisco: Freeman; and Ormrod, J. (2000). *Educational psychology: Developing learners.* Upper Saddle River, NJ: Merrill/Prentice-Hall.

## InSight 3.3
## Gagné's Principles: Providing Tools for Teachers

Gagné built on the work of behavioral and information-processing theorists by translating principles from their learning theories into practical instructional strategies that teachers could employ with directed instruction. He is best-known for three of his contributions in this area: the events of instruction, the types of learning, and learning hierarchies.

• **Events of instruction.** Gagné used the information-processing model of internal processes to derive a set of guidelines that teachers could follow to arrange optimal "conditions of learning." His set of nine "Events of Instruction" was perhaps the best-known of these guidelines (Gagné, Briggs, & Wager, 1988):

1. Gaining attention
2. Informing the learner of the objective
3. Stimulating recall of prerequisite learning
4. Presenting new material
5. Providing learning guidance
6. Eliciting performance
7. Providing feedback about correctness
8. Assessing performance
9. Enhancing retention and recall

• **Types of learning.** Gagné identified several types of learning as behaviors students demonstrate after acquiring knowledge. These differ according to the conditions necessary to foster them. He showed how the Events of Instruction would be carried out slightly differently from one type of learning to another (Gagné, Briggs, & Wager, 1988):

1. Intellectual skills
   - Problem solving
   - Higher-order rules

   - Defined concepts
   - Concrete concepts
   - Discriminations
2. Cognitive strategies
3. Verbal information
4. Motor skills
5. Attitudes

• **Learning hierarchies.** To develop "intellectual skills," Gagné believed, requires learning that amounts to a building process. Lower-level skills provide a necessary foundation for higher-level ones. For example, to learn to work long division problems, students first would have to learn all the prerequisite math skills, beginning with number recognition, number facts, simple addition and subtraction, multiplication, and simple division. Therefore, to teach a skill, a teacher must first identify its prerequisite skills and make sure the student possesses them. He called this list of building block skills a learning hierarchy.

**Implications for education.** Gagné's events of instruction and learning hierarchies have been widely used to develop systematic instructional design principles (see InSight 3.4). Although his work has had more impact on designing instruction for business, industry, and the military than for K-12 schools, many school curriculum development projects still use a learning hierarchy approach to sequencing skills.

**Implications for technology integration.** Gagné, Wager, and Rojas (1981) showed how Gagné's Events of Instruction could be used to plan lessons using each kind of instructional software (drill, tutorial, simulation). They said that only a tutorial could "stand by itself" and accomplish all of the necessary events of instruction; the other kinds of software required teacher-led activities to accomplish events before and after software use.

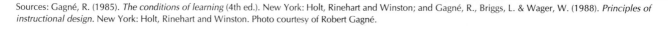

Sources: Gagné, R. (1985). *The conditions of learning* (4th ed.). New York: Holt, Rinehart and Winston; and Gagné, R., Briggs, L. & Wager, W. (1988). *Principles of instructional design.* New York: Holt, Rinehart and Winston. Photo courtesy of Robert Gagné.

### Characteristics of Directed Instruction

Teaching methods based primarily on behaviorist and information-processing learning theories usually are associated with more traditional, teacher-directed forms of instruction. Robert Gagné (see InSight 3.3) is considered a leader in developing instructional guidelines for directed instruction that combine the behavioral and information-processing learning theories. He asserted that teachers must accomplish at least three tasks to link these learning theories with teaching practices:

1.  **Assure prerequisite skills.** Teachers must make sure that students have all the prerequisite skills they need to learn a new skill. This may involve identifying component skills and the order in which they should be taught. Gagné referred to this group of skills as a *learning hierarchy.*

2.  **Supply instructional conditions.** Teachers must arrange for appropriate instructional conditions to support the internal processes involved in learning; that is, they must supply sequences of carefully structured presentations and activities that help students understand (process), remember (encode and store), and transfer (retrieve) information and skills.

3.  **Determine the type of learning.** Finally, teachers must vary these conditions for several different kinds of learning. (The kinds of learning, along with brief descriptions of related instructional conditions, are shown in InSight 3.3.)

Behaviorist and information-processing theories not only have helped establish key concepts such as types of learning and instructional conditions required to bring about each type; they also laid the groundwork for more efficient methods of creating directed instruction. These methods, known as systematic instructional design or systems approaches (see InSight 3.4), incorporated information from learning theories into step-by-step procedures for preparing instructional materials. Systematic methods came about largely in response to logistical problems in meeting large numbers of individual needs. They were adopted more often by military and industrial trainers, however, than by K-12 classroom teachers (Saettler, 1990; Wager, 1992).

Systems approaches contribute to courseware development primarily through the design of self-contained tutorial packages. However, when teachers plan their own directed instruction with technology, thinking about instruction as a system may help them develop guidelines to evaluate their own teaching effectiveness and the usefulness of their computer-based resources. For example, they may pose and answer the following kinds of questions about the components of their instructional systems to evaluate and improve their plans and materials:

- **Instructional goals and objectives.** Am I teaching what I intended to teach? Do the goals and objectives of the courseware materials match my own?

- **Instructional analysis (task analysis).** Do my students have all of the lower-level skills they need to learn successfully what I want to teach them? Does the courseware require skills my students lack?

- **Tests and measures.** Do the tests I will use measure what I will teach? Do the items included in the courseware materials match my own measures?

- **Instructional strategies.** Are my instructional activities carefully structured to provide appropriate conditions (instructional events) for the kind of learning involved (supplying examples and explanation as well as gaining attention)? What part do chosen courseware resources play in the activities and why?

- **Evaluating and revising instruction.** Have I successfully presented the instruction I envisioned? How could I improve it to make it more effective? Has the courseware successfully played the part I envisioned for it? Do I need better strategies for using it? Do I need better courseware?

## Directed Methods: Problems Raised versus Problems Addressed

The learning theories and instructional design approaches associated with directed instruction have profoundly affected American curriculum and classroom practices over the past five decades. Some would say that at least part of the impact has been negative. Programmed instruction, an early method based on behavioral principles and systematic methods, usually was successful, but students found it boring. During the 1970s, the behavioral emphasis on observable outcomes was translated into performance objectives and individual skill testing in K-12 schools—requirements often

unpopular among teachers. In many cases, schools did not follow systematic design with systematic methods; for example, many school districts required specific performance objectives for all curricula but never linked them to any instructional materials or tests. In other cases, widespread "teaching to the tests" made curriculum dry and apparently disconnected from any application outside the classroom. Constructivism is, in part, a backlash against the perceived regimentation arising from this emphasis.

**Criticisms of directed methods.** The greatest current criticisms of directed methods focus on their irrelevance to the needs of today's students. Critics of directed instruction cite several problems:

- **Students cannot do problem solving.** Many parents and educators feel that traditional methods focus too narrowly on breaking topics into discrete skills and teaching them in isolation from how they are applied. They blame this limitation for poor national test scores on more global skills of problem solving and reasoning (Cognition and Technology Group at Vanderbilt [CTGV], 1991b). The CTGV report says that, "The thinking activities that are of concern include the ability to write persuasive essays, engage in informal reasoning, explain how data relate to theory in scientific investigations, and formulate and solve moderately complex problems that require mathematical reasoning" (p. 34).

- **Students find directed instruction activities unmotivating and irrelevant.** Some critics of directed methods feel that teaching isolated skills tends to isolate students from each other and from the authentic situations they find motivating and relevant. This makes learning repetitive and predictable—what the CTGV call an industrial assembly line approach to transmitting knowledge. The CTGV repeatedly cited Corey's (1944) article, *Poor Scholar's Soliloquy,* in which a student of obvious intelligence and capability describes how he performs poorly in school because he cannot relate to the tasks his teachers assign. The CTGV said that this 55-year-old article highlighted an old, ongoing problem: "Many students seem to learn effectively in the context of authentic, real-life activities yet have great difficulty learning in the decontextualized, arbitrary-task atmosphere of schools" (p. 9). They also felt that students' lack of interest in school tasks leads directly to higher drop-out rates.

- **Students cannot work cooperatively.** Observers of economic trends in this country and throughout the world seem to feel that national economic survival depends, in large part, on how well workers work together to solve problems of mutual concern. Cooperative group work has rarely been emphasized in American schools, especially at secondary levels. Directed instruction seems geared toward individual learning, so it has been accused of isolating learners from each other and neglecting much-needed social skills.

**Current uses of directed methods.** In modern classrooms, teachers do not use programmed instruction to teach skills, nor do they design many individual lessons with specific objectives and tests for each one. Teachers use lesson plans primarily to communicate clearly to supervisors or substitutes what will happen in the classroom, but lesson plans

## InSight 3.4
## Systems Approaches and the Design of Instruction: Managing the Complexity of Teaching

Although there are many versions of the systematic design process, Bradens (1996) describes the steps of this model in the accompanying diagram. His article also gives a comprehensive discussion of the ongoing controversies surrounding the terms instructional design and systems approaches.

Saettler (1990) says that the development of "scientifically based instructional systems" precedes this century, but he also points out that modern instructional design models and methods have their roots in the collaborative work of Robert Gagné and Leslie Briggs. These notable educational psychologists developed a way to transfer "laboratory-based learning principles" gleaned from military and industrial training to create an efficient way of developing curriculum and instruction for schools.

Gagné specialized in the use of instructional task analysis (see steps 4 and 5 in Braden's model) to identify required sub-skills and conditions of learning for them. Briggs's expertise was

in systematic methods of designing training programs to save companies time and money in training their personnel. When they combined the two areas of expertise, the result was a set of step-by-step processes known as a systems approach to instructional design, or systematic instructional design, which came into common use in the 1970s and 1980s.

One component of a systematic instructional design process was the use of learning hierarchies to develop curriculum maps (Gagné, Briggs, & Wager, 1988, p. 24). According to Saettler (1990), "the 1960s produced most of the major components of the instructional design process." Names associated with this era include Robert Mager (instructional objectives), Glaser (criterion-referenced testing), and Cronbach and Scriven (formative and summative evaluation). Other major contributors to modern instructional design models include David Merrill (Component Display Theory) and Charles Reigeluth (Elaboration Theory).

### Braden's 1996 Instructional Design Model

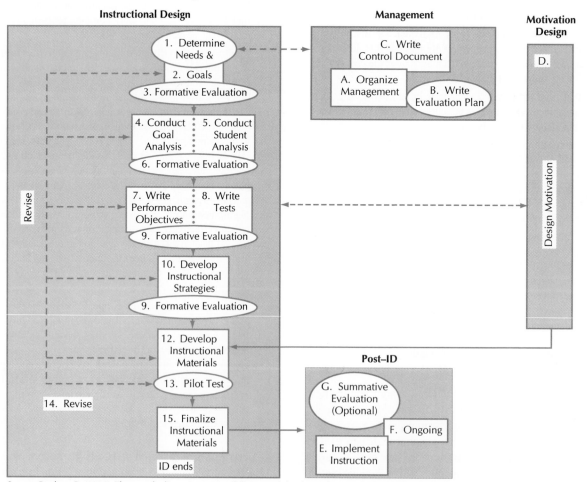

Source: Bradens, R. (1996). The case for linear instructional design and development: A commentary on models, challenges, and myths. *Educational Technology, 36*(2), 5–23.

*Continued*

<table>
<tr><td>

**Implications for education.** Systems approaches to designing instruction have had great influence on training programs for business, industry, and the military, and somewhat less influence on K-12 education. However, identifying performance objectives and sequences for instructional activities still are widely used. Most lesson planning models call for performance objectives (sometimes called behavioral objectives) to be stated in terms of measurable, observable behaviors.

</td><td>

**Implications for technology integration.** Most directed models for using technology resources are based on systems approaches, that is, teachers set objectives for a lesson, then develop a sequence of activities. A software package or an Internet activity is selected to carry out part of the instructional sequence. For example, the teacher may introduce a principle of genetics, then allow students to experiment with a simulation package to "breed" cats in order to see the principle in action.

</td></tr>
</table>

Sources: Gagné, R., Briggs, L. & Wager, W. (1988). *Principles of instructional design.* New York: Holt, Rinehart and Winston; and Saettler, P. (1990). *The evolution of American educational psychology.* Englewood, CO: Libraries Unlimited.

usually are not considered strict sequences to be followed exactly. Methods other than or in addition to objective test items are used to determine what students have learned.

But teachers still must arrange conditions of learning, and they are still largely responsible for answering the question, "What behaviors will I look for in my students to show me they have learned what I expected them to learn?" Teachers may find these traditional methods the best choice when they identify students who need more structured learning than others, or that certain prerequisite skills can best be learned through directed instruction. Although behaviorism may be viewed as an archaic and outmoded theory (Bradens, 1996), a considerable body of research indicates that teaching methods based on it work well for certain situations. Carnine, Silbert, and Kameenui (1997) and Stein, Silbert, and Carnine (1997) document its effectiveness in teaching reading and mathematics skills. A special issue of *Educational Technology* (October 1993) gives additional examples:

- Fluency practice in precision teaching of basic reading and math skills to young learners (Spence & Hively, 1993)
- Performance management contingencies to improve the study habits and achievement of college students (Mallott, 1993)
- Structured, teacher-directed techniques to teach problem solving and higher-order thinking skills to at-risk students (Carnine, 1993)
- Proposed application of behavioral techniques to teach the required behaviors leading to creativity (Epstein, 1993)

Raspberry (1998) and others find that directed or "scripted" programs such as DISTAR, which were developed many years ago based on behavioral principles, continue to be highly effective in many schools.

## Theoretical Foundations of Constructivism

Molenda (1991) has said that "constructivism comes in different strengths … from weak to moderate to extreme" (p. 47). Phillips (1995) referred to constructivism as made up of many "sects, each of which harbors some distrust of

its rivals" (p. 5). The differences among those who think of themselves as constructivists makes it difficult to settle on a single definition for constructivism. However, these differences may be explained by examining the variations in learning theories that underlie constructivist approaches.

### Learning Theories Associated with Constructivism

Constructivist strategies are based on principles of learning derived from branches of cognitive science. This area focused specifically on student motivation to learn and ability to use what they learn outside the school culture. Constructivist strategies try to respond to perceived deficiencies in behaviorist and information-processing theories and the teaching methods based on them. In addition, constructivists try to inspire students to see the relevance of what they learn and to prevent what the CTGV (1990) call inert knowledge, or student failure to transfer what is already known to the learning of other skills that require prior knowledge.

These theories are based on the ideas of revered educational philosophers such as John Dewey and renowned educational psychologists such as Lev Vygotsky, Jerome Bruner, Jean Piaget, and Howard Gardner. Later work by educational theorists such as Seymour Papert and educational psychologists and practitioners such as John Seely Brown, the Cognition and Technology Group at Vanderbilt, Rand Spiro, D. N. Perkins, Ann Brown, Joe Campione, Carl Bereiter, and Marlene Scardamalia expand on these principles and develop specifications for translating these theories of cognition into teaching practices.

### The Contributions of Early Cognitive Learning Theories

Educators credit theorists such as John Dewey, Lev Vygotsky, Jean Piaget, and Jerome Bruner with some of the fundamental premises of constructivist thinking.

**Dewey's social constructivism.** John Dewey is well-known for laying the theoretical groundwork for many characteristics of today's educational system. He was responsible for the progressive movement in American education, many principles that are now being re-examined for possible applications in school restructuring efforts. Several of

## InSight 3.5
## The Contributions of Lev Vygotsky: Building a Scaffold to Learning

For many years, the writings of Russian philosopher and educational psychologist Lev Semenovich Vygotsky had more influence on the development of educational theory and practice in America than in his own country. Davydov (1995) notes that Vygotsky's landmark book, *Pedagogical Psychology,* though written in 1926, was not published in Russia until 1991. Davydov attributes this lack of attention to the nature of the Russian government up until the time of *perestroika.* "… Vygotsky's general ideas could not be used for such a long time in the education system of a totalitarian society—they simply contradict all of its principles" (p. 13). What were these educational concepts that were so threatening to a communistic state but found such a warm reception in a democracy?

Vygotsky felt that cognitive development was directly related to and based on social development (Gage & Berliner, 1988; Ormrod, 1998). What children learn and how they think are derived directly from the culture around them: "… children begin learning from the world around them, their social world, which is the source of all their concepts, ideas, facts, skills, and attitudes.… [O]ur personal psychological processes begin as social processes, patterned by our culture" (Gage & Berliner, 1988, p. 124). An adult perceives things much differently than a child does, but this difference decreases as children gradually translate their social views into personal, psychological ones. Vygotsky's theories, with their emphasis on individual differences, personal creativity, and the influence of culture on learning, were discordant with the aims of the USSR, a government designed to "subjugate the education of young people to the interests of a militarized state that needed citizens only as devoted cogs" (Davydov, 1995, p. 12).

Vygotsky referred to the difference between these two levels of cognitive functioning (adult/expert and child/novice) as the *zone of proximal development.* He felt that teachers could provide good instruction by finding out where each child was in his or her development and building upon the child's experiences. He called this building process "scaffolding." Ormrod (2000) said that teachers promote students' cognitive development by presenting some classroom tasks that "they can complete only with assistance, that is, within each student's zone of proximal devel-

opment" (p. 59). Gage and Berliner (1988) feel that problems occur when the teacher leaves too much for the child to do independently, thus slowing the child's intellectual growth. "In the zone of proximal development, social knowledge—knowledge acquired through social interaction—becomes individual knowledge and individual knowledge grows and becomes more complex" (Gage & Berliner, 1988, p. 126).

**Implications for education.** Davydov (1995) found five basic implications for education in Vygotsky's ideas (p. 13):

1. Education is intended to develop children's personalities.

2. The human personality is linked to its creative potential, and education should be designed to discover and develop this potential to its fullest in each individual.

3. Teaching and learning assume that students master their inner values through some personal activity.

4. Teachers direct and guide the individual activities of the students but they do not force their will on them or dictate to them.

5. The most valuable methods for student learning are those that correspond to their individual developmental stages and needs; therefore, these methods cannot be uniform across students.

These ideas had heavy influence on constructivist thought; Vygotsky's works were very much in tune with constructivist concepts of instruction based on each child's personal experiences and learning through collaborative, social activities.

**Implications for technology integration.** Many constructivist models of technology use the concepts of scaffolding and developing each individual's potential. Many of the more visual tools, from Logo to virtual reality, are used under the assumption that they can help bring the student up from their level of understanding to a higher level by showing graphic examples and by giving them real-life experiences relevant to their individual needs.

Sources: Davydov, V. (1995). The influence of L. S. Vygotsky on education theory, research, and practice. *Educational Researcher, 24*(3), 12–21; Gage, N. & Berliner, D. (1988). *Educational psychology* (4th ed.). Boston: Houghton Mifflin; and Ormrod, J. (2000). *Educational psychology: Developing learners.* (3rd ed.). Upper Saddle River, NJ: Merrill/Prentice-Hall.

Dewey's ideas support constructivist models of teaching and learning. Among these ideas is the need to center student instruction around relevant, meaningful activities. Prawat (1993) recalled Dewey's label of "worse than useless" any instruction that did not center around problems already stirring in the child's experience (p. 6).

**Vygotsky's scaffolding.** The work of renowned human development theorist Lev Vygotsky (see InSight 3.5) also contributed key support for constructivist approaches. His twin concepts of *scaffolding* and the *zone of proximal*

*development* are important for constructivists. Prawat (1993) observed that "Vygotsky emphasized the importance of social relations in all forms of complex mental activity" (p. 10); likewise, constructivists feel that teachers can most effectively provide scaffolding or help in acquiring new knowledge through collaboration with others.

**Piaget's stages of development.** The internationally famous developmental psychologist Piaget (see InSight 3.6) is generally regarded as a major contributor of theoretical principles for constructivist thinking. While some edu-

## InSight 3.6
# Jean Piaget's Theories: Cognitive Development in Children

As Flavell (1985) observed, "Piaget's contributions to our knowledge of cognitive development have been nothing short of stupendous" (p. 4). His examination of how thinking and reasoning abilities develop in the human mind began with observations of his own children and developed into a career that spanned some 60 years. He referred to himself as a "genetic epistemologist," or a scientist who studies how knowledge begins and develops in individuals. Both believers in and critics of Piagetian principles agree that his work was complex, profound, sometimes misunderstood, and usually oversimplified. However, at least two features of this work are widely recognized as underlying all of Piaget's theories: his stages of cognitive development and his processes of cognitive functioning.

Piaget believed that all children go through four stages of cognitive development. While the ages at which they experience these stages vary somewhat, he felt that each developed higher reasoning abilities in the same sequence:

- **Sensorimotor stage (from birth to about 2 years).** Characteristics of children:
  - Explore the world around them through their senses and through motor activity. In the earliest stage, they cannot differentiate between themselves and their environments (if they cannot see something, it does not exist).
  - Begin to have some perception of cause and effect; develop the ability to follow something with their eyes.

- **Preoperational stage (from about age 2 to about age 7).** Characteristics of children:
  - Develop greater abilities to communicate through speech and to engage in symbolic activities such as drawing objects and playing by pretending and imagining
  - Develop numerical abilities such as the skill of assigning a number to each object in a group as it is counted
  - Increase their level of self-control and are able to delay gratification, but are still fairly egocentric
  - Unable to do what Piaget called conservation tasks (tasks that call for recognizing that a substance remains the same even though its appearance changes, e.g., shape is not related to quantity)

- **Concrete operational stage (from about age 7 to about age 11).** Characteristics of children:
  - Increase in abstract reasoning ability and ability to generalize from concrete experiences
  - Can do conservation tasks

- **Formal operations stage (from about age 12 to about age 15).** Characteristics of children:
  - Can form and test hypotheses, organize information, and reason scientifically
  - Can show results of abstract thinking in the form of symbolic materials (e.g., writing, drama)

Piaget believed that a child's development from one stage to another takes place through a gradual process of interacting with the environment. Children develop as they confront new and unfamiliar features of their environment that do not fit with their current views of the world. When this happens, he said, a "disequilibrium" occurs that the child seeks to resolve through one of two processes of adaptation. The child either fits the new experiences into his or her existing view of the world (a process called assimilation) or changes that schema or view of the world to incorporate the new experiences (a process called accommodation). Though recent research has raised questions about the ages at which children's abilities develop, and it is widely believed that age does not determine development alone, Ormrod (2000) summarizes Piaget's basic assumptions about children's cognitive development in the following way:

1. Children are active and motivated learners.
2. Children's knowledge of the world becomes more integrated and organized over time.
3. Children learn through the processes of assimilation and accommodation.
4. Cognitive development depends on interaction with one's physical and social environment.
5. The processes of equilibration (resolving disequilibrium) help to develop increasingly complex levels of thought.
6. Cognitive development can occur only after certain genetically controlled neurological changes occur.
7. Cognitive development occurs in four qualitatively different stages.

**Implications for education.** Educators do not always agree on the implications of Piaget's theories for classroom instruction. One frequently expressed instructional principle based on Piaget's stages is the need for concrete examples and experiences when teaching abstract concepts to young children who may not yet have reached a formal operations stage. Piaget himself repeatedly expressed a lack of interest in how his work applied to school-based education, calling it "the American question." He pointed out that much learning occurs without any formal instruction, as a result of the child interacting with the environment. However, constructivist educators tend to claim Piaget as the philosophical mentor that guides their work.

**Implications for technology integration.** Many technology-using teachers feel that using visual resources such as Logo and

*Continued*

simulations can help raise children's developmental levels more quickly than they would have occurred through maturation; thus children who use these resources can learn higher-level concepts than they normally would not have been able to understand until they were older. However, research evidence to support their belief still is being gathered. Other educators feel that young children should experience things in the "real world" before seeing them represented in the more abstract ways they are shown in software, for example, computer simulations.

Sources: Flavell, (1985). *Cognitive development* (2nd ed.). Englewood Cliffs, NJ: Prentice-Hall; and Ormrod, J. (2000). *Educational psychology: Developing learners.* (3rd ed.). Upper Saddle River, NJ: Merrill/Prentice-Hall. Photo from Corbis-Bettman.

cators feel that Piaget's ideas have been applied inappropriately, some of his basic premises seem related to constructivist approaches.

**Bruner relevance principle.** Some of the principles associated with educational theorist Jerome Bruner (see InSight 3.7) seem to coincide with those of Vygotsky and Piaget, providing further theoretical support for constructivist theory. Like Piaget, Bruner believed children go through various stages of intellectual development. But unlike Piaget, Bruner supported intervention. He was primarily concerned with making education more relevant to student need at each stage, and he believed that teachers could accomplish this by encouraging active participation in the learning process. Active participation, he felt, was best achieved by providing discovery learning environments that would let children explore alternatives and recognize relationships between ideas (Bruner, 1973).

**Theoretical foundations of constructivism.** From these theorists, constructivists derived the premise that educational experiences should foster a child's progress through stages of development. Constructivists tend to perceive much of today's education as too structured and geared to activities that are inappropriate for children's current developmental levels. These experiences, they say, can actually slow students' progress by inhibiting their innate desire to make sense of the world at each stage of their cognitive development. Like Bruner, most constructivists call for instructional intervention, that is, for teachers to provide learning activities designed not only to match but to accelerate movement through these stages. They also feel that education should provide children with more opportunities for cognitive growth through exploration, unstructured learning, and problem solving.

### The Contributions of Later Work Based on Cognitive Principles

Several lines of research and development based on principles from cognitive science have profoundly affected educational practice, particularly instructional applications of technology. This section discusses some major contributors to this research.

**Papert's microworlds.** Seymour Papert, a mathematician and pupil of Piaget, (see InSight 3.8) was one of the first vocal critics of using technology in the context of traditional instructional methods. In his 1980 book *Mindstorms,* he became one of the first to raise national consciousness about the potential role of technology in creating alternatives to what he perceived as inadequate and harmful educational methods. Bass (1985) observed that "In many ways, the development of Logo has paralleled the recent development of Piagetian theory" (p. 107). However, even Bass admitted that while the focus of Piaget's colleagues may have changed, Piaget himself was never "particularly concerned with what he called 'the American question' of how to influence [children's] development through planned learning environments" (p. 113).

**John Seely Brown and cognitive apprenticeships.** Brown and his colleagues at the Institute for Research on Learning focused on the work of cognitive psychologists who built on Vygotsky's hypotheses (Brown, Collins, & Duguid, 1989). Brown et al. were especially concerned with the relationship between this work and a problem they observed throughout much school learning. They refer to this problem as *inert knowledge,* a term introduced in 1929 by Whitehead. Brown et al. found that many school practices reduce the likelihood that children will transfer learned skills to later problem solving that requires those skills. The researchers observe that "it is common for students to acquire algorithms, routines, and decontextualized definitions that they cannot use and that, therefore, lie inert" (p. 33). They say this is because skills often are taught in abstract ways and in isolation from actual, authentic application. For example, students often learn multiplication facts and procedures, but fail to recognize applications of these skills to real-life problems or to word problems that require multiplication. Students often feel that activities like multiplication are something done in a school culture with no real utility or application outside school.

*What* students learn, Brown et al. argue, should not be separated from *how* they learn it. Students must come to understand how to transfer knowledge, they say, by learning it at the same time as they apply it in meaningful ways. This can best be accomplished by providing *cognitive apprenticeships,* activities that call for authentic problem solving, that is, problem solving in settings that are familiar and useful to the student. Such tasks require students to use knowledge in content areas as tools, much as an apprentice tailor would use a sewing machine and scissors.

## InSight 3.7
# The Contributions of Jerome Bruner: Learning as Discovery

Like Piaget, Jerome Bruner was interested in children's stages of cognitive development. Bruner described development in three stages (Gage & Berliner, 1988):

- **Enactive stage (from birth to about age 3).** Children perceive the environment solely through actions that they initiate. They describe and explain objects solely in terms of what a child can do with them. The child cannot tell how a bicycle works, but can show what to do with it. Showing and modeling have more learning value than telling for children at this stage.

- **Iconic stage (from about age 3 to about age 8).** Children can remember and use information through imagery (mental pictures or icons). Visual memory increases and children can imagine or think about actions without actually experiencing them. Decisions are still made on the basis of perceptions, rather than language.

- **Symbolic stage (from about age 8).** Children begin to use symbols (words or drawn pictures) to represent people, activities, and things. They have the ability to think and talk about things in abstract terms. They can also use and understand what Gagné would call "defined concepts." For example, they can discuss the concept of toys and identify various kinds of toys, rather than defining them only in terms of toys they have seen or handled. They can better understand mathematical principles and use symbolic idioms such as "Don't cry over spilt milk."

Bruner also identified six indicators or "benchmarks" that revealed cognitive growth or development (Owen, Froman, & Moscow, 1981, p. 49; Gage & Berliner, 1988, p. 121–122). He said they:

1. Respond to situations in varied ways, rather than always in the same way
2. Internalize events into a "storage system" that corresponds to the environment
3. Have increased capacity for language
4. Can interact systematically with a tutor (parent, teacher, or other role model)
5. Use language as an instrument for ordering the environment
6. Have increasing capacity to deal with multiple demands

**Implications for education.** Unlike Piaget, Bruner was very concerned about arrangements for school instruction that acknowledged and built upon the stages of cognitive development. The idea of discovery learning is largely attributed to him. Discovery learning is "an approach to instruction through which students interact with their environment—by exploring and manipulating objects, wrestling with questions and controversies, or performing experiments" (Ormrod, 2000, p. 442). Bruner felt that students were more likely to understand and remember concepts they had discovered in the course of their own exploration. However, research findings have yielded mixed results for discovery learning, and the relatively unstructured methods recommended by Bruner have not found widespread support (Eggen & Kauchak, 1999; Ormrod, 2000). Teachers have found that discovery learning is most successful when students have prerequisite knowledge and undergo some structured experiences.

**Implications for technology integration.** Many of the more "radical constructivist" uses of technology employ a discovery learning approach suggested by Bruner. For example, rather than telling students how logic circuits work, a teacher might allow students to use a simulation that lets them discover the rules themselves. Most school uses of technology, however, use what Eggen and Kauchak (1999) call a guided discovery learning approach. For example, a teacher may introduce a problem scenario such as those in the *Adventures of Jasper Woodbury* videodiscs, then help students develop their approaches to solving the problem.

Source: Eggen, P. & Kauchak, D. (1999). *Educational psychology: Windows on classrooms*. (4th ed.). Upper Saddle River, NJ: Merrill/Prentice Hall; Gage, N. & Berliner, D. (1988) *Educational psychology* (4th ed.). Boston: Houghton Mifflin; Goetze, E., Alexander, P., & Ash, M. (1992). *Educational psychology: A classroom perspective*. New York: Merrill; Bruner, J. (1966). *Toward a theory of instruction*. Boston: Little, Brown; Ormrod, J. (2000). *Educational psychology: Developing learners*. (3rd ed.). Upper Saddle River, NJ: Merrill/Prentice Hall; and Owen, S., Froman, R., & Moscow, H. (1981). *Educational psychology*. Boston: Little, Brown. Photo courtesy of Jerome Bruner.

For example, the researchers suggest teaching multiplication in the context of coin problems "because in the community of fourth grade students, there is usually a strong, implicit, shared understanding of coins" (p. 38). Through these kinds of activities, multiplication becomes useful and real beyond the school culture. They refer to this kind of teaching and learning as *situated cognition,* and like Vygotsky, they feel it can best be accomplished through collaborative (group) learning.

**Vanderbilt's cognition and technology group and anchored instruction.** A group of researchers at Vanderbilt's Learning and Technology Center built on the concepts of situated cognition and collaborative learning introduced by Brown et al. as well as Vygotsky's concept of scaffolding (see InSight 3.9). They recommended anchoring instruction in situations where students not only create answers to problems, but also generate many aspects of the problem statements. The researchers referred to this

## InSight 3.8
## Seymour Papert: Turtles and Beyond

One of Piaget's most famous American pupils, Seymour Papert, has influenced profoundly the field of educational technology. Papert began his career as a mathematician. After studying with Jean Piaget in Geneva from 1959 to 1964, Papert became impressed with Piaget's way of "looking at children as active builders of their own intellectual structures" (Papert, 1980, p. 19). Papert subsequently joined the Artificial Intelligence Laboratory at the Massachusetts Institute of Technology and began experimenting with Logo, a new programming language, and its use with young children. One of his colleagues was also working with children, teaching them to control a robot in the shape of a turtle. The MIT team decided to combine the two concepts, integrating an on-screen "turtle" into the Logo language. This addition provided the vital link that Papert felt would allow children to move more easily from the concrete operations of earlier stages of Piaget's hypothesis to more abstract (formal) ones. In 1980, Papert published his theories in a book entitled *Mindstorms: Children, Computers, and Powerful Ideas*. This book challenged then-current instructional goals and methods for both mathematics and educational technology, and it became the first widely recognized constructivist statement of educational practice with technology resources.

**Implications for education and technology integration.** As Papert himself observed, "I make a slightly unorthodox interpretation of [Piaget's] theoretical position and a very unorthodox interpretation of the implications of his theory for education" (Papert, 1980, p. 217). Piaget himself was not concerned with instructional methods or curriculum matters, and he had no interest in trying to accelerate the stages of cognitive development. Papert, on the other hand, felt that children could advance in their intellectual abilities more quickly with the right kind of environment and assistance. He described the requirements of such an environment in his 1980 book.

• **Discovery learning and "powerful ideas."** Although he never used the term discovery learning, Papert felt that children should be allowed to "teach themselves" with Logo. Reflecting the Piagetian concept of disequilibrium, he explained that "in a Logo environment, new ideas are often acquired as a means of satisfying a personal need to do something one could not do before" (Papert, 1980, p. 74). He felt that children need great flexibility to develop their own "powerful ideas" or insights about new concepts.

• **Logo and the microworlds concept.** Papert perceived Logo as a resource with ideal properties for encouraging learning. Since Logo is graphics-oriented, it allows children to see cause-and-effect relationships between the logic of programming commands and the pictures that result. This logical, cause-and-effect quality of Logo activities makes possible "microworlds," or self-contained environments where all actions are orderly and rule-governed. He called these microworlds "incubators for knowledge" where children could pose and test out hypotheses.

When research studies on educational applications of Logo failed to yield the improvements expected by educators, many of Papert's concepts became even more controversial. Papert criticized these research efforts as "technocentric," saying that they focused more on Logo itself than on the methods used with it. However, Logo as an "instructional method" dropped out of common use in the early 1990s.

Although Logo is not in common use today, Papert's constructivist emphasis has had a distinct influence on the use of newer technology resources. Until Papert's work, the quality of software and media were judged almost solely on how well they reflected systematic design principles. After Logo, technology resources began to be evaluated according to how they could be used as "microworlds" and "incubators for knowledge" in which learners could generate their own knowledge.

Source: Papert, S. (1980). *Mindstorms: Children, computers, and powerful ideas.* New York: Basic Books. Photo courtesy of Scholastic, Inc.

active involvement in problem solving as *generative learning* and pointed out that video-based technologies have unique qualities to support these kinds of problem-solving environments.

**Cognitive flexibility theory and radical constructivism.** Rand Spiro and a group of researchers that included Feltovich, Jacobson, Coulson, Anderson, and Jehng developed a constructivist theory in reaction to a perceived failure of many current instructional approaches—including some constructivist ones. Spiro et al. say that current classroom methods are more suited to learning in well-structured knowledge domains, while much of what stu-

dents should learn lies in "ill-structured domains." For example, "... basic arithmetic is well-structured, while the process of applying arithmetic in solving word problems drawn from real situations is more ill-structured" (Spiro et al., 1991, p. 26). For learning in these ill-structured domains, Spiro et al. say, students need a different way of thinking about learning. "The interpretation of constructivism that has dominated much of cognition and educational psychology for the past 20 years or so has frequently stressed the retrieval of organized packets of knowledge, or schemas, from memory.... We argue that ... ill-structured knowledge domains often render [these] schemas inadequate" (p. 28).

## InSight 3.9
## The Cognition and Technology Group at Vanderbilt (CTGV): Tying Technology to Constructivism

A research team located at the Learning Technology Center at Vanderbilt University has helped establish some practical guidelines for integrating technology based on constructivist principles. This team, known as the Cognition and Technology Group at Vanderbilt (CTGV), proposed an instructional approach based on concepts introduced by Vygotsky; Whitehead; and Brown, Collins, and Duguid (1989). It has also developed several technology products modeling this approach that have achieved widespread use in American education. Several related concepts provide the theoretical foundation for the CTGV team's approach:

*   **Preventing inert knowledge.** The CTGV hypothesized without a direct relationship to children's personal experience, often resulting in their acquiring what Whitehead referred to as inert knowledge. That is, students never actually applied the knowledge they had learned because they could not see its relationship to problems they encountered. Inert knowledge is "knowledge that can usually be recalled when people are explicitly asked to do so, but is not used spontaneously in problem solving even though it is relevant" (CTGV, 1990).

*   **The nature of situated cognition and the need for anchored instruction.** Brown, Collins, and Duguid (1989) suggested that teachers could prevent the problem of inert knowledge by situating learning in the context of what they called authentic experiences and practical apprenticeships—activities that learners considered important because they emulated the behavior of experts (adults) in the area. In this way, students see the link between school learning and real-life activities. The CTGV felt that teachers can meet the criteria for situated cognition by anchoring instruction in highly visual problem-solving environments. "Anchored instruction provides a way to recreate some of the advantages of apprenticeship training in formal educational settings involving groups of students" (CTGV, 1990, p. 2).

*   **Building knowledge through generative activities.** Like Vygotsky, the CTGV believes that learning is most meaningful to students when it builds (scaffolds) on experiences they have already had. Students are also more likely to remember knowledge that they build or "generate" themselves, rather than that which they simply receive passively (CTGV, 1991).

**Implications for education and technology integration.** The CTGV proposed that the best way of providing instruction that would meet all the required criteria was to present it as videodisc-based scenarios posing interesting but difficult problems for students to solve. The first of these technology-based products, the *Jasper Woodbury Problem Solving Series*, focused on mathematics problems. Another, *The Young Children's Literacy Series,* addressed reading and language skills (CTGV, 1993). Both of these products were designed to build on children's existing knowledge in a way that would emphasize knowledge transfer to real-life situations.

Sources: Brown, J. S., Collins, A. & Duguid, P. (1989). Situated cognition and the culture of learning. *Educational Researcher 18*(1), 32–41; Cognition and Technology Group at Vanderbilt (1990). Anchored instruction and its relationship to situated cognition. *Educational Researcher 19*(6), 2–10; Cognition and Technology Group at Vanderbilt (1991). Technology and the design of generative learning environments. *Educational Technology 31*(5), 34–40; and Cognition and Technology Group at Vanderbilt (1993). The Jasper experiment: An exploration of issues in learning and instructional design. *Educational Technology Research and Development 40*(1), 65–80. Photo courtesy of Billie Kingsley, Vanderbilt University, photographer David Crenshaw.

Spiro et al. say that the new constructivism of their Cognitive Flexibility Theory is "doubly constructive." That is, it calls for students to generate not only solutions to new problems, but also the prior knowledge needed to solve the problems. This kind of constructivism demands even less direct teaching and even more exploration on the part of students than those of Brown et al. and CTVG. Perkins (1991) calls this the difference between "BIG (beyond the information given) instruction" and "WIG (without the information given) instruction" (p. 20). Because they call for an even greater departure from directed instruction methods than other constructivists, those who hold views

similar to those of Spiro et al. are sometimes referred to as *radical constructivists.*

**Gardner's theory of multiple intelligences.** Gardner's theory (see InSight 3.10) that many kinds of intelligence exist is not strictly constructivist. But it does coincide with the constructivist emphasis on group work, both as a function of distributed intelligence and as a necessary social skill. According to Gardner, since students may vary greatly in strength and aptitude, each can make a unique and valuable contribution to a group product. Many teachers find Gardner's theory intuitively appealing; it reinforces

# InSight 3.10
## Gardner's Theory of Multiple Intelligences

Of all the learning and developmental theories embraced by constructivists, Howard Gardner's is the only one that attempts to define the role of intelligence in learning. His work is based on Guilford's pioneering work on the structure of intellect (Eggen & Kauchak, 1999) and Sternberg's view of intelligence as influenced by culture (Ormrod, 2000). Gardner's theory (1983) is that at least eight different and relatively independent types of intelligence exist (see table below).

**Implications for education.** If Gardner's theory is correct, then IQ tests (which tend to stress linguistic and logical-mathematical abilities) may not be the best way to judge a given student's ability to learn, and traditional academic tasks may not be the best reflection of ability. Ormrod (2000) points out that "to the extent that intelligence is culture-dependent, intelligent behavior is likely to take different forms in children from different ethnic backgrounds" (p. 156). Teachers, then, should try to determine which type or types of intelligence each student has and direct the student to learning activities that capitalize on these innate abilities. Gardner and Hatch (1989) give suggestions for how best to do this. Also, teachers may consider learning activities based on distributed intelligence, where each student makes a different, but valued contribution to creating a product or solving a problem.

**Implications for technology integration.** Gardner's theory meshes well with the trend toward using technology to support group work. When educators assign students to groups to develop a multimedia product, they can assign students roles based on their type of intelligence. For example, those with high interpersonal intelligence may be the project coordinators, those with high logical-mathematical ability may be responsible for structure and links, and those with spatial ability may be responsible for graphics and aesthetics.

| Types of Intelligence | Description | Reflected in Activities |
|---|---|---|
| Linguistic | Uses language effectively<br>Is sensitive to the uses of language<br>Writes clearly and persuasively | Writer, journalist, poet |
| Musical | Understands musical structure and composition; communicates by writing or playing music | Composer, pianist, conductor |
| Logical-mathematical | Reasons logically in math terms<br>Recognizes patterns in phenomena<br>Formulates and tests hypotheses and solves problems in math and science | Scientist, mathematician, doctor |
| Spatial | Perceives the world in visual terms<br>Notices and remembers visual details<br>Can recreate things after seeing them | Artist, sculptor, graphic artist |
| Bodily-kinesthetic | Uses the body skillfully<br>Manipulates things well with hands<br>Uses tools skillfully | Dancer, athlete, watchmaker |
| Intrapersonal | Is an introspective thinker<br>Is aware of one's own motives<br>Has heightened metacognitive abilities | Self-aware/self-motivated person |
| Interpersonal | Notices moods and changes in others<br>Can identify motives in others' behavior<br>Relates well with others | Psychologist, therapist, salesperson |
| Naturalist | Can discriminate among living things | Botanist, biologist |

Sources: Eggen, P. & Kauchak, D. (1999). *Educational psychology: Windows on classrooms.* Upper Saddle River, NJ: Merrill/Prentice Hall; Gardner, H. (1983). *Frames of mind.* New York: Basic Books; Gardner, H. (1989). Multiple intelligences go to school: Educational implications of the theory of multiple intelligences. *Educational Researcher, 18*(8), 4–10; Ormrod, J. (2000). *Educational psychology: Developing learners.* Upper Saddle River, NJ: Merrill/Prentice Hall; Photo courtesy of C. Jerry Bauer, 1994.

their own observations and experiences with students. Perhaps more important, however, it helps justify having different goals and criteria for success for each student, rather than a one-size-fits-all set for everyone.

## Characteristics of Constructivism

Constructivism challenges the traditional goals of education and proposes restructured, innovative teaching approaches. Constructivist goals focus on students' ability to solve real-life, practical problems, and its methods call for students to construct knowledge themselves rather than simply receiving it from knowledgeable teachers. As Figure 3.3 indicates, students typically work in cooperative groups rather than individually. They tend to focus on projects that require solutions to problems rather than on instructional sequences that require learning certain content skills. In contrast to directed instruction, where the teacher sets the goals and delivers most of the instruction, the job of the teacher in constructivist models is to arrange for required resources and act as a guide to students while they set their own goals and "teach themselves."

For example, rather than teaching an isolated objective such as identifying animals by phylum and genus, teachers may arrange for students to carry out cooperative projects that investigate the behavior of animals in the local environment.

Sometimes instructional activities based on constructivist models are more time-consuming, since they may call for teachers to organize and facilitate group work and to evaluate in authentic ways. By comparison, paper-and-pencil tests are both quicker to develop and easier to administer. Many commercially available instructional materials based on constructivist models are recent designs. Since these materials may have been in use only briefly, teachers often have limited information available on how to smooth classroom implementation or what problems to anticipate. This is especially true with activities involving newer technologies such as interactive video and multimedia. The knowledge base on these kinds of classroom activities is growing, but teachers still are adapting classroom strategies and coping with the logistics of setting up and using such equipment and media.

It also is important to recognize potential contradictions in theorists' views on how teachers should carry out constructivist approaches. As Spiro, et al. (1991) observe, there are many variations on what is meant by constructivist (p. 22). For example, Papert feels that learning activities should be fairly unstructured and open-ended, frequently with no goal in mind other than discovery of powerful ideas. Spiro et al. also call for varied opportunities for exploration when learning in ill-structured knowledge domains, but they seem to advocate at least some acquisition of specific skills and information. The guidelines set forth by CTGV are still more goal-oriented and call for students to generate solutions to specific problems.

Teachers must analyze the needs of their students and decide which constructivist strategies seem most appropriate for meeting these needs.

The work of researchers and theorists such as Papert, Brown et al., CTGV, and Perkins have contributed especially important guidelines on how to develop instructional activities according to constructivist models. Since these guidelines do not always agree, teachers cannot usually follow all of them within the same instructional activity. But each of the following principles is still considered characteristic of constructivist purposes and designs:

**Problem-oriented activities.** Most constructivist models focus on students solving problems, either in a specific content area such as mathematics or using an interdisciplinary approach. For example, such a problem might require a combination of mathematics, science, and language arts skills. Jungck (1991) says that constructivist methods frequently combine problem posing, problem solving, and persuasion of peers (p. 155). Problems may be posed in terms of specific goals (e.g., how to develop an information package to help persuade classmates to stop littering the beach), as "what if" questions (e.g., what would life be like on earth if we had half the gravity we now have?), or as open-ended questions (e.g., in light of what you know about the characters and the times in which they lived, what is the best ending for this story?). These kinds of problems are *usually* more complex than those associated with directed instruction and they require students to devote more time and more diverse skills to solve them.

**Visual formats and mental models.** CTGV is especially concerned that instructional activities help students build good "mental models" of problems to be solved. They feel that teachers can promote this work most effectively by posing problems in visual, as opposed to written, formats. These researchers say that "Visual formats allow students to develop their own pattern recognition skills, and they are dynamic, rich, and spatial" (1990, p. 3). This degree of visual support is felt to be particularly important for low-achieving, at-risk students who may have reading difficulties and for students with little expertise in the area in which the problems are posed.

**Rich environments.** Many constructivist approaches seem to call for what Perkins (1991) terms "richer learning environments" (p. 19) in contrast to the minimalist classroom environment that usually relies primarily on the teacher, a textbook, and prepared materials. Perkins observes that many constructivist models are facilitated by combinations of five kinds of resources: information banks such as textbooks and electronic encyclopedias to access required information; symbol pads such as notebooks and laptop computers to support learners' short-term memories; construction kits, including Legos, Tinkertoys, and Logo to let learners manipulate and build;

phenomenaria (e.g., a terrarium or computer simulation) to allow exploration; and task managers like teachers and electronic tutors to provide assistance and feedback as students complete tasks.

**Cooperative or collaborative (group) learning.** Most constructivist approaches heavily emphasize work in groups rather than as individuals to solve problems. This arrangement achieves several aims that advocates of constructivism and directed instruction alike consider important. CTGV observes that gathering students in cooperative groups seems to be the best way to facilitate generative learning. Perkins (1991) points out that cooperative learning illustrates distributive intelligence at work. In a distributive definition of intelligence, accomplishment is not a function simply of individual capabilities but the product of individuals and tools, each of which contributes to achieving desired goals. Finally, cooperative learning seems an ideal environment for students to learn how to share responsibility and work together toward common goals, skills they will find useful in a variety of settings outside school.

**Learning through exploration.** All constructivist approaches call for some flexibility in achieving desired goals. Most stress exploration rather than merely getting the right answer and a high degree of what advocates of directed instruction call *discovery learning*. Constructivists differ among themselves, however, about how much assistance and guidance a teacher should offer. Only a few constructivists feel that students should have complete freedom and unlimited time to discover the knowledge they need. Perkins (1991) says, "Education given over entirely to WIG (without any given) instruction would prove grossly inefficient and ineffective, failing to pass on in straightforward ways the achievements of the past" (p. 20).

**Authentic assessment methods.** When the goals and methods of education change in the ways described here, teachers also need new methods of evaluating student progress. Thus, constructivist learning environments exhibit more qualitative assessment strategies rather than quantitative ones. Some popular assessment methods center on student portfolios with examples of students' work and products they have developed (Bateson, 1994; Young, 1995); narratives written by teachers to describe each student's work habits and areas of strength and weakness; and performance-based assessments in combination with checklists of criteria for judging student performance (Linn, 1994).

## Constructivist Methods: Problems Raised versus Problems Addressed

**Criticisms of constructivist methods.** Despite the current popularity of constructivism, its principles and practices have stimulated a variety of criticisms. Two issues of *Educational Technology* magazine (May and September

1991) provided a forum for describing and debating the merits of constructivist learning strategies. Discussion focused on the following issues:

*   **How can one certify skill learning?** Reigeluth (1991) pointed out that, although constructivists deplore formal tests or objective measurements, schools must sometimes certify that students have learned key skills. "It is not sufficient to know that a doctor was on a team of medical students that performed the operation successfully; you want to know if the doctor can do it without the team" (p. 35).

*   **How much prior knowledge is needed?** Constructivist strategies often call for students to approach and solve complex problems. But both Tobias (1991) and Molenda (1991) point out that, regardless of their motivation, many students may lack the prerequisite abilities that would allow them to handle this kind of problem solving.

*   **Can students choose the most effective instruction?** Constructivist tasks often require students to learn how to teach themselves, that is, to choose methods by which they will learn and solve problems. But Tobias quotes a study by Clark (1982) that indicates that students often learn the least from instructional methods they prefer most.

*   **Which topics suit constructivist methods?** Many educators feel that constructivist methods serve some purposes more effectively than others. For example, constructivist activities frequently seek to teach the problem-solving methods used by experts in a content area (thinking like a historian), rather than to learn any specific content or skills such as historical facts. Molenda points out that constructivists may be surprised to learn that this is not what many parents and educators have in mind. "Parents and school people [are] ... much more interested in communicating our cultural heritage to the next generation. Facts are viewed as powerful ends in themselves" (Molenda, 1991, p. 45). Tobias notes that constructivists often favor depth of coverage on one topic over breadth of coverage on many topics: "Students taught the first term of American history from a constructivist perspective may have a very profound understanding of the injustices imposed by taxation without representation.... however, would they learn anything about the War of 1812, Shay's Rebellion, the Whiskey Rebellion, or the Monroe Doctrine?" (Tobias, 1991, p. 42).

*   **Will skills transfer to practical situations?** Constructivists assume that problem solving taught in authentic situations in school will transfer more easily to problems that students must solve in real life. Yet Tobias (1991) found little evidence from related research to indicate that such transfer will occur. He decries "esoteric jargon which is unsubstantiated by research findings" (p. 42) and says that "Perhaps the time has come to devote more attention to the conduct of research" (p. 42).

**Current constructivist trends.** Despite these criticisms, interest in constructivist methods is on the rise, and research is increasing to measure the impact of learning based on student problem solving and product development (CTGV, 1995). It is possible that the next decade will witness some dramatic shifts in curriculum goals and methods that largely follow constructivist principles. An increasing number of schools and districts already are emphasizing alternative assessments such as portfolios and group projects, either in addition to or in place of traditional testing.

In recent years, the movement in education to integrate technology into teaching has become closely identified with the restructuring movement. Many educators believe they cannot make curriculum reflect constructivist characteristics *without* technology. Constructivists offer this combination of problem-oriented activities, cooperative group work, tasks related to students' interests and backgrounds, and highly visual formats provided by technology resources as components of a powerful antidote to some of the country's most pervasive and recalcitrant social and educational problems.

## Technology Integration Strategies: Directed, Constructivist, and Combined Approaches

Subsequent chapters in this book describe and give examples of integration strategies for various types of courseware materials and technology media. However, all of these strategies implement a group of general integration principles. Some draw on the unique characteristics of a technology resource to meet certain kinds of learning needs. Others take advantage of a resource's ability to substitute for materials lacking in schools or classrooms. Teachers may use many or all of the following strategies at the same time. However, it is important to recognize that each of the integration strategies described here addresses a specific instructional need. They are not employed to make students computer literate or because technology is the wave of the future or because students should occasionally use computers because it is good for them. The authors advocate making a conscious effort to match technology resources to problems that educators cannot address in other, easier ways.

### Integration Strategies Based on Directed Models

**Integration to remedy identified weaknesses.** One premise of constructivist, whole-language approaches is that students will be motivated to learn prerequisite skills if they see their relevance when the need arises in the context of group or individual projects. However, experienced teachers know that even the most motivated students do not always learn skills as expected. These failures occur for a variety of reasons, many of which are related to learners' internal capabilities and not all of which are thoroughly understood. Curriculum is currently moving toward allowing students to acquire skills on more flexible schedules. But when the absence of prerequisite skills presents a barrier to higher-level learning, directed instruction usually is the most efficient way of providing them. For example, if a student does not learn to read when it is developmentally appropriate, research has shown great success in identifying

and remedying specific weaknesses among the component skills (Torgeson, Waters, Cohen, & Torgeson, 1988; Torgeson, 1993). Materials such as drills and tutorials have proven to be valuable resources that help teachers provide this kind of individualized instruction. Well-designed resources like these not only can give students effective instruction but also are frequently more motivating and less threatening than teacher-delivered instruction to students who find learning difficult.

**Integration to promote fluency or automaticity of prerequisite skills.** Some kinds of prerequisite skills benefit students more if they can apply the skills without conscious effort. Gagné (1982) and Bloom (1986) referred to this as *automaticity of skills,* and Hasselbring and Goin (1993) call it *fluency* or *proficiency.* Students need rapid recall and performance of a wide range of skills throughout the curriculum, including simple math facts, grammar and usage rules, and spelling. Some students acquire automaticity through repeated use of the skills in practical situations. Others acquire this automatic recall more efficiently through isolated practice. Drill and practice courseware provides an ideal means of practice tailored to individual skill needs and learning pace.

**Integration to make learning efficient for highly motivated students.** Current educational methods are sometimes criticized for failure to interest and motivate students because activities and skills are irrelevant to students' needs, experiences, and interests. However, some students' motivation to learn springs from internal rather than external sources. These internally motivated students do not need explicit connections between specific skills and practical problems. These students may be motivated more by desire to please parents or other authority figures or by long-range goals of going to particular colleges or pursuing specific vocations. In addition, interest in a subject kindled originally by a cooperative class project may spur students to learn everything they can about the field. Self-motivated students pursue skills they believe are related to their topics or provide foundations for later concepts. For such learners, the most desirable method of learning is the most efficient one. Directed instruction for these students can frequently be supported by self-instructional tutorials and simulations—assuming the teacher can locate high-quality materials on the desired topics.

**Integration to optimize scarce personnel and material resources.** Anyone associated with public schools will readily admit that current resources and personnel are not optimal. For example, real problems result from schools having too many students and not enough teachers. Many of the courseware materials described in later chapters can help make up for the lack of required resources in the school or classroom—from consumable supplies to qualified teachers. For example, drill and practice programs can replace worksheets, a good tutorial program can offer instruction in topics for which teachers are in short supply, and a simulation can let students repeat a experiments without using chemicals or other materials.

**Integration to remove logistical hurdles.** Some technology tools offer no instructional sequence or tasks but help students complete learning tasks more efficiently. These tools support directed instruction by removing or reducing logistical hurdles to learning. For example, word processing programs do not teach students how to write but let students write and rewrite more quickly, without the labor of handwriting. Computer-assisted design (CAD) software does not teach students how to design a house but allows them to try out designs and features to see what they look like before building models or structures. A videodisc may contain only a set of pictures of sea life but can let a teacher illustrate concepts about sea creatures more quickly and easily than with books. Part II addresses tools that make learning more efficient and less laborious for students.

## Integration Strategies Based on Constructivist Models

**Integration to generate motivation to learn.** Teachers who work with at-risk students often point to the need to capture students' interest and enthusiasm as a key to success and frequently as their most difficult challenge. Some educators assert that today's television-oriented students are increasingly likely to demand more motivational qualities in their instruction than students in previous generations. As an important part of their rationale, constructivists argue that instruction must address students' affective needs as well as their cognitive ones, hypothesizing that students will learn more if what they are learning is interesting and relevant. Whenever a teacher needs stronger student motivation, the highly visual and interactive qualities of videodisc and multimedia resources have been shown to be valuable.

**Integration to foster creativity.** Although creative work is not usually considered a primary goal of education, many educators and parents consider it highly desirable. Some argue that students can be educated without being creative, but few schools want to graduate students who cannot think or act creatively. Resources such as Logo, problem-solving courseware, and computer graphics tools require neither consumable supplies nor any particular artistic or literary skill. They also allow students to revise creative works easily and as many times as desired. These qualities have provided uniquely fertile, nonthreatening environments for fostering development of students' creativity.

**Integration to facilitate self-analysis and metacognition.** If students are conscious of the procedures they use to go about solving problems, perhaps they can more easily improve on their strategies and become more effective problem solvers. Consequently, teachers often try to get students to analyze their procedures to increase their effi-

ciency. Resources such as Logo, problem-solving courseware, and multimedia applications often are considered ideal environments for constructivist activities that get students to think about how they think.

**Integration to increase transfer of knowledge to problem solving.** The CTGV team points out unique capabilities of certain technology resources to address the problem of inert knowledge. They observe that this problem often occurs when students learn skills in isolation from problem applications. When students later encounter problems that require the skills, they do not realize how the skills could be relevant. Problem-solving materials in highly visual videodisc-based formats allow students to build rich mental models of problems to be solved (CTGV, 1991a). Students need not depend on reading skills, which may be deficient, to build these mental models. Thus, supporters hypothesize that teaching skills in these highly visual, problem-solving environments help to assure that knowledge will transfer to higher-order skills. These technology-based methods are especially desirable for teachers who work with students in areas such as mathematics and science where inert knowledge is frequently a problem.

**Integration to foster group cooperation.** One skill area currently identified as an important focus for schools' efforts to restructure curriculum (U.S. Department of Labor, 1992) is the ability to work cooperatively in a group to solve problems and develop products. Although schools certainly can teach cooperative work without technology resources, a growing body of evidence documents students' appreciation of cooperative work as both more motivating and easier to accomplish when it uses technology. For example, descriptions of students who develop their own multimedia products and presentations are more common in current literature on teaching cooperative skills to at-risk students.

**Integration to allow for multiple and distributed intelligence.** Integration strategies with group cooperative activities also give teachers a way to allow students of widely varying abilities to make valuable contributions on their own terms. Since each student is seen as an important member of the group in these activities, the activities themselves are viewed as problems for group—rather than individual—solution. This strategy has implications for enhancing students' self-esteem and for increasing their willingness to spend more time on learning tasks. It also helps students see that they can help each other accomplish tasks and can learn from each other as well as from the teacher or from media.

**Integration to develop technological and visual literacy.** Some of the most popular and common technology integration strategies simply give students practice in using modern methods of communicating information. For example, when students use presentation software instead of cardboard charts to give a report, they gain experience for college classrooms and business offices where computer-based presentations are the norm. When they develop multimedia book reports, instead of a paper ones, they use more visually complex methods that are commonplace in our media-permeated culture. Using technology to communicate visually represents Information Age skills students will need both for higher education and in the workplace.

## Combining Integration Strategies in Curriculum Planning

This chapter and subsequent chapters describe an established, well-documented knowledge base on how to integrate technology resources effectively into both directed instruction and constructivist activities. This chapter proposes that directed and constructivist models each address specific classroom needs and problems and that both will continue to be useful.

But the authors of this text go one step further in this description; they propose that neither model in itself can meet the needs of all students in a classroom. Teachers must merge directed and constructivist activities to form a new and more useful school curriculum. Even Gagné, a leader in promoting systematic, directed methods, proposes that effective, useful instruction sometimes calls for *integration of objectives* in the context of a complex, motivational learning activity that he refers to as an *enterprise* (Gagné & Merrill, 1990). His description of the nature of this enterprise sounds much like the kinds of activities often proposed by constructivists. In fact, one of his three kinds of enterprises calls for a *discovering schema*.

At this time, however, teachers find few practical guidelines for combining directed and constructivist approaches and integration strategies into a single curriculum. The concept of combining them at all is currently in an exploratory stage. Although teachers across the country are probably combining approaches in classroom activities, formal descriptions of effective applications are rare and lack detail. Given here are some recommended guidelines and two examples that indicate how this curriculum development might occur; both are derived from teachers' writings, discussions, and examples.

## Recommended Guidelines for Developing a Technology-Integrated Lesson

Very often, technology can help with "small problems" in teaching specific topics. Teachers who know the capabilities of various technology resources are skilled at looking for matches between these problems and specific resources that help resolve them.

## Recommended Guidelines for Developing a Technology-Integrated Curriculum

**Plan for a grading period (6 to 9 weeks, a semester, or a school year).** Curriculum that includes constructivist activities requires a long-term view of skills development. Ideally, students experience a combination of teacher-directed and self-directed work throughout their time in school. Curriculum planned for short, discrete lessons leaves little of the flexibility that both teachers and students need to accomplish curriculum goals.

**Allow enough time.** When constructivist strategies are new to teacher and students, learning activities often take more time than the familiar routines of directed instruction would require. Teachers who are beginning to introduce these kinds of activities may find that it takes a while to learn the management techniques they need to guide and facilitate learning. Students also need enough time to complete their tasks and follow up on newly discovered interests.

**Match the assessment to the activity.** It is especially important to measure students' accomplishments in a way that suits the kinds of learning activities they have done. For example, a teacher should not guide students through a problem-solving activity based on the Optical Data Corporation's *Adventures of Jasper Woodbury* and then give a multiple-choice test on how to solve mathematics word problems. Students know they must earn grades of some kind. As with all classroom learning, they should understand from the start the criteria by which the teacher will measure performance.

**Be flexible.** Although planning is essential to successful technology integration, plans should be flexible. If the teacher notices in the middle of a mathematics problem-solving project that students lack prerequisite skills, the lesson may have to stop to allow some direct teaching before it can proceed.

**Don't be afraid to experiment.** Despite the demands on teachers to prepare their students well, they should have the same opportunity for exploration and risk taking that they give to students. Teachers will not develop new and more effective methods without making some mistakes along the way. Combining directed and constructivist curriculum requires a delicate balance of informal and formal situations, problem solving and drill and practice, and generated and memorized knowledge. It is a difficult balance to strike—but is worth the effort.

## Examples of Technology-Integrated Units

### The CCCnet Inventorium: An Online Invention Project

**Rationale.** Mr. Washington is a fourth-grade teacher in an inner-city elementary school. His own interests are in science, and he believes strongly that students' interests in science as a potential college major and job area begin at an early age. He wants to give his students a good foundation in what he calls scientific creativity skills. He wants them to be more creative, but in an inquiry-based, scientific way. He decides to subscribe to CCCnet, a Computer Curriculum Corporation Web site that has a program for elementary children called the Inventorium. This project has a combination of structured, guided learning activities and opportunities for inquiry and exploration.

**Stage 1: Introduction.** He uses his classroom Internet connection with a computer and large monitor to demonstrate how to use the Phase-Into-Invention activity, a step-by-step CCCnet Web tutorial on how to develop an invention. Then he takes the class to the computer lab and lets them work in pairs through the tutorial. They do the following sequence:

1. **Why Invent?** Examples and descriptions of other children's inventions
2. **Find an Idea.** Explanation of what an invention is and example patents
3. **Research and plan.** Planning steps, questions to ask, and a Web search for existing inventions like ones under consideration
4. **Develop and test.** Follow the planning steps developed above
5. **Tell about the invention.** Publishing the invention

**Stage 2: Demonstrations and brainstorming.** Back in the classroom, the students look at more example inventions in the Inventorium's Invention Idea Gallery and Link Tank that provide links to other invention Web sites. They talk about some of their ideas.

**Stage 3: Learning stations.** Mr. Washington sets up four learning stations to help students work through the invention process: an Internet station to browse through links to more ideas; a worksheet station to review basic invention concepts, planning steps, and vocabulary; a station with materials to read on various inventors and inventions; and one with printouts of the Inventorium Web site describing past winning inventions.

**Stage 4: Invention development.** After everyone has worked through the learning stations and has an invention idea in mind, Mr. Washington hands out copies of the Inventorium Strategy Sheet on which students may plan their own invention. He works with the students to complete these sheets and they share them by presenting them to the class. The students discuss and critique each others' work and make any necessary revisions based on the feedback. They spend several class periods working to develop examples of their invention.

**Stage 5: Publishing the inventions.** The students go back to the computer lab and work on entering their inventions in the Inventorium Web site. Also, Mr. Washington

arranges for his class to present their invention models and Web site descriptions at a school PTO meeting.

### Improving French Language Skills: Combining Drills, Tutorials, and Online Activities

**Rationale.** A high school French teacher has a group of students who have had a previous course in French but are at varying levels of proficiency. Some have problems because they have a relatively small French vocabulary; some have a good grasp of vocabulary but have minor grammatical and structure problems; and some are fairly proficient with the language. The teacher would like to involve all the students in an activity that will give them practical application of their skills while letting each work from where they are to build proficiency with the language.

**Stage 1: Introducing the lesson.** The teacher explains to students that, through her involvement in an online Internet listserv, she has established contact with a teacher of English in Paris. They have decided to do a joint project in which the students will do a "language exchange" activity resulting in a product. The project will revolve around exploring each other's language as a reflection of their culture. The teacher explains that they will do one such project each semester. This semester, the American group gets to choose the product. The next semester, the French group decides.

**Stage 2: Deciding on the group product.** She asks the students to think about how our use of language shows things about where we live, what we consider important, and how we think as a culture. She asks them to consider these aspects and suggest products that might help demonstrate similarities and differences between themselves and their French counterparts. After much discussion, they decide to create a dictionary of expressions for various emotions (surprise, anger, affection, disgust) and publish their findings on the school Web site. The American group will supply an introduction in French; the Paris class will supply one in English.

**Stage 3: Assigning groups.** The teacher forms groups and assigns roles that represent an area of expertise these students have with the language:

- **Vocabulary.** These are the students who need work on their French vocabulary. She assigns these students to brush up on their basic vocabulary with a drill and practice program she has tailored to meet their needs and placed in the language lab. If the class needs any vocabulary words, this group is in charge of locating them and spelling them correctly. Also, they will prepare a glossary of major vocabulary words used in the booklet.

- **Grammar and usage.** Students who need some help with syntax and usage work with a HyperStudio tutorial the teacher has prepared. The tutorial reviews the most common language syntax problems for beginners in French. For the class project, this group will oversee the development of the booklet's introduction and description statements.

* **E-mails.** Students with the highest level of proficiency with the language are assigned to exchange background information, favorite activities, etc. with their counterparts by writing a series of e-mail messages.

**Stage 4: Building language skills.** For the first two weeks, the groups spend the first 10–15 minutes of each class meeting doing their assigned tasks. Then the groups meet for the remainder of the period to work on the production tasks. The whole class then reviews the products of the e-mail group by viewing them on a large computer monitor. Each group lends its expertise in editing the final messages for vocabulary and syntax before the messages are sent.

**Stage 5: Completing and displaying the product.** The following three weeks are spent working together to structure the booklet and exchange information with the French students. The final two weeks are spent on production tasks. Students prepare their summary and post it on the school's Web site. Also, they make a printout and the teacher works with them to prepare a bulletin board to display their work.

## Exercises

### Record and Apply What You Have Learned

**Activity 3.1: Chapter 3 Self-Test** To review terms and concepts in this chapter, take the Chapter 3 self-test. Select Chapter 3 from the front page of the companion Web site (located at http://www.prenhall.com/roblyer), then choose the *Multiple Choice* module.

**Activity 3.2: Portfolio Activities** The following activities will help you add to your professional portfolio. To complete these activities online and save or submit the materials electronically, select Chapter 3 from the front page of the companion Web site (http://www.prenhall.com/roblyer), then choose the *Portfolio* module.

*Overview of Learning Theories* Prepare a chart that summarizes the learning theorists and theories that support directed model and constructivist models. Use the following headings in the format shown in the chart below (a first entry is already in the chart as an example).

*Contrasts between Directed and Constructivist Models* Create a diagram, chart, or caricature (for an example, see Figure 3.1) that shows the differences between the two models described in this chapter. Contrast them according

to language they use, teaching/learning problems they address, and/or the methods they use.

**Activity 3.3: Questions for Thought and Discussion** These questions may be used for small group or class discussion or may be subjects for individual or group activities. To take part in these discussions online, select Chapter 3 from the front page of the companion Web site (http://www.prenhall.com/roblyer), then choose the *Message Board* module.

* Seymour Papert (1987) criticized traditional experimental research methods because they are "... based on a concept of changing a single factor in a complex situation while keeping everything else the same ... (which is) radically incompatible with the enterprise of rebuilding an education system in which nothing will be the same" (p. 22).

  What aspects of the current education system do you think need to be changed? How do constructivist methods propose to change them? If we do not use experimental research, what methods will we use to determine our changes have improved the education system?

**Activity 3.4: Collaborative Activities** The following may be developed in small group work. Each group should present the findings to the class in a format they know how to

|  | Name of Theorist(s) | Name of Theory | Three Major Terms Used in the Theory | Applications/ Related Names |
|---|---|---|---|---|
| **Directed Model** | B. F. Skinner | behaviorism | learning contingencies reinforcement observable behaviors | mastery learning (Benjamin Bloom) programmed instruction |
| **Constructivist Model** |  |  |  |  |

use (word processed report, presentation software, multimedia product). *Each summary should have a graphic representation with it.* Completed group products may be copied and shared with the entire class and/or included in each person's Personal Portfolio:

***The Directed/Constructivist Debate*** Prepare a debate on the benefits of using directed versus constructivist models for teaching and learning. Each small group should gather evidence to support arguments on *one* of the following aspects of *one* of the models: real, practice problems they address; the soundness of their underlying theories; and the usefulness in preparing students for future education and work. The group members working on the directed models comprise the panel arguing for directed strategies, while the members working on constructivist models comprise the opposite panel. Present the debate in class, with the instructor acting as moderator.

***Directed and Constructivist Examples*** Use Internet resources and software company catalogs to locate an example of a directed learning activity such as drills and tutorials and a constructivist activity such as group projects. Develop a presentation that describes each one and shows why it is a good reflection of the directed or constructivist model.

***Example Integration Strategies*** Each group chooses or is assigned one of the types of technology integration strategies described earlier in this chapter. Each group locates or develops a classroom example that reflects this strategy and presents it to the class *without telling the class the strategy.* The class members identify the strategy being used.

**Activity 3.5: Integrating Technology Across the Curriculum Activities** Use the *Integrating Technology Across the Curriculum* CD-ROM packaged with this textbook to complete the following exercise:

What is the difference between a directed and constructivist integration strategy? You can get an idea of the answer to this question by doing a search on the Teaching and Learning Strategies descriptor. Go to *Find Lesson Plan* and click on *Find by Criteria.* Under the *Teaching and Learning Strategies* descriptor, select Constructivist, Directed, or Combination, and click *Search,* and compare the examples for each.

# References

Alessi, S. & Trollip, S. (1991). *Computer-based instruction: Methods and development.* Englewood Cliffs, NJ: Prentice-Hall.

Atkinson, R. & Shiffrin, R. (1968). Human memory: A proposed system and its control processes. In K. Spence & J. Spence (Eds.). *The psychology of learning and motivation: Vol. 2.* New York: Academic Press.

Ausubel, D. (1968). *Educational psychology: A cognitive view.* New York: Holt, Rinehart and Winston.

Barker, T., Torgeson, J., & Wagner, R. (1992). The role of orthographic processing skills in five different reading tests. *Reading Research Quarterly, 27*(4), 335–345.

Bass, J. (1985). The roots of Logo's educational theory: An analysis. *Computers in the Schools, 2*(2–3), 107–116.

Bateson, D. (1994). Psychometric and philosophic problems in "authentic" assessment: Performance tasks and portfolios. *Alberta Journal of Educational Research, 40*(2), 233–245.

Bereiter, C. (1990). Aspects of an educational learning theory. *Review of Educational Research, 60*(4), 603–624.

Bloom, B. (1986). Automaticity. *Educational Leadership, 43* (5), 70–77.

Branden, R. (1996). The case for linear instructional design and development: A commentary on models, challenges, and myths. *Educational Technology, 36*(2), 5–23.

Bringuier, J. (1980). *Conversations with Jean Piaget. Translated by Basia M. Gulati.* Chicago, IL: University of Chicago Press.

Brown, J. S., Collins, A., & Duguid, P. (1989). Situated cognition and the culture of learning. *Educational Researcher, 18*(1), 32–41.

Bruner, J. (1973). *The relevance of education.* New York, NY: W. W. Norton & Company.

Carnine, D. (1993). Effective teaching for higher cognitive functioning. *Educational Technology, 33*(10), 29–33.

Carnine, D., Silbert, J., & Kameenui, E. (1997). *Direct instruction reading (3rd. ed.).* Columbus, OH: Merrill Publishing Company.

Clark, R. E. (1982). Antagonism between achievement and enjoyment in ATI studies. *Educational Psychologist, 17*(2), 92–101.

Cognition and Technology Group at Vanderbilt (1990). Anchored instruction and its relationship to situated cognition. *Educational Researcher, 19*(6), 2–10.

Cognition and Technology Group at Vanderbilt (1991a, May). Integrated media: Toward a theoretical framework for utilizing their potential. Proceedings of the Multimedia Technology Seminar, Washington, DC.

Cognition and Technology Group at Vanderbilt (1991b). Technology and the design of generative learning environments. *Educational Technology, 31*(5), 34–40.

Cognition and Technology Group at Vanderbilt (1993). The Jasper experiment: An exploration of issues in learning and instructional design. *Educational Technology Research and Development, 40*(1), 65–80.

Cognition and Technology Group at Vanderbilt (1995). Looking at technology in context: A framework for understanding technology and education research. In D. C. Berliner (Ed.). *The handbook of educational psychology.* New York: Macmillan.

Corey, S. M. (1944). Poor scholar's soliloquy. *Childhood Education, 33,* 219–220.

*Educational Technology* (May 1991), *31*(5); and (September 1991), *31*(9). Special issues on constructivist versus directed approaches.

*Educational Technology* (October 1993), *32*(10). Special issue on current uses of behavioral theories.

Eggen, P. & Kauchak, D. (1999). *Educational Psychology: Windows on Classrooms.* Upper Saddle River, NJ: Merrill/Prentice Hall.

Epstein, R. (1993). Generativity theory and education. *Educational Technology, 33*(10), 40–45.

Gagné, R. (1982). Developments in learning psychology: Implications for instructional design. *Educational Technology, 22*(6), 11–15.

Gagné, R. (1985). *The conditions of learning.* New York: Holt, Rinehart & Winston.

Gagné, R., Briggs, L., & Wager, W. (1988). *Principles of instructional design.* New York: Holt, Rinehart & Winston.

Gagné, R. & Merrill, R. (1990). Integrative goals for instructional design. *Educational Technology Research and Development, 38*(1), 23–30.

Gagné, R., Wager, W., & Rojas, A. (1981). Planning and authoring computer-assisted instruction lessons. *Educational Technology, 21*(9), 17–26.

Gardner, H. (1983). *Frames of mind.* New York: Basic Books.

Gardner, H. (1989). Multiple intelligences go to school: Educational implications of the theory of multiple intelligences. *Educational Researcher, 18*(8), 4–10.

Hasselbring, T. & Goin, L. (1993). Integrated technology and media. In Polloway & Patton (Eds.). *Strategies for teaching learners with special needs.* New York: Merrill Publishing Co.

Jungck, J. (1991). Constructivism, computer exploratoriums, and collaborative learning: Construction scientific knowledge. *Teaching Education, 3*(2), 151–170.

Linn, R. (1994). Performance assessment: Policy promises and technical measurement standards. *Educational Researcher, 23*(9), 4–14.

Mallott, R. (1993). The three-contingency model of performance management and support in higher education. *Educational Technology, 33*(10), 21–28.

Molenda, M. (1991). A philosophical critique on the claims of "constructivism." *Educational Technology, 31*(9), 44–48.

National Commission on Excellence in Education. (1983). *A nation at risk.* Washington, DC: U.S. Department of Education.

Ormrod, J. (2000). *Educational psychology: Developing learners.* Upper Saddle River, NJ: Merrill/Prentice Hall.

Papert, S. (1980). *Mindstorms: Children, computers, and powerful ideas.* New York: Basic Books.

Papert, S. (1987). Computer criticism vs. technocentric thinking. *Educational Researcher, 16*(1), 22–30.

Perkins, D. (1991). Technology meets constructivism: Do they make a marriage? *Educational Technology, 31*(5), 18–23.

Phillips, D. C. (1995). The good, the bad, and the ugly: The many faces of constructivism. *Educational Researcher, 24*(7), 5–12.

Prawat, R. (1993). The value of ideas: Problems versus possibilities in learning. *Educational Researcher, 22*(6), 5–16.

Raspberry, W. (1998, March 30). Sounds bad, but it works. *Washington Post,* Section A, p. 25.

Reigeluth, C. (1991). Reflections on the implications of constructivism for educational technology. *Educational Technology, 33*(10), 34–37.

Saettler, P. (1990). *The evolution of American educational technology.* Englewood, CO: Libraries Unlimited.

Sfard, A. (1998). One-two metaphors for learning and the dangers of choosing just one. *Educational Researcher, 27*(2), 4–13.

Skinner, B. F. (1938). *The behavior of organisms.* New York: Appleton.

Skinner, B. F. (1968). *The technology of teaching.* New York: Appleton.

Spence, I. & Hively, W. (1993). What makes Chris practice? *Educational Technology, 35*(6), 5–23.

Spiro, R., Feltovich, P., Jacobson, M., & Coulson, R. (1991). Knowledge representation, content specification, and the development of skill in situation-specific knowledge assembly: Some constructivist issues as they relate to cognitive flexibility theory and hypertext. *Educational Technology, 31*(9), 22–25.

Stein, M., Silbert, J., & Carnine, D. (1990). *Designing effective mathematics instruction: Direct instruction mathematics (3rd. ed.).* Columbus, OH: Merrill Publishing Company.

Sulzer, B. & Mayer, R. (1972). *Behavior modification procedures for school personnel.* Hinsdale, IL: Dryden Press.

Taylor, R. (1980). *The computer in the school: Tutor, tool, tutee.* New York: Teachers College Press.

Tennyson, R. (1990). Integrated instructional design theory: Advancements from cognitive science and instructional technology. *Educational Technology, 30*(7), 9–15.

Tinker, R. (1998, Winter). Teaching and learning in the knowledge society. *The Concord Consortium Newsletter,* 1–2, 14.

Tobias, S. (1991). An eclectic examination of some issues in the constructivist-ISD controversy. *Educational Technology, 31*(9), 41–43.

Torgeson, J. (1986). Using computers to help learning. Disabled children practice reading: A research-based perspective. *Learning Disabilities Focus, 1*(2), 72–81.

Torgeson, J., Waters, M., Cohen, A., & Torgeson, J. (1988). Improving sight word recognition skills in learning disabled children: An evaluation of three computer program variations. *Learning Disabilities Quarterly, 11,* 125–133.

U.S. Department of Labor (1992). SCANS (The Secretary's Commission on Achieving Necessary Skills) report. Washington, DC: U.S. Government Printing Office.

Wager, W. (1992). Instructional systems fundamentals: Pressures to change. *Educational Technology, 33*(2), 8–12.

Willis, J. (1995). A recursive, reflective model based on constructivist-interpretivist theory. *Educational Technology, 33*(10), 15–20.

Young, M. (1995). Assessment of situated learning using computer environments. *Journal of Science Education and Technology, 4*(1), 89–96.

# Part II

## Using Software and Media Tutors and Tools: Principles and Strategies

### The chapters in this part will help teachers learn:

1. To identify the various teaching and learning functions that instructional software can fulfill

2. The unique capabilities of each of the resources known as software tools

3. The capabilities and educational applications of multimedia and hypermedia systems

4. To match specific kinds of instructional software and technology tools to classroom needs

5. To design lesson integration strategies for instructional software, technology tools, and multimedia/hypermedia

### Introduction

As Part I illustrated, the field of educational technology is characterized by controversy and change, and the dynamic nature of computer technology has only reinforced this characteristic. Lack of consensus about the terminology of instructional technology reflects this changing and evolving nature. As with the terms used to describe directed and constructivist methods (see Part I Overview), no agreement has ever emerged about the terms for various educational computing resources or how to categorize them.

Until microcomputers entered schools, classroom computing resources usually were classified under three general headings: computer-assisted instruction (CAI), computer-managed instruction (CMI), and other. CAI usually referred mainly to drill and practice, tutorial, and simulation software; CMI encompassed testing, recordkeeping, and reporting software. During the 1980s, other authors began using many more inclusive terms to refer to instructional uses of computers such as computer-based instruction (CBI), computer-based learning (CBL), and computer-assisted learning.

In 1980, Taylor proposed a classification system for instructional technology that grouped computer resources according to their functions. This classification system consisted of three terms: tutor, tool, and tutee. The tutor functions included those in which the "computer [was] programmed by experts in both programming and in a subject matter ... and the student [was] then tutored by the computer" (p. 3). In its tool functions, the computer "had some useful capability programmed into it such as statistical analysis ... or word processing" (p. 3). Tutee functions helped the student learn about logic processes or how computers worked by "teaching" (programming) computers to perform various activities in languages like BASIC or Logo.

Although many technology-oriented educators still observe these categories by broadening the definitions of *tutor* and *tools* (and dropping the tutee designation), the field has produced no neat classification system for technology resources. There simply are too many different resources and applications, and experts have found no feasible way to agree on terminology. The authors of this textbook recommend that *teachers prepare themselves for this lack of consensus on terms and labels so they can recognize the functions of technology products under any name or in any medium.* After teachers recognize the functions of each resource, they will be ready to match functions with their own instructional and productivity needs.

The three chapters in Part II deal with technology resources that involve a computer program or software. Some resources such as probeware, music editor, or a graphing calculator combine software with hardware, such as a probe or a music synthesizer, in order to accomplish their functions. The resources in Part II are addressed in three chapters: instructional software or courseware, software tools, and multimedia/hypermedia. Each of these chapters describes resources and suggests integration strategies for them based on directed and constructivist models.

## Chapter 4: Using Instructional Software in Teaching and Learning

This text usually substitutes the term *courseware* for *instructional software*. Most people think of instructional software as performing a tutor function. However, it functions as a tool in integration strategies based on constructivist models. Software described in this chapter fulfills the following instructional roles:

* Tutorial
* Drill and practice
* Simulation

* Instructional game
* Problem solving

Chapter 4 also covers networked delivery systems that provide these resources and keep track of students' usage of them. In directed models, these systems usually are termed *integrated learning systems (ILSs)*. Those who implement constructivist models also may refer to ILSs, but they mean to indicate different resources and uses of those resources.

## Chapter 5: Using Productivity Software and Other Software Tools in Teaching and Learning

Most people think of the word *tool* as an all-encompassing term describing any implement used to help accomplish an activity. Thus, software tools could include any technology resource that teachers use to accomplish the activities of teaching. But this definition is probably too broad to be helpful. A more limited and useful definition would identify the tools described in Chapter 5 as resources that help primarily with the mundane, mechanical operations of teaching. Computer tools can help learners with many mechanical operations such as:

* Handwriting, when the focus of instruction is writing a story or a composition
* Arithmetic calculations, when the purpose of the lesson is solving algebra problems
* Organizing information, when the purpose of the lesson is showing how to classify animals according to common features
* Presenting information clearly and attractively, when the purpose of the presentation is showing the results of a research project

Chapter 5 looks at technology tools as resources that can ease the logistics of the more mechanical activities involved in learning, so that teachers and students may concentrate more on achieving learning objectives. Such tools contribute to teaching in the same way that power tools contribute to designing and building a house as compared to using hand tools. The more advanced tools make it easier to carry out the mechanics of building the house, but they can also profoundly affect the complexity of the designs that builders may attempt. Similarly, technology tools not only make learning faster and easier, they also allow it to employ more complex, higher-level methods than would be possible without such tools.

Chapter 5 describes and gives integration strategies for three of the most commonly discussed computer programs under the category of classroom technology tools: word processing, spreadsheet, and database software. The popularity of these tools probably results from two facts. They were among the first tools to be developed and used in education, especially with microcomputers; thus, the literature documents more uses and classroom integration strategies for them than for most of the tools developed later. Also, these three functions are commonly found as components of so-called *integrated software packages* or *software suites*. (These are different from the integrated learning systems or ILSs discussed in Chapter 4.) As parts of a single integrated software package, the products of these tools may be used separately or "cut and pasted" from one to the other. For example, a teacher may prepare an illustration of a budget on a spreadsheet program, copy it, and paste it into a word-processed handout that describes the contents of budgets and how to prepare them. Although word processing, spreadsheet, and database programs usually are discussed and taught together as a group, each has a distinct set of characteristics and range of applications in education.

Even though these three tools have come to be known as productivity software, Chapter 5 describes and illustrates both productivity and instructional applications for them. Both types of applications are necessary classroom activities, but each fulfills a different purpose to support and enhance teachers' activities:

### Productivity Uses

These activities may have little to do with actual teaching (e.g., explaining or illustrating new concepts, or making information clearer or learning activities more enjoyable), but they do help teachers use their time more efficiently so that their subsequent interaction with students can be more meaningful. For example, teachers may record and calculate grades and track club budgets on a spreadsheet; they can then redirect the time they save on this activity to allow more contact with their students. Teachers may keep track of classroom instructional resources suitable for various instructional levels and purposes in a database, which can help them select materials targeted to the needs of each of their students. Productivity applications earn their name because they help make teachers more productive in accomplishing their professional tasks in the same way that

technology tools can make office staff more productive for the companies in which they work.

### Instructional Uses

Many of the same tools that improve teacher productivity also enhance instruction. For example, a spreadsheet helps students keep track of data during an experiment or predict the effects on sums or averages of changing numbers in a column or row. Students can be taught to develop their own databases to help them learn how to organize and search for information. These tools are called *instructional applications* because they serve valuable purposes in direct learning activities, even though they may not deliver information in the same way a tutorial, drill, or simulation program does.

In addition to these tools, Chapter 5 describes the features and applications of many more software tools that support teaching and learning tasks. These include resources to save teacher time, products to enhance and support production and presentation tasks, tools for managing data, and other support tools specific to the needs of certain disciplines.

## Chapter 6: Using Multimedia and Hypermedia in Teaching and Learning

The final chapter in Part II focuses on some of the most exciting technology resources in education today. Multimedia and hypermedia applications can be done with a variety of different hardware and software combinations ranging from simple uses of videodiscs to sophisticated authoring systems. Perhaps more than any other technology resources, these applications help teachers and students reflect and draw from the diversity of images and motion that characterize the world around us. To do this, they use resources that range from pre-drawn, still pictures to full-motion video. This chapter describes each of the configurations that can be used in classrooms, including interactive videodisc (IVD) systems, CD-ROM and DVD systems, and multimedia/hypermedia authoring software systems.

# Chapter 4

## Using Instructional Software in Teaching and Learning

The fact that individuals bind themselves with strong emotional ties to machines ought not to be surprising. The instruments [we] use become ... extensions of [our] bodies.

Joseph Weizenbaum in *Computer Power and Human Reason* (1976, p. 9)

## This chapter covers the following topics:

- Definitions, issues, integration strategies, and example lesson activities based on a directed instructional model for:

- Drill and practice functions
- Tutorial functions

- Definitions, issues, integration strategies, and example lesson activities based on both directed and constructivist models for:

- Simulation functions
- Instructional game functions
- Problem-solving functions

- Characteristics and uses of integrated learning systems (ILSs) and other technology-oriented learning systems

- Criteria and methods for software selection

# Objectives

1. For each description of a classroom need for instructional materials, identify one or more types of instructional technology functions that could meet the need.

2. Plan lesson activities that integrate technology resources using a directed learning strategy.

3. Plan lesson activities that integrate technology resources using a constructivist learning strategy.

# Introduction

### What Is Instructional Software?

From the time when people began to recognize the potential power of computers to do tasks quickly and systematically, they also began exploring and experimenting with its capability to emulate and improve on the functions of a human teacher. If computer programs could be written to do essentially anything, why could computers not be programmed to teach? Many educators and developers pursued this goal of the computer as teacher during the 1960s and 1970s. Some, like William Norris who developed Control Data's PLATO teaching systems, believed that computer-based education was the only logical alternative to education's "outdated, labor-intensive ways" (1977, p. 451). Norris believed that education could become more productive if computers were to take over much of the traditional role of teachers.

Today, after about 30 years of development and experimentation, there is less talk of computers replacing teachers, but programs still exist that perform various teaching functions. While these programs are not alternatives to human teachers, as envisioned by Norris, they can enhance teaching and learning in many ways.

Programs written in computer languages such as BASIC, Assembler, and C++ can perform tasks called *applications software* or *programs*. Instructional software (or courseware) delivers all or part of a student's instruction on a topic or assists with learning in some key way. Although software such as word processing, database, and spreadsheet programs also enhance instructional activities, this textbook differentiates between such tools and instructional software. Software tools serve a variety of purposes other than teaching; instructional software are programs developed for the sole purpose of delivering instruction or supporting learning activities.

### Problems in Identifying and Classifying Software Functions

*Computer-assisted instruction (CAI)* originated in the early days of educational technology as a name for instructional software, and the term is still in common use. However, some kinds of instructional software are designed with more constructivist purposes in mind and do not actually deliver instruction *per se;* therefore many people consider the term CAI outdated and misleading. Teachers may hear instructional software referred to as *computer-based instruction (CBI), computer-based learning (CBL),* or *computer-assisted learning* along with more generic terms such as *software learning tools*. Names for the types of instructional software functions also vary, but they are usually identified as:

- **Drills (or drill and practice).** Allow learners to work problems or answer questions and get feedback on correctness
- **Tutorials.** Act like tutors by providing all the information and instructional activities a learner needs to master a topic (information summaries, explanation, practice routines, feedback, and assessment)
- **Simulations.** Model real or an imagined systems to show how those systems or similar ones work
- **Instructional games.** Designed to increase motivation by adding game rules to learning activities; usually either drills or simulations
- **Problem solving.** Teach directly, through explanation and/or practice, the steps involved in solving problems or help learners acquire problem-solving skills by giving them opportunities to solve problems

Much of today's software complicates or defies easy classification of software packages. For one thing, developers have reached no consensus on the above terms or on the characteristics that define them. For example, some developers refer to a drill program that gives extensive feedback as a *tutorial*. Others refer to games as *drill programs*. Some packages contain several different activities, each of which serves a different purpose. For example, a program like *Millie's Math House* has a number of straight drill activities along with some problem-solving and game activities.

In light of these issues, educators who use software for instruction should analyze all of the activities in a package and classify each one according to its instructional function. For example, one may not be able to refer to an entire package as a tutorial or a drill, but it is possible and desirable to identify a particular activity according to whether it provides practice or opportunities for solving problems. As this chapter will show, each software function serves different purposes during learning and, consequently, has its own integration strategies.

### Programming Languages as Instructional Software

This chapter focuses on classroom uses of instructional software, while Chapter 5 addresses productivity and instructional uses of the resources known as software tools. However, programming languages may be considered a hybrid software, merging the capabilities of both instructional software and tools. Programming languages were created to develop computer programs that make computers do various tasks. For example, word processing programs

**Example Lesson 4.1**
**Using Programming Languages**

| | |
|---|---|
| **Lesson Plan:** | Problem Solving à la vos Savant |
| **Developed by:** | Patricia Wagner |
| **Content Area/Topic:** | Logic and organizational skills |
| **Instructional Resources:** | Programming software; word processing software |

**Lesson Purposes.** Analyze a probability problem and show the solution in a flowchart or algorithm.

**Instructional Activities**

*Introduction.* For many high school students, beginning programming is a way to gain practice in organizational skills. To write a program, they must be able to analyze a problem and show the solution in a flowchart or algorithm. Even if students never actually write a program, the activity of analyzing the problem and describing the solution in an algorithm can be helpful in developing their critical thinking skills.

This activity is an example of a problem that students find interesting and motivating and that lends itself to algorithm development. It was based on a problem from Marilyn vos Savant's *Parade Magazine* column "Ask Marilyn." The column posed this question:

"Suppose you are on a game show and you're given a choice of three doors. Behind one is a car; behind the others, goats. You pick a door—say No. 1—and the host, who knows what's behind the other doors, opens another door—say No. 3—which has a goat. He then says to you, 'Do you want to pick door 2?' Is it to your advantage to switch your choice?" (p. 12)

Marilyn vos Savant asserted that the odds of winning the car increase from 1-in-3 to 2-in-3 by switching doors. Ask students if they agree with this assessment.

*Exploring the Problem.* Marilyn challenged students around the country to test her conclusion by acting out the game. One student plays the host, another the contestant. Label three paper cups 1, 2, and 3. While the contestant looks away, the host tosses a die until 1, 2, or 3 comes up, then hides a penny under the cup of that number. Then the contestant chooses a cup by throwing a die in the same way and the host lifts up a losing cup from the two unchosen. Finally, the contestant lifts up the original cup to see if it contains the penny. They repeat this 200 times and record the results each time. Then they test the "switching" strategy 200 times in the same fashion. Point out that another way to do the same activity is to write a program that lets the computer do the "game" in this way.

*Whole-class Planning.* Get the students to discuss the procedure that Marilyn suggests and help them develop a sequence for doing the activity. Use word processing to write the sequence so that the whole class can see it, on a computer with a large screen or one connected to a projection device. After they develop this verbal description of the activity, point out that this is an algorithm.

*Small-group Work.* Before students begin work in small groups to develop their programs, review random number formulas and be sure they understand how variables and subroutines work. Have them begin work on the first part of the program, staying with the initial choice of doors. Help the groups work through the statements required to carry out their algorithms. Have them run the program to see how they can make it work better and be easier for others to follow and understand. After this part works, have them develop the second part of the program: the door-switching strategy.

*Extension Activities.* Challenge the students to come up with their own problems to solve. They can design the algorithms and programs to carry out the solution and, if they desire, share their problems with Marilyn vos Savant by writing her a letter.

Source: Based on Wagner, P. (1992). Gamer 1, 2, 3: The vas (sic) Savant challenge. *The Computing Teacher, 19*(5), 12–14.

are written in programming languages as are drills, tutorials, and other forms of instructional software. However, teachers also use programming languages as a tool to teach as well as to develop programs (see Example Lesson 4.1).

One of the most widely known of the programming languages used for instruction is Logo. The work of Seymour Papert (see Chapter 3) and his colleagues at the Massachusetts Institute of Technology made Logo "widely used throughout the world as an introductory programming language and mathematical learning environment for students in elementary and secondary schools" (p. 615). Papert hoped that it would become "a context which is to learning

**Figure 4.1  Example Software with Drill and Practice Functions: Millie's Math House**

Source: Used by permission of Edmark Corporation.

**Figure 4.2  Example Software with Drill and Practice Functions: Milliken Phonics Sequences**

Source: Courtesy of Milliken Publishing Co.

mathematics what living in France is to learning French" (Papert, 1980, p. 6).

Although not as popular as it was in the 1980s, Logo is still a good example of how programming languages can be used in education for a variety of purposes. It often introduces very young children to programming concepts and has been used successfully both for programming and to explore concepts in content areas such as mathematics and language arts.

## Drill and Practice Activities

### Drill and Practice: Definition and Characteristics

Drill and practice activities provide exercises in which students work example items, usually one at a time, and receive feedback on their correctness. Programs vary considerably in the kind of feedback they provide in response to student input. They range from a simple display like "OK" or "No, try again" to elaborate animated displays or verbal explanations. Some programs simply present the next item if the student answers correctly.

Types of drill and practice are sometimes distinguished by the sophistication with which the program tailors the practice session to student needs (Merrill & Salisbury, 1984). The most basic drill and practice function often is described as a *flashcard activity*. A student sees a set number of questions or problems on the screen and answers one at a time. Examples of instructional software that reflect this type of function are shown in Figures 4.1 and 4.2.

A more sophisticated form of drill and practice moves students on to advanced questions after they get a number of questions correct at some predetermined mastery level; it may also send them back to lower levels if they answer a certain number wrong. Some programs automatically review questions that students get wrong before going on to other levels. Movement between levels often is transparent to students since the program may do it automatically with-

out any indication. Sometimes, however, the program may congratulate students on good progress before proceeding to the next level, or it may allow them to choose their next activities.

In addition to meeting general criteria for good instructional courseware (see Figure 4.14 on pages 106–107), well-designed drill and practice programs should also meet other criteria:

- **Control over the presentation rate.** Unless the questions are part of a timed review, students should have as much time as they wish to answer and examine the feedback before proceeding to later questions. If the program provides no specific feedback for correct answers, it usually is acceptable to present later questions without any further entries from students.

- **Appropriate feedback for correct answers.** Although some courseware designers stress the importance of positive feedback for correct answers, not all programs provide it. If students' answers are timed, or if their session time is limited, they may find it more motivating simply to move quickly to later questions. Positive feedback should not be so elaborate and time-consuming that it detracts from the lesson's purpose. No matter how attractive the display, students tend to tire of it after a while and it ceases to motivate them.

- **Better reinforcement for correct answers.** Some programs inadvertently motivate students to get wrong answers. This happens when a program gives more exciting or interesting feedback for wrong answers than for correct ones. The most famous example of this design error occurred in an early version of a popular microcomputer-based math drill series. Each correct answer got a smiling face, but two or more wrong answers produced a full-screen, animated crying face that students found very amusing. Consequently, many students tried to answer incorrectly to see it. The company corrected this flaw, but this classic error still exists today in other programs.

### Issues Related to Drill and Practice

Drill and practice courseware activities were among the earliest and most well-recognized instructional uses of computers and are still used extensively in schools. These activities have frequently been shown to allow the effective rehearsal students need to transfer newly learned information into long-term memory (Merrill & Salisbury, 1984; Salisbury, 1990). However, drill and practice is also the most maligned of the courseware activities, sometimes informally referred to among its critics as "drill and kill." This derision results, in part, from perceived overuse. Many authors have criticized teachers for presenting drills for overly long periods or for teaching functions that drills are ill-suited to accomplish. For example, teachers may expose students to drill and practice courseware as a way of introducing new concepts rather than just practicing and reinforcing familiar ones.

But probably the most common reason for the virulent criticism of drill and practice courseware is its identification as an easily targeted icon for what many people consider an outmoded approach to teaching. Critics claim that introducing isolated skills and directing students to practice them directly contradicts the trend toward restructured curriculum in which students learn and use skills in an integrated way within the context of their own projects that specifically require the skills.

Although curriculum increasingly emphasizes problem solving and higher-order skills, teachers still give students on-paper practice (e.g., worksheets or exercises) for many skills to help them learn and remember correct procedures. Many teachers feel that such practice gives students more rapid recall and use of basic skills as prerequisites to advanced concepts. They like students to have what Gagné (1982) and Bloom (1986) call *automaticity* or *automatic recall* of these lower-order skills to help them master higher-order ones faster and more easily. The usefulness of drill programs in providing this kind of practice has been well-documented, but the programs seem especially popular among teachers of students with learning disabilities (Hasselbring, 1988; Okolo, 1992; Higgins & Boone, 1993). The following examples cite basic skills that are prerequisite to higher-order skills:

- Automatic recall of multiplication facts is required for most higher-level mathematics ranging from long division to algebra.

- Keyboard proficiency is a prerequisite for assignments that require extensive typing.

- Graded compositions require rapid recall and application of correct sentence structure, spelling, and principles of grammar and usage.

- Many schools still require students to memorize facts such as states and capitals.

Despite the increasing emphasis on problem solving and higher-order skills, it is likely that some form of drill and practice courseware probably will be useful in many classrooms for some time to come. Such programs address needs for these and other required skills. Rather than ignoring drill and practice software as outmoded, teachers should seek to select and use these kinds of programs for uses they can best accomplish.

## How to Use Drill and Practice in Teaching

**Benefits of drill functions.** Drill and practice programs may be used whenever teachers feel the need for on-paper exercises such as worksheets. Drill courseware provides several acknowledged benefits as compared to paper exercises:

*Immediate feedback.* When students practice skills on paper, they frequently do not know until much later whether or not they did their work correctly. To quote a common saying, "Practice does not make perfect; practice makes permanent." As they complete work incorrectly, students may actually be memorizing the wrong skills. Drill and practice courseware informs them immediately whether or not their responses are accurate, so they can make quick corrections. This helps both "debugging" (identifying errors in their procedures) and retention (usually necessary to place the skills in long-term memory for ready access later).

*Motivation.* Many students refuse to do the practice they need on paper, either because they failed so much that the whole idea is abhorrent; or they have poor handwriting skills; or simply dislike writing. In these cases, computer-based practice may motivate students to do the practice they need. Computers don't get impatient or give disgusted looks when a student gives a wrong answer.

*Saving teacher time.* Since teachers do not have to present or grade drill and practice, students may do this activity essentially on their own while the teacher addresses other student needs.

**Classroom applications of drill functions.** On some occasions, even the most creative and innovative teacher may take advantage of the benefits of drill and practice courseware to have students practice using isolated skills.

*To supplement or replace worksheets and homework exercises.* Whenever students have difficulty with higher-order tasks ranging from reading and writing to mathematics, teachers may have to stop and identify specific prerequisite skills that these students lack and provide the instruction and practice they need to go forward. In these cases, learning may require a rehearsal activity to make sure information is stored in long-term memory so students can retrieve it easily. Drills' motivation, immediate feedback, and self-pacing can make it more productive for students to practice required skills on the computer rather than on paper.

*In preparation for tests.* Despite the new emphasis on student portfolios and other authentic assessment measures, students can expect to take several kinds of objective examinations in their education careers. When they need to prepare to demonstrate mastery of specific skills in important examinations (e.g., for end-of-year grades or for college

**Example Lesson 4.2**
**Integration of Drill and Practice Courseware**

| | |
|---|---|
| **Lesson:** | Traffic Officer (Elementary level) |
| **Developed by:** | Doris Murdoch, Webster Elementary School (St. Augustine, Florida) |
| **Courseware:** | *Muppet Word Book* (Sunburst) |
| **Content Area/Topic:** | Language arts-Letter cases |

**Instructional Resources.** In addition to computer and software, the lesson plan employs the following constructed materials: upper/lowercase letter cards mounted as necklaces for each student; stop sign and patrol belt or a large, handheld Kermit graphic; printout of traffic officer worksheet.

**Lesson Purposes.** Identify given letters of the alphabet. Tell whether letters are upper or lower case.

**Instructional Activities**
*First Day.* Each student is given either an upper- or lowercase letter card. Students identify letters as a full group. One child is chosen as the traffic officer. Two areas are designated as parking lots, one for uppercase letters and one for lowercase letters. The traffic officer directs the other students' "cars" to the correct parking lot according to letter case. Students will be guided through this activity by the teacher. After letters are sorted ("cars are parked"), the class counts the number of letters in each group. The teacher introduces the class to the parking lot activity on the Muppet Word Book disk.

*Second Day.* At centers or workshops, individual students or small groups of students practice classifying letter cases with the Muppet Word Book parking lot activity and the traffic officer game.

*Third Day.* Students complete the traffic officer worksheet as an assessment activity.

Source: Based on Cobb, L., Dunn, A., & Henry, G. (1991). Name games. *The Florida Technology in Education Quarterly, 3*(2), 63–66.

entrance), drill and practice courseware can help them focus on their deficiencies and correct them.

An example integration strategy for drill functions is shown in Example Lesson Plan 4.2

**Guidelines for using drill and practice.** Observe the following guidelines when designing integration strategies for drill and practice functions:

*Set time limits.* Teachers should limit the time devoted to drill assignments to 10–15 minutes per day. This ensures that students will not become bored and that the drill and practice strategy will retain its effectiveness. Also, teachers should be sure students have been introduced previously to the concepts underlying the drills; drill courseware should serve mainly to debug and to help students retain their grasp of familiar concepts.

*Assign individually.* Since self-pacing and personalized feedback are among the most powerful benefits of drills, these activities usually work best for individual computer use. However, some teachers with limited technology resources have found other, ingenious ways to capitalize on the motivational and immediate feedback capabilities of drills. If all students in a class benefit from practice in a skill using a drill program, the teacher may divide them into small groups to compete with each other for the best group scores. The class could even be divided into two

groups for a "relay race" competition over which group can complete the assignment the fastest with the most correct answers.

*Use learning stations.* If not all students need the kind of practice that a drill provides, the teacher may make courseware one of several learning stations to serve students with identified weaknesses in one or more key skills. The key to using drill and practice appropriately is to match its inherent capabilities with the identified learning needs of individual students.

## Tutorial Activities

### Tutorials: Definition and Characteristics

Tutorial courseware uses the computer to deliver an entire instructional sequence similar to a teacher's classroom instruction on the topics. This instruction usually is expected to be complete enough to stand alone; the student should be able to learn the topic without any help or other materials from outside the courseware. Unlike other courseware activities, tutorials are true teaching courseware. Gagné, Wager, and Rojas (1981) stated that tutorial courseware should address all instructional events. (See the discussion of Gagné's events of instruction in Chapter 3.) Gagné et al. show how a tutorial may vary its strategies to accomplish events for different kinds of learning ranging from verbal information to complex applications of rules and problem solving.

People may confuse drill activities with tutorial activities for two reasons. First, drill courseware may provide elaborate feedback that reviewers may mistake for the tutorial explanations required by Gagné's Events 4 and 5. Even courseware developers may claim that a package is a tutorial when it is, in fact, a drill activity with detailed feedback. Second, a good tutorial should include one or more practice sequences to address Events 5 through 7, so reviewers easily become confused about the primary purpose of the package.

Tutorials often are categorized as linear and branching tutorials (Alessi & Trollip, 1991). A simple, linear tutorial gives the same instructional sequence of explanation, practice, and feedback to all learners regardless of differences in their performance. A more sophisticated, branching tutorial directs learners along alternate paths depending on how they respond to questions and whether or not they show mastery of certain parts of the material. Even branching tutorials can range in complexity by the amount of branching they allow and how fully they diagnose the kinds of instruction a student needs.

Some tutorials also have computer-management capabilities; teachers may "tell" such a program at what level to start for a student and get reports on each student's progress through the instruction. Although a tutorial program does not need these components, data collection and management features often make it more useful to teachers.

As the description of events of instruction implies, tutorials are most often geared toward learners who can read fairly well, usually older students or adults. Since tutorial instruction is expected to stand alone, it is difficult to explain or give appropriate guidance on-screen to a non-reader. However, some tutorials aimed at younger learners have found clever ways to explain and demonstrate concepts with graphics, succinct phrases or sentences, or audio directions coupled with screen devices.

Some of the best tutorial courseware activities are in packages that accompany newly purchased computers or applications software, for example, *Tour of the Macintosh* or *Introduction to Microsoft Works*. While tutorials are found more frequently on mainframe or file server systems than on microcomputers, some good tutorials are available on standalone systems. An example of a microcomputer tutorial sequence is shown in Figures 4.3.

Being a good teacher is a difficult assignment for any human, let alone a computer. However, courseware must accomplish this task to fulfill a tutorial function. In addition to meeting general criteria for good instructional courseware, well-designed tutorial programs should also meet several additional standards:

- **Extensive interactivity.** The most frequent criticism of tutorials is that they are "page-turners," that is, they ask students to do very little other than read. Good tutorials, like good

teachers, should require students to give frequent and thoughtful responses to questions and problems and they should supply appropriate practice and feedback to guide students' learning.

- **Thorough user control.** *User control* refers to several aspects of the program. First, students should always be able to control the rate at which text appears on the screen. The program should not go on to the next information or activity screen until the user presses a key or gives some other indication of completing necessary reading. Next, the program should offer students the flexibility to review explanations, examples, or sequences of instruction or move ahead to other instruction. The program should also provide frequent opportunities for students to exit as desired.

- **Appropriate and comprehensive teaching sequence.** The program's structure should provide a suggested or required sequence of instruction that builds on concepts and covers the content adequately. It should provide sufficient explanation and examples in both original and remedial sequences. In sum, it should compare favorably to an expert teacher's presentation sequence for the topic.

- **Adequate answer-judging and feedback capabilities.** Whenever possible, programs should allow students to answer in natural language and should accept all correct answers and possible variations of correct answers. They should also give appropriate corrective feedback when needed, supplying this feedback after only one or two tries rather than frustrating students by making them keep trying indefinitely to answer something they may not know.

Although some authors insist that graphics form part of tutorial instruction (Baek & Layne, 1988), others emphasize judicious use of graphics to avoid interfering with the purpose of the instruction (Eiser, 1988). Eiser is among those who recommend online evaluation and recordkeeping on student performance as part of any tutorial.

## Issues Related to Tutorials

Tutorials attract the same criticism as drill and practice for teacher-directed methods; that is, they deliver traditional instruction in skills rather than letting students create learning experiences through generative learning and development projects. Also, since good tutorials are difficult to design and program, critics charge that tutorials represent trivial or even counterproductive uses of the computer. A number of tutorials fail to meet criteria for good programs of this kind, thus contributing to this perception.

Tutorials are difficult to find, even for those who want to use them. Software publishers describe fewer packages as tutorials than any other kind of microcomputer courseware. Part of the reason for this comes from the difficulty and expense of designing and developing them. A well-designed tutorial sequence emerges from extensive research into how to teach the topic well, and its requirements for programming and graphics can become fairly involved. Designers must know what learning tasks the topic requires, what sequence students should follow, how best to explain and demonstrate essential concepts,

**Figure 4.3   Example Software with Tutorial Functions from Advanced Learning Systems (A+LS) Algebra Series**

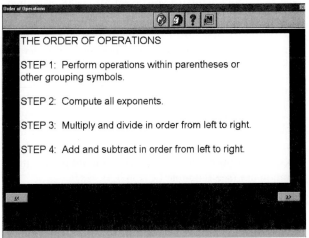

THE ORDER OF OPERATIONS

STEP 1:  Perform operations within parentheses or other grouping symbols.

STEP 2:  Compute all exponents.

STEP 3:  Multiply and divide in order from left to right.

STEP 4:  Add and subtract in order from left to right.

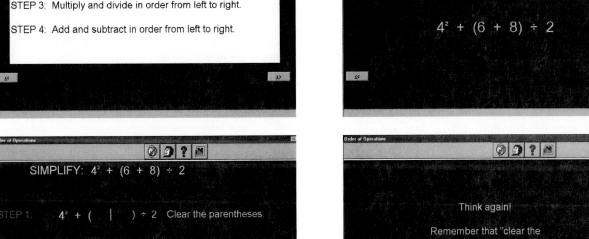

It's your turn again!

We will solve this problem together using the order of operations.

$$4^2 + (6 + 8) \div 2$$

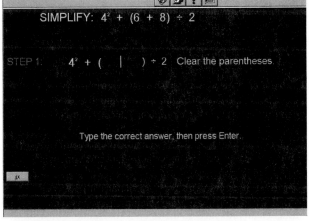

SIMPLIFY:  $4^2 + (6 + 8) \div 2$

STEP 1:      $4^2 + ( \ | \ ) \div 2$   Clear the parentheses.

Type the correct answer, then press Enter.

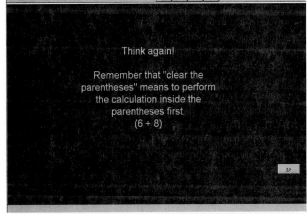

Think again!

Remember that "clear the parentheses" means to perform the calculation inside the parentheses first.
$(6 + 8)$

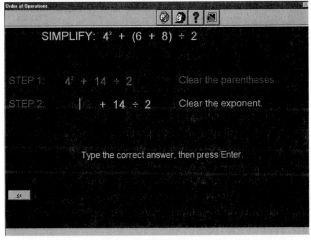

SIMPLIFY:  $4^2 + (6 + 8) \div 2$

STEP 1:      $4^2 + 14 \div 2$        Clear the parentheses.

STEP 2:      $| \ + 14 \div 2$        Clear the exponent.

Type the correct answer, then press Enter.

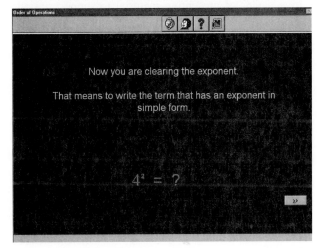

Now you are clearing the exponent.

That means to write the term that has an exponent in simple form.

$$4^2 = ?$$

Source: From the Advanced Learning System® published by The American Education Corporation. Reprinted by permission.

common errors that students are likely to display, and how to provide instruction and feedback to correct those errors. Tutorials can be large, so they often work slowly on microcomputers. Larger tutorials must be delivered via integrated learning systems or other networked systems, making them expensive.

These problems become still more difficult because teachers frequently disagree about what they should teach for a given topic, how to teach it most effectively, and in what order to present learning tasks. A teacher may choose not to purchase a tutorial with a sound instructional sequence because it does not cover the topic the way he or she presents it. Not surprisingly, courseware companies tend to avoid programs that are problematic both to develop and market.

### How to Use Tutorials in Teaching

**Benefits of tutorial functions.** It is unfortunate that microcomputer tutorials are so rare; a well-designed tutorial on a nontrivial topic can be a valuable instructional tool. Since a tutorial can include drill and practice routines, helpful features include the same ones as for drills (immediate feedback to learners and time savings) plus the additional benefit of self-contained, self-paced substitutes for teacher presentations.

**Classroom applications of tutorial functions.** Self-instructional tutorials should in no way threaten teachers, since few conceivable situations make a computer preferable to an expert teacher. However, the tutorial's unique capability of presenting an entire interactive instructional sequence can assist in several classroom situations:

*Self-paced reviews of instruction.* On many occasions, students need repeated instruction on a topic after the teacher's initial presentation. Some students may be slower to understand concepts and need additional time on them. Others seem to learn better in a self-paced mode without the pressure to move at the same pace as the rest of the class. Still others may need review before a test. Teachers can help these students by providing tutorials at learning stations to review previously presented material while the teacher works with other students.

*Alternative learning strategy.* Tutorials also provide alternative means of presenting material to support various learning strategies. Some students, typically advanced ones, prefer to structure their own learning activities and proceed on their own. A good tutorial allows students to glean much background material prior to meeting with a teacher or others to do assessment and/or further work assignments.

*Instruction when teachers are unavailable.* Some students have problems when they surge ahead of their class rather than falling behind. The teacher cannot leave the rest of the class to provide the instruction that such an advanced student needs. Many schools, especially those in rural areas, may not offer certain courses because they cannot justify the expense of hiring a teacher for comparatively few students who will need physics, German, trigonometry, or other lower-demand courses. Well-designed tutorial courses, especially in combination with other methods such as distance learning, can help meet these students' needs.

**Guidelines for using tutorials.** Like drill and practice functions, tutorial functions are designed primarily to serve individuals. Depending on which of the above strategies it promotes, a tutorial may form a classroom learning station or may be available for checkout at any time in a library/media center. Several successful uses of tutorials have been documented (Murray et al., 1988; Kraemer, 1990; CAI in Music, 1994; Graham, 1994), but microcomputer tutorials that fulfill the functions listed rarely are found in classroom use. Although they have considerable theoretical value and are somewhat popular in military and industrial training, schools and colleges have never fully tapped their potential as teaching resources. The expense of developing them and difficulty of marketing them may be to blame for this situation. However, recent trends toward combining tutorial courseware with video media and distance education may bring tutorial functions into more common use (see Example Lesson 4.3).

## Simulation Activities

### Simulations: Definition and Characteristics

A simulation is a computerized model of a real or imagined system designed to teach how a system works. Simulations differ from tutorial and drill and practice activities by providing learner-structured activities. The person using the courseware usually chooses tasks and the order in which to do them. Alessi and Trollip (1991) identify two main types of simulations: "those that teach about something and those that teach how to do something" (p. 119). They further divide the "about" simulations into physical and process types and they divide the "how to" simulations into procedural and situational types.

- **Physical simulations.** Users manipulate objects or phenomena represented on the screen. For example, students see selections of chemicals with instructions to combine them to see the result or they may see how various electrical circuits operate.

- **Process simulations.** These speed up or slow down processes that usually either take so long or happen so quickly that students could not ordinarily see the events unfold. For example, courseware may show the effects of changes in demographic variables on population growth or the effects of environmental factors on ecosystems. Biological simulations like those on genetics are popular, since they help students experiment with natural laws like the laws of genetics by pairing animals with given characteristics and showing the resulting offspring.

- **Procedural simulations.** These activities teach the appropriate sequences of steps to perform certain procedures. They include diagnostic programs, in which students try to identify the sources of medical or mechanical problems, and flight simulators, in which students simulate piloting an airplane or other vehicle.

- **Situational simulations.** These programs give students hypothetical problem situations and ask them to react. Some simulations allow for various successful strategies such as letting students play the stock market or operate businesses. Others have most desirable and least desirable options such as choices when encountering a potentially volatile classroom situation.

---

**Example Lesson 4.3**
**Integration of Tutorial Courseware**

| | |
|---|---|
| **Lesson:** | Interactive Algebra (Middle-high school level) |
| **Developed by:** | M. D. Roblyer (University of West Georgia) |
| **Courseware:** | *A+LS Algebra 1*(American Education Corporation) |
| **Content Area/Topic:** | Mathematics/Algebra |

**Instructional Resources.** Computer and software

**Lesson Purposes.** Students can use the Study Guide, Practice, and Test components in this software as a review after the material has been introduced in class. This helps ensure that they understand the concepts and are prepared for taking end-of-year exams.

**Instructional Activities.** Concepts at this level of Algebra I begin with using variables and end with solving quadratic equations by factoring. Teachers introduce each of the concepts at this level in their usual way. However, instead of assigning worksheets or other practice to make sure students understand and remember the concepts, the teacher assigns each student to go through the software tutorial sequence on the topic. After all students go through this individual activity, the teacher holds a cooperative roundtable review. This review is especially important for more complex concepts such as "What do the slope and x-y coordinates in a linear equation mean?" As students state one thing they remember about the topic, the teacher or one of the students enters the contribution into a computer connected to a projection system for all to see. Students continue adding information, asking questions, and giving comments about the topic, until the teacher believes that they have an adequate comprehension of the concepts.

Source: Based on ideas taken from the American Education Corporation's *Advanced Learning System Teacher Resource Guide* (1998).

---

These types only clarify the various forms a simulation might take. *Teachers need not classify a given simulation into one of these categories.* They need to know only that all simulations show students what happens in given situations when they choose certain actions. Simulations usually emphasize learning about the system itself, rather than learning general problem-solving strategies. For example, a program called *The Factory* has students build products by selecting machines and placing them in the correct sequence. Since the program emphasizes solving problems in correct sequence rather than manufacturing in factories, it should probably be called problem-solving activity rather than a simulation. Programs such as *SimCity* (Brøderbund), which let students design their own cities, provide more accurate examples of building simulations.

Since simulations promote such widely varied purposes, it is difficult to provide specific criteria for selecting high-quality ones. By one frequently cited criterion, *fidelity*, a more realistic and accurate representation of a system makes a better simulation (Reigeluth & Schwartz, 1989). However, even this is not a criterion for judging all simulations (Alessi, 1988). Reigeluth and Schwartz (1989) describe some design concerns for simulations based on instructional theory. They list important simulation components including a scenario, a model, and an instructional overlay that lets learners interact with the program. Since the screen often presents no set sequence of steps, simulations—more than most courseware—need good accompa-

nying documentation. A set of clear directions helps the teacher learn how to use the program and show the students how to use it rapidly and easily.

## Issues Related to Simulations

Most educators acknowledge the instructional usefulness of simulations; however, some are concerned about the accuracy of the programs' models. For example, when students see simplified versions of these systems in a controlled situation, they may get inaccurate or imprecise perspectives on the systems' complexity. Students may feel they know all about how to react to situations because they have experienced simulated versions of them. Many educators feel especially strongly that situational simulations must be followed at some point by real experiences. Many teachers of very young children feel that learners at early stages of their cognitive development should experience things first with their five senses rather than on computer screens.

Some simulations are viewed as complicated ways to teach very simple concepts that could just as easily be demonstrated on paper, with manipulatives, or with real objects. For example, students usually are delighted with the simulation of the food chain called *Odell Lake,* a program that lets students see what animal preys on what other animals in a hypothetical lake. However, some wonder whether or not such a computer simulation is necessary or even desirable to teach this concept. Hasselbring and Goin

(1993) point out that students can often master the activities of a simulation without actually developing effective problem-solving skills; on the contrary, such applications actually can encourage counterproductive behaviors. For example, some simulations initially provide little information with which to solve problems, and students are reduced to "trial-and-error guessing rather than systematic analysis of available information" (p. 156). Teachers must carefully structure integration strategies so that students will not use simulations in inappropriate ways.

Simulations are considered among the most potentially powerful computer courseware resources; however as with most courseware, their usefulness depends largely on the program's purpose and how well it fits in with the purpose of the lesson and student needs. Teachers are responsible for recognizing the unique instructional value of each simulation and using it to best advantage.

## How to Use Simulations in Teaching

**Benefits of simulation functions.** Simulations have long been recognized for their unique teaching capabilities. Depending on the topic, a simulation can provide one or more of the following benefits (Alessi & Trollip, 1991):

- **Compress time.** This feature is important whenever students study the growth or development of living things (e.g., pairing animals to observe the characteristics of their offspring or other processes that take a long time (e.g., the movement of a glacier). A simulation can make something happen in seconds that normally takes days, months, or longer. Consequently, feedback is faster than in real life and students can cover more variations of the activity in a shorter time.

- **Slow down processes.** Conversely, a simulation can also model processes normally invisible to the human eye because they happen so quickly. For example, physical education students can study the slowed-down movement of muscles and limbs as a simulated athlete throws a ball or swings a golf club.

- **Get students involved.** Simulations can capture students' attention by placing them in charge of things and asking that most motivating of questions: "What would *you* do?" The results of their choices can be immediate and graphic. It also allows users to interact with the program instead of just seeing its output.

- **Make experimentation safe.** Whenever learning involves physical danger, simulations are the strategy of choice. This is true any time students are learning to drive vehicles, handle volatile substances, or react to potentially dangerous situations. They can experiment with strategies in simulated environments that might result in personal injury to themselves or others in real life.

- **Make the impossible possible.** This is the most powerful feature of a simulation. Very often, teachers simply cannot give students access to the resources or the situations that simulations can. Simulations can show students what it would be like to walk on the moon or to react to emergencies in a nuclear power plant. They can see cells mutating or hold

**Figure 4.4 Example Software with Simulation Functions: Operation Frog (a)**

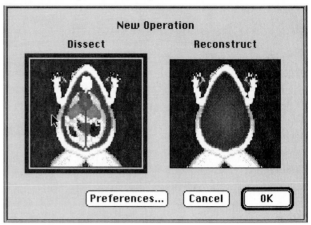

Source: From Scholastic's Operation Frog. Used by permission of Scholastic Inc.

countrywide elections. They can even design new societies or planets and see the results of their choices.

- **Save money and other resources.** Many school systems are finding dissections of animals on a computer screen much less expensive than on real frogs or cats and just as instructional. (It also is easier on the animals!) Depending on the subject, a simulated experiment may be just as effective as a learning experience but at a fraction of the cost.

- **Repeat with variations.** Unlike real life, simulations let students repeat events as many times as they wish and with unlimited variations. They can pair any number of cats or make endless airplane landings in a variety of conditions to compare the results of each set of choices.

- **Make situations controllable.** Real-life situations often are confusing, especially to those seeing them for the first time. When many things happen at once, students have difficulty focusing on the operation of individual components. Who could understand the operation of a stock market by looking at the real thing without some introduction? Simulations can isolate parts of activities and control the background noise. This makes it easier for students to see what is happening later when all the parts come together in the actual activity (see Figures 4.4 and 4.5).

**Classroom applications of simulation functions.** Real systems are usually preferable to simulations, but a simulation can suffice when a teacher considers the real situation too time-consuming, dangerous, expensive, or unrealistic for a classroom presentation. Simulations should be considered in the following situations, keeping in mind that the real activity is preferable:

*In place of or as supplements to lab experiments.* When adequate lab materials are not available, teachers should try to locate computer simulations of the required experiments. Many teachers find that simulations offer effective supplements to real labs, either to prepare students for making good use of the actual labs, or as follow-ups with

**Figure 4.5  Example Software with Simulation Functions: Operation Frog (b)**

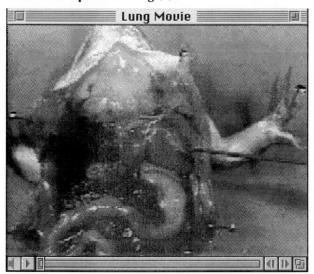

Source: From Scholastic's Operation Frog. Used by permission of Scholastic Inc.

variations on the original experiments without using up consumable materials. Some simulations actually allow users to perform experiments that they could not otherwise manage or that would be too dangerous for students (see Example Lesson 4.4).

***In place of or as supplements to role playing.*** When students take on the roles of characters in situations, computer simulations can spark students' imaginations and interests in the activities. However, many students either refuse to role play in front of a class or get too enthusiastic and disrupt the classroom. Computerized simulation can take the personal embarrassment and logistical problems out of the learning experience and make classroom role playing more controllable.

***In place of or as supplements to field trips.*** Seeing an activity in the real setting can be a valuable experience, especially for young children. Sometimes, however, desired locations are not within reach of the school and a simulated experience of all or part of the process is the next best thing. As with labs, simulations provide good introductions or follow-ups to field trips.

In addition to these integration strategies, which represent directed methods, simulations may also promote constructivist strategies:

***Introducing a new topic.*** Courseware that allows students to explore the elements of an environment in a hands-on manner frequently provides students' first in-depth contact with a topic. This seems to accomplish several purposes. First, it is a nonthreatening way to introduce new terms and unfamiliar settings. Students know that they are not being graded, so they feel less pressure than usual to learn everything right away. A simulation can become simply a get-acquainted look at a topic. Simulations can also build students' initial interest in a topic. Highly graphic, hands-on activities draw them into the topic and whet their appetite to learn more. Finally, some software helps students see how certain prerequisite skills relate to the topic; this may motivate students more strongly to learn the skills than if the skills were introduced in isolation from the problems to which they apply. An example of this is *Decisions! Decisions!* software by Tom Snyder on Social Studies topics such as urbanization and elections.

***Fostering exploration and process learning.*** Teachers often use content-free simulation/problem-solving software as motivation for students to explore their own cognitive processes. Since this kind of courseware requires students to learn no specific content, it is easier to get them to concentrate on problem-solving steps and strategies. However, with content-free products, it is even more important than usual that teachers draw comparisons between skills from the courseware activities and those in the content areas to which they want to transfer the experience. For example, *The Incredible Laboratory* (Sunburst) brings an implicit emphasis on science process skills that the teacher may want to point out. These kinds of activities may be introduced at any time, but it seems more fruitful to use them just prior to content area activities that will require the same processes.

***Encouraging cooperation and group work.*** Sometimes a simulated demonstration can capture students' attention quickly and effectively and interest them in working together on a product. For example, a simulation on immigration or colonization might be the "grabber" a teacher needs to launch a group project in a social studies unit (see Example Lesson 4.5).

**Guidelines for using simulation functions.** Simulations offer more versatile implementation than tutorials or drills. They usually work equally effectively with a whole class, small groups, or individuals. A teacher may choose to introduce a lesson to the class by displaying a simulation or to divide up the class into small groups and let each solve problems. Because they instigate discussion and cooperative work so well, simulations usually are considered more appropriate for pairs and small groups than for individuals. However, individual use certainly is not precluded.

The market offers many simulations, but it often is difficult to locate one on a desired topic. The field of science seems to include more simulations than any other area (Andaloro, 1991; Richards, 1992; Ronen, 1992; Smith, 1992; Mintz, 1993; Simmons & Lunetta, 1993), but use of simulations is also popular in social sciences topics (Clinton, 1991; Allen, 1993; Estes, 1994). However, more simulations currently are in development and feature videodisc and online supplements to combine the control, safety, and interactive features of computer simulations with the visual impact of pictures of real-life devices and processes.

## Example Lesson 4.4
## Directed Integration of Simulation Courseware

| | |
|---|---|
| **Lesson:** | Earthquake! (Elementary level) |
| **Developed by:** | Karen Smith, McArthur Elementary School (Pensacola, Florida) |
| **Courseware:** | *Science Toolkit: Earthquake Module* (Brøderbund) |
| **Content Area/Topic:** | Science-Earth concepts |
| **Instructional Resources:** | In addition to a computer and software, a laserdisc player and laserdisc: Windows on Science, Intermediate-Earth Science, Vol. 1 (Optical Data) |

**Lesson Purposes.** Learn to work cooperatively with a group to perform an experiment. Identify fault lines and explain the movement of an earthquake.

**Instructional Activities**

*Reviewing Earthquake Information.* To begin this lesson, the teacher should start with a basic review of an earthquake, asking questions such as: What is an earthquake? What happens when an earthquake occurs? What causes earthquakes? Review the layers of the earth using a visual aid showing the crust, mantle, and core. Discuss plates in the crust. Explain that the earth's crust is divided into sections called plates. The plates fit together like a puzzle. Show a world map with the plates defined. If possible, have a world map sectioned off showing the plates. Cut them apart and apply magnetic tape on the back to form a visual puzzle to pull apart, reinforcing the concept. Explain that the plates are constantly moving, perhaps interjecting a videodisc clip of the plates on Windows on Science: Earth Science, Volume 1. Use Frame 17984, which shows an explanation and the movement of the plates. Be sure students understand that an earthquake is the sudden moving and shaking of the earth due to pressure buildup within the plates causing plates to rise and fall.

*Earthquake Demonstrations.* Have a child build a simulated building using paper cups and plates. Show what happens during an earthquake by gently bumping the base of the structure. Explain ways of recording movement through a machine called a seismograph. Explain the seismograph and its function. Talk about its importance for recording data constantly and monitoring movement for possible predictions of major earthquakes. Show the laser disc again, choosing frames related to your level. This shows an earthquake and explains what is happening. Explain the use of the Science Toolkit Earthquake Lab to create an earthquake and better understand how seismographs work.

*Doing the Experiment.* Start up the software and set up the seismoscope according to directions in the instruction manual. Make sure the interface box is plugged into the computer and the photocell probe is in the correct slot. The seismoscope will measure light movement as the source of earthquake activity. Set the light source (flashlight) on the table. Make sure the light is directed toward the photocell. The least movement of the light will create movement of the seismograph needle on the screen. Try three variables. First, have a student hit the table with the flashlight lightly. The computer will begin recording data as soon as it detects movement. Notice the needle jumping each time the student hits the table. Repeat the procedure with a large earthquake by pounding on the table with your fist and recording. The last part of the experiment will show a seismograph reading a severe earthquake; shake the table with the light source to create movement.

*Analyzing the Data.* Review data gathered by using arrow keys to read the graph backward and forward. To get a hard copy of the experimental data, press Escape until you reach the Earthquake Lab menu. (You may elect to save the data and print later.) Select EXPERIMENT PLOTTER. If you want to print the whole experiment, press RETURN. Your experiment should print. You may choose to print only one section of the experiment by following the directions in the manual. End this experiment by going back to the Main menu.

Source: Based on Smith, K. (1992). Earthquake! *The Florida Technology in Education Quarterly, 4*(2), 68–70.

**Example Lesson 4.5**
**Constructivist Integration of Simulation Courseware**

| | |
|---|---|
| **Lesson:** | Community Planning Projects with *SimCity* (Seventh grade) |
| **Developed by:** | Marianne Teague and Gerald Teague, Northern Middle School (Calvert County, Maryland) |
| **Courseware:** | *SimCity* (Maxis Software) |
| **Content Area Topic:** | Social studies-Citizenship/group cooperation in social projects |
| **Instructional Resources:** | Computer, software, and local community contacts |

**Lesson Purposes.** Raising awareness of responsibility to become informed citizens and participate in local decision making. Learning to work cooperatively with a group to carry out a social project.

**Instructional Activities.** This software and the idea for the project tied in with a current event of concern to the whole community: the development of a comprehensive plan for the township. (Many communities across the country are involved in this kind of plan.) After a representative from the county planning and zoning office talked with the students about factors of concern to community development, the social studies teacher helped introduce a group of about 50 students to the *SimCity* software. This program served to demonstrate the concepts that the representative had talked about with them. The group of students formed teams of 4 to 5 students each and started their own community planning projects with *SimCity*. Each group met for an hour every week for about three months to discuss and develop its plan. As a group, they decided how to select and place features such as roads, homes, and utilities. After recording their decisions on paper, they entered them into the program and observed the results. They discussed feedback that the program gave them on areas such as taxes, crime rates, and public opinion. They videotaped their meetings, discussions, and computer work to document them.

After their plans were completed, each group presented its plan to the teacher and the media specialist. Some of the groups that were most successful in meeting the preset criteria of low crime rates, low pollution levels, reasonable costs, and public approval were asked to prepare formal presentations. These teams presented their designs via the computer and printouts. Members of the local county planning and zoning office helped review the final products. Students had to present their designs and explain and defend their choices.

Source: Based on Jacobson, P. (1992). Save the cities! SimCity in grades 2–5. *The Computing Teacher, 20*(2), 14–15.

# Instructional Games

## Instructional Games: Definition and Characteristics

Instructional games are courseware whose function is to increase motivation by adding game rules to learning activities. Even though teachers often use them in the same way as drill and practice or simulation courseware, games usually are listed as a separate courseware activity because their instructional connotation to students is slightly different. When students know they will play a game, they expect a fun and entertaining activity because of the challenge of the competition and the potential for winning (Randel, Morris, Wetzel, & Whitehill, 1992). Naturally, classroom instruction should not consist entirely of these kinds of activities, no matter how instructional or motivational they are. Teachers intersperse games with other activities to hold attention or to give rewards for accomplishing other activities.

As with simulations, the categories described here merely illustrate the various forms an instructional game may take. Teachers should not feel that they have to classify specific games into categories. But it is important to recognize the common characteristics that set instructional games apart from other types of courseware: game rules, elements of competition or challenge, and amusing or entertaining formats. These elements generate a set of mental and emotional expectations in students that make game-based instructional activities different from nongame ones.

Since instructional games often amount to drills or simulations overlaid with game rules, the same criteria, such as better reinforcement for correct answers than for incorrect ones, should apply to most games. When Malone (1980) examined the evidence on what makes things fun to learn, he found that the most popular games included elements of adventure and uncertainty and levels of complexity matched to learners' abilities. However, teachers should examine instructional games carefully for their value as both educational and motivational tools. Teachers should also assess the amount of physical dexterity that games require of students and make sure that students will not be frustrated instead of motivated by the activities. Games that call for violence or combat need careful screening, not only to avoid parent criticism, but also because girls often perceive the attraction of these activities differently than boys and because such games sometimes depict females as targets of violence.

### Issues Related to Instructional Games

A classroom without elements of games and fun would be a dry, barren landscape for students to traverse. In their review of the effectiveness of games for educational purposes, Randel, Morris, Wetzel, and Whitehill (1992) found "[the fact] that games are more interesting than traditional instruction is both a basic for using them as well as a consistent finding" (p. 270). They also observed that retention over time favors the use of simulations/games. Yet many educators believe that games, especially computer-based ones, are overused and misused (McGinley, 1991). Other teachers believe games convince students that they are escaping from learning, and that they draw attention away from the intrinsic value and motivation of learning. Critics also feel that winning the game becomes a student's primary focus and the instructional purpose is lost in the pursuit of this goal. Observers disagree whether getting lost in the game is a benefit or a problem. Some teachers believe that any time they can sneak learning in under the guise of a game, it is altogether a good thing (McGinley, 1991). Other teachers believe that students can become confused about which part of the activity is the game and which part is the skill; they may then have difficulty transferring their skill to later nongame situations. For example, the teacher's manual for Sunburst's *How the West Was One + Three × Four* reminds teachers that some students can confuse the math operations rules with the game rules and that teachers must help them recognize the need to focus on math rules and use them outside the game.

Although students obviously find many computer games exciting and stimulating, educational value sometimes is difficult to pinpoint. Teachers must try to balance the motivation that instructional games bring to learning against the classroom time they take away from nongame strategies. For example, students may become immersed in the challenge of the *Carmen Sandiego* series, but more efficient ways to teach geography may be just as motivating. Successful uses of games have been reported in many content areas (Trotter, 1991; Flowers, 1993).

### How to Use Instructional Games in Teaching

Several kinds of instructional opportunities invite teachers to take advantage of the motivational qualities of games (see Figure 4.6).

- **In place of worksheets and exercises.** This role resembles that of drill and practice (see Example Lesson 4.6).

- **To foster cooperation and group work.** Like simulations, many instructional games serve as the basis for or introduc-

### Figure 4.6    Example Software with Instructional Game Functions: *How the West Was One + Three × Four*

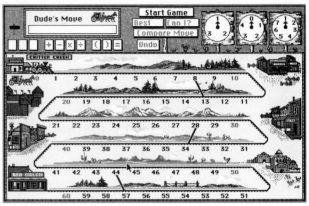

Source: Used by permission of Sunburst Communications.

tions to group work. A game's interactive and motivational qualities help interest students in the topic and present opportunities for competition among groups.

- **As a reward.** Perhaps the most common use of games is to reward good work. This is a valid role for instructional courseware, but teachers should avoid overuse of it. Otherwise, the game can lose its motivational value and become an "electronic babysitter." Some schools actually bar games from classrooms for fear that they will overemphasize the need for students to be entertained.

## Problem-Solving Courseware

### Problem-Solving Courseware: Definition and Characteristics

Teachers may find the topic of problem solving both alluring and perplexing. No goal in education seems more important today than making students good problem solvers, yet no area is as ill-defined and difficult to understand. Even scientists have difficulty defining problem solving. Funkhouser and Dennis (1992) quoted an earlier author as saying that "Problem solving [means] the behaviors that researchers who say they are studying problem solving, study" (p. 338). Sherman (1987–1988) was somewhat more specific, claiming that all problem solving involves three components: recognition of a goal (an opportunity for solving a problem), a process (a sequence of physical activities or operations), and mental activity (cognitive operations to pursue a solution). Sherman said that problem solving is a relatively sophisticated mental ability that is difficult to learn and that it is highly idiosyncratic. That is, problem-solving ability depends on "knowledge, prior experience, and motivation, and many other attributes" (Sherman, 1987–1988, p. 8).

This definition of problem solving covers a wide variety of desired component behaviors. The literature mentions such varied subskills for problem solving as metacognition, observing, recalling information, sequencing, analyz-

## Example Lesson 4.6
## Integration of Instructional Game Courseware: Practicing Math Rules of Operation

**Lesson:** Please! Please! Remember My Dear Aunt Sally! (Middle school)
**Developed by:** Gla Culpeper and Elaine Meyers (Jacksonville, Florida)
**Courseware:** *How the West Was One + Three × Four* (Sunburst Communications)
**Content Area/Topic:** Mathematics - Order of mathematics operations

**Instructional Resources.** Computer and courseware; worksheets in Sunburst, Davidson, and SRA Manuals; overhead transparency; chalkboard

**Lesson Purposes.** Use the order of operations rule to solve mathematical problems. Use correct math terminology.

**Instructional Activities**

*Reviewing Prerequisite Skills.* Before beginning instruction, use worksheets to assure that all students know basic math operations and symbols (+, −, ×, ÷); reteach if necessary. Remaining students practice basic math skills with *Math Blaster Plus,* leaving the teacher available to work with remedial students.

*Motivating Students.* Demonstrate the software to the students and let them play the game as a group activity. Point out how using parentheses, powers, and roots can expand the number of moves and tell the class they will be learning skills to help them solve mathematical problems using order of operations. Make sure the students know that the order of operations is a mathematical rule that always applies and not a game rule applicable only to this program.

*Presenting New Information and Learning Guidance.* Explain the mnemonic "Please, Please Remember My Dear Aunt Sally" and the meaning of the order of operations (Parentheses, Powers, Roots, Multiplication, Division, Addition, Subtraction from left to right). Point out that not all operations are used in this program. Show the rules for *How the West Was One + Three × Four* (HTWWO) on an overhead transparency. Demonstrate (+, −, ×, ÷) problems with and without parentheses and give examples of problems for students to do as a group. Worksheets help students practice and remember these rules; the teacher checks and assists with their work.

*Practice Activities.* When all students seem able to work the problems, demonstrate HTWWO and review the rules. Students practice one game as a group. Make arrangements for students to practice their skills on the game in the classroom or computer lab for a large group activity. Students help each other play the game against the computer. Give special recognition to students who win the most games in a period.

*Assessment and Followup.* After students have had an opportunity to practice, give a test to evaluate their knowledge and applications of basic order-of-operations (multiplication, division, addition, subtraction, from left to right). The teacher continues working with students who have problems and encourages them to continue using the software to get their names on the Top 10 players list and as a reward for finishing regular work.

Source: Based on Culpeper, G., Myers, E., & Roblyer, M. D. (1991). Please, please remember my dear Aunt Sally! *The Florida Technology in Education Quarterly, 3*(2), 87–88.

ing, finding and organizing information, inferring, predicting outcomes, making analogies, and formulating ideas. Since even the definition of problem solving inspires ongoing controversy in education, it is not surprising that opinions differ dramatically about the proper role of courseware and other technology products in helping to foster this important capability. The positions lean toward two general ways in which teachers can view problem solving. Which of these views a teacher uses will determine the

strategy for teaching problem solving and the application of related technology resources.

**Two views on fostering problem solving.** Some teachers view problem solving as a high-level skill that can be taught directly, at least in part, by specific instruction and practice in its component strategies and subskills. Others suggest placing students in problem-solving environments and, with some coaching and guidance, letting them develop their own heuristics for attacking and solving problems. Although the purposes of the two views overlap somewhat, one is directed more toward supplying prerequisite skills for specific kinds of problem solving. The other view aims more toward motivating students to attack problems and to recognize solving problems as an integral part of everyday life. Blosser (1988) confirms this dichotomy, saying that "Problem solving includes … an attitude or predisposition toward inquiry as well as the actual processes by which individuals … gain knowledge." Students need to combine these two elements; teachers must make ongoing adjustments to the amount of time they spend on each kind of approach in each of several content areas.

**Two types of problem-solving courseware for directed instruction.** Two distinct types of courseware purport to teach problem-solving skills. One is specific to teaching content area skills, primarily in mathematics. (For example, *The Geometric Supposer* by Sunburst encourages students to learn strategies for solving geometry problems by drawing and manipulating geometric figures.) The other type of problem-solving software focuses on general, content-free skills such as recalling facts, breaking a problem into a sequence of steps, or predicting outcomes. Sunburst's *Memory Castle* is designed to help students remember instructions and follow directions.

Most courseware is specifically designed to focus on one of these two approaches; however, some authors point out that programs can help teach problem solving without being specifically designed to do so (Gore, 1987–1988). Courseware implements numerous approaches to teach each of these kinds of skills. Some use challenge strategies (*The King's Rule* by Sunburst); others use puzzle games (*Safari Search* by Sunburst), adventure-games (*Carmen Sandiego* by Brøderbund), or simulation approaches (*The Factory* by Sunburst).

### Issues Related to Problem-Solving Courseware

**Names versus skills.** As mentioned earlier, courseware packages use many terms to describe problem solving and their exact meanings are not always clear. Terms that appear in courseware catalogs as synonyms for problem solving include thinking skills, critical thinking, higher-level thinking, higher-order cognitive outcomes, reasoning, use of logic, and decision making. In light of this diversity of language, teachers can identify the skills that a courseware package addresses by looking at its activities. For example, a courseware package may claim to teach inference skills. One would have to see how it defines *inference* by examining the tasks it presents, which may range from determining the next number in a sequence to using visual clues to predict a pattern.

**Courseware claims versus effectiveness.** It would be difficult to find a courseware catalog that did not claim that its

products foster problem solving. However, few publishers of courseware packages that purport to teach specific problem-solving skills have data to support their claims. When students play a game that requires skills related to problem solving, they do not necessarily learn these skills. They may enjoy the game thoroughly and even be successful at it without learning any of the intended skills. Teachers may have to do their own field testing to confirm that courseware is achieving the results they want.

**Possible harmful effects of directed instruction.** Some researchers believe that direct attempts to teach problem-solving strategies actually can be counterproductive for some students. Mayes (1992) reports on studies that found "teaching-sequenced planning to solve problems to high ability learners could interfere with their own effective processing" (p. 243). In a review of research on problem solving in science, Blosser (1988) also found indications that problem-solving instruction may not have the desired results if the instructional strategy does not suit certain kinds of students. For example, students with high math anxiety and low visual preference or proportional reasoning abilities will profit from instruction in problem solving only if it employs visual approaches.

**The problem of transfer.** Although some educators feel that general problem-solving skills such as inference and pattern recognition will transfer to content-area skills, scant evidence supports this view. In the 1970s and 1980s, for example, many schools taught programming in mathematics classes under the hypothesis that the planning and sequencing skills required for programming would transfer to problem-solving skills in math. Research results never supported this hypothesis. In general, research tends to show that skill in one kind of problem solving will transfer primarily to similar kinds of problems that use the same solution strategies. Researchers have identified nothing like "general thinking skills," except in relation to intelligence (IQ) variables.

### How to Use Problem-Solving Courseware in Teaching

**Benefits, applications, and guidelines for using directed strategies with problem-solving courseware.** Integration of courseware into direct teaching of problem-solving skills places even more responsibility than usual on teachers. Usually, teachers want to teach clearly defined skills. To teach problem solving, they must decide which particular kind of problem-solving ability students need to acquire and how best to foster it. With clearly identified skills and a definite teaching strategy, problem-solving courseware has unique abilities to help focus students' attention on required activities. This kind of courseware can get students to apply and practice desired behaviors specific to a content area or more general abilities in problem solving (see Figures 4.7–4.9).These six steps can help teachers to integrate courseware for these purposes:

**Figure 4.7   Example Software with Problem-Solving Functions: *King's Rule***

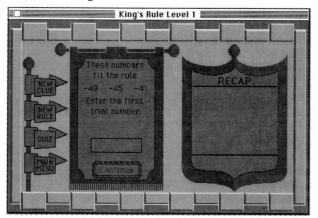

Source: Used by permission of Sunburst Communications.

**Figure 4.8   Example Software with Problem-Solving Functions: *Math Shop***

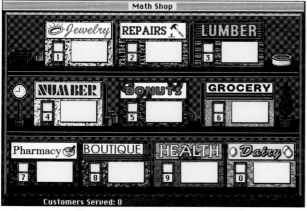

Source: From Scholastic's Math Shop. Copyright © 1995 by Scholastic, Inc. Used by permission. SCHOLASTIC MATH SHOP is a registered trademark of Scholastic Inc.

1. Identify problem-solving skills or general capabilities to build or foster skills in:

   a. solving one or more kinds of content-area problems (building algebra equations);

   b. using a scientific approach to problem solving (identifying the problem, posing hypotheses, planning a systematic approach); and

   c. components of problem solving such as following a sequence of steps or recalling facts.

2. Decide on an activity or a series of activities that would help teach the desired skills (see Example Lesson 4.7).

3. Examine courseware to locate materials that closely match the desired abilities, remembering to not judge capabilities on the basis of vendor claims alone.

4. Determine where the courseware fits into the teaching sequence (for example, to introduce the skill and gain attention or as a practice activity after demonstrating problem solving or both).

5. Demonstrate the courseware and the steps to follow in solving problems.

**Figure 4.9   Example Software with Problem-Solving Functions: *The Factory***

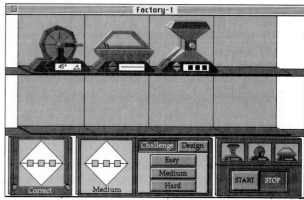

Source: Used by permission of Sunburst Communications.

6. Build in transfer activities and make students aware of the skills they are using in the courseware.

**Benefits, applications, and guidelines for using constructivist strategies with problem-solving courseware.** Like many technology resources, some software with problem-solving functions can be employed in directed ways, but are designed for implementation using more constructivist models. These models give students no direct training in or introduction to solving problems; rather they place students in highly motivational problem-solving environments and encourage them to work in groups to solve problems.

Constructivists believe this kind of experience helps students in three ways. First, they expect that students will be more likely to acquire and practice content-area, research, and study skills for problems they find interesting and motivating. For example, to succeed in the *Carmen Sandiego* software series, students must acquire both some geography knowledge and some ability to use reference materials that accompany the package. Also, they must combine this learning with deductive skills to attack and solve detective-type problems (Robinson & Shonborn, 1991).

Second, constructivists claim that this kind of activity helps keep knowledge and skills from becoming inert because it gives students opportunities to see how information applies to actual problems. They learn the knowledge and its application at the same time. Finally, students gain opportunities to discover concepts themselves, which they frequently find more motivating than being told or, as constructivists might say, *programmed* with the information (McCoy, 1990).

**Guidelines for using problem-solving software.** Seven steps help teachers integrate problem-solving courseware according to constructivist models:

1. Allow students sufficient time to explore and interact with the software, but provide some structure in the form of directions, goals, a work schedule, and organized times for sharing and discussing results.

## Example Lesson 4.7
## Problem-Solving Courseware Activity:
## Addressing Confirmation Bias when Determining Number Rules in Mathematics

| | |
|---|---|
| **Lesson:** | Could Your Answer Be Wrong? (Middle school) |
| **Developed by:** | James Johnson, Pennsylvania State University (University Park, PA) |
| **Courseware:** | *King's Rule* (Sunburst Communications) |
| **Content Area/Topic:** | Mathematics-Testing hypotheses in problem-solving strategies |
| **Instructional Resources:** | Computer and software |

**Lesson Purposes.** Drawing students' attention to the problem of confirmation bias in problem solving

**Instructional Activities.** Have students play the Hidden Rule Game, in which the program generates three numbers and students have to give their own sets of three numbers that follow the same rule. The program tells them whether or not their sets follow the rule.

As students consider the numbers, the teacher must ask questions to help them form alternative hypotheses about the rule and generate evidence to support their positions. For example, suppose the numbers are 16, 18, 20. Students must be encouraged to gather confirming evidence and submit their rules carefully. They may jump to the conclusion that the rule is "Jumps of two," when it may be "all even numbers" or "ascending numbers." For example:

**Student enters:**
4,6,8
**Computer responds:**
"Yes"
**Student reacts:**
"Numbers jump by 2."

**Teacher says:**
"Could it be something else? Try a set that is not numbers jumping by 2."

**Student enters:**
4,8,12
**Computer responds:**
"Yes"
**Student reacts:**
"It's not numbers jumping by 2. Maybe ascending numbers?"

**Teacher says:**
"What numbers could you try in order to eliminate that rule?"

**Student enters:**
5,7,9
**Computer responds:**
"Yes"
**Student reacts:**
"It's not ascending numbers or constant jumps. Maybe it's even numbers."

**Teacher says:**
"Are you sure? What can you try to find out?"

When students feel confident they have grasped good strategies well enough to take a quiz in rule-ascertaining, they select the program's quiz function. The program presents five sets of numbers for students to try.

Source: Based on Johnson, J. (1987). Do you think you might be wrong? Confirmation bias in problem solving. *Arithmetic Teacher, 34*(9), 13–16.

2. Vary amount of direction and assistance, depending on each student's needs.

3. Promote a reflective learning environment; let students talk about their work and the methods they use.

4. Stress thinking processes rather than correct answers.

5. Point out the relationship of courseware skills and activities to other kinds of problem solving.

6. Let students work together in pairs or small groups.

7. For assessments, use alternatives to traditional paper-and-pencil tests.

Problem solving and simulation activities work so similarly in constructivist models that it usually is difficult to differentiate between them. Integration strategies for either usually are the same.

## Integrated Learning Systems (ILSs) and Other Networked Products

### Integrated Learning Systems (ILSs): Definition and Characteristics

Integrated learning systems (ILSs) are the most powerful—and the most expensive—of the courseware products, primarily because they are more than just courseware and because they require more than one computer to run them. An ILS is a network, a combination of instruction and management systems that runs on microcomputers connected to a larger computer. An ILS offers a combination of drill and practice, tutorial, simulation, problem solving, and tool courseware integrated into a total curriculum support package. In addition, it is capable of maintaining detailed records on individual student assignments and performance data and supplying printouts of this information to teachers. Bailey and Lumley (1991, p. 21) list the following general characteristics of an ILS:

* Instructional objectives specified, with each lesson tied to those objectives

* Lessons integrated into the standard curriculum

* Courseware that spans several grade levels in comprehensive fashion

* Courseware delivered on a networked system of microcomputers or terminals with color graphics and sound

* Management systems that collect and record results of student performance

ILS courseware and management software are housed on a computer called a *file server,* which is connected via a network to a series of microcomputers. As each student signs onto a microcomputer station, the file server sends, or downloads, student assignments and courseware to the station and proceeds to keep records on what the students do during time spent on the system. The teacher makes initial assignments for work on the system, monitors student progress by reviewing ILS printouts, and provides additional instruction or support where needed.

The first ILSs on the market were primarily drill and practice delivery systems designed to improve student performance on the isolated skills measured by standardized tests. These self-contained, mainframe-based systems predated the microcomputer era, and they did not run any software besides their own. Usually housed in labs, they were designed for use in pull-out programs to supplement teachers' classroom activities, that is, students were pulled out of classrooms daily or weekly and sent to ILS labs for remedial or reinforcement work. However, these systems have evolved into multipurpose products that can run software and courseware other than their own; they can now provide a variety of instructional support from enrichment to complete curriculum. As with other media such as videodiscs, school districts view ILSs as alternatives to traditional classroom materials such as textbooks.

**ILSs compared with other networked courseware products.** ILSs are characterized by their "one-stop shopping" approach to providing courseware. Each one offers a variety of instructional techniques in one place, usually as a package complete with technical maintenance and teacher training. They present strengths like prepared curricula and ease of use so that school personnel need not know a great deal about technology to use them. Consequently, they usually simplify integration decisions by defining schoolwide curriculum rather than individual lessons. Teachers now ask when their classes will use the ILS rather than where they will integrate it into their other classroom activities.

ILSs represent one of the major courseware delivery system choices for schools. Aside from standalone microcomputer products, schools can also choose *multiple media systems,* which combine several kinds of media such as CD-ROMs, microcomputers, videodiscs, or networked products, which deliver separate courseware packages to students via networks.

ILSs usually are considered part of directed rather than constructivist environments. Companies that provide networked systems to support constructivist approaches object to the classification of their products under the ILS rubric.

**The courseware component of an ILS.** Instructional activities available on an ILS range from simple drill and practice to extensive tutorials. Most ILSs are moving toward complete tutorial systems intended to replace teachers in delivering entire instructional sequences. An ILS usually includes instruction on the entire scope and sequence of skills in a given content area; for example, it may cover all discrete mathematics skills typically presented in Grades 1 through 6.

**The management system component of an ILS.** The capability that differentiates ILSs from other networked systems is the emphasis on individualized instruction tied

**Figure 4.10  Sample ILS Student History Report**

Green River School District
Jostens Elementary School

| Student History Report | | | | Page 1 of 2 |

1 —

| Name: | Kovak, Paula |
| Group: | Ms. Bartlett's Bluebirds |
| Date Range: | 09/01/95 – 09/29/95 |
| Date: | September 29, 1995    11:49 am |

2 —

| Assignment: | Second Grade Math | | | | 4–6 |

| Activity | | Raw Score | % Score | Time | Date |
| --- | --- | --- | --- | --- | --- |
| 02EM0301 | Telling Time: Hours and Half | 16/22 | 73% | 0:10 | 09/06/95 |
| 02EM0302 | Telling Time in 5-Minute Units | 15 (16) | 95% | 0:15 | 09/06/95 |
| 02EM0303 | Reviewing Hours and Minutes | 100/100 | 100% | 0:14 | 09/11/95 |
| MT-ADD21D3 | Practice | 15 (16) | Mastered | 0:10 | 09/11/95 |
| MT-ADD22D3 | Sort | 15 (17) | Mastered | 0:06 | 09/13/95 |
| MT-ADD23C3 | Meanings | 100/100 | 100% | 0:08 | 09/13/95 |
| MT-ADD24D3 | Practice | 15 (16) | Mastered | 0:11 | 09/18/95 |
| MT-ADD25D3 | Pan Balance | 15 (16) | Mastered | 0:07 | 09/18/95 |
| MT-SUB20C3 | Meanings | 95/100 | 95% | 0:05 | 09/20/95 |
| 02EM0304 | Days and Months | 28/32 | 88% | 0:18 | 09/20/95 |
| 02EM0305 | Introducing the Calendar | - - - | Bookmrkd | 0:13 | 09/27/95 |

3 — (activities) — 7

8–9 —

| Average | | | 92% | 0:10 | |
| Total Completed Activities: | 10 | | | Total Time: | 1:57 |

| Assignment: | Reading Placement | | | | |

| Activity | | Raw Score | % Score | Time | Date |
| --- | --- | --- | --- | --- | --- |
| RD-PLC001 | Placement Test | 3.5 | Done | 0:36 | 09/05/95 |

10 —

| Average | | | | 0:36 | |
| Total Completed Activities: | 1 | | | Total Time: | 0:36 |

**Assignment Information**

1.  Date range when the student worked on the assignment

2.  Name of the assignment covered in this section of the report

**Activity Data**

3.  List of activities the student completed within the date range, in order by the date of completion

4.  The student's raw score for each activity, showing the number correct out of the total possible (for scored activities) or out of the number attempted (for "Mastered" activities)

5.  Student's score for the activity shown as a percent or status

6.  Time, in hours and minutes, that the student worked in the activity

7.  Date the student last worked in the activity

**Averages and Totals**

8.  Average percentage score and time spent to complete an activity

9.  Total number of activities completed (including failures) and time spent in the assignment

10. Placement test results

Source: From *Reports Guide* by Jostens Learning Corporation. © 1995 by Jostens Learning Corp. Used by permission.

to records of student progress. A typical ILS gives teachers progress reports across groups of students as well as the following kinds of information on individual performance:

*   Lessons and tests completed
*   Questions missed on each lesson by numbers and percentages
*   Numbers of correct and incorrect tries
*   Time spent on each lesson and test
*   Pretest and posttest data

An example of one report is shown in Figure 4.10. In addition, sample screens from an integrated learning system are shown in Figures 4.11, 4.12, and 4.13.

## Issues Related to ILSs

**The costs of ILSs.** The primary criticism of ILSs centers on their expense compared to their impact on improving learning. Bentley (1991) warns that ILS benefits are largely theoretical and that most studies on their effectiveness have been done by companies with much to gain from positive reports. "The ILS could prove to be the biggest money pit in a school's budget, sapping large amounts of resources earmarked for other educational needs ... The multitude of individual costs is staggering and each cost that is paid usually opens up further costs ... The search for less expensive alternatives to the ILS is only logical considering how difficult it would be to find options that are *more* expensive" (p. 25).

**Figure 4.11**  **Example Screen from Jostens ILS (a)**

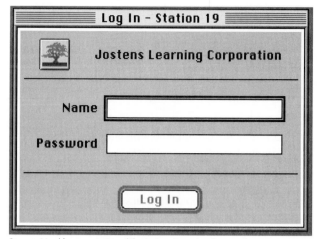

Source: Used by permission of the Jostens Learning Corporation.

**Figure 4.12**  **Example Screen from Jostens ILS (b)**

Source: Used by permission of the Jostens Learning Corporation.

ILS proponents, on the other hand, feel that the students who experience the most success with ILSs are those whose needs are typically most difficult to meet (Bender, 1991; Bracy, 1992; Shore & Johnson, 1992). ILS proponents say there is value in any system that can help potential dropouts stay in school or help remedy the deficiencies of learning-disabled students. They point to studies and personal testimony from teachers over the years that attest to the motivational qualities of allowing students to work at their own pace and experience success each time they work on the system.

When Becker (1992) reported his summary of some 30 studies of ILS effectiveness, he found widely varied results with various implementation methods and systems. Students generally tend to do somewhat better with ILSs than with other methods, and results were sometimes substantially superior to non-ILS methods. But Becker found

**Figure 4.13**  **Example Screen from Jostens ILS (c)**

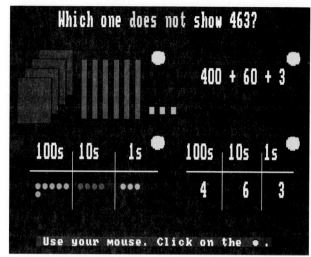

Source: Used by permission of the Jostens Learning Corporation.

no predictable pattern for successful and unsuccessful ILSs. He concluded that data were not sufficient either to support or oppose the purchase of an ILS in a given school or district.

**Concerns about the role of ILSs.** Another criticism of ILSs reflects a current fear rather than reality. Many educators worry that the cost of ILSs combined with the comprehensive nature of their curricula will cause schools to view them as replacements for teachers. White (1992) asks if ILSs will take over all teaching, as some fear. Maddux and Willis (1993) describe a slightly different version of this problem. They warn that ILSs can have the effect of shaping or driving a school's curriculum rather than responding to it. The best way to address these kinds of concerns may be through a careful, well-planned purchasing process for an ILS. Smith and Sclafani (1989) and Chrisman (1992), among others, have offered guidelines to potential ILS purchasers. The list below summarizes the recommendations of Smith and Sclafani (1989):

- Clearly identify the problem the ILS is supposed to solve.
- Understand the instructional theory upon which the system is based.
- Determine whether the ILS is a closed system (one that provides 80 percent or more of the instruction for a given course) or an open system (one linked to the school's resources).
- Find out if the system's scope and sequence are matched to that of the school.
- Determine the target population for which the system was designed and whether or not it closely matches the characteristics of students with whom the ILS will be used.
- Consider the adequacy of the reporting and management system for the school's needs.
- Consider how much of its resources the school must spend on hardware and software.

- Project the educational benefits to the school from the system and compare them with the costs.

Chrisman (1992) provided another set of recommendations:

- Carefully review each vendor's educational philosophy and compare it to that of the school.
- Request that vendors inform the school on ILS updates.
- Carefully evaluate the grade-level courseware, management system, customization, and online tools and be sure they match the school's expectations.
- Set up reasonable terms of procurement.
- Calculate the personnel and fiscal impact of the ILS.
- Consider all the characteristics of the system that will affect day-to-day operations such as student time required to log on and off and the fit of the system with the district master plan for technology, etc.

Factors other than quality determine the fate of an ILS. Bailey and Lumley (1991) describe eight issues facing administrators who supervise teachers using ILSs:

1. **Use by special and regular populations.** Although many ILSs are purchased for Chapter I populations, they can be helpful for other students as well. However, administrators must know how the technology can best serve each population.

2. **ILS integration into school/teacher culture.** Administrators and teachers should work together to decide how the ILS can benefit students in combination with other resources and curricula. Since teachers will implement an ILS, administrators should consider teacher input as vital to its success.

3. **Research on students with varied abilities.** Administrators must keep current on ILS research with various kinds of students and be sure that teachers have this information. This will help them make the best use of ILS capabilities.

4. **Software development, selection, and adoption processes.** Adoptions of other materials must be coordinated with ILS adoption, but the ILS must not prescribe the total curriculum. Administrators and teachers must accomplish the necessary coordination without letting the ILS guide the entire process.

5. **Role and control of teachers in ILS instruction.** An ILS requires changes in the teacher's role from source of information to facilitator. Administrators must assist in this transition and help teachers become comfortable with their new roles.

6. **Financial considerations.** The expense of ILSs requires principals from individual schools to work together to develop strategic plans for purchase and implementation.

7. **Staff development.** Past research has shown neglect of teacher training in ILS use (Sherry, 1992). More and better teacher training is required to realize the potential of ILS capabilities.

8. **Technology planning.** All technology purchases must be part of the district's short- and long-range plan for technology use. The purchase of an ILS represents only one step in a total blueprint for technology applications to improve the quality of education.

The staff of the Texas Center for Educational Technology (1991) has developed a comprehensive booklet that describes how to plan technical details of an optimal implementation of an ILS. The booklet also details how to evaluate the success of an ILS in a school setting.

### How to Use ILSs in Teaching

Since an ILS creates a combination of the materials already described here, its potential benefits are quite similar. The highly interactive, self-pacing features of an ILS can help to motivate students who need highly structured environments; these activities free up the teacher's time for students who need personal assistance. Also, teachers can personalize instruction for each student by reviewing the extensive information on student and class progress provided by the ILS management system.

Successful uses of ILSs have been reported for two different kinds of teaching approaches: directed and constructivist.

**Directed applications for ILSs.** In a directed teaching approach, an ILS system can be used for remediation and as a mainstream delivery system.

*For remediation.* Although ILSs are expensive alternatives to other kinds of delivery systems, White (1992) observes that "they will probably play an increasing role in the large urban systems that have faced achievement test scores that seem intractable to the usual classroom solutions" (p. 36). However, schools still must determine how ILS functions coordinate and complement those of the classroom teacher. Most ILS uses serve target populations that have typically presented the most difficult problems for traditional classroom activities: Chapter I groups, ESOL students, special education students, and at-risk students. Schools have tried and usually failed to reach these students with other methods.

*As a mainstream delivery system.* Rather than using an ILS only as a backup system to address educational problems, a school may let an ILS do the initial job of teaching whole courses for all students in a grade level. In light of the expense of ILSs, these uses are more rare. However, some alternative projects, like the Edison Project, predict that the costs of using technology in this way will amount to substantially less over time than teacher salaries. Using ILSs to increase student-to-teacher ratios has stimulated ongoing debate and study.

In either of these uses, teachers still have important roles to play. As Blickman (1992) puts it, "ILSs allow teachers a comfortable transition from the role of deliverer of instruction to manager of instruction ... [T]eachers are still actively engaged in the teaching process but as 'guides' or facilitators as opposed to distributors of information" (p. 46). American educators generally assume that ILSs

## Example Lesson 4.8
## Directed Instruction with an ILS

**Lesson:** One-Step Linear Equations (Secondary)
**Developed by:** Curriculum specialists at The Jostens Learning Corporation
**Courseware:** Jostens Middle School Mathematics Curriculum: Algebra Expressions
**Content Area/Topic:** Mathematics-Algebra
**Instructional Resources:** Computer, ILS software, chalkboard, overhead projector, and erasable overheads

**Lesson Purposes.** This is the third algebra lesson in Jostens' standard sequence for grade 8. Students learn to solve and graph linear equations.

**Instructional Activities**
*Preparation.* Review on the chalkboard various algebra expressions the students have covered previously. Have students take turns solving problems involving order of operations. If necessary, have students review online assignments in MT-ALG06-Algebra Expressions before going on to the next activity.

*On-computer.* Use the first activity in MT-ALG10C8-Algebra Expressions to allow students to do intuitive equation problem solving to find the value of a variable that makes the equation true. Provide additional practice in the Learning Center for students having difficulty with this activity.

*Reinforcement.* The next four activities in the sequence provide various forms of practice for the skills in the previous activity.

*Extension.* MT-ALG15C8 is a tutorial on graphing in which students are asked to identify the equation when given the graph of a line and to graph the line of a given equation. Have students use an overhead projector and erasable overheads to illustrate to each other how they solved some of the problems.

Source: Based on ideas taken from the Jostens Learning Corporation's *Directed Classroom Integration Activities* manuals, 1990.

should not be seen as "teacher proof" but rather "teacher enhancing." Teachers must still assign initial levels of work, follow up on student activities on the system, and give additional personal instruction when needed (see Example Lesson 4.8).

**Constructivist applications for ILSs.** Just as an integrated learning system combines several kinds of courseware to create a skill-based, directed learning environment, a network can also combine several kinds of technology resources to support the goals of constructivist learning approaches. When networks provide technology resources of constructivist design and use, the resulting products are sometimes labeled with terms other than ILS to differentiate them from what some educators consider more traditional uses of technology. For example, they may be called *integrated technology systems (ITSs), integrated learning environments, multimedia learning systems,* or *open learning systems* (Hill, 1993, p. 29).

The technology of an ITS resembles that of an ILS, but the products, as well as the ways that schools integrate them into instruction, are very different. Integrated technology systems usually provide wide varieties of unstructured tools on the same networked system. Typically, an ITS will include some kind of information bank (electronic encyclopedias), symbol pads (word processing and/or desktop publishing software), construction kits (Logo or other graphic languages or tools), and phenomenaria (computer simulations and/or problem-solving resources). They also usually have data-collection systems to track student usage of the system (Mageau, 1990). Thus, this kind of networked product can provide what Perkins (1991) called a "rich environment." (See Example Lesson 4.9).

## Evaluating and Selecting Instructional Software

In the 1980s, microcomputer courseware began to flood the educational market from such diverse sources as state projects, major publishing houses, and even cottage industries. This torrent made educators increasingly aware that

## Example Lesson 4.9
## Constructivist Activities with an ILS

| | |
|---|---|
| **Lesson:** | The Cat That Walked by Himself (Elementary) |
| **Developed by:** | Curriculum specialists at The Jostens Learning Corporation |
| **Courseware:** | Jostens Elementary Reading Expansions |
| **Content Area/Topic:** | Reading and literature |
| **Instructional Resources:** | Computer, ILS software, and related Jostens text materials such as teacher's edition, student textbooks, and supplementary handouts. The Directed Classroom Integration Activities manual also supplies detailed notes on how to set up the classroom and how to use the software as one component in a reading/literature unit. |

**Lesson Purposes.** This is one of several literature-based activities, each of which is designed to be the hub of an integrated lesson.

**Instructional Activities**

*Preparation.* Talk about the author Rudyard Kipling and some of the stories he wrote for children. Show the students the story in the book and explain that this on-computer activity introduces this story and helps them read a portion of it. Say that once this activity is complete, they will be doing other in-class activities related to the story.

*On-computer.* Let students do the on-computer reading activity.

*Reinforcement.* Discuss the main ideas mentioned in the on-computer activity such as:

- How would you describe the setting for this part of the story?
- What is the meaning of the word "Nenni"?
- What did the dog want when he visited the cave?

*Extension.* Use the web of activities shown here to identify components of a classroom unit centered around the story. Begin to read portions of the book to the class and use activities from the web that correspond to the portion of the book to extend the reading activity into other areas of the curriculum.

Source: Based on ideas taken from the Jostens Learning Corporation's *Directed Classroom Integration Activities* manuals, 1990.

simply putting instructional routines on the computer did not assure that they would take advantage of its potential power as an instructional tool. Indeed, some of the products were so bad that they could be worse than no instruction at all.

Courseware quality became a major issue in education and courseware evaluation evolved into a popular and highly publicized practice. Many professional magazines created sections to report the results of product evaluations; indeed, whole magazines like *Courseware Review* were developed to publish such evaluations. The Northwest Regional Lab's Microsoft Project and the Educational Products Information Exchange (EPIE) were just two of the many organizations that sprang up for the sole purpose of reviewing and recommending good instructional courseware.

As the field of educational technology matured and educators refined their attitudes toward computer use, the mys-

tique of courseware faded and assumed more of the mundane aspects of purchasing any good instructional material. During the 1980s, teachers primarily evaluated and selected their own courseware. Now, state- and school district-level personnel increasingly control these purchases. Thus, the evaluation procedures and criteria have changed considerably from the early days of microcomputers. Regardless of who chooses the products, teachers should recognize that just because courseware addresses certain topics or skills, it does not mean that it will meet their needs.

## The Need for Evaluation

Courseware quality is less troublesome now than it was in the early days of microcomputers when technical soundness frequently caused problems. For example, courseware programming did not anticipate all possible answers a student might give and did not account for all possible paths through a sequence of instruction. Consequently, programs frequently would "break" or stop when these unusual situations occurred. The early courseware also strongly emphasized entertainment, giving less attention to educational value.

Courseware producers have obviously learned much from their early errors and problems, and overall quality has improved considerably. But educators still have good reasons for spending some time reviewing and/or evaluating courseware before selecting it for classroom use. Computerized instruction is not necessarily effective instruction, and eye-catching screen displays should not be the primary criteria for selecting materials.

Teachers should review courseware even after prescreening by committees or experts. Very often, state- or district-level committees are responsible only for selecting courseware that does not have gross problems and reaches the desired general level in a general content or topic area. Each teacher must then determine which specific curriculum needs and specific grade levels the package addresses and whether or not courseware functions fit with planned teaching strategies. It cannot be emphasized enough that courseware must match clearly identified instructional needs. It should *not* be used simply because it is available at a discount or supplied free by the state or district.

### Courseware Evaluation Procedures: A Recommended Sequence

Evaluation procedures and criteria vary dramatically depending on whether a teacher is selecting courseware for a single classroom or is part of a district-level committee screening materials for use by many schools. One major difference is that committees generally must justify decisions to purchase one package over another by using weighted criteria checklists and assigning total point scores to individual packages. Small groups or individual teachers use much less formal procedures and criteria.

This section is designed primarily for individual teachers or small organizations like individual schools that (1) do not have large organizations purchasing courseware for them, (2) wish to supplement resources purchased for them by others, or (3) want to review preselected courseware to determine its usefulness for their immediate needs. These procedures are intended to help teachers anticipate and deal with problems related to courseware quality and to assist them in matching courseware to their classroom needs. The following sequence is recommended when selecting courseware for classroom use:

1.   **Begin with an identified need.** Know what topics and skills you want to address and how you think you will use technology. This will require some knowledge of what kinds of instructional support technology has to offer.

2.   **Locate titles.** As mentioned earlier in this section, teachers should probably not base their courseware purchasing decisions on descriptive reviews. Recommendations from colleagues and professional magazines and journals should serve primarily as leads. Once teachers discover a package they find interesting, they should use one or both of the next two general procedures to determine its usefulness.

3.   **Complete hands-on reviews.** There is no substitute for running the courseware. Teachers should also avoid reviewing demo packages, abbreviated versions of actual courseware. These are inadequate, frequently misleading substitutes for the real thing. A typical hands-on review consists of two or three passes through a program. A teacher usually goes through it the first time just to assess its capabilities and what it covers. During the second pass, the teacher tries to make incorrect responses and press keys that aren't supposed to be pressed in order to determine the program's ability to handle typical student use. Depending on its capabilities, the teacher may choose to go through the program again to review the usefulness and/or quality of particular demonstrations or presentations.

4.   **Collect student reviews.** Experienced teachers usually can tell from their own hands-on reviews when instructional materials are appropriate for their students. Even so, they are sometimes surprised at student reaction to courseware. Students sometimes encounter unexpected problems, or they may not seem to get out of the activity what the teacher expected they would. If at all possible, it is beneficial to field test courseware by observing students using it, getting their reactions, and, if possible, collecting data on their achievement. Gill, Dick, Reiser, and Zahner (1992) describe a detailed method for evaluating software that involves collecting data on student use.

### Courseware Evaluation Procedures: Recommended Criteria

The set of recommended evaluation criteria in Figure 4.14 represents a synthesis from many sources (Roblyer, 1983; Sharfmeyer, 1990; Hoffman & Lyons, 1997). In addition to this comprehensive list, teachers may want to use the Minimum Criteria Checklist shown in Figure 4.15.

### Selecting Software for Constructivist versus Directed Uses

Nearly all references to courseware evaluation and methods in the literature emphasize products that will be used with directed instruction. Although many criteria are appropriate for software designed for both uses, additional details are lacking on what to look for in software that will be used with constructivist methods. Constructivist activities emphasize multimedia and distance learning products rather than software. For example, Litchfield (1992) lists criteria for "inquiry-based science software and interactive multimedia programs." Other criteria and methods for evaluating multimedia products will be discussed further in Chapter 6.

## Figure 4.14

## Recommended Courseware Evaluation Criteria

Many sets of courseware criteria and checklists are available; they vary widely depending on the educational philosophy of the evaluator and the type of courseware being reviewed (Roblyer, 1983; Shaefermeyer, 1990). Courseware criteria may be divided into two types: those that should be considered essential and those that are sometimes applicable and sometimes not, depending on the user's needs.

**Minimum criteria.** Certain criteria may be used to discriminate between acceptable and unacceptable courseware materials. Criteria specific to each of the types of courseware have already been discussed in previous sections. The following additional criteria that apply to all courseware, regardless of type, are shown on the minimum criteria checklist in Figure 4.15.

### I. Required Instructional Design and Pedagogy: Does It Teach?

- **Appropriate teaching strategy, based on best-known methods**—This covers a wide range of possible problems, from little or no interactivity to insufficient examples for concept development. One program had no graphics at all, even though it was a mathematics package intended for very young children. Learners at early stages of development are known to need concrete examples rather than text only.

- **Presentation on screen contains nothing that misleads or confuses students**—One particularly blatant error of this type was in a courseware package intended to teach young children about how the human body works. It depicted the human heart as a square box. Another, a math program, displayed a number of objects based on what the student answered, but never bothered to change the number of objects if it was a wrong answer. Thus, the student could be seeing the corrected numeral but the wrong number of objects.

- **Comments to students that are not abusive or insulting**—Programs must be sensitive to student's feelings, even if comments are intended humorously. One program based on a well-known cartoon cat with an acerbic personality belittled the student's name, saying "What kind of name is that for a worthy opponent?" It also commented on the student's "lack of mental ability" when a wrong answer was supplied. Although this was in keeping with the cat's persona, it was still inappropriate.

- **Readability at an appropriate level for students who will use it**—Although this may apply to any use of language in any program, it is particularly applicable to tutorials, which may require many explanations. For example, one tutorial for second-grade math skills had explanations at a fourth-grade reading level. This would probably not be an appropriate expectation for students who have trouble with this level of math.

- **Graphics fulfill important purpose and are not distracting to learners**—Pictures and animation are considered motivational to students, but this is not always true. For example, animated feedback may be charming the first ten times the students see it, but may achieve just the opposite effect after that. Also, some courseware attracts students' attention by flashing text or objects on the screen. This can be distracting when one is trying to focus on other screen text. Early courseware used a device called "scrolling" which had text moving up the screen as the student tried to read it, but this was quickly identified as a distracting mechanism and is rarely seen now.

### II. Required for Content: Is It Correct?

- **No grammar, spelling, or punctuation errors on the screen**—Even though a program may be on a nonlanguage topic, it should reflect accurate language since students learn more than just the intended skills from instructional materials. One early release on punctuation skills misspelled the word "punctuation" three different ways in the program!

- **All content accurate and up-to-date**—Many people do not associate errors such as these with courseware material; they seem to trust content presented on a computer, as if the computer would correct the text itself if it spotted a problem! Content inaccuracies have been observed in a number of packages. For example, one program referred to blood as a "red substance," which, of course, is not always true. Instructional materials in social studies should be carefully screened for inaccurate reflections of country names, which are changing rapidly.

- **No racial or gender stereotypes**—Look for diversity in names and examples used. Are they all for "Dick and Jane" and are they always in the suburbs? Also review examples for gender stereotypes. Are all doctors men? Are all homemakers women?

- **Social characteristics**—Does courseware exhibit a sensitive treatment of moral and/or social issues? For example, do games and simulations avoid unnecessary violence?

### III. Required for User Flexibility: Is It "User Friendly"?

- **User has some control of movement within the program**—Depending on the purpose of the program, the students should normally be able to go from screen to screen and read each screen at a desired rate. They should also have exit options available at any time.

- **Can turn off sound, if desired**—Since courseware may be used in classrooms, the teacher should have the ability to make the courseware quiet so it will not disturb others.

*Continued*

## IV. Required Technical Soundness: Does It Work Correctly?

* **Program loads consistently, without error**—A common problem in early courseware, problems of this kind are not seen very often now.

* **Program does not break, no matter what the student enters**—Again, this was a more common problem in early courseware. Programs should be designed to expect any possible answer, not just the correct or most obvious ones. When unexpected answers are entered, they should give an appropriate response to get the student back on track.

* **Program does what the screen says it should do**—If the screen indicates the student should be able to exit or go to another part of the program, this capability should be allowed as stated.

**Optional criteria.** Teachers reviewing courseware may consider a great many other criteria depending on their needs, the program's purpose, and the intended audience. These are detailed in Roblyer (1983), Lockard et al. (1990), and Merrill et al. (1992). Many of these criteria, which are listed below, are subjective in nature; it is up to the teacher to decide whether or not the courseware meets them.

### Optional Instructional Design Criteria

* **Stated objectives**—Does the courseware state its objectives?

* **Prerequisite skills**—Are skills specified that students will need to do the courseware activities?

* **Presentation logic**—Do instructional units follow a logical sequence based on skill hierarchies?

* **Tests**—Do tests match stated skills and are they good measures of the skill?

* **Significance**—Are stated skills "educationally significant" (e.g., in the curriculum)?

* **Use of medium**—Does courseware make good use of the medium?

* **Field testing**—Is there evidence the courseware has been field-tested with students and revised based on this feedback before its release?

### Optional Student Use Criteria

* **Student ease of use**—Is the program easy to use for the intended students? Does it require physical dexterity to answer items the students may not have even though they know the correct answers? Is a lot of typing required?

* **Required keys**—Are the keys required to input answers easy to remember (e.g., pressing "B" for going "back")?

* **Input devices**—Are alternate input devices allowed to make courseware more usable for special populations?

* **Directions**—Are there on-screen directions on how to use it?

* **Support materials**—Are there print support materials to support on-screen activities?

* **Optional assistance**—Is a "HELP" feature available if the student runs into difficulty?

* **Optional directions**—Can students skip directions, if they desire, and go straight to the activities?

* **Creativity**—Do materials foster creativity rather than just rote learning?

* **Summary feedback**—Are students given an on-screen summary of performance when they finish working?

### Optional Teacher Use Criteria

* **Teacher ease of use**—Can teachers figure out, with minimum effort, how to work the program?

* **Management**—Does courseware contain adequate record-keeping and management capabilities?

* **Teacher manuals**—Are clear, nontechnical teachers manuals available with the courseware?

* **Ease of integration**—Are courseware materials designed to integrate easily into other activities the teacher is doing?

* **Teacher assistance**—Does courseware improve the teacher's ability to teach the subject?

* **Adaptability**—Can teachers adapt the courseware for their needs by changing content (e.g., spelling words) or format (e.g., animated versus written feedback)?

### Optional Presentation Criteria

* **Graphics features**—Are graphics, animation, and color used for instructional purposes rather than flashiness?

* **Screen layout**—Are screens so "busy" or cluttered that they interfere with reading?

* **Speech capabilities**—Is speech of adequate quality so students can understand it easily?

* **Required peripherals**—Does the program require peripherals the schools are likely to have (e. g., light pens, speech synthesizers)?

### Optional Technical Criteria

* **Response judging**—Does the response judging allow for ALL possible correct answers and disallow ALL possible incorrect ones?

* **Timing**—Does the program present itself quickly so displays and responses are accomplished without noticeable delays?

* **Portability**—Can teachers transfer the courseware from one machine to another?

* **Compatibility**—Does courseware run on more than one platform?

* **Technical manuals**—Do teacher or user manuals contain technical documentation on program operation and any technical features or options?

**Figure 4.15   Minimum Criteria Checklist for Evaluating Instructional Courseware**

Title _____   Publisher _____

Content Area _____   Hardware Required _____

**Courseware functions:**

| | |
|---|---|
| _____ Drill and practice | _____ Instructional game |
| _____ Tutorial | _____ Problem solving |
| _____ Simulation | _____ Other: _____ |

Many characteristics should be considered when selecting courseware for use in one's classroom or lab, but the following should be considered *essential qualities* for any instructional product on the computer. If courseware does not meet these criteria, it should not be considered for purchase. For each item, indicate *Y* for yes if it meets the criterion, or *N* for no if it does not.

**I.   Instructional Design and Pedagogical Soundness**

_____ Teaching strategy appropriate for student level and is based on best-known methods

_____ Presentation on screen contains nothing that misleads or confuses students

_____ Readability and difficulty at an appropriate level for students who will use it

_____ Comments to students not abusive or insulting

_____ Graphics fulfill important purpose (motivation, information) and not distracting to learners

**Criteria specific to drill and practice functions:**

_____ High degree of control over presentation rate (unless the method is timed review)

_____ Appropriate feedback for correct answers (none, if timed; not elaborate or time-consuming)

_____ Feedback is more reinforcing for correct than for incorrect responses

**Criteria specific to tutorials:**

_____ High degree of interactivity (not just reading information)

_____ High degree of user control (forward and backward movement, branching upon request)

_____ Comprehensive teaching sequence so instruction is self-contained and standalone

_____ Adequate answer-judging capabilities for student-constructed answers to questions

**Criteria specific to simulations:**

_____ Appropriate degree of fidelity (accurate depiction of system being modeled)

_____ Good documentation available on how program works

**Criteria specific to instructional games:**

_____ Low quotient of violence or combat-type activities

_____ Amount of physical dexterity required appropriate to students who will use it

**II.   Content**

_____ No grammar, spelling, or punctuation errors on the screen

_____ All content accurate and up-to-date

_____ No racial or gender stereotypes

_____ Exhibits a sensitive treatment of moral and/or social issues

**III.   User Flexibility**

_____ User normally has some control of movement within the program (can go from screen to screen at desired rate; can read text at desired rate; can exit program when desired)

_____ Can turn off sound, if desired

**IV.   Technical Soundness**

_____ Program loads consistently, without error

_____ Program does not break, no matter what the student enters

_____ Program does what the screen says it should do

**Decision:**

_____ Is recommended for purchase and use

_____ Is not recommended

## Exercises

## Record and Apply What You Have Learned

**Activity 4.1: Chapter 4 Self-Test**  To review terms and concepts in this chapter, take the Chapter 4 self-test. Select Chapter 4 from the front page of the companion Web site (located at http://www.prenhall.com/roblyer), then choose the *Multiple Choice* module.

**Activity 4.2: Portfolio Activities**  The following activities will help you add to your professional portfolio. To complete these activities online and save or submit the materials electronically, select Chapter 4 from the front page of the companion Web site (http://www.prenhall.com/roblyer), then choose the *Portfolio* module.

- **Instructional software examples.** From instructional software packages, select at least one that represents each function described in this chapter. Using word processing or multimedia software, prepare a description of the software that focuses on which functions it fulfills.

- **Instructional software in a content area.** On the Internet, do a search for software examples in your content area or grade level. Prepare a list of the sites with good examples of each type of software function.

**Activity 4.3: Questions for Thought and Discussion**  These questions may be used for small group or class discussion or may be subjects for individual or group activities. To take part in these discussions online, select Chapter 4 from the front page of the companion Web site (http://www.prenhall.com/roblyer), then choose the *Message Board* module.

- The tendency to refer to drill and practice software by the derogatory term "drill and kill" is growing. Is this because the number of situations is diminishing in which drill and practice software would be the strategy of choice?

- Some schools, like those with a college preparatory focus, do not allow the use of instructional games of any kind. Is there a compelling case to be made for allowing the use of instructional game software to achieve specific educational goals? That is, can games do something in an instructional situation that no other strategy is able to do? If so, what?

**Activity 4.4: Collaborative Activities**  The following may be developed in small group work. Completed group products may be copied and shared with the entire class and/or included in each person's Personal Portfolio. Remember that most hypermedia authoring systems provide a free player that can play these student-produced products:

- **Courseware evaluation.** Each small group selects one of the types of software functions described in this chapter. Using the Minimum Criteria Checklist in Figure 4.15, the groups locate and evaluate a courseware package with that function. They prepare a description and demonstration of the software and present it to the class.

- **Lesson plans for instructional software.** Each small group selects one of the types of software functions described in this chapter. They locate a courseware package and prepare a lesson that integrates it into classroom activities in one of the ways described in this chapter. They present the final product to the class.

**Activity 4.5: Integrating Technology Across the Curriculum Activities**  Use the *Integrating Technology Across the Curriculum* CD-ROM packaged with this textbook to complete the following exercise:

Simulations generally are considered some of the most powerful and versatile of the instructional software functions. Most simulations are used in science and social studies, but the ways they are integrated differ greatly between the two content areas. Locate an integration lesson plan for science and for a social studies area; compare and contrast the integration strategies used in the two lessons. To locate each lesson, go to *Find Lesson Plan* and click on *Find by Criteria.* Under the *Technologies* descriptor, select *Simulation,* and under the *Content Area* descriptor, select *Science;* click *Search.* To locate a social studies lesson, repeat this process and select *Social Studies* under the *Content Area* descriptor. Repeat this comparison several times and see if you can come to any general conclusions about the differences in integration strategies between science simulations and social studies simulations.

## References

### Introduction

Norris, W. (1977). Via technology to a new era in education. *Phi Delta Kappan, 58*(6), 451–459.

Papert, S. (1980). *Mindstorms: Children, computers, and powerful ideas.* New York: Basic Books.

Taylor, R. (1980). *The computer in the school: Tutor, tool, and tutee.* New York, NY: Teachers College Press.

Weizenbaum, J. (1976). *Computer power and human reason.* San Francisco: W. H. Freeman & Co.

## Drills

Alessi, S. & Trollip, S. (1991). *Computer-based instruction: Methods and development.* Englewood Cliffs, NJ: Prentice-Hall.

Bloom, B. (1986). Automaticity. *Educational Leadership, 43*(5), 70–77.

Gagné, R. (1982). Developments in learning psychology: Implications for instructional design. *Educational Technology, 22*(6), 11–15.

Gagné, R. & Merrill, M. D. (1990). Integrative goals for instructional design. *Educational Technology Research and Development, 38*(1), 23–30.

Hasselbring, T. (1988). Developing math automaticity in learning handicapped children. *Focus on Exceptional Children, 20*(6), 1–7.

Higgins, K. & Boone, R. (1993). Technology as a tutor, tools, and agent for reading. *Journal of Special Education Technology, 12*(1), 28–37.

Merrill, D. & Salisbury, D. (1984). Research on drill and practice strategies. *Journal of Computer-Based Instruction, 11*(1), 19–21.

Okolo, C. (1992). The effect of computer-assisted instruction format and initial attitude on the arithmetic facts proficiency and continuing motivation of students with learning disabilities. *Exceptionality: A Research Journal, 3*(4), 195–211.

Salisbury, D. (1990). Cognitive psychology and its implications for designing drill and practice programs for computers. *Journal of Computer-Based Instruction, 17*(1), 23–30.

## Tutorials

Baek, Y. & Layne, B. (1988). Color, graphics, and animation in a computer-assisted learning tutorial lesson. *Journal of Computer-Based Instruction, 15*(4), 31–35.

CAI in music. (1994). *Teaching Music, 1*(6), 34–35.

Eiser, L. (1988). What makes a good tutorial? *Classroom Computer Learning, 8*(4), 44–47.

Gagné, R., Wager, W., & Rojas, A. (1981). Planning and authoring computer-assisted instruction lessons. *Educational Technology, 21*(9), 17–26.

Graham, R. (1994). A computer tutorial for psychology of learning courses. *Teaching of Psychology, 21*(2), 116–166.

Kraemer, K. (1990). SEEN: Tutorials for critical reading. *Writing Notebook, 7*(3), 31–32.

Murray, T., et al. (1988). An analogy-based computer tutorial for remediating physics misconceptions (ERIC Document Reproduction No. ED 299 172).

## Simulations

Alessi, S. (1988). Fidelity in the design of computer simulations. *Journal of Computer-Based Instruction, 15*(2), 40–47.

Alessi, S. & Trollip, S. (1991). ibid.

Allen, D. (1993). Exploring the earth through software. Teaching with technology. *Teaching PreK-8, 24*(2), 22–26.

Andaloro, G. (1991). Modeling in physics teaching: The role of computer simulation. *International Journal of Science Education, 13*(3), 243–254.

Clinton, J. (1991). Decisions, decisions. *The Florida Technology in Education Quarterly, 3*(2), 93–96.

Estes, C. (1994). The real-world connection. *Simulation and Gaming, 25*(4), 456–463.

Hasselbring, T. & Goin, L. (1993). Integrating technology and media. In Polloway & Patton (Eds.). *Strategies for teaching learners with special needs (5th ed.).* New York: Merrill.

Mintz, R. (1993). Computerized simulation as an inquiry tool. *School Science and Mathematics, 93*(2), 76–80.

Reigeluth, C. & Schwartz, E. (1989). An instructional theory for the design of computer-based simulations. *Journal of Computer-Based Instruction, 16*(1), 1–10.

Richards, J. (1992). Computer simulations in the science classroom. *Journal of Science Education and Technology, 1*(1), 67–80.

Ronen, M. (1992). Integrating computer simulations into high school physics teaching. *Journal of Computers in Mathematics and Science Teaching, 11*(3–4), 319–329.

Simmons, P. & Lunetta, V. (1993). Problem-solving behaviors during a genetics computer simulation. *Journal of Research in Science Teaching, 30*(2), 153–173.

Smith, K. (1992). Earthquake! *The Florida Technology in Education Quarterly, 4*(2), 68–70.

## Instructional Games

Alessi, S. & Trollip, S. (1991). ibid.

Flowers, R. (1993). New teaching tools for new teaching practices. *Instructor, 102*(5), 42–45.

Malone, T. (1980). *What makes things fun to learn? A study of intrinsically motivating computer games.* Palo Alto, CA: Xerox Palo Alto Research Center.

McGinley, R. (1991). Start them off with games! *The Computing Teacher, 19*(3), 49.

Randel, J., Morris, B., Wetzel, C., & Whitehill, B. (1992). The effectiveness of games for educational purposes: A review of recent research. *Simulation and Gaming, 23*(3), 261–276.

Trotter, A. (1991). In the school game, your options abound. *Executive Educator, 13*(6), 23.

## Problem Solving

Blosser, P. (1988). Teaching problem solving—Secondary school science (ERIC Document Reproduction No. ED 309 049).

Funkhouser, C. & Dennis, J. (1992). The effects of problem-solving software on problem-solving ability. *Journal of Research on Computing in Education, 24*(3), 338–347.

Gore, K. (1987–1988). Problem solving software to implement curriculum goals. *Computers in the Schools, 4*(3–4), 7–16.

Johnson, J. (1987). Do you think you might be wrong? Confirmation bias in problems solving. *Arithmetic Teacher.*

Mayes, R. (1992). The effects of using software tools on mathematics problem solving in secondary school. *School Science and Mathematics, 92*(5), 243–248.

McCoy, L. (1990). Does the Supposer improve problem solving in geometry? (ERIC Document Reproduction No. ED 320 775).

Robinson, M. & Schonborn, A. (1991) Three instructional approaches to Carmen Sandiego software series. *Social Education, 55*(6), 353–354.

Sherman, T. (1987–1988). A brief review of developments in problem solving. *Computers in the Schools, 4*(3–4), 171–178.

### ILSs

Bailey, G. & Lumley, D. (1991). Supervising teachers who use integrated learning systems. *Educational Technology, 31*(7), 21–24.

Becker, H. (1992). Computer-based integrated learning systems in the elementary and middle grades: A critical review and synthesis of evaluation reports. *Journal of Educational Computing Research, 8*(1), 1–41.

Bender, P. (1991). The effectiveness of integrated computer learning systems in the elementary school. *Contemporary Education, 63*(1), 19–23.

Bentley, E. (1991). Integrated learning systems: The problems with the solution. *Contemporary Education, 63*(1), 24–27.

Blickman, D. (1992). The teacher's role in integrated learning systems. *Educational Technology, 32*(9), 46–48.

Bracy, G. (1992). The bright future of integrated learning systems. *Educational Technology, 32*(9), 60–62.

Chrisman, G. (1992). Seven steps to ILS procurement. *Media and Methods, 28*(4), 14–15.

Hill, M. (1993). Chapter I revisited: Technology's second chance. *Electronic Learning, 13*(1), 27–32.

Maddux, C. & Willis, J. (1993). Integrated learning systems: What decision-makers need to know. *ED TECH Review.* Spring/Summer, 3–11.

Mageau, T. (1990). ILS: Its new role in schools. *Electronic Learning, 10*(1), 22–24.

Perkins, D. (1991). Technology meets constructivism: Do they make a marriage? *Educational Technology, 31*(5), 18–23.

Robertson, Stephens, & Company. (1992). ibid.

Sherry, M. (1992). Integrated learning systems: What may we expect in the future? *Educational Technology, 32*(9), 58–59.

Shore, A. & Johnson, M. (1992). Integrated learning systems: A vision for the future. *Educational Technology, 32*(9), 36–39.

Smith, R. A. & Sclafani, S. (1989). Integrated teaching systems: Guidelines for evaluation. *The Computing Teacher, 17*(3), 36–38.

Texas Center for Educational Technology (1991). *ILS assessment and evaluation kit.* Denton, TX: University of North Florida, Texas Center for Educational Technology.

White, M. (1992). Are ILSs good for education? *Educational Technology, 32*(9), 49–50.

### Evaluating and Using Types of Courseware

Gill, B., Dick, W., Reiser, R., & Zahner, J. (1992). A new model for evaluating instructional software. *Educational Technology, 32*(3), 39–48.

Hoffman, J. L. & Lyons, D. L. (1997). Evaluating instructional software. *Learning and Leading with Technology, 25*(2), 52–56.

Litchfield, B. (1992). Science: Evaluation of inquiry-based science software and interactive multimedia programs. *The Computing Teacher, 19*(6), 41–43.

Lockard, J., Abrams, P., & Many, W. (1994). *Microcomputers for educators (2nd ed.).* Glenview, IL: Scott, Foresman & Co.

Merrill, P., Hammons, K., Tolman, M., Christensen, L., Vincent, B., & Reynold, P. (1992). *Computers in education (2nd ed.).* Boston: Allyn & Bacon.

Roblyer, M. (1983). How to evaluate software reviews. *Executive Educator, 5*(9), 34–39.

Roblyer, M. (1986). Careers in courseware evaluation. *Educational Technology, 26*(5), 34–35.

# Chapter 5

## Using Productivity Software and Other Software Tools in Teaching and Learning

Hence, could a machine be invented which would instantaneously arrange on paper each idea as it occurs to us, without any exertion on our part, how extremely useful would it be considered.

Henry David Thoreau, as quoted by David Humphreys, in *Computers in English and the Language Arts* (1989)

[T]he notion that computers are neutral and just another technological tool may seem quite a reasonable one.... But ... think of the influence the automobile and television have had on our culture. The evidence is accumulating that computers are having a decided impact on the way our schools and society organize, communicate, and make decisions.

Joe Nathan, from *Micro-Myths,* 1985

### This chapter covers the following topics:

- Definition and characteristics of word processing, spreadsheets, and databases and a variety of other software tools

- Unique advantages of these tools for various classroom activities

- Example classroom uses for each tool

## Objectives

1. Use correct terminology to identify features and capabilities of word processing, spreadsheet, database, and several other software tool programs.

2. Describe specific kinds of teaching and learning tasks for both teachers and students that each kind of tool can support.

3. Identify applications for software tools that educators would find valuable in making their work more efficient and productive.

4. Develop lesson activities that integrate the functions and capabilities of each of several software tools.

## Introduction to Technology Support Tools

### Why Use Technology Support Tools?

In education and, indeed, in most other areas of our information society, the three most widely used software support tools are word processing, spreadsheet, and database programs. However, a wide variety of other computer-based products exist that can support teachers and students in a multitude of teaching and learning tasks. These tools vary greatly in their purposes, the kinds of benefits they offer, and their utility for teachers. Some, such as electronic gradebooks and CMI tools, are designed to organize and analyze information; they are fast earning an image as indispensable aids for teachers struggling to cope with increasing amounts of data related to student performance and achievement. Other tools, such as certificate makers and clip art packages, serve merely to improve the appearance of instructional products and make it easier for teachers and students to produce attractive, professional-looking materials that inspire pride.

The tools described in this chapter range in importance from nearly essential to nice to have and in function from presenting instruction to supporting background tasks that make a classroom function smoothly. However, each one has unique and powerful features. As Nathan (1985) emphasized, these tools, if used wisely and creatively, have the potential not only to support classroom activities, but also to transform the very nature of the way people learn and work.

Each tool described in this chapter requires additional classroom resources and time to learn and to implement. Teachers should choose them for the qualities and benefits they bring to the classroom, rather than simply because they are available on the market. Depending on the capabilities of a particular tool and the needs of the situation, a technology support tool can offer several benefits:

- **Improved productivity.** Many of the tools described in this chapter make it faster to get organized, produce instructional materials, or accomplish paperwork tasks. Using a technology tool to do these tasks can free up valuable time that can be rechanneled toward working with students or designing learning activities.

- **Improved appearance.** Many tools help teachers to produce polished-looking materials that resemble the work of professional designers. In fact, these tools frequently are the same ones used by professional designers. The quality of classroom products is limited only by the talents and skills of the teachers and students using the tools. Students appreciate receiving attractive-looking materials and find it rewarding and challenging to produce handsome products of their own.

- **Improved accuracy.** Several tools make it easier to keep precise, accurate records of events and student accomplishments. More accurate information can support better instructional decisions about curriculum and student activities.

- **More support for interaction.** Some products have capabilities that promote interaction among students or allow input from several people at once. These qualities can encourage many creative, cooperative group-learning activities.

### Types of Software Support Tools

This chapter divides software support tools into seven general categories or functions:

- **Productivity software tools.** Word processing, databases, and spreadsheets typically are thought of as supporting teacher and student productivity, thus the term productivity software. However, this chapter illustrates that they also enhance instructional activities in many important ways.

- **Materials generators.** Help teachers produce instructional materials

- **Data collection and analysis tools.** Help teachers collect and organize numerical information that indicates student progress

- **Graphics tools.** Allow production of images and illustration of documents

- **Planning and organizing tools.** A variety of tools that help teachers and students conceptualize their work before they begin

- **Research and reference tools.** Electronic versions of encyclopedias, atlases, and dictionaries, usually stored on CD-ROM

- **Tools to support specific content areas.** Assist with activities associated with certain content areas

### Software Suites versus Integrated Packages

In the late 1980s, software companies began to sell combinations of several software tools in one package; this trend has increased in recent years. Since they usually are cheaper than buying each tool separately, these packages are becoming increasingly popular in education and business. Keizer (1997) differentiates between *integrated packages,* which usually include word processor, spreadsheet, database, and graphics tools; and *software suites,* which usually contain one or more additional programs and may come in a variety of versions or combinations tailored to meet certain kinds of needs. For example, *ClarisWorks* and

Figure 5.1   **Types of Word Processing Software in Education**

| By screen appearance | Text-based, WYSINWYG | WYSIWYG |
|---|---|---|
| By packaging | Single application | Integrated package |
| By student level | Young students (support for beginning writers) | Older students (support for later writers) |

*Microsoft Works* are integrated packages containing productivity software tools, while *Corel Office Professional* includes a dozen or so separate applications. Since suites usually are more expensive and more memory intensive, educators tend to use integrated packages over suites. However, either may be useful, depending on the needs of the classroom and the types of software included in the suite.

### Software Support Tools Covered in Other Chapters: Web Tools and Multimedia Authoring

The purpose of this chapter is to provide a comprehensive overview of software tools used in education, but two categories of tools are addressed in other parts of this textbook. Software used with the Internet, either to develop materials for use on the Internet or to allow people to use the Internet, is covered in Chapter 8. Authoring software and other software tools associated with developing multimedia and hypermedia products are described in Chapter 6.

## Using Word Processing Software in Teaching and Learning

### Introduction to Word Processing

**Word processing defined.** Word processing is, simply put, typing on a computer. The term *word processor* can refer either to a computerized machine set up primarily to do word processing (an electronic typewriter) or to a general-purpose computer that can use word processing software. This chapter describes how to use microcomputers with word processing software, since this is the kind of word processing resource that educators usually use in classrooms.

Word processing can support nearly any kind of task or teaching activity that was previously done by handwriting or typewriter, but offers more capability and versatility than either of these methods. Since a word processing document is prepared on-screen before being printed onto paper, the writer can correct errors, insert or delete words or sentences, and even move lines or paragraphs around before printing the document. The writer can easily change the words or appearance because the document is stored in the computer's memory and, hopefully, on a disk or a hard drive. Once stored or saved, documents can be changed or reprinted later. Subsequent sections of this chapter describe and illustrate word processing capabilities and

benefits for both teacher productivity and for teaching and learning tasks.

**Types of word processing software.** Figure 5.1 illustrates that word processing software can be classified in several ways. One current classification depends on a document's appearance on the screen, a classification that will probably disappear in time since it concerns the capabilities of older versus newer word processing software. The first word processing programs presented documents that looked different on-screen from the printed copy. Instead of showing words or phrases that would be underlined, boldfaced, or centered on the page, the screen showed symbols before and after words or phrases to indicate how they look when printed. Today's word processing software has a *"what you see is what you get" (WYSIWYG)* document display. Some older word processing programs such as *Word Perfect 5.1* still are in use which have text-based displays (*WYSINWYG—what you see is not what you get*).

Another way to classify word processing software is according to how it is packaged. Users can interact with either a single application; part of an integrated package that also includes database, spreadsheet, and often telecommunications and/or graphics software; or part of a total writing instruction package that also includes aids such as prewriting assistance or language analyzers.

Teachers also can separate word processing capabilities by their intended users. Word processors have been designed to support student writing at various grade levels. For example, *Kidwriter Gold* is ideal for use with young children, while *Research Paper Writer* focuses on assisting writing instruction for older students; it provides a variety of prewriting and language analysis features. This type of software frequently includes other materials such as prepared activity files that have been developed to help teachers use word processing software for various writing exercises. Teachers must select word processing software with capabilities that match their needs.

**General word processing features and capabilities.** Word processing represents a significant improvement over typing on a typewriter. Although word processing capabilities and procedures vary from program to program, most programs have several features in common:

- **Storing documents for later use.** The most powerful advantage of word processing over typewriters is the ability to handle documents more than once without reentering the same text. Once created on the screen, a document can be stored on

Figure 5.2    **Illustration of Fonts and Styles**

| Fonts | Typestyles |
|---|---|
| This is an example of the Palatino font. | *This is Palatino in italics.*<br>**This is Palatino in boldface.** |
| This is an example of the Avant Garde font. | *This is Avant Garde in italics.*<br>**This is Avant Garde in boldface.** |

disk, re-loaded into the computer's memory later, and either modified or printed out again.

- **Erasing and inserting text.** Changes to typed documents require physical erasing or simply starting over; word processing allows a writer to insert additional letters, spaces, lines, or paragraphs easily into a document.

- **Search and replace.** If an error is repeated throughout a document, a word processing program can easily correct the error by searching the document for all occurrences and changing them as specified.

- **Moving or copying text.** Sometimes a writer decides that a paragraph would sound better or seem more logical in a different location, or perhaps a given line will be repeated several times throughout a document. Word processing allows users to cut and paste, that is, specify a block of text and either move it or repeat it in the places specified.

- **Word wraparound.** Typists usually must place "carriage returns" (a legacy term from the typewriter era) at the ends of lines. Word processing software does this automatically with a feature called *word wraparound.* Most word processors also allow users to do automatic hyphenation of words at line breaks.

- **Change style and appearance easily.** Word processing allows a writer to employ a variety of fonts, typestyles, margins, line spacings, and indentations in a single document. Figure 5.2 illustrates some fonts and typestyles.

- **Justification.** The trademark feature of a word processing document is the justification of both right and left margins, sometimes referred to as *full justification.* However, users also can easily specify that a given line or block of text be centered

or right or left justified. Figure 5.3 shows examples of various justifications.

- **Automatic headers, footers, and pagination.** Word processors can automatically place a title at the top (header) or bottom (footer) of each page in a document with or without page numbering (pagination).

- **Inserting text prepared on other word processors.** Each word processing program has software commands to apply formatting; these commands are specific to the package. Therefore, one program cannot usually read a document prepared in another. However, many word processors can store documents as text or ASCII (American Standard Code for Information Interchange) files. This process removes formatting commands, so another word processor can read a file stored in this way. Some word processors also have filters or program functions that will accept regular files originally prepared and stored on other word processors.

- **Checking and correcting spelling.** Spell checking is a word processing capability that compares words in a document to those stored in its dictionary files. The program identifies words in the document that it cannot find in the dictionary and suggests possible corrections.

- **Suggesting words.** In addition to a spell checking dictionary, a program may include access to a thesaurus. A user can request a synonym or an alternate suffix for a given word.

- **Reviewing style and grammar.** Some word processing software can check text features such as sentence length, frequency of word use, and subject-verb agreement. This function may also suggest changes or corrections to the text.

Figure 5.3    **Illustration of Text Justifications**

| Left Justification | Full Justification | Centered |
|---|---|---|
| "What did I ever do before word processing? Now I am a word processing evangelist!" said the English teacher. "It has made all of my work so much easier! My students love not having to rewrite everything to make one or two corrections." | "What did I ever do before word processing? Now I am a word processing evangelist!" said the English teacher. "It has made all of my work so much easier! My students love not having to rewrite everything to make one or two corrections." | An Ode to<br>Word Processing<br><br>by<br><br>Ima Convert |

- **Allowing insertion of graphics.** Some programs allow users to insert pictures stored as graphics files within their documents; others also have draw features that allow users to create and place their own pictures within their documents.

- **Merging text with database files.** Finally, some word processing programs can place database fields within documents such as letters. When it prints the letter or other document, the program automatically inserts information from the database as directed. Thus, a teacher could write one parent letter and merge it with a student database to print a personalized letter for each parent.

### The Impact of Word Processing in Education

**Advantages of word processing.** Perhaps no other technology resource has had as great an impact on education as word processing. Not only does this tool offer a great degree of versatility and flexibility, it also is "model-free" instructional software, that is, it reflects no particular instructional approach. A teacher can use it to support any kind of directed instruction or constructivist activity. Since its value as an aid to teaching and learning is universally acknowledged, word processing has become the most commonly used software in education. It offers many general advantages to teachers and students:

- **Time savings.** Word processing helps teachers use preparation time more efficiently by letting them modify materials instead of creating new ones. Writers can also make corrections to word processing documents more quickly than they could achieve on a typewriter or by hand.

- **Better appearances.** Materials from word processing software look more polished and professional than handwritten or typed materials. It is not surprising that students seem to like the improved appearance that word processing gives to their work (Harris, 1985).

- **Sharing methods.** Word processing allows a means of sharing materials easily among writers. Teachers can exchange lesson plans, worksheets, or other materials on disk and modify them to fit their needs. Students can also share ideas and products among themselves.

**Issues related to word processing in education.** Educators seem to agree that word processing is a valuable application, but some aspects of its use in education are controversial.

- **When to introduce word processing.** The development of word processing software designed for young children has allowed schools to introduce word processing to students as young as 4 or 5 years old. Although some educators feel that word processing will free students from the physical constraints of handwriting and enable them to advance more quickly in their written expression skills, others wonder about the impact of this early use on students. It may affect their willingness to spend time developing handwriting abilities and other activities requiring fine motor skills.

- **The necessity of keyboarding skills.** Another ongoing discussion in education asks whether students need to learn keyboarding, or typing on the computer, either prior to or in conjunction with word processing activities. Some educators feel that students will never become really productive on the computer until they learn ten-finger keyboarding. Others feel that the extensive time spent on keyboarding instruction and practice could be better spent on more important skills.

- **Effects on handwriting.** While no researchers have conducted formal studies of the impact of frequent word processing use on handwriting legibility, computer users commonly complain that their handwriting isn't what it used to be, ostensibly because of infrequent opportunities to use their handwriting skills.

- **Impact on assessment.** Some organizations have students answer essay-type tests questions with word processing, rather than by handwriting or even typing them. This practice introduces several issues. Roblyer (1997) reviewed research that found students' word processed compositions tend to receive *lower* grades than handwritten ones. This surprising finding indicates that educational organizations that allow students to choose either handwriting or word processing must be careful to establish guidelines and special training to ensure that raters do not inadvertently discriminate against students who choose word processing.

Teachers and administrators are still deciding how best to deal with these issues. Since word processing is becoming an increasingly pervasive presence in both home and classroom writing activities, more information should soon become available to help educators make informed decisions about how best to employ its capabilities.

**Benefits of word processing: Findings from research.** Research on the benefits of word processing in education yield contradictory findings. Results of studies of the effects of word processing on quality and quantity of writing are mixed (Bangert-Drowns, 1993). Three different reviews of research (Hawisher, 1989; Bangert-Drowns, 1993; and Snyder, 1993) found that these differences in findings may reflect differences in researchers' choices of types of word processing systems, prior experience and writing ability of students, and types of writing instruction to evaluate. Generally, word processing seems to improve writing and attitudes toward writing only if it is used in the context of good writing instruction and if students have enough time to learn word processing procedures before the study begins. Figure 5.4 summarizes some of the findings of the three research reviews.

Generally, studies seem to conclude that students who use word processing in the context of writing instruction programs tend to write more, revise more (at least on a surface level), make fewer errors, and have better attitudes toward their writing than students who do not use word processing. Teachers who use word processing with their students should not expect writing quality to improve automatically. Improvements of that kind depend largely

Figure 5.4    **Findings from Reviews of Word Processing in Education**

|  | Hawisher (26 studies) (1989) | Snyder (57 studies) (1993) | Bangert-Drowns (32 studies) (1993) |
|---|---|---|---|
| Better quality of writing | No conclusion | No conclusion | Positive results |
| Greater quantity of writing | Positive results | Positive results | Positive results |
| More surface (mechanical) revisions | No conclusion | Positive results | No conclusion |
| More substantive (meaning) revisions | No conclusion | No improvement | No conclusion |
| Fewer mechanical errors | Positive results | Positive results | Not reviewed |
| Better attitude toward writing | Positive results | Positive results | No improvement |
| Better attitude toward word processing | No conclusion | Positive results | Not reviewed |

on factors such as the type of writing instruction. A review by Reed (1996) found that the type of word processor students use may have an impact. Younger, less able writers may profit from word processing software with more prompts, while this kind of word processor may actually inhibit the writing of older, more able writers who prefer learner-controlled word processing. But the *potential* value of word processing has been established, making it one of the most validated uses of technology in education.

### Word Processing in the Classroom

**When to use word processing: Teacher productivity.** Word processing can help teachers prepare classroom materials they previously typed or wrote out by hand. These include handouts or other instructional materials, lesson plans and notes, reports, forms, letters to parents or students, flyers, and newsletters. Word processing benefits these tasks by saving preparation time, especially if the teacher prepares the same documents each school year. For example, a teacher may send the same letter to parents every year simply by changing the dates and adding new information. Teachers may want to keep files of templates or model documents that they can easily update and reuse with minimal effort. Here are some suggestions for additions to this file of reusable documents:

* Beginning of the year welcome letter
* Permission letters for field trips and other events
* Request for fee payments letter
* Fundraising letter
* List of class rules
* Flyers and other announcements
* Periodic student progress letters to parents
* Frequently-used worksheets and exercises
* Student information sheets and handouts

* Annual reports for the school
* Lesson plans and notes
* Newsletters and letterhead stationeries

**When to use word processing: Teaching and learning activities.** Students can also use word processing for almost any written work, regardless of subject area, that they would otherwise write by hand. Research shows that word processing alone cannot improve the quality of student writing, but can help them make corrections more efficiently; this can motivate them to write more and take more interest in improving their written work. Some current word processing applications:

* **Writing processes.** Students can use word processing to write, edit, and illustrate stories; to produce reports in content areas; to keep notes and logs on classroom activities; and for any written assignments (see Example Lessons 5.1–5.3).
* **Dynamic group products.** Teachers can assign group poems or letters with various students, adding and changing lines or producing elements of the whole document in a word processing program (see Example Lessons 5.4–5.6).
* **Individual language, writing, and reading exercises.** Special word processing exercises allow individual students to work on-screen combining sentences, adding or correcting punctuation, or writing sentences for spelling words. Word processing may also make possible a variety of reading/language-related activities ranging from decoding to writing poetry and enjoying literature. Viau (1998) points out that adding colors to text can be the basis for activities to enhance critical thinking during writing instruction (see Example Lessons 5.7–5.10).
* **Encouraging writing across the curriculum.** A recent trend in education is to encourage writing skills in courses and activities other than those designed to teach English and language arts. This practice of writing-through-the-curriculum is in keeping with the new emphasis on integrated, interdisciplinary, and thematic curricula. Word processing can encourage these integrated activities (see Example Lessons 5.11–5.13).

## Example Lesson 5.1
## Writing through Webbing for Elementary Students

**Developed by:**          Mrs. Curran, first-grade teacher, Aldie Elementary School (Aldie, West Virginia)

**Lesson Purposes.** Teachers use word processing in a five-step process to help students learn writing skills.

**Instructional Activities.** This lesson addresses the problem very young students have with beginning writing. They have a lot to say, but often it is difficult for them to get started. The authors propose a five-step writing curriculum:

Think → Draw → Tell → Write → Share

Through the following activities, teachers introduce students to this five-step process and encourage them to to use it to start writing.

1. **Preparing to write.** This activity is used at the beginning of the school year when students are excited about meeting new people. Each teacher takes photos of the students in the class and inserts them in their written documents. Students are encouraged to think about what they will write by describing themselves to the class in terms of their favorite food, sports, TV shows, and pets. The discussion may branch out to other areas such as vacations and future plans.

2. **Planning through webbing.** Students enter the information about themselves into a "webbing" template designed using *ClarisWorks*. Each student's picture is scanned into a "pict file" and placed in the center of the student's web. A copy is printed out for each student. The chart serves to graphically organize students' ideas that they may draw on for their writing. See the accompanying CD for an example of a student web.

3. **Writing activities.** Using the information in the web, students begin composing a summary about themselves. Students choose the font and size and color of type for their document, and teachers enter the information into a word processing file as the students dictate it. Students work with the adults to correct spelling and prepare a final copy to print out and share with the whole class. Also, the *ClarisWorks* Slideshow option is used to present the final products on the screen.

Source: Etchinson, C. (1995). A powerful web to weave—Developing writing skills for elementary students. *Learning and Leading with Technology, 23*(3), 14–15.

## Example Lesson 5.2
## Process Writing and Word Processing (high school juniors and seniors)

**Developed by:**          Lee VerMulm, Cedar Falls High School (Cedar Falls, Iowa)

**Lesson Purposes.** Students use word processing for all aspects of the writing process in a one-semester elective writing course. A networked lab is used for the writing activities.

**Instructional Activities.** Students write several small assignments and one 500- to 700-word essay in each of four units. In the final unit, they write longer (25-page) research papers that combine text and graphics. In addition to writing and revising their work, students maintain writing logs in which they record what they accomplish each day. They also complete lessons on the basic skills of analytical and persuasive writing. These lessons are downloaded to students from the file server as needed. Students can access several word processing programs; graphics programs; a bibliographic citations database; a note-taking program; several writing analysis programs; and online help in grammar, word usage, and punctuation in the form of a thesaurus and various desk accessories. They also use an electronic bulletin board and fax machine to support information searches. Students' writing is reviewed daily by the teacher and writing groups. They review completed drafts with a teacher and decide on appropriate revisions. When a draft is revised and completed, the teacher evaluates it based on the criteria and makes notes on any areas that need improvement.

Source: VerMulm, L. (1993). The Christa McAuliffe Writing Center: Process writing with a networked Mac lab. *The Computing Teacher, 20*(7), 48–53.

### Example Lesson 5.3
### Cartoon Commentaries on the Computer

**Developed by:**          Rose Reissman

**Lesson Purposes.** This activity uses cartoons and comic strips to focus on two different skill areas that often present problems to middle school students and their teachers.

**Instructional Activities.** Write persuasive essays or position papers and analyze current affairs.

*Preparation.* The teacher asks students to complete a Pre-Comic Commentary Assessment. Two computers are set up—one with drawing software and one with word processing software. The class is divided into small groups of 3–4 students each. See the accompanying CD for an example assessment.

*Activities.* The teacher distributes newspapers to the groups. The students go through the papers, selecting at least two comic strips and/or editorial cartoons. They "write the story" or idea of the comic using either a dialog, narrative, or essay form. One person in the group is designated the recorder. This person enters what the group agrees on. If one of the group feels motivated to draw out their own picture or cartoon showing the group's conclusions about the comic, the student uses the monitor with the drawing software. After they create their reactions, they print them out and use them as the basis for their group discussions. Each group reports to the class on its analysis.

The teacher asks the groups to add another paragraph to their write-ups to express their own opinions about the comic's purposes. To initiate their responses, the teacher asks questions such as: Do you support the purpose and point of view of the person doing the cartoon? Why or why not? and What mix of images and text does the person use to make his point? Is this mix effective?

Again, these write-ups are shared with the class and used as the basis for discussions.

*Assessment and Follow-up.* Finally, the teacher asks students to fill out the Commentaries Assessment again and review their initial assessments.

Source: Reissman, R. (1994). Computer cartoon commentaries. *The Computing Teacher, 21*(5), 23–25.

### Example Lesson 5.4
### A Class Literary Paper

**Developed by:**          Mary Schenkenberg, Nerinx Hall High School (St. Louis, Missouri)

**Lesson Purposes.** The teacher uses word processing to let students develop a literary paper as a group in order to model the process.

**Instructional Activities.** A computer is attached to a large monitor so all students can see. The class creates a class essay on William Faulkner's "A Rose for Emily," which they are reading and discussing. They first brainstorm a list of ideas and the class selects "Emily" as their theme. They look through the story, searching for images or words illustrating Emily's connection with the Old South, and fill the monitor with their ideas. By the end of the class, students develop a thesis, an outline, and a substantial amount of content for the essay. More importantly, they have a clearer grasp of the process for writing such a paper.

Source: Wresch, W. (1991). Collaborative writing projects for the information age. *The Computing Teacher, 18*(2), 19–21.

## Example Lesson 5.5
## A Class Poem (grade 8)

**Developed by:**        Joan Hamilton, Emerson School (Bolton, Massachusetts)

**Lesson Purposes.** A connection between reading and writing is built by having students write a class poem modeled after Walt Whitman's "Song of Myself."

**Instructional Activities.** After students read the original poem, the teacher sets up six stations in the computer lab. Each is labeled with a beginning line from the poem:

I hear … I understand … I saw … I want … Injustices … and Who are you?

Students move from computer to computer adding one idea to each category. For example, at the "Who are you?" station, students are encouraged to add words, phrases, or ideas that describe a typical eighth-grade student. The resulting lists are then saved, printed, and made available to all students for use in writing their own poems. When the individual poems are completed, students have the option of combining their efforts into a class poem. Groups of students decide which parts of individual poems should be included and in what order. The final poem is printed, used as a choral reading, and displayed on bulletin boards.

Source: Wresch, W. (1991). Collaborative writing projects for the information age. *The Computing Teacher, 18*(2), 19–21.

## Example Lesson 5.6
## A Class Novel (high school)

**Developed by:**        Lee Sebastiani (University Park, Pennsylvania)

**Lesson Purposes.** The class explores the genre of science fiction by creating its own science fiction novel on the word processor.

**Instructional Activities.** The class begins by imagining possible sites for the novel. After creating a fictional planet and city, they decide to focus on one period in the planet's history. They then develop character outlines, with each student contributing one character for the novel. The teacher encourages students to let the characters reflect their own personalities and interests. Each student is asked to imagine an incident in the planet's history and describe it in a 3-to-5 page story; word processing is used for all phases of this process. Students also use graphics programs to illustrate their stories and provide detail for the imaginary planet and its events.

Source: Wresch, W. (1991). Collaborative writing projects for the information age. *The Computing Teacher, 18*(2), 19–21.

## Example Lesson 5.7
## Investigating Sentence Variety (grades 5 and up)

**Lesson Purposes.** This exercise helps students focus on making sentences vary in length and structure. The word processor is used to set off sentences in paragraphs so they can be more easily read and reviewed.

*Continued*

**Instructional Activities.** Have students select an essay they have already written and revised. Ask them to load the file into the computer, select their longest single paragraph, and set it off from the others by inserting blank lines before and after it. If the word processor allows a Return or Enter in its search and replace function, search for periods in the paragraph and replace them with a period and a Return or Enter. Otherwise, do a Find function for periods, and press Return or Enter after each one. Sentences will be isolated from each other in a list. Encourage students to determine whether or not all sentences have the same structure and/or length. If so, then edit in the following ways:

- Combine sentences, especially those that have overlapping meanings. Omit ones that do not communicate meaning clearly.
- Add new sentence beginnings.
- Rearrange word order within sentences to vary rhythm and structure.

Source: Elder, J., Schwartz, J., Bowen, B., & Goswami, D. (1989). *Word processing in a community of writers.* New York: Garland, 117–132.

## Example Lesson 5.8
## Creating Coherence between Sentences (grades 5 and up)

**Lesson Purposes.** This exercise gets students to focus on the relationships between sentences. The word processor is used to scramble sentences and then put them back together in order to examine how they fit together to communicate meaning.

**Instructional Activities.** Students begin the exercise in the same way as in Example Lesson 5.7 on Investigating Sentence Variety. They isolate the sentences in a list. Then they use cut and paste functions to scramble the sentences in random order in the list. Now have them look carefully at the sentences like pieces of a puzzle and look for clues that signal where they go together, that is, which words "link back" or "forecast ahead" (p. 132). In the best test of coherence, each student should have a partner who uses the cut and paste function to rearrange the sentences in their intended order. If the person cannot put them in the desired order, the links between the sentences may not be explicit enough. If this is the case, students will have to make the connections clearer.

Source: Elder, J., Schwartz, J., Bowen, B., & Goswami, D. (1989). *Word processing in a community of writers.* New York: Garland, 117–132.

## Example Lesson 5.9
## Appreciating Punctuation (grades 5 and up)

**Lesson Purposes.** This exercise encourages students to look at the important role of punctuation in writing. The word processor is used first to remove punctuation and capitalization and then to restore them.

**Instructional Activities.** Students load or type a paragraph onto the screen, removing all punctuation marks and all capital letters as well as all extra spaces at the ends of sentences. The teacher points out how difficult it is to read without these "clues" to meaning. Students trade computers and try to restore all the punctuation marks, capital letters, and spaces in their partners' paragraphs. They save their files to different names, load the original versions at the same time, and compare their versions with the originals. If the versions differ, students examine whether or not other punctuation or capitalization is necessary for meaning and change it as needed.

Source: Elder, J., Schwartz, J., Bowen, B., & Goswami, D. (1989). *Word processing in a community of writers.* New York: Garland, 117–132.

**Example Lesson 5.10**
**Writing Poetry to Develop Literacy (all ages)**

**Developed by:**          Marguerite Nelson

**Lesson Purposes.** Students use the word processor to write several styles of poems that focus on sounds. These poetry exercises become a way of practicing and improving fluency in decoding skills.

**Instructional Activities.** The students are introduced to a variety of forms of "experimental poetry," which is "an attempt to express writers' frustration with the limitations of language to describe the rapid changes in culture.... The writers tried to obliterate meaning by replacing traditional rules for writing poetry with randomness" (Nelson, 1994, p. 39). The results are forms of poetry that emphasize sound as opposed to meaning. Writing these poems gives students motivational opportunities to practice decoding without relying on context while they exercise their own creativity. In each of the following forms, students use the unique capabilities of the word processor to facilitate the development of their poems.

**Dada.** Students use banks of newspaper articles or headlines saved on disk. A student loads a story and uses the Move function to go to random places in the document. Each word where the cursor stops is cut and pasted until the whole article is rearranged randomly. The resulting *Dada* is saved and printed out.

> Example:          Day   Spending   Work   Flexible   Striking
> (Stephanie, grade 2)

**Sound Poems.** These are created with nonsense syllables that make certain desired sound effects. Students use sources of vowel combinations, consonant blends, and digraphs saved on disk. They use the word processor's Replace function to replace a specified vowel or blend. The result is a sound poem.

> Example:                    ick   phick   snick
>                          twick   blick   click
> (Anthony, grade 3)

**Optophonetic Poems.** Sounds take on a visual form in these poems. The word processor is used to generate letters with varying typefaces for students to read aloud.

**Oulipo.** Students use various alphabetical algorithms to specify which vowels will be included or left out or to arrange words alphabetically. The word processor's Move function can be used to alphabetize words as desired.

> Example: Only I or E Vowels:    I like mice/In white pies
> (Daniel, grade 4)

**Snowballing Iceograms.** Poems are written by starting with a single letter and then adding one letter to each subsequent line to make series of real words.

> Example:                    O
>                             No
>                             Now
>                             Know
>                             Known
> (Reid, grade 3)

**Iterative Poetry.** Students begin with a famous line or quote and replace the nouns or other parts of speech in it according to a certain algorithm (replace a noun with the word that falls seven words after it in the dictionary). The word processor's Replace function is used after the word is located in the dictionary.

*Continued*

Example:        I heard it through the grapevine/I heard it through the grassland
(Tony, grade 5)

*Transformations.* In these poems, words are replaced with their definitions. The Replace or Edit functions are used to delete and insert text.

Example:        I saw a girl with a bow in her hair. I saw a female child with a knot with loops
                in it in her fine threadlike structure growing from the skin of most mammals.
(Laura, grade 3)

After writing the poems, students are allowed to read them aloud and share with each other.

Source: Nelson, M. H. (1994). Processing poetry to develop literacy. *The Computing Teacher, 22*(3), 39–41.

# Example Lesson 5.11
# Word Processing in Early Foreign Language Learning (grades 7–8)

**Developed by:**        Pam Lewis

**Lesson Purpose.** Word processing is used to help young foreign language students get more interested in writing and pay more attention to detail in word usage, agreements, and verb conjugations. Although the activities described here focus on use with middle school students, similar ones could be adapted for upper elementary and high school or adult levels.

**Instructional Activities.** Beginning language students need the practice of writing simple compositions in the language they are studying. Yet students who have limited vocabulary and grammar mastery frequently find it difficult and tedious to accomplish this. Word processing lets them make corrections more quickly; combining writing with graphics makes the activity more exciting and helps students convey complex thoughts they are not yet able to express. Using fancy fonts with authentic punctuation and characters is helpful. The following are some suggested writing projects that incorporate these resources for French language learning.

*Autobiographies.* Have students do a self-portrait in writing. In an assignment presented to them in French, ask them to incorporate items such as name, age, birthday, family members, grandparents and their nationalities, friends, what they like to do on weekends, religion, favorite TV programs, what they like to eat, favorite sports, places they have visited, remarks about their school, and languages they speak.

*Menus.* Introduce the class to vocabulary on French foods and the cultural experiences related to them. Have them form small groups and make up a dialogue about "The Restaurant" in which they role-play a server and client as they order from a menu they create, eat the food, and pay the check. They use word processing and graphics to prepare and illustrate their menu. The groups make a rough draft and critique each other's work. Then they memorize and present their dialogue, along with their prepared menus.

*Developing Comic Strips.* Ask students to draw or adapt existing cartoon or comic strip characters to develop their own comic or cartoon and present it in a computer slide show.

*Family Albums.* Ask students to make a book or album about their family using at least 15 French sentences to describe the family. They use scanned-in photographs or pictures to illustrate their album.

Source: Lewis, P. (1997). Using productivity software for beginning language learning. *Learning and Leading with Technology, 24*(8), 14–17.

## Example Lesson 5.12
## Using Technology to Study Biospheres (junior high)

**Developed by:** Rose Reissman
**Instructional Resources:** Computers with Internet and e-mail access; books, magazines, and other materials on biospheres; word processing software; electronic encyclopedias; scanner

**Lesson Purpose.** Junior high students use a variety of technology tools to learn about the design and uses of biospheres. Biospheres offer a rich environment in which students can collaborate with others as they practice their research and inquiry skills.

**Instructional Activities**

*Background Research.* Begin by having students form small group cooperative teams. They can use newspapers, magazines, books, and electronic encyclopedias to gather information on biospheres and begin to learn about biosphere design. They record their facts and design aspects in a word processor file.

*Online Work.* The students use online resources such as Internet searches to locate experts in biosphere design and e-mail questions to them. By posting open messages on listservs and bulletin boards, they may locate other schools and classrooms who are also interested in this topic and begin to work with them.

*Biosphere Design.* Students begin collecting visuals of biosphere designs. Each team has access to both word processing and drawing software as well as a scanner. Each team exchanges visuals with one other team and critiques the scientific accuracy of the designs. Their analysis should consider elements such as enclosed greenhouse, self-sufficient structure, resource management system, and subsystems.

After the teams complete their critiques, they review all the various team critiques. Then the teams begin using the scanned images to create their own final biosphere designs.

*Presentations.* After teams complete their work, the products can be shown in a number of ways. For example, teams can print out and post the images or they can develop a slide show using multimedia software.

Source: Reissman, R. (1992). A biosphere research expedition. *The Computing Teacher, 20*(1), 32–33.

## Learning Word Processing: Common Mistakes and Misconceptions

Beginning users of word processing experience some common problems. Teachers may want to review them before beginning the exercises. If students encounter problems, they may want to review this list again:

**Forgetting to move the cursor before typing.** The computer does not automatically place text as desired. The user must indicate a spot for new text using the mouse or command keys to place the cursor at the desired location. Beginners often have their eyes on the place they want to insert a letter or word but forget to move the cursor there first. They are surprised when their typing appears somewhere other than where they had intended.

**Forgetting to highlight before changing a format.** The same kind of problem occurs when beginners want to change the appearance of text (centering a title or inserting an automatic paragraph indent). The computer will not change the correct part of the text unless the user highlights the text *first* and *then* selects the option. If the selected option doesn't work, be sure to indicate which part of the text the format should change.

**Losing part of the document.** Unless a computer system has a large (19-inch) screen, an entire document may not fit on one screen. As the user types, the top of the document scrolls up the screen and out of view. Beginners sometimes become distressed because they cannot see all they have typed and think it may be lost. They should use the scroll box or scroll arrows to bring the missing part of the document into view on the screen.

**Forgetting automatic wraparound at the ends of lines.** Beginners sometimes use the typewriter convention of hitting the Return key at the end of each line. This will make large spaces appear in the text when the document prints out on paper. Remember to press Return or Enter *only* at the ends of paragraphs.

---

**Example Lesson 5.13**
**Exploring Political Parties (middle school)**

**Developed by:**          Rose Reissman

**Lesson Purpose.** Students use research skills along with word processing and graphics software to explore what it means to be a Democrat, Republican, or Independent.

**Instructional Activities.** This activity focused on the 1992 presidential election, but a similar one could be done on any local or national election. The following steps can be used to carry out this exploration of the political process.

*Start-up.* The words "Democrat," "Republican," "Independent," "Third Party," and "None of the Above" are typed on a computer with a large monitor so the whole class can see. The class is divided into Party Probe teams of 3–4 students each with two side-by-side computers. One computer has a word processing program on the screen; the other has a graphics program.

*Identifying Party Associations.* The teacher asks the students to take 10 minutes to come up with as many visual and verbal associations as they can for each party. To assist them, she distributes some cartoons and newspaper articles on political events. One member of the team is appointed the sketch artist for the visual images, and another is the recorder for the verbal associations.

*Discussing the Findings.* After time is up, the teacher selects one student from the class to compile the visual images across groups and another student to compile the verbal associations. Two computers with large screen monitors are set up for this purpose. The two recorders lead the discussions as results are compiled. In the 1992 presidential election activity, students came up with the following associations.

- **For Democrats.** Verbal associations included liberals, women's rights, student loans, single mothers, and child care. Visual associations included a donkey and a single mother.

- **For Republicans.** Verbal associations included "read my lips," "family values," and "a thousand points of light." Visual associations included an elephant, two lips with "read mine" on them, and a picture of a potato with the spelling "potatoe" on it.

- **For Independent or third party.** Verbal associations included time for a change, deficit plan, and early withdrawal (with reference to Perot's withdrawal from the race). Visual associations included a podium with a "Perot for President" banner on it, but no one behind it.

As they discussed these results, the students checked off associations that had been on more than one list. They talked about where they had gotten their findings and where they could get more information.

*More Research.* Students can use additional sources such as history books, online discussion groups, and encyclopedias to gather more information. They can discuss the extent to which these sources confirm their original associations or change them as a result of their new findings.

*Follow-up.* The teacher prepares a collection of political cartoons and uses them to discuss parties further. She asks a colleague representing each party to come and share their views with the students. The students analyze the cartoons and comments from the colleagues. Then they proceed to do critical analyses of party coverage they see on T.V. and other media.

Source: Reissman, R. (1994). Party probe: A technology-supported introduction to political parties research. *The Computing Teacher, 21*(7), 21–22.

---

**Problems with naming and saving files.** Word processing is frequently the first application that beginning computer users learn. Thus, this may provide their first experience with the concepts of storing and replacing documents in computer memory. The most common error is forgetting to save a document before closing it. Novice users may think they need to save only once and are surprised to open a document later and find that some of what has been typed is missing. Always remember to save a document before closing it.

**Incorrect spacing at the top or bottom of the document.** Beginners are sometimes surprised when their printed documents have different top and bottom margins than what they saw on a WYSIWYG screen. This can be caused by two problems:

- **Setting paper in the printer.** The printer is a separate machine from the computer. When it receives a command to print from the computer, it will begin printing wherever the paper is positioned, even if the paper is already positioned halfway up the page. If unexpectedly large or small spaces fall at the top of a document, students must check to see if the paper is positioned in the printer at the top of the sheet.

- **Extra blank lines in the document.** Even though blank lines do not always appear on the word processing screen, the computer knows they are there and allows space for them on the printed page. Beginners do not always realize that when they press Return or Enter, they insert a blank line that is as real to the program as text lines. If the paper is set at the top of the page and unexpected blank spaces still appear at the end of a printed document, see if blank lines appear in the document itself. If so, delete them by highlighting them and pressing the Delete key.

**Problems with search and replace.** This handy feature is easy to misuse and can result in unexpected changes to the document. Seasoned users joke about the accountant who wanted to change the wording in all his letters from TO CUSTOMERS to BY CUSTOMERS. He instructed the word processor to automatically search and replace all text from "TO" to "BY." The computer changed everything to BY CUSBYMERS. Before changing all instances of some text, be sure you can predict the result accurately.

## Using Spreadsheet Software in Teaching and Learning

### Introduction to Spreadsheet Software

**Spreadsheet defined.** Electronic spreadsheet programs organize and manipulate numerical data. The term *spreadsheet* comes from the pre-computer word for an accountant's ledger: a book for keeping records of numerical information such as budgets and cash flow. Unlike the term *word processing,* which refers only to the computer software or program, the term spreadsheet can refer either to the program itself or to the product it produces. Spreadsheet products are sometimes also called *worksheets.* Information in a spreadsheet is stored in rows and columns. Each row–column position is called a *cell,* which may contain numerical values, words or character data, and formulas or calculation commands.

A spreadsheet helps users manage numbers in the same way that word processing helps manage words. Bozeman (1992) described spreadsheets as a way to "word process numbers" (p. 908). Spreadsheets were the earliest application software available for microcomputers. Some people credit them with starting the microcomputer revolution, since the availability of the first spreadsheet software, *Visicalc,* motivated many people to to buy a microcomputer.

Teachers today typically use electronic spreadsheets for work that involves keeping track of and calculating numerical data such as budgets and grades. Spreadsheets process calculations faster, more accurately, and with more visual feedback than other tools such as calculators. For example, if a worksheet is set up to add a column of expense items, the cell showing the sum will change automatically in response to any change to one of the expense items. If a worksheet is set up to calculate a student's grade average, the cell showing the cumulative average will be updated if the points change for any of the grades. These capabilities allow both teachers and students to play with numbers and see the results. This section of the chapter helps teachers to define both the capabilities and the classroom applications of spreadsheets. It will describe capabilities and benefits of spreadsheets for teacher productivity and teaching and learning.

**Types of spreadsheet programs and products.** Like word processing software, a spreadsheet program can form an application of its own or be part of an integrated package such as *Microsoft Works* that also contains word processing and database software. Sometimes spreadsheet capabilities are also combined with a database program to create a powerful, multipurpose product such as *Lotus 1-2-3* or *QuattroPro.* Teachers usually select a program like *Lotus 1-2-3* to present business education concepts to high school students or to handle more complex recordkeeping tasks than simple gradekeeping. These combination spreadsheet/database programs have more capabilities than self-contained spreadsheets or integrated packages and are more complicated to learn and use.

Teachers also use spreadsheet derivatives. Gradebooks or gradekeeping packages are special-purpose spreadsheets designed exclusively to store and calculate grades. Some software publishers also sell spreadsheet templates, predesigned worksheets for special instructional purposes such as demonstrating concepts of budgeting.

**General spreadsheet features and capabilities.** Spreadsheet packages offer significant improvements over calculating values by hand or with a calculator. Like word processing documents, spreadsheets can easily be edited and stored for later use. Although spreadsheet capabilities and procedures vary from program to program, most programs have the following features in common:

- **Calculations and comparisons.** Spreadsheets calculate and manipulate stored numbers in a variety of ways through formulas. In addition to adding, subtracting, multiplying, and dividing specified in formulas, spreadsheets also manipulate data in many more complex ways through function commands. These include mathematical functions such as logarithms and roots, statistical functions such as sums and averages, trigonometric functions such as sines and tangents, logical functions such as Boolean comparisons, and financial functions such as periodic payments and rates. Most spreadsheets also offer special-purpose functions such as lookup tables. These are sets of

**Figure 5.5    Charts and Graphs Prepared with Spreadsheets**

Weight/Planets SS (SS)

| | A | B | C | D | E | F | G | H |
|---|---|---|---|---|---|---|---|---|
| 1 | WEIGHT ON MOON AND VARIOUS PLANETS | | | | | | | |
| 2 | | | | | | | | |
| 3 | | | | | | | | |
| 4 | PLANET/MOON | GRAVITY | WEIGHT ON EARTH | WEIGHT ON PLANET | | | | |
| 5 | | vs. Earth's gravity | Pounds | Pounds | | | | |
| 6 | | | | | | | | |
| 7 | Our Moon | 0.17 | 75 | 13 | | | | |
| 8 | Mercury | 0.38 | 75 | 29 | | | | |
| 9 | Venus | 0.91 | 75 | 68 | | | | |
| 10 | Earth | 1.00 | 75 | 75 | | | | |
| 11 | Mars | 0.38 | 75 | 29 | | | | |
| 12 | Jupiter | 2.64 | 75 | 198 | | | | |
| 13 | Saturn | 1.13 | 75 | 85 | | | | |
| 14 | Uranus | 1.17 | 75 | 88 | | | | |
| 15 | Neptune | 1.19 | 75 | 89 | | | | |
| 16 | Pluto | 0.43 | 75 | 32 | | | | |

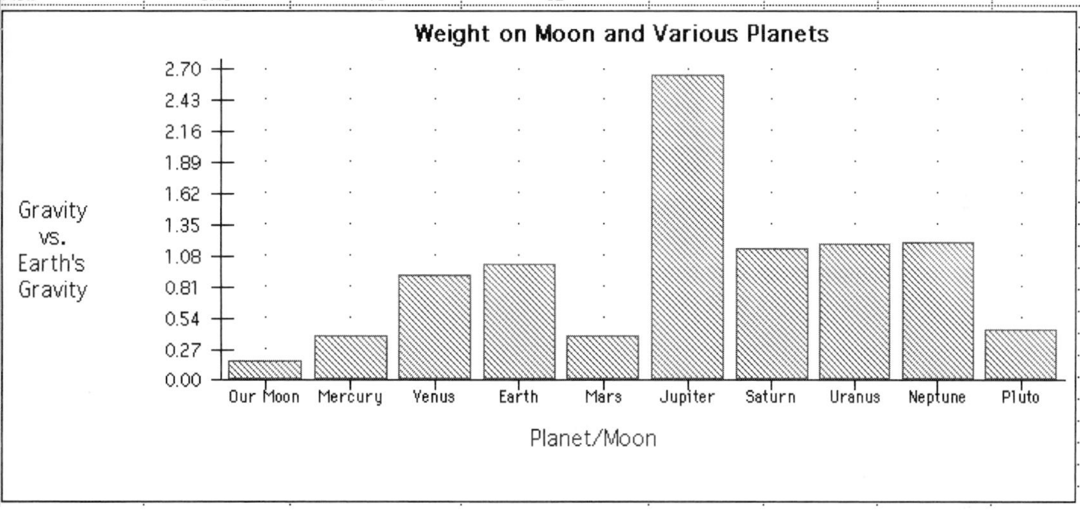

numbers that are automatically compared with those in the spreadsheet and assigned a value if they match. For example, a teacher might have a lookup table to assign letter grades based on students' final numerical grades. Formulas also allow users to weight given grades.

- **Automatic recalculation.** This is the most powerful advantage that spreadsheets offer. When any number changes, the program updates all calculations related to that number.

- **Copying cells.** Once a user enters a formula or other information into a cell, it can be copied automatically to other cells. This can save time, for example, when placing a long formula at the end of each of 20 rows; the user can simply copy the information from the first row to other rows.

- **Line up information in columns.** Spreadsheets store data by row–column positions, a format that makes information easy to read and digest at a glance.

- **Create graphs that correspond to data.** A spreadsheet program displays entered and calculated data in a chart or graph such as a pie chart or bar graph. Figure 5.5 shows an example spreadsheet and a bar chart derived from its data.

- **Use worksheets prepared on other programs.** Spreadsheet programs have software commands, invisible to the user, that perform formatting features such as centering text in columns. Since these program commands vary from package to package, one spreadsheet program cannot usually read and manipulate a worksheet prepared on another program.

However, many spreadsheet programs allow a document to be saved as a text, ASCII, or SYLK file. When stored in this way, a whole worksheet or specific parts can be brought in (imported) and used in another spreadsheet program.

## The Impact of Spreadsheets in Education

**Advantages of spreadsheets.** Spreadsheet programs are in widespread use in classrooms at all levels of education. Teachers use them primarily to present mathematical topics but sometimes for other purposes. They can help teachers and students in several ways:

- **Time savings.** Spreadsheets save valuable time by allowing teachers and students to complete essential calculations quickly. They save time not only by making initial calculations faster and more accurate, but their automatic recalculation features make it easy to update products such as grades and budgets. Entries also can be changed, added, or deleted easily, with formulas that automatically recalculate final grades.

- **Creating charts.** Although spreadsheet programs are intended for numerical data, their capability to store information in columns makes them ideal tools for designing informational charts such as schedules and attendance lists that may contain few numbers and no calculations at all.

- **Answering "what if" questions.** Spreadsheets help people visualize the impact of changes in numbers. Since values are

Figure 5.6    **Example Gradebook Using Spreadsheets**

| | A | B | C | D | E | F | G | H | I | J | K | L | M | N | O | P |
|---|---|---|---|---|---|---|---|---|---|---|---|---|---|---|---|---|
| 1 | Fall 1994 Grades  -  PERIOD 4 Social Studies | | | | | | | | | | | | | | | |
| 2 | | | | | | | | | | | | | | | | |
| 3 | | | Individual Assignments | | | | | | Prod. | Prod. | | Test | Test | | Final | FINAL |
| 4 | | | 1 | 2 | 3 | 4 | 5 | | 1 | 2 | | #1 | #2 | | Avg. | GRADE |
| 5 | | | 8% | 8% | 8% | 8% | 8% | | 20% | 20% | | 10% | 10% | | | |
| 6 | | | | | | | | | | | | | | | | |
| 7 | Adams, Alma | | 89 | 92 | 84 | 96 | 80 | | 88 | 95 | | 54 | 70 | | 84.28 | B |
| 8 | Betts, Lee | | 95 | 84 | 81 | 77 | 90 | | 91 | 95 | | 90 | 100 | | 90.36 | A |
| 9 | Bradley, Brindell | | | | | | | | | | | | | | | |
| 10 | Brush, Jason | | 86 | 95 | 96 | 90 | 90 | | 91 | 95 | | 87 | 45 | | 86.96 | A |
| 11 | Dirk, Dwan | | 80 | 97 | 90 | 83 | 90 | | 97 | 100 | | 75 | 100 | | 92.10 | A |
| 12 | Gretsky, Gerald | | 72 | 75 | 90 | 97 | 90 | | 77 | 76 | | 81 | 50 | | 77.62 | C |
| 13 | Howard, Kay | | 84 | 89 | 79 | 97 | 100 | | 91 | 90 | | 78 | 80 | | 87.92 | B |
| 14 | Johnson, Betty | | 89 | 98 | 96 | 96 | 90 | | 94 | 90 | | 94 | 100 | | 93.72 | A |
| 15 | Jones, Natalie | | | | | | | | | | | | | | | |
| 16 | Lane, Michael | | 83 | 85 | 72 | 50 | 76 | | 91 | 95 | | 76 | 80 | | 82.08 | B |
| 17 | McBur, Yolanda | | 96 | 100 | 96 | 96 | 77 | | 91 | 90 | | 81 | 100 | | 91.50 | A |
| 18 | McClellan, Will | | 45 | 100 | 92 | 95 | 100 | | 97 | 100 | | 99 | 100 | | 93.86 | A |
| 19 | Morrison, Addie | | 97 | 93 | 92 | 96 | 90 | | 88 | 95 | | 93 | 100 | | 93.34 | A |
| 20 | Moultrie, Fred | | 98 | 91 | 88 | 89 | 100 | | 91 | 90 | | 56 | 80 | | 87.08 | B |
| 21 | Sanders, Lillie | | 97 | 90 | 88 | 85 | 100 | | 94 | 90 | | 83 | 100 | | 91.90 | A |
| 22 | Shepherd, April | | | | | | | | | | | | | | | |
| 23 | Williams, Peter | | 93 | 65 | 92 | 82 | 56 | | 80 | 70 | | 71 | 100 | | 78.14 | C |
| 24 | | | | | | | | | | | | | | | | |
| 25 | | | | | | | | | | | | | | | | |

automatically recalculated when changes are made in a worksheet, a user can play with numbers and immediately see the result. This capability makes it feasible to pose "what if" questions and answer them quickly and easily.

• **Motivation.** Many teachers feel that spreadsheets make working with numbers more fun. Collis (1988) described spreadsheets as "sufficiently enjoyable and interesting in themselves that students can sometimes be experiencing the pleasure of exploring math at the same time as they are doing math" (p. 264). Students sometimes perceive mathematical concepts as dry and boring; spreadsheets can make these concepts so graphic that students express real delight with seeing how they work.

**Issues related to spreadsheets.** One of the few disagreements related to spreadsheets in education is whether to use them to keep grades or to rely instead on gradekeeping packages (gradebooks) designed especially for this purpose. Spreadsheets usually offer more flexibility in designing formats and allowing special-purpose calculation functions, while gradebooks are simpler to use and require little setup other than entering students' names and assignment grades. Teachers appear to be about evenly divided on which is better; the choice comes down to personal preference.

Since spreadsheet use creates no researchable issues of the kind word processing does, there are no research results to report in this area. Studies show, however, that spreadsheets can be useful tools for teaching topics ranging from problem solving (Sutherland, 1993) to statistical analysis methods (Klass, 1988). The literature contains numerous testimonials by teachers who have used spreadsheets suc-

cessfully in teaching topics ranging from mathematics (Baugh, 1995) to social studies (Voteline, 1992).

### Spreadsheets in the Classroom

**Applications of spreadsheets: Teacher productivity.** Teachers can use spreadsheets to help them prepare classroom materials and complete calculations that they would otherwise have to do by hand or with a calculator. An example spreadsheet a teacher might use for keeping grades is shown in Figure 5.6. They help with many activities and products in education, including:

• Gradekeeping to keep records and to prepare grade charts for posting

• Club and/or classroom budgets

• Computerized checkbooks for clubs or other organizations

• Attendance charts

• Performance assessment checklists

**Applications of spreadsheets: Teaching and learning activities.** The literature reflects an increasing variety of applications for spreadsheets. Although their teaching role focuses primarily on mathematics lessons, spreadsheets have also effectively supported instruction in science, social studies, and even language arts. Teachers can use spreadsheets in many ways to enhance learning:

• **Demonstrations.** Whenever concepts involve numbers and concrete representation can clarify the ideas, spreadsheets contribute to effective teaching demonstrations. Spreadsheets offer

**Example Lesson 5.14**
**Using Spreadsheets to Demonstrate Concepts (grade 5)**

**Developed by:**            Kenneth Goldberg, New York University (New York)

**Lesson Purposes.** A spreadsheet is used to display data from a U.S. presidential election to show how popular votes and electoral votes differ and how it is possible for a person to win the popular vote and still lose the election.

**Instructional Activities.** This lesson was used just prior to the 1988 U.S. presidential election but can illustrate the concepts involved in any U.S. presidential election. The class held a mock election and assigned electoral votes to each class in the school based on enrollment numbers. (A class with 10 or fewer students got one vote, one with 11 to 20 students got two votes, and one with 21 or more got three votes.) The spreadsheet was set up to match the list of classes and their popular and electoral votes. Data on election results were entered after the election was held and the spreadsheet was displayed on a large monitor so the whole class could see the results as they were entered. Some facts became clear when students began to see the data. It was evident that George Bush would win; the popular vote was fairly close; the electoral vote was not close; and, if very few of the popular votes in key areas were changed, the results of the election would be reversed. The class discussed these results as well as the possibility that a candidate could win the popular vote and lose the electoral vote.

Source: Goldberg, K. (1991). Bringing mathematics to the social studies classroom: Spreadsheets and the electoral process. *The Computing Teacher, 18*(1), 35–38.

an efficient way of demonstrating numerical concepts such as multiplication and percentages and numerical applications such as the concept of electoral votes versus popular votes. A worksheet can make a picture out of abstract concepts and provide a graphic illustration of what the teacher is trying to communicate (see Example Lesson 5.14).

• **Student products.** Students can use spreadsheets to create neat timelines, charts, and graphs as well as products that require them to store and calculate numbers (see Example Lesson 5.15).

• **Support for problem solving.** Spreadsheets take over the task of doing arithmetic functions so students can focus on higher-level concepts (Ploger, Rooney, & Klingler, 1996). By answering "what if?" questions, spreadsheets help teachers encourage logical thinking, develop organizational skills, and promote problem solving (see Example Lessons 5.16 and 5.17).

**Example Lesson 5.15**
**Using Spreadsheets for Student Products (middle-high school)**

**Developed by:**            John Beaver, SUNY College at Buffalo (Buffalo, New York)

**Lesson Purposes.** Students use a spreadsheet to generate charts and graphs of data they have gathered.

**Instructional Activities.** The teacher introduces graphing concepts by having students interpret some commercially produced charts and graphs. Then they assign charts to do without benefit of spreadsheet software. (This gives concrete experience that teaches both the benefit of using a spreadsheet to produce these items and the procedures for generating them.) Then the teacher demonstrates how to use spreadsheet software to create charts and graphs. Students generate and conduct a brief class survey on a topic of interest. They use the spreadsheet to collect the data and display it in chart or graph form. The products are displayed on a bulletin board as "A Profile of the Class." If additional surveys of other classes are done, the results can be posted on a bulletin board and compared across classes.

Source: Beaver, J. (1992). Using computer power to improve your teaching—Part II: Spreadsheets and graphing. *The Computing Teacher, 19*(6), 22–24.

---

### Example Lesson 5.16
### Using Spreadsheets to Teach Problem Solving (middle and junior high school)

**Developed by:**　　　　　Richard Sgroi, SUNY (New Paltz, New York)

**Lesson Purposes.** Students use spreadsheets to do calculations as they learn a four-step sequence for problem solving.

**Instructional Activities.** The teacher prepares students to learn the problem-solving approach by reviewing the contradiction strategy. This procedure attacks a problem by identifying clues to aid in the solution and then answering questions about which solutions are possible and not possible. When students are comfortable with this approach, the teacher introduces spreadsheet use in the context of two types of problems: coin problems and ratio problems. In a coin problem, students know a certain number of coins and a total sum and must determine how many of each coin could give the sum. In the ratio problem, students must find three 3-digit numbers that use all of the digits 1 through 9 only once; the ratio of the first number to the second number must be 1:2 and the ratio of the first number to the third number must be 1:3 (a 1:2:3 ratio). For each kind of problem, the teacher presents a prepared spreadsheet to support the necessary calculations. Then, the four-step problem-solving procedure is introduced: Understand the problem, devise a plan, carry out the plan, and look back. The class works through these problems in small groups and then discusses procedures and solutions together.

Source: Sgroi, R., (1992). Systematizing trial and error using spreadsheets. *The Arithmetic Teacher, 39*(7), 8–12.

---

### Example Lesson 5.17
### Using Spreadsheets to Teach Problem Solving (elementary school)

**Developed by:**　　　　　James R. M. Paul

**Lesson Purposes.** Students use a spreadsheet to help do numerical calculations involved in problem solving.

**Instructional Activities.** "Primary school children think big" (Paul, 1995, p. 65). They talk about and attack many math-oriented problems that require arithmetic skills that they lack. Spreadsheets can help with the calculations involved in solving such problems and can support the conceptual development related to these activities.

　　With the first problem, students visit a pizza parlor with three different size pizzas (small, medium, and large) and divide them into 4, 6, and 8 portions. Students discuss whether individual portions are equal across all three sizes. They talk about whether it is more cost-effective to buy two small pizzas of four portions each, or one large pizza with eight portions. They make initial estimates and then measure the pizzas. After discussion of the best methods to use and after making some initial calculations, they form initial hypotheses, look at the kind of calculations necessary to solve the problems, and enter the data and formulas into the spreadsheet. After determining the solution to their problem, they change the pricing parameters to answer "what if?" questions. Then they change the radii of the pizzas until the cost for all sizes is equal.

Source: Paul, J. (1995). Pizza and spaghetti. *The Computing Teacher, 22*(7), 65–67.

---

- **Storing and analyzing data.** Whenever students must keep track of data from classroom experiments, spreadsheets help organize these data and perform required descriptive statistical analyses (see Example Lesson 5.18).

- **Projecting grades.** Students can be taught to use spreadsheets to keep track of their own grades. They can do their own "what if?" questions to see what scores they need to make on their assignments to project desired class grades. This

---

### Example Lesson 5.18
### Using Spreadsheets to Store and Analyze Data (grade 3)

**Developed by:**          Scarlet Harriss, Webster Elementary School (St. Augustine, Florida)

**Lesson Purposes.** Students use a spreadsheet to record the results of their M&Ms count and do various activities with estimation and prediction.

**Instructional Activities.** The teacher must prepare for this activity by developing a paper M&M Record Form for each student and a spreadsheet for use by the whole class. Each student pair receives a bag of M&Ms and a form. They count and separate by color the M&Ms in their bag. Given what they know about the contents of their own bags, students use estimation and prediction to project what they will find by color and number for the whole class. Each student pair fills out their M&M Record Form. The pairs take turns entering their data into the spreadsheet. When all data are in the spreadsheet, the students reevaluate their predictions. The teacher shares the spreadsheet sums and averages using an overhead projector and LCD panel and the class compares predictions with the actual totals and averages. The teacher ends by summarizing the prediction and estimation processes the class has used. As an extension activity, the class may discuss how these processes can be used in various ways in everyday life.

**Problems to Anticipate.** Teachers need to make sure students understand concepts such as sums, averages, estimating, and predicting before beginning this activity.

Source: Harriss, S. (1992). M&M count. *Florida Technology in Education Quarterly, 4*(2), 60–61.

---

simple activity can play an important role in encouraging them to take responsibility for setting goals and achieving them.

### Learning to Use Spreadsheets: Common Mistakes and Misconceptions

Many beginning spreadsheet users encounter some common problems. If you are having problems, look over this list to see if you can find a solution:

**Forgetting to highlight cells to be formatted.** The computer cannot format a cell in the spreadsheet until the user highlights the affected cells *first* and *then* selects the option. If a chosen formatting option doesn't work for the cells you were formatting, be sure you first indicate the part of the worksheet where the format should apply.

**Difficulties in developing formulas.** Perhaps the most common problems in spreadsheet use have to do with creating formulas. This results from failing to complete the first step in the procedure for creating formulas: placing the cursor in the correct cell. The next most common problem results from pressing the right arrow key (instead of the Return or Enter key) to leave the cell while creating a formula. Rather than moving the pointer, this action adds something to the formula. Many students become confused when they see a formula grow as they struggle to leave the cell. Another common problem with formulas is accidentally including the formula cell itself in the formula's calculation. This is sometimes called a *circular reference*

*error.* Even if an error message does not appear, this error usually is spotted quickly because the formula results in much larger numbers than expected.

## Using Database Software in Teaching and Learning

### Introduction to Database Software

**Database defined.** Databases are computer programs that allow users to store, organize, and manipulate information, including both text and numerical data. Database software can perform some calculations but their real power lies in allowing the user to locate information through keyword searches. Unlike word processing software, which can be compared to a typewriter, or a spreadsheet, which can be compared to a calculator, a database program has no electronic counterpart. It is most often compared to a file cabinet or a Rolodex card file. Like these precomputer devices, the purpose of a database is to store important information in a way that makes it easy to locate later. This capability becomes increasingly important as society's store of essential information continues to grow in volume and complexity.

People often use the term *database* to refer both to the computer program and the product it creates; however, database products are also sometimes called *files*. While a spreadsheet stores an item of data in a cell, a database stores one item of data in a location usually called a *field.*

**Figure 5.7  Example Database for Instruction: Genetic Characteristics**

Source: "Microsoft Access" from *Productivity Tools in the Classroom* by Microsoft Corporation. © Microsoft Corp.

Although each field represents one item of information in a database, perhaps the more important unit of information is a record, since it relates directly to the designated purpose of the database file. For example, in a database of student records, each record corresponds to a student and it consists of several fields of information about the student such as name, address, age, and parents' names. In a database of information on a school's inventory of instructional resources, each record represents one resource and consists of several fields describing such resources as title, publisher, date published, and location.

Database software packages vary considerably in the format and appearance of information. Figure 5.7 shows an example database file on genetic traits observed in students (Revenaugh, 1997). Designed to help teach about heredity and how genetics determines human characteristics, the database holds a record for each student in the class and each item about a student (such as age, eye color, and height) appears in a field.

**The importance of databases.** Teachers face a challenge in trying to do justice to the usefulness of database software in a classroom or curriculum. Unlike word processing or spreadsheet programs, instruction using databases may require a fairly dramatic shift in the way a teacher thinks and teaches. Some cite the database program's potential for facilitating new, constructivist teaching strategies as the source of its reputation as an indispensable classroom tool.

Heine (1994) said that "A database is one of the computer tools that students should be able to use by the end of elementary school" (p. 39). Teachers have long recognized the unique capabilities of database software to support instruction in problem solving, research skills, and information management. Teachers also have found databases useful for teaching higher-level concepts such as classification and keyword searching to young students (Hollis, 1990; Jankowski, 1993–1994). Students as young as 6 or 7 can begin to learn how to classify and group people or animals according to characteristics and how to locate entries that match a certain description.

The productivity uses of databases have not earned them the same widespread popularity with teachers as tools such as word processing. Teachers may not have any existing filing system that a database could facilitate. For example, they may not have a special system—other than looking along shelves—to search for instructional resources that could help them teach a topic. They might not keep any personal classroom records on student performance, relying instead on those in the main office for vital information. Those who do not use databases may view the work required to create and/or use personal databases for these purposes as more time-consuming and difficult than existing mechanisms for dealing with information. However, as examples will show later in this chapter, a classroom database also gives teachers new capabilities and options for information management that they would not otherwise have.

**Types of database programs and products.** Figure 5.8 presents several ways to categorize database programs. The first classification separates packages according to purpose. As with word processing and spreadsheet programs, a database program is an application on its own like *dBase* or part of an integrated package like *Microsoft Works* or *ClarisWorks* that also contains software for word processing, spreadsheets, graphics production, and/or telecommunications. The figure also notes a difference between database software intended to allow people to prepare their own database files to store their own data and prepared database files such as Dialog's *ERIC on Disc* or Sunburst's *Animals Data Bases,* which give access to existing collections of information. Prepared databases usually are

**Figure 5.8  Types of Database Programs**

|  | **First Type** | **Second Type** |
|---|---|---|
| By packaging | Single application (*dBase, Microsoft Word*) | Integrated package (*ClarisWorks, Microsoft Works*) |
| By purpose | Database software (*dBase, Microsoft Works*) | Prepared database (*ERIC on Disc*) |
| By filing type | Flat filing system (*ClarisWorks, Microsoft Works*) | Relational filing system (*dBase, Fox Pro, Oracle*) |
| By capability | Nonprogrammable systems (*ClarisWorks, Microsoft Works*) | Programmable DBMS systems (*dBase, Fox Pro, Oracle*) |

designed to support learning of curriculum topics or make research tasks more efficient. Sometimes these collections are available on media such as CD-ROM, microdisk, or online via telecommunications.

Another way to categorize database products is according to their schemes for storing and organizing information. A flat file database program produces a single file consisting of records, each with several fields. Another kind of database program, a *relational database,* links or relates separate files through a common field called a *key field.* For example, a student database containing personal background data may be linked to another student database with course and grade histories. These files are linked through a common field such as student name or Social Security number. The database program can draw reports from either file through the key field.

A final way to categorize database products is according to their levels of capability. More capable systems are also more complex to use, but some complex systems provide Database Management Systems (DBMSs) that give users helpful interfaces to the databases. This interface is a language, either a structured query language (SQL) or an actual programming language, which makes it easier to select items from the database for reports of various kinds. Most, but not all, relational database systems also have DBMSs.

**General database features and capabilities.** Database programs offer several kinds of capabilities for handling information that could not be used for information stored in a noncomputer format such as on paper in file folders in a file cabinet. Although capabilities and procedures vary from program to program, most programs have the following features:

- **Allowing changes to information.** To make changes to paper documents, one must locate documents from each of the file folders that contain copies of the information. One must then retype or otherwise alter the sheets of paper. Computer users can access information stored in a database from a number of locations (either via disk or at a terminal), no matter where it is physically stored. Changing data usually means simply calling up the file and editing information on-screen in one or more fields or giving a command to search and update all the information that meets certain criteria.

- **Sorting information alphabetically or numerically.** The computer's ability to put data in order is handy when information is stored in a database. The program can sort or order records according to data in any one of the fields. For example, student records could be printed out alphabetically according to the Last Name field, or the same information could sort student information from youngest to oldest by the Age field.

- **Searching for information.** All database programs allow users to search for and compare information according to keywords. For example, a teacher might want to locate the records of all teenaged students in a certain grade. If the information were stored in file folders, the teacher would have to go through each one, look up the person's birthday, and check to see if it fell before a certain date. With a database, the teacher

could simply give a command to display all records whose Age field contained a number higher than 12 or whose Birthdate field contained a year lower than a certain year.

- **Automatically retrieving reports or information summaries.** Storing information in databases makes it easier to prepare summaries across all data elements. For example, a teacher may want to group students for work outside class on group projects; the database could indicate when each student could meet outside class time. The teacher could search for all students who had free periods at the same time and assign these students to work together.

- **Merging with word processing documents.** A user can insert information stored in a database automatically in several letters or other word processing documents simply by preparing one document and putting field names in it instead of actual names or other information. The information stored in those fields for each record is automatically inserted as each copy of the document is printed out. This process is called *merging* the database with the word processing document.

## The Impact of Databases in Education

**Advantages of databases.** Database programs and products are in widespread use in classrooms at all levels of education. They can help teachers and students in the following ways:

- **Reducing data redundancy.** In education, as in business and industry, many organizations need access to the same kinds of information on the same people or resources. In pre-computer days, each organization had to maintain its own stores of information that were often identical to those of other organizations. For example, each school office and school district office might have duplicate files on teachers and students. Nowadays, since databases can be accessed from multiple locations, an organization needs to keep only one actual copy of these kinds of information. This cuts down on both the expense and the physical space needed to store the information.

- **Saving time locating and/or updating information.** People need to locate information and keep it accurate—time is money. It takes time to find the information and keep it updated for everyone who needs it. Since a database stores information in a central computer instead of in several different file folders in various offices, users can find information more quickly and they can more easily make changes whenever updates are needed. For example, if a student's address or legal guardian changes, updating the information in a database is both quicker and easier than locating and changing it in many file folders.

- **Allowing comparisons of information through searches across files.** Electronic databases also offer an important capability of locating information that meets several criteria at once. For example, a teacher may want to locate all of the resources in video format at a certain grade level that focus on a certain topic. A database search would make locating these materials an easy task as compared to a search of library shelves. For a large collection of information, this kind of search is possible *only* if information is stored in a database.

**Issues related to databases.** Databases are permanent and pervasive parts of life in the information age. They allow users to locate bits of important data in a landscape crowded with information; they support decisions with confirmed facts rather than assumptions; and they put the power of knowledge at our fingertips. Yet this power is not without its dangers, and knowing how to find information is not the same as knowing what to do with it.

***Simplifying access versus safeguarding privacy.*** Each of our names is listed, along with much of our personal information, on literally dozens of databases. This cataloging begins when we are born—even before we are named—when we appear on the hospital's patient database. Our doctors and schools—even our places of worship—have our names and other notes about us in their databases. Whenever we apply for credit cards, driver's licenses, or jobs, we enter still more databases. These information entities reside on computers that can communicate and exchange notes, so information in one database can be shared with many information systems. Education, like other systems in our society, has come to depend on ready access to these information sources.

However, easy access to information about people long has been recognized as a threat to personal privacy. If information is easy to access, it may also be easy for unauthorized people to obtain and possibly misuse or for organizations to use it in ways that violate basic human rights. In the Privacy Act of 1974, Congress formally recognized the problems presented by government access to information on private citizens. This law requires that federal agencies identify publicly the records they maintain on U.S. citizens. It also limits the kinds of information that can be kept and requires that people be told what information the government keeps on them.

As teachers begin to keep student information in classroom databases and use information from school and district databases, they must recognize their responsibility to safeguard this private information and protect it from unauthorized access. Sometimes this means keeping disks in secure places; sometimes it means making sure passwords remain secret. It may also mean deleting information if parents or students request it. It always means being sensitive to who is looking at screens or printouts containing personal student information.

***Instructional uses of databases.*** The literature reflects extensive applications of databases for instructional purposes. There are several reasons for this popularity. First, databases are a completely philosophy-free technology resource. They can be used in teacher-directed ways or to support student-directed projects. Second, databases are a relatively inexpensive type of software, with a wide range of capabilities; thus, they can be used effectively in ways ranging from very simple to very complex. Hunter (1983) and Collis (1988) were among the first to document the uses of microcomputer databases for instructional purposes. Their books contain many varied lesson plans and demonstrate that databases could underlie teaching and learning

activities for many content areas and grade levels. Early database applications were frequently offered to teachers as good ways to teach problem-solving skills (Watson, 1993). However, some 10 years of use and research on the instructional applications of databases has shown that simply having students use them does not ensure learning of desired research and problem-solving skills.

Collis (1990) summarized six different studies on instructional uses of databases. She found that students can use databases to acquire useful skills in searching for and using information, but they need guidance to ask relevant questions and analyze results. If allowed to proceed on their own, students may regard a simple printed list of results a sufficient measure of success. Studies by Maor (1991) in science and Ehman, Glenn, Johnson, and White (1992) in social studies yielded essentially the same results. Databases offer the most effective and meaningful help when they are embedded in a structured problem-solving process and when the activity includes class and small-group discussion of search results.

## Using Databases in the Classroom

**When to use databases: Teacher productivity.** Teachers can use databases to help them prepare classroom materials and to do tasks that they would otherwise have to do by hand or could not do at all. The appearance of the screen display may change greatly depending on the software package, so it is not possible to show a standard example. However, Figure 5.9 shows an example database display from one software package that a teacher might use. Teachers rely on databases to make their work more efficient and productive in several ways:

- **Inventorying and locating instructional resources.** Teachers can store titles and descriptions of instructional resources in a database to help them identify materials that meet certain instructional needs. If a school has a large collection of resources used by all of the teachers, the school's library/media center probably catalogs this collection on a database designed for this purpose. Some teachers like to keep databases of their own materials so they can match available resources with specific instructional needs quickly and easily.

- **Using information on students to plan instruction and enhance motivation.** Whether a teacher designs and keeps a personal information database or uses one from the school or school district office, this information suggests many ways to meet individual student needs. For example, a teacher might keep information on student reading levels or particular learning problems. Information on each child's favorite sport or hobby could influence designs of motivating activities and selection of materials that would attract attention. Personal touches for each student are easier to accomplish when all the information is on a database. A teacher might begin each week with a birthday search of the student database to give special congratulations or a banner for each student's birthday.

- **Using information on students to respond to questions or perform required tasks.** Teachers often are asked to

**Figure 5.9    Example Database for Teacher Productivity: Classroom Inventory**

| Title | Content Area | Topic | Grade Level | Type | Docs | Publisher |
|---|---|---|---|---|---|---|
| Compton's Multimedia Encyclopedia | Misc. | Encyclopedia | All grades | Tool | | Compton's NewMedia |
| Computer Inspector | Misc. | Computer Programs | All levels | Utility Tool | X | MECC |
| Conduit: Algebra Drill & Practice II | Math | Algebra | Middle School | Drill & Practice | X | Conduit |
| Conduit: Coexist | Social Studies | Population Dynamics | Secondary | Simulation | X | Conduit |
| Conduit: Discovery in Trigonometry | Math | Trigonometry | 9th & up | Tutorial | X | Conduit |
| Conduit: Evolut | Science | Evolution/Natural Sci. | Secondary | Simulation | X | Conduit |
| Conduit: Surfaces for Multi-Variables Calculus | Math | Calculus | College level | Tutorial | X | Conduit |
| Conquering Decimals (+,–) | Math | Decimals (+, –) | 4th – 8th | Drill/Game | X | MECC |
| Conquering Decimals (x, /) | Math | Decimals (x, /) | 3rd – 8th | Drill/Game | X | MECC |
| Conquering Fractions (+, –) | Math | Fractions (+, –) | 4th – 8th | Drill/Game | X | MECC |
| Conquering Fractions (x, /) | Math | Fractions | 5th – 8th | Game | X | MECC |
| Conquering Math Worksheet Generator | Math | Worksheets | Teachers (3–8) | Utility | X | MECC |
| Conquering Percents | Math | Percents | 5th – 8th | Drill/Game | X | MECC |
| Conquering Ratios & Proportions | Math | Ratios & Proportions | 5th – 8th | Drill/Game | X | MECC |
| Conquering Whole Numbers | Math | Whole Numbers (+, –, x) | 3rd – 6th | Drill & Practice | X | MECC |
| Coordinate Math | Math | Charts, diagrams | 4th – 9th | Drill & Practice | X | MECC |
| Counting Critters | Math | Counting | Pre K – K | Drill & Practice | X | MECC |
| Creative Writer | Lang. Arts | Writing | Ages 8 – 14 | Word Processing | | Microsoft |
| Database in the Classroom: Dataquest Sampler | S.S./Science | Database | 5th – 12th | Database | X | MECC |
| Decimal Concepts | Math | Decimals | 3rd – 6th | Game | X | MECC |
| Decision, Decisions: Immigration | Social Studies | Problem Solving | 8th – 12th | Game/Simul. | X | Tom Snyder Productions |

supply personal information on students or deal with situations relating to their personal needs, yet it is difficult to remember everything on dozens of students. For example, some students require special medication; the teacher is responsible for reminding them to take it. A teacher might need to decide quickly whether a particular adult is authorized to take a child from the school. A database with these kinds of information can be very helpful.

• **Sending personalized letters to parents and others.** The capability to merge database information with a word processing document is convenient whenever the teacher wants to send personalized notes to parents or to the students themselves. The teacher can create only one letter or note; the database program takes care of the personalizing.

**When to use databases: Teaching and learning activities.** When database software became available for microcomputers in the 1980s, instructional activities with these tools quickly became popular. Thus, the literature reflects an increasing variety of applications for databases. The heaviest uses seem to be in social studies, but effective applications have been designed for topics in content areas from language arts to science. Here are some ways teachers use databases to enhance learning:

• **Teaching research and study skills.** Skills in locating and organizing information to answer questions and learn new concepts have always been as fundamental as reading and writing skills. Students need good research and study skills not only for school assignments, but also to help them learn on their own outside school. As the volume of information in our society increases, the need to learn how to locate important information quickly also grows. Before computers, families strived to buy reference tools such as a good dictionary and a set of encyclopedias so that children could do research for their school reports and other assignments. Today, these and other sources are stored on electronic media and students need to know how to do computer searches of these references (see Example Lessons 5.19 and 5.20).

## Example Lesson 5.19
### A Database Journal for Mathematics (grade 4)

**Developed by:**        Deborah Getties, Des Moines Public Schools (Des Moines, Iowa)

**Lesson Purposes.** In this activity, students keep a mathematics journal to enhance their learning and help them remember and apply what they learn. They use a database to help them record and manage information on what happened in class each day, what they learned, and how to apply it in real life.

**Instructional Activities.** This activity can be helpful both to students and teachers. Some sample uses for students include the following.

1. Students frequently feel they have not learned much in a mathematics class. To give them a more concrete picture of mathematics skills they have acquired, ask them to review what

*Continued*

they have learned about a specific topic under the "Today I Learned" field. Although they may feel they have not learned a lot, their own notes will show them what they have accomplished.

2.    Have them sort the "Feeling" field to identify and tell the teacher the topics they enjoyed most and least.

3.    Ask them to determine how the topic they are about to learn relates to what they've already learned. Have them use one or more keywords to search the "Summary" field. For example, if they are about to begin a unit on measurement, have them do a search on the word "measure" and see what turns up.

Some sample uses for teachers include the following.

1.    Gather reactions on how well your lesson went by looking at the notes in students' "Summary" fields. Copy these summaries, paste them into a word processing document, and use the notes to review and revise your approaches to the topics.

2.    Identify what you have covered for a certain time period by using the "Date" field. This helps in planning the next steps because it tells what has been covered and makes it easier to see what remains to be done.

3.    Sort by the "Date" field to identify what a student has done for a given time period. Print a collection of comments from the "Summary" field. This is useful during parent conferences to show what the student has accomplished in the class.

4.    Determine what the students enjoyed and which instructional approaches might need improvement by obtaining summary information from the "Feeling" field. Topics with consistently low scores across students may need a different approach. Also, the teacher can use these scores to help spot areas where individual students are experiencing problems.

5.    Sort by the "Materials Used" field, then sort records within a given material by the "Feeling" field. This can help spot which materials did not appeal to students.

Source: Gettys, D. (1994). Journaling with a database. *The Computing Teacher, 22*(2), 37–40.

## Example Lesson 5.20
## Surveying Activities (all grades)

**Developed by:**    Jamie Judd-Wall

**Lesson Purpose.** Curriculum blending or curriculum overlapping is the practice of having students at all ability levels—including those with physical or learning disabilities—work on the same activities, but grading them differently. The authors propose that having students do surveys and analyze the data are ideal activities for this purpose. The article proposes doing one survey activity per month, although teachers may do as many as they feel appropriate for their classrooms.

**Instructional Activities**
*Getting Started.* The teacher selects a topic for the survey. The topic in this article was "favorite fruits." Older students may gather more types of data (e.g., on characteristics of people surveyed), while younger students may collect fewer types of data. A typical survey "script" for younger or less able students might be:

**Opening:**
"Hello, can do you my survey?"
**Question:**
"What is your favorite fruit?"

*Continued*

**Response:**
"Apples."
**Closing:**
"Thank you for your help. Goodbye."

For students with physical disabilities, you may set up a station to support asking the questions and recoding the responses. For example, you may need a multiple input modification access device (MIMAD) consisting of an adaptive firmware card or Ke*nx (from Don Johnson, Inc.); an input device such as OverlayMaker or IntelliKeys (from IntelliTools); and voice-input, word processing software such as *IntelliTalk* (from IntelliTools) or *Write OutLoud* (from Don Johnson, Inc.).

*Doing the Survey.* Select a location and time of day students will do the surveying. (Be sure to get approval from the administration.) It should be a location with enough traffic to gather data easily, but so that you will not create a traffic jam. (A location near the library or at the back of the line in a cafeteria can be a good site.) Younger students or those with physical disabilities can begin the survey script by touching the "Can you answer our survey question?" icon. If the person agrees to participate, the student asks the questions by touching the correct icon, and the computer gives both typed and voice responses. Older or more physically able students may simply use a computer keyboard rather than the alternate one to enter responses. Have students rehearse the sequence in advance, so it will move quickly when they actually begin the survey.

*Analyzing the Results.* There are many different kinds of analysis activities you may do, depending on students' ages and abilities.

- **For primary students.** Have students guess what the most popular fruit will be. Then have them print out and cut apart the response sheets. Ask them to sort and count the responses. Make the responses into a bar graph by gluing them down. If there are demographic data such as age or grade levels, print out responses for each on different colored paper to make it easier to compare the graphs.

- **For secondary students.** Have students do some comparison shopping on the costs of fruit and which is more economical (fresh or canned, fruits with or without peels). Have them calculate percentages such as What percentage of the eighth grade prefers apples? and query the data: "Do older students prefer different fruits than younger ones?" Older students might create statistics and algebraic equations to answer questions such as "Do female tenth-graders have different fruit preferences than male twelfth-graders?"

Source: Judd-Wall, J. (1996). Curriculum blending: Computerized surveying activities for everyone. *Learning and Leading with Technology, 23*(8), 61–64

In one sense, electronic formats make it easier to access information; thus, they support student learning and make it easier to acquire study skills. However, because of the unique capabilities offered by databases, looking up information in electronic formats is a far different activity than doing research in books. To take advantage of the new information resources available to them, students must learn new skills such as using keywords and Boolean logic (looking for references with the keywords Macintosh AND Apple but NOT fruit). They must also learn skills in operating computer equipment and using procedures and commands required by database software. Many database activities are designed to introduce these kinds of searches along with information for a report or a group project.

- **Teaching organization skills.** Students need to understand concepts related to handling information. To solve problems, they must locate the right information and organize it in such a way that they can draw relationships between isolated elements. One way to teach these skills is to have students devel-

op and use their own databases; many examples of this kind of activity have been reported. Even very young students can learn about organizing information by creating databases of information about themselves, including birth dates, heights, weights, eye colors, pets, and parents' names. They can then do simple searches of their databases to summarize information about the members of their class. These kinds of activities help students understand what information is and how to use it. In later grades, students can design and create databases related to areas of study. For example, a class might create a database of descriptive information on candidates running for office in their state or in a national election (see Example Lessons 5.21 and 5.22).

- **Understanding the power of information "pictures."** Students need to understand the persuasive power of information organized into databases. Sometimes a database can generate an information "picture" that may not be visible in any other way. Although these pictures may or may not be completely accurate, many decisions are based on them. For

## Example Lesson 5.21
## A Database Yearbook (grade 2)

**Developed by:**     Ruth Hollis, Peru Central School (Plattsburg, New York)

**Lesson Purposes.** Information on all students in the second grade is placed in a database to organize it for a class yearbook and support various classroom activities.

**Instructional Activities.** The second-grade teachers introduce the yearbook project to students by talking about the district's curricular theme ("Beginnings") and about the things students would like to know about each other. Each class brainstorms the 10 most important kinds of information about themselves. Then all the second-grade teachers consolidate the areas into the final 10 to be included in the database. The computer teacher creates a database template and models for the teachers how to collect the information with their classes by using butcher paper on the wall. Once the classes collect the information, students work in pairs to enter it into the database in their own classrooms. When the database is completed, teachers help the students use it to answer questions about themselves, e.g., "How many kids like pizza?" and "What is the class's favorite color?" Teachers then create the yearbooks by printing out the database records for their classes and adding a picture for each student, a graphic cover, and an introduction. Many kinds of learning activities can be designed based on this information. When students enter information in the database, encourage them to have a doer and a helper and exchange roles halfway through the task. The helper should assist by holding the paper rather than touching the keys.

Source: Hollis, R. (1990). Database yearbooks in the second grade. *The Computing Teacher, 17*(6), 14–15.

## Example Lesson 5.22
## For the Record: A Personal Music Database (middle school)

**Developed by:**     Microsoft Corporation

**Lesson Purposes.** Students learn how to organize and manage data by creating a database that catalogs their music collection of CDs and tapes. They sort, analyze, and print selected database records in answer to questions about their favorite music recordings and performing artists.

**Instructional Activities**

*Introduce the Project.* Ask students how they keep track of important birthdays, addresses, telephone numbers, and appointments. Have students discuss the advantages (inexpensive) and disadvantages (easy to lose) of conventional paper-based memory boosters. Talk about what a computer database is and what it does. Encourage students to think about electronic database's advantages such as information is stored in a single place, it's readily available, it can't be misplaced, it's easy to update, it's always neat and legible, and they can search for records in a variety of different ways.

Explain to students that they will build a database to catalog either their home music collection of audio CDs, records, and cassette tapes or the collection available in the school music room/library. Provide a glossary of terms that students are likely to encounter as they create a database such as table, record, field, query, filters, sort, layout, database wizard, design view, form view, datasheet view, and preview mode.

Tell students that they will learn how to manage information by creating numbered records that they arrange, retrieve, sort, and print. They will use *Microsoft Access* to catalog their collection of music CDs, records, and cassette tapes, storing information about recording artists, music styles, and music tracks. They will learn how to display this information in a datasheet (table format) or on a custom-designed form. They will also learn how to retrieve information from the database using the software's Find command. By employing a variety of sorting techniques to examine their data, they

*Continued*

will try to find patterns or trends. The goal is to develop a "wish" list of CDs or tapes for distribution to friends and family, so that everyone knows exactly what to get for their next birthday. Finally, they will write a report using Microsoft Word, evaluating the significance of this activity.

*Prepare a Database Template.* Students use the *Microsoft Access* "Music Collection.mdz" wizard to create a music collection database. (Note: If they use the database module in *Microsoft Works,* they can use WorksWizard to create a database template. Works does not have a Music Collection TaskWizard.) When the Music Collection Database Wizard appears on screen, choose the fields students want to include in the various database tables. Decide whether they want to include any optional fields (the ones listed in italics) or any sample data. Students choose a style for the screen display of their database form and a style for their printed reports. Finally, name the database and decide whether students want to include a picture on all reports. When they click Finish, their music database will be ready to accept data.

*Enter Data.* Information is entered about each recording artist, record, track, track title, and track length by tabbing from one field to another to move through the list.

*Sort Data.* New insights are developed about students' music collection by rearranging, sorting, and filtering the data. After they've entered a few records, students can make them easier to find by putting the records in alphabetical order.

*Find Data.* If they can't remember the name of a particular recording, but know the name of its recording artist, students can use the *Microsoft Access* Find command to locate the required information.

*Reporting the Results.* Once they have database information in *MS Word,* students can report on the results. Who's their favorite artist? What's their favorite music category? What's their favorite musical instrument? Would any of their other data collections benefit from database management?

*Extension Activities.* Browse these recommended web sites:

* Music Central Online (http://musiccentral.msn.com/)
* The Ultimate Band List (http://www.ubl.com)

Source: Based on a lesson from *Productivity in the Classroom.* © 1997 Microsoft Corporation. For a detailed copy of this lesson, visit this Microsoft Web site: http://www.microsoft.com/education/k12/resource/lessons.htm.

example, the U.S. government uses information databases on those who have been convicted of past income tax offenses to generate descriptive profiles of people who may be likely to try to defraud the government in the future. Students can learn to use database information to generate these pictures, either with existing databases or their own (see Example Lesson 5.23).

* **Posing and testing hypotheses.** Many problem-solving activities involve asking questions and locating information to answer them. Therefore, using databases is an ideal way to teach and provide practice with this kind of problem solving. Students can either research prepared databases full of information related to a content area, or they may create their own databases. Either way, these activities encourage them to look for information that will support or refute a position. In lower grades, the teacher may pose the question and assign students to search databases to answer it. Later, the activity may call for students to both pose and answer appropriate questions. For example, the teacher may ask students to address popular beliefs concerning artistic or gifted people. The students formulate questions, form debate teams, and design searches of databases on famous people to support their positions (see Example Lessons 5.24 and 5.25).

## Learning to Use Databases: Common Mistakes and Misconceptions

Beginning users of databases often encounter some common problems. If you are having problems, look over this list to see if you can find a solution:

**Confusing spreadsheet and database features.** Depending on the software package, a spreadsheet or worksheet may look similar to a database listing. Sometimes learners get confused about what they see on the screen and which of their activities call for which kind of software. Some spreadsheet software has many database-like capabilities in the same package. But other packages have separate software components for spreadsheet and database functions and they produce separate outputs for each one. When a spreadsheet is a separate package or component, it normally can be identified by its characteristic row numbers and column letters. Use a spreadsheet for anything that calls for extensive calculations; to organize information so it can be searched, you

**Example Lesson 5.23**
**Getting a Clearer Focus on History (high school)**

**Developed by:**      Rick Thomas (Eugene, Oregon)

**Lesson Purposes.** Students use a database of 1835 census information on Cherokee citizens of the United States to gain a more accurate historical perspective on the Cherokee lifestyle and culture than is available from traditional written sources.

**Instructional Activities.** This activity is designed to impress social studies students with the power of database information for finding a truer picture of people or events than they can get in sources such as public papers, letters, and diaries. For example, much information about the lives of long-dead people can be gleaned from information such as tax rules, census reports, and church and business records—information that is difficult to manage without a database.

The example in this lesson is a study of the Cherokee nation in the 1800s. The documents of the time paint a picture of a savage and uncultivated people. Even speeches by famous politicians of the time such as Andrew Jackson support this view. Students begin by reviewing this traditional information and discussing the rationale for the removal of the Cherokee from Georgia, Tennessee, North Carolina, and Alabama by 1839 in what came to be known as the "Trail of Tears." Then students begin to pose questions such as "What kind of people were the Cherokee?" and "How will our understanding of their lives affect our perspective on their removal?"

Students begin their review of the database of 1835 census information on the Cherokee nation by exploring the contents and organization of the file. Then they begin to pose questions that evaluate the generalizations about the Cherokee that are evident in documents of the time. Ask them to formulate conclusions about the Cherokee lifestyle. Make an assignment for students to write a summary of their findings and whether or not their beliefs about the events of the time have changed as a result of their findings.

Source: Thomas, R. (1991). A focus on history. *The Computing Teacher, 18*(6), 30–33.

**Example Lesson 5.24**
**Investigating Graveyard Data with Spreadsheets (middle school)**

**Developed by:**      James R. M. Paul and Colette Kaiser (Grahamstown, South Africa)

**Lesson Purpose.** Students visit local graveyards, gather headstone data, enter them into a database, and answer questions about lifespan through database queries.

**Instructional Activities.** Readers should note that this activity was done in Grahamstown, South Africa, and concentrated on a graveyard with many graves from the 1800s and early 1900s. However, this approach could be used for other time periods and locations in the world.

*Collecting the Data.* Students worked together in pairs, first dividing up the rows they would work on so that all would be covered and none duplicated. They used a data collection sheet to gather surnames, first names, dates of death, ages at death, and other details they thought relevant. They used math skills to calculate the age at death from the headstone data on birth date and date of death.

*Inputting Data.* After they collected all the data, the class was divided into three groups, and each group entered the data in 2-hour sessions. (The database had been set up previously to mirror the data sheet.)

*Continued*

*Querying the Database.* Students scrolled through the data to get a feel for what was covered and how it looked in summary form. They sorted data alphabetically by surname to see what families were represented. Teachers asked students to form some questions to ask about the data and what it showed. Some questions developed by students were:

- Do women live longer than men?
- Did people live longer in the 20th century than they did in the 19th century?

They sorted data by date of death and by age to count occurrences in specific age or year categories. Students worked in pairs to make tables and graphs to represent their findings. After they drew their graphs, the whole class held a discussion on findings.

Source: Paul, J. & Kaiser. C. (1996). Do women live longer than men? Investigating graveyard data with computers. *Learning and Leading with Technology, 23*(8), 13–15.

need database capabilities. A spreadsheet can produce a simple chart with nicely formatted straight rows and columns more easily than a database.

**Difficulties with keyword searches.** The most useful feature of databases also presents the most difficulties for new users. A keyword search automatically reviews the whole database and selects only those records that contain certain words, phrases, or numbers. A user can combine several different keywords using the principles of Boolean logic. New users make the most mistakes with database searches when they do not understand how this logic works. When constructing a search, it is sometimes helpful to create a diagram or picture that shows graphically the results expected.

**Decisions about which fields to include.** Most people who have never before used databases have difficulty conceptualizing just what fields to include to make a helpful database file. For example, a teacher who wants to do mail merges to send personal letters to students may include a separate field for first name only. The teacher may find it helpful to discuss with others the purpose of the database and how it will be used when it is complete. The teacher may also want to review some examples of similar databases done by others.

## Example Lesson 5.25
## A Rock Database Project (grades 3–8)

**Developed by:** Thalia Hartson (Alberta, Canada)

**Lesson Purposes.** A unit of study on rocks forms the basis for learning science inquiry skills. A database of information on rocks helps organize the information for use in supporting these problem-solving activities.

**Instructional Activities.** The National Geographic filmstrip "Rocks and Minerals" supplies background information on the unit. This stimulates students' natural interest in rocks and minerals and they spontaneously begin to collect rock samples to sort, observe, and classify. The teacher introduces the three main types of rocks and the rock formation cycle. Laserdisc pictures supplement reference book pictures. Students each select one mineral to research. They enter the information they find into a database. The teacher and student then develop questions and use the database to answer them. Typical questions are Which crystal structures are the most common? and What makes certain minerals valuable? A printed set of questions can be used later as a consolidating exercise. They use the MECC simulation, "Murphy's Minerals," to follow up this technique of testing and identifying minerals according to characteristics.

It usually is best that students enter their data in separate files that the teacher later consolidates. This helps prevent errors and unintentional deletions.

Source: Hartson, T. (1993). Rocks, mineral, databases, and simulations. *The Computing Teacher, 21*(1), 48–50.

# Using Materials Generators

### Desktop Publishing Software

**Definitions: Desktop publishing versus desktop publishing software.** It is perhaps ironic that one of the most useful and widely used of the technology tools is one that communicates information in a traditional medium: the printed page. By allowing teachers and students to design elaborate printed products, however, desktop publishing tools give them the important advantage of complete control over a potentially powerful form of communication. This control over the form and appearance of the printed page defines the activity of desktop publishing. Norvelle (1992) reported that the term *desktop publishing* was coined in 1984 by Paul Brainerd, founder of the Aldus Corporation, to focus on the role of personal computers and laser printers in making the individual-as-publisher a viable concept.

Like word processing software, desktop publishing software allows manipulation of text; the capabilities and classroom applications of these two products overlap. According to many accounts in educational technology literature, the tasks of desktop publishing are performed with many available word processing software packages; the key element in such an activity is control over the design and production of a document. Both kinds of tools allow users to mix text and graphics on each page.

The primary difference between software designed for word processing and that designed for desktop publishing is that the latter is designed to display documents page by page. It also allows easier flexibility over the placement and formats of both text and graphics on individual pages. Word processing is designed to flow text from page to page as it is typed in. Text boxes can appear anywhere on a desktop-designed page. As a result, classroom products created with desktop publishing software can be as eye-catching and professional-looking as those produced by the most prestigious ad agency in New York, Chicago, or San Francisco. The impact of a desktop published product is limited only by the capabilities of the person creating it. Just as the quality of a word processed article depends on the skill of the writer, the quality of a newsletter or brochure from a desktop publishing system depends on the creativity and expertise of the designer. Thus, desktop publishing software focuses on designing communications through a combination of written words and page appearance, while word processing communicates the message primarily through words (McCain, 1993; Williams, 1994).

**Elements of desktop publishing.** Desktop publishing software gives power to users by allowing them to control three elements: page setup, text format, and graphics. They can create text boxes of any size and place them anywhere on the page. Users can manipulate text format by changing type font, size, style, and color. As noted earlier, software offers *fonts* in an ever-increasing array from plain, type-writer-looking Courier to fancy Boulevard. Font size, measured in points (1 point equals about 1/72 inch), ranges from very small to as large as will fit on a page. (The type size for text in most books is about 10 points.) *Type style* refers to appearance changes such as **boldface**, *italics,* outlining, and underlining. Desktop publishing software also allows users to choose colors of type. For example, many documents use the special effect of white type on black backgrounds. Graphics of any kind can be designed using drawing tools provided by the software or the user can import existing pictures and diagrams into the document.

**Types of desktop publishing software.** Teachers can choose from a wide range of desktop publishing software for classroom use. Several packages, such as Microsoft's *Publish It!,* are designed especially for education or for simple newsletter production. For more sophisticated work, teachers may select one of the higher-end packages used in professional design offices like *Quark XPress* or *PageMaker.* Naturally, the more capable packages take more time to learn. Schools usually choose these for more complicated design tasks that require advanced page design features such as creating complex graphics and rotating graphic and text elements on the page.

**Making the most of desktop publishing software: Skills and resources.** Like other technology tools, desktop publishing is most effective if the user knows something about the activity before applying the tool. Designing effective print communications is an entire field of expertise in itself with its own degree programs. Graduates frequently are in high demand in business and industry. As Knupfer and McIsaac (1989) observe, many aspects of page design can influence reading speed and comprehension. They describe four different categories of variables that have been researched: graphic design, instructional text design, instructional graphics, and computer screen design. While the last category focuses on reading from a computer screen, Knupfer and McIsaac note that some of its features apply to both electronic and print-based research (p. 129), including factors like text density and uppercase versus lowercase type.

However, even with this in mind, teachers and students need not be professional designers to create useful desktop publishing products, and their skills will improve with practice. According to Parker (1989) and Rose (1988), desktop publishing products have greater impact and communicate more clearly if they reflect some fairly simple design criteria. Beginners may want to keep the following suggestions in mind:

- **Select and use typefaces (fonts) carefully.** Unusual typefaces can help direct the eye toward text, but too many different fonts on a page are distracting and some fancy fonts can be difficult to read. A *serif font,* a font with small curves or "hands and feet" that extend from the ends of the letters, is easier to read in paragraphs; use it for text in the main body of the document. Use *sans serif type,* a font without extensions, for titles and headlines. Make type large enough to assist the reader. For example, younger readers usually need large point sizes.

* **Use visual cueing.** When specific information on the page is important, attract readers toward it by cueing them in one of several ways. Desktop publishing allows users to employ cueing devices like frames or boxes around text, bullets or arrows to designate important points, shading the part of the page behind the text, and changing the text in some way such as **boldface** or *italic* type. Captions for pictures, diagrams, and headings also help to guide the reader's attention.

* **Use white space well.** There is a saying in advertising that "white space sells." Don't be afraid to leave areas in a document with nothing in them at all; this will help focus attention on areas that do contain information.

* **Create and use graphics carefully.** Use pictures and designs to focus attention and convey information, but remember that too many elaborate pictures or graphic designs can be distracting.

* **Avoid common text format errors.** Parker (1989) describes ten desktop design pitfalls to avoid. These include irregularly shaped text blocks, angled type, excessive underlining, widows and orphans (leftover single words and phrases at the tops of pages), unequal spacing, excessive hyphenation, exaggerated tabs and indentations, grammatical errors, cramped logos and addresses, and too many typefaces.

To take full advantage of desktop publishing software, a system needs the right hardware and additional software. Remember some helpful resource hints:

* **Recommended hardware.** With any design elements, desktop publishing products always are more professional looking if printed on a laser printer rather than on a dot matrix printer. An optical scanner also is useful for importing existing pictures and other graphics into a document.

* **Recommended software tools.** Predesigned graphic tools can be very useful. One such tool is clip art packages, computer files of drawings and logos. These are available on disk or CD-ROM and can be combined with each other or with original drawings to produce a desired picture. Some people buy clip art books and scan the pieces of art into files as needed. Whenever a document will be reused with modifications, it is helpful to save it in a file of templates or predesigned products.

**Example classroom applications.** Desktop publishing software can be used for many of the same classroom activities and products as word processing software. Desktop publishing is the tool of choice, however, to produce elaborate, graphic-oriented documents. Teachers can use desktop publishing software to help them produce notices and documents for parents, students, or faculty members. Desktop publishing also can support some highly motivating classroom projects. Hermann (1988), McCarthy (1988), Newman (1988), and Willinsky and Bradley (1990) have reported instructional benefits of these uses for both students and teachers. These include increases in children's self-esteem when they publish their own work, heightened

**Figure 5.10  Example of Desktop Published Product**

Source: Courtesy of the Florida Design Initiative, Florida A&M University, School of Architecture.

interest in and motivation to write for audiences outside the classroom, and improved quality of instruction through teacher collaboration. A list of common classroom applications and ideas for implementing them include:

* **Letterhead.** Teachers can design their own individual stationery and encourage students to do the same for themselves or for the class. Students can design letterheads for their clubs or even for the school.

* **Flyers and posters.** Whenever teachers or students must design announcements, desktop publishing can turn the chore into an instructional adventure. A simple notice of an upcoming event can become an opportunity to learn about designing attractive and interesting communications. Teachers can smuggle in instruction in grammar and spelling.

* **Brochures.** For more extensive information than a simple flyer can convey or for information to be in a series, student projects can revolve around creating brochures. Popular examples of such classroom projects include travel brochures that report on student exploration during field trips, descriptions of the local region, and creative descriptions of organizations or activities.

* **Newsletters and magazines.** The literature has reported many examples of classroom projects built around student-designed newsletters or magazines. Sometimes this activity represents the culmination of a large project such as a series of science experiments or a social studies research unit; sometimes it simply is a way for every student to contribute writing for a class project. All these projects are highly motivational to students, and they attract "good press" for the teacher and the school. Figure 5.10 shows a cover page from a newsletter.

* **Books and booklets.** Even very young students are thrilled to produce and display their own personal books, which sometimes represent work produced over the course of a school year. Sometimes the books show creative works resulting from a competition; frequently, examples of students' best work is collected for a particular topic or time period. Students can sell their publications as a fund-raising activity, but this kind of project reaps other benefits for students of all abilities. One teacher of low-achieving students found that "making these

**Example Lesson 5.26
In the News (middle school)**

| | |
|---|---|
| **Developed by:** | Connie Skinner, Gla Culpepper, and Marsha Wiggam (Duval County, Florida); Elaine Myers, Florida Diagnostic Learning Resources System; NEFEC; and Jack Wright, Florida Diagnostic Learning Resources System/Crown Region |

**Lesson Purpose.** These activities show students the components of a news publication and how to produce a text and graphics layout for a publication.

**Instructional Activities.** Begin by discussing the project with students and showing them examples of the kind of publication they will produce. Focus on the parts of a news story by having them preview a local TV broadcast looking for specific facts in each news story (who, what, when, where, why). Go on field trips to the local newspaper and TV and radio stations to talk to the professionals at these locations. Have guest speakers from the local area such as newspaper reporters and TV and radio news reporters. Discuss the terminology of the newspaper (which students should have been hearing about in their field trips and from speakers). Do a hands-on exploration of example newspapers, identifying the parts of each one. Teach students how to use the desktop publishing program to produce each part of one of the example layouts. Then have students move on to designing their own newspaper. They form small groups, with each group working on a section of the publication, writing their own stories, laying them out, and editing the final product. Students who have artistic talent produce the graphics, emulating the examples they have seen in other newspapers.

Source: Skinner, C., Culpepper, G., Wiggam, M., Myers, E. & Wright, J. (1991). In the news. *The Florida Technology in Education Quarterly, 3*(2), 73–74.

books has really turned the kids around…. Getting published … had an enormous positive impact on … self confidence and self-esteem" (McCarthy, 1988, p. 25). (See Example Lesson 5.26.)

### Test Generators and Test Question Banks

Software tools help teachers with what many consider one of the most onerous and time-consuming of instructional tasks: producing on-paper tests. The teacher creates and enters the questions and the program prepares the test. The teacher either may print out the required number of copies on the printer or print only one copy and make the required copies on a copy machine. These tools have several advantages, even over word processing programs (Gullickson & Farland, 1991). For one, they produce tests in a standard layout; the teacher need not worry about arranging the spacing and format of the page. For another, such a program can automatically produce various forms or versions of the same test upon request. Changes, deletions, and updates to questions are also easy to accomplish, again without concern for page format. The features of test generators vary, but the following capabilities are common:

- **Test creation procedures.** The software prompts teachers to create tests item-by-item in formats such as multiple-choice, fill-in-the blank, true/false, matching, and—less often—short answer and essay.

- **Random generation of questions.** Test items are selected randomly from an item pool to create different versions. This

is especially helpful when a teacher wants to prevent "wandering eye syndrome" as students take a test.

- **Selection of questions based on criteria.** Programs usually allow teachers to specify criteria for generating a test. For example, items can be requested in a specific content area, matched to certain objectives, or in a certain format such as short answer items only.

- **Answer keys.** Most programs automatically provide an answer key at the time the test is generated. This is helpful with grading, especially if different versions of the test must be graded.

- **On-screen testing and grading.** Most test generators offer only on-paper versions of tests, but, as Figure 5.11 illustrates, some allow students to take the test on-screen after it is prepared. These programs usually also provide automatic test grading and performance summary statistics for each question. Many test generators allow use of existing question pools, or test question banks, and some offer these banks for purchase in various content areas. Some programs also import question banks prepared on word processors.

### Worksheet Generators

Teachers also use software to produce worksheets, which are very similar in many ways to test generators. *Worksheet generators* help teachers produce exercises for practice rather than tests. Like the test generator, the worksheet generator software prompts the teacher to enter questions of various kinds, but it usually offers no options for completing exercises on-screen or grading them. The most common worksheet generators deal with lower-level skills such as

**Figure 5.11   Sample Screen: Test Generator Software**

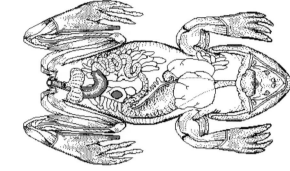

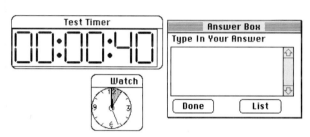

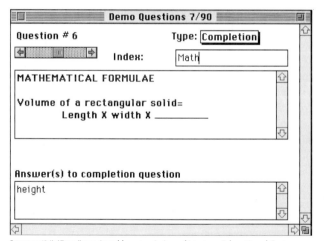

Source: "VisiFrog" reprinted by permission of Ventura Educational Systems.

math facts, but other programs are available to generate activities such as Cloze exercises. In many cases, test generator software and worksheet generator software are similar enough to be used interchangeably and some packages are intended for both purposes.

## Puzzle Generators

Tools that automatically format and create crossword and word search puzzles fall under a general category of tools called *puzzle generators*. The teacher enters the words and/or definitions and the software formats the puzzle. Children often are fascinated by word search puzzles, but

**Figure 5.12   Sample Screen: Bar-code Generator Software**

Source: Murdoch, N. (1992). BioSci babies. *The Florida Technology in Education Quarterly, 4*(2), 30–32.

these materials may have little instructional value other than reviewing spelling of new words. Crossword puzzles, on the other hand, can be used as exercises to review words and definitions or even low-level concepts.

## Bar-code Generators

One technological advancement that has provided great benefits to education is the ability to store large numbers of pictures and documents on optical media such as videodiscs and CD-ROMs. Collections of still and motion video images and pictures of important documents are available in a wide variety of topics ranging from science and history to art and music. However, teachers need more than availability to incorporate these resources into instruction; they must have a way to access them quickly as needed. This is the function of bar-code generating software. A bar-coded frame number can identify the location of each of the items stored on optical media. These bar codes look like the UPC codes on grocery items, as Figure 5.12 shows. Bar-code generating programs allow teachers to prepare pages of bar codes for pictures and information that relates to a given topic.

A science teacher can use this technology to show students examples of various transformations of energy by displaying images stored on a physical sciences videodisc. Before class, the teacher uses a bar-code generator program to prepare a page of bar codes designating the locations where the examples are stored. During class, the teacher runs a bar-code reader across each bar code and the desired picture displays on the screen. Students can also use this technique to generate their own project presentations or reports (see Example Lesson 5.27).

**Example Lesson 5.27**
**BioSci Babies (kindergarten)**

**Developed by:**        Doris Murdoch, Webster Elementary School (St. Augustine, Florida)

**Lesson Purposes.** Students identify various animals by name, compare them, and sort them according to whether or not they are hatched from eggs or born from their mothers.

**Instructional Activities.** The class reads *Baby Animals,* by Podendorf, or a similar book on baby animals. Using prepared bar-code sheets, show clips from the BioSci II Elementary videodisc (Videodiscovery) of various animals that hatch from eggs. Then show clips of animals that were born from their mothers. Ask, "How do these animals differ?" "How are they alike?" Pass out example stuffed animals to each of the children. Have them identify the animals and tell whether they think the animals were hatched or born. When all animals have been discussed, ask the children to draw a general conclusion about which animals are hatched and which give birth to their young. Follow up the lesson with other books such as *Are You My Mother?* (Eastman), *Horton Hatches an Egg* (Dr. Seuss), and *Baby Animals* (Kuchalla).

Source: Murdoch, D. (1992). BioSci babies. *The Florida Technology in Education Quarterly, 4*(2), 30–32.

## IEP Generators

The current restructuring movements in education have brought increasing emphasis on school and teacher accountability. With this comes an increase in paperwork on student progress. Teachers of special students, however, still seem to have the most paperwork requirements. Federal legislation such as PL 94–142 and the Americans with Disabilities Act require that schools prepare an individual educational plan, or IEP, for each special student. These IEPs serve as blueprints for each special student's instructional activities and teachers must provide documentation that such a plan is on file and that it governs classroom activities. Software is available to assist teachers in preparing IEPs (Lewis, 1993). Like test and worksheet generators, IEP generators provide on-screen prompts that remind users of the required components in the plan. When a teacher finishes entering all the necessary information, the program prints out the IEP in a standard format. Some IEP generation programs also accept data updates on each student's progress, thus helping teachers with required record-keeping as well as IEP preparation.

## Certificate Makers

Recognizing achievement is a powerful means of motivation. Teachers have found certificates to be a useful form of this recognition. Certificates congratulate students for accomplishments and the students can take them home and share them with parents and friends. Certificate makers simply provide computerized help with creating such products. Most certificate makers include templates for various typical achievements. The teacher selects one appropriate for the kind of recognition desired (completing an activity or first-place winner) and enters the personalizing information for each student. This software helps teachers produce certificates quickly and easily, so they can award them frequently.

## Form Makers

Like desktop publishing, form design is a special area of expertise that software can facilitate. Teachers must frequently create forms to collect information from students, parents, or faculty. Sometimes these forms are as simple as permission for students to participate in a class event, but they can become much more complicated. For example, a teacher may need forms to collect personal information from students for student records or to enter information on software packages as they are evaluated. Formatting even the simplest form can be time-consuming on a word processor. Form maker software structures the process and makes the design simple to accomplish. Most such packages have some graphic abilities, allowing users to add lines and boxes for desired information. As teachers create these forms, they can store them as templates for later use, perhaps with revisions.

## Groupware Products

Groupware is one of the newest technology tools. The term itself has been in the educational technology lexicon only since around 1991. It refers to software products designed to promote cooperative learning among groups of students by helping them document their work as they progress. Groupware usually resembles a special-purpose word processor that allows students to enter the results of work sessions and their contributions to the development of a product. Some packages allow links via modem, so students in more than one location can work on a cooperative project. Pearlman (1994) says that these products "stimulate group activity in a one-computer or sometimes no-computer classroom" (p. 1). Cowan (1992) describes three groupware products and gives some suggestions for using them effectively with students:

- Set and communicate ahead of time well-structured rules and procedures for using the groupware. These guidelines keep the students on task and prevent collaborative activities from becoming chaotic. Teachers should participate in and monitor sessions to enforce these rules.

- Make sure that all students have opportunities to express themselves so that one or two students do not control the process of entering information.

- Groupware takes teacher time and computer resources to use. Identify ahead of time places in the curriculum that seem likely to profit from groupware as opposed to word processing software. Use groupware to improve communication and collaboration skills.

## Using Data Collection and Analysis Tools

### Gradebooks

Although many teachers prefer to keep their grades on flexible spreadsheet software, some also prefer special software designed exclusively for this purpose. A gradebook (electronic gradekeeping) program allows a teacher to enter student names, test/assignment names, data from tests, and weighting information for specific test scores. The program then analyzes the data and prints out reports based on this information. Some gradebooks even offer limited-purpose word processing capabilities to enter notes about tests. The software automatically generates averages and weighted averages for each student and averages across all students on a given test. Gradebooks require less teacher set-up time than spreadsheets, but also allow less flexibility on format options. Wager (1992) describes the process and criteria one group of teachers used to select a gradebook for use throughout the school. Important criteria included:

- Capacity to track many tests/assignments
- Flexibility in report formats such as sorting by name and individual and group reports
- Wide range of peripheral support (use with various printers, networks)
- Ease of setup and use
- Use on multiple platforms

Stanton (1994) also reviewed gradebook packages according to a list of criteria. He noted some new capabilities to look for in an electronic gradebook, including generating graphs, making seating charts, and tracking attendance.

### Statistical Packages

As Gay (1993) joked, many teachers believe that the field of statistics should be renamed *sadistics*. Yet several kinds of instructional situations may interest teachers in statistical analyses. Brumbaugh and Poirot (1993), among others, maintain that teachers should take advantage of opportunities to do research in their classrooms. If teachers do choose to do classroom research, they must follow data collection with data analysis. Depending on the type of research, several typical analyses yield helpful information, including descriptive statistics such as means and standard deviations to inferential statistics such as t-tests and analyses of variance.

Software can also help with qualitative data collection and analysis. Teachers may perform statistical analysis of student performance on tests. Question analysis procedures help them analyze test questions they intend to use more than once. By changing and improving questions, teachers can make their tests more accurate and reliable. Finally, teachers may have to teach beginning statistics to their own students, for example, in a business education course.

Statistical software packages perform the calculations involved in any of these kinds of procedures. Naturally, a teacher must have considerable knowledge of the proper applications of various statistical procedures; the software merely handles the arithmetic. But this alone can save considerable time. Webster (1992) reviewed several statistical software packages for use in business education courses and found that the packages varied considerably in their usefulness for this purpose.

### Data Management (CMI) and Testing Tools

**Definitions: CMI versus data management.** The term *computer managed instruction,* or *CMI,* is left over from when nearly all education technology software could be classified as CMI or CAI (see Chapter 1). As early as 1978, Baker admitted that a precise description of CMI did not exist because of "definitions that are as diverse as the number of existing systems" (p. 11). Baker gave examples of several such systems that were popular at the time, noting widely varying characteristics. Among these systems were the Teaching Information Processing System (TIPS), the Sherman School System, and the Program for Learning in Accordance with Needs (PLAN). At that time, there was a burgeoning interest in mastery learning in which teachers specified a sequence of objectives for students to learn and prescribed instruction to help the students master each objective. Clearly, the teacher had to keep track of each student's performance on each objective—a mammoth recordkeeping task. CMI systems running on large, mainframe computers were designed to support teachers in these efforts.

Today's teachers emphasize mastery learning less than keeping students on task and monitoring their progress to make sure their work is challenging, not frustrating. Some educators feel the term CMI has always been a misnomer for a recordkeeping routine within an instructional system rather than a type of instructional delivery. However, software

Figure 5.13  **Example ILS Data Report**

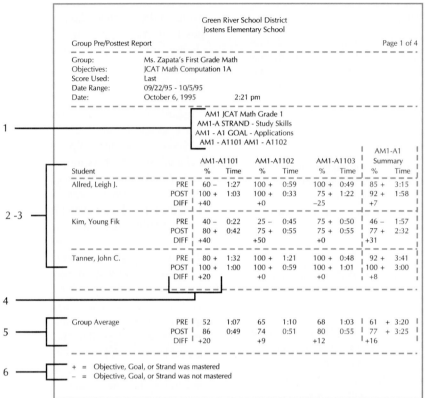

Source: *Reports Guide* by Jostens Learning Corporation. © 1991 by Jostens Learning Corp. Used by permission.

**Objectives**

1. Objectives on this report shown in their hierarchical structure

**Individual Student Data**

2. Names of selected students

3. For each student, percentage scores and mastery status on two administrations of a test, including total time in minutes and seconds (optional)

4. For each objective, pretest scores (PRE), posttest scores (POST), and the difference between them (DIFF)

**Group Data**

5. Group averages showing percentage correct, time, and difference between pretest and posttest for each objective

**Legend**

6. Codes used on the report:
   + for mastered objectives
   – for non-mastered objectives

tools still are available—now on microcomputers and networks—to store and analyze data on student progress during instruction and to provide summary progress reports. The purpose for collecting the data may be different, but the recordkeeping task is still considerable. Although some people still call this software CMI, others refer to it simply as *data management software.*

**Types and functions of data management tools.** Roblyer (1992) identified three different kinds of computerized data management tools: components of computer-based learning systems, computerized testing systems, and test scoring and data analysis systems.

*Components of computer-based learning systems.* These tools allow teachers to enter names and other student information. When each student types in his or her name, the system presents a sequence of activities tailored to that student's needs. The system also collects data as students go through the instruction. Reports show the teacher what students have accomplished and point out areas where they may still need assistance and off-line work. Although some standalone microcomputer-based packages have these tools built into the software, these systems are more commonly seen as components of networked integrated learning systems (ILSs) and integrated technology systems. These systems have the power and capacity to handle large amounts of data on student performance.

***Computerized testing systems.*** With these tools, students receive actual instruction elsewhere, usually by noncomputer media. Computers facilitate on-screen testing and recordkeeping after instruction. Sometimes known as *computer-assisted testing (CAT),* these tools generate test forms and process performance data. They differ from test generators, which allow on-screen testing but do not give detailed reports on results for individuals and groups. Some of the major standardized tests such as the SAT and GRE are now given on computerized testing systems. These systems offer many benefits, including immediate knowledge of results. Tests can also be shorter, since the systems assess each person's ability level with fewer questions. This is because the software continuously analyzes performance and presents more or less difficult questions based on the student's performance, a capability known as *computer adaptive testing* (CAT) (Strommen, 1994). CAT is used more and more frequently for testing in professional courses like those in nursing education. The capabilities of computerized testing systems let educators go beyond the limits of multiple-choice tests and make possible alternative assessments. These systems also simplify test scheduling, since everyone need not take tests at the same time.

***Test scoring and data analysis systems.*** These types of data management tools accept test data input either through the keyboard or by optically scanning bubble sheets. Tests are automatically scored and reports on the results are generated. Both devices and sheets are available from companies such as National Computer Systems (NCS) or Scantron.

All of these data management systems serve two primary purposes. First, they provide clerical support for all of the calculation and paperwork tasks required to track student progress. Second, they help teachers to match instruction to the needs of each student. Each type of system provides various kinds of reports about student progress. ILS management systems usually provide the most extensive reporting. They include a wealth of feedback ranging from the number of test questions answered correctly and incorrectly on a student's test to summary data on the performance of whole classes in a topic area. One example of these reports is shown in Figure 5.13.

## Using Graphics Tools

### Print Graphics Packages

These software tools have a limited purpose, but one that many teachers find indispensable. Print graphics packages essentially are simple word processors designed especially

**Figure 5.14   Example Print Graphics Product**

for quick and easy production of one-page signs, banners, and greeting cards. One graphics program, *Print Shop Deluxe* (Brøderbund), has become one of the best-selling software packages in education. Teachers can find hundreds of uses for the products of print graphics software ranging from door signs to decorations for special events. Some schools have even held contests to design the most creative signs or banners using this program. The graphics and other options in the program are selected from menus, making the programs so easy to use that anyone can sit down and create a product in a matter of minutes. One example print product is shown in Figure 5.14.

### Draw/Paint and Image Programs

To produce more complex hard-copy graphics, draw/paint programs are the technology tool of choice. These tools usually are used to create designs and pictures that are then imported into desktop publishing systems or desktop presentation tools, as described in the following section. Just as print graphics programs are known for their simplicity and limited options, draw/paint programs are known for their sophistication and wide-ranging capabilities. Many of these packages such as *Aldus Freehand* or *Adobe PhotoShop* require considerable time to learn and implement. But some, like *Kid Pix* in Figure 5.15, are designed specifically for children to use without formal training. Catchings and MacGregor (1998) are among those who believe that draw/paint programs allow many students to develop their visual-verbal literacy and creativity. Example

**Figure 5.15    Example Draw/Paint Software Screen**

Source: Reproduced using Kid Pix®; ©1992, Brøderbund Software, Inc. All Rights Reserved. Used by Permission.

Lessons 5.28–5.30 illustrate some of the many instructional uses for draw/paint programs.

## Presentation Software and Computer Projection Systems

**Definitions and types.** Presentation software packages help users create on-screen descriptions, demonstrations, and summaries of information. Presentation tools represent a notable example of a technology that migrated from business and industry to education. These tools were first adopted by business executives and salespeople who used them to give reports at meetings and presentations to clients. Their capabilities to demonstrate, illustrate, and clarify information became evident and presentation tools began to make their way into K-12 and university classrooms.

The programs allow more flexibility than print graphics programs in the selection of features, allowing a user to choose from an array of text, graphics, and animation. Hoffman (1994) reported that presentation tools began exclusively as "electronic slide shows," but have evolved into an additional kind of presentation product: *multimedia authoring tools,* which allow users to incorporate motion sequences from CD-ROM and other video media into their presentations (see Figure 5.16). Therefore, hypermedia software (discussed in detail in Chapter 8) are used frequently as presentation software.

**Making the most of presentation software: Skills and resources.** As with desktop publishing, the effectiveness of a presentation tool depends largely on the communications skills of the presenter. For large classes and other groups, presentation software products usually are used in conjunction with computer projection systems. These may be devices such as LCD panels that fit on top of overhead projectors or systems that operate as standalone devices. All of these devices enlarge the image produced by the software by projecting it from a computer screen onto a wall screen.

**Example classroom applications of presentation software.** These are especially useful for teacher presentations

---

### Example Lesson 5.28
### Map Skills with *Kid Pix* (grade 3)

**Developed by:**    Dennis Day, Westhill Elementary School (Bothell, Washington)

**Lesson Purposes.** Students use the *Kid Pix* drawing program to design a map as an introduction to a unit on basic geography skills.

**Instructional Activities.** This activity is the beginning of a 4-week unit on geography skills. It begins with a whole-class demonstration of *Kid Pix* on the computer projection system. Students are given handouts describing the requirements of the project they will do and giving an example product. The map they produce should include a compass rose with an arrow and an N for North, a map title, a date, and seven map symbols of their choice. After a session for hands-on exploration of *Kid Pix,* they are given time to design and produce their own maps. If certain students have trouble getting organized, the teacher might try assigning elements and symbols for them to use in their maps. Students may also find it better to use the mini-word processor in *Kid Pix* to label their maps rather than pointing and dragging individual letters from the alphabet menu.

Source: Day, D. (1994). Active mapping. *The Computing Teacher, 21*(5), 27–28.

### Example Lesson 5.29
### Exploring Tessellations with Computer Art (high school)

**Developed by:**  Rick Wigre

**Lesson Purposes.** This lesson combines art and mathematics by focusing on how to draw *tessellations*—the complete covering of a plane by one or more figures in a repeating pattern, with no overlapping of the figures. The author points out that this kind of lesson can be carried out in various ways, including math and art teachers exchanging classes for two weeks or both teachers integrating math and art into their instruction.

**Instructional Activities**

*Preparation.* Begin by helping students see that tessellations are one of the "building blocks of nature and the visual arts" (p. 15). Show students presentations of various artists' work such as Cole, Rickwell, Varsarlly, and Escher. Show examples of tessellations in art and nature by using slides, pictures, and nature objects; by looking at examples of art works by Escher; by looking at the use of patterns in the folk art works of various cultures; and by using books such as *Creating Escher-type Drawings,* by Ranucci and Teeters and *Tessellations: The Geometry of Patterns,* by Bezuszka, Kenney, and Silvey.

*Introducing the Drawing Software.* Show students drawing/painting software features such as paint and pencil tools, erase, and zoom in and zoom out and basic computer operations such as copy/cut/paste and save. Introduce basic vocabulary:

- **Tessellation.** The complete covering of a plane by one or more figures in a repeating pattern, with no overlapping of the figures.
- **Transformations.** The figure slides across the plane so that all points are parallel.
- **Rotations.** The figure rotates so that all points may rotate from the center or from any point on the plane.
- **Reflections.** The figure rotates at 180°.

(See example figures in the lesson on the accompanying CD.)

*Using Tiling.* Ask students to use one of the following shapes to create a tiled design: equilateral triangles, squares, rectangles, or hexagons. Show them how to create the tessellation by combining polygons and by using transformations of each shape. After they cover the page with their design, students can use shading or colors to get a more finished look.

*Introducing the Mathematics of Tessellations.* Use one of the following geometric shapes to create a tessellation:

- **Equilateral triangle.** Use an equilateral triangle to create an interlocking figure and use the figure to create a tessellation.
- **Rectangle.** Alter at least one side of a rectangle so that it will interlock with itself and use the resulting figure to create a tessellation.
- **Hexagon.** Alter at least one side of a hexagon so that it will interlock with itself and use the resulting figure to create a tessellation. One can make a transformation of a hexagonal shape by moving the newly created lines left to right and up to down or rotating diagonally. Develop a hexagonal tessellation with an even more complex look by drawing the shapes, removing the hexagon, and letting the form interlock with itself.

*Tessellations with Images.* Select an equilateral triangle, a square rectangle, or a hexagon and create a tessellation by using transformations, rotations, and reflections of each shape. Within these shapes, create an image. Finish it by using color or shading.

*Hexagonal Kaleidocycles.* Create shapes that interlock with tessellated images and turn these into a three-dimensional form by pasting the images onto hexagonal kaleidocycles.

Source: Wigre, R. (1993–1994). Reflections on tessellations. *The Computing Teacher, 21*(4), 15–16.

**Example Lesson 5.30**
**Drawing in the Art Curriculum (high school)**

**Developed by:**          Rick Wigre, Everett High School (Everett, Washington)

**Lesson Purposes.** Students use drawing programs in an introductory art course to pave the way for integrating art into other curriculum areas.

**Instructional Activities.** Students are first introduced to draw/paint programs in an introductory art course taught in the freshman year. This course is also a good base for computer art courses, which are designed to integrate with other disciplines. Students use visual communication skills they learn through the draw/paint programs to develop products and assignments for many other courses. For example, they may use computer images to present reports in history or science. The computer art course begins with two weeks of introduction to an array of computer art and graphics in which students write and talk about what they see. They refer back to visual concepts taught in the introductory art class. During this time, students also become familiar with looking up visual images in the library and using them as resources. They spend the rest of the course learning basic drawing features such as tiling (creating a design and covering a page with it) and use of clip art, as well as more advanced skills that combine a variety of drawing features. They also learn use of other equipment, such as the camcorder and laserdisc to design presentations. The art teacher works closely with teachers in other disciplines to develop assignments that make use of these drawing/presentation skills.

Source: Wigre, R. (1993–1994). Reflections on tessellations. *The Computing Teacher, 21*(4), 15–16.

to whole classes of students but can also be used to enhance conference presentations or talks to large groups. They can enhance instruction in traditional large-group lecture courses (Bolduc, Hale, & Webb, 1994) or increase the effectiveness of a distance learning curriculum (Joiner & Alvarez, 1994). Presentation software is not just for teachers; Granning (1994) describes how student skills with presentation tools have become the focal point for a high

**Figure 5.16    Example Presentation Screen: Presentation Software**

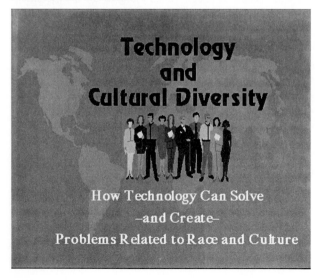

school program to develop communications skills. Every student in the program is required to put together presentations that combine computer-generated graphics, audio, and video (see Example Lesson 5.31).

### Charting/Graphing Software

Charting and graphing software tools automatically draw and print out desired charts or graphs from data entered by users. The skills involved in reading, interpreting, and producing graphs and charts are useful both to students in school and adults in the workplace. However, those with limited artistic ability face special challenges in learning and using these skills. Fortunately, charting and graphing software take the mechanical drudgery out of producing these useful "data pictures." If students do not have to labor over rulers and pencils as they try to plot coordinates and set points, they can concentrate on the more important aspects of the graphics: the meaning of the data and what they represent. As Duren (1990–1991) observed, this kind of activity supports students in their efforts at visualizing mathematical concepts and engaging in inquiry tasks. Graphing activities in science, social studies, and geography also profit from applications of these kinds of software tools. Moersch (1995) lists and gives example instructional applications for 10 kinds of software-produced graphs: bar, pie, stacked bar, X/Y, scatter, box, stem and leaf, best fit, and normal curve (see Example Lesson 5.32).

**Example Lesson 5.31**
**Book Reports with Presentation Software (grade 5)**

**Developed by:**    Dan Lake

**Lesson Purposes.** Book reports take on new motivation and interest—both to those giving them and those hearing them—when these reports are given in a slide show format with presentation software.

**Instructional Activities**
*Choosing the Events.* Students begin by selecting 10–15 events from the textbook that were most exciting or most important in shaping the story. They briefly write down summaries of the events.

*Creating the Slides.* The teacher shows the students how to use the software to insert text and graphics on a slide. The students develop a title page and one frame or slide per event. The teacher works with them to use shortcuts from frame to frame to make the work go faster.

*Presenting the Reports.* The students print a hard copy of all the frames from their report in smaller versions on one or two pages. Below each frame, they make notes on what they want to say about it. They use this to guide their report as they project and go through the slides. After the classroom presentations, the reports also can be set up to run at a PTA meeting or parent's night or in the library.

Source: Lake, D. (1990). Patrick's visual: A book report using presentation software. *The Computing Teacher, 17*(8), 54–55.

**Example Lesson 5.32**
**A Project with Teeth (elementary)**

**Developed by:**    Diana Boehm, Principal, Internet Schoolhouse

**Lesson Purposes.** Teachers use e-mail to connect their K-3 students with "keypals" around the world in order to exchange information on how many teeth children lose during the year. This activity is used as a springboard for learning geography (locations of the keypals), literature and culture (tooth fairy traditions and other stories from their regions), art (creating pictures or murals illustrating tooth fairy traditions), creative writing (e-mail messages to participants, poems and rhymes on teeth), and mathematics (graphing data on lost teeth).

**Instructional Activities.** Begin by preparing a bulletin board to stay in the classroom throughout the length of the project. Place on it a large happy face and 13 large "teeth" made out of paper, cardboard, or tag board. The first twelve teeth should each be labeled with a month of the year and the last should say, "I still have all of my teeth." Each time a student loses a tooth, write the name of the student on the "tooth" with the month in which it was lost. Find out from parents which students have lost teeth prior to the beginning of the project and label the appropriate months for them. Names of students who have lost no teeth are put on the "I still have all of my teeth" sign.
   Do the following activities as part of the unit:

1.   **The introductory e-mail message.** With the students' input, write a letter describing the project. Include a time line (a semester or a school year); how you will communicate your results to each other (e-mail, snail-mail, graphs); and information you would like to have them send each month (their locations, number of teeth participating students have lost, local traditions about lost teeth, and items of information about their regions).

2.   **A class story.** After you have gathered stories from other students, begin a class story on tooth traditions and legends. You can assign each student to write a part of the story and enter the text into a word processing file as students dictate their paragraphs to you.

*Continued*

3.  **Locating participants.** Give each student a world map. As participants send their responses, have students mark and/or color the location on the map from where the message was sent. Also have globes and wall maps around the room for students to examine as responses come in.

4.  **Tooth fairy mural.** Have students use art media or a graphics program such as *KidPix* to create illustrations for the tooth fairy stories and tooth traditions they have gathered. They can also add their own poems and rhymes to the mural.

5.  **E-mail letters.** Show students how to create, send, receive, and print e-mail messages. Students may work individually or in small groups to prepare their messages.

6.  **Graphing lost tooth data.** After you have at least three months of data on lost teeth, show students how to use a spreadsheet or graphing program to compile the data and prepare line or bar graphs. Each student or small group may choose a part of the data to graph; then compose a letter explaining the results to their keypals. As a cumulative or final whole-class activity, students may use a calculator to add up all the teeth data for each month from all the schools and then enter all the data into one common spreadsheet. Results may be shared among the participants through e-mail.

Source: Boehm. D. (1997). I lost my tooth! *Learning and Leading with Technology, 24*(7), 17–19.

### Clip Art Packages, Video Collections, and Sound Collections

Clip art packages are collections of still pictures drawn by artists and graphics designers and placed in a book or on a disk for use by others. When teachers prepare presentations with desktop publishing or presentation tools, they need not use draw/paint programs to draw original pictures. A wealth of pictures is available in the form of clip art. Most word processing and desktop publishing systems can import clip art stored on disk into a document. Draw/paint programs can also import clip art for use in designing other pictures and graphic images. Clip art from a book may be optically scanned into a computer file and stored on a disk for use with these programs. When more realistic depictions are desired, actual pictures stored on video media such as CD-ROM and videodisc may be imported in the same way.

Clip art packages and video collections are invaluable tools to help both teachers and students illustrate and decorate their written products. Teachers find that such pictures help make flyers, books, and even letters and notices look more polished and professional. Some teachers feel that students are more motivated to write their own stories and reports when they can also illustrate them.

For teachers and students who want to develop their own multimedia presentations, collections of sound effects and movie clips are also becoming more common. A system may need special hardware such as sound cards or synthesizers or software such as *Quicktime,* a movie-making software, in order to incorporate these elements.

### Digitizing Systems and Video Development Systems

Several other kinds of tools help users prepare graphics for both print and on-screen presentations. Digitizing programs are software tools that handle pictures scanned into the computer and stored as picture files. Users can edit these pictures as needed or include them as they are. With Apple's QuickTake camera and similar devices, teachers can take pictures as they would with any camera, storing the images on disk instead of on film. They can then import the photos into video presentations or desktop publishing products. Kodak's Photo CD is a unique product that digitizes images from 35mm film and stores them on CDs (Jones, 1994). The number of products that assist with graphics production is increasing and new capabilities to develop and import images are constantly being developed. Teachers and students can even use movie-making software in their graphics productions.

## Using Planning and Organizing Tools

### Outlining Tools and Other Writing Aids

Several kinds of technology tools are available to help students learn writing skills or to assist accomplished writers in setting their thoughts in order prior to writing. Outlining tools are designed to prompt writers as they develop outlines to structure documents they plan to write. For example, the software may automatically indent and/or supply the appropriate number or letter for each line in the outline. Outliners are offered either within word processing packages or as separate software packages for use before word processing.

Other writing aids include software designed to get students started on writing reports or stories: a *story starter*. This kind of program provides a first line and invites students to supply subsequent lines. Other tools give students topic ideas and supply information about each topic they can use in a writing assignment. Sometimes a software package combines outlining tools and other writing aids.

### Brainstorming and Concept Mapping Tools

These might also be called *conceptualizing tools*, since they help people think through and explore ideas or

Figure 5.17   **Example Concept Map**

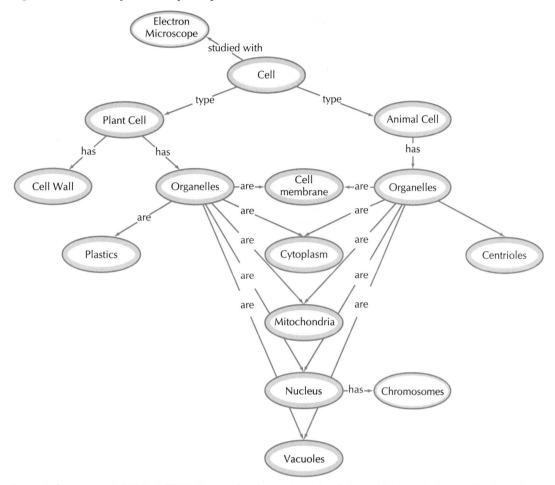

Source: Anderson-Inman, L. & Zeitz, L. (1993). Computer-based concept mapping: Active studying for active learners. *The Computing Teacher, 21*(1), 6–8, 10–11. Used by permission of ISTE.

topics. One such tool, *Idea Fisher,* provides semantic connections with given words. For example, if a user were to click on the word *whale,* the program might display several words associated with whales such as *ocean* and *sea life* as well as some less obvious connections such as *endangered species.* The program can also ask probing questions to provoke thoughts about each topic selected. Another program, *Inspiration,* assists brainstorming by helping people develop concept maps. Concept maps are visual outlines of ideas that can offer useful alternatives to the strictly verbal representations provided by content outlines (see Figure 5.17). Anderson-Inman and Zeitz (1993) and Kahn (1997) give good examples of classroom applications for concept mapping tools (see Example Lesson 5.33).

## Lesson Planning Tools

Most teachers do not rely heavily on written lesson plans to guide their teaching activities. However, many occasions demand some form of documentation to show what teachers are teaching and how they are teaching it. Tools that help teachers develop and document their descriptions of

lessons are sometimes called *lesson makers* or *lesson planners.* Most of these programs simply provide on-screen prompts for specific lesson components such as objectives, materials, and activity descriptions. They also print out lessons in standard formats, similar to the way test generators format printouts of tests.

## Schedule/Calendar Makers and Time Management Tools

Several kinds of tools have been designed to help teachers organize their time and plan their activities. Schedule makers help formulate plans for daily, weekly, or monthly sequences of appointments and events. Calendar makers are similar planning tools that actually print out graphic calendars of chosen months or years with the planned events printed under each day. Other time management tools are available to help remind users of events and responsibilities. The teacher enters activities and the dates on which they will occur. Then, when he or she turns on the computer each day, the software displays on the screen a list of things to do. Some integrated packages combine all these tools.

---

**Example Lesson 5.33**
**Concept Mapping (grade 11)**

**Developed by:**          Lynn Anderson-Inman and Leigh Zeitz

**Lesson Purposes.** This activity introduces concept mapping as a way to represent a specific knowledge domain in graphic form. Concept-mapping software eases the logistics of constructing and modifying the maps.

**Instructional Activities.** Student-created concept maps (also called semantic maps or webs) can help learners construct knowledge by providing a vehicle for integrating new information with that learned previously. Because the learner plays an active role in creating and modifying the concept map, this study strategy promotes active learning and student involvement. Prior to reading an assigned chapter, students are asked to create a concept map for a set of terms. Then while reading the chapter, the students revise their maps to include newly learned information and clarify newly understood relationships. After classroom instruction and discussion, they might modify their maps again. Depending on the complexity of the material, this process might be modified several times. An example is an assignment in biology. Students are asked to learn about the structure of cells; they are given 11 important vocabulary words. They create a concept map showing how they feel these terms are related. Using *Inspiration* concept mapping software, each term is placed in a node and the lines linking the nodes are labeled. After reading the chapter on "Cell Structure," students revise their maps. After a classroom discussion of the topic, students are given another opportunity to revise their maps. On the last day of the unit, the teacher suggests augmenting the concept maps once again in preparation for the test. More detailed information for some concepts is placed into note windows linked to each node.

---

Source: Anderson-Inman, L. & Zeitz, L. (1993). Computer-based concept mapping: Active study for active learners. *The Computing Teacher, 12*(1), 6–8, 10–11.

## Using Research and Reference Tools

### Electronic Encyclopedias

For many years, American families kept sets of encyclopedias to support their children's education. Young people used these books for research on school projects and parents used them to take advantage of "teachable moments" when their children required more than quick answers. Now most major encyclopedias come on CD-ROM with some kind of database structure. CD-ROM encyclopedias have several advantages over books. Users can search to locate one specific item or all references on a given topic. They usually offer multimedia formats that include sound and/or film clips as well as hypertext links to related information on any topic. Chapters 7 and 8 present more information on and examples of disc-based encyclopedia applications.

### Atlases

Like encyclopedias, atlases are popular educational reference tools for families as well as schools. They summarize geographic and demographic information ranging from population statistics to national products. CD-ROM versions of these atlases are especially helpful since they are so interactive. Students can see information on a specific country or city or gather information on all countries or cities that meet certain criteria (see Figure 5.18). Some atlases even play national songs on request!

### Dictionaries (Word Atlases)

Sometimes called *word atlases,* CD-ROM dictionaries specify pronunciation, definition, and example uses for

**Figure 5.18    Example Screen from an Atlas**

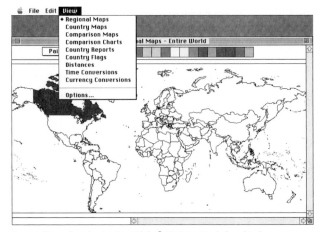

Source: Reproduced using MacGlobe®; ©1992, Brøderbund Software, Inc. All Rights Reserved. Used by Permission.

each word entry. They also offer many search and multimedia features similar to those of encyclopedias and atlases. Many CD-ROM dictionaries can play an audio clip of the pronunciation of any desired word, a capability of special help to young users and others who cannot read diacritical marks.

## Using Tools to Support Specific Content Areas

### CAD and 3-D Modeling/Animation Systems

A *computer-assisted design (CAD)* system is a special kind of graphics production tool that allows users to prepare sophisticated, precise drawings of objects such as houses and cars. Like presentation tools, CAD systems began to appear in classrooms after their introduction in business and industry. This kind of software is usually employed in vocational-technical classrooms to teach architecture and engineering skills. However, some teachers use CAD software to teach drawing concepts in art and related topics. More advanced graphics students may use 3-D modeling and animation software systems to do fancy visual effects such as morphing. (See Figure 5.19 for a sample of CAD software.)

### Music Editors and Synthesizers

Music editor software provides blank musical bars on which the user enters the musical key, time, and individual notes that constitute a piece of sheet music. This software is designed to help people develop musical compositions on-screen, usually in conjunction with hardware such as a musical instrument digital interface (MIDI) keyboard and music synthesizer. This hardware allows the user to either hear the music after it is written or create music on the keyboard and automatically produce a written score. Steinhaus (1986–1987) explained that music editors offer powerful assistance in the processes of precomposing, composing, revising, and even performing. Forest (1993) offers examples of these activities in a school setting as well as a list of good music-related software and media. Ohler's (1998) thorough review of MIDI technology and its current applications for teaching music reminds us that technology tools can help students "flex the musical muscle that (Howard) Gardner reminds us has always been there" (p. 10). (See Chapter 14 for more classroom uses of these tools.)

### Reading Tools

Both reading teachers and teachers of other topics occasionally need to determine the approximate reading level of specific documents. A teacher may want to select a story or book for use in a lesson or to confirm that works are correctly labeled as appropriate for certain grade levels. Several methods are available for calculating the reading

**Figure 5.19   Sample Screen from CAD Software**

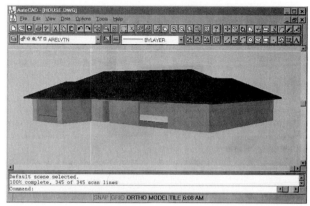

Source: Courtesy of Bill Wiencke.

level of a written work; all of them are time-consuming and tedious to do by hand. Readability analysis software automates calculations of word count, average word length, number of sentences, or other measures of reading difficulty.

Another software tool related to reading instruction, Cloze software, provides passages with words missing in a given pattern, for example, every fifth word or every tenth word. Students read the sentences and try to fill in the words. Cloze passages have been found to be good measures of reading comprehension. Some teachers also like to use them as exercises to improve reading comprehension.

Many books for children as well as adults are available in interactive CD-ROM versions (Truett, 1993). Some of these allow children to hear narrations in English or Spanish. Others, like the Living Books series (*Just Grandma and Me*), let children explore the screen, activating animations and sounds when they click in various locations. These books are designed to provide an interesting, interactive way to read and increase reading fluency.

### MBLs (Probeware)

A technology tool that has proven particularly useful in science classrooms is the microcomputer-based labs (MBL), sometimes referred to as *probeware*. When these probes are connected to a graphing calculator as opposed to a computer (as described in the following section), they also are called Calculator-Based Labs (CBLs). MBL packages consist of software accompanied by special hardware probes designed to measure light, temperature, voltage, and/or speed (see Figure 5.20). The probes are connected to the microcomputer and the software processes the data collected by the probes. Bitter, Camuse, and Durbin (1993) said that microcomputer probeware actually can replace several items of lab equipment such as oscilloscopes and voltmeters because MBLs outperform this traditional equipment. Ladelson (1994) points out that probeware achieves a dual purpose of gathering empirical data and revealing the relationship between science and

**Figure 5.20    Example Probeware**

Source: Courtesy of Vernier Software.

**Figure 5.21    TI Graphing Calculator**

Source: Courtesy of Texas Instruments.

math. Stanton (1992) describes a variety of MBLs, covering their capabilities and prices along with grade levels and science subjects they can help teach (see Figure 5.20 and Example Lessons 5.34 and 5.35).

### Graphing Calculator

For many years, calculators have played a widespread— and often controversial—role in mathematics education. Currently, even more capable, software-programmed devices called graphing calculators (see Figure 5.21) are becoming prominent in both mathematics and higher-level

science curriculum. Albrecht and Firedrake (1997) describe uses in Physics instruction using these devices in conjunction with the Internet and what they call "data-grabbing devices" (probeware, MBLs, or CBLs). Borenstein (1997) reviews uses of graphing calculators to make possible various experiments and concept demonstrations in algebra.

---

### Example Lesson 5.34
### Exploring the Relationship between Science and Mathematics (high school)

**Developed by:**        Louis Nadelson

**Lesson Purposes.** Students use the line equation in the software that is intended for calibrating the probes in the MBL probeware to explore mathematical concepts underlying the general linear equation $y = mx + b$ (where $m$ = slope and $b$ = the $y$ intercept).

**Instructional Activities.** Many different probeware setups require users to calibrate prior to using it for data collection. This process establishes a relationship between the input to the computer from the probe and the value that the measurement represents. The software also gives instruction on how to do the calibration. For example, if the MBL is measuring voltage, the probe is calibrated by connecting it to a AA battery previously confirmed by a multimeter to output 1.5 volts. The computer registers 215 counts for 1.5 volts. The beginning point of 0 counts and the ending point of 215 defines a line. This line is used to calibrate the probe.

After the probe is calibrated, an equation is developed for the line (0, 0 and 215, 1.5). Students sketch the graph of the line defined by these points using either paper or graphing software. They predict values for counts given specific voltages using their graph by locating the value on the $x$ axis and finding the corresponding $y$ value for counts. They use the general linear equation $y = mx + b$ to discuss the slope of the line as the rise (vertical distance between the two points) divided by the run (horizontal distance between the points). The teacher has the students calculate the slope for their lines. They enter the value for the slope into the general linear equation and do the final equation for the example calibration. Once the equation has been determined, students calculate counts for specific voltages. When the probe is ready to be used, students bring in samples to be tested.

Source: Nadelson, L. (1994). Calibrating probeware: Making a line. *The Computing Teacher, 21*(6), 46–47.

**Example Lesson 5.35**
**The Magnetic Field in a Slinky® (middle–high school)**

Developed by:                 Vernier Software (www.verniwer.com)

**Lesson Purposes.** Students use the Vernier magnetic field sensor to determine the relationship between (a) magnetic field and the current in a solenoid and (b) the magnetic field and the number of turns per meter in a solenoid.

**Instructional Activities.** Connect the Vernier magnetic field sensor to the universal lab interface on a Macintosh or Windows PC computer and set the switch on the sensor to high. Stretch the Slinky® until it is about 1 meter in length. Set up the equipment. (See the Setup for Probeware Experiment lesson on the accompanying CD.)

Wires with clips on the end should be used to connect to the Slinky®. Turn on the power and set the ammeter to read "2.0 A" when the switch is held closed. (Warn students not to leave the power on continuously or the current going through them will make the wires and Slinky® very hot.)

Prepare the computer for data collection and have students begin the testing to answer the following questions:

- Which direction in the Slinky® gives the largest magnetic field reading?
- How does the magnetic field inside the solenoid seem to vary along its length?

To determine the relationship between magnetic field and the current in a solenoid, hold the switch closed and place the magnetic field sensor between the coils of the Slinky® near the center. Rotate the sensor to find the direction that gives the largest magnetic field reading. Check the magnetic field intensity in various locations of the Slinky®, as well as just outside it. Collect the data on these observations and analyze the data to answer the question.

Next, gather data to determine how the relationship between a magnetic field in a solenoid is related to the spacing of the turns. Change the length of the Slinky® to 0.5 m, 1.5 m, and to 2.0 m to change the number of turns per meter. Adjust the power supply to "1.5 A" when the switch is closed and collect data on each length to address the question.

Students can discuss their findings and the implications for other experiments with magnetic fields.

Source: Contributed by Vernier Software.

# Exercises

## Record and Apply What You Have Learned

**Activity 5.1: Chapter 5 Self-Test** To review terms and concepts in this chapter, take the Chapter 5 self-test. Select Chapter 5 from the front page of the companion Web site (located at http://www.prenhall.com/roblyer), then choose the *Multiple Choice* module.

**Activity 5.2: Portfolio Activities** The following activities will help you add to your professional portfolio. To complete these activities online and save or submit the materials electronically, select Chapter 5 from the front page of the companion Web site (http://www.prenhall.com/roblyer), then choose the *Portfolio* module.

*Software Tools List* Prepare a list of each of the software tools described in this chapter with which you have had hands-on experience. For each one, describe how you plan to use it in your classroom.

*Tool Templates* Choose an appropriate software tool and develop a template you can use from year-to-year for each of the following purposes:

a.   Classroom letterhead

b.   Records (names, addresses, birthdates) for students in your classes

c.   Gradekeeping

d.   Event announcement flyer

e.   Test item form and item bank for your subject area

**Activity 5.3: Questions for Thought and Discussion** These questions may be used for small group or class discussion or may be subjects for individual or group activities. To take part in these discussions online, select Chapter 5 from the front page of the companion Web site (http://www.prenhall.com/roblyer), then choose the *Message Board* module.

- Word processing is a software valued by many teachers but is criticized by some who feel it is ruining our handwriting and making us over-reliant on technology to do our writing. How would you respond to these critics?

- The increasing use of databases in our society, combined with pervasive use of the Internet, is making it very easy to get access to personal information about anyone. What implications arise regarding the safety and privacy of students in our schools? What is the teacher's role in these privacy and security issues?

**Activity 5.4: Collaborative Activities** The following may be developed in small group work. Completed group products may be copied and shared with the entire class and/or included in each person's Personal Portfolio.

*Create a Newsletter* Use desktop publishing software to create a newsletter for the school, classroom, or student organization. Each small group can create a section or page of the newsletter such as Notes from the Faculty, Principal Page, Music Events, and so on.

*Flyer Competition* The class works in pairs to develop a flyer announcing a school event or advocating a position on a topic of current interest to the school or community. Each pair uses draw/paint software in conjunction with available clip art and scanned photos. After all flyers are printed, ask faculty members and/or parents to be judges to select the ones with the greatest impact. Post the winner and runners-up on a school bulletin board. Discuss what qualities made the winners the best.

*Create a Test* Make a list of all the tools described in this chapter and have each small group select one or two. Have them develop five descriptions of applications teachers might do with each one. Place these descriptions in a test generator and create several versions of a review in which students must match tools appropriate for the applications. Have student groups work on these for homework.

*Software Tools Lesson Plans* Each small group selects one of the following tools and integration strategies and develops a lesson plan based on it:

1. **Word processing development.** Develop a classroom lesson activity that integrates word processing functions into instruction in one or more of these ways:

   a. Writing processes

   b. Dynamic group products

   c. Language and writing exercises

2. **Spreadsheet development.** Develop a classroom lesson activity that integrates spreadsheet functions into instruction in one or more of the following ways:

   a. Presenting demonstrations

   b. Developing student products

   c. Supporting problem solving

   d. Storing and analyzing data

   e. Projecting grades

3. **Database development.** Develop a classroom lesson activity that integrates database functions into instruction in one or more of the following ways:

   a. Teaching research and study skills

   b. Teaching information organization skills

   c. Creating information pictures

   d. Posing and testing hypotheses

The lesson activity will be evaluated according to the following criteria. It should:

- Have a realistic time frame, so students can learn to use the software before applying it;

- Use the unique capabilities of the software to support instructional activities; and

- Save instructional time, support the logistics involved in the lesson, and/or make possible instructional activities that would be impossible otherwise.

**Activity 5.5: Integrating Technology Across the Curriculum Activities** Use the *Integrating Technology Across the Curriculum* CD-ROM packaged with this textbook to complete the following exercises:

- Word processing is a software tool that teachers can use to encourage writing across the curriculum. Look at lesson plans that demonstrate some of the ways word processing can foster writing skills in content areas such as mathematics, science, and social studies. Go to *Find Lesson Plan* and click on *Find by Criteria.* Under the *Technologies* descriptor, select word processing, and under the *Content Area* descriptor, select a content area; click *Search.* Review the types of lessons designed for use in each content area.

- Of the four most common tools in integrated software packages (word processing, spreadsheets, databases, and graphics), which is the most popular?

Hypothesize an answer to this question, then check your hypothesis against the number of plans you find on the CD for each one. Go to *Find Lesson Plan* and click on *Find by Criteria*. Under the *Technologies* descriptor, select word processing and check the number of plans. Continue with the other three software types. Explain why there are so many more for this software.

# References

Keizer, G. (1997). Which software works? *FamilyPC, 4*(5), 117–121.

Revenaugh, M. (1997). *Productivity in the classroom.* Redmond, WA: Microsoft Corporation (http://www.microsoft.com/education/k12/resource/lessons.htm).

## Word Processing

Bangert-Drowns, R. (1993). The word processor as an instructional tool: A meta-analysis of word processing in writing instruction. *Review of Educational Research, 63*(1), 69–93.

Elder, J., Schwartz, J., Bowen, B., & Goswami, D. (1989). *Word processing in a community of writers.* New York: Garland.

Harris, J. (1985). Student writers and word processing. *College Composition and Communication, 36*(3), 323–330.

Hawisher, G. (1986, April). The effects of word processing on the revision strategies of college students. Paper presented at the Annual Meeting of the American Educational Research Association, San Francisco, CA (ERIC Document Reproduction Service No. ED 268 546).

Hawisher, G. (1989). Research and recommendations for computers and compositions. In G. Hawisher & C. Selfe (Eds.). *Critical perspectives on computers and composition instruction.* New York: Teachers College Press.

Humphries, D. (1989). A computer training program for teachers. In C. Selfe, D. Rodrigues, & W. Oates (Eds.). *Computers in English and the Language Arts.* Urbana, IL: National Council of Teachers of English.

King, R. & Vockell, E. (1991). *The computer in the language arts curriculum.* Watsonville, CA: Mitchell McGraw-Hill.

Kuechle, N. (1990). Computers and first grade writing: A learning center approach. *The Computing Teacher, 18*(1), 39–41.

Levin, J. A., Boruta, M. J., & Vasconcellos, M. T. (1983). Microcomputer-based environments for writing: A writer's assistant. In A. C. Wilkinson (Ed.). *Classroom computer and cognitive science.* New York: Academic Press.

Levin, J. A., Riel, M., Rowe, R., & Boruta, M. (1984). Muktuk meets Jacuzzi: Computer networks and elementary school writers. In S. W. Freeman (Ed.). *The acquisition of written language: Revision and response.* Hillsdale, NJ: Ablex.

Lockard, J., Abrams, P., & Many, W. (1994). *Microcomputers for 21st century educators (3rd ed.).* New York: HarperCollins.

Mehan, H., Miller-Souviney, B., & Riel, M. (1984, April). Knowledge of text editing and the control of literacy skill. Paper presented at the Annual Meeting of the American Educational Research Association, New Orleans, LA.

Morehouse, D., Hoaglund, M., & Schmidt, R. (1987, February). *Technology demonstration program final evaluation report.* Menomonie, WI: Quality Evaluation and Development.

Nelson, M. H. (1994). Processing poetry to develop literacy. *The Computing Teacher, 22*(3), 39–41.

Reed, W. M. (1996). Assessing the importance of computer-based writing. *Journal of Research on Computing in Education, 28*(4), 418–437.

Roblyer, M., Castine, W., & King, F. J. (1988). *Assessing the impact of computer-based instruction: A review of recent research.* New York: Haworth Press.

Roblyer, M. D. (1997). Technology and the oops! effect: Finding a bias against word processing. *Learning and Leading with Technology, 24*(7), 14–16.

Schramm, R. (1989). The effects of using word processing equipment in writing instruction: A meta-analysis. Unpublished doctoral dissertation, Northern Illinois University, DeKalb.

Schwartz, E. & Vockell, E. (1989). *The computer in the English curriculum.* Watsonville, CA: Mitchell.

VerMulm, L. (1993). The Christa McAuliffe writing center: Process writing with a networked Mac lab. *The Computing Teacher, 20*(7), 48–53.

Viau, E. (1998). Color me a writer: Teaching students to think critically. *Learning and Leading with Technology, 25*(5), 17–20.

Wresch, W. (1990). Collaborative writing projects: Lesson plans for the computer age. *The Computing Teacher, 18*(2), 19–21.

## Spreadsheets

Baugh, I. (1995). Tool or terror? *The Computing Teacher, 22*(5), 14–16.

Beaver, J. (1992). Using computer power to improve your teaching, Part II: Spreadsheets and charting. *The Computing Teacher, 19*(6), 22–24.

Bozeman, W. (1992). Spreadsheets. In G. Bitter (Ed.). *Macmillan encyclopedia of computers.* New York: Macmillan.

Collis, B. (1988). *Computer, curriculum, and whole-class instruction.* Belmont, CA: Wadsworth.

Edwards, J. (1992). What's in our trash? *Florida Technology in Education Quarterly, 4*(2), 86–88.

Goldberg, K. (1990). Bringing mathematics to the social studies class: Spreadsheets and the electoral process. *The Computing Teacher, 18*(1), 35–38.

Harriss, S. (1992). M&M count. *Florida Technology in Education Quarterly, 4*(2), 60–61.

Klass, P. (1988, April). Using microcomputer spreadsheet programs to teach statistical concepts (ERIC Document Reproduction Service No. ED 293 726).

Paul, J. R. M. (1995). Pizza and spaghetti: Solving math problems in the primary classroom. *The Computing Teacher, 22*(7), 65–67.

Ploger, D., Rooney, M., & Klingler, L. (1996). Applying spreadsheets and draw programs in the classroom. *Tech Trends, 41*(3), 26–29.

Sgroi, R. (1992). Systematizing trial and error using spreadsheets. *Arithmetic Teacher, 39*(7), 8–12.

Sutherland, R. (1993). A spreadsheet approach to solving algebra problems. *Journal of Mathematical Behavior, 12*(4), 353–383.

Voteline: A project for integrating computer databases, spreadsheets, and telecomputing into high school social studies instruction. (1992). Report of a statewide North Carolina project (ERIC Document Reproduction Service No. ED 350 243).

## Databases

Coe, M. & Butts, T. (1991). Keeping up with technology. *The Computing Teacher, 18*(5), 14–15.

Collis, B. (1988). *Computer, curriculum, and whole-class instruction.* Belmont, CA: Wadsworth.

Collis, B. (1990). *The best of research windows: Trends and issues in educational computing.* Eugene, OR: International Society for Technology in Education (ERIC Document Reproduction No. ED 323 993).

Ehman, L., Glenn, A., Johnson, V., & White, C. (1992). Using computer databases in student problem solving: A study of eight social studies teachers' classrooms. *Theory and Research in Social Education, 20*(2), 179–206.

Hartson, T. (1993). Rocks, minerals, databases, and simulations. *The Computing Teacher, 21*(1), 48–50.

Heine, E. (1994). The world at their fingertips. *The Florida Technology in Education Quarterly, 7*(1), 38–42.

Hollis, R. (1990). Database yearbooks in the second grade. *The Computing Teacher, 17*(6), 14–15.

Hunter, B. (1983). *My students use computers.* Alexandria, VA: Human Resources Research Organization.

Jankowski, L. (1993–1994). Getting started with databases. *The Computing Teacher, 21*(4), 8–9.

Magee, D. (1991). Carmen Sandiego and world geography. *The Computing Teacher, 19*(3), 31–32.

Maor, D. (1991, April). Development of student inquiry skills: A constructivist approach in a computerized classroom environment. Paper presented at the Annual Meeting of the National Association for Research in Science Teaching, Lake Geneva, WI, April 7–10, 1991 (ERIC Document Reproduction No. ED 326 261).

Strickland, A. & Hoffer, T. (1990–1991). Integrating computer databases with laboratory problems. *The Computing Teacher, 18*(4), 30–32.

Thomas, R. (1991). A focus on history. *The Computing Teacher 18*(6), 30–33.

Watson, J. (1993). *Teaching thinking skills with databases* (Macintosh version). Eugene, OR: ISTE.

Wetzel, K. & Painter, S. (1994). *Microsoft Works 3.0 for the Macintosh: A workbook for educators.* Eugene, OR: ISTE.

## Other Software Tools

Albrecht, B. & Firedrake, G. (1997). New adventures in hands-on and far-out physics. *Learning and Leading with Technology, 25*(2), 34–37.

Anderson-Inman, L. & Zeitz, L. (1993). Computer-based concept mapping: Active studying for active learners. *The Computing Teacher, 21*(1), 6–8, 10–11.

Baker, F. (1978). *Computer-managed instruction: Theory and practice.* Englewood Cliffs, NJ: Educational Technology Publications.

Bitter, G., Camuse, R., & Durbin, V. (1993). *Using a microcomputer in the classroom (3rd ed.).* Boston: Allyn & Bacon.

Bolduc, R., Hale, M., & Webb, J. (1994). Multimedia for presentations in large-lecture classrooms. *The Florida Technology in Education Quarterly, 6*(2), 65–68.

Borenstein, M. (1997). Mathematics in the real world. *Learning and Leading with Technology, 24*(7), 30–39.

Brumbaugh, K. & Poirot, J., (1993). The teacher as researcher: Presenting your case. *The Computing Teacher, 20*(6), 19–21.

Catchings, M. & MacGregor, K. (1998). Stoking creative fires: Young authors use software for writing and illustrating. *Learning and Leading with Technology, 25*(6), 20–23.

Cowan, H. (1992). The art of group communication. *Electronic Learning, 11*(8), 38–39.

Duren, P. (1990–1991). Enhancing inquiry skills with graphing software. *The Computing Teacher, 20*(3), 23–25.

Ferrington, G. & Loge, K. (1992). Making yourself presentable. *The Computing Teacher, 19*(5), 23–25.

Forest, J. (1993). Music and the arts: Keys to a next-century school. *The Computing Teacher, 21*(3), 24–26.

Gay, L. R. (1993). *Educational research: Competencies for analysis and application (4th ed.).* Columbus, OH: Merrill.

Granning, M. Presentation technologies enhance students' communication skills at Lakewood High School. *The Florida Technology in Education Quarterly, 6*(2), 37–43.

Gullickson, A. & Farland, D. (1991). Using micros for test development. *Tech Trends, 35*(2), 22–26.

Hermann, A. (1988). Desktop publishing in high school: Empowering students as readers and writers (ERIC Document Reproduction No. ED 300 837).

Hoffman, E. (1994). Overview of presentation software: What every teacher needs to know. *The Florida Technology in Education Quarterly, 6*(2), 11–15.

Joiner, D. & Alvarez, D. (1994). Presentation software in distance learning: Marion County's MacAir project. *The Florida Technology in Education Quarterly, 6*(2), 16–24.

Jones, P. (1994). Photo CD: Implications for Florida education. *The Florida Technology in Education Quarterly, 6*(2), 44–49.

Kahn, J. (1997). Well begun is half done: Teaching students to use concept mapping software. *Learning and Leading with Technology, 24*(5), 39–40.

Knupfer, N. & McIsaac, M. (1989). Desktop publishing software: The effects of computerized formats on reading speed and comprehension. *Journal of Research on Computing in Education, 22*(2), 127–136.

Ladelson, L. (1994). Calibrating probeware: Making a line. *The Computing Teacher, 21*(6), 46–47.

Lewis, R. (1993). *Special education technology.* Pacific-Grove, CA: Brooks-Cole.

McCain, T. (1993). *Designing for communication: The key to successful desktop publishing.* Eugene, OR: ISTE.

McCarthy, R. (1988). Stop the presses: An update on desktop publishing. *Electronic Learning, 7*(6), 24–30.

Moersch, C. (1995). Choose the right graph. *The Computing Teacher, 22*(5), 31–35.

Nathan, J. (1985). *Micro-myths: Exploring the limits of learning with computers.* Minneapolis: Winston Press.

Newman, J. (1988). Online: Classroom publishing. *Language Arts, 65*(7), 727–732.

Norvelle, R. (1992). Desktop publishing. In G. Bitter (Ed.). *Macmillan encyclopedia of computers.* New York: Macmillan.

Ohler, J. (1998). The promise of MIDI technology: A reflection on musical intelligence. *Learning and Leading with Technology, 25*(6), 6–15.

Parker, R. C. (1989). Ten common desktop design pitfalls. *Currents, 15*(1), 24–26.

Pearlman, B. (1994). Designing groupware. *ISTE Update, 6*(5), 1–2.

Roblyer, M. (1992). Computers in education. In G. Bitter (Ed.). *Macmillan encyclopedia of computers.* New York: Macmillan.

Rose, S. (1988). A desktop publishing primer. *The Computing Teacher, 15*(9), 13–15.

Stanton, D. (1992). Microcomputer-based labs. *Electronic Learning Special Edition (Buyers Guide), 12*(1), 16–17.

Stanton, D. (1994). Gradebooks, the next generation. *Electronic Learning, 14*(1), 54–58.

Steinhaus, (1986–1987). Putting the music composition tool to work. *The Computing Teacher, 14*(4), 16–18.

Strommen, E. (1994). Can technology change the test? *Electronic Learning, 14*(1), 44–53.

Truett, C. (1993). CD-ROM storybooks bring children's literature to life. *The Computing Teacher, 21*(1), 20–21.

Wagner, W. (1992). Evaluating grade management software. *The Florida Technology in Education Quarterly, 4*(3), 59–66.

Webster, E. (1992). Evaluation of computer software for teaching statistics. *Journal of Computers in Mathematics and Science Teaching, 11*(3/4), 377–391.

Williams, R. (1994). *The non-designer's design book: Design and typographic principles for the visual novice.* Berkeley, CA: Peachpit Press, 1994.

Willinsky, J. & Bradley, S. (1990). Desktop publishing in remedial language arts settings: Let them eat cake. *Journal of Teaching Writing, 9*(2), 223–238.

# Chapter 6

## Using Multimedia and Hypermedia in Teaching and Learning

Multimedia learning is not something new. It is woven into the fabric of our childhood ... Educational multimedia design ... creates something that is dazzling new and deeply familiar.

Tom Boyle in *Design for Multimedia Learning* (1997)

### This chapter covers the following topics:

- Definitions and characteristics of multimedia and hypermedia systems

- Unique advantages and uses of interactive videodisc (IVD) systems and CD-ROM/DVD multimedia/hypermedia systems

- Procedures for using multimedia/hypermedia authoring systems

- Educational applications of multimedia/hypermedia authoring systems

# Objectives

1. Define multimedia and hypermedia from historic and current perspectives.

2. Design classroom lesson activities appropriate for each kind of multimedia/hypermedia product.

3. Identify the components of a product developed with a hypermedia authoring program.

4. Use an authoring system to develop a product that meets visual, navigation, and instructional criteria for an effective hypermedia system.

5. Design lesson activities appropriate for student development of hypermedia products.

## Introduction to Multimedia and Hypermedia

We live in a multimedia world, surrounded by complex images, movement, and sound. So perhaps it is not surprising that part of our human evolution has focused on making our technology reflect the color and clamor of our surroundings. In educational technology, multimedia has been a steadily growing presence for some time. As discussed in Chapter 1, computer-based multimedia learning stations have been used since 1966, and noncomputer multimedia methods have been around even longer. This chapter looks at current classroom uses of multimedia and its companion concept, hypermedia.

### Multimedia and Hypermedia: How Do They Differ?

Like other educational technology concepts, definitions for multimedia and hypermedia defy consensus (Moore, Myers, & Burton, 1994; Tolhurst, 1995); people find the two concepts either too close to distinguish between or too slippery to get words around. Tolhurst quoted one source as saying, "By its very nature, (multimedia) is invertebrate. You poke it and it slithers away" (p. 21). Definitions used in this chapter come to us from two paths that were separate initially but have converged over time.

*Multimedia* simply means "multiple media" or "a combination of media." The media can be still pictures, sound, motion video, animation, and/or text items combined in a product whose purpose is communicating information.

*Hypermedia* are "linked media" that have their roots in a concept developed by Vannevar Bush (1945) in his landmark article "As We May Think" (1945). Bush proposed a "memex" machine that would let people quickly access items of information whose meanings were connected but which were stored in different places. In the 1960s, Ted Nelson coined the term "hypertext" to describe a proposed database system called Xanadu based on Bush's idea (Boyle, 1997). In this system, items of information from all

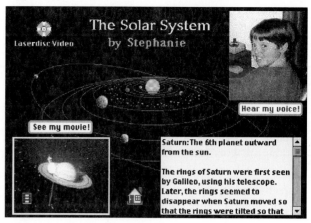

Figure 6.1   **Example of a Hypermedia Product with** *HyperStudio*

Source: From HyperStudio®, courtesy of Roger Wagner Publishing, Inc.

over the world were to be logically connected with "hypertext" links. For example, one could select "apple" and get information on all related concepts such as trees, fruit—even the Garden of Eden. The technology at that time was inadequate to produce Xanadu, but the idea was the forerunner of today's hypermedia systems in which information stored in various media are connected, thus the term *hypermedia*.

In current technologies such as browsers (see Chapter 8) and authoring systems, most multimedia products also are hypermedia systems. That is, the combination of media elements are linked with buttons to click on or menus from which to select. Clicking or selecting one item sends the user to other, related items. This chapter gives many examples of hypermedia products, but the student-produced *HyperStudio* product shown in Figure 6.1 introduces the concept of hypermedia. Note that clicking on the laserdisc button sends the user to a videodisc clip; clicking on "Hear My Voice" plays a recording of Stephanie, and so on. The combination of media makes this product multimedia; the ability to get from one media/information element to another makes it hypermedia.

### Types of Multimedia and Hypermedia Systems

Multimedia and hypermedia systems come in a variety of hardware, software, and media configurations but usually are classified according to their primary storage equipment: interactive videodiscs (IVD), CD-ROMs (compact disc-read only memory), digital versatile disc (DVD), and other technologies, including CD-I (compact disc-interactive), DVI (digital video interactive), and photo CDs (photographic compact discs). This chapter focuses on IVD and CD-ROM technologies, since they have the most powerful current impact on K-12 education; we will touch on DVD, since it is an emerging technology that will likely play a significant role in future multimedia/hypermedia systems.

These technologies all share a single core technology: laser beams heat light-sensitive material on a disc so that a chemical reaction causes the area to either remain opaque or reflect light, thus revealing encoded information. In contrast, magnetic storage units, such as hard disks and tape devices, store data as magnetic pulses, which are read or altered by the disk drive (Mathisen, 1991; Walkenbach, 1992). Generally accepted style in the industry has adopted the spelling *disk* for magnetic storage systems and *disc* for optical devices.

Hypermedia systems published as web page documents also represent a powerful technology of the future. Hypermedia systems used in distance communications and learning are described in Chapter 8.

### Current and Future Impact of Multimedia and Hypermedia on Education

The current widespread educational uses of multimedia and hypermedia systems augur an even heavier reliance on these products in classrooms of the future. Educators recognize and use these systems when they see the strengths they offer.

**Unique capabilities of multimedia and hypermedia systems.** These systems offer some of the most powerful capabilities technology has to offer, including motivation, flexibility, development of creative and critical thinking skills, and improved writing and process skills.

*Motivation.* Hypermedia programs offer such varied options that most people seem to enjoy using them. Students who usually struggle to complete a project or term paper often will tackle a hypermedia project enthusiastically. McCarthy (1989) believes the most important characteristic of hypermedia is its ability to encourage students to be proactive learners.

*Flexibility.* Hypermedia programs can draw on such diverse tools that they truly offer something for students who excel in any of what Gardner calls "intelligences" (see Chapter 3). For example, a student who may not be good at written expression but has visual aptitude can document things with sound or pictures.

*Development of creative and critical thinking skills.* The tremendous access to hypertext and hypermedia tools opens up a multitude of creative avenues for both students and teachers. Marchionini (1988) refers to hypermedia as a fluid environment that constantly requires the learner to make decisions and evaluate progress. He asserts that this process forces students to apply higher-order thinking skills. Turner and Dipinto (1992) report that the hypermedia environment encourages students to think in terms of metaphors, to be introspective, and to give free rein to their imaginations.

*Improved writing and process skills.* Turner and Dipinto (1992) also find that exposure to hypermedia authoring tools helps students by giving them a new and different perspective on how to organize and present information

and a new insight into writing. Instead of viewing their writing as one long stream of text, students now see it as chunks of information to be linked together.

The use of hypermedia tools in the learning process has important implications for schools. Dede (1994) sees uses of hypermedia tools beyond simple presentations of information:

- They offer new methods of structured discovery.
- They address varied learning styles.
- They motivate and empower students.
- They accommodate nonlinear exploration, allowing teachers to present information as a web of interconnections rather than a stream of facts.

Our society's heavy reliance on hypertext/hypermedia to communicate information seems likely to expand in the future. The accelerating number of World Wide Web pages on the Internet is evidence that linking data together with hypertext and hypermedia is an effective way to present and add value to large bodies of information. Millions of people already publish hypermedia documents on the information highway in the hope of attracting viewers, readers, and listeners.

Hypermedia tools also may permit sophisticated evaluations of learning. In the process of using hypermedia, people are said to "leave a track" (Simonson & Thompson, 1994), which may help analyze how students approach learning tasks. Future hypermedia systems might apply pattern-recognition techniques from the field of artificial intelligence to help schools assess student mastery of higher-order cognitive skills (Dede, 1994). Bagui (1998) says multimedia "may have unique capabilities to facilitate learning because of the parallels between multimedia and the natural way people learn" (p. 4), that is, through visual information and imagery.

**Research on the impact of multimedia and hypermedia systems.** While some reviewers have tried to capture the unique contributions of these systems on achievement (McNeil & Nelson, 1991; Adams, 1992), Lookatch (1997) echoes Clarks's warning (see Chapter 1) that instructional strategies—not media—will make the difference in achievement. Two recent research reviews attempt to document other kinds of findings that could guide future educational uses of multimedia/hypermedia.

Swan and Meskill (1996) examined how effectively current hypermedia products support the teaching and acquisition of critical thinking skills in reading and language. They reviewed hypermedia products as to how well they made possible response-based approaches to teaching and learning literature, that is, instructional activities that "place student-generated questions at the center of learning ... (and encourage) a problem-finding as well as a problem solving approach to critical thinking" (p. 168). They evaluated 45 hypermedia literature programs using criteria in three areas: technical items, response-based concerns, and classroom issues. The majority of the 45 products used a CD-ROM format, but 10 used a combination of CD-ROM and videodisc, and four used computer software. They found that most products were technically sound and linked well with classroom topics, but few were designed to promote the response-based methods that promote critical thinking. "Programs designed for elementary students ... equated literature education with reading instruction; programs designed for high school ... generally adopted a traditional text-centered approach" (p. 187). These findings indicate that teachers who want to use multimedia/hypermedia products specifically to promote higher-level skills must select products judiciously and warily.

**Research on the design of multimedia and hypermedia systems.** Stemler (1997) reviewed findings on various multimedia/hypermedia characteristics that could have an impact on the potential effectiveness of these systems: screen design, learner control and navigation, use of feedback, student interactivity, and video and audio elements. Her findings are too extensive to give adequate treatment here, but educators who are committed to high-quality multimedia development should review the full text of her article.

*Instructional design.* Stemler recommends that developers analyze each element in a multimedia product to determine which of Gagné's Nine Events of Instruction (see Chapter 3) it aims to achieve and how well it achieves it.

*Screen design.* Well-designed screens focus learners' attention, develop and maintain interest, promote processing of information, promote engagement between learner and content, help students find and organize information, and support easy navigation through lessons (p. 343).

*Interaction and feedback.* Keep feedback on the same screen with the question and student response and provide immediate feedback. Verify correct answers and give hints and another try for incorrect ones. Tailor feedback to the response and provide encouraging feedback, but do not make it more entertaining for wrong answers than for correct ones. If possible, let students print out the feedback (p. 345).

*Navigation.* Support navigation with orientation cues, clearly-defined procedures, clearly labeled back-and-forth buttons, and help segments (pp. 346–347).

*Learner control.* In general, give older and more capable students more control over the sequence; younger, less experienced students should have less control (p. 348).

*Color.* Use color sparingly and employ it primarily for cueing and highlighting certain elements to bring them to the learner's attention. Use a consistent color scheme throughout to promote ease of use (pp. 350–351).

*Graphics.* Use graphics as well as text to present information to serve students who prefer one kind of presentation over the other. Use graphics sparingly for other purposes (to entertain or amuse) (p. 351).

*Animation.* Use animation sparingly and only to present dynamic processes or to highlight key information (p. 352).

*Audio.* Use audio for short presentations of program content, but do not let it compete with video presentation. Do not require long readings on each screen. Separate material into chunks on each of several screens (p. 353).

*Video.* Use video sequences for broader, abstract material (that with emotional impact) and for advance organizers rather than for presenting detailed information (p. 354).

### Emerging Developments in Multimedia Systems: Digital Versatile Disc (DVD) and Virtual Reality (VR)

As storage media continue to evolve in capability and decrease in price, they will have a significant impact on the kinds of multimedia/hypermedia that teachers can develop. DVD technology is projected to become an important storage medium in the future, taking the place of current CD-ROMs and even hard drives (Arthur & Mizer, 1998). This will allow educators to include more multimedia elements, especially video sequences, which currently take up more room than may be available.

*Virtual reality (VR)* environments (see Chapter 9) have great potential for use in instructional hypermedia systems. Imagine a hypermedia environment for teaching students how geometry is reflected in the world around them. With VR, they can "walk through" a building, see shapes highlighted, and be able to touch them and hear descriptions of what they are and how they relate to the structures in the building. Developments in storage media such as DVD also will make it possible for educators to take advantage of VR technology in their own hypermedia development.

### Issues Related to Multimedia and Hypermedia Use in Education

Educators already have voiced several concerns about our media-driven culture and its role in education. A few of these are described here.

**The critical importance of media literacy.** As Mergendollar (1997) warns, technologies such as multimedia are an equivocal blessing. They help us communicate information more expeditiously but do not help us analyze whether or not information is accurate, relevant, or current. The more information we have, the more important it becomes to learn critical analysis, visual literacy, and information literacy skills.

**The need for multimedia communication standards.** Galbreath (1997) discusses the need to develop consistent standards to govern the information compression, transmission, distribution, and storage that make multimedia possible and useful. He gives a good technical overview of these standards and the likelihood they will occur in the future.

**Effective integration strategies.** Like most technology resources, the impact of multimedia systems will depend heavily on how well teachers integrate them into classroom activities. Blissett and Adkins (1993) suggest the following strategies for teachers to employ when integrating interactive multimedia into the classroom:

- Provide guidance and further explanation on the nature of the task when a group gets stuck or, worse, misunderstands what to do.
- Check that the software package provides advance organizers for its conceptual content.
- Individualize the learning experience by assessing learning as it occurs and then intervening to link and relate or extend and consolidate concepts to meet the needs of particular pupils or groups.
- Ask open-ended questions that require pupils to verbalize their thought processes and review their understanding of the conceptual subject matter.
- Challenge and provoke thinking, leading to more abstract and conceptual discussions.
- Help the group to review its problem-solving strategies and direct them toward more powerful ones.
- Before assigning hypermedia projects, do training in group-work skills.

**Limitations of hypermedia.** Although multimedia/hypermedia systems truly represent the communication method of choice both now and in the future, education's use of these resources is hampered by several problems.

*Hardware intensity.* To take full advantage of the benefits of hypermedia technology, students need ample online development time. This presents a problem in most classroom settings due to insufficient numbers of computers. The problem is exacerbated when available computers are not configured for hypermedia authoring. For example, they may lack the capacity to digitize sound or to input video.

*Lack of training.* Although hypermedia programs are becoming easier to use, they still require extensive training. Unfortunately, training is not a top priority in most school districts. One survey showed that staff development makes up only about 8 percent of technology budgets (Siegel, 1995). The toughest challenge instructional personnel face is not learning to use a particular program, but learning to integrate it within the curriculum. To help alleviate this problem, hypermedia training needs to go beyond just learning how to make an authoring program work. Training must also give serious consideration to effective curriculum integration. In addition, to ensure quality products, hypermedia training should extend to the areas of media, design, and the arts.

*Difficulty of projecting.* Teachers often want to project students' hypermedia projects onto large screens so that others can see the results. This is still a somewhat cumbersome task that requires the teacher to hook up an LCD panel or a video projector. Both of these pieces of hardware also are quite expensive, so every classroom cannot have a projection setup. A compromise solution may be to use a converter that can project the computer signal onto a television/monitor.

*Integration problems.* Integration of hypermedia technology into the curriculum presents some major problems. To assure quality projects, students need sufficient time to focus, build, and reflect. The conventional school schedule, often broken into 50-minute blocks, does not lend itself to serious project development. If hypermedia authoring is to have a major impact on learning, educators will need to look at ways of infusing more flexibility into students' daily schedules. One step in the right direction might be more integration of subject matter.

*Data compression.* A hypermedia project can fill a tremendous amount of storage space on a computer's hard drive; digitized video and sound files are the major culprits. Until the compression techniques promised by DVD improve and become more cost effective, this problem will persist. Another component of this problem is the difficulty of transferring a file from one computer to another, since even very small hypermedia files will exceed the capacity of a single data disk.

There are some ways of getting around these problems. Students can store files on external hard drives or zip disks. These add another cost element, but the prices are dropping rapidly. Another way of dealing with large files is to employ a program that splits a large file into a number of smaller ones, each of which fits on a microdisk. Using this method, a student can copy a project from the hard drive onto a number of 3 ½-inch microdisks.

## Interactive Videodisc (IVD) Systems

Videodiscs are optical storage media for random-access storage of high-quality audio and analog information. Laser videodiscs store text, audio, video, and graphics data in analog format. *Interactive videodisc (IVD)* technology was first released in the 1970s and now has applications in both the education and business worlds. A videodisc resembles an audio CD disc, except it is generally larger in diameter. Most videodiscs are 12 inches in diameter (Figure 6.2) and hold 54,000 still frames or the equivalent of 675 carousel slide trays. They represent a durable medium for storing and displaying visual information. Videodiscs are read by a laser beam, and the mechanism allows random access to any part of the disc. The random access feature is important because it avoids the need to fast forward or rewind to find a particular image as is necessary with a videotape.

**Figure 6.2    A Videodisc**

Source: Scott Cunningham/Merrill.

**Figure 6.3    Features of CLV and CAV Formats**

| Attribute | CLV | CAV |
|---|---|---|
| Random access | yes | yes |
| Still frame | no | yes |
| Frame search | no | yes |
| Time search | yes | no |
| Chapter search | yes | yes |
| Scan | yes | yes |
| Multispeed | no | yes |
| Minutes per side | 60 | 30 |
| Straight play | yes | yes |
| Two audio tracks | yes | yes |

Although not generally considered cutting-edge technology, videodiscs have remained popular teaching tools among many educators. The quantity, and particularly the quality, of applications are expanding rapidly. The wide variety of software linked to videodiscs encompasses programs that should appeal to just about any teaching style.

### IVD Formats and Levels of Interactivity

Optical disc technology was first introduced by the Dutch firm NV Philips in 1972, leading to the release of a commercial product in 1976. Videodiscs were initially marketed as media to show movies at home. Soon after they got started in the consumer market, however, relatively low-cost VCR technology became available and emerged as the medium of choice for consumers.

**IVD formats.** Currently videodiscs come in two formats: constant angular velocity (CAV) and constant linear velocity (CLV). CAV discs permit interactive applications by enabling users to access randomly any of 54,000 frames on each side in only a few seconds. This format permits a user to display a single frame continuously, treating images as individual slides. To make this process easy, each frame on the disc has its own number ranging from 1 to 54,000. Laser videodisc players offer the following features with CAV discs: frame search, chapter search, single frame stepping, scanning (fast forward or fast reverse), slow motion, and triple speed. All of these features can function in forward or reverse mode. The total video capacity of a CAV disc is 60 minutes (30 minutes on each side).

CLV videodiscs are used for linear applications, sometimes called *extended play applications,* such as movies or television specials. The CLV discs have limited interactive possibilities; for example, the players do not provide random access to individual frames and freeze frame images. CLV discs are indexed by time rather than frame numbers, so players provide random access to exact seconds on CLV discs. The total running time of video on a CLV disc is approximately 60 minutes per side. Figure 6.3 summarizes the features of CLV and CAV formats.

All videodisc players can can be used in both CLV and CAV formats. Of the two formats, CAV is considered more appropriate for education since it offers more options for access and interactivity.

**IVD levels of interactivity: Function, hardware, and software.** A videodisc player connects to a television set or computer monitor in much the same way as a VCR does. Both generally are configured to use either RF or RCA connectors. Remote controls and bar-code readers are not difficult to use but do require some training and practice. To take full advantage of the interactivity in IVD technology, the teacher must handle the mechanics of its operation smoothly. The level of interactivity of a videodisc program refers to the amount of control the program gives the user and what kinds of software and hardware the user needs to achieve control. Videodisc programs are referred to as Level I, Level II, Level III, and Level IV.

*Level I.* In Level I interactive video, the user controls the program directly without the computer's involvement. The necessary hardware for Level I interactive video includes a videodisc player, a monitor, and a method of controlling the player—either the control panel on the machine, a remote control device, or a bar-code reader. (Not all videodisc players are equipped for bar-code control.) The user also needs a computer and appropriate software to make customized bar codes. The videodisc provides the only software needed for this level. The user also needs a special software package such as Pioneer's *Bar'n'Coder* to generate customized bar codes (see Figure 6.4). Level III interactivity requires an appropriately configured videodisc player, a monitor, a computer, and an RS-232 cable. (Some videodisc players will function only at Level I.) It is important to note that Level I video represents a multimedia,

**Figure 6.4    Screen from _Bar'n'Coder_ Software**

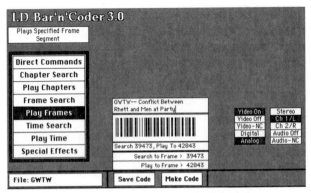

Source: Used by permission of Pioneer New Media Technologies.

rather than a hypermedia environment. Although frame numbers let users get to any location on the disc, there are no hypertext links to allow users to link to related concepts.

_Level II._ Level II videodiscs never came into common use. The videodisc player needed an internal microprocessor that read the computer program stored along with other data on the videodisc. This level of interactivity was replaced by digital technologies such as CD-ROM.

_Level III._ Level III interactivity requires the use of a computer connected to a videodisc player. A computer program operates the player via a cable by running appropriate driver software. As Figure 6.5 shows, Level III interactivity requires an appropriately configured videodisc player, a monitor, a computer, and an RS-232 cable. (Some videodisc players will function only at Level I.) Level III software programs include drivers for most videodisc players. This combination offers the user the advantage of simultaneous access to computer data and videodisc data. This level gives the user several software options: a curriculum program like Tom Snyder's _The Great Ocean Rescue,_ a slide show generating program

**Figure 6.5    Level III Videodisc Setup**

Source: Joseph H. Bailey, ©1991 National Geographic Society. Used by permission.

such as Videodiscovery's _Media Max,_ or a hypermedia authoring program like Roger Wagner's _HyperStudio_ or Alchemidia's _Multimedia Scrapbook._

_Level IV._ This term refers to Level III interactivity with a single monitor to display all material. Some industry experts think of Level IV interactivity as programs that apply artificial learning techniques to create expert learning systems. Level IV systems often include sophisticated devices for user interfaces, such as touch screens, speech recognition apparatuses, and virtual reality peripherals. In a broad sense, Level IV also refers to future developments in interactive multimedia (Skolnik & Kanning, 1994). Because they remain relatively undeveloped at this time, Level IV applications are not covered in this text.

When schools introduced IVD technology a number of years ago, its advocates focused their excitement on the potential of Level III interactivity. It's easy to see why. Smooth interaction between the user and the technology developed an almost magical quality. Some even predicted that Level III interactive technology would revolutionize education. They tended to dismiss Level I technology as inferior to Level III, mainly because it involved no computer.

As often happens, the experts did not read accurately the pulse of the schools or the teachers. Level III interactivity required more hardware than schools could afford to implement on any scale. In addition, one station in a classroom did not fit in well with the directed instruction styles of most teachers. Instead, Level I usage has proven very popular with teachers and software developers have begun to take notice. As more compatible technology becomes available in schools, Level III usage is increasing along with Level I. In order to try to meet the needs of both sets of customers, developers often ship videodisc programs with bar codes for Level I and software for Level III.

### Advantages of IVD Technology

**Flexibility.** IVD supports a variety of applications for teachers and students. The control options, as well as the unlimited creative potential of repurposing videodiscs, allow this tool to integrate effectively into most curricula.

**Dual audio tracks.** Developers often use the second track to play program audio in a second language (usually Spanish) or to include a simpler or more detailed version of the presentation. The teacher can then let some students listen to one track through headphones while the rest of the class listens to the other track through the monitor.

**Ease of use.** Most teachers and students feel comfortable enough to begin using this technology with only a few hours of training. However, they may become fully comfortable only after many hours of use. Some schools have encouraged teachers to check out videodisc players for practice at home, making them much more likely to use the equipment in their classrooms.

**Quality.** High-resolution video images and audio clips stored on videodiscs provide much higher quality than videocassette tapes. Videodiscs also beat the quality of digitized video displayed directly on computer monitors.

**Durability.** Since videodiscs are read with a laser beam, they suffer no real wear and tear with normal use. Discs are coated with plastic that generally protects them from small scratches or fingerprints. They are certain to last longer than videotapes or films.

**Standards.** Videodisc manufacturers have adopted a worldwide standard for the technology. As a result, any videodisc will play on any player. Videodiscs also adhere to the LB and LB2 bar-code standards, which means that all videodisc bar codes work with all bar-code readers.

### Disadvantages of IVD Technology

**Cost.** The cost of some videodisc programs can be quite high, as much as $300 to $500 or more. This presents a big problem when a school's media purchasers see these programs simply as videos. Someone who can pay $49.95 for a videotape may balk at the cost of a videodisc. Schools should evaluate these higher-end videodisc programs as curriculum packages, rather than just discs.

**Read only.** The videodisc is a read-only technology, which means that users cannot record information. This is an obvious disadvantage compared to the VCR or writable CDs.

**Lack of interface standards.** No industry standards regulate interface between videodisc players and computers. This means that different brands of players require different cables, and some software programs are incompatible with some players. To guard against incompatibility, it would be wise for a school to settle on one brand of player.

**Hardware intensive systems for Level III.** A Level III setup includes a videodisc player, monitor, computer, and cables. Teachers often find it burdensome to gather all of this equipment in one place. Some schools have opted to create portable multimedia stations that can easily be transported from one classroom to another. Level III interactivity also presents a cumbersome interface for the user who must pay attention to two monitors—the computer screen and the television screen.

**Maintenance costs.** Videodisc players can be expensive to repair, and users should handle them with care. However, the industrial type of players sold to schools are designed to be more durable than home players.

**Limited video capacity.** Although videodiscs provide tremendous storage capacity for still frames, when played as continuous video, the CAV format offers only 30 min-

### Figure 6.6 Bar-Code Reader and Bar Code

Source: Anthony Magnacca/Merrill.

utes per side. A complete movie can fill three, four, or even five separate discs.

**Uncertain future.** The explosion of CD-ROM technology has been predicted to eclipse videodiscs, but these dire predictions may be premature. Teachers still find Level I IVD technology an easy-to-use and effective tool (Shields, 1994). Schools will not likely decide simply to drop videodiscs and switch to CD-ROMs, especially since Level I use does not require a computer and videodisc players can easily be moved and set up. However, the future of Level III is somewhat uncertain because of its awkward hardware configuration versus the simplicity of CD-ROM and CD-I systems; schools will likely prefer the simpler interactive multimedia platform. Level III may be relegated to the role of a presentation tool, which takes advantage of its real strength—delivering high-quality, full-motion video on a TV screen, without the necessity of a scan converter. The choice between videodisc and CD technology need not settle on one over the other; instead, schools must choose how to prioritize expenditures.

### Level I Capabilities and Applications for Education

**Using bar codes.** Users can scan bar codes to access chapters, individual frames, or segments of video on both CLV and CAV discs. The bar codes look like UPC codes on commercial-use products. The bar-code reader that interprets the patterns of stripes resembles the technology in many stores (see Figure 6.6).

Bar codes are considered the easiest way to access information from videodisc. They simplify control of the technology so the teacher can concentrate on interacting with the students without worrying about entering frame or chapter numbers with a remote control device. Vendors have taken advantage of these capabilities and now include bar codes with most Level I programs. A good example of the power of bar codes emerged when Optical Data Corporation upgraded its *Windows on Science* program. By indexing discs with bar codes, the company turned a potentially cumbersome program into one that teachers find both exciting and easy to use.

A number of software packages for Macintosh, Windows, and DOS systems (*Bar'n'Coder 3.0, Barcode Maker, Lesson Maker*) enable users to create bar codes for videodiscs. Most of these programs work similarly. The user enters the frame or time numbers to display and then types in a descriptor for the code. At the user's command to make the code, the program either prints it out or exports it to a word processing document.

Once the bar code is generated, it can be used in many ways. A teacher might create bar codes that access data on a videodisc dealing with geography and then glue the bar codes on appropriate parts of maps. This becomes an exploration center for students. Another instructor might use the computer to paste the bar code into a word processing file and then scan it during a teacher-directed activity. Bar-code software can also make bar codes for an audio CD. Videodisc players sold since 1992 support the LB2 standard. They can play audio CDs under control of bar codes that match the standard. The "address" for the audio CD shows up on the TV monitor hooked up to the videodisc player. Users can enter this information into the bar-code program as they do for a videodisc frame to get to a specific part of the audio CD.

**Repurposing videodiscs for Level I.** Videodisc producers and developers have specific uses in mind for it. Depending on the program, these can range from home entertainment to very structured, directed-instruction lessons.

*Repurposing* refers to an originally unintended application of a videodisc via a control program (Barron & Orwig, 1993, p. 43). In other words, the user, perhaps a teacher or student, can display a portion of a videodisc to serve a completely different purpose than what the developers had in mind. This represents one of the most powerful uses of IVD in schools (Porter, 1995; Sullivan, 1995). It opens up the door to tremendous opportunities for students and teachers to develop their creative potentials. Also, it gives teachers and students a perspective on video through the eyes of a director and helps to prepare teachers and students for the time in the near future when they will have tremendous editing capabilities with digital video.

**Types of Level I uses.** Regular and repurposed videodiscs give teachers a variety of types of products for classroom use.

*Interactive curriculum.* Perhaps the most ambitious use of videodisc technology comes from Optical Data Corporation, which has developed entire curriculum packages around Level I technology. The company has followed its *Windows on Science* program, now in wide use, with *Windows on Math* and *Windows on Social Studies*. Some states now allow school districts to adopt these programs in lieu of textbooks. D. C. Heath's *Interactions* program uses video technology to bring interactive examples of math applications in real-world settings.

*Problem solving.* Discs such as Videodiscovery's *Science Sleuths* and *Math Sleuths* provide students with mysteries to solve. The videodisc programs offer clues in the form of interviews, textual and numeric data, photographs, and diagrams. The teacher plays an active role in guiding students via questioning techniques and just-in-time teaching.

*Simulations.* Optical Data's *Adventures of Jasper Woodbury* teaches middle-school math with a series of simulated scenarios. Students solve real-world applied math problems by retrieving data embedded in the stories. Barcode technology comes in handy, since it enables students to review segments from the story as needed. It is designed so that the teacher can stop the action and teach certain math techniques just when needed to solve techniques problems.

*Visual databases.* Visual databases are collections of individual pictures and short video segments. *BioSci II* was one of the earliest examples of this type of program. These databases are perhaps most useful in the areas of science and art and provide a wealth of resources for both teacher presentations and student projects.

*Movies and documentaries.* Schools can choose from thousands of movies, documentaries, and other general-use videodiscs at reasonable prices. These resources can yield tremendous educational benefits. Through the search feature controlled by the remote control, a teacher can access any frame or segment of a disc almost instantly. The random access capability of the technology holds great promise for encouraging sound pedagogical uses of video as opposed to playing movies straight through.

*Student presentations.* Videodiscs allow students to create their own illustrated presentations on topics they have researched or books they have read (Thorpe, 1993). This is a kind of repurposing, in which students present selected frames to support and enhance their reports.

**Level III Capabilities and Applications for Education**

**Hypermedia.** In probably its most powerful use, Level III technology incorporates videodisc resources into interactive hypermedia programs. These resources include video, audio, animation, photographic, and text data. The most common resources accessed from a videodisc are video and still images.

Figure 6.7 shows an example screen from a hypermedia program that utilizes Level III interactive video.

**Figure 6.7    Screen from a Level III Software Curriculum Package**

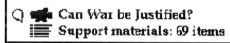

> ## Can War be Justified?
> Virtually all of the world's great philosophies declare that people should treat each other with dignity, justice and respect. To Christians, Muslims and Jews, who follow faiths that consider the Old Testament to be a sacred text, "Thou Shalt Not Kill" is believed to be one of the **ten commandments** given by God to Moses on Mount Sinai.
>
> Despite the moral and religious prohibitions against violence, war and violence have continued throughout human history. One of the challenges of philosophers has been to explain why wars continue, and to determine under what circumstances war can be justified. The concepts of fairness and justice that all cultures share have also resulted in a body of customs and agreements that have become **international law**. These laws of nations also establish the circumstances under which nations may claim that waging war is justified.
>
> Q  Can War be Justified?
> Support materials: 69 items

Source: From ABC News Interactive Lessons of War. Reprinted by permission of Glencoe Publishing Co.

**Presentation tool.** Level III interactive videodiscs also act as components of presentation tools integrated into educational programs. Some curriculum programs, like those in the *ABC Interactive* series and *BioSci II*, have built-in tools that allow teachers and students to develop their own presentations by drawing on the videodisc resources.

**Types of Level III uses.** Though not as popular as Level I uses, Level III IVD offers several kinds of activities for classroom use.

- **Databases.** Level III software allows easy access to the contents of visual databases. For example, the *Living Textbook* series from Optical Data offers a vast collection of visual resources to enhance science instruction.

- **Hypermedia exploration.** A number of Level III programs are designed to let users choose their own pathways through large bodies of information. IBM's *Illuminated Manuscript, STV: Human Body,* and *GTV: A Geographic Perspective on American History* are examples of this type of program. Some

educators believe that hypermedia represents the best and highest use of videodisc technology.

- **Simulations.** IBM's *Exploring Chemistry* series simulates an interactive laboratory that a provides a safe, efficient, and effective way for students to do experiments. Tom Snyder's *The Great Ocean Rescue* and *The Great Solar System Rescue* invite teams of students to analyze visual data and solve problems. Both Snyder programs are for whole-group instruction in a one-computer classroom.

- **Problem solving.** Apple Computer's *TLT: Teaching, Learning, and Technology* is a Level III tool intended to help schools work through the school improvement process. The videodisc component provides interviews with experts in the field and numerous examples of teachers and students in action. A presentation program interfaces with CD-ROM drives as well as videodisc players.

### Example Lessons Using IVD Multimedia/ Hypermedia Systems

The Example Lessons, 6.1 through 6.3, illustrate how to use IVD at both Level I and Level III interactivity.

---

### Example Lesson 6.1
### A Persuasive Presentation with Level I IVD (grades 5–12)

**Lesson Purpose.** Use Level I interactive videodisc technology to create a persuasive presentation.

**Instructional Activities.** Pass out a copy of the following scenario to the students. Ask them to read it.

*Scenario.* The Salt Quest. Military commands all over the world are in a state of high alert. A fleet of alien spacecraft has been lurking just outside earth's atmosphere for the past two days. An organization called "What's Up"—a think tank composed of highly educated men and women who for years

*Continued*

have been convinced that extraterrestrial life exists—was asked to contact the aliens to see what they wanted. The spacecraft are from a planet called Nacl, which is in another solar system. The inhabitants of Nacl require tremendous amounts of salt to exist. They are getting close to depleting their own supplies and have been on a long search for new supplies. They have noticed that the earth's oceans are full of salt, so they thought that they would help themselves to this huge supply.

You are a committee of "What's Up" members that must persuade the Naclites that it would not be a good idea to mine the salt from the oceans. The Naclites are reasonable beings who, it is thought, will move on to other places if they realize that mining the oceans would kill off millions of beautiful creatures. "What's Up" is charged with putting together a presentation that will convince the Naclites that the sea life on earth is too magnificent to be sacrificed just to satisfy their need for salt. The members decide that the presentation must have visuals, and Level I interactive video would be the best media to use.

To tap the creative resources of as many members as possible, the group has divided into subgroups that will each develop a 5-minute presentation. The group will then decide which presentation to use with the Naclites. The individual presentations will be evaluated according to the following criteria: persuasiveness, creativity, and entertainment value. Provide the groups at least one videodisc that contains images of sea creatures. The groups then need to scan through the videodisc and select still frames or video segments that they can use in their presentation. They will then develop the actual presentations, keeping in mind the criteria for evaluation.

Source: Jack Edwards.

## Example Lesson 6.2
## Critical/Creative Listening with Level I IVD (grades 3–12)

**Lesson Purpose.** To develop the creative and critical listening skills of the students. Specifically, students will determine a speaker's purpose or point of view.

**Instructional Activities.** The teacher selects a videodisc that may be suitable for this activity. The academic level of the students and the availability of discs should determine this choice. The teacher chooses some exemplary segments from the disc that model speakers expressing points of view or demonstrating clear purposes. The teacher then plays a segment and asks students to surmise the speaker's purpose or point of view. The videodisc player enables the teacher to show the segment over and over again. This activity often leads to lively discussion in the class. The videodisc player can also support student assessment. For example, a segment could be shown, and students could write their responses. The teacher can select a student objective from the following list:

- Determine the main idea of what the speaker is saying.
- Identify details that support the main idea.
- Determine the speaker's purpose or point of view.
- Adapt information to one's own needs or experiences, or both.
- Indicate cause-and-effect relationships among the speaker's ideas.
- Evaluate continuity or logic in what the speaker says.
- Visualize a scene the speaker describes.
- Judge the validity or veracity of what the speaker says.
- Relate what the speaker says to one's own experiences.
- Determine whether additional meanings are hidden behind the speaker's words.
- Anticipate what the speaker will say next.
- Sort out relevant information from the irrelevant and fact from opinion.
- Identify propaganda techniques the speaker may be using.

Source: Jack Edwards.

**Example Lesson 6.3**
**Innovative Ideas for Level III IVD (grades 5–12)**

**Lesson Purpose.** The ideas outlined here are based on a description of various classroom videodisc uses given by Sherwood (1994). Each calls for using an authoring program such as *HyperStudio* to create a series of clickable buttons on the screen to show the frames of the videodiscs specified in these lesson activities:

**Instructional Activities**

*A Lesson on Ecosystems.* Use discs such as *Science Essentials* and *Wild Places,* Volumes 2 and 3. Let students select and report on an aspect of ecosystems in general such as ecosystems definitions, deserts, and rain forests. Each student is responsible for writing a word processed introduction to their reports as well as a presentation of videodisc images and clips to support their topics. Have them work in pairs to create buttons to run the videodisc sequences. After they complete their projects, the students present their products to several classes and the school board.

*A Solar Systems Lesson.* Let students use a disc such as *Beyond the Solar System.* Have them create buttons to display and describe each of several kinds of heavenly bodies like planets, comets, and stars. Have them write an introduction and directions for using the stack and include them on the title page.

*Learning about Insects.* The students use a disc on insects such as Smithsonian's *Insects* to structure a lesson for younger students. The students who create the lesson can use the multimedia authoring software to include questions and answers with the materials. The younger students use the product as a review of the physical characteristics and behaviors of various insects.

*Colonial America.* Make history come alive by using a disc such as the *Colonial America 1760's* in conjunction with role playing. Have students create buttons that allow users to look at various colonist occupations. After viewing and discussing the segments, the students can act out the roles of colonists, the Royal governor, a colonial assembly member, and a British magistrate.

Source: Jack Edwards.

## Interactive CD-ROM and DVD Systems

CD-ROMs as music media have become as commonplace in the lives of young people as phonograph records were to their parents and grandparents. But CD-ROMS have additional capabilities undreamed of in the days of record albums and turntables. Commonly called *compact discs* or *CDs,* CD-ROMs are made of the same material as videodiscs but are smaller in size, just 4.72 inches (12 cm) in diameter. In appearance, CD-ROMs look identical to audio CDs. The main practical difference between an audio CD and a CD-ROM is what they can store and how they are used. Both store data in digital form. But audio CDs store sound, while CD-ROMs store text, audio, video, animation, and graphics information. CD-ROMs are known for their huge storage capacity, up to 650 MB of data, which equates to the equivalent of 250,000 pages of text, or five hundred 500-page novels. Computer systems get access to CD-ROMs through either internal or external CD-ROM players (see Figure 6.8).

DVDs look like CD-ROMs but have much greater storage capacity: currently 4.7 GB and from 8.5–17 GB in the future (DVD Coming Soon, 1998). Like CD-ROMs, DVDs began with a read-only format but are predicted to take the place of computer disks, hard drives, and even videodiscs and CD-ROMs. They will be able to store high-quality video as well as audio and text data, thus making

**Figure 6.8    CD-ROM and DVD Player with Discs**

Source: Anthony Magnacca/Merrill.

them valuable to multimedia developers in education and elsewhere.

## CD-ROM and DVD System Capabilities and Applications

The technical information provided in this section about the design and use of CD-ROMs and DVDs will help educators understand when and how to use them.

**Hardware.** Internal, or built-in, CD-ROM drives are housed inside computer cases. External drives connect to computers by cables. In recent years, more and more machines have been sold with built-in CD-ROM drives. Some CDs play audio information only through external speakers or headphones. Another hardware consideration is the size of the computer's monitor; some programs that include video will require 13-inch or larger monitors. The fine print in catalogs of CD-ROM programs usually list the hardware requirements.

**Software.** The special software a computer must run to communicate with a CD-ROM player is commonly referred to as CD-ROM *drivers*. This usually is not an issue with a built-in CD-ROM drive, since the manufacturer installs the software along with the hardware. Some CD-ROM programs require users to install additional software on the hard drive to expedite the use of the program on the CD.

**Drive speed.** Many of the newer CD-ROMs include video segments. To play video segments successfully, a CD-ROM player should have access time of 280 milliseconds (ms) or less. A quicker access time (smaller number of milliseconds) is faster and more desirable.

**Platform.** CD-ROMs typically fit under one of four platform types: Macintosh, MS-DOS, Windows, and MPC. MPC (multimedia PC) is a multimedia standard agreed upon by hardware and software producers in the PC industry. It provides enhanced audio and video, but only for MS-DOS computers. When ordering, it's important to request the correct type of disc for your machines. Many CD-ROMs are produced as *hybrid* CDs, or those that contain software for two or more platforms (usually Macintosh and Windows) on a single disc.

### Advantages of CD-ROM and DVD Technologies

- **Large storage capacity.** CD-ROMs provide an excellent way of storing large quantities of text, audio, and video information. Floppy disks do not have the capacity to take advantage of the potential of multimedia.
- **Durability.** Discs are durable enough to hold up well under constant handling by students.

- **Cost.** Once content is developed, the cost of replicating CD-ROMs is low.
- **Search speed.** Although CD drives read information more slowly than hard drives, they provide a fast way of searching through large collections of information.
- **CD availability.** Thousands of titles are available, many educational.
- **Audio CD capability.** CD-ROM players can play tracks from audio CDs. This is convenient for hypermedia authoring. Students can add segments of music or sound effects to a hypermedia product by accessing a disc in the CD-ROM drive, an advantage that alleviates copyright concerns. A word of caution: Never try to play a CD-ROM disc on an audio CD player; it will ruin the CD-ROM.
- **DVD capability.** These discs will remedy many of the limitations presented by CD-ROMs. They will store more information—including full-motion video—and offer faster access.

### Disadvantages of CD-ROM and DVD Technologies

- **Access speed.** CD-ROM drives access data slowly compared to hard drives. However, DVD offers faster speeds.
- **Shortage of hardware.** The aging computers in many schools still prevent them from taking advantage of CD-ROM technology. As time passes, this should become a less serious problem. If at all possible, schools should buy machines with built-in CD-ROM drives.

### Classroom Applications for CD-ROM and DVD Multimedia/Hypermedia Systems

The number of titles in the CD-ROM market has increased at a phenomenal rate over the past few years and will continue to grow. Eventually, CD-ROMs will store and display motion sequences, a role currently filled by IVD and DVD. At this time, IVD primarily is used for applications that require video clips, while CD-ROMs are used more for database products such as encyclopedias. In the meantime, CD-ROM technology has adapted to allow users to store data on them as well as use them for pre-stored applications. Since CD-ROMs hold so much more information than disks, they are becoming valuable additions to schools' collections of storage devices, and readable/writable CD-ROM drives are becoming commonplace. Consequently, there are several popular categories of classroom uses.

- **Interactive storybooks.** These on-screen stories have become extremely popular with primary teachers and students (Glasgow, 1996, 1996–1997, and 1997; Kahn, 1997). On the audio tracks, narrators read pages as the words are highlighted on screen. If a student needs to hear a word again, just clicking on it with the mouse pointer will activate the audio. Some teachers prefer the straightforward approach of the *Discus Books* series, while others are more drawn to the Brøderbund titles because students tend to find them more engaging. Other formats are likely to emerge as educators learn more about the instructional value of these books.

- **Instructional software.** A single CD-ROM can store the equivalent of 800 3½-inch microdisks. This makes CD-ROM a wonderful technology for distributing instructional software. Some companies have taken advantage of this added capacity by enhancing successful programs with new multimedia features, for example, *The Oregon Trail* by MECC and Brøderbund's *Adventures of Carmen Sandiego.*

- **Reference materials.** CD-ROM technology meets the needs of students and teachers in this area more than any other. A plethora of reference materials is available at reasonable costs. To add still more value, these resources are accompanied by software that makes searching for information both easy and efficient. Below are just a few of the categories and titles.

  - **Encyclopedias.** *Compton's Encyclopedia, Encarta* by Microsoft, *The Aircraft Encyclopedia,* and *Encyclopedia of Science and Technology.*

  - **Almanacs.** *Illustrated Facts, The CIA World Factbook, The KGB World Factbook,* and *The Time Almanac.*

  - **Atlases.** *U.S. Geography, Picture Atlas of the World, U.S. Atlas,* and *Small Blue Planet: The Real Cities Atlas.*

- **Collections of development resources.** A wide variety of resources are now shipped on CD-ROM. These include collections of clip art, sound effects, photographs, video clips, fonts, and document templates. Some major conferences, like the National Educational Computing Conference (NECC), distribute to each registrant proceedings, presenter handouts, vendor samples, and shareware on CD-ROM.

- **Future uses of DVD for multimedia/hypermedia.** As Arthur and Mizer (1998) observe, DVD technology currently is limited to "linear motion pictures, replacing VHS tapes with better sound and picture quality, but without taking advantage of the medium" (p. 24). However, they anticipate that many non-entertainment applications should be available by the year 2000, including several for education, including encyclopedias, museum tours, and books on DVD.

### Example Lessons Using CD-ROM Multimedia/Hypermedia Systems

Example Lessons 6.4 and 6.5 illustrate how to use resources typically stored on CD-ROM-based multimedia systems.

---

### Example Lesson 6.4
### A "Tracking Down Trivia" Scavenger Hunt (grades 3–12)

**Lesson Purpose.** This activity is designed to improve student skills in using CD-ROM-based encyclopedias and databases for research.

**Instructional Activities.** Pass out copies of a list of questions like the following to the class. Have students work in pairs on a "scavenger hunt" for information. Using an atlas and/or encyclopedia as resources, have them look up the answers to the questions. If appropriate, inject an element of competition in the activity by offering incentives to all those who answer the most questions correctly during class.

1. What is the capital city of Sweden?
2. What was E. B. White's first name?
3. Who won the Nobel Prize for Peace in 1985?
4. When did the Japanese bomb Pearl Harbor?
5. How did John Paul Jones die?
6. What is the state flower of Utah?
7. What does illiterate mean?
8. What gases make up the atmosphere of Jupiter?
9. What movie won the Academy Award for best picture in 1985?
10. What is a synonym for the word *supercilious?*
11. What is the chemical formula for sulfuric acid?
12. If Babe Ruth had lived 20 years longer, how old would he have been when he died?

## Example Lesson 6.5
## Research Detectives (grades 7–12)

**Lesson Purpose.** This activity can help develop student skill at locating and analyzing historical information.

**Instructional Activities.** Distribute copies of the following scenario to small groups of students. Provide access to a CD-ROM player and a variety of CD-ROM reference tools. Microsoft's *Bookshelf* is excellent for this activity since it contains an encyclopedia, dictionary, almanac, atlas, and other resources—all on one CD-ROM. Some high-level vocabulary and ambiguous facts have been deliberately included in the scenario; this requires students to use the reference resources to read up on the history cited, locate discrepancies in the suspects' stories, and analyze them to determine which suspect must be lying. Another way to do this type of project is to have students write their own scenarios which could then be published and shared with other classes to develop their research and analytical skills.

*Scenario 1: The Case of the Missing CD-ROM.* The staff, parents, and students of Luke Bean High School have worked for the past year to develop a comprehensive technology plan for their school. They have collected a vast quantity of data to present to the school board in the hope that the board will fund their proposal. The LBHS technology plan has been transferred to a CD-ROM in order to present it in a multimedia/hypermedia format; this should enable the board members to sort easily through the wealth of resources: interviews, sample lessons, and research reports—all intended to inform and persuade.

A major glitch developed last night, however, when somebody stole the only CD-ROM master. The police have narrowed down the list of suspects to three individuals: a teacher, a student, and a parent; for different reasons, all are opposed to the use of technology in school. Summaries of the police interviews with the three suspects follow. Your job is to find out who stole the CD-ROM. If you find out which one is telling lies in the interview, then you will find the thief. Therefore, you must fully research their statements made during the interviews.

*Suspect 1.* Beeso Bidmee has been a faculty member at Luke Bean High School for the past 19 years. He was born on July 14, 1923, as Mr. Bidmee pointed out, the same date as former U.S. Senator Bob Dole. He teaches advanced math and driver education. Mr. Bidmee does not believe that schools need to spend money on advanced technology. He sees nothing wrong with the way schools have been teaching; the problem is the kids. He would like to use the money earmarked for technology to hire a full-time person to staff an ongoing in-school suspension program. "There is no way that I could have taken that CD-ROM last night," said Beeso. "My consort, Brenda, and I were watching a theatrical representation about the 21st president of the United States, Teddy Roosevelt. Plus, the police said that the disc was stolen between the hours of 10:00 p.m. and 9:00 a.m. and I didn't get up this morning until after the time that the Japanese bombed Pearl Harbor in 1941."

*Suspect 2.* Alice B. Cokeless is a child of the 1960s. She was born on May 9, 1945, the day after V-E Day. She has matured over the years and now is a responsible parent who has put her wild years behind her. She still holds on to some of her anti-establishment beliefs, however, and she steadfastly opposes the use of instructional technology in schools. She complains that big business is pushing the use of technology in schools as a way to make money; in the process, it is depleting schools of precious fiscal resources. Alice denies any involvement in the theft of the CD-ROM. She was at the library working on her book about the civil rights movement. Last night, she was researching an incident in 1972 when the governor of Alabama was shot.

*Suspect 3.* Raul Fernandez, a student at LBHS, is a football player who thinks that technology is taking money away from more important needs such as athletic equipment. Raul was born during the time that the 1980 Olympics were being held in Lake Placid, New York. He was busy last night doing schoolwork; he was working on a report that covered the United States invasion of Grenada in 1983. This subject interests Raul, he says, since the U.S. troops invaded in order to evict the troops of a noted anti-religious dictator, Fidel Castro.

Source: Jack Edwards.

## Hypermedia Authoring Systems

One of the most amazing aspects about multimedia systems is that people who are fairly non-technical can develop their own complex, capable hypermedia products. Perhaps most importantly for schools, hypermedia authoring may play a major role in preparing students for the information-intensive and visually-oriented world of the future. In tomorrow's digital world, powerful personal computers and ubiquitous electronic networking will allow people to incorporate a variety of media into their communications. Indeed, hypermedia publishing may eventually supersede paper publishing in importance. People will transfer information and knowledge using a combination of video, animation, music, graphics, and sound effects. To prepare for this information-intensive environment, students and teachers alike will need an array of skills in hypermedia authoring.

### Characteristics of Hypermedia Authoring Systems

Although different hypermedia programs may employ different terminology for their structure, most follow a similar metaphor: that of a stack of cards (see Figure 6.9). This text will use the card terminology, which is employed in *HyperCard* and *HyperStudio,* but readers should understand and be able to transfer the general concepts behind this terminology to other hypermedia environments.

**Characteristic 1: Stacks made up of cards.** Each screen of information in a hypermedia product is called a *card.* A group of cards is called a *stack.* The hypermedia author need not arrange these cards in conventional manner, such as alphabetically or chronologically, since stacks don't have clearly defined beginning or ending points. They are linked together with interactive *hotspots* or *buttons.* Buttons define places on the screen that initiate actions when clicked with the mouse pointer. Since invisible buttons can be placed on top of graphics or text, they can adopt almost any appearance. Buttons represent the most powerful component of the hypermedia metaphor; they are the engines that drive hypermedia and hypertext interactivity.

Cards also contain *graphics items* and *text fields.* Graphics items, or computer drawings, may be placed on a card using the paint tools included in the hypertext authoring program, by importing pre-made computer-generated graphics, or by using a scanner to digitize a paper copy. Large collections of graphics covering many subjects are commercially available on both floppy disk and CD-ROM at reasonable prices.

Text may also be added to a card using a text tool within the program's graphics function or with a text field. A text field is essentially a small word processing screen that can be formatted, sized, and placed on a card as the author sees fit. One card can contain multiple text fields. The author

Figure 6.9  **Sample Multimedia Stack**

can easily edit text placed in a text field. The text tool is useful for labeling items, but they are difficult to edit later. Large blocks of text must be added by creating a text field.

Depending on a program's complexity, the author can control button actions in two ways: through pre-made buttons or by scripting. In the most common control method, the author selects from a number of pre-programmed options for the most common button actions. This feature enables the author to develop hypermedia stacks efficiently and is so easy to use that even elementary students can become hypermedia authors. However, buttons also can be programmed through scripting.

**Characteristic 2: Scripting.** Most hypermedia authoring programs allow the author to program button actions in simple programming languages such as *HyperLogo.* Once the only way to select button actions, this method now is used primarily by advanced authors to develop more sophisticated projects. However, some teachers choose to have their students script regularly as a way to encourage development of basic programming skills.

### Hypermedia Authoring Resources

As hypermedia programs have evolved, they have become more powerful and more user-friendly. Authors now can draw on a wide variety of resources to put a full range of sound and motion in their hypermedia products. This section describes some common resources available in hypermedia authoring.

**Audio resources.** Hypermedia authoring programs offer users a number of ways to incorporate audio clips.

- **CD audio.** Cards include segments of audio CDs in CD-ROM drives or videodisc players that use the LB2 standard. CDs provide digitized music, speech, or sound effects.

- **Videodiscs.** Rather than playing both the video and audio tracks of a videodisc, authors may choose to leave the video and access the audio track alone.

- **Recorded sounds.** Hypermedia programs usually allow authors to record sound into their programs. This can include voice, as when an author records his/her reading of a poem.
- **Prerecorded sounds.** Many hypermedia authoring programs come with built-in selections of sound effects. Authors can also add sounds from packaged collections stored on microdisks or CD-ROMs, sometimes called "clip sounds."

**Video resources.** Videoclips can add a whole new dimension to a program and provide authors with many new communication possibilities. As with audio, authors can incorporate video displays into a program in many ways.

- **Digitized videos.** By using a video digitizer, a hypermedia author can import video images from external sources such as a VCR, a videodisc, or a camcorder. Programs such as *Quicktime* allow authors to create and edit their own short videoclips (movies) and place them on cards. Teachers and students need to observe copyright laws when importing video in this manner. Digitized video also consumes a great deal of hard drive storage space, thus limiting the amount of video that can realistically be incorporated into a program. An external hard drive offers one solution to this problem; removable cartridge systems are very effective in this role, although the costs for the individual cartridges can be quite high. In the future, more efficient video compression routines promise greater latitude for hypermedia authors.
- **Videodiscs.** Most hypermedia programs enable authors to access either individual slides or segments of video from videodiscs. This can prove a big advantage due to the high quality of audio and video recordings from videodiscs.
- **Prerecorded videos on CD-ROMs.** Authors can buy collections of short videoclips on CD-ROM to incorporate into hypermedia programs. No copyrights inhibit use of these images, giving authors much more leeway in their presentations.

**Photographs.** A picture is worth a thousand words in hypermedia, as much as elsewhere. Photographs provide a powerful resource for authors in all subject areas.

- **Scanned photos.** Authors can digitize traditional photographs using scanners and then incorporate these images into hypermedia stacks.
- **Captured from video sources.** By using a video digitizer, an author can freeze images from a VCR, camcorder, or videodisc player and then import them.
- **Digital cameras.** These cameras take digitized, color pictures that can be added to hypermedia cards. Pictures can be downloaded directly from the camera to the computer's hard drive.
- **Imported from CD-ROMs.** Collections of photographs on CD-ROMs are marketed expressly for inclusion in hypermedia programs.

**Graphic images.** Graphics or drawings offer another tool for authors to communicate their ideas. Often an illustration will demonstrate a point that is difficult to get across with words. This aspect of hypermedia authoring is particularly appealing to artistically inclined users.

- **Created by authors.** Virtually all hypermedia programs offer basic collections of tools that let users draw or paint graphics. These tools enable users with even limited artistic talents to create credible designs and drawings.
- **Imported from clip art collections.** A vast array of clip art collections are available for purchase. These pre-made graphics cover a wide assortment of subject areas.
- **Scanned images.** As another alternative for accessing graphics, an image can be scanned from either a book of clip art or a drawing done in conventional art media such as pencils or paintbrushes. Since computer access often is limited, some teachers prefer students to draw their pictures off the computer and then digitize them using scanners.

**Animation.** Animation is a highly effective tool for illustrating a concept; a student might create an animation of a seed germinating as part of a project on plants. The sources of these displays are familiar.

- **Imported from CD-ROMs.** Collections of animation are also available on CD-ROM. Like other media, these premade collections allow authors to rapidly add effective and professional animations to a project.
- **Created using animation tools.** Hypermedia programs have improved dramatically in their animation capabilities. A novice animator can now easily generate sophisticated and effective animations.

**Text.** In spite of the attention paid to other components of hypermedia, text still remains one of the most powerful ways of communicating ideas.

- **Writing as project develops.** All hypermedia programs offer standard word processing features that enable users to write text. In addition, text may also be added as a graphic item. This feature lets the user easily drag text around the screen and is handy for adding labels to pictures.
- **Importing from word processing files.** Most programs also let authors import text created separately in word processors. This can be a boon for an author who has saved a great deal of writing in a large collection of word processing files.

### Hypermedia Authoring Software Packages

Since the late 1980s, teachers have had access to hypermedia authoring programs like *HyperCard* for Macintosh, *LinkWay* for MS-DOS machines, and *TutorTech* for Apple II. These early programs represented a major jump forward in technology, but their use was limited. Authors had to make major time commitments to learn the software, and developing projects of any length took a long time. Their major limitation resulted from the need to include extensive scripting, or programming commands. Although the scripting language was easy to learn compared to more traditional computer languages, its complexity still limited its popularity.

Things began to change when Roger Wagner's *Hyper-Studio* was released for Apple IIGS. This program used the same basic metaphor as *HyperCard* but eliminated much of the need for scripting. In recent years, a number of programs have become available that emulate *HyperStudio's* easy-to-use format. As computer power increases and becomes more affordable, even more sophisticated and easy-to-use programs than the ones described here will become available. However, teachers also can choose simpler products such as Brøderbund's *KidPix* or the slideshow option in *AppleWorks.*

- **HyperCard.** Apple has only slowly upgraded this product; however, at press time, a major upgrade was planned. *HyperCard* still has a large user base and remains one of the most powerful programs.

- **HyperStudio.** One of the most innovative products on the market for Mac and *Windows* computers, this product has developed a large following among teachers. Roger Wagner Inc. has focused its efforts on *HyperStudio* and upgrades it regularly.

- **MicroWorlds Project Builder (LCSI).** The unique emphasis on Logo gives users experience at simple programming. Separate packages are also sold as *Math Project Builder* and *Language Arts Project Builder.*

- **Multimedia Toolbook by Asymetrix.** This *Windows* program features video editing software, support for many file formats, and a Media Packager that gathers and compresses multimedia elements for a given product.

- **Digital Chisel.** A powerful product for the Macintosh by Pierian Spring Software, this program supports full text-to-speech capability and includes question templates for developing tests.

- **Macromedia Authorware.** This authoring package has features ranging from animations to streaming video.

- **Macromedia Director.** This very capable and complex full-featured system is for developing multimedia products and includes video.

## Hardware Requirements for Hypermedia Authoring

Though hypermedia authoring can be accomplished with a fairly minimal computer system, more complex products require additional hardware and software capabilities.

- **Computer with keyboard and monitor.** Hypermedia development may be done on any platform as long as the system has a hard drive and 12–16 MB of RAM. The minimum requirements to utilize programs like *HyperStudio* or *LinkWay Live* are much more realistic for the average classroom than higher-end programs.

- **Digital camera.** These cameras, like the Canon XapShot or Apple QuickTake, let users take digital photographs and store them as digital files. The images can then be incorporated into hypermedia projects. Students of all ages enjoy using their own digital photographs in projects.

- **Scanner.** If no digital camera is available, scanners can be used to digitize photos so they can be saved to a disk. Scanners also can capture still images from magazines or books.

- **Video digitizer.** Video digitizers, also known as *digitizing boards,* capture full-motion video from video cameras, VCRs, videodisc players, or live TV. The video segments are then stored as computer files and can be edited using software like *Adobe Premier.* Both teachers and students should recognize copyright restrictions when digitizing and editing video.

- **Video input.** To implement motion or still video in a production, access to the source of these images is needed. Video cameras, VCRs, videodiscs, or CD-ROMs are among the possible sources.

- **Audio card.** To incorporate sound, an audio capture, playback card, and audio source such as a microphone are needed. Many computer systems sold in recent years have had built-in audio cards.

- **CD-ROM drive.** CD-ROMs are essential elements in multimedia technology, and, because of their huge storage capacity, CD-ROMs are the only technology for storing large quantities of digitized video or audio. Hypermedia authors can also buy large collections of digitized video, audio, and still image resources on CD-ROM.

- **Audio speakers.** In order to monitor quality and simply to hear the audio parts of a program, speakers are mandatory for hypermedia development. Many newer computers are shipped with either external or internal speakers.

- **Videodisc players.** Videodisc players with Level III capabilities provide excellent resources for hypermedia authors. High-quality video or audio input can easily be accessed from any videodisc. With thousands of videodisc titles on the market and existing videodisc players in many schools, this technology will prove to be a valuable resource for years to come.

## Hypermedia Authoring Procedures

Whether teachers are developing their own skills or those of their students, they must remember that the hypermedia authoring process involves two distinct phases. Initially, authors need to learn the mechanics of the programs and develop their understanding of the concept of hypermedia. No one can develop a quality product without first being reasonably comfortable with the tools. However, at the next level, hypermedia authors must develop insights on the complexities of the various media and knowledge of visual and navigation design. This is a long-term process that will emerge through a great deal of experience. A number of strategies can aid the classroom teacher in helping students use their time efficiently and focus on developing quality products.

**An optimal development sequence.** Consider the following steps when students do hypermedia development:

1. **Review others' products.** An effective way of developing authoring skills for beginners is to look at what others have done. This is particularly true with scripting. Evaluating the scripts of existing programs can give insight into how to write scripts for new projects. Through the Internet or commercial on-line services, teachers can download stacks. This opens up a world of low-cost or free hypermedia resources for both teachers and students. It is also helpful to examine some effective uses of media; Ken Burns's series on the Civil War, for example, demonstrates the power of images and sound when melded together in the context of a story.

2.    **Do research first.** Most hypermedia development projects require research to locate materials and data, analyze their findings, and summarize them in a format for use in the hypermedia product. It is important to allow adequate time for this research phase for it is the heart of the learning activity.

3.    **Storyboard.** Storyboarding helps students make better use of valuable computer time. On index cards or sticky notes, students can lay out what they want on each individual frame. But planning is the most difficult thing for students; they want to get right to the "fun stuff." Most students prefer to develop only online. Teachers must insist that on-paper planning be done first. It may help to explain that professional media creators practice storyboarding and that even famous movie directors such as Steven Spielberg storyboard their entire movie before doing a single camera shot because it saves time in the long run.

4.    **Develop individual frames.** Before adding links or graphics, students should develop each frame, including text fields.

5.    **Insert graphics.** Add clip art, photos, animations, movies, and other media onto each card as needed to carry out the design.

6.    **Add links and/or scripts.** Only after all the cards have been developed and decorated should links be added. Most authoring software allows a storyboard format to see most or all of the cards at one time. This and the card or sticky-note storyboards help students keep links organized among cards.

7.    **Test and revise the product.** After it is drafted, students should test their products, preferably with the help of others who have not been involved in its development. The aim is to revise their products and meet criteria outlined in a later section of this chapter, Evaluating Hypermedia Products.

Rembelinsky (1997–1998) offers a development sequence designed specifically for creating multimedia summaries of project-based research. She recommends students do steps in each of the following general headings: written summary, historical background, creative narrative, scanned images, video, and self-evaluation.

**Authoring skills to develop over time.** The beauty of hypermedia authoring is that students can create products with skills that range from basic to extraordinarily complex and sophisticated. Students may begin with "the basics" and teachers can help them move on to advanced techniques in several areas.

*Media literacy.* Given the complexities and proliferation of different media, an understanding of media basics will become a fundamental skill for the information age. Since most people will have tremendous capabilities to adapt and alter existing media in the near future, a critically important part of instruction in hypermedia authoring will focus on how to be critical and ethical producers and consumers of media (Roblyer, 1998).

*Using music and art.* Visual arts and music play major roles in the effectiveness of hypermedia products. As students gain more knowledge in the theory and aesthetics of music and art, they will use these resources more productively in the authoring process.

*Design principles.* Many principles of desktop publishing also apply to hypermedia designs. When students first see the array of graphics and sound options available, they typically overindulge and use so many colors, graphics, and sounds that content is overshadowed. Some of the design principles that can help guide more judicious use of these options are described later in this chapter, Evaluating Hypermedia Products.

*Creativity and novel thinking.* When assessing student projects, look for and encourage creative uses of the potential of hypermedia. Too many student projects resemble glorified paper-based projects; they do not take advantage of the true power of this medium. Classroom activities that encourage creative and critical thinking in all subject areas help develop skills and a mindset that naturally enhances the authoring process.

*Considering audience.* Whenever possible, teachers should try to give students an opportunity to display their projects. Students will be much more motivated if they believe their work is valued. Research on writing has shown that students will invest more effort in the writing process when they know others will read their writing. Turner and Dipinto (1992) and others have observed that this sense of audience carries over to hypermedia authoring. However, teachers sometimes find that components of a student project make sense only to the author. Younger students in particular should be reminded constantly that they need to think of their projects from the user's point of view. Encourage them to test their projects on other students, family, or friends.

## Evaluating Hypermedia Products

Dipinto and Turner (1995) suggest that student self-assessment of hypermedia projects may be the most important component of the assessment process, saying that perhaps it enables students to construct a microworld where assessment becomes a feedback mechanism, leading to further exploration and collaboration (p. 11).

**Criteria for evaluating products.** Several authors have developed criteria and rubrics for assessing the quality of hypermedia products. Litchfield (1995), Brunner (1996), and Clark (1996) describe qualities to look for in effective products. These are summarized in Figure 6.10. In addition, McCullen and Alexander (McCullen, 1998) have developed the rubric shown in Figure 6.11 for evaluating hypermedia products.

**Electronic portfolios.** Hypermedia projects are valuable additions to student portfolios used for assessment purposes. Many authoring programs include player files that run program files without the application itself. This is particularly useful when a student wants to take a project home and run it on the family computer or to take it to a college or job interview.

**Figure 6.10    Criteria for Evaluating Multimedia Projects**

> **Language**
> _____ No ethnic, slang, or rude names; content presented in a professional way
> _____ Correct spelling, punctuation, and grammar
> _____ No questionable vocabulary, slang terms, or curse words
>
> **Type and Font**
> _____ Controlled use of fonts and type sizes (no more than 2–3 in product)
> _____ Type large enough to read when projected
> _____ Color contrasts with background for easy reading
> _____ Bold or plain for writing main text; avoid shadow and outline for more than a few words
> _____ Have only brief main ideas in each frame; do not have paragraphs of text; save explanations for your presentation
>
> **Graphics, Visuals, and Sound**
> _____ Content includes text, graphics, visuals, and sound; each frame contains text and graphics
> _____ Graphics, visuals, and sound are appropriate to the topic, add to your project, and help communicate the information relevant to the topic
> _____ No obscene or rude graphics or visuals
> _____ Controlled, non-distracting use of screen changes such as wipes, zooms, and fades
> _____ Buttons on each card; each works as indicated
> _____ Pictures and sounds associated with buttons are appropriate to purpose and content of the card(s)
>
> **Content**
> _____ All information is current
> _____ All information is factually accurate

Source: Based on Litchfield, 1995; Brunner, 1996; and Clark, 1996.

## Classroom Applications of Hypermedia Authoring

Multimedia and hypermedia development projects are taking the place of many traditional activities to accomplish the same purposes. Some common classroom applications of multimedia and hypermedia are described here.

- **Multimedia slideshows.** Although slideshow projects frequently call for presentations that are linear in format, they can be useful to help younger students develop beginning multimedia creation skills, since the focus is on the basic skills of writing text and screen design. Monahan and Susong (1996) describe how students developed simple slideshows to display their findings on wildlife.

- **Book reports.** Instead of presenting book reports verbally or as written summaries, it is becoming increasingly common for students to report on their reading through multimedia slideshows or as hypermedia products. Teachers often design a standard format and students fill in the required information and add their own illustrations.

- **Research presentations.** Scholten and Whitmer (1996), Bennett and Diener (1997), and Stuhlmann (1997) point out that hypermedia presentations not only let students present their findings attractively and with impact, the act of producing and sharing what they have learned serves to help students learn even more about the topics and enhance their research, study, and communication skills.

- **Created tours.** Hypermedia products are an effective way to document field trips because they let others take virtual "trips" to the locations.

- **Interactive storybooks.** Fredrickson (1997) describes a use that builds on the book report purpose. Students document existing stories or write their own so they can be read interactively by others. Those reading these hypermedia stories can click on various places on screen to hear or see parts of a story. This format also lets students go beyond one basic sequence and create their own branches and endings to stories.

- **School yearbooks.** Although still a relative novelty, more and more schools are developing their yearbooks as hypermedia products (Kwajewski, 1997).

## Example Lessons Using Hypermedia Authoring

Teachers must prepare students well for hypermedia authoring activities by teaching them technical skills they need and by setting well-defined parameters for the project. This is especially true for younger students and for all students doing such projects for the first time. In addition to some project ideas, Example Lessons 6.6 through 6.9 include activities designed to foster development of students' visual and information literacy skills.

**Figure 6.11  Rubric for Evaluating Multimedia Projects**

| | 1 | 2 | 3 | 4 | Total |
|---|---|---|---|---|---|
| **Curriculum Alignment** (*Objectives to be listed on Entry Form*) | No evidence of relationship to target curriculum; no reference to facts and properly documented resources. Users are not likely to learn from this product. | Some evidence of connection to target curriculum; a few references to facts and properly documented resources. Users find it difficult to learn from this product. | Adequate evidence of connection to target curriculum; clear references to facts and properly documented resources. Users can learn from this product. | Clear evidence of connection to target curriculum; frequent references to facts and properly documented resources. Users are likely to learn from this product. | |
| **Work Completed in the Classroom** (*To be listed on Entry Form*) | Less than 65% of the work was completed in the classroom. | 65–79% of the work was completed in the classroom. | 80–94% of the work was completed in the classroom. | 95–100% of the work was completed in the classroom. | |
| **Teamwork** (*To be listed on Entry Form*) | One or two people did all or most of the work. | Most team members participated in some aspect of the work, but workloads varied. | Most team members contributed their fair share of the work. | The work load was divided and shared equally by all team members. | |
| **Organization of Content** | No logical sequence of information; menus and paths to information are not evident. | Some logical sequence of information, but menus and paths are confusing or flawed. | Logical sequence of information. Menus and paths to more information are clear and direct. | Logical, intuitive sequence of information. Menus and paths to all information are clear and direct. | |
| **Originality** | The work is a minimal collection or rehash of other people's ideas, products, images, and inventions. There is no evidence of new thought. | The work is an extensive collection and rehash of other people's ideas, products, images, and inventions. There is no evidence of new thought or inventiveness. | The product shows evidence of originality and inventiveness. While based on an extensive collection of other people's ideas, products, images, and inventions, the work extends beyond that collection to offer new insights. | The product shows significant evidence of originality and inventiveness. The majority of the content and many of the ideas are fresh, original, inventive, and based upon logical conclusions and sound research. | |
| **Subject Knowledge** | Subject knowledge is not evident. Information is confusing, incorrect, or flawed. | Some subject knowledge is evident. Some information is confusing, incorrect, or flawed. | Subject knowledge is evident in much of the product. Information is clear, appropriate, and correct. | Subject knowledge is evident throughout (more than required). All information is clear, appropriate, and correct. | |
| **Graphical Design** | Exaggerated emphasis upon graphics and special effects weakens the message and interferes with the communication of content and ideas. | Graphical and multimedia elements accompany content but there is little sign of mutual reinforcement. There is no attention paid to visual design criteria such as balance, proportion, harmony and restraint. There is some tendency toward random use of graphics. | Design elements and content combine effectively to deliver a high impact message with the graphics and the words reinforcing each other. | The combination of multimedia elements with words and ideas takes communication and persuasion to a very high level, superior to what could be accomplished with either alone. The mixture brings about synergy and dramatic effects which reach the intended audience. | |
| **Mechanics** | Presentation has four or more spelling errors and/or grammatical errors. | Presentation has three or more misspellings and/or grammatical errors. | Presentation has fewer than two misspellings and/or grammatical errors. | Presentation has no misspellings or grammatical errors. | |
| **Screen Design** | Screens are either confusing and cluttered or barren and stark. Buttons or navigational tools are absent or confusing. | Screens are difficult to navigate, but some buttons and navigational tools work. Users can navigate a few screens. | Screens contain adequate navigational tools and buttons. Users can progress through screens in a logical path to find information. | Screens contain all necessary navigational tools and buttons. Users can progress intuitively through screens in a logical path to find information. | |
| **Use of Enhancements** | No video, audio, or 3-D enhancements are present or use of these tools is inappropriate. | Limited video, audio, or 3-D enhancements are present. In most instances, use of these tools is appropriate. | Some video, audio, or 3-D enhancements are used appropriately to entice users to learn and to enrich the experience. In some cases, clips are either too long or too short. | Appropriate amounts of video, audio, or 3-D enhancements are used effectively to entice users to learn and to enrich the experience. Clips are long enough convey meaning. | |

Source: Developed for ISTE by Caroline McCullen, Instructional Technologist, SAS Institute. Published by *MidLink Magazine*, http://longwood.cs.ucf.edu/~MidLink.

**Example Lesson 6.6**
**Animation and Science**

This activity offers students an opportunity to develop animation skills by incorporating science into the animation process. Students view a video segment that illustrates an aspect of science, for example, a time-lapse view of a plant flowering. The students then develop an animation of the sequence. An animation program or a hypermedia program with animation capabilities may be used. If possible, use a videodisc player to show the video segment; this allows students to easily view the segment as many times as needed. If technology is not available, students can still create the animation using pencils and paper to make flip books. These skills are directly transferable to the computer animation process.

Source: Jack Edwards.

**Example Lesson 6.7**
**Choral Reading**

This activity is designed to develop student skills at effectively utilizing sound effects or music in a presentation. Sound can play an important role in determining the quality of a hypermedia product and teachers should not assume that students will automatically know how to properly utilize sounds. For this activity, students use a videodisc player configured for the LB2 standard, which enables users to access segments from an audio CD. In conjunction with a bar-code program, these tools give students a great deal of editing capability with sounds or music.

Tell the students that they will be doing an activity to read a poem and add sound effects or music to embellish the reading. Students may either write a poem or use existing poetry. They then need to select segments from an audio CD that somehow add to the reading. Music stores often carry compact discs with short segments of sound effects. For example, a CD of horror sounds could be used with a Halloween reading. Once the segments have been selected, a bar-code program can be used to create bar codes for the audio clips. It is advisable to have students work in pairs on a project like this, so one can read while the other operates the bar codes. A tape recording can be made of the presentation for authentic assessment.

Source: Jack Edwards.

**Example Lesson 6.8**
**Developing a Hypertext Database**

This activity gives students practice at linking information together effectively. This is a good activity to use in situations that lack access to many peripherals such as video and audio sources. It also is suitable when the teacher wants to focus on effective and creative linking without distracting students with flashy media. Students can work most effectively in pairs. A partner provides support and a simple checks-and-balances system. Students either choose or are assigned topics on which to collect data. This might be something like the rosters of their favorite sports teams. The students then work to create links within their beginning bodies of information. For example, the developer might link a player's year of birth with a list of major news stories of that year. The linking possibilities are almost limitless. In the course of this project, students will demonstrate imagination and gain a great deal of research experience.

Source: Jack Edwards.

---

**Example Lesson 6.9**
**A Student Autobiography**

This activity begins with students researching their backgrounds. This activity should employ a questionnaire that students help generate. They then take it home and get help from relatives with filling out details of their lives. The teacher may suggest or require that the projects contain some or all of the following information:

- Events that happened the year that they were born; these may be drawn from newspapers, almanacs, magazines, or parents' recollections.
- Their interests and hobbies
- Information about the town where they were born
- Family tree diagrams
- Top-ten lists, including books, foods, movies, songs, people, and sports teams
- Scanned-in photos

Culminate the project in an open-house for relatives to view the class projects.

---

Source: Jack Edwards.

# Exercises

## Record and Apply What You Have Learned

**Activity 6.1: Chapter 6 Self-Test**  To review terms and concepts in this chapter, take the Chapter 6 self-test. Select Chapter 6 from the front page of the companion Web site (located at http://www.prenhall.com/roblyer), then choose the *Multiple Choice* module.

**Activity 6.2: Portfolio Activities**  The following activities will help you add to your professional portfolio. To complete these activities online and save or submit the materials electronically, select Chapter 6 from the front page of the companion Web site (http://www.prenhall.com/roblyer), then choose the *Portfolio* module.

*Defining Multimedia and Hypermedia*  Develop a chart, diagram, or presentation that compares and contrasts multimedia and hypermedia. List or describe the defining qualities they share and those that make them different from each other.

*Hypermedia Professional Self-Description*  Use a hypermedia authoring program to develop a presentation that introduces your professional background, skills, and plans for the future. Use storyboards or Post-It notes to develop the design and layout for your presentation. Review your product and make sure it meets the criteria given in this chapter.

**Activity 6.3: Questions for Thought and Discussion**  These questions may be used for small group or class discussion or may be subjects for individual or group activities. To take part in these discussions online, select Chapter 6 from the front page of the companion Web site (http://www.prenhall.com/roblyer), then choose the *Message Board* module.

Mergendollar (1997) said that multimedia environments are an "equivocal blessing" because they give us a bounty of information without indicators of its quality, accuracy, or usefulness. What are the possible consequences to education of our increasing wealth of unevaluated multimedia information?

Boyle said that, "Multimedia learning is not something new. It is woven into the fabric of our childhood" (1997, p. ix). What do you think Boyle meant by that, and what implications might his observation have for enhancing children's learning experiences?

**Activity 6.4: Collaborative Activities**  The following may be developed in small group work. Completed group products may be copied and shared with the entire class and/or included in each person's Personal Portfolio. Remember that most hypermedia authoring systems provide a free player that can play these student-produced products:

*Create a Level I Presentation*  Use a videodisc to design and present a persuasive presentation. The topic will depend on the disc, e.g.:

- **Drug and tobacco use:** Teenagers should not start smoking

- **Solar system/space travel:** The U.S. government should expand its space program

- **American history:** The United States should/should not have dropped the bomb on Hiroshima

***Develop a Hypermedia Teaching System***  The class divides into small groups to create a hypermedia stack to teach others about hypermedia authoring. Each group takes a topic and the class puts the products together at the end. For example, groups may select one of the one following topics:

- What topics lend themselves to hypermedia? Ideas and examples

- An overview of the components of a hypermedia product

- A review of development steps

- Screen design procedures

- Adding graphics images

- Adding motion sequences: movies, animation, and videoclips

- Criteria for judging hypermedia products

***Multimedia/Hypermedia Lesson Plans***  Using the lesson plans in this chapter as models and idea sources, develop a classroom integration lesson plan to teach content area skills using one of the following resources:

- Level I videodisc curriculum package

- Level III videodisc curriculum package

- CD-ROM or DVD encyclopedia or database package

- Hypermedia authoring system such as *HyperStudio*

**Activity 6.5: Integrating Technology Across the Curriculum Activities**  Use the *Integrating Technology Across the Curriculum* CD-ROM packaged with this textbook to complete the following exercise:

Hypermedia/multimedia resources can help make mathematics learning less abstract for students by making it a more visual experience. Look at two different ways of doing this by comparing these two lessons: *HyperCard Helps Teach Word Problems in Mathematics* and *Math on the Job with KidPix*. How are these approaches the same? Different? Which do you think is more powerful? Which do you think would be more doable in your classroom?

# References

Arthur, P. C. & Mizer, R. A. (1998). What is the future of DVD? *Syllabus, 11*(8), 24–28.

Bagui, S. (1998). Reasons for increased learning using multimedia. *Journal of Educational Multimedia and Hypermedia, 7*(1), 3–18.

Barron, A. & Orwig, G. (1993). *New technologies for education: A beginner's guide.* Englewood, CO: Libraries Unlimited.

Bennett, N. & Diener, K. (1997). Habits of mind: Using multimedia to enhance learning skills. *Learning and Leading with Technology, 24*(6), 18–21.

Blissett, G. (1993). Are they thinking? Are they learning? A study of the use of interactive video. *Computers and Education, 21*(1–2), 31–39.

Boyle, T. (1997). *Design for multimedia learning.* London, England: Prentice Hall.

Brunner, C. (1996). Judging student multimedia. *Electronic Learning, 15*(6), 14–15.

Bush, V. (1986). As we may think. In Lambert & S. Ropiequte (Eds.). *CD-ROM: The new papyrus.* Redmond, WA: Microsoft Press. [Reprinted from *The Atlantic Monthly,* (1945, July). 101–108.]

Clark, J. (1996). Bells and whistles … but where are the references: Setting standards for hypermedia projects. *Learning and Leading with Technology, 23*(5), 22–24.

Dede, C. (1994). *Making the most of multimedia. Multimedia and learning: A school leader's guide,* Alexandria, VA: NSBA.

Dipinto, V. & Turner, S. (1995). Zapping the hypermedia zoo: Assessing the students' hypermedia projects. *The Computing Teacher, 22*(7), 8–11.

DVD: Coming soon to your desktop. (1998). *Syllabus, 11*(6), 18–20.

Frederickson, S. (1997). Interactive multimedia storybooks. *Learning and Leading with Technology, 25*(1), 6–10.

Galbreath, J. (1997). Multimedia communications: An update on standards. *Educational Technology, 39*(2), 49–55.

Glasgow, J. (1996). Part I: It's my turn! Motivating young readers. *Learning and Leading with Technology, 24*(3), 20–23.

Glasgow, J. (1996–1997). Part II: It's my turn! Motivating young readers using CD-ROM storybooks. *Learning and Leading with Technology, 24*(4), 18–22.

Glasgow, J. (1997). Keep up the good work! Using multimedia to build reading fluency and enjoyment. *Learning and Leading with Technology, 24*(5), 22–25.

Gustafson, K. & Smith, M. (1995). Using a bar-code reader with interactive videodiscs. *TechTrends, 40*(1), 29–32.

Kahn, J. (1997). Scaffolding in the classroom: Using CD-ROM storybooks at a computer reading center. *Learning and Leading with Technology, 25*(2), 17–19.

Karlin, M. (1994). Videodiscs and CD-ROM: Impact on a history lesson. *Media and Methods, 30*(5), 12–15.

Kwajewski, K. (1997). Memories in living color: Multimedia yearbooks. *Learning and Leading with Technology, 25*(2), 20–21.

Litchfield, B. (1995). Helping your students plan computer projects. *The Computing Teacher, 22*(7), 37–43.

Luskin, B. (1993). CD-I from boob tube to teacher's assistant—The smart TV. *Journal of Instructional Delivery Systems, 7*(1), 3–5.

Malhotra, Y. & Erikson, R. (1994). Interactive educational multimedia: Coping with the need for increasing data storage. *Educational Technology, 34*(4), 38–46.

Marchionini, M. (1988). Hypermedia and learning: Freedom and chaos. *Educational Technology, 28*(11), 8–12.

Mathisen, R. (1991). Interactive multimedia and education: Specifications, standards, and applications. *Collegiate Microcomputer, 5,* 93–102.

McCullen, C. (1998). Multimedia mania: Multimedia presentation rubric. *Midlink Magazine* (http://longwood.cs.ucf.edu/~Midlink).

Monahan, S. & Susong, D. (1996). Author slide show and Texas wildlife. *Learning and Leading with Technology, 24*(2), 6–16.

Moore, M., Myers, R., & Burton, J. (1994). What multimedia might do … and what we know about what it does. In *Multimedia and learning: A school leader's guide.* Alexandria, VA: NSBA.

Parham, C. (1995). CD-ROM storybooks revisited. *Technology and Learning, 15*(6), 14–18.

Porter, S. (1995). Waving the magic wand: Making books using laserdisc bar codes. *The Computing Teacher, 22*(7), 21–23.

Rembelinsky, I. (1997–1998). Us and them: Multimedia explorations of prejudice and intolerance in American history. *Learning and Leading with Technology, 25*(4), 42–47.

Roblyer, M. D. (1998). Visual literacy: Seeing a new rationale for teaching with technology. *Learning and Leading with Technology, 26*(2), 51–54.

Scholten, B. & Whitmer, J. (1996). Hypermedia projects: Metastacks increase content focus. *Learning and Leading with Technology, 24*(3), 59–62.

Sherwood, S. (1994). Student laser projects. *The Computing Teacher, 22*(2), 32–33.

Shields, J. (1994). Getting the big picture on videodiscs. *Technology and Learning, 15*(2), 48–52.

Siegel, J. (1995). The state of teacher training. *Electronic Learning, 14*(8), 43–53.

Simonson, M. R. & Thompson, A. (1994). *Educational computing foundations.* New York: Merrill.

Stemler, L. (1997). Educational characteristics of multimedia: A literature review. *Journal of Educational Multimedia and Hypermedia, 6*(3/4), 339–359.

Stuhlmann, J. (1997). Butterflies! Using multimedia to capture a unique science project. *Learning and Leading with Technology, 25*(3), 22–27.

Sullivan, J. (1995). Exciting ways to use videodiscs. *Media and Methods, 31*(3), S8–S10.

Swan, K. & Meskill, C. (1996). Using hypermedia in response-based literature classrooms: A critical review of commercial applications. *Journal of Research on Computing in Education, 29*(2), 167–192.

Thorpe, B. (1993). Kids can create videodisc reports. *The Computing Teacher, 20*(2), 22–23.

Tolhurst, D. (1995). Hypertext, hypermedia, multimedia defined? *Educational Technology, 35*(2), 21–26.

Truett, C. (1994). CD-ROM, videodiscs, and new ways of teaching information and research skills. *The Computing Teacher, 21*(6), 42–43.

Turner, S. V. & Dipinto, V. M. (1992). Students as hypermedia authors: Themes emerging from a qualitative study. *Journal of Research on Computing in Education, 25*(2), 187–199.

Walkenbach, J. (1992). Optical storage comes up to speed. *New Media, 10,* 26–30.

# Part III

# Linking to Learn—Principles and Strategies

**The chapters in this part will help teachers learn:**

1. To identify available distance learning resources and recognize the teaching and learning functions they can fulfill

2. To identify the role that Internet resources and strategies can play in teaching and learning

3. To identify five trends in emerging technologies likely to have profound influences on educational practices in the future

4. To develop integration strategies for each of these current and future technologies that match their capabilities to classroom needs

## Introduction

Our entry into the millennium marks nearly a half-century of computer use in society. Computers have been used in education since the beginning of their existence. But thanks to microcomputers, the last 15 years have seen an explosion of computer technology-related activity in schools and classrooms. The emergence of a graphically-oriented Internet in 1994 suddenly and dramatically shifted the spotlight from standalone microcomputers to the importance of linking with others: other computers, other people, and other "worlds." Other developments combine with these distance resources to shape the future of educational technology. The chapters in this section focus on the resources that link us with each other as well as with our future as a civilization.

## Chapter 7: Distance Learning Opportunities and Options

Distance learning, a means of providing courses and workshops for industry training and higher education, continues to increase in popularity and the range of applications grows steadily. This chapter reviews a variety of distance learning resources and methods to link learners with each other and with needed resources at distant sites.

## Chapter 8: Integrating the Internet into Education

The information superhighway has become a pervasive metaphor for technology in modern culture, but educators are just beginning to develop integration strategies for the Internet. This chapter focuses on current and anticipated uses of the Internet, both in schools and in the context of other learning communities.

## Chapter 9: A Link to the Future—Where Is Education Going with Technology?

Technologies such as virtual reality make the future seem to have landed on our doorstep. This chapter describes technologies whose practical applications are just emerging, but whose potential power promises to shape the future of education and society. These include developments in networking, visualization, human-to-computer interfaces, artificial intelligence (AI), and various types of computer-related equipment.

# Chapter 7

## Distance Learning Opportunities and Options

It is obvious that both teaching and learning … will be influenced in varying ways by "the death of distance."

Michael G. Moore, in an editorial for *The American Journal of Distance Education*, 1995

This chapter covers the following topics:

- Definitions and descriptions of various distance learning options available to educators

- Implementation issues to consider when using distance learning

- Impact distance learning has had and is expected to have on education

- How to select and implement broadcast and computer-based distance learning resources

- Teaching and learning activities that make use of distance learning technologies

# Objectives

1. Compare and contrast how distance technologies have affected education in the past with how they affect them now and in the future.

2. Describe current educational benefits and applications of various types of broadcast/terrestrial systems.

3. Describe current educational benefits and applications of computer-based resources.

4. Describe a plan for each of five ways distance learning can be integrated into education: classroom lesson activities, course delivery, degree delivery, communications, and teaching preparation.

## Introduction: Reaching Out to a World of Resources

Technology has changed no aspect of society more quickly and dramatically than its communications capabilities. Children today regard revolutionary technologies such as fax machines, cellular phones, and the Internet as normal, everyday parts of the electronic landscape in which they live. Even in the rapid environment of technological evolution, these remarkable changes in communications have come about with incredible speed; some resources have developed from possible to pervasive in only a few years. These changes are by no means completed or even slowing down. The primary reason for this breathtaking revolution in communications is society's recognition of the importance of ready access to people and resources. If knowledge is power, as Francis Bacon said, then communication is freedom—freedom for people to reach information they need in order to acquire knowledge that can empower them. This heady freedom permeates the atmosphere of an information society.

Rapid developments in communication technologies have brought about what Moore (1995), quoting an issue of *The Economist,* called "the death of distance" which happens "when the cost of communications comes down to next to nothing, as seems likely in the first decade of the next century" (p. 1). But the death of distance seems to have given new life to education. Distance learning (DL) has not only changed how quickly educators and students can exchange and access information, it has altered the educational equation in fundamental ways. Thanks to distance technologies such as broadcast systems and the Internet, learning has escaped the physical boundaries of the classroom and the school, and students and teachers have become part of a virtual classroom they share with counterparts around the world. Our society is just beginning to understand and take advantage of the potential of this new classroom.

This chapter begins by exploring the terms and concepts used to define distance learning and by examining the physical configurations available to education and major implementation concerns involved in selecting them. Subsequent sections provide detail on ways to implement distance learning and how distance learning can be integrated in various ways depending on educational needs.

### What Is Distance Learning?

The changing definition of distance learning is a clue to the kind of impact it has had on the definition of education itself. Most past definitions of distance learning had the following key components:

- Instructor and learner separated by time and/or geographic distance, and
- Electronic, print resources, voice communications, and combinations of them are used to bridge the gap.

Some authorities feel the definition of distance learning is changing too quickly to have a formal definition (Zenor, 1998). However, in 1998, the United States Distance Learning Association (USDL) went on record to define distance learning as:

> … the acquisition of knowledge and skills through mediated information and instruction, encompassing all technologies and other forms of learning at a distance.

This definition leaves open the door to more constructivist views of learning, including the possibility that, though learning is taking place, there may not be an instructor at all and no formal or organized instruction may be offered. The USDL definition says simply that learning may take place where learners are connected with information resources, with each other, with instructors, or with any combinations of these resources.

But the 1998 USDL definition should not be considered the final word—or even the only one. Proponents of directed and constructivist methods (see Chapter 3) may disagree as to how this or other definitions should be interpreted. Furthermore, future definitions may serve to omit any learning activities that rely exclusively on non-electronic forms of communications such as print. Other changes in definitions include distance learning versus distance education and telecommunications.

**Distance learning versus distance education.** Many authors used to differentiate between *distance education* and *distance learning,* referring to the former as the role of the instructor and the latter as the role of the learner. Now, they typically are used interchangeably.

**Telecommunications.** Although the most precise definition of telecommunications is communication at a distance, it is evolving into a general term for any electronic technologies (broadcast/terrestrial, computer-based, or combinations of the two) used for linking people for communications purposes. Some education articles still use telecommunications, distance education, and distance learning interchangeably; but most educators now refer to distance learning/distance education as a learning process and telecommunications as the communications mechanism for making this process possible. Harris (1994) uses the term *telecomputing* coined by Kearsley, Hunter, and Furlong (1992) to describe activities in which classroom computers link groups with each other and with educational resources. However, this term is in limited use by others.

## Distance Learning Directions: Past, Present, and Future

As the changes in definitions show, the past decade has brought about dramatic changes in the goals and purposes of distance learning, many of which have come about as a result of technological developments. Over the years, the rationale for distance learning activities has changed and expanded, as have the mechanisms for accomplishing them.

**Past rationales and methods.** The rationale for distance learning first was based on access for students and cost-savings for organizations. Correspondence courses were very popular among rural and military students who needed credits for certification or graduation but who could not travel to and/or reside at educational institutions. Later, when print materials were supplemented with videotapes and instructional television (ITV), businesses found they could train workers more cheaply than having an instructor at every site. Post-secondary institutions discovered they could increase the number of students a professor could teach in one course by having the instructor broadcast lectures to students in a number of sites. Whole institutions grew up around this distance learning rationale, and many large businesses and universities used this method to some extent.

**Current rationales and methods.** Today's distance learning has evolved a broader and more diverse rationale for its existence, but increased student access and costs of education and training still are very much at the heart of it. Distance learning activities today are driven by a two-fold focus: to increase student access to information and people, and to compete for the "education dollar" of those needing certification and degrees. With the help of what seems to be every business, school, and college in the world, the Internet has become a way to obtain any information anytime and from any location. Many institutions are working toward developing courses and degree programs students can complete without ever entering a formal classroom or seeing a live instructor. Also, although many correspondence courses in print and/or video formats still are in use, they rapidly are being replaced by electronic means. Organizations that stay with the "old" formats or that do not provide students with distance learning alternatives and options may be threatened with extinction (Sherritt, 1996).

**Future rationales and methods.** In the future, distance learning seems likely to focus on a new rationale: making learning environments increasingly life-like. Ready access to information resources and alternatives to traditional learning strategies will be taken for granted and print/video correspondence courses will be a distant memory. The emphasis will be on developing better quality systems to simulate "being there" and being face-to-face with the teacher/trainer and the other students. Distance learning will become interactive video-and-audio and virtual reality systems that allow people to exchange information as if they were in the same location. If this rationale becomes reality, distance may, indeed, be dead.

## Overview of Current Distance Learning Configurations and Applications

The number and types of linking methods used in education are growing daily. This is partly because communication technologies are expanding rapidly and because teachers and students constantly are finding new ways of combining these technologies to solve problems and meet needs that arise from distance or lack of access to resources. However, not all options are always available to a given teacher or school. For example, distance learning options that deliver whole courses usually involve expensive resources and time-consuming implementation strategies and require changes to the traditional classroom structure. Decisions to integrate these kinds of distance learning activities often are made by a school, district, or state department rather than by an individual teacher.

On the other hand, some distance learning activities are less expensive and require less restructuring of the classroom delivery system; teachers can initiate these and use them to supplement their traditional classroom instruction. Regardless of who makes the decisions, the information in this section can help teachers and administrators build a basic understanding of current distance learning options as well as emerging options.

At this stage, distance learning takes place through three kinds of physical configurations: *broadcast/terrestrial, computer-based,* and hybrids of the two. These are summarized in Figure 7.1.

**Broadcast and terrestrial systems.** These systems are made possible by:

- broadcast technologies that use satellite links or microwaves to send video;
- terrestrial (land) lines such as telephone lines, cable lines, and other transmission lines to send audio and/or video; or
- combinations of broadcast and terrestrial systems.

**Figure 7.1  Current Distance Learning Configurations, Components, and Uses***

| Types of Systems | Description of System and Transmission Methods | Types of Uses |
|---|---|---|
| **Broadcast/Terrestrial** | | |
| Audio only | Instructor and students talk via telephones connected with telephone lines | Talking and leaving messages during courses |
| Audio via phone plus fax | Instructor and students talk via telephones, transmit written messages via fax | Talking plus exchanging documents during courses |
| Broadcast video/audio (one-way, taped or live) | Instructor broadcasts to students using satellite/microwave/land lines; students need television and access to cable channel | Video instruction |
| Broadcast video/audio (one-way live) | Instructor broadcasts to students using satellite/microwave/land lines; students need satellite downlink or microwave dish | Video instruction and teleconferences |
| Broadcast one-way video and two-way audio | Instructor broadcasts to students using satellite or microwave; students need satellite downlink or microwave dish; communications are supplemented with telephone lines | Video instruction and teleconferences |
| Broadcast video out, compressed video in, plus two-way audio | Instructor broadcasts to students using satellite or microwave; students need satellite downlink or microwave dish via TV quality broadcast; instructor sees students via compressed video on T1 line; students see TV-quality video, but instructor sees video with some lag | Video instruction |
| Two-way compressed video plus audio | Video and audio transmitted each way over T1 lines; students and instructor see each other, but quality of video not as good as broadcast video | Video instruction and teleconferences |
| Two-way broadcast with audio | Instructor and students see each other through broadcast video and audio; very expensive system requires satellite uplink and downlink or microwave dishes at both sites plus cameras and production equipment and audio equipment | Video instruction and teleconferences |
| Videoconferencing systems | Instructor and students see each other through point-to-point video and audio; very capable, expensive systems range from desktop to full group communications between two sites, or among two or more sites, each connected via T1 or other lines (also see desktop videoconferencing below in computer-based systems) | Videoconferencing, video instruction, and visual communications |
| **Computer-based Systems** | | |
| Microcomputer with modem | Instructor and students communicate among themselves via e-mail and/or file transfers; each user needs computer, modem, telephone line, and communications software | Written communications and Internet use (including e-mail, chatrooms, Web courses) |
| Microcomputer connected to network | Instructor and students communicate among themselves via e-mail and/or file transfers; each user needs computer, communications software, and wiring to the network | Written communications and Internet use (including e-mail, chatrooms, Web courses) |
| Microcomputer and camera | Microcomputer with modem or network connection, plus camera and videoconferencing software (future systems will have camera, software, and modem built in); many courses also make use of computer bulletin boards so students and instructors can communicate among themselves during course activities | Desktop videoconferencing (also see videoconferencing above in broadcast/terrestrial systems) |
| **Examples of Hybrid Systems** | | |
| One-way audio plus computer | Students, teachers, and parents leave messages on computer-managed telephone systems | Voice-mail messaging; telephone "meetings" |
| Broadcast video plus computer | Instructor broadcasts to students using satellite or microwave; students need satellite downlink or microwave dish; communications are supplemented with e-mail and file transfer; instructional activities supplemented on computer | Video instruction, written communications, Internet use |

*These are the major types of configurations, but many more combinations are possible and are being developed and used.
This chart was developed with the assistance of Melinda Crowley of the Florida Department of Education, Florida Distance Learning Network (FDLN) Office in Tallahassee, Florida.

**Computer systems.** Some configurations use microcomputers—both individual workstations and more capable servers—to communicate among sites. These links are made possible through modems, network connections from schools or districts, or a combination of the two.

**Hybrid systems.** As costs of various communications components decrease and as people think of ways to combine broadcast/terrestrial systems with computer-based systems, it will be increasingly difficult to categorize a given distance learning system as one or the other. The future will see an increasing number of combination or hybrid systems designed to meet distance learning needs at the lowest cost.

Examples of these configuration options range from inexpensive to very expensive depending on whether or not they have video and on the video's quality. The most common applications for these systems are listed below.

*Written communications.* Although in-person communication often is preferred, e-mail is becoming a staple for written forms of communication. In fact, by far the most common use of the Internet is e-mail (Roblyer, 1997). People frequently need to leave private messages to a person or group, and e-mail is the current method of choice. Some written communications also take place through real-time "chat rooms," which allow users immediate viewing of messages as they are entered or bulletin boards, which are used for public posting of messages.

*Video instruction.* Both broadcast/terrestrial and computer-based systems can make possible the delivery of scheduled video courses and workshops. These range from one-way video broadcasts to fully interactive simulations of face-to-face activities.

*Teleconferences.* These are live events that simulate meetings or conferences. *Teleconferences* usually are held on a one-time basis and sometimes include one-way video and two-way audio. People at the delivering site talk to people at one or more other sites; listeners can then ask questions via audio.

*Videoconferencing.* Both broadcast/terrestrial and computer-based systems can make possible what used to be called videoteleconferencing. *Videoconferencing,* as it is now called, allows live interaction among users at various distant sites. It is used for delivery of scheduled courses or for intermittent communications.

*Internet activities.* Computer-based systems allow access to the *Internet,* a major need in every educational organization. The rich array of resources available on the Internet offers educators a unique combination of full-text documents; graphics, motion, and sound presentations; and up-to-the-moment information on a variety of topics such as weather, current events, and legislative hearings.

## Major Implementation Issues with Distance Learning

As excitement about distance learning grows, the race to compete in the distance learning marketplace is intensifying. Universities especially feel pressure to develop a distance learning program and course offerings in order to retain or increase their share of the student market. Lucas (1998) said that, based on projections from an earlier survey, about 60 percent of all U.S. post–secondary institutions offered distance learning courses as of 1998. "Virtual high schools" also appear with great frequency, but many kinds of issues will determine the potential for success of distance learning.

**Positive and negative impact on education reform.** Many educators predict that distance learning will reform teaching methods and increase access to quality education; however, support for distance learning is not unanimous. Even ardent advocates point out pitfalls. Van Dusen (1997) is optimistic that the distance learning movement will alter traditional, "professor-centered" methods and bring about more constructivist ones, but he emphasizes that this shift will not happen without intensive professional development. Also, he feels there is a danger that quality of undergraduate education could suffer unless universities renew their commitment to core values. Meanwhile a backlash to distance learning-based reform methods is growing. One statement of protest drafted at the University of Washington said that while distance learning programs present "… a mouth-watering bonanza to … corporate sponsors, what they bode for education is nothing short of disastrous" (Monaghan, 1998, June 8).

**Reform of top-level policy/planning.** Federal and state governments will play increasingly key roles in helping assure that distance learning succeeds. The responsibility for public education rests with state education departments, and government agencies disburse federal funds earmarked for communications, technology, and distance learning. Top-level involvement also helps assure that distance learning systems meet the needs of the entire educational system in a cost-effective way. Today's education, communication, and information policies and regulations were developed long before the major technological breakthroughs that made distance learning possible. Some lawmakers, remembering the "improprieties" involving several correspondence schools in the 1990s (Selingo, 1998, June 5, p. A30), are fearful of giving financial support to distance learning programs. However, if distance learning is to be successful, the federal government, states, districts, and schools must develop far-sighted plans and policies that can supply financial support and remove logistical obstacles to distance learning.

**Costs and funding.** Few schools and colleges can afford the distance learning configurations and applications they would like. However, several recent state and federal initiatives have been designed to help them get the resources and training they need in order to implement distance learning activities. One such initiative is "retrofitting grants," designed to get schools re-wired and networked for modern communications methods. Another initiative is providing a lower-cost rate called the "e-rate" (Kimball & Sibley, 1997–98; Crowley, 1998), so educators can afford to install and use more telephone lines. Obtaining the computers, other equipment, training, and support schools need for distance learning is an ongoing problem (see Chapter 2). Boettcher (1998) points out that costs of distance learning vary dramatically, depending on the kind of system and the way it is used. One variable is the type of instruction being offered. For example, estimates for developing instruction for a distance learning system vary from 3–10 hours for videotaped lectures to 300 hours for interactive video (p. 58).

**Infrastructure and policy needs.** Retrofitting and e-rate help in providing some, but by no means all, of the foundation resources needed for distance learning. In addition to these, a school's basic infrastructure must include ready access to technical support personnel and maintenance procedures. Esquivel (1998) gives an excellent summary of these infrastructure requirements. Budgeting for these resources and periodical updates to equipment and materials will become as important as initial purchases.

**Teacher involvement and training.** For any educational innovation to succeed, it must attract early involvement of classroom teachers. Teacher concerns about implementing (or being replaced by) new technologies must be determined and addressed. The most successful strategies involve teachers in early planning stages and then consistently seeking meaningful teacher input and participation. Educators need to learn how to operate and integrate the new technology tools, to implement radically different curricular approaches and associated classroom management strategies, and to become facilitators of learning. Professional development in technology applications has never kept pace with the purchase and distribution of equipment (Hawkins & Macmillan, 1993).

**Communications innovations.** The development of better distance learning systems, as to connection options, relies on communications becoming faster, more reliable, and more flexible. Old copper wiring is being replaced by fiber optic cabling and by faster lines such as T1 and ISDN. A technology called *switches* is frequently added to these lines to compress data, which allows information to be transmitted at higher speeds no matter what line or cable is used. Asynchronous transfer mode (ATM) switches will be important in speeding up communications on all types of lines. As communications become more digital, telephone companies still will have wires in place that require analog transmission. So they will rely increasingly on switching methods like ATM to make the transition between lines that allow only analog data and those that can send digital

data. Other new technologies will make it possible to do all kinds of communications (e. g., voice, video, and fax) at the same time, thus making communications more flexible and versatile. ISDN was the first technology to accomplish this, but not the last. New developments in transmission capabilities are exciting news for technicians trying to make links work; but, ultimately, these technical improvements will be completely transparent to teachers and students.

**Rapidly changing technologies.** Both computer technology and communications technology are changing and evolving rapidly. New, as yet undreamed-of technologies may emerge on the horizon and change drastically the options, capabilities, and costs described here. Many schools lease equipment and lines instead of buying them in order to remain flexible for emerging developments in communications and other technologies that support distance learning.

**Logistical problems.** Projects that involve links with other schools or classrooms call for careful planning and elaborate coordination among members. Equipment must be compatible and technical problems must be worked out as they arise. Students must have access to equipment when they need it. Participants in a linking project must agree among themselves about a time frame for the activities. Working across different time zones adds another dimension; sometimes interaction cannot be in the form of real-time chats, since one group of students may be in class while the other is getting a good night's sleep. Finally, class and course schedules must be made more flexible to permit students time to complete collaborative projects.

**School-level administrative support.** A 1992 study by Henry Jay Becker, a sociologist at the University of California at Irvine, suggests that a chief factor found in exemplary computer-using teachers is the administrative support that such teachers enjoy within their schools. By adopting appropriate policies, "school administrators ought to be able to develop many more similarly skilled teachers" (Leslie, 1993, p. 93). Principals and other administrators who advocate the use of technology in their offices and schools without using that technology make teachers skeptical. Administrators need not be experts, but they do need to understand the various technologies and their good and bad features so they can be effective leaders and managers. To do this, they must share the same intensive training opportunities and peer support networks that teachers enjoy.

## Present and Potential Impact of Distance Learning

Due in large part to the popularity of the Internet, distance learning activities currently enjoy a wellspring of support unprecedented in the history of educational technology.

Fortunately, this trend is not just a fad; years of research have confirmed the effectiveness of some forms of distance learning, and studies on other strategies seem to be on the increase. Furthermore, educators at all levels are predicting that distance learning has the potential to revolutionize education in the next century (Bybee, 1996; Imel, 1996; Roblyer, 1998a). This section captures some current research and activity that indicate how distance learning is helping shape the future of teaching and learning.

### Research Evidence on Various Distance Learning Activities

In the past, the most popular kind of research compared a distance learning method with a traditional one. However, several other kinds of questions also are proving useful in shaping the impact of distance learning:

- Are certain types of distance learning resources or delivery systems more effective than others?

- What are characteristics of effective distance learning courses?

- What are characteristics of students who choose distance learning?

- What are characteristics of students who are effective distance learners?

- What are characteristics of effective distance instructors?

- What cost factors enter into preparing and implementing distance education programs, and how do we determine cost-effectiveness?

**Effectiveness of distance learning for course delivery.** Some distance learning methods are among the most well-studied in education. For example, course delivery with instructional television has long been considered equivalent to face-to-face instruction in its impact on achievement and on attitudes of students (Russell, 1992). In addition, hundreds of studies conducted from 1954 through 1996 consistently found no significant difference between instruction delivered through traditional classroom methods and instruction delivered over one or more distance technologies (Schlosser & Anderson, 1994; Russell, 1997). Although no current studies have compared the effectiveness on different types of students of instruction delivered via distance learning, evaluation from the federally funded Star Schools Program indicates that distance learning students enrolled in high school courses function slightly better than comparable students in traditional classes (Withrow, 1992). There is no reason to believe that courses done on other delivery systems such as the Internet or videoconferencing will achieve different results, since the determining variable is course quality rather than delivery system (Driscoll & Kirby, 1997). Some studies attempted to capture benefits that are unique to distance learning formats, such as increased awareness and appreciation of cultural diversity (Roblyer, 1992), but these studies are not as common.

**Effectiveness of specific distance learning resources.** Similarly, although there has been substantially less research on the impact of specific distance learning products, such as e-mail, or videoconferencing, past research in other educational technology areas makes it likely that the technologies themselves will be less important than how they are used (see Clark's studies described in Chapter 2).

**Course characteristics that affect success.** Since specific course features have great impact on both student achievement and attitudes, substantial research has been directed toward identifying factors that make for an effective distance learning course. Though some studies focus on course factors that correlate directly to dropout rates in distance learning courses (Bernard & Amundsen, 1989; Gibson & Graff, 1992), many researchers agree with Wilkes and Burnham (1991) that course success should be measured by more than just endurance and achievement, since "highly motivated learners may be willing to endure almost (anything) to achieve a passing grade" (p. 43). Therefore, the majority of studies in this area focus on attitudes of students who complete distance learning courses. Cheng, Lehman, and Armstrong (1991), Biner (1993), and Hardy and Boaz (1997) agree that the handful of factors described here are the major contributors to course satisfaction. These include the following.

- **Degree of interaction.** Though some studies find that the convenience distance learning offers means more to students than teacher interaction (Klesius, Homan, & Thompson, 1997), the single greatest determinant of satisfaction across studies is the amount of interaction between instructor and students (Thompson, 1990; Fulford & Zhang, 1993; Zirken & Sumler, 1995; Smith, 1996; Furst-Bowie, 1997; and Wetbrook, 1997). McHenry and Bozik (1997) found that lack of "classroom community" among distance learners can decrease interaction and affect course satisfaction. But as is typical of distance learning and traditional classes alike, smaller class size can determine student perception of interactivity and, therefore, satisfaction with distance learning instruction (Biner, Welsh, Barone, Summer, & Dean, 1997). Riddle (1990) suggests that meeting students face-to-face for the first class meeting helps establish a rapport that can lead to better interaction throughout the course. However, Smith's (1996) study found that about 30 percent of the nearly 400 respondents would never choose distance learning because they felt it could never provide the degree of interaction in a face-to-face course.

- **Support during course.** Many studies show that students value and profit from support during their course experiences, from registration through course activities and evaluation (Gibson & Graf, 1992; Hardy & Boaz, 1997). McHenry and Bozik (1997) find that lack of library resources and slow transfer of paperwork are among the support problems that affect course satisfaction.

- **Technical problems.** Consistent evidence exists that technical problems can doom the best-planned course (Cheng, Lehman, & Armstrong, 1991; Thomerson & Smith, 1996). Successful courses are those that minimize problems.

**Characteristics of people who choose distance learning.** Moore and Kearsley (1996) and Hardy and Boaz (1997) find that, in the past, most distance learners have been working adults: between 25–50 years old, married, and employed full-time while taking courses; about two-thirds have been female. However, Wallace (1996) and Guernsey (1998) report that these demographics may be changing as distance learning becomes more mainstream than alternative education, and that typical distance learners soon may be more like traditional students: younger and full-time. Guernsey (1998) found that 500 of the 608 students taking distance learning courses at the University of Colorado also are taking regular, face-to-face courses there.

**Student characteristics that affect success with distance learning.** Some researchers have tried to identify certain student capabilities or other factors that could predict whether or not a student might drop out, be less satisfied with, or do less with than others in an on-line activity. These characteristics include self-motivation and ability to structure one's own learning (Gibson & Graf, 1992; Hardy & Boaz, 1997), previous experience with technology (Richards & Ridley, 1997), good attitude toward course subject matter (Coussement, 1995), and self-choice of distance learning rather than having no other option (Roblyer, 1999).

**Characteristics of effective distance learning instructors.** Cyrs (1997) emphasizes that distance learning instructors need different skills than instructors for traditional courses. His review of research reveals several areas of unique competence, all of which require experience with distance learning environments: course planning and organization that capitalize on distance learning strengths and minimize constraints; verbal and nonverbal presentation skills specific to distance learning situations; collaborative work with others to produce effective courses; ability to use questioning strategies; and ability to involve and coordinate student activities among several sites. Moskal, Martin, and Foshee (1997) refer to these skills in general as instructional design skills specific to distance learning. Dillon, Hengst, and Zoller (1991) find that these skills do not come naturally even among instructors who are effective in non-distance learning settings; and Gross (1997) and Wolcott (1997) find that few faculty are willing to learn these new skills because they are not rewarded for doing so.

**Research on cost-effectiveness of distance learning.** The University of Idaho's Engineering Outreach home page (http://www.uidaho.edu/evo) posted a list taken from Threlkeld and Brzoska (1994) on several categories of cost factors of offering a distance learning course:

- **Technology.** Hardware and software
- **Transmission.** Ongoing expenses of leasing transmission access (e.g., T-1, satellite)

- **Maintenance.** Repairing and updating equipment
- **Infrastructure.** Foundational network and telecommunications infrastructure located at originating and receiving sites
- **Production.** Technical and personnel support to develop/adapt teaching materials
- **Support.** Expenses needed to keep the system working successfully, for examples, administrative costs, registration, advising/counseling, local support costs, facilities, and overhead costs
- **Personnel.** Instructors and support staff

Although studies show that initial costs of starting distance learning programs are high, research also suggests that as programs become more efficient and used over more courses, program costs should decrease (Ludlow, 1994).

## How Distance Learning Is Changing the Face of Education

Recent surveys show that about three-quarters of all U.S. schools at the K-12 level and most post-secondary institutions have Internet access. Most schools and colleges have some electronic form of distance learning with the Internet, videoconferencing, or other interactive visual medium. In some areas, the predicted revolution of the education system seems well under way. Clearly, the general expectation of many educators is that distance learning will be key to raising and maintaining the quality of American education. Some of these anticipated improvements are described here.

**Structural changes to educational systems.** In his book about the coming transformation of media and American life, futurist George Gilder said that distance learning technologies have the power to transform public education by making the nation's best teachers available to students anywhere (Gilder, 1992). This transformation is taking place to a degree that perhaps even Gilder could not have imagined. Distance learning is beginning to restructure diploma, degree, and certification programs across the world by offering alternatives to face-to-face classroom instruction. Several states are experimenting with Virtual High School degree programs (Elbaum, 1998) in which the core curriculum is completely online. Many colleges and universities offer courses in distance learning formats; others are offering whole virtual degree programs or ones with major online components. This new option promises to make significant changes to the economic and academic structure of schools, districts, and post-secondary institutions. It is unclear at this time how much of the current system will be replaced or revised by distance learning options, but the potential for impact is enormous.

**Increased access to educational opportunities.** Removing the obstacle of distance is making it possible for many people, who were not able to do so before, to take advantage of educational opportunities. However, there are no figures yet on how many people constitute this new learning population. Learning activities that are readily available and can be done any time of day or night have special implications for disabled students, students in rural areas, and working adults.

**Changes to curriculum and activities.** Like people everywhere, students are profiting from the tremendous array of information resources—both documents and people—available through the Internet. Project research has taken on a whole new aspect as students search online for articles to read and experts to talk to on any desired topic. As teachers learn about these sources, the knowledge is changing the nature of student assignments and how they are asked to show their products. Also, as access to information increases, curriculum needs to focus much more on information literacy and visual literacy skills to cope with the "information avalanche" (Roblyer, 1998a and 1998b).

**Changing roles of teacher and learner.** One effect of the increasing use of educational technology in general and distance technologies in particular has been a change in the culture of the classroom. For example, the Apple Classrooms of Tomorrow (ACOT) project (Ringstaff, 1993) saw a gradual evolution of a "student expert" structure in which teachers began to capitalize on the technical expertise of their students. In this environment, slower students blossomed, less popular students were sought out for advice and assistance, and formerly unmotivated students became excited and involved. Increased access to distance learning technologies may accelerate and expand this trend toward "shared expertise" and the teacher as facilitator rather than deliverer of information.

**Creating learning communities.** In a learning community, education plays a critical part in the lifelong transformation of the human personality. In today's ever-changing and increasingly global world, that transformation is continual, necessary for economic survival, and an important part of our cultural growth. A community of learners fosters a fundamental commitment to learning and a recognition that the most important asset of any community is the people within it (Education Imperative, 1992). Distance learning technologies play a major role in creating and sustaining learning in such communities because such activities tend to blur social distinctions. Race, gender, disabilities, physical appearances, even social status, lose their significance when all that matters is one's capacity for expression (Leslie, 1993, p. 90). The same technologies that allow for universal access to learning also foster a growing sense of community and relationship among people throughout the world. As a result, distance no longer impedes either learning or a sense of community that extends to individuals who may never meet and to neighborhoods that are never visited.

## Broadcast/Terrestrial Audio and Video Options and Uses

### Audio-based Systems

Audio systems have limited usefulness for actual instruction, but one-way audio systems that combine telephone and computer technology are currently used in many states as student-teacher and parent-teacher information sources (Bauch, 1993). One example, originated by Jerold Bauch at Peabody College of Vanderbilt University, is the TransParent School Model, which uses computer-based voice messaging to enhance teacher-parent interaction over the telephone.

Each teacher writes a short script and records a classroom message into a voice-mail message box in a site-based computer. All parents can call and hear the message at any time from any touch-tone telephone. A school can also record a message to be sent automatically to any or all parents. When the model is fully implemented, parents call one number and learn everything they need to know to help their children with home learning. They also find information on meeting schedules, sports events, lunch menus, and special school-sponsored functions.

As of late 1993, this model was used in more than 400 schools in 27 states, leading to increases of up to 800 percent in school-parent involvement. Documented side effects include student grade improvements, increasingly positive parent attitudes toward schools, and even improved attendance rates (Bauch, 1993).

In another new use of an older technology, college instructors are giving tests, providing feedback, and assigning homework using computerized voice-mail systems accessed by telephone from home or other remote locations. Future applications will expand voice-mail systems to deliver audio messages over computer networks. Audioconferencing systems, which allow many telephone callers to participate in a shared conversation, are used frequently for professional development activities as well. For example, when introducing a new and potentially controversial health curriculum, school-level curriculum coordinators in one district met daily via telephone to discuss implementation issues and share individual concerns.

### Video-based Systems

As we become an increasingly visual society, video-based distance learning systems are increasing in popularity. Applications like instructional television and teleconferences have been around for some time and still are commonly used. But other methods described in this section are now available that allow increased interaction among participants, and it seems likely they will gradually replace the older methods.

**Video courses.** Although the current distance learning emphasis is on "Web courses" (discussed in the following section) and videoconferencing, other ways to deliver course material in visual formats include televised video, broadcast one-way video, interactive "realtime" video courses, teleconferencing, and videoconferencing.

*Televised video.* The "instructional television" format still is in widespread use around the United States, probably because of its flexibility. Televised courses can be delivered to students who have access to a television, and programs can be taped for later viewing. These types of video courses are not interactive but deliver information visually and can be supplemented with print materials and telephone or e-mail communication with the instructor.

*Broadcast one-way video.* This format requires the instructor to have a satellite uplink, and students must be in a conferencing center with a downlink. This method, too, offers flexibility, since the programs can be taped at the downlink site and viewed later by students.

*Interactive "realtime" video courses.* Less frequently, organizations (usually universities) offer live courses via satellite links and telephone lines or interactive television systems. For example, Old Dominion University offers live video classes at several sites in Virginia and surrounding states as well as to Navy ships at sea (McCollum, 1998, April 17). This is the format most similar to face-to-face courses, but also is the most expensive arrangement. East Carolina University offers successful interactive television courses via a compressed video system (Wheatley & Greer, 1995).

*Teleconferencing.* Teleconferencing generally employs one-way video and two-way audio, although increasing access to satellite uplink facilities allows more sites to become completely interactive. Teleconferences are delivered live (in real time); however, like broadcast courses, they may be taped for later viewing by other audiences. The technology for teleconferencing is decades old, dating back to an AT&T demonstration during the 1964 World's Fair in New York. With teleconferencing, a satellite uplink facility transmits a signal up to a satellite, which rebroadcasts to desired receiver sites. For planned and scripted teleconferences, the combination of studio and/or transmission expenses and satellite costs can make make total production/transmission costs for teleconferencing somewhat high. Also, teleconferencing works best when the flow of information is one-way; this medium is not suited to programs requiring high levels of response or interaction.

The main difference between interactive, video-based instruction and teleconferencing activities is the content or subject of the transmission; one-time programs or series of programs on specific topics are standard fare for teleconferences. These sessions frequently serve as staff development for professionals. Other types of teleconferences are intended to keep people updated on rapidly-breaking events. For example, the NASA Teaching from Space Program at Oklahoma State University, in cooperation with OSU's Educational Television Services, presents a series of live educational teleconferences broadcast via satellite to thousands of schools across the country. NASA ... On the Cutting Edge is described as "a series of exciting, interactive educational live shows that take students and educators on electronic field trips to laboratories, classrooms, NASA Centers, and remote sites across the country to experience science, mathematics, geography, and technology in real-world settings" (1998, http://www.okstate.edu/aesp/VC.html).

*Videoconferencing.* Two-way video systems based on broadcast and land-line technologies that make possible "live action" interactive two-way video/audio interaction have become known as videoconferencing. Teleconferencing and videoconferencing (also sometimes known as video teleconferencing) sound alike but are two different technologies. Teleconferencing uses one-way video (one participant could broadcast to the others) with two-way interaction via the telephone among all participants. Videoconferencing is a point-to-point closed communications system connected by CODECs (coder-decoder) that are each equipped with video. These systems need expensive dedicated lines in order to operate. Anyone with a satellite dish to pull down the signal can *see* a teleconference, but no one except the participants connected with these dedicated lines can see videoconferencing transmissions. (Also see desktop videoconferencing with computers later in this section.) Some current examples of these systems are Picture-tel and V-tel, and they range from one-instructor-to-one-group arrangements to more complex multiple-group uses.

## Computer-based Options and Uses

**Internet uses.** Most computer-based distance learning applications involve some Internet resource or activity and many rely exclusively on Internet materials. Some important options involved with computer-based systems are how students get access to the Internet (modem or network) and whether or not they have videoconferencing capability. Since the Internet figures so prominently in many distance learning activities, Chapter 8 will focus on this rapidly-growing and evolving force in education and society.

**Desktop videoconferencing.** The increasing availability of telephone switching technologies allows completely interactive communication between desktop computers. Computers adapted for two-way interaction are becoming common in schools and classrooms across the country. A typical desktop videoconferencing system has a video camera and microphone; speakers at each workstation or learning station allow learners to be seen and heard by the teacher or learner at the remote site. Signals are transmitted using modems and telephone lines. Teachers can use presentation technologies such as LCD projection panels connected to the computers to expand the number of persons who may observe the on-screen video. Learners may communicate directly with teachers, peers, and experts who use compatible systems.

Current applications of desktop videoconferencing are limited by several factors. First, the cost of transmitting video data over telephone lines is high because of the large amount of bandwidth those signals require. Second, current video transmissions must deal with analog signals, making them difficult to manipulate. However, videoconferencing is on the increase, especially as equipment and line costs become cheaper and resources get easier to use (Jerram, 1995; Walsh & Reece, 1995).

## Overview of Distance Learning Integration Strategies

The descriptions of distance learning configurations given earlier in this chapter included a few example distance learning applications; this section provides more detail on ways of using these resources to meet educational needs. Like other technologies described in this text, schools and teachers may integrate distance learning resources into their work in instructional ways and through productivity applications.

### Integration for Instruction: Virtual Lessons, Courses, and Degrees

Distance learning instruction is conducted in individual lessons, credit courses, and whole degree programs.

**Virtual lessons.** Since most individual lessons use the Internet, types of directed and constructivist lesson integration strategies and examples of each type are given in Chapter 8, Integrating the Internet into Education.

**Virtual courses.** Most current distance learning offerings are courses, rather than full degree programs (Lucas, 1998). Pilsik (1997) gives useful criteria for evaluating the quality of existing online courses and Kubla (1998) describes effective activities and strategies for those designing such a course. Although his course is at the college level, the integration methods he describes are useful for courses at any level.

*Course preparation.* Courses given completely or primarily via distance learning require more advance preparation than traditional courses because teachers must provide alternate ways to give detail (either in writing or in video) and assure the interaction is comparable to a face-to-face class. Kubla found that a textbook and set of handouts and readings was especially helpful to structure course activities.

*Preparing students for distance methods.* Many distance learning courses have no in-person, face-to-face meetings at all, but Kubla recommends one initial in-person orienta-

tion session. At this time, the instructor makes sure everyone knows how to use the equipment and understands how the course will operate. Kubla arranged to have each student's picture taken and posted in a Student Listing, along with their e-mail addresses to help assure interaction among them. He discussed the "canons" of distance learning to help them stay on task and get the most out of their course experience, including a review of "netiquette" (see Chapter 8).

*Technical support.* No matter which distance learning technology is used, it would be a rare course in which there were not even a few equipment problems, software glitches, or students having technical problems. Technical personnel must be readily available to troubleshoot these problems and answer questions for students experiencing difficulties.

*Assignments and exams.* Course activities can take many forms, including presenting material to read or watch online, giving links to Internet sites, having students do collaborative projects through e-mail, and holding discussions on questions posed by the instructor. Kubla did not incorporate live chats; he felt they were too difficult to coordinate and carry out effectively. Instead, he held threaded discussions in an online area called the Course Forum. Students also had to do "reaction papers" and e-mail them to him. Quizzes were done by e-mail, and the final exam, worth 35 percent of the grade, had to be done in person at the university or at a designated, proctored site.

Wolcott (1996) has additional recommendations to minimize the psychological distance that she feels can make a distance learning experience different from a face-to-face one. She recommends a "learner-centered approach" to address three main factors: building rapport, decreasing isolation, and enhancing interaction. She recommends the strategies discussed below.

- **Attitudes.** Instructors should examine their own beliefs about distance learning and about learning, in general. The view, for example, that distance learning is "second-best" to face-to-face instruction can create a self-fulfilling prophesy. Instructors also should reflect on their practices and attitudes toward students. If our teaching methods demoralize students, rather than challenge them, "… there is little dignity in being a learner" (Wolcott, 1996, p. 26), no matter what the delivery system.

- **Policies.** Work to remove restrictive policies in tuition, registration, communications, and support services that increase distance between the institution and its students.

- **Instructional practices.** Use methods that minimize psychological distance in all phases of the course (see Figure 7.2).

**Virtual degrees.** New virtual degree programs at all levels of education are springing up every day. Elbaum (1998) describes some virtual high schools around the country, including John F. Kennedy HS, Fremont, CA; Shrewsbury HS, Shrewsbury, MA; Marlborough HS, Marlborough,

**Figure 7.2   Wolcott's Matrix of Strategies for Minimizing Psychological Distance in Distance Learning Courses**

| Build Rapport | Decrease Isolation | Enhance Interaction |
|---|---|---|
| **Pre-active** | | |
| • Distribute information about the course prior to the first class meeting.<br>• Gather information about enrolled students—their goals, expectations, and previous experiences; create student profiles.<br>• Write course objectives to define what students will do, not what you will do.<br>• Provide students with choices in objectives and activities.<br>• Plan instructional activities that require students to collaborate. | • Plan collaborative activities.<br>• Use small groups; vary group configurations to include students from different sites.<br>• Assign responsibility for specific activities/content to groups or individuals.<br>• Think visually; provide students with common graphics and visual images.<br>• When feasible, plan a general in-person meeting or visit and/or originate from different sites.<br>• Design activities and supporting materials which help students learn how to learn. | • Incorporate active learning techniques such as role playing, discussion groups, and case studies.<br>• Plan a variety of activities which include listening, reflecting, and discussing.<br>• Build in time for questions and answers.<br>• Design activities that address higher order objectives such as application, synthesis, and problem solving. |
| **Interactive** | | |
| • Use ice-breaker or get-acquainted activities such as introductions.<br>• Learn and use students' names.<br>• Listen; be respectful and open to students' opinions and concerns.<br>• Present an approachable demeanor, e.g., smile and make eye contact.<br>• Show enthusiasm for teaching/learning, for content, and the method of delivery.<br>• Play up commonalties among students and between you and the students.<br>• Emphasize personal responsibility for learning. | • Have students share their experiences and use students' experiences to draw individuals into discussions.<br>• Try to address each student or site at least once during each class session.<br>• Make connections between various aspects of the content and between the content and students' goals and expectations.<br>• Encourage students to talk to each other both informally and through cross-group discussions. | • Assume student participation.<br>• Brief students on the use of the telecommunications equipment.<br>• Minimize "teacher talk"; alternate lecture with student activity.<br>• Ask questions; make it easy for students to answer and to ask questions of their own.<br>• Pause to allow students to think and to formulate questions. |
| **Post-active** | | |
| • Communicate with students outside of class, e.g., initiate calls to check on student progress.<br>• Engage in informal conversations before/after class and during breaks.<br>• Share class lists, student profiles, and/or photos of students. | • Work with the library staff to facilitate access to resources.<br>• Provide information about support services such as advising and counseling.<br>• Encourage study groups.<br>• Make it easy for students to contact you outside of class, e.g., through office hours, home phone number, voice mail, or electronic mail. | • Provide timely feedback; respond to questions and "turn-around" assignments promptly.<br>• Provide air-time before and after class for questions. |

Source: Wolcott, L. (1996). Distant, but not distanced. A learner-centered approach to distance education. *Tech Trends, 41*(4), 23–27.

MA; Allen HS, Allen, TX; and Alcanes HS, Lafayette, CA. In his "ecology" of distance learning, Lucas (1998) describes the types of post–secondary distance learning degree programs currently in place. The most successful programs, he finds, are those in which an institution "develops its distance curriculum programmatically" (p. 14), and has an office in place to coordinate articulation agreements and reciprocal credit exchanges among institutions.

### Integration for Teacher Productivity: Support for Communication and Course Preparation

Distance technologies can help educators use their time more efficiently as they prepare instructional lessons and projects and communicate among themselves and with students.

**Support for communications.** Fetterman (1998) describes some of the ways distance technologies help educators communicate among themselves and with students. Distance technologies make an educator's work more efficient if used consistently as an integral part of a teachers' professional "toolbox." Strategies Fetterman (1998) recommends include the following.

- **E-mail.** Use whenever possible for written communications with other teachers, experts, students, and parents. For quick access, keep an online e-mail directory of people with whom you communicate frequently.

- **Virtual office.** Set up space on a Web site to exchange documents and messages with colleagues working on the same activity such as team teaching.

- **Videoconferenced meetings.** To save travel time, hold videoconferencing "meetings" with colleagues, where each person involved can see the others. Fetterman recommends this only with people you know well.

**Support for course preparation.** Finally, educators can use the Internet in combination with software tools to help them prepare for teaching and deal with the logistics of many complex instructional activities. For example, a middle school teacher who wants to do a project on the rain forest can use a search engine (see Chapter 8) with the keywords "rain forest," "school," and "project" to find information and links to many materials, resources, and projects-in-progress. The only problem teachers have when looking for materials and experts on a particular topic is deciding which to use from the wealth of possibilities they find.

## Exercises

### Record and Apply What You Have Learned

**Activity 7.1: Chapter 7 Self-Test** To review terms and concepts in this chapter, take the Chapter 7 self-test. Select Chapter 7 from the front page of the companion Web site (located at http://www.prenhall.com/roblyer), then choose the *Multiple Choice* module.

**Activity 7.2: Portfolio Activities** The following activities will help you add to your professional portfolio. To complete these activities online and save or submit the materials electronically, select Chapter 7 from the front page of the companion Web site (http://www.prenhall.com/roblyer), then choose the *Portfolio* module.

*Distance Learning Characteristics* Using information in this chapter and other materials, develop and fill in a chart that lists the important characteristics of distance learning and describes how these characteristics have changed and are changing. An example format:

| Past | Current | Future |
| --- | --- | --- |

Distance learning characteristics that will change:

1._____
2._____
3._____

Distance learning characteristics that will stay the same:

1._____
2._____
3._____

*Overview* Based on the information in this chapter and your other readings and discussions, prepare a prediction scenario for how distance learning will appear and how it will affect our educational systems in the year 2050. Be specific about the kinds of equipment that will be in place, what kinds and numbers of students and institutions will use distance learning, how student learning opportunities and options will be affected, and what role teachers will play as a result of the changes.

**Activity 7.3: Questions for Thought and Discussion** These questions may be used for small group or class discussion or may be subjects for individual or group activities. To take part in these discussions online, select Chapter 7 from the front page of the companion Web site (http://www.prenhall.com/roblyer), then choose the *Message Board* module.

- Sherritt (1996) said that, "... some institutions are getting into distance (education) for the wrong reasons, primarily to solve budget problems" (p. 7).

- A letter to the president of the University of Washington signed by some 700 faculty members said, in part: "While costly fantasies of this kind present a mouth-watering bonanza to software manufacturers and other corporate sponsors, what they bode for education is nothing short of disastrous.... Distance learning should be a supplement to higher education ... not a central feature of it."

**Activity 7.4: Collaborative Activities**  The following may be developed in small group work. Completed group products may be copied and shared with the entire class and/or included in each person's Personal Portfolio:

*Overview of Distance Learning Options*  Divide this project up into tasks so that it may be done in small groups. The purpose is to develop a graphic overview, using diagrams, charts, or images, of the distance learning options available to educators under the major headings: broadcast/terrestrial and computer-based. Once the whole project is completed, the groups can work together to combine the products into one overview. For each distance learning option, identify required equipment, benefits and limitations, and at least one real-world example of a program using that system. (Hint: Use the Internet and do a keyword search to link to places using this type of system.)

*Distance Learning Integration Strategies*  Each group can prepare one of the following:

- **Plan a distance learning course.** Identify a local need for a distance learning course and develop a plan for how the course should be structured and taught. Be sure to address the kind of distance learning configuration you will use, learning activities that take

advantage of the distance learning resources, and strategies to decrease psychological distance and keep students on task.

- **Plan a distance learning degree program.** Imagine you are a school, district, or college administrator; identify a local need for a distance learning degree program. Plan what courses should comprise the curriculum for the program. Search the Internet for existing courses and prepare a plan for how you would use them and other courses you would develop and offer.

- **Distance learning designs for teacher productivity.** Imagine you are a teacher at the elementary, middle school, or secondary level. Describe ways you feel distance learning resources will make you more productive in your communications with others and your ability to prepare effectively for teaching. Be specific about the kinds of resources you will use and how they will help you.

**Activity 7.5: Integrating Technology Across the Curriculum Activities**  Use the *Integrating Technology Across the Curriculum* CD-ROM packaged with this textbook to complete the following exercise:

The use of e-mail can support learning activities in all content areas. Go to *Find Lesson Plan* and click on *Find by Criteria*. Under the *Technologies* descriptor, select "e-mail" and click *Search*. Of the lessons listed, select ones that use e-mail in each of three different content areas. Compare the strategies. Develop your own lesson modeled after the strategy you feel is most powerful.

# References

Bauch, J. (1993). Telephones in classrooms: An unsung technology revolution. *Inventing Tomorrow's Schools, 3*(4), 5–7.

Bernard, R. & Amundsen, C. (1989). Antecedents to dropout in distance education: Does one model fit all? *The Journal of Distance Education, 4*(2), 25–46.

Biner, P. (1993). The development of an instrument to measure student attitudes toward televised courses. *The American Journal of Distance Education, 7*(1), 62–73.

Biner, P., Welsh, K., Barone, N., Summers, M., & Dean, R. S. (1997). The impact of remote-site group size on student satisfaction and relative performance in interactive telecourses. *The American Journal of Distance Education, 11*(1), 23–32.

Boettcher, J. (1998). How much does it cost to develop a distance learning course? It all depends.... *Syllabus, 11*(9), 56–58.

Bybee, D. (1996). Congress passes telecommunications act of 1996. *ISTE Update, 8*(5), 1.

Cheng, H., Lehman, J., & Armstrong, P. (1991). Comparison of performance and attitude in traditional and computer

conferencing classes. *The American Journal of Distance Education, 5*(3), 51–64.

Clark, R. E. (1983). Reconsidering research on learning from media. *Review of Educational Research, 53*(4), 445–459.

Coussement, S. (1995). Educational telecommunication: Does it work? An attitude study (ERIC Document Reproduction No. 391 465).

Crowley, M. (1998). E-rate to enhance connectivity at Florida schools and libraries. *T.H.E. Journal, 25*(11), 26A–27A.

Cyrs, T. E. (1997). Competence in teaching at a distance. In T. E. Cyrs (Ed.). *Teaching and learning at a distance: What it takes to effectively design, deliver, and evaluate programs.* San Francisco: Jossey-Bass.

Dillon, C., Hengst, H., & Zoller, D. (1991). Instructional strategies and student involvement in distance education: A study of the Oklahoma televised instruction system. *Journal of Distance Education, 6*(1), 28–41.

Driscoll, M. & Kirby, E. (1997). Facilitator and student roles and performance in a high school distance education course. Paper presented at the Annual Meeting of the American

Educational Research Association, Chicago, Illinois (ERIC Document Reproduction No. 406 966).

Education Imperative (1992). *The Present Futures Report, 2*(9), 1–8.

Elbaum, B. (1998, Winter). Is the virtual high school "educational reform"? @ *Concord.Org: Newsletter of the Concord Consortium.* Concord, MA, pp. 10–11.

Esquivel, E. (1998). Infrastructure requirements for schools. *T.H.E. Journal, 25*(11), 14A–16A.

Fetterman, D. (1998). Webs of meaning: Computer and Internet resources for educational research and instruction. *Educational Researcher, 27*(3), 22–30.

Fulford, C. & Zhang, S. (1993). Perceptions of interaction: The critical predictor in distance education. *The American Journal of Distance Education, 7*(3), 8–21.

Furst-Bowie, J. (1997). Comparison of student reactions in traditional and videoconferencing courses in training and development. *International Journal of Instructional Media, 24*(3), 197–205.

Gibson, C. & Graf, A. (1992). Impact of adults' preferred learning styles and perception of barriers on completion of external baccalaureate degree programs. *Journal of Distance Education, 7*(1), 39–51.

Gilder, G. (1992). *Life after television.* New York: W. W. Norton.

Gross, P. (1997). Engaging the disengaged: How is it different when using distance education? In Walking the tightrope: The balance between innovation and leadership. Proceedings of the Annual International Conference of the Chair Academy, Reno, NV, pp. 56–60 (ERIC Document Reproduction No. 407 008).

Guernsey, L. (1998, March 27). Colleges debate the wisdom of having on-campus students enroll in online classes. *The Chronicle of Higher Education Online.*

Hardy, D. W. & Boaz, M. H. (1997). Learner development: Beyond the technology. In T. E. Cyrs (Ed.). *Teaching and learning at a distance: What it takes to effectively design, deliver, and evaluate programs.* San Francisco: Jossey-Bass.

Harris, J. (1994). Teaching teachers to use telecomputing tools. *The Computing Teacher, 22*(2), 60–63.

Hawkins, J. & Macmillan, K. (1993). So what are teachers doing with this stuff? *Electronic Learning, 13*(2), 26.

Imel, S. (1996). Distance education: Trends and issues alerts (ERIC Document Reproduction No. ED 399 383).

Jerram, P. (1995). Videoconferencing gets in sync. *New Media, 5*(7), 48, 50–55.

Kearsley, G., Hunter, B., & Furlong, M. (1992). *We teach with technology.* Wilsonville, OR: Franklin, Beedle, & Associates, Inc.

Kember, D., Murphy, D., Siaw, I., & Yuen, K. S. (1991). Towards a causal model of student progress in distance education. *The American Journal of Distance Education, 5*(2), 3–15.

Kimball, C. & Shibley, P. (1997–1998). Am I on the mark? Technology planning for the e-rate. *Learning and Leading with Technology, 25*(4), 52–55.

Klesius, J., Homan, S., & Thompson, T. (1997). Distance education compared to traditional instruction: The students' view. *International Journal of Instructional Media, 24*(3), 207–220.

Kubla, T. (1998). Addressing student needs: Teaching on the Internet. *T.H.E. Journal, 25*(8), 71–74.

Leslie, J. (1993). Kids connecting. *Wired, 1*(5), 90–93.

Lucas, R. (1998). An ecology of distance learning. *Syllabus, 11*(10), 14–16, 22.

Ludlow, B. L. (1994). A comparison of traditional and distance education models. Proceedings of the Annual National Conference of the American Council on Rural Special Education, Austin, TX (ERIC Document Reproduction No. ED 369 599).

McCollum, K. (1998, April 17). All MBAs on deck! *The Chronicle of Higher Education, 44*, A27–A28.

McHenry, L. & Bozik, M. (1997). From a distance: Student voices from the interactive video classroom. *TechTrends, 42*(6), 20–24,

Moore, M. G. (1995). Editorial: The death of distance. *The American Journal of Distance Education, 9*(3), 1–4.

Moore, M. G. & Kearsley, G. (1996). *Distance education: A systems view.* Belmont, CA: Wadsworth Publishing Co.

Moskal, P., Martin, B., & Foshee, N. (1997). Educational technology and distance education in central Florida: An assessment of capabilities. *The American Journal of Distance Education, 11*(1), 6–22.

Pilsik, G. (1997). Is this course instructionally sound? A guide to evaluating online training courses. *Educational Technology, 37*(4), 50–59.

Richards, C., and Ridley, D. (1997). Factors affecting college students' persistence in online computer-managed instruction. *College Student Journal, 31*, 490–495.

Riddle, J. (1990). Measuring affective change: Students in a distance learning class. Paper presented at the Annual Meeting of the Northern Rocky Mountain Educational Research Association, Greeley, CO (ERIC Document Reproduction No. ED 325 514).

Ringstaff, C. (1993). Trading places: When students become the experts. *Apple Education Review, 3.*

Roblyer, M. (1992). Electronic hands across the ocean: The Florida-England connection. *The Computing Teacher, 19*(5), 16–19.

Roblyer, M. D. (1998a). Is distance ever really dead? Comparing the effects of distance learning and face-to-face courses. *Learning and Leading with Technology, 25*(8), 32–34.

Roblyer, M. D. (1998b). Visual literacy: Seeing a new rationale for using technology. *Learning and Leading with Technology, 26*(2), 51–54.

Roblyer, M. D. (1999). Why do students choose distance learning? A study of participation in virtual courses at high school and community college levels. Paper presentation at the American Educational Research Association Annual Meeting, Montreal, Canada.

Russell, T. L. (1992). Television's indelible impact on distance education: What we should have learned from comparative research. *Research in Distance Education, 4*(4), 2–4.

Russell, T. L. (1997). *The "no significant difference" phenomenon as reported in research reports, summaries, and papers.* Raleigh, NC: Office of Instructional Telecommunications, North Carolina State University.

Selingo, J. (1998, June 5). Congress moves cautiously on aid for students in distance education. *The Chronicle of Higher Education, 44*(39), A30.

Sherritt, C. (1996). A fundamental problem with distance programs in higher education (ERIC Document Reproduction No. ED 389 906).

Smith, C. K. (1996). Convenience vs. connection: Commuter students' views on distance learning. Paper presented at the Annual Forum of the Association for Institutional Research, Albuquerque, NM (ERIC Document Reproduction No. ED 397 725).

Thomerson, D. & Smith, C. (1996). Student perceptions of the affective experiences encountered in distance learning courses. *The American Journal of Distance Education, 10*(3), 37–48.

Thompson, G. (1990). How can correspondence-based distance learning be improved? A survey of attitudes of students who are not well disposed toward correspondence study. *Journal of Distance Education, 5*(1), 53–65.

Threlkeld, R. & Brzoska, K. (1994). Research in distance education. In B. Willis (Ed.). *Distance education: Strategies and tools.* Englewood Cliffs, NJ: Educational Technology Publications, Inc.

Van Dusen, G. (1997). The virtual campus: Technology and reform in higher education. ERIC Digest. Washington, DC: ERIC Clearinghouse on Higher Education (ERIC Document Reproduction No. ED 412 815).

Wallace, L. (1996). Changes in the demographics and motivations of distance education students. *Journal of Distance Education, 11*(1), 1–31.

Walsh, J. & Reese, B. (1995). Distance learning's growing reach. *T.H.E. Journal, 22*(11), 58–62.

Westbrook, T. (1997). Changes in students' attitudes toward graduate business instruction via interactive television. *The American Journal of Distance Education, 11*(1), 55–69.

Wheatley, B. & Greer, E. (1995). Interactive television: A new delivery system for a traditional reading course. *The Journal of Technology and Teacher Education, 3*(4), 343–350.

Wilkes, C. & Burnham, B. (1991). Adult learner motivations and electronic distance education. *The American Journal of Distance Education, 5*(1), 43–51.

Withrow, F. (1992). Distance learning: Star Schools. *Metropolitan Universities, 3*(1), 61–65.

Wolcott, L. (1996). Distant, but not distanced. A learner-centered approach to distance education. *TechTrends, 41*(4), 23–27.

Zenor, S. (1998, June). Telephone conversation with AECT President Stanley Zenor.

Zirkin, B. & Sumler, D. (1995). Interactive or non-interactive: That is the question!!! An annotated bibliography. *Journal of Distance Education, 10*(1), 95–112.

# Chapter 8

---

## Integrating the Internet into Education

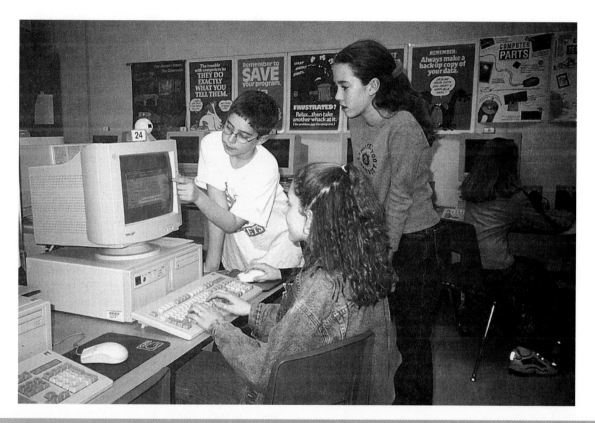

But the Net, I guarantee you, really is fire. I think it's more important than the invention of moveable type.

Brad Ferren, as quoted by David Remnick in "Future Perfect," *The New Yorker* (October 1997)

## This chapter covers the following topics:

- Background on past, present, and future Internet uses

- Definitions and descriptions of various Internet resources available to educators

- Implementation issues to consider when using the Internet

- Teaching and learning activities that use Internet and the World Wide Web technologies

# Objectives

1. Describe the purpose of each of the following Internet resources: Web browsers, search engines, gophers, e-mail, listservs, bulletin boards, chatrooms, FTP and streaming video/audio, Web authoring tools, push technologies, site capturing (local HTML), intranets, Internet TV, and avatars.

2. Identify an Internet resource that would meet a specific written or visual communications need.

3. Select and use an appropriate Web authoring tool to meet a specific need.

4. Identify recent developments on each of several ethical issues related to Internet use.

5. Develop a plan for an Internet project designed according to a directed or a constructivist model.

## Introduction: Enter the Internet

The Internet burst on the scene in our society and in education only a few years ago, but quickly set fire to the interest and imagination of even the least technical teachers, students, and parents. Now most computer-based distance learning applications involve some Internet resource or activity, and many rely exclusively on Internet materials. With computer-based systems, the only option is how students get access to the Internet (modem or network) and whether or not to have videoconferencing capability. Since the Internet figures so prominently in many distance learning activities, this chapter focuses on this rapidly-growing and evolving force in education.

### Where Did the Internet Come From?

Today's educational uses of the Internet bear little resemblance to its original purpose. Yet learning something about its original design can help educators understand how the Internet works today. The U.S. Department of Defense (DOD) developed the first version of the Internet during the 1970s to allow quick communication among researchers working on DOD projects in about 30 locations. The DOD also saw it as a way to continue communications among these important defense sites in the event of a worldwide catastrophe such as a nuclear attack. Since these projects were funded by the DOD's Advanced Research Projects Agency (ARPA), the network was originally called ARPAnet.

In the 1980s, just as desktop computers were becoming common, the National Science Foundation (NSF) funded a high-speed connection among university centers based on the ARPAnet structure. By connecting their individual networks, universities could communicate and exchange information in the same way DOD's projects had. However, these new connections had an additional, unexpected benefit. A person accessing a university network from home or school could also get access to any site connected to that network. This connection began to be called a *gateway* to all networks, and what we now call the Internet was born.

### What Is the Internet Now?

Networks connect computers to allow users to share resources and exchange information easily. The Internet has been called the ultimate network or "the mother of all networks" because it is a network of networks. It is a way for people in network sites all over the world to communicate with each other as though they were on the same local area network. The name means literally "between or among networks." Though most people think of the Internet as synonymous with the World Wide Web (WWW), the latter really is a subset of the Internet system. The WWW is an Internet *service* that links sites around the world through hypertext documents. By bringing up a hypertext or Web page document in a program called a *Web browser,* one can click on text or graphics linked to other pages in other sites. In this way, one "travels" around the Internet from site to site.

Our use of the Internet depends on common procedures or protocols that allow computers to communicate with each other, despite differences in programs or operating systems. Two important protocols are Internet protocol (IP) addresses and uniform resource locators (URLs).

**IP addresses.** Internet exchanges are possible because everyone uses a common communications system called an Internet protocol, which assigns a number designation to each Internet address. To navigate the Internet, you must have an account on a computer connected to it. Most users connect their computers to the Internet through large, high-powered computer systems (servers) running the Unix operating system. An Internet address is the combination of your account name (*user id*) and the Internet-registered name of the computer (*host name*). For example, look at the components of the following Internet e-mail address:

mroblyer@westga.edu

- The name *roblyer* represents the user id.

- The @ symbol sets off the *host name,* in this case, *mail* (a server for the main organization, FIRN). The periods are essential parts of the address as well because they separate key elements of the host name. Usually the institution or company follows the machine name.

- The *edu* identifies the type of company or institution, in this case, an educational organization. Other common types are *org* (organization), *com* (company), and *gov* (government). Users in countries outside the United States append two-character codes to indicate their origins. For instance, *uk* identifies England and *au* is Australia.

InterNIC (Internet Network Information Center), a cooperative service of the National Science Foundation and a Virginia company called Network Solutions, serves as a registry for Internet addresses, ensuring that no two Internet addresses or IP numbers are identical. Think of it as a database similar to that maintained by the Social Security Administration, which ensures that no two people have identical Social Security numbers. In 1998, the U.S. Congress provided funds allocated to improve this system and to help large universities who act as providers for educators to pay for high-speed Internet connections (Biemiller & Young, 1998, May 15).

**Uniform resource locators (URLs).** Every Web page or Web site has an address called a uniform resource locator (URL). A URL starts with the prefix HTTP, which stands for HyperText Transfer Protocol—an Internet standard that defines how messages are sent and what actions servers and browsers should take in response to commands. A URL entered into a browser sends an HTTP command to the Web server directing it to transmit the requested Web page. The standard format for a URL is:

http://www.prenhall.com/roblyer

## Why Has the Internet Become So Popular?

Educators, like just about everyone in the civilized world, either seem to be on the Internet or trying to get on it. It has become a symbol for our era of technology's power to shape our lives. A major benefit of the Internet is the comprehensive nature of its information and services. Once connected, educators and students can use the Internet to exchange messages and files among themselves and with others anywhere in the world. Also, they can use it to locate information virtually from any place in the world. A person or site with the desired information need only be connected to the Internet and willing to provide an online listing of available resources. But the Internet's popularity does not spring merely from its wealth of information, but from three other characteristics that give widespread appeal to technical and non-technical people alike. It is widely available, easy to use, and highly visual and graphic.

**Widely available.** Anyone in the world can access the Internet and use it to communicate with others. In this sense, it is as popular as the telephone and is, in fact, combining with telephone service to broaden the usefulness of both.

**Easy to use.** The Internet is based on a simple and intuitive "point-and-click" activity. Anything on an Internet page, such as a word or picture, can be a link to another location. One link may be to another place on the same Web page; another link can connect to another place in the world. Both are equally easy to do. A brief demonstration has made many noncomputer users into Internet enthusiasts. The terms "surfing" and "browsing" indicate just how popular it has become to follow these links from site to site, gathering information along the way.

**Highly visual and graphic.** When the Internet was strictly a text-based system, it was not nearly as popular with "non-techies." It was when images became a primary means of communication on Web pages that the Internet caught on. This graphic quality appealed to society's growing dependency on visual forms of communication fostered by television and video games.

Despite these features, educational use of the Internet is not yet as widespread as its popularity. In 1994, Honey observed that the vast majority of educators were not tapping the Internet's potential, and Roberts (1996) later said that full effects of such technologies are rarely felt in the classroom. The same logistical problems that hamper use of any technology (lack of training, time, and access to resources) also limit educators' use of the Internet; however, interest continues to grow.

## How Do Schools Get Connected?

There are two different types of gateways to the Internet: a direct connection or an account with a service provider or other organization with a direct connection.

**Direct connection.** Larger schools and other organizations usually have direct connections to the Internet and allow any of their members to use these connections, usually free of charge. For example, if a school has an Internet connection, anyone working there may acquire an account that becomes, in effect, an Internet address. The connection with the Internet is so transparent to these users that they frequently have the illusion that their connections are free; however, they actually are paid for by the organization.

**A service provider account.** A variety of service providers has sprung up to sell accounts to those who do not have free access in some other way. Perhaps the best-known are international companies such as America Online and CompuServ, but hundreds of regional and local companies also sell Internet access. Users of these accounts usually pay by the amount of time they spend connected. Service providers typically give users various software tools in addition to user IDs that act as addresses for sending and receiving information. Also, anyone can get an Internet account with a local Freenet, if available.

Larger schools and higher education institutions usually provide their faculty and students with a direct Internet connection through their own network. Schools with no network can give teachers two connection options as shown in Figures 8.1a and 8.1b, while schools with a network usually choose the option shown in Figure 8.2. See Ryder and Hughes (1998) for more information.

**Figure 8.1a    Internet Connection Option 1: Basic Home Connection**

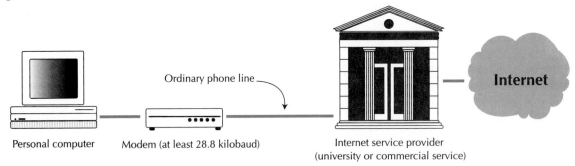

Source: Ryder, R. & Hughes, T. (1998). *Internet for educators (2nd ed.)*. Reprinted by permission of Prentice-Hall, Inc., Upper Saddle River, NJ.

**Figure 8.1b    Internet Connection Option 1: ISDN Setup**

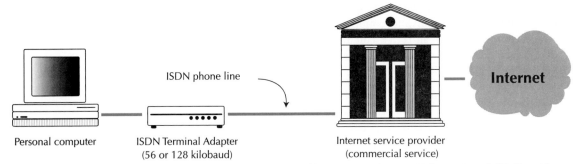

Source: Ryder, R. & Hughes, T. (1998). *Internet for educators (2nd ed.)*. Reprinted by permission of Prentice-Hall, Inc., Upper Saddle River, NJ.

**Figure 8.2    Internet Connection Option 2: Connecting a School LAN to the Internet**

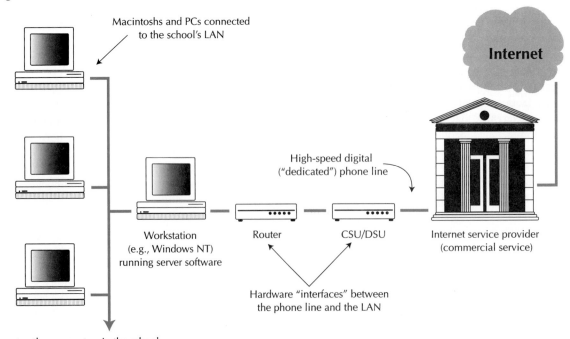

Source: Ryder, R. & Hughes, T. (1998). *Internet for educators (2nd ed.)*. Reprinted by permission of Prentice-Hall, Inc., Upper Saddle River, NJ.

# Web Browsing and Searching

Using the Internet in its earliest form required familiarity with the commands used in a technical system called Unix. Today, very little needs to be known about Unix to use the Internet effectively. Several user-friendly programs called *clients* have been designed to carry out various user activities such as browsing and searching. These programs are called clients because they work through the host computers or servers on which they reside; in a sense the server "works for" them. The most popular clients are browsers, search engines, and gophers.

## Using Web Browsers

Web browsers allow users to move freely and effortlessly from one site to another through a text-based linking system known as *hypertext.* Browsers make using the Internet as easy as point-and-click because they let users access all available resources on the Web to search for information. The first browser, *Mosaic,* appeared on the market in 1993 and began to attract attention to the Internet. But the two browsers that appeared subsequently, *Netscape Communicator* and *Internet Explorer,* now are the most commonly used browsers (see Figure 8.3).

When a browser is first installed on a computer, it must be set up with options such as which Web site will appear automatically as the *home page* when the user connects to the Internet. The most common choices for teachers to designate as a browser home page are:

- A teacher's personal home page or school home page;
- The Netscape site or Internet Explorer site;
- A news service such as a local newspaper's home page; or
- A "push technology" site that sends customized news to users' desktops on topics they specify are of most interest to them.

Browsing is considered a wandering, unstructured tour through whatever path of Internet links the user follows. However, if teachers want a more structured search for information specific to a certain topic, they usually use a search engine.

## Using Search Engines

Roberts (1997) gives a succinct and valuable summary of search engines and methods to use with them. Some good search engines for teachers include:

- Alta Vista, from the Digital Equipment Corporation
- Excite, from Excite, Inc.
- InfoSeek, from the Infoseek Corporation
- Lycos, now owned by Excite, which takes its name from the Portuguese explorer who navigated the Strait of Magellan in 1520

**Figure 8.3** **Images of Netscape and Internet Explorer Home Pages**

**Netscape Communicator™**

Source: Courtesy of Netscape.

**Internet Explorer 4.0**

Source: Icon reprinted with permission from Microsoft Corporation.

- WebCrawler, from America Online
- Yahoo! (short for "Yet Another Hierarchical Officious Oracle"), which was started by David Filo and Jerry Yang at Stanford University

## Using Gophers

Gopher is a search system developed at the University of Minnesota and named after the school's mascot. Developed before the advent of more graphic browsers, a server with Gopher shows its contents as a hierarchically structured menu of files. Two Gopher resources, Veronica and Jughead, allow people to search the Internet for resources stored in Gopher systems.

# Communicating in Writing on the Internet

Computer-based written forms of communication are becoming as common as telephone calls.

## E-mail

*Electronic mail (e-mail)* is the most common way to exchange personal, written messages between individuals or small groups. It is possible to send e-mail via an internal network, rather than the Internet, but most people with e-mail accounts also send e-mail outside their systems via the Internet. Abilock (1996) discusses how powerful e-mail can be for communications among teachers, students, and resource experts.

## Listservs

*Listservs* are discussion groups on the Internet that feature ongoing "conversations" via e-mail between groups of people who share common interests. When e-mail is addressed to a listserv mailing list, it is automatically duplicated and sent to everyone on the list.

### Bulletin Boards

*Bulletin boards,* like listservs, serve as electronic message centers but usually are used to post notices of interest rather than hold ongoing conversations. (An exception to this is the use of bulletin boards in a distance learning course.) Most bulletin boards serve specific interest groups. They allow members to review messages left by others, and leave their own messages. There are tens of thousands of bulletin board services in the United States alone.

### Chatrooms

*Chatrooms* are Internet locations that allow "live," real-time communications between two or more users. As users in a chatroom type in their comments, what they type is seen by everyone in the "room." Chatrooms are considered more interactive than any of the other written communications options. The chats held in them are sometimes known as "threaded discussions."

## Communicating Visually on the Internet

Although written communications retain their importance, visual communications are an emerging standard. Our society relies increasingly on images to communicate information, which means that both students and teachers must become adept at developing and using visual forms of communication in distance learning.

### Images and Animations

Some of the graphics tools referred to in Chapter 6 are used to develop Internet resources. Clip art, photos, and animations are standard fare on most Web pages. Clip art and clip photo packages are banks of prepared images that may be inserted into Web pages; a scanner can also be used to prepare an image from an original photograph or picture for use on a page. Animations are motion sequences made up of individual pictures put together to form the illusion of continuous motion. Prepared animation packages also are available.

### Regular and Streaming Video/Audio

Students and teachers need tools that allow development of audio and development and viewing of full-motion video. The programs that play the prepared audio and video are known as *plug-ins* and generally are available for downloading free from the Internet. Currently, there are two kinds of full-motion video on the Internet: downloaded movies and streaming (compressed) video.

**Downloaded movies.** One kind of full-motion video is designed to play in a window on the computer screen after it is downloaded from the Internet to a computer. Programs such as Apple's *QuickTime* are used to create these movies, which usually are shot with a camcorder and stored in a Moving Picture Experts Group (MPEG) format. To see them, one needs an MPEG player plug-in.

**Streaming video.** This term applies to movies that have been compressed and transmitted in the form of real-time video via the Internet. Just as an MPEG player is needed to view digitized movies, a streaming video player such as RealVideo is needed to see streamed video. A streamed video file begins loading from a remote Web site when the user clicks on it but does not wait until the video is downloaded; it starts almost immediately after the download begins. This is especially useful for large videos that take a long time to download. However, video quality is dependent on the quality and speed of the line connecting the computer to the Internet. For more information on streaming video, see: http://www.streamingvideos.com.

### Desktop Videoconferencing

As described in Chapter 7, the increasing availability of telephone switching technologies allow completely interactive communication among desktop computers. Today, computers adapted for complete two-way interaction are becoming common in schools and classrooms across the country. A typical desktop videoconferencing system has equipment—video camera, microphone, and speakers—at each workstation or learning station that allows the learner to be seen and heard by the teacher or learner at the remote site. Signals are transmitted using modems and telephone lines. Teachers can use presentation technologies such as LCD projection panels connected to the computers to expand the number of persons who may observe the on-screen video. Learners may communicate directly with teachers, peers, and experts who use compatible systems.

Current applications of desktop videoconferencing are limited by several factors. First, the cost of transmitting video data over telephone lines is high because of the large amount of bandwidth those signals require. Second, current video transmissions must deal with analog signals, making them difficult to manipulate. However, videoconferencing is on the increase, especially as equipment and line costs become cheaper and resources get easier to use (Jerram, 1995; Walsh & Reece, 1995).

## File Transfer Options

The Internet is useful for transferring large written documents, graphic files, and programs from one computer to another. Documents, images, and movies can be sent to a computer and displayed with the appropriate software. Many plug-ins and other useful programs are available free when downloaded from the Internet. These programs usually are sent in compressed (stuffed) format and the user must decompress (unstuff) them before they may be used. Many of the new Internet e-mail programs automatically compress and decompress these files before and after downloading if a utility program such as *Stuffit* (Aladdin Software) is stored on the computer's hard drive. Although transferring files is rapidly getting easier, there are a few technical issues to deal with concerning compatibility of files prepared in one program and sent to another. Bull, Bull, and Sigmon (1997b) describe some common problems with compatibility of transferred files and suggest some practical ways to deal with them.

### E-mail Attachments

One easy way to send files is merely to attach them to e-mail messages. Browsers have built-in options for selecting files to send as attachments. Usually, it's as easy as selecting the attachment option from a menu while preparing an e-mail message.

### FTPing

An acronym for File Transfer Protocol, FTP is a common procedure for sending files on the Internet. The FTP servers that house full-text documents also have built-in search engines to allow searches for them. FTP software is needed to send or receive FTP files.

### Gophering

Since Gopher servers are designed to display things in text, rather than graphic, format, they are well-suited for locating and transferring documents.

## Web Page and Web Site Development: Languages and Web Development Programs

Developing personal, professional, school, and project Web pages and Web sites has become an excellent way for both teachers and students to learn the power of the Internet, to participate in cooperative projects, and to display the project results.

### Web Languages and Tools

Only a few years ago, Web pages could not be developed without programming and scripting tools. Now, thanks to Web page development software, it is possible to develop whole sites without writing a line of code or script. However, even if one uses a Web authoring program, it is good to know enough about each of the major languages to

make minor adjustments or additions to developed pages. In addition to the tools described here, which are used primarily in Web development and use, several general purpose programming languages are in common use by more developers. These include C++, Visual Basic, and Practical Extraction and Report Language (PERL), a popular text-processing language used for writing CGI scripts.

**Hypertext markup language (HTML).** HTML is the Internet standard for how Web pages are formatted and displayed. Many books and online sources are available to help people learn and use HTML effectively. An example of HTML and the beginning of the page it generates is shown in Figure 8.4. (Note that the example displays only the beginning of the complete code.) Ryder (1998) has an excellent HTML tutorial, and beginners can find a variety of other HTML tips and tools on the Internet.

**Java.** Originally called OAK, Java is a high-level programming language developed by Sun Microsystems. An object-oriented language similar to C++, it was developed originally for more general use but has become popular for its ability to do interactive graphic and animation activities on Web pages. Many already-developed Java applications called *Java applets* are available for downloading from a Web server and can be run on any computer that has a Java-compatible Web browser. The example applet in Figure 8.5 shows a counter that keeps track of the number of times the page is accessed.

**Virtual Reality Modeling Language (VRML).** Although not commonly used by Web page developers at this time, VRML develops and displays 3-D objects on Web pages. These objects give the illusion of being "real" much more than videos or animations and can create *virtual worlds*. VRML has great potential for making Web pages even more interactive and life-like (Skipton, 1997, May 5). Skipton notes that most VRML packages let developers create basic shapes (primitives) like cubes, spheres, and cylinders and include polygon-based modeling tools for creating more complex objects. Some offer further modeling features—freeform or cutouts—that enable users to extrude or cut out shapes to create more complicated models. Skipton adds that, in combination with other programs, VRML can create "a multi-user avatar space" like that in the science fiction novel *Snow Crash* (Stephenson, 1992). See Chapter 9 for further explanation of this capability.

**Common Gateway Interface (CGI).** CGI is not a language, but a specification for how data will be collected. Developers can use PERL or another language to write CGI programs that create "dynamic documents." That is, Web page users can insert their comments or answers into active Web pages as they run on a server. Many Web pages contain forms that use a CGI program to process the form's data once submitted. Figure 8.6, a page from

**Figure 8.4    Example of HTML Code and Web Page Created By It**

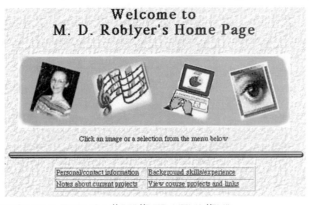

```
<!DOCTYPE HTML PUBLIC "-//IETF//DTD HTML//EN">
<!—This file created 4/5/98 9:20 PM by Claris Home Page version 2.0—>
<HTML>
<HEAD>
  <TITLE>Home Page</TITLE>
  <META NAME=GENERATOR CONTENT="Claris Home Page 2.0">
  <X-SAS-WINDOW TOP=54 BOTTOM=582 LEFT=109 RIGHT=740>
<meta http-equiv="Content-Type"
content="text/html; charset=iso-8859-1"><meta name="FORMATTER"
content="Microsoft FrontPage 2.0">
</HEAD>
<BODY BGCOLOR="#FFFFFF" background="Gray_Textured000CC147.gif">
<P><CENTER><STRONG><FONT SIZE="+3" COLOR="#000080">Welcome
to<BR clear="right">
M. D. Roblyer's Home Page</FONT></STRONG></CENTER></P>
```

**Figure 8.5    Counter: A Java Applet**

Source: Courtesy of Chami.com.

Pacific Bell's videoconferencing information Web site (http://www.kn.pacbell.com/wired/vidconf/), allows users to enter their comments and sign a *guestbook*. All informa- tion entered at this site is processed by a CGI server, which prepares a summary of the information for later review by those who want to read the guestbook comments.

**Figure 8.6 Example CGI Application**

**Guest Book**

If you're interested in classroom or library videoconferencing, sign the videoconferencing guestbook to let others know!

If you'd like to find guests with specific interests, select an interest and click the "Find" button below.

○ K-12 Schools ○ Higher Education ○ Libraries ○ Community
○ Government ○ Business ○ Health Care/Telemedicine

[Reset Values] [Find]

## Web Development Programs and Procedures

A variety of alternatives exists for educators and students who want to develop Web pages but do not want to write their own codes and/or scripts. Web development packages are authoring systems that create Web pages using a point-click-and-drag strategy, very much like developing a word processed document with images. As words are typed and graphics are inserted, the authoring program generates automatically the HTML required for the pages to be placed on the WWW. Ryder and Hughes (1998) say it is no longer necessary for teachers to learn HTML because these packages are "the future of home page creation software" (p. 155). Currently, there are two levels of Web development software packages.

**Web page development software.** Web page development software is available as a standalone package (Adobe *PageMill,* Microsoft *FrontPage,* and Claris *HomePage*); as part of word processing software (Microsoft *Word*); or as a software option on a browser or search engine site.

**Web course development systems.** More complex and capable than authoring programs, these systems are designed to develop whole Web courses with tools and resources on a company's site. Examples of these systems are *Web CT* (Figure 8.8), *Web in a Box,* and

**Figure 8.7 Example Web Page Development Software: Claris *HomePage***

**Claris Home Page**

**Figure 8.8 Example Web Course Development Software: *Web CT***

*LearningSpace.* In addition to Web page development tools, these systems include resources such as conferencing systems, on-line chat spaces, student progress tracking, grade maintenance and distribution, course calendar, student home pages, and search engines that look for course content.

**Web page development procedures.** Cafolla and Knee (1996) say that "many Web pages are poorly designed because they are so easy to create" (p. 8). They give recommendations for creating Web sites to help ensure they are easy-to-navigate, attractive, and useful to others (1996, 1996–1997, and 1998). Following are a suggested sequence of steps for developing a Web site.

Step 1 **Plan and storyboard.** Without a doubt, planning and design are the most difficult—and most important—first steps in developing a Web page or Web course. Most people want to get to the fun of development; they do not want to spend time mapping out the structure and contents of the site. Yet planning is critical to a well-designed Web site. Some people use storyboard frames or cognitive mapping software to sketch out their designs. Others use 3" × 5" sticky notes placed on large pieces of posterboard. Mapping software or sticky notes offer more flexibility to move things around. Bailey and Blythe (1998) offer procedures for how to design Web page content and structure systematically. These steps include outlining (either in linear or the more flexible "mindmapped" form), diagramming, and storyboarding.

Step 2 **Develop pages with text.** The next step is creating blank pages and inserting the text elements such as a title, paragraphs of description, and any text labels that will serve later as links (e.g., "Go back home"). From a structural standpoint, there are three general designs for pages: basic, basic with anchors on same page, and frame pages.

Step 3 **Insert images and sounds.** Pictures, animations, and movies come next. Images and animations must be in GIF or JPEG format; movies and sounds must be in MPEG format. (See Chapter 6 for description of various formats for saving graphic images.) If movies or audio are to be streamed, the page should inform the user and provide a way to obtain the plug-in needed to see or hear the item.

Step 4 **Insert links and frames.** After all pages are designed, set "hot spots" or links from text and images to other locations.

Figure 8.9  **Criteria for Evaluating Web Sites**

Check each of the following criteria *before* and *after* designing a page.

**Content**

___ All information is accurate; plan to update the page periodically. The "last time updated" date is given.

___ Information is complete but not excessive or redundant.

___ Information is well-organized and clearly labeled.

___ Information is interesting, informative, and worthwhile.

___ Information is not redundant to many other sources; there is a reason to put it on the Web.

___ All text has correct spelling, grammar, and punctuation.

___ Level of content and vocabulary are appropriate for intended audience.

___ Content is free from stereotyping, coarse or vulgar language, or matter that could be offensive to typical users.

___ Author(s) of the page are clearly identified.

___ The page gives an e-mail address or other way to contact authors.

**Visual and Audio Design**

___ The site has a consistent look.

___ Graphics, animations, videos, and sounds make an important contribution; each serves a purpose.

___ Pages have only one or two fonts.

___ Each page uses a limited number of colors, especially for text.

___ Colors have been selected to be compatible with the Netscape 216 color palette.

___ Type colors/styles and text-to-background contrast have been selected for good readability.

___ Each graphic is designed to fit 640 × 480 pixel screens, allowing for scroll bars/toolbars.

___ Each page is limited to 2–3 screens; the most important information is at the top.

___ The pages are simply and attractively designed; they make a user want to read the information.

**Navigation**

___ Pages load quickly.

___ Pages have simple, consistent navigation scheme to let users get to desired places quickly and easily.

___ The first page indicates clearly how the site is organized and how to get to items of interest.

___ Links (text and icons) are easy to identify. Graphics and sounds are clearly identified.

___ Icons clearly represent the information they link to.

___ Each supporting page has a link back to the home page.

**Miscellaneous (for larger sites and pages)**

___ Requests for private information are secured.

___ Page information is kept short enough so that it can be printed out quickly.

___ The user can choose to load alternate versions of the page such as text only or smaller images.

___ The site has its own search engine for locating items within the pages.

___ Branching is organized so that all content is no more than three clicks away from the home page.

Use the following tips to make your sites and pages easier to design and use:

___ Organize the site on paper ahead of time before putting it on the computer.

___ To speed loading, limit graphics to no more than 50K and re-use images whenever possible.

___ Use GIFs for line art or graphics with limited colors and sharp edges; use JPEGs for photos with many colors and smooth gradients. Avoid PICT and other formats that must be converted by users.

___ Test out your page with a real browser.

___ Use a GIF spacer (1 × 1 transparent GIF) to space paragraphs, indents, or alignments on pages.

Source: Based on criteria by Gray (1997), Everhard (1997), and McClelland (1997).

**Step 5** **Insert interactive elements.** Bull, Bull, and Sigmon (1997a) describe how a Web page can be made "interactive" by inserting applets, CGI scripts, and mail-tos to gather comments from users.

**Step 6** **Test in a browser.** Many development programs have a built-in preview system, but McClelland (1997) and others recommend testing the site with an actual browser to observe how it will work when it is published on the Web.

**Step 7** **Publish the site.** For others to see created Web pages, developers must send or place them on a server. This is called publishing the site. If the user can sit down at the keyboard of the computer acting as the server, the files may be moved over from a disk to the hard drive. For servers that are not nearby, the user may upload the pages to the server as FTP files.

**Step 8** **Gather evaluation comments, revise, and maintain the site.** The best Web sites are those that are updated regularly based on user comments and the continuing insights of the developers. This may be done through CGI programs built into the page or simply through inviting e-mailed comments.

More useful tips for Web page developers are listed below (McClelland, 1997).

- **Observe naming conventions.** Extensions such as *.html* and *.gif* must used on the Web. Aside from the period before these suffixes, avoid punctuation in the file names; this can cause confusion to the server.

- **Have graphics in GIF or JPEG format.** Although some development packages convert images automatically from PICT and TIFF formats, the program may place them in an unexpected place on the hard drive, creating problems later. Therefore, McClelland recommends they be in correct format before they are inserted.

- **Have a GIF spacer handy.** A GIF spacer is an empty GIF file that is just a few pixels wide and tall and is created in a program such as *Adobe PhotoShop* with a white transparent background. "It comes in handy for paragraph spacing, indents, and alignment tweaks" (p. 107).

### Web Page Criteria

The set of Web page evaluation criteria shown in Figure 8.9 has been synthesized and compiled from those recommended by Gray (1997), Everhart (1997), and McClelland (1997). Also, Pilsik (1997) gives a comprehensive description of qualities and features to look for in online courses.

## Optimizing Web Power

Anyone who "surfs" the Internet regularly knows that it can be time-consuming. The sheer amount of information to peruse can be confusing and factors such as traffic and line speed can slow progress. Methods are continually developed to cope with these problems and to help people use the Internet's power more efficiently.

### Push Technologies

Information sent out electronically—whether requested or not—is known as a "push technology." E-mail and broadcast television are examples of push technologies. The World Wide Web, on the other hand, usually is considered a "pull technology" because a Web page must be requested before it is sent. However, one push technology that helps teachers keep up with the latest news from the WWW on their topics of interest is a news service like PointCast, Inc.'s *PointCast* or Davidson's *EduCast*. This free service is obtained by going to a company's Web site, downloading the required software, and specifying what topics should be monitored. Every time a user logs on the WWW, a summary of the news for those topics automatically appears.

### Bookmarking

Once a good Internet site is found, a quick way to get back to it later is to "bookmark" the URL (address). Each browser has a pull-down bookmark menu; the first item on it is to add a bookmark. Selecting this option when at the URL adds a bookmark for that URL to the bookmark list. To get to the URL later, the bookmarked name is selected from the menu list; the browser then automatically goes there. Harris (1998) says that well-prepared bookmark files are great resources for teachers and should be shared with others who have similar interests.

### Site Capturing

On a high traffic day, the Internet can be as slow as a highway traffic jam. Slow-moving screens can play havoc with teachers and students trying to carry out classroom activities. An alternative is to use a product such as ForeFront's *Web Whacker,* software that downloads pages or sites to a computer's hard drive where they later can be run through a browser without benefit of Internet connection. The popularity of this software created the term "whacking."

### Intranets

Another way to speed up access to the Internet is through an internal network called an *intranet.* This network, like the Internet, is based on TCP/IP protocols, but belongs only to an organization and can be accessed only by the organization's members. An intranet's Web sites look and act just like any other Web sites, but the network has a firewall that will not allow unauthorized access. A school might maintain its own intranet of selected sites while allowing access to the larger Internet for less-used sites (D'Ignazio, 1996). More information about creating and maintaining intranets is available from online magazines such as

*Intranet Design Magazine* (http://www.innergy.com/index.html) and *Intranet Journal* (http://www.intranet journal.com).

## Internet-TV, Avatars, and Other Aspects of the Future

The Internet has opened up a world of new development tools and applications as well as a wealth of resources for education. Some current developments will have a future impact on how the Internet is used.

### Internet-TV Products

Products and technologies that let users connect to the Internet through their TVs are referred to collectively as Internet-TV products. Most such products, for example WebTV, consist of a small box that connects to a telephone line and television. The box makes a connection to the Internet via telephone service, downloads Web pages, and converts the downloaded Web pages to a format that can be displayed on a TV. Internet-TV products also come with a remote control device that permits navigation through the Web. These products may become very useful in schools, especially when they can access the Internet directly through the cable TV lines, rather than telephone lines. Other Internet-based products may be on the horizon as companies look for ways to meet the growing demand for Internet access.

### Avatars

The future of the Internet will be increasingly visual, and certain features seem likely to evolve. One such development is the use of *avatar* spaces. The widespread use of avatars on the Internet were proposed in Neal Stephenson's 1992 science fiction novel *Snow Crash*. Avatars are 3-D figures that serve as moving icons to represent people in virtual reality environments. These figures can be made to look much like the person they represent or may be complete fantasy figures, selected by a user to project a certain aura or point of view. Avatar spaces already are used in some Internet chatrooms and e-mail systems. Their uses in education still are limited, but have great potential for fostering visual literacy, motivating students to develop writing and other communication skills, and helping teach skills that involve visual design.

## Internet Integration Strategies and Issues

As it has become a society-wide tool, the Internet also has spawned its share of society-wide debates and problems. In many ways, it is a reflection of the best and worst qualities of our society. Books by Virginia Shea (1994) and Donald Rose (1994) discuss many of these problems. Teachers must be prepared to deal with ethical, behavioral, and privacy issues as they use the Internet and offer its use to children.

### Ethical Issues and Problems

People are spending increasing amounts of time communicating with each other and obtaining information online, and some problems with human behavior (and misbehavior) have already begun to emerge. These include objectionable materials, predators, viruses, and copyright violations.

**Objectionable materials and predators.** The contents of messages and Web sites are difficult to monitor in resources like the Internet and may contain language or information not appropriate for the public or for minors (Elmer-Dewitt, 1995, July; Carpenter, 1996). Yet the Internet is designed to make information easily obtainable, and, unfortunately, such materials can be accessed all too easily by accident. Educational organizations should have mechanisms and safeguards in place to keep users from getting to these materials either accidentally or intentionally. Munro (1998, March 24) gives a comprehensive listing of filtering utilities that set up firewalls or codes to block access to sites based on keywords and/or site names.

Ryder and Hughes (1998) emphasize that students should be told that the same rules about strangers in the real world apply in cyberspace and for the same reasons. Some people get on the Internet to seek out and take advantage of vulnerable young people. Students should be told never to provide their complete names, addresses, or telephone numbers to any stranger they "meet" on the Internet, and they should report to teachers any people who try to get them to do so. Schools should never give names of students on Web pages.

**Viruses and copyright violations.** Discussed in Chapters 1 and 2 as ethical issues related to general computer use, viruses and copyright violations also present special problems in an online environment. If host servers or individual computers do not have security software to guard against viruses, logic bombs, worms, and Trojan horses, hackers can send them as users download seemingly harmless files or utilities from the Internet. Much of the information on Web sites is for public access and use, but much of it also is copyrighted. Teachers and students should look for copyright statements on the site, and, if there is any doubt, contact the author before copying and using images or verbatim material.

**"Netiquette" behavior.** The etiquette guidelines that govern behavior when communicating on the Internet have become known as *netiquette*. Netiquette covers not only rules on behavior during discussions, but also guidelines that reflect the unique electronic nature of the medium.

Netiquette usually is enforced by fellow users who are quick to point out infractions to rules of netiquette. Thomas W. Kosma, a systems analyst at Wayne State University, published a summary called Cyberlore No. 1: Netiquette 101 at his Web site (http://www.pass.wayne.edu/~twk/netiquette.html). Some points based on this summary are described here.

*Good electronic manners.* Use the following courtesy guidelines in e-mails and other communications:

- **Identify yourself.** Begin messages with a salutation and end them with your name. Most mail programs let you include a signature footer at the end of a message, but a signature twice the size of the message itself is considered bad form.

- **Include a subject line.** Give a descriptive phrase in the subject line of the message header that tells the topic of the message (not just "Hi, there!").

- **Avoid sarcasm.** People who don't know you may misinterpret its meaning.

- **Respect others' privacy.** Do not quote or forward personal e-mail without the original author's permission.

- **Acknowledge and return messages promptly.**

- **Copy with caution.** Don't copy everyone you know on each message.

- **No "junk mail" (spam).** Don't contribute to worthless information on the Internet by sending or responding to mass postings of chain letters, rumors, etc. (The slang term for electronic junk mail is *spam.*)

- **Be concise.** Keep your messages brief—about one screen, as a rule of thumb.

- **Use appropriate language.** Avoid coarse, rough, or rude language, and observe good grammar and spelling.

*Convey emotion and intensity.* Some conventions have been developed to convey emotion in an electronic format. These include:

- **Emoticons or smileys.** Use punctuation such as ":-)" to convey happy and ":-(" for sad.

- **Intensifiers.** Words in capital letters convey emphasis, but sentences typed this way are considered yelling or "flaming." Flaming, like spamming, is considered rude behavior. Asterisks surrounding words indicate italics used for emphasis (*at last*), and words in brackets such as <grin> show one's state of mind.

**Privacy issues.** As Ross and Bailey (1996) note, "Student privacy in public education is a credo enforced by the Family Rights and Privacy Act" (p. 51). In their Web products, teachers should be careful not to identify students with last names, addresses, and other personal information. Another privacy issue surrounds the use of "cookies," or small text files placed on a hard drive by a Web server contacted on the Internet. The purpose of cookies is to provide the server with information that can help personalize Web activity to your needs. For example, the cookie gives a password automatically for a secure site you subscribe to.

But cookies also may track behavior on the Internet in ways that violate privacy. Though browsers come with some built-in defenses against cookies, Randall (1998, March 24) recommends programs called "cookie managers" to control the information given to these cookies.

**Socialization issues.** Spending too much time on computers, especially when used for delivering on-line courses, is considered by many to be harmful to children's development of relationships and social skills. Also, because anyone can put anything on a Web page, some information is inaccurate or misleading. Students must learn to critically analyze Web information.

## Activities and Examples of Internet Integration Activities

So many distance learning resources have been developed and are emerging every day that it is difficult to know how to start. This section offers a summary and examples for teachers to integrate various distance learning resources into teaching and other professional activities. Integration strategies are described for lesson activities, course delivery, support for teacher and student communications, and support for educators conducting or participating in research.

Some of the most exciting distance learning applications call for student collaboration via technology to address significant problems or issues or to communicate with people in other cultures throughout the world. In a series of articles written for *Learning and Leading with Technology* (formerly *The Computing Teacher*), Judi Harris refers to these as "educational telecomputing activities" (Harris, 1994, 1997–1998, 1998) and describes three general types of models: interpersonal exchanges (students communicating via technology with other students or with teachers/experts); information collection and analysis (using information collections that provide data and information on request); and problem solving (student-oriented, cooperative problem-solving projects). Harris (1998) lists a total of 18 different strategies, several under each model, referring to these as "wetware," or activity structures that guide teachers' actions in the project from planning through product development. Detailed descriptions of these structures may be found in her book. Some forms these models can take and some examples of each are given here.

**Electronic penpals.** The simplest instructional activity in which distance technologies play a role is linking each student with a partner or penpal in a distant location to whom the student writes letters or diary-type entries. This kind of writing assignment has been shown to be very motivating to students (Cohen & Riel, 1989). Writing to communicate something to real people—rather than writing for teacher evaluations—encourages students to write more and with better grammar, spelling, and usage. This makes electronic correspondence an ideal activity for English and/or writing classes. Networking in this way also eliminates social bias regarding gender, race, age, and physical appearance. Without social and cultural cues to color interactions, two people who may never have communicated to one another in person are able to build positive electronic relationships. Though not a substitute for face-to-face activities in multi-cultural education, e-mail is an important way to begin building awareness of and appreciation for other cultures.

**Individual and cooperative research projects.** Students can research a problem online working either by them-selves or in groups, gathering information from electronic and paper-based sources. These research activities usually culminate in a presentation to the class and subsequent dis-cussion of the findings. For example, students may be asked to tap various online databases for articles and reports on contributions by the space program to people's lives and modern culture. They may supplement this infor-mation with online conversations with experts they locate on the Internet. When the research is completed, the class report might include actual examples of these contributions as well as summaries delivered via multimedia or presenta-tion software.

**Electronic mentoring (telementoring).** Dyrli (1994) refers to subject matter experts who volunteer to work closely with students online as "electronic mentors" (p. 34). One source of aid in these activities—the Electronic Emissary Project at the University of Texas—links up classes across the country with mentors on topics ranging from Greek literature to life support in space (p. 35). The Center for Children and Technology (CCT, 1996) describes three kinds of telementoring activities it set up to encourage young women to enter science, engineering, and other tech-nology professions. However, they are useful strategies for all student mentoring activities and include guidance, dis-cussion forums, and peer lounges.

*One-to-one guidance.* Young people have private, individ-ual "discussions" via e-mail links with professionals who give advice and guidance related to a particular field. CCT says that before these discussions begin, mentors and stu-dents participate in separate online sessions to prepare for establishing these relationships. Mentors and students, for example, are asked to craft introductory biographies and set goals for their relationships (p. 3).

*Discussion forums.* Students and mentors are linked in a mailing list that supports large group discussions on topics of mutual interest. These are particularly useful in provid-ing students with information and encouragement related to career pursuits.

*Peer lounges.* These are smaller mailing lists set up to share information and ideas for dealing with problems and issues during large projects. A "lounge" is set up for men-tors, one for students, and one for teachers. Mentors use the lounges to talk among themselves about mentoring tech-niques and how to deal with common problems or issues.

**Figure 8.10    Electronic Field Trips to the Jason Site**

Source: Copyright © 1999 Jason Foundation for Education. Reprinted by permission.

Students use the lounge to discuss their projects and class-room issues. Teachers use the lounge to discuss their pro-grams with other teachers. Each is considered a type of peer mentoring (see Example Lesson 8.1).

**Electronic field trips.** As Figure 8.10 shows, an electronic field trip in its simplest form fills classroom screens with visual images of a place considered to offer some educa-tional value and to which students would not routinely be able to travel. Virtual trips are designed to explore unique locations around the world, and, by involving learners at those sites, to share the experience with other learners at remote locations. Trips may use only video programs or may include prepared curriculum guides, suggested prepa-ration and follow-up activities, and discussion questions to help correlate experiences with specific curriculum objec-tives. Learners can interact with peers via telephone, com-puter, broadcast transmission, fax, and mail. Some typical examples of electronic field trips include a visit to the Great Wall of China, a walking tour of Washington, D.C., an exploration of an archeological dig, and a trip to a state capitol during a legislative session. Through electronic field trips, many students imagine themselves leaving their neighborhoods and cities; they experience in some fashion the excitement and wonder of new places and faces—and they learn from the experience.

**Group development of products.** Teachers have devel-oped many variations on group development of products. For example, students may use e-mail to solicit and offer feedback on an evolving literary project, sometimes involv-ing advice from professional authors. Students may work independently toward an agreed-upon goal, each student or group adding a portion of the final product. This is sometimes called *chain writing* (also described in Chapter 5 under word processing). For example, two different Missouri schools linked electronically to write and video-tape a play. At one school, students developed a list of characters and a general plot outline and wrote Scenes 1

## Example Lesson 8.1
## Telementoring: Partners Online

**Developed by:**   Jan Sims, Hickory Grove Elementary School (Bloomfield Hills, Michigan)
and Bruce Simms, Della Lutes School (Waterford, Michigan)

**Level:**   Grades 3–5

**Lesson Purposes.** Students become aware of and comfortable with technology integrated into the curriculum; students develop intergenerational relationships.

**Instructional Activities.** Students are paired with senior citizens for communication through telecommunications: messages are sent and received through local bulletin board systems. Students begin the activity by becoming familiar with the computer keyboard and certain key functions. They then begin working on questions to develop biographies that they subsequently share with other students as well as their older partners. Instructors prepare the senior citizens and assist them in logging on and off, entering passwords and user names, downloading messages, answering student questions, and sending and receiving files. Students use their questionnaires to interview the senior citizens to stimulate communication and obtain information needed to develop biographies. At the end of the activity, instructors arrange for students to meet their partners and present the biographies to them. Academic subjects are integrated into many parts of this activity. Students spend time on language arts, history, math, geography, and science skills. Intergenerational relationships developed through this activity are meaningful to both sets of partners. Teachers observe an increase in student's self-esteem, leadership, cooperative learning skills, and academic achievement.

***Problems to Anticipate.*** The external partners need much of the same support provided to the classroom students, making careful preparation and teacher accessibility important parts of the activity.

Source: From Simms, J. & Simms, B. (1994). The electronic generation connection. *The Computing Teacher, 21*(7), 9–11.

and 2. Students at the other school selected the topic for the play; developed the personalities, physical characteristics, and backgrounds of the characters; and wrote Scenes 3 and

4. Together the students developed the final story line and produced the play, exchanging the videotaped portions that they produced independently (see Example Lesson 8.2).

## Example Lesson 8.2
## Group Development Activity/Information Exchange

**Developed by:**   Hillel Weintraub

**Level:**   Grades 10–11

**Lesson Purposes.** Students use telecommunications to explore the concept of humor from personal, cultural, and intercultural perspectives.

**Instructional Activities.** Within individual classes, students begin to search for things they find humorous and discuss what and why they find particular situations, jokes, or people funny. In class and online with other schools/classes involved in the project, students then begin to look for cultural features of humor, discussing and sharing insights using e-mail as well as print materials prepared by the students. As the activity progresses, classes are encouraged to create products to send to other schools: original plays, interviews, original drawings, or jokes. Several final activities are suggested, but not planned in advance, giving students and teachers the opportunity to select their own culminating student, class, intraschool, or interschool activities. This activity helps deepen student understanding of humor and cultural differences in humor as well as to provide specific practice with computer interaction and collaborative project development. (Sharing information that is interesting to students is also an excellent international telecommunications activity.)

Source: From Harris, J. (1994). Information collection activities. *The Computing Teacher, 21*(6), 32–33.

---

**Example Lesson 8.3**
**Parallel Problem Solving: Integrated Science**

**Developed by:**  Star Bloom and Larry Rainey, University of Alabama, Integrated Science Project
**Level:**  Teachers

**Lesson Purposes.** Students and teachers share science discovery projects via competition between classrooms in several states with results shared online and via broadcast as part of the regularly scheduled integrated science curriculum segment for a specific grade level. Networked teachers discuss challenges, resources, and results while the activities are in progress.

**Instructional Activities.** Science projects are assigned via text and television broadcast and then tackled by individual students or groups of students. Teachers engage in discussion with other science teachers using the curriculum and with project developers to clarify activities, check results, and share data collected. Student projects are sometimes sent to project headquarters for exhibition or as part of regular competitions among schools. Teachers also are supported online with assessment materials and strategies, suggestions for further activities or alternate assignments, materials lists, and references for more information or research activity. Although students themselves are only beginning to use the telecommunications technologies available to the integrated science project to gather or share information, the teacher connectivity and ongoing online support make this project an exciting example of teacher collaboration and support using broadcast video and telecommunications technologies.

Source: Contributed by Mary Anne Havriluk.

---

**Parallel problem solving.** Through technological links, students in a number of different locations can work on similar problems (Harris, 1994). They solve the problem independently and then compare their methods and results or build a database or other product with information gathered during the activity. Students in one school collaborating on a joint air quality project were surprised when they discovered through comparisons that their classroom air quality failed to meet minimum public health standards (see Example Lesson 8.3).

**Simulated activities.** In this type of problem-solving exercise, students participate in structured activities in which they carry out specific duties or responsibilities on which depends some aspect of the project outcome. One example is the Simulated Space Shuttle Program, in which different schools prepare for various missions that will take place during a specified launch period. Success of the simulated mission depends on a series of smaller successes and appropriate student participation (see Example Lesson 8.4).

**Social action projects.** Online communication gives students access to people in other countries that can support social problem solving. In this type of project, students are responsible for learning about and addressing important global social, economic, political, or environmental conditions. For example, students collaborating on a peace project write congressional representatives to voice concerns and present their viewpoints (see Example Lesson 8.5).

Many other examples based on these categories of integration strategies are given in *Telecommunications in the*

*Classroom* (Armstrong, 1995) and the series of booklets from *Classroom Connect: Lessonplan.net* (1997 and 1998) and the *Teaching with the Internet Lesson Plan* series (1998).

## Web Site Support for Classroom Projects

Harris (1997) gives an excellent description with examples of ways to use Web sites to support some types of distance learning activities. The following section summarizes Harris' work and shows that Web sites can serve any of several functions or combination of functions.

**Project overview, announcement, and application.** Sites can introduce the goals and purposes of a project and invite people to participate (see Figure 8.11). A global project, Canadian Kids from Kantata, gives a description designed to "encourage communication among indigenous peoples and later immigrants" (Harris, 1997, p. 17). The page gives a history, an explanation of how the groups involved are organized, a list of organizations and people who support the project, and links to complete an application to become a participant. The British Chatback Project's "Memories from 1945" gives information on how to subscribe to an e-mail discussion list or listserv.

**Project instruction.** A site gives participants actual instruction and information on how to do project activities. For example, the I*EARN Learning Circle global classroom project gives a "linked set of hypertextually rich Web pages that provide step-by-step instruction for project participation" (Harris, 1997, p. 18).

---

### Example Lesson 8.4
### A Simulated Activity

**Developed by:** Jamie Fagan, Christ Church Grammar School (Claremont, Perth, Western Australia, Australia)
**Level:** Grades 6–7

**Lesson Purposes.** To teach students about finding positions using a real situation, accessing information, geography, math, and lifestyles of people from different countries

**Instructional Activities.** Students are assigned a specific yacht to participate in an annual race around the world. They are responsible for accessing computer databases of information giving latitude, longitude, elapsed time, and place. Each morning during the race, a student or group of students accesses a remote database and downloads information on the assigned yacht. Students keep daily records of their yacht's progress from the beginning of the race until the boats arrive at a nearby harbor. Students ultimately presents each real skipper with a map of that yacht's progress and has the opportunity to discuss the race in person with some of the crew. The activity incorporated several curriculum areas. Students learn how to use distance technologies, how to locate positions using latitude and longitude, and how to calculate distance by comparing positions from one day to the next. In addition, students use the situation to develop writing assignments. Students devote at least 30 minutes to 1 hour a day to this activity.

---

Source: From Fagan, J. (1993). Telecomputing activity plan contest. *TIE News 5*(2), 14. Reprinted by permission of the International Society for Technology in Education.

---

### Example Lesson 8.5
### Social Action: The Trashy Project

**Developed by:** Joyce Kutney, Orange Glen School (Escondido, California)
**Level:** Grades 5–7

**Lesson Purposes.** To gather and compare data regarding the collection and dispersion of trash to see if one region conserves better than others and to assess grade level and day of the week differences

**Instructional Activities.** Students collect information on the number of ounces of paper trash collected each day in their classroom. In addition to collecting data on the trash, students record the number in attendance each day to analyze the relative proportion of trash to the number of students. The data collected are then electronically transmitted to a central classroom where the information is pooled for distribution. The students hypothesize about what the data might show and discuss local and collective data.

---

Source: Kelly, M. G. & Wiebe, J. (1994). Telecommunications, data gathering, and problem solving. *The Computing Teacher, 21*(7), 23–25. Reprinted by permission of the International Society for Technology in Education.

**Information repository and exchange.** Students use Web sites to add information to a collection that will be shared with others (see Figure 8.12). KIDLINK's Multicultural Calendar database is a collection of descriptions written by students of holidays and festivals around the world. Students use the site to enter summaries and can search the resulting database by month, holiday, country, and author.

**Project-related communication.** Students working with others in distant sites share a Web site to support their cooperative work. For example, a Colorado meteorologist posted a picture on a shared Web site of a device students

could build to help them complete an experiment in radiative processes (Harris, 1997, p. 19). These co-development Web sites can be even more helpful if they build in streaming video and/or videoconferencing.

**Project support.** Web sites serve as links to resources to support project activities and make gathering information for project work more efficient.

**Example project activities.** "Chronology sites" exhibit an ongoing description of past, current, and planned project activities. In the GlobaLearn project, visitors to the site

Figure 8.11    **Web Site for Project Overview/Announcement—Youth Net**

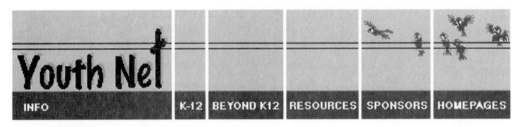

*Learning is part of youth, and life-long learning is the fountain of youth for the mind.*

This server is a place where youth (of all ages) around the world can safely meet each other, and participate in discussions, interactive learning projects, and activities that meet their needs.

- Interactive Projects for Grades K-12
- Youth Net's Life-Long Learning Program
- Youth Net Supporters
- More Information about Youth Net
- Resources and Other Projects for K-12 Educators and Students
- Homepages of Schools and Youth Net Participants

Source: Courtesy of Youth Net.

view artifacts found by explorers as they travel to various countries, "reporting" their findings on the Web site.

**Displays of student work.** Students use sites to show off the products of their learning activities. Many Internet Web sites show examples of students' poems, stories, pictures, and multimedia products.

**Project-development centers.** Finally, Web sites sometimes are set up for the specific purpose of inviting new distance learning projects. Five current ones are:

- Global SchoolNet Foundation (http://www.gsh.org)
- The Intercultural E-mail Classroom Connection (http://www.stolaf.edu/network.iecc/)
- KIDPROJ (http://www.kidlink.nodak.edu)

- KIDSPHERE (kidsphere@vms.cis.pitt.edu)
- Pitsco's Ask an Expert site (http://www.askanexpert.com/askanexpert/ask.html)

### Directed versus Constructivist Approaches to Integrating the Internet

The Web-based activities described here may be implemented with a directed and systematic approach or one with a more constructivist strategy. With directed distance learning projects, teachers tell students the purpose and objectives of the project and structure the learning activities. With constructivist projects, students develop their own goals and activities and the learning activities are more open-ended. Steps in the two types of strategies are described here.

Figure 8.12    **The KIDLINK Multicultural Calendar Database**

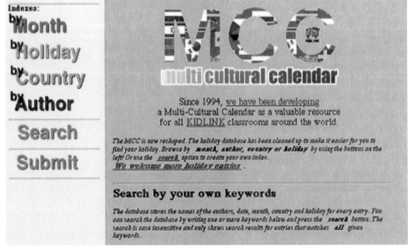

Source: Reprinted by permission of Kidlink, Kidlink at http://www.kidlink.org.

**Directed lesson integration strategies.** Many educators prefer a highly-structured approach to Internet projects. Systematic planning helps assure more efficient use of Internet resources and Royer (1997) gives a sequence for carrying out directed types of collaborative development activities. The steps she recommends are described here.

**Step 1 Plan and prepare.** The teacher defines a project by specifying the purpose, objectives, unit activities, specifications, timeline, number of participants allowed, and logistical considerations.

**Step 2 Post the project information.** Advertise the project on the Internet and invite participants. Include a registration form so that people can respond in a standard way with needed information. Respond to everyone who replies and, if the project is full, be sure to inform people quickly that they will not be part of this activity. As people register, post a listing of everyone registered and how many spaces are left.

**Step 3 Carry out activities.** The teacher is responsible for ensuring that participants build motivation, keep on track, and complete products on time. Begin by having students introduce themselves and describe their backgrounds and current activities. They may build Web pages to accomplish this. Break the project into small components and set weekly or bi-weekly deadlines. Host a chatroom, listserv, or e-mail exchange where people can discuss the project.

**Step 4 Publish the product(s).** After the products are completed, send copies to everyone, both on paper and on the Web. Send certificates of completion to each participating school.

**Step 5 Evaluate the project.** The teacher should do a personal evaluation—documenting what went well and what didn't—and send questionnaires asking for comments to help make the next project better.

**Constructivist lesson integration strategies.** Constructivist models call for less structure set up by the teacher and more conceptual work done by students. Educators who try to get students to think critically about the world around them prefer this approach; they feel this kind of activity helps foster higher level skills in problem solving and analyzing information. Lamb, Smith, and Johnson (1997) describe steps to follow in a more open-ended, constructivist approach. They call their model for community-based learning on the Web the "8 Ws." The steps include the following.

1. **Watching.** Have students begin by observing their environment in order to develop a purpose for their project. Ask them questions that lead them to think about social issues around them. Students keep journals to answer these questions and share their answers later with classmates. Then they begin to narrow the focus of their topic.

2. **Wondering.** Through brainstorming, discussing, and reflecting on their questions and ideas, students explore topics and focus on specific issues or concerns. For example, if the general topic is homeless people, the teacher poses questions to narrow the topic, "Where are homeless people in our town? What do they look like?"

3. **Webbing.** Students use a variety of electronic resources such as Internet sites as well as print resources to locate information and connect ideas.

4. **Wiggling.** In this phase, students look for clues, ideas, and perspectives by evaluating the quality of the information they have found. Students consider whether each information source is authoritative, objective, reliable, and relevant.

5. **Weaving.** This phase requires a high level of critical thinking as students begin to put together their ideas. They compare information from different sources, select information that seems most useful, organize the information into a solution, and decide on a way to express the results (a picture or chart).

6. **Wrapping.** Students "wrap" or package the information and solutions in a format (video, Web site, or multimedia package) that will appeal to their intended audience.

7. **Waving.** In this phase, students publicize their involvement in the project and decide how to carry out the solutions they have developed. For example, they might decide to help alleviate homelessness by making a presentation to a county board or volunteering in a homeless shelter.

8. **Wishing.** In the final stage, students reflect on how the project went and what they have learned. They also analyze the impact of their work. For example, if they sent a report to a local legislator, did they get a response?

# Exercises

## Record and Apply What You Have Learned

**Activity 8.1: Chapter 8 Self-Test** To review terms and concepts in this chapter, take the Chapter 8 self-test. Select Chapter 8 from the front page of the companion Web site (located at http://www.prenhall.com/roblyer), then choose the *Multiple Choice* module.

**Activity 8.2: Portfolio Activities** The following activities will help you add to your professional portfolio. To complete these activities online and save or submit the materials electronically, select Chapter 8 from the front page of the companion Web site (http://www.prenhall.com/roblyer), then choose the *Portfolio* module.

*An Internet Resource Map* Develop a chart, diagram, multimedia presentation, or Web page that documents in an easy-to-read format the names and purposes of each of the following Internet resources described in this chapter: Web browsers, search engines, gophers, e-mail, listservs, bulletin boards, chatrooms, FTP and streaming video/audio, Web authoring tools, push technologies, site capturing, intranets, Internet TV, and avatars. Label or present the purpose of each resource. Give URL links to examples of each resource. (Hint: You can use the subheadings given in the chapter to group the resources into types. Make a graphic or a hotspot for each type, list or present graphically the resources under each heading, and connect the major types in a chart or multimedia stack.)

***Personal Web Page***   Look at personal home pages on the Internet. Use storyboards or sticky notes to develop a design for your own home page. If you have access to Web page development software, develop your home page from your own design. Review your page and make sure it meets the criteria given in this chapter.

**Activity 8.3: Questions for Thought and Discussion**
These questions may be used for small group or class discussion or may be subjects for individual or group activities. To take part in these discussions online, select Chapter 8 from the front page of the companion Web site (http://www.prenhall.com/roblyer), then choose the *Message Board* module.

In a 1998 debate in *TIME* magazine, powerful representatives of two sides squared off. The following quotes are in response to the question: *Should schools be wired to the Internet?* Using information in this chapter combined with other readings, how would you respond to each of these statements?

***Vice President Al Gore***   "Access to the basic tools of the information society is no longer a luxury for our children. It is a necessity…. We must give our children … the chance to succeed in the information age, and that means giving them access to the tools that are shaping the world in which they live."

***David Gelernter***   "First learn reading, writing, history, and arithmetic. Then play Frisbee, go fishing, or surf the Internet. Lessons first, fun second…. If children are turned loose to surf, then Internet in the schools won't be a minor educational improvement, it will be a major disaster."

**Activity 8.4: Collaborative Activities**   The following may be developed in small group work. Completed group products may be copied and shared with the entire class and/or included in each person's Personal Portfolio:

***Internet Ethical Issues***   Select one of the following issues related to Internet use and do an Internet search for recent information and developments on the subject. Develop a summary of the findings to present to the class:

- Objectionable materials and/or predators

- Viruses

- Copyright

- Netiquette

- Student privacy

- Accuracy of Internet information

***Directed or Constructivist Internet Lesson***   Design and prepare a lesson that uses Internet resources and follows procedures outlined in the chapter for an effective directed or constructivist lesson.

**Activity 8.5: Integrating Technology Across the Curriculum Activities**   Use the *Integrating Technology Across the Curriculum* CD-ROM packaged with this textbook to complete the following exercise.

Developing Web pages can be a powerful learning activity for students. Review an example of this activity in the lesson entitled "Creating Your Own Web Site." Go to *Find Lesson Plan* and click on *Find by Keyword*. Type the lesson name. Adapt this lesson to create one of your own in another content area or grade level.

## References

Abilock, D. (1996). Integrating e-mail into the curriculum. *Technology Connection, 3*(5), 23–25.

Armstrong, S. (1995). *Telecommunications in the classroom.* Palo Alto, CA: Computer Learning Foundation and Eugene, OR: ISTE.

Bailey, G. & Blythe, M. (1998). Outlining, diagramming, and storyboarding, or how to create great educational web sites. *Learning and Leading with Technology, 25*(8), 6–11.

Biemiller, L. & Young, J. R. (1998, May 15). Spending bill provides $37 million for improving the Internet. *The Chronicle of Higher Education, 44*(36), A31.

Bull, G., Bull, G., & Sigmon, T. (1997a). Interactive web pages. *Learning and Leading with Technology, 24*(6), 13–17.

Bull, G., Bull, G., & Sigmon, T. (1997b). Common protocols for shared communities. *Learning and Leading with Technology, 25*(1), 50–53.

Cafolla, R. & Knee, R. (1996). Creating world wide web sites. *Learning and Leading with Technology, 24*(3), 6–9.

Cafolla, R. & Knee, R. (1996–1997). Creating world wide web sites: Part II—Implementing your site. *Learning and Leading with Technology, 24*(4), 36–39.

Cafolla, R. & Knee, R. (1997). Creating educational web sites: Part III—Refining and maintaining the site. *Learning and Leading with Technology, 24*(5), 13–16.

Carpenter, C. (1996). Online ethics: What's a teacher to do? *Learning and Leading with Technology, 23*(6), 40–41, 60.

Center for Children and Technology. (1996). Telementoring: Using telecommunications to develop mentoring relationships. *CCT Notes, 4*(1), 1–3.

Cohen, M. & Riel, M. (1989). The effect of distant audiences on children's writing. *American Educational Research Journal, 26*(2), 143–159.

D'Ignazio, F. (1996). Think intranet. *Learning and Leading with Technology, 24*(1), 62–63.

Dyrli, O. (1994). Riding the Internet schoolbus: Places to go and things to do. *Technology and Learning, 15*(2), 32–40.

Elmer-Dewitt, P. (1995, July). On a screen near you: Cyberporn. *TIME, 146,* 1.

Everhart, N. (1997). Web page evaluation: Views from the field. *Technology Connection, 4*(3), 24–26.

Gelernter, D. (1998, May 25). Should schools be wired to the Internet: No: Learn first, surf later. *TIME, 151*(20), 55.

Gore, A. (1998, May 25). Should schools be wired to the Internet: Yes, it's essential to the way kids learn. *TIME, 151*(20), 54.

Gray, T. (1997). No crazy gods. *Learning and Leading with Technology, 25*(1), 43–45.

Harris, J. (1994a). Opportunities in work clothes: Online problem-solving project structures. *The Computing Teacher, 21*(7), 52–55.

Harris, J. (1994b). Teaching teachers to use telecomputing tools. *The Computing Teacher, 22*(2), 60–63.

Harris, J. (1997). Content and intent shape function: Designs for web-based educational telecomputing activities. *Learning and Leading with Technology, 24*(5), 17–20.

Harris, J. (1997–1998). Wetware: Why use activity structures? *Learning and Leading with Technology, 25*(4), 13–17.

Harris, J. (1998). Assistive annotations: The art of recommending web sites. *Learning and Leading with Technology, 25*(6), 58–61.

Harris, J. (1998). *Virtual architecture: Designing and directing curriculum-based telecomputing.* Eugene, OR: ISTE.

Honey, M. (1994). NII roadblocks: Why do so few educators use the Internet? *Electronic Learning, 14*(2), 14–15.

Jerram, P. (1995). Videoconferencing gets in sync. *New Media, 5*(7), 48, 50–55.

Lamb, A., Smith, N., & Johnson, L. (1997). Wondering, wiggling, and weaving: A new model for project- and community-based learning on the Web. *Learning and Leading with Technology, 24*(7), 6–13.

Making connections with telecommunications (1993). *Technology & Learning, 13*(8), 33–34; 36.

McClelland, D. (1997, August). Web publishing made easy. *MacWorld, 1*(8), 104–110.

Munro, K. (1998, March 24). Monitor a child's access. Internet parental filtering utilities. *PC Magazine, 17,* 185–194.

Pilsik, G. (1997). Is this course instructionally sound? A guide to evaluating online training courses. *Educational Technology, 37*(4), 50–59.

Randall, N. (1998, March 24). Defend against invaders. Internet desktop security utilities. *PC Magazine, 17,* 177–182.

Roberts, L. (1996). The Clinton administration's educational technology initiatives. In *An educator's guide to the Internet in the classroom.* Tustin, CA: *T.H.E. Journal.*

Roberts, L. (1997). Web searching made easy. *Learning and Leading with Technology, 24*(8), 60–62.

Roblyer, M. (1992). Electronic hands across the ocean: The Florida-England connection. *The Computing Teacher, 19*(5), 16–19.

Roblyer, M. D. (1998). Is distance ever really dead: Comparing the effects of distance learning and face-to-face courses. *Learning and Leading with Technology, 25*(8), 32–34.

Rose, D. (1994). *Minding your cybermanners on the Internet.* Indianapolis: Alpha Books.

Ross, T. W. & Bailey, G. D. (1996). Creating safe Internet access. *Learning and Leading with Technology, 24*(1), 51–53.

Royer, R. (1997). Teaching on the Internet: Creating a collaborative project. *Learning and Leading with Technology, 25*(3), 6–11.

Ryder, R. & Hughes, T. (1998). *Internet for educators (2nd. ed.).* Columbus, OH: Prentice Hall/Merrill.

Shea, V. (1994). *Netiquette.* San Francisco: Albion Books.

Skipton, C. (1997, May 5). As the worlds turn: VRML authoring and modeling software. *New Media, 7*(6).

Stephenson, N. (1992). *Snow crash.* New York: Bantam Books.

# Chapter 9

## A Link to the Future—
## Where Is Education Going with Technology?

Contributed by William R. Wiencke, University of West Georgia.

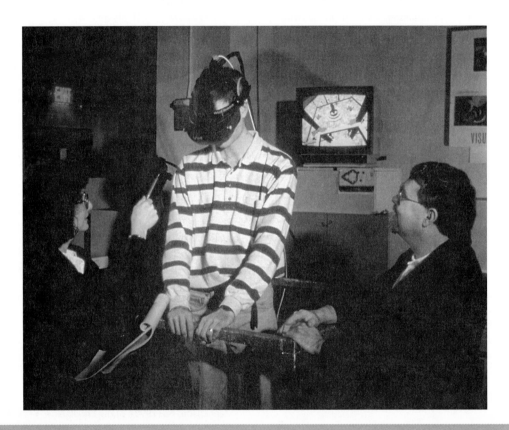

In the evenings on the planet Mars, when the fossil sea is warm and motionless, Mr. K sits in his room, listening to his book ...

From *The Martian Chronicles,* a screenplay based on the book by Ray Bradbury

The best way to predict the future is to create it.

Peter F. Drucker

Any technology sufficiently advanced in comparison to the society in which it appears would seem like magic.

Unknown

**This chapter covers the following topics:**

- Five kinds of technology trends that will shape learning environments in the future

- Capabilities, applications, benefits, and limitations of emerging technologies in five areas

# Objectives

1. Identify emerging technologies in each of five areas:

   * Networking
   * Visualization
   * Human-to-Computer Interfaces
   * Artificial Intelligence and Intelligent CAI
   * Innovative Equipment

2. Identify applications of these technologies for education.

3. Based on predictions of developments in technical resources, develop a personal vision for the kind of role technology will play in shaping a future education system.

4. Describe professional skills required by educators and students who wish to benefit from, cope with, and help direct emerging technology developments.

## Introduction: Classrooms and Other Learning Environments of the Future

A wise observer once remarked that today's science fiction is tomorrow's reality. The "audible texts" that sang to Ray Bradbury's futuristic Martians are now the interactive storybooks our children use at school and the books-on-tape we listen to in our cars. Soon we will listen to our interactive e-books and speak to our electronic librarians. Visions of the future are suffused with images of technologies that may seem magical and far-fetched now, just as cellular phones and fax machines seemed only a few decades ago. And, though the technology images we see when we look into the future of education are murky and ill-defined, we know that they will mirror current technical trends and the goals and priorities we set today for tomorrow's education.

Peter Drucker's observation has never seemed so relevant as when we consider the potential of technology for education. The "futuristic" developments described in this chapter either already exist or will likely become commonplace in the near future, and they have nearly unlimited potential for altering educational opportunities. As with so many "miraculous" technologies, the question is how we will take advantage of their capabilities to bring about the kind of future education systems our society wants and our economy needs.

The purposes of this chapter are to describe the trends in hardware, software, and applications development that drive societal uses of technology and to present a vision for how these trends could be reflected in a restructured educational system in the near future. Each of the futuristic

technologies that are likely to play an important role is described, along with current integration strategies and those that may develop. Since teachers will play a critically important role in shaping this future, we end the chapter by describing some skills and sense of mission teachers must acquire in order to take part in this activity.

### Historical Reinvention: A Technology-Infused History Curriculum Unit in the Not-Too-Distant Future

Kay is sitting in the Local Learning Lab (LLL), listening to her e-book. She is reviewing videos of the historical period 1774–1776 that she downloaded from the library as well as summaries she wrote and recorded about these events in her English classes. These activities are preparing Kay for her role in the first of five virtual reality (VR) simulations in a unit called *Historical Reinvention,* a component of her virtual American history class. The VR activities in the unit are described here.

* **Part 1. 1776: Decisions Past, Decisions Possible.** What key decisions were made in 1776? Who helped make them? Why were they made? What impact did they have on subsequent American history? What would have been different if different decisions had been made?

* **Part 2. 1860: Uncivil War.** What impact did the decisions of 1776 have on events of a century later? What would have been different at this time if other decisions had been made in 1776?

* **Part 3. 1900: Industrious America.** What would our country's entry into the industrial age have been like if different decisions had been made in 1776?

* **Part 4. 1945: Our World at War.** How would the world be today if different decisions had been made in 1776? Would there have been a world war? If so, would our role in it have been different?

* **Part 5. Current Day: The Past as Prologue.** What would our world have been like today if different decisions had been made in 1776?

In the first VR activity, Kay plays the role of Lyman Hall, one of the signers of the Declaration of Independence. It is her job to represent Hall's opinions and concerns as they would have been at that time, and make the decisions for him in the first series of meetings held in 1775–1776 to discuss the controversial topic of American liberty.

Kay is not happy about having to play the part of a man in this simulation, but she already has learned from her research and discussion groups that there were no women in the Philadelphia congress. She knows she can play a female in each of the other four simulations because they take place at various time periods after 1776. She has worked hard to prepare for this VR role-playing activity by reading the materials her teacher has introduced, participating in videoconferencing discussion groups, researching the online history databases, and writing analyses of the decisions made at these historical meetings. At first, it was a little overwhelming, but she is beginning to understand her Lyman Hall character and see how his background and that of his Georgia associates helped shape his decisions in 1776. Since the students have the power to make different decisions from those made by the men in Philadelphia, she has decided to do one thing differently from what Hall actually did. She is determined to vote against allowing slavery in this new country and, through her research, she thinks she has found a way to make a case for Hall taking this position. If everyone agrees with her and slavery is prohibited in the Declaration of Independence, she is interested to see what impact this will have on the subsequent VR simulations.

The LLL is in the community center near her home, and soon Kay is joined there by several classmates and an American history resource teacher. They all don their VR gear, headsets, and arm covers that allow them to join students and teachers in a virtual environment that includes students at two schools and three other LLLs in various locations in the school district. All students in the county high schools are taking this American history course together in what the state calls "distributed learning environments." These are several "congresses" like hers whose members are connected by high-speed network to each other. Each meets in the virtual class using the avatars they developed in their art class using graphics toolkits. Kay's art teacher helped her make her avatar look like the pictures she found of Lyman Hall. The VR environment created by computer science classes looks like the room in Philadelphia where the pioneers of American liberty met in 1775. Kay is excited and eager to start the simulation; she is ready to make history.

### Five Trends Driving the Evolution of Technology

Trends in emerging technologies and new developments in older technologies hold promise for making fundamental changes in our society and its education systems. Some of these trends are apparent to us right now; some will become clearer in the next few years.

Education's use of "magical" technological developments on the horizon are not without problems and controversies. Several issues will shape the impact of these trends on teaching and learning.

**Hardware development will continue to outstrip software abilities to take advantage of them.** This has been the case since computer development began its race in the 1970s, and shows no tendency to alter this course. Computer processors continue to be smaller, faster, and more capable, but operating systems often are years behind in their ability to take advantage of these qualities.

**Education's response to new technologies.** Most of the developments discussed in this chapter come to us by way of military applications and the entertainment industry.

Business tends to profit first from these developments, followed much later by education. This trend of the better-funded areas of our society driving technology innovation seems unlikely to change. Education typically uses technological methods well past the time that newer, more capable tools become available. Integrating technology into instructional methods has traditionally been a long, slow process—a trend unlikely to change even as society changes around it.

**Lack of access means lack of educational opportunities.** Now and for some time to come, there will be students whose families and schools cannot afford access to the technologies discussed here. As these resources become more central to education, this lack of access will translate ever more quickly into limited learning opportunities unless special efforts are made to provide them.

## Trend 1: Emerging Developments in Networking

### Increased Capability and Use of Home Systems

Most American families currently connect to the Internet via modems; the trend is toward ever better connectivity becoming as ubiquitous as telephones. Long-distance carriers such as Sprint's integrated on-demand network (ION) (Sprint, 1998) are gearing up to provide digital access that combines communication channels that have been separate in the past. With ION, one telephone line carries multiple signals such as voice, high-speed data, fax, and video. Law and corporate decisions, rather than technology, will determine how these systems are implemented. For example, the courts must interpret current telecommunication laws governing access rates. However, some experts are predicting that all households someday will have one line coming in that carries all necessary communication channels: Internet, radio, television, and telephone.

### Higher-speed Connections

Communications are becoming faster due to competition between telephone and cable companies. Cable companies currently use installed cable network, and cable modems can make possible data access speeds of 10 Mbs (Derfler, 1998). This allows fast transmission of large graphic files such as movies and animations that has been prohibitive with today's analog modem rates. Impediments to this system are not technology based, but mired in debates over standardization of communication protocols.

### Rewiring of Educational Facilities

More schools are updating their infrastructures to expand connectivity with each other and with Internet-delivered resources; new schools are being built with these features. This wiring not only increases communication among

**Figure 9.1  Angel Technologies Web site**

Source: Courtesy of Angel Technologies.

members of the educational community, it opens windows to a variety of networked learning resources available through the Internet.

### Wireless Communications

With the advent of small hand-held computers and personal digital assistants (PDAs), mobile communications though cellular and digital formats will increase the ability to network anytime and anyplace (O'Donovan, 1998). Cost-effective alternatives to satellite communications will increase with the advent of high-altitude planes replacing low-orbit, high-cost satellite systems. Technologies similar to Angel Technologies' Halo system (1998) will use aircraft, which circle a geographic area, to uplink and downlink information (see Figure 9.1).

### Implications of Networking for Education

Use of online systems for reference and help with learning assignments will likely increase in the future. Students will use these systems as readily as they now use books and teachers. Networking for education will likely result in other changes as well, including increased communication in distance learning and new definitions of distance education.

**Collaboration at different physical sites.** Since it will be easier to communicate with others in distant locations (and communication will be more visual, as the section below describes), teachers and school administrators can communicate with students and parents via e-mail and school Web site announcements. Advances in networking will make it more feasible for students to take advantage of the goal-based scenario learning described by Schank and Lass (1996), the "collaboratory notebook" ideas offered by Edelson, Pea, and Gomez (1996), and the student communities hypothesized by Scardamalia and Bereiter (1996).

**Changing definitions of distance education.** As widespread access becomes more commonplace, we will move from a delivery paradigm to a communications model. For example, students on a field trip will carry portable devices that link to the Internet or the school's server. They could look up references related to the field trip and e-mail their reports back to school. With reduced costs of such equipment comes an increased possibility of grants or loaner systems for home use, thus increasing connectivity and access for even the poorest schools and students.

## Trend 2: Emerging Developments in Visualization

### Advances in 3-D Visualization

Advances in computer design will allow graphic processing to be incorporated within the main CPU. Intel began this inclusion with the introduction of MMX technology and will expand the architecture within their new 64-bit chip, code-named Mercer (Jerome, 1998; Mace, 1998). The processing power will allow full 3-D graphic manipulations, or the illusion of moving around inside a model. For example, when students walk around a room, they experience a real, three-dimensional environment. 3-D graphics allow students to "walk around" inside models of rooms (Ozer, 1998).

### Virtual Environments

The ability to process 3-D objects will make possible the development of *virtual environments*—full immersion systems that create the illusion of interacting with people, places, and things from the past, far away, or never existed. Interfaces currently under development include *surround-goggles* (see Figure 9.2) with *data gloves* and whole rooms such as the Cave Automatic Virtual Environment (C.A.V.E.) (see Figure 9.3) on whose walls images are projected, providing an environment that surrounds a person "standing" inside it (Cruz-Neira, Czernuszenko, & Pape, 1997). Educational applications of virtual environments have been explored for several years (Brown, Kerr, & Wilson, 1997; Gaddis, 1997; Pantelidis, 1997;

**Figure 9.2  Virtual Reality Equipment**

Source: Courtesy of Victor Maxx Technologies, Inc.

**Figure 9.3    Cave Automatic Virtual Environment (C.A.V.E.)**

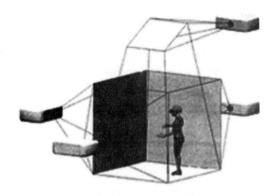

Source: Electronic Visualization Lab, University of Illinois.

Taylor, 1997), but currently are still in the demonstration stage.

## Use of Avatars

People will become a more visual and functional part of virtual environments by creating and using avatars—3-D images of themselves. These already are used on the Internet to represent people in online 3-D environments and are becoming popular in e-mail systems.

## Implications of Visualization for Education

Educational applications of virtual environments are limited only by imagination—and the funds to implement them.

**Virtual field trips.** Students can "travel" to other countries, other planets, or other periods in history to observe and take part in activities there. They can go as themselves or as the persona their avatars represent.

**Models as learning tools.** Instead of building one model, students can build and manipulate many models in 3-D environments. For example, students could build a house and walk around in it, observing its structure and components, measuring things, taking readings of temperatures and densities, and removing and changing things as they go.

**Visual data.** Students can compare data such as changes in ocean temperatures and inland rainfall by observing them and discovering visual relations and patterns.

**Freedom for handicapped learners.** Virtual environments have unique benefits for learners whose physical limitations make movement difficult or impossible (Kulen & Doyle, 1995; Andrae, 1996; Rose et al., 1998; Latash, 1998). Virtual environments also have been useful for students with mental handicaps (Darrow, 1995), allowing them to practice skills and social behaviors in private, controlled environments.

## Trend 3: Emerging Developments in Interfaces

### Voice/Audio and Voice Recognition

Voice/audio interfaces (the way people communicate with computers) will begin to allow partial or full hands-free interactions with computer applications (Editors, 1998; Morris, 1998). Voice interfaces have been in development for several years, but with the advent of smaller hand-held systems, the need for voice processing in lieu of typed input has increased dramatically. Many software application packages now include voice recognition software. Examples include word processors that allow direct dictation into a document; operating systems that accept voice commands for copying and moving files or formatting disks; e-mail systems on which people can leave voice message; and automobile computers that check e-mail, make phone calls, and give directions.

### Physical Log-in

Devices that identify users through fingerprints or retina scans are becoming common. This development could be used for taking attendance and verifying the presence of distance students for evaluation purposes (Bott, 1998).

### Implications of Interface Developments for Education

New kinds of interfaces could have a profound impact on communications and computer uses across society. The differences between dictating text and writing characters on paper require entirely different processing skills. This change in communication techniques could enhance or deter student writing ability. E-mail already is more visual and voice-activated, allowing students and teachers to communicate more easily with each other over distances.

## Trend 4: Emerging Developments in Artificial Intelligence (AI)

Artificial intelligence (AI) is a relatively old "emerging" technology, dating back to a 1956 conference at Dartmouth (Golob & Brus, 1990), though it has had limited use in education. AI usually is defined as having a computer perform in ways comparable to behavior governed by a human brain. Types of AI include technical classifications such as fuzzy logic (logic systems designed to parallel human decision making by accounting for subjectivity and uncertainty) and neural networks (programs that can "learn" from their mistakes) (Patton, Swan, & Arikara, 1993). Types of AI systems with educational applications are described here.

## Expert Systems

Expert systems are programs that computerize human expertise in a narrow field of knowledge (Orwig & Baumbach, 1991–1992). An expert system acts as an advisor and offers suggestions to assist the user's decision-making process, just as a human expert would. The multimedia tutoring system *The Cardiac Tutor* described by Woolf (1996) is an example of an expert system.

## Coaches

Artificial intelligent assistants, or coaches, currently are incorporated into various tool programs (Moursund, 1998). The most common coaches are used in word processing and spreadsheet programs that step you through the development of a document. Intelligent coaches can be incorporated into courseware to provide assistance during tutorial, simulation, and problem-solving packages.

## Intelligent Agents

Salvadore (1995) described intelligent agents as software packages that do various jobs for students. For example, the programs may "search online systems for information tailored to a user's needs and interests" (p. 14). Intelligent agents learn by observing a user's actions and noting patterns of behavior such as reading preferences. The programs then present articles based on revealed preferences. In the future, intelligent agents may be programmed to search libraries and archives for specific information or to give suggestions on the most efficient way to learn or to do a desired task.

## Implications of Artificial Intelligence for Education

Current applications of artificial intelligence in education make possible several kinds of educational strategies, discussed below.

**Intelligent computer assisted instruction (ICAI).** Knowledge-based, or intelligent computer assisted instruction (ICAI), takes the idea of coaching to a higher level (Moursund, 1998). ICAI monitors and creates a profile for each student and then tailors the instruction to meet individual student needs and modifies the profile as progress is made.

**Problem solving.** AI systems are designed to help solve difficult mathematics problems (Mission Accomplished, 1993). One expert system for math can review a problem and display a solution set of equations. The user can then implement or override the program's solution.

**Personal tutoring systems.** One example of an intelligent tutoring system adapted for microcomputers is the Smithtown (Raghavan & Katz, 1989) system, which uses an AI routine to tutor students in beginning economics

courses. Schank's (1997) software case studies are another example of this use.

**Student performance feedback.** Schools use expert systems to integrate the accumulated knowledge of a subject area for self-testing. One expert system allows students to test their comprehension in a basic accounting course (Fogarty & Goldwater, 1993).

**Critical-thinking skills.** Another expert system program, ES, helps high school students develop their own expert systems (Dillon, 1994). The thought process involved in developing an expert system can provide an extremely productive student learning experience.

# Trend 5: Emerging Developments in Equipment

Miniaturization of components continues to enhance the production of powerful handheld devices (see Figure 9.4). Initially, these miniature components focused on specialized "niche" markets such as Personal Digital Assistants (PDAs) (Venezia, 1998), which house an electronic business planner and phone book and can be connected to a desktop for coordination of records. The latest systems have moved beyond PDAs to provide a window onto data residing on a PC, a corporate server, and/or the Internet for personal productivity as well as business and educational applications. Advances in voice recognition will augment or replace the small keypads and pens on today's handheld devices.

## Wearable Systems

An extension of handheld devices are computer system components that can be worn. Typical wearable systems

**Figure 9.4 The Palm III™ Connected Organizer**

Source: Courtesy of Palm Computing, Inc., a 3Com Company.

**Figure 9.5   Softbook®**

today consist of small displays that fit over one eye or glasses that provide "heads-up" see-though displays similar to military fighter pilot helmets; hip-pocket CPU and storage; voice recognition and audio feedback; and "data gloves" that enable the transfer of data between other people through a simple handshake (Metz, 1998).

### Electronic Books (E-Books)

Electronic books such as the Softbook®, RocketBook®, and EveryBook® will provide a new dimension to visual interaction. E-books are capable of storing dozens of books, documents, and course packs all within a lightweight, portable reading device. Companies such as Softbook are currently marketing electronic books that allow readers to access multiple books and information.

### Implications of Equipment Developments for Education

**Handheld devices.** These devices can be used to locate books or other references in a library. The system not only will search for the item but also determine if and where it was shelved and give directions to the shelf.

**Wearable components.** These components offer students great flexibility in collecting data, looking up references, and communicating information to others at distant sites. Lost children would not be a problem anymore; wearable devices on children could coordinate with global positioning systems (GPS) to identify their location.

**E-book uses.** Electronic libraries could check out books by downloading them to a student's e-book. Students could connect to holdings from anywhere, and the downloaded text could delete itself at the end of the loan period. In addition, books would no longer have static presentations; they could incorporate multimedia references similar to today's electronic encyclopedias. For example, if a student is reading about how cells divide, a short movie could show a visual of the event.

## Future Challenges for Teachers

### Visions of Technology's Role in Restructuring Education

Many educators maintain that technology is essential to curriculum reform and school restructuring needed to improve the educational system (Bruder, Buchsbaum, Hill, & Orlando, 1992; Hill, 1993; Wiburg, 1995–1996; Salisbury, 1996). The proper role for computers and related technology in education has stimulated continued, often intense debate for some years. Although computers captured the imaginations of educational innovators early in the 1960s, no commonly held vision ever emerged to show how technology would enhance—let alone change—education. Even now, with a growing dissatisfaction of traditional teaching and learning systems and a consensus on the need to change or restructure American education, considerable disagreement persists over the role technology will play in a restructured system.

**Replacing teacher functions versus changing teacher roles.** In educational technology's early days, when resources were available only through centrally controlled computer systems, some foresaw technology eventually replacing the teacher as the primary instructional delivery system (Norris, 1977). When microcomputers placed the power of technology directly in the hands of teachers, the image of technology shifted from replacing teachers to supplementing and enhancing teacher-based instruction. Criticized as expensive, inefficient, and outdated, technology again is proposed as an alternative to delivering instruction primarily through teachers (Reigeluth & Garfinkle, 1992). This proposal assumes that technology-based delivery systems will achieve better results by standardizing instructional methods and decreasing personnel costs (Reigeluth & Garfinkle, 1992; *U.S. News and World Report,* 1993). Some critics advocate technology replacing traditional roles of both schools and teachers (Perelman, 1993). Others feel that teachers and schools must remain an important part of the instructional process, but that technology tools will empower them to teach better and use their time more productively. As requests for curricular reform increase, far-reaching changes in traditional teacher roles seem an inevitable part of the total restructuring package.

**Enhancing existing methods versus changing the nature of education.** Even if teachers retain an important role, considerable debate remains over how technology will *change* those roles. Even the new technologies described in this chapter are only mirrors that either can reflect a vision to restructure a school's fundamental operations and educational goals or one that supports existing structures.

**The role of distance learning.** New developments in distance learning technologies promise to alter drastically our traditional concepts of what constitutes education, teaching, and learning. Some innovative course delivery systems made possible by distance technologies already are bringing about a radical restructuring of learning opportunities at all levels (Owston, 1997; Elbaum, 1998). Dede (1996) offers several new forms of expression that may reform traditional methods even further in the future. These include *knowledge webs* for distributed online conferences, links to information and experts, and virtual exhibits to duplicate real-world settings; *virtual communities* to complement face-to-face classroom activities; experiences in *synthetic environments* to "extend learning by doing in real world settings" (p. 25); and *sensory immersion* in virtual reality environments. All of these "futuristic technologies," which the Internet has made more accessible than ever before, give new life and practicality to restructuring efforts.

Literature on technology's role in restructuring yields some common principles (Foley, 1993; *U.S. News and World Report,* 1993; Muffoletto, 1994; Luterbach & Reigeluth, 1994; Chesley, 1994; Reigeluth & Garfinkle, 1994; Jostens Learning Corporation, 1995; Dede, 1996; Gonzales & Roblyer, 1996). The following recurring themes are central to building a more effective system of education:

* **Teachers will retain a key role.** Although teacher roles will undergo radical changes, few consider replacing teachers with technology-based delivery systems. Even where teachers are not available or are in short supply, such as in rural schools and highly technical subject areas, the technology strategy of choice to optimize the power of available teachers is networking or distance learning. Technology resources also will help teachers shift their emphasis from delivering information to facilitating learning.

* **Interdisciplinary approaches will flourish.** Curriculum will change from a disjointed collection of isolated skills training to integrated activities that incorporate many disciplines and call for teacher collaboration. The theme-based projects described in Part IV of this book illustrate how technology resources can both focus and facilitate these cross-disciplinary activities.

* **Research and problem-solving skills will gain attention.** Pure constructivist principles may prove difficult to implement under current constraints and resource limitations, but educational goals already are undergoing two kinds of shifts. First, an increasing emphasis on general-purpose study

and research skills seeks to help learners in any content area. Use of databases, online information services, and hypermedia systems will promote success in this new direction of studies. Second, the emphasis is shifting from learning isolated skills and information within each content area to learning how to solve problems specific to each area. Again, the engaging qualities of technology resources such as videodiscs, multimedia, and distance learning help teachers to focus students on such complex goals that call for underlying basic skills.

* **Assessment methods will change to reflect the new curriculum.** New calls for "authentic assessment" methods mirror the need to make both instruction and evaluation of progress more relevant to student needs. Assessment of performance is shifting from paper-and-pencil tests to performance-based methods and student portfolios. Technology-based production tasks can help accomplish this kind of assessment goal and help track acquisition of component skills.

* **Distance learning will play a large role.** The number of educators and organizations in distance learning shows that it has already altered our educational system. Nearly all colleges and universities either offer courses or degrees via distance technologies or plan to do so in the near future. Also, there is a thriving "virtual high school" movement in progress (Elbaum, 1998). In this sense, the "death of distance" (Moore, 1995) already has made our educational system a different place than it was at the beginning of this century. The challenge for educators is not just to use technology, but to use it in ways that acknowledge its benefits and limitations. Clearly, 21st-century educators will have to deal with many issues their predecessors could not even have imagined.

## Future Skills for the Technology-Savvy Teacher

In addition to the demanding requirements listed in Chapter 1, educators must prepare for a technology-permeated future by keeping up with change. They must learn to adopt effective strategies, such as reading technical and educational publications, attending training sessions, and perusing Internet Web sites, for keeping as current as possible on the new and anticipated technologies described in this chapter, as well as methods of using them. If technology is to make a real difference in their work, teachers must have a vision of what they are working toward, recognize the kind of infrastructure necessary to bring about their vision, and be active in building what is needed for change and growth. Esquivel (1998) outlines some of these essential infrastructure requirements.

These activities must become part of the repertoire of the future educator. Teachers must adopt an outlook that their pre-service preparation is only a first step in what must be a lifelong exploration of ways to use technology and other resources to improve education. Technology is coming to represent both a constant resource and a continual reminder that educators never can become satisfied with their methods, skill levels, or results.

# Exercises

## Record and Apply What You Have Learned

**Ⓦ Activity 9.1: Chapter 9 Self-Test** To review terms and concepts in this chapter, take the Chapter 9 self-test. Select Chapter 9 from the front page of the companion Web site (located at http://www.prenhall.com/roblyer), then choose the *Multiple Choice* module.

**Ⓦ Activity 9.2: Portfolio Activities** The following activities will help you add to your professional portfolio. To complete these activities online and save or submit the materials electronically, select Chapter 9 from the front page of the companion Web site (http://www.prenhall.com/roblyer), then choose the *Portfolio* module.

***Technology Impact on Content Areas*** Prepare your personal visual summary of the five areas of development described in this chapter by naming at least one technology in each of the areas, along with your own description of how it will impact teaching and learning practices in your area.

***In-depth Impact*** Prepare a list of five resources (publications, Web sites) or activities (attendance at certain meetings) that will help you keep up with important developments of technology in your area of interest.

**Ⓦ Activity 9.3: Questions for Thought and Discussion** These questions may be used for small group or class discussion or may be subjects for individual or group activities. To take part in these discussions online, select Chapter 9 from the front page of the companion Web site (http://www.prenhall.com/roblyer), then choose the *Message Board* module.

- In William Clark's 1994 article about the "high-tech classroom of the future," he says that the evolution of the classroom "will be characterized by the steady replacement of traditional basal programs by multiple media programs and collections of supplemental materials. Some of these materials will be classroom resident. Others will flow through various manifestations of the information highway" (p. 38). Do you agree with Clark's predictions? Do you feel the impact of these changes will be beneficial or not?

- Baines (1997) said that "the frenetic race to acquire and use technology in the schools is often attributed to … the demands of corporate leaders who want competent workers. However, when Fortune 500 companies were surveyed about the ideal education for children of the 21st century, (they emphasized) the need for analytical, logical, higher-order, conceptual, and problem solving skills, along with proficiencies in writing, reading, and … communication" (p. 495). Do you think these two statements are contradictory? Give examples from this chapter about how one can help bring about the other.

**Activity 9.4: Collaborative Activities** The following may be developed in small group work. Each group should present the findings to the class in a format they know how to use such as a word processed report, presentation software, or multimedia product. Each summary should have a graphic like the one in Figure 1.6 or a table to help communicate the information. Completed group products may be copied and shared with the entire class and/or included in each person's Personal Portfolio:

- **Scenarios of the future.** Prepare your own scenario of how a future curriculum unit that incorporates "technologies of the future" (similar to *Historical Reinvention*) would be structured and carried out.

- **Impact of future technology.** Have the groups exchange curriculum scenarios they have developed. Each group identifies the new technological innovations in the scenario and discusses the impact of each innovation on reshaping education in the future in the way the scenario shows.

**Activity 9.5: Integrating Technology Across the Curriculum Activities** Use the *Integrating Technology Across the Curriculum* CD-ROM packaged with this textbook to complete the following exercise:

How will some of the developments described in this chapter change the way some of the lessons on the CD will be carried out? For example, review the lessons that require use of "probeware/MBL" technologies. Go to *Find Lesson Plan* and click on *Find by Criteria*. Under the *Technologies* descriptor, select "probeware/MBL" and click *Search*. Develop a summary of how smaller, more portable data-gathering computer equipment will change the way these lessons are done. For each of the other trends, select a lesson and describe the impact an emerging technology may have for enhancing this activity.

# References

Andrae, M. H. (1996). Virtual reality in rehabilitation. *British Medical Journal International, 312*(7022), 4–5.

Angel Technologies. (1998). Angel's HALO network (http://www.angelcorp.com/description.htm).

Baines, L. (1997). Future schlock. *Phi Delta Kappan, 78*(7), 494–497.

Bott, E. (1998). Windows 2008. *PC Computing, 11*(9), 174–175.

Brown, D., Kerr, S., & Wilson, J. (1997). Virtual environments in special-needs education. *Communications of the ACM, 40*(8), 72–75.

Bruder, I., Buchsbaum, H., Hill, M., & Orlando, L. (1992). School reform: Why you need technology to get there. *Electronic Learning, 11*(8), 22–28.

Chesley, G. (1994). The engineering of restructuring: What do we do and how do we do it? *NASSP Bulletin, 78*(565), 21–27.

Clark, W. (1994, October). The high-tech classroom of the future: What will it be like? *Curriculum Product News, 38*, 62.

Cruz-Neira, C., Czernuszenko, M., & Pape, D. (1997). CAVE user's guide (http://evlweb.eecs.uic.edu/pape/CAVE/CAVEGuide.html).

Dede, C. (1996). Distance learning-distributed learning: Making the transformation. *Learning and Leading with Technology, 23*(7), 25–30.

Derfler, F. J. (1998). Internet connectivity. *PC Magazine, 17*(11), 187–188.

Dillon, R. (1994). Creating an expert system. *The Computing Teacher, 21*( 7), 17–20.

Dragan, R. (1998). Software agents. *PC Magazine, 17*(11), 166.

Edelson, D., Pea, R., & Gomez, L. (1996). The collaboratory notebook. *Communications of the ACM, 39*(4), 32–33.

Editors. (1998). PC computing 10th anniversary time capsule. *PC Computing, 11*(8), 197–212.

Elbaum, B. (1998, Winter). Is the virtual high school "educational reform"? *Concord.Org: Newsletter of the Concord Consortium.* Concord, MA, 10–11.

Foley, D. (1993). Restructuring with technology. *Principal, 72*(3), 22, 24–25.

Gaddis, T. (1997). Using virtual reality to bring your instruction to life. Paper presented at the League for Innovation Conference on Information Technology, Atlanta, GA, October 15–17 (ERIC Document No. 413 961).

Golob, R. & Brus, E. (1990). *The almanac of science and technology.* Boston: Harcourt Brace Jovanovich.

Gonzales, C. & Roblyer, M. D. (1996). Rhetoric and reality: Technology's role in restructuring education. *Learning and Leading with Technology, 24*(3), 11–15.

Hill, M. (1993). Math reform: No technology, no chance. *Electronic Learning, 12*(7), 24–32.

Jerome, M. (1998). Mercer. *PC Computing, 11*(9), 172–173.

Jostens Learning Corporation. (1995). *Educating Jessica's generation.* San Diego, CA: Author.

Kuhlen, T. & Doyle, C. (1994). Virtual reality for physically disabled people. *Computing in Biological Medicine, 25*(2), 205–211.

Latash, M. (1998). Virtual reality: A fascinating tool for motor rehabilitation: To be used with caution. *Disability and Rehabilitation, 20*(3), 104–105.

Luterbach, K. & Reigeluth, C. (1994). School's not out yet. *Educational Technology, 34*(41), 47–54.

Mace, J. (1998). Mainstream graphics. *PC Magazine, 17*(11), 122.

Metz, C. (1998). MIT: Wearable PCs, electronic ink, and smart rooms. *PC Magazine, 17*(11), 192–193.

Mission accomplished. (1993). *NASA Tech Briefs, 17*(9), 14.

Moore, M. G. (1995). The death of distance. *The American Journal of Distance Education, 9*(3), 1–4.

Morris, J. (1998). User interfaces. *PC Magazine, 17*(11), 162–163.

Moursund, D. (1998). Software trends. *Learning and Leading with Technology, 25*(5), 4–5.

Norris, C. & Reigeluth, C. (1991). A national survey of systemic school restructuring experiences (ERIC Document Reproduction No. ED 335 001).

Norris, W. (1977). Via technology to a new era in education. *Phi Delta Kappan, 58*(6), 451–453.

O'Donovan, E. (1998). Notebooks and PDAs: Pint-sized computing powerhouses. *Technology and Learning, 18*(9), 63–66.

Orwig, G. W. & Baumbach, D. (1991–1992). Artificial intelligence. *SIGTC Connections, 8*(2), 11–12.

Owston, R. (1997). The World Wide Web: A technology to enhance teaching and learning? *Educational Researcher, 26*(2), 27–33.

Ozer, J. (1998). 3-D computing. *PC Magazine, 17*(11), 118.

Pantelidis, V. (1997). Virtual reality and engineering education. *Computer Applications in Engineering Education, 5*(1), 3–12.

Patton, A., Swan, D. M., & Arikara, M. (1993). Modeling car batteries with neural networks. *Machine Design, 65*(21), 133–134.

Perelman, L. (1993). *School's out: Hyperlearning, the new technology, and the end of education.* New York: William Morrow.

Powers, D. & Darrow, M. (1994). Special education and virtual reality: Challenges and possibilities. *Journal of Research on Computing in Education, 27*, 111–121.

Raghavan, K., and Katz, A. (1989). Smithtown: An intelligent tutoring system. *Technological Horizons in Education Journal, 17*(1), 50–53.

Reigeluth, C. & Garfinkle, R. (1992). Envisioning a new system of education. *Educational Technology, 22*(11), 17–22.

Reigeluth, C. & Garfinkle, R. (1994). Systemic change in education (ERIC Document Reproduction No. ED 367 055).

Salisbury, D. (1996). *Five technologies for educational change.* Englewood Cliffs, NJ: Educational Technology Publications.

Salvadore, R. (1995). What's new in artificial intelligence? *Electronic Learning, 14*(4), 14.

Scardamalia, M. & Bereiter, C. (1996). Student communities for the advancement of knowledge. *Communications of the ACM, 39*(4), 36–37.

Schank, R. (1997). *Virtual learning.* New York: McGraw-Hill.

Schank, R. & Lass, A. (1996). A goal-based scenario. *Communications of the ACM, 39*(4), 28–29.

Softbook Press. (1998). Softbook. (http://www.softbook.com/softbook_sys/softbook.html).

Sprint. (1998). Sprint ION, Integrated On-Demand Network. (http://www.sprintbiz.com/ion/trends.html).

Strommen, E. & Lincoln, B. (1992). Constructivism, technology, and the future of classroom learning. *Education and Urban Society, 24*(4), 466–476.

Taylor, W. (1997). Student responses to their immersion in a virtual environment. Paper presented at the Annual Meeting of the American Educational Research Association, Chicago, Illinois, March 24–28 (ERIC Document No. 407 931).

*U.S. News and World Report.* (1993, January 11). The perfect school: Nine reforms to revolutionize American education.

Venezia, C. (1998). Hand-held devices. *PC Magazine, 17*(11), 126.

Wiburg, K. (1995–1996). Changing teaching with technology. *Learning and Leading with Technology, 23*(4), 46–48.

Woolf, (1996). Intelligent multimedia tutoring systems. *Communications of the ACM, 39*(4), 30–31.

Wright, R. (1996). Can machines think? *Time, 147*(13), 50–57.

# Part IV

## Integrating Technology into the Curriculum

---

### The chapters in this part will help teachers learn:

1. To identify some of the current issues in various subject-area instruction that may impact the selection and use of technology

2. To describe some popular uses for technology in today's curricula

3. To identify exemplary Internet sites for subject-area instruction

4. To create instructional activities that successfully model subject-area integration strategies

## Introduction

Part IV addresses the use of technology in various subject areas. In an effort to model subject-area integration, the disciplines have been grouped by chapter as follows:

## Chapter 10: Technology in Language Arts and Foreign Language Instruction

English and foreign language technology applications are grouped together in Chapter 10 because they are both language-related topics. Language arts in this chapter includes the communications skills (reading, listening, speaking), addressed primarily in the elementary grades, as well as English topics (writing and literature), which are the focus at secondary levels. Foreign language topics include the learning of foreign languages and English for Speakers of Other Languages (ESOL).

# Chapter 11: Technology in Science and Mathematics Instruction

Science and mathematics topics are considered closely related and curricula for them are often intertwined. This chapter looks at how technology applications help integrate the teaching of these topics and how they address the special curriculum needs of each.

# Chapter 12: Technology in Social Studies Instruction

Technology applications covered in Chapter 12 include those for history, social studies, civics, and geography. Social sciences may be one of the subject areas most influenced by recent technological advances.

# Chapter 13: Technology in Art and Music Instruction

This chapter focuses on technology applications for the topics in arts instruction to which the majority of K-12 students are exposed: music (appreciation, theory and performance) and art (drawing, painting, and image production).

# Chapter 14: Technology in Physical Education and Health

The closely related subjects of physical education and health are generally not allocated the status of the more "academic" subject areas. However, the quality of the teaching of these subjects may play a major role in the future success of our students. Instructional technology provides a number of resources that may maximize the effectiveness of the limited time that typically is given to these subjects.

# Chapter 15: Technology in Special Education

Chapter 15 is the only chapter identified by population rather than by topic. Technology applications for students with special needs are addressed in Part IV because the curriculum for them has many unique characteristics. Needs of special students addressed in this chapter include those for learners with mental disabilities and behavioral/emotional disorders as well as those with physical disabilities (e.g., hearing impaired, visually impaired, nonspeaking, wheelchair-bound), and gifted and talented students.

## Structure of Each Chapter

**Issues and problems related to technology use in the content area.** Chapters in this part provide information to support both single-subject and interdisciplinary integration strategies. Each chapter has a brief description of current issues that affect the use of instructional technology in a specific content area. Most teachers do not ask *whether* they should use technology, but *when, how, and for what* they should use it. Considering how quickly technologies and their applications develop, answers to these questions are bound to change. However, one of the greatest benefits of the infusion of technology into schools is an increased reflection about teaching and learning strategies; these chapters are designed to promote this reflection.

**How technology is integrated into the content area.** Each chapter suggests general resources and applications for its subject area. Specific examples are provided of how these technologies are used in the classroom setting. The examples are then linked to one or more of the integration strategies offered in the text.

**Useful Web sites for subject-area instruction.** A selection of exemplary Web sites is given for each subject area. The selection usually includes one from a national organization in the field and others that provide either teacher or student resources.

**Sample integration lessons for subject-area education.** Activities in Chapters 10 through 15 provide both resources and models for curriculum integration. Teachers are encouraged to use these activities and elaborate on them, customizing them to meet students' needs and to match facility resources. The *Integrating Educational Technology Across the Curriculum* lesson plan CD-ROM that accompanies this book has additional examples to illustrate how technology is integrated into each content area.

**Chapter activities to record and apply what you have learned.** Exercises at the end of each chapter give students and instructors a number of options for applying what has been learned. Suggestions are provided for both individual and teams projects as well as prompts to stimulate group discussions.

# Chapter 10

## Technology in Language Arts and Foreign Language Instruction

Literacy is one of the devices society uses to reproduce itself and to adapt to social changes. The form of literacy emphasized in schools is an effort to align school subjects with new markets and tools in the workplace....

Miles Meyers

Language and communication are at the heart of the human experience.

Statement of Philosophy: Foreign Language Standards

## This chapter covers the following topics:

- Current issues and problems in language arts and foreign language instruction

- How technology is integrated into language arts and foreign language instruction

- Example World Wide Web site resources for language arts and foreign language instruction

- Example activities for a variety of integration strategies in language arts and foreign language instruction

# Objectives

1. Identify some of the current issues in language arts and foreign language instruction that may impact the selection and use of technology.

2. Describe some popular uses for technology in language arts and foreign language curricula.

3. Identify exemplary World Wide Web sites for language arts and foreign language.

4. Create instructional activities for language arts and foreign language instruction that successfully model integration strategies.

## Introduction

Communications skills—reading, listening, and speaking—generally are considered fundamental qualifications for basic literacy; most educators identify these skills as prerequisites to adequate performance in all other content areas. Curricula for the elementary to middle grades often group these skills together as "language arts" instruction, while later grades often cover them in combination or separately within English, literature, or writing courses. Many activities and technology resources are common to both levels and this chapter discusses them together, giving example lesson activities for each level. In an effort to model integration of all subject areas, the chapter also addresses foreign language instruction. The crossover between language arts and foreign language instruction is unavoidable, especially as English as a second language (ESOL) programs operate in many school systems.

## Issues and Problems in Language Arts Education

### Phonics versus Whole Language

The role of technology in teaching language arts has been shaped in large part by ongoing discussions and controversies about the best pedagogical strategies for this area. The "phonics versus whole language" debate has been played out in the media over the last 25 years and has become a political issue, showing no sign of resolution. Educators and parents often take a position that one of the following models should be emphasized:

- **Competencies model.** This model assumes that "language arts skills can be broken down into components" (Mandel, 1980, p. 6) and taught sequentially.
- **Whole language model.** This approach focuses on deriving meaning, rather than individual skills, in speech and literacy activities. It encourages children to learn reading in the context of self-expression in all forms.

The following sections recommend resources that have general applications for both models and some that suit each one. However, the current trend is toward a balanced approach for language arts instruction that includes both approaches. In a study by Weisendanger and Roberts (1998), 427 teachers were surveyed concerning their preferences for literacy instruction. Results indicated most teachers prefer a combined approach. Findings by Cunningham, Hall, and Defree (1998) agree with this perception, finding that elementary students need to spend equal time on word study, writing, self-selected reading, and guided reading to be successful readers.

Teachers should be prepared to address several issues prior to implementing any of the resources discussed in this chapter. Careful attention to some important guidelines will help to smooth efforts to incorporate technology resources into language arts and English instruction. When teachers neglect these concerns, promising resources can actually impede the instructional process.

### Standards in Language Arts

The Standards for Language Arts issued in 1996 stress the following points (Chin, 1996).

- Students must be capable readers and writers. As they grow as readers, students must learn and develop effective learning strategies for dealing with challenging materials.

- Students must organize their ideas logically and write and speak clearly and effectively.

- Students must read often, interpreting and evaluating a broad range of classic and contemporary literature.

- Students should be active and critical users of media and technology.

- Students must be able to communicate effectively in many different situations, including those requiring standard English (see Example Lesson 10.1 on page 249).

- As they answer questions and explore issues, students must be able to find many sources of information. They should know how to evaluate information, summarize it, and communicate their conclusions clearly to others.

- They should work successfully in teams, using their language skills to solve problems.

- Students should use their English language arts education to become lifelong learners.

### Keyboarding

The controversy over whether or not to require keyboarding skills as prerequisite to computer use has inspired vigorous, ongoing debates. Whole language proponents in elementary schools seem to emphasize these skills less than business education teachers do, for example, but this is not always the case. This controversy affects teachers in language arts and English especially, since word processing software and other resources commonly used in these areas usually require much typing. Teachers must decide whether to assign keyboarding practice based on knowledge of their students and the goals they are trying to achieve. If word processing is introduced in language arts activities at early grade levels, students usually acquire sufficient keyboarding skills by later grades to use software. However, ten-finger typing is commonly considered a desirable skill to develop at some point in a student's education.

### Prerequisite Technical Skills

Perhaps more than any other content area, language teachers must allow students enough time to become proficient at using equipment and software before assigning tasks. Schwartz and Vockell (1988) emphasize this need especially for word processing activities. They advise teachers to introduce word processing features patiently and gradually using readily available guides and assistants. Also, teachers should not expect that students' proficiency in one word processing package will automatically enable them to use another application. Students need time and practice to acquire a general facility that transfers to new resources.

**Internet technology and composition.** The emergence of the Internet and the ease in which information may be accessed has created questions for the language arts community to consider. What are the possibilities of such access to information? What are the emerging definitions of authorship? In what ways are composing processes and modes of discourse changing in an increasingly technological world? What are the possibilities and constraints of technology (Kline, 1998)? The NCTE likely will be addressing and re-addressing these questions for years to come.

**Media literacy.** There is a growing societal concern across the ideological spectrum about the negative impact of various media on youth. Often such concerns result in a backlash reaction that leads to censorship. Many believe that media literacy should be an integral part of schooling but are not sure where it should lie in the curriculum (Porter, 1998). Some view language arts as a natural place for this subject to be taught; however, the NCTE has not taken a position on including media literacy as basic in English language arts instruction.

## How Technology Is Integrated into Language Arts Education

### Word Processing and Desktop Publishing

Generally viewed as the most versatile and powerful software for teaching language topics, a word processing package may have various features depending on its purpose

and intended users. For example, word processing software designed for early elementary students may include draw features, easily imported graphics, and text-to-speech capabilities. For upper elementary students, programs often include a spell checker and a thesaurus, and screen displays often look more mature. Middle and high school students usually use word processing packages designed for adult use. The latter software often comes with activity files and exercises to help learn the software.

Desktop publishing software features more powerful formatting capabilities than word processing software. It enables users to develop documents such as newsletters and brochures that require more complicated layout and graphics. Desktop publishing functions usually differ from those of word processors in that they lay out and format the text and graphics of each page, rather than creating files of continuous text and then dividing them into pages; desktop publishing packages also tend to have more graphics and draw capabilities. In recent years, much of the distinction between word processing software and desktop publishing software has all but disappeared since word processors now include more desktop publishing features.

Some teachers believe that the quick editing capabilities of word processors actually are an impediment to good writing. Students stop and correct mistakes as they type; this constant editing impairs the "flow" that is often necessary for creativity. As a way of dealing with this dilemma, teachers choose to have their students turn down the contrast on the screen, thus darkening it, while they write their drafts. This is an example of integrating to foster creativity. Other ideas for word processing integration are described here.

- Students develop a publicity campaign for a school-wide event. They create announcements, flyers, invitations, special calendars, and banner advertisements.

- Students use desktop publishing or word processing software to create a class or school newspaper.

- When writing journals, students use graphics to illustrate points.

- When learning to write business letters, students fax letters to local business partners to be critiqued.

- Students take a product that must be assembled, like a new toy, and write a technical manual for assembling the product.

### The Internet

The capability of communicating via computer with other students has provided unexpectedly powerful support for language arts and English activities. Students frequently are more motivated to write well. For example, they communicate more clearly and use better spelling and grammar when they write for audiences at other sites (Cohen & Riel, 1989). Writing often takes the form of letters, but several teachers have designed successful telecommunications projects around creative writing themes such as developing and comparing reports, poems, and stories. The rapid growth in the quantity and quality of World Wide Web sites provides another major resource for educators and their students. However, teachers also must help students become consumers of the Internet's information (Marcovitz, 1997). The Internet can be integrated in additional ways, described here.

- E-mail or chats to gather information from experts.
- Virtual tours of students' own local history, art, or science museum.
- Models for doing information searches and analyzing and using the results.
- Groups collaborate to develop a survey to gather data on the characteristics of participating students.
- Student participants write a poem or essay as a "verbal postcard" to tell others about some aspect of the local community. Then students communicate these products with each other through e-mail and chatrooms set up for the project.
- Students send questions to their favorite authors; many now have Web sites (see Figure 10.1).
- Students collect book reviews from other students. These reviews are then used in a book review database.
- Information about cultures represented in literature can be researched.
- Teachers use the misinformation on the Web to develop their students' information literacy skills.

## Video

Language arts teachers use video technology primarily in reading and literature. Some of these programs present the film versions of classic stories on videodisc and provide the user with bar codes to access scenes that support analysis of the story. They offer supplemental material such as interviews with authors, illustrators, or critics. A number of major textbook publishers now market videodiscs as supplements to their reading series. These resources differ in their approaches but most offer comprehensive support materials to make the materials user-friendly. Many great films on videodisc provide an excellent resource for teachers and students. Students can incorporate segments of video into activities that foster critical analysis of the film. The examination of video can also extend to instruction in media literacy, which many identify as a basic skill for the information age. Some other uses include the following.

- Students produce their own video news program.
- Teachers develop a lesson that uses bar-code software to edit clips from a popular film. The class views segments that exemplify a principle of visual literacy.
- Student teams use a camcorder to record visuals of a particular scene, perhaps a simulated crime scene. At the same time, they must provide a narrative describing the action. This activity helps students develop precise language skills.

**Figure 10.1    Site for Collaboration Projects**

- Secondary students develop a "how to" video targeted toward elementary students. A final product is then sent to schools as a resource.

## Instructional Software and Software Tools

In addition to word processing, which underlies many whole language and process writing activities, several other kinds of software support and encourage correct language and sentence structure in students' writing. Software to support skill building within process writing includes spell checkers and grammar checkers, style analyzers, and other language analyzers. A new genre of more comprehensive language and reading programs also is widely used. Some use both CAI and word processing software to offer a comprehensive early reading and writing program.

Most software devoted to teaching reading subskills is based on the more traditional types of computer-assisted instruction like drill and practice, instructional games, and tutorials. Programs also are available that analyze text readability levels to help teachers assign appropriate reading materials for students.

As with reading skills, grammar, usage, spelling, and punctuation skills also are addressed through traditional drill and practice, instructional games, and tutorial software. These packages frequently induce students to spend more time practicing subskills on the computer than they would spend on pencil-and-paper activities.

Simulation programs for writing have also begun to emerge. One such program guides student teams through the creation of a class newspaper. The students actually produce the paper on a desktop publishing program of their choice. The simulation program serves as a resource that teaches individuals and teams writing and resource skills as needed. Software like this helps to foster group cooperation and optimize scarce resources (see Figure 10.2).

**Figure 10.2    Tom Snyder Classroom Newspaper Project**

Source: Reprinted with permission from Tom Snyder Productions.

Other software tools are available to support reading and language instruction, although they do not deliver any actual instruction. One of the most popular of these is *Accelerated Reader (AR)* by Advantage Learning Systems (Keller, 1999). *AR* was introduced in 1986 and has enjoyed phenomenal acceptance in schools. It is basically a Computer Managed Instruction (CMI) program that allows students to take quizzes on stories they have read, keeps track of their scores, and provides reports to teachers. Keller says that AR's broad choice of stories at varying levels makes it popular with students of all types, including ESL, Title I, learning disabled, and gifted.

The increasing supply of critical-thinking and problem-solving software programs represents another source of instructional material closely aligned with language arts. Many of these programs cover skills essential for reading comprehension, writing, information literacy, and visual literacy. Other uses of instructional software in language arts instruction include:

* Interactive books to teach reading to primary-grade children.
* Teaching students prewriting skills such as outlining and concept mapping.
* Guiding students through the revision process.
* Teaching research skills.
* Pre-K students learning the alphabet by using a simplified keyboard and specialized software.
* Primary students learning letter sounds by using a program that links pictures of common objects with the first letter of the word and the sound.
* Secondary students using a simulation program that uses a "story" to guide the user through the process of developing a research paper.
* A number of reading programs, developed primarily for network implementation, that usually offer management systems to record scores and reading levels.

## Hypermedia Authoring

Hypermedia authoring rapidly is becoming a mainstream activity due to the tremendous growth of the Internet. In time, the definition of authoring may expand to include a wide variety of media as well as text. Although the technical teaching of hypermedia skills may fall under another discipline, much of the quality will derive from language arts principles. With a quick glance at the language arts standards, it is easy to see how they can be extrapolated to the use of hypermedia tools. One way of using this technology is having students develop large group presentations with software used for visuals. This type of integration helps develop student creativity and visual literacy skills.

* Students use authoring software to develop Web pages.
* Elementary students develop slideshow book reports.
* Student teams develop a Level III program that analyzes a film.
* Elementary students create their own versions of interactive storybooks that include dialogue between the characters.
* By using the electronic publishing features of hypermedia authoring programs, traditional poetry can be embellished with sounds and animation.

## Useful Web Sites for Language Arts Instruction

- **National Council of Teachers of English**
  (http://www.ncte.org/)

  The National Council of Teachers of English (NCTE) is the leading professional organization for improving the teaching of English and language arts at all grade levels. The site presents information of value to K-12 classroom teachers.

- **Teachers and Writers Collaborative**
  (http://www.twc.org/)

  Teachers and Writers Collaborative, a nonprofit organization of writers and educators, explores the connections between writing and reading literature. The site also includes links to related resources.

- **Word Play**
  (http://www.wolinskyweb.com/word.htm)

  Word Play includes "student friendly" links such as: Acronym Finder, Alan Cooper's Homonym List, The Amazing Run-On Sentence Page, American Slanguages, Anagram Hall of Fame, The Big List of Clichés and Other Fun But Stupid Things to Say, Brain Bait—The Creative Writing Site, Broken Rules Page, and Common Errors in English.

- **Rensselear Writing Center**
  (http://www.rpi.edu/dept/llc/writecenter/web/handouts.html)

  The Rensselear Writing Center provides guidance in writing abstracts, cover letters, laboratory reports, memos, and resumes; plus gives suggestions on revising prose and writing using gender-fair language.

**Figure 10.3   KidPub Web Site**

Source: KidPub Copyright © 1999 KidPub Worldwide Publishing. Reprinted courtesy of KidPub.

- **Guide to Grammar and Good Writing**
(http://webster.commnet.edu/HP/pages/darling/grammar.htm)

This site includes sentence level, paragraph level, and essay level help and has "Interactive Quizzes," "Ask Grammar!" and a "Grammar Log" of past questions and answers plus the humorous—"Anomalous Anonymies."

- **The Children's Literature Web Guide**
(http://www.acs.ucalgary.ca/~dkbrown/index.html)

The Children's Literature Web Guide is an attempt to gather together and categorize the growing number of Internet resources related to books for children and young adults. This site includes such features as "Best Books," "Web-Traveller's Toolkit: Essential Kid Lit Websites," and "What We're Reading: Commentary on Children's Books."

- **KidPub**
(http://www.launchsite.org/meeting/meet02.html)

This site has a collection of more than 11,000 stories and poems written by young people (see Figure 10.3). Here students can publish their own writing on the Internet. "KidMud" and "Keypals" are areas in KidPub where young students meet other young writers.

## Issues and Problems in Foreign Language Education

### Foreign Language Education Standards

The following National Foreign Language standards were published in 1996.

- **Communication in Languages Other than English**

*Standard 1.1:* Students engage in conversations, provide and obtain information, express feelings and emotions, and exchange opinions.

*Standard 1.2:* Students understand and interpret written and spoken language on a variety of topics.

*Standard 1.3:* Students present information, concepts, and ideas to listeners or readers on a variety of topics.

- **Gain Knowledge and Understanding of Other Cultures**

*Standard 2.1:* Students demonstrate an understanding of the relationship between the practices and perspectives of the culture studied.

*Standard 2.2:* Students demonstrate an understanding of the relationship between the products and the perspectives of the culture studied.

- **Connect with Other Disciplines and Acquire Information**

*Standard 3.1:* Students reinforce and further their knowledge of other disciplines through foreign language.

*Standard 3.2:* Students acquire information and recognize the distinctive viewpoints available only through foreign language and its cultures.

- **Develop Insight into the Nature of Language and Culture**

*Standard 4.1:* Students demonstrate understanding of the nature of language through comparisons of the language studied with their own.

*Standard 4.2:* Students demonstrate understanding of the concept of culture through comparisons of the culture studied with their own.

- **Participate in Multilingual Communities at Home and around the World**

*Standard 5.1:* Students use foreign language both within and beyond the school setting.

*Standard 5.2:* Students show evidence of becoming lifelong learners by using foreign language for personal enjoyment and enrichment.

### Skills versus Language Immersion

Foreign language instruction traditionally followed the same basic pattern that dominated the teaching of English: the competencies model. Students spent most of their time in foreign language classes learning the rules of grammar, memorizing vocabulary, or translating text. Over the past two decades, a new school of thought—commonly called communicative language teaching—has emerged. Although this trend has produced no clearly defined single model of communicative teaching (Whitley, 1993), the term conveys "a broad ability to use language appropriately in natural situations" (p. 40). This translates to less classroom emphasis on rules of grammar and much more time immersing students in speaking and listening to the second language, especially within the context of relevant dialogue.

### The Impact of Distance Learning

With demand for foreign language instruction increasing and shortages of qualified teachers in many areas, distance education through satellites has become extremely important. This method has provided a way for students to study some of the more exotic languages like Chinese, Japanese, and Russian despite local scarcity of qualified instructors.

However, the technology remains expensive and many question its cost-effectiveness. Communications via the Internet seem to hold greater promise than these methods.

## Teaching Foreign Language in Elementary Schools

Despite the evidence that foreign language expertise provides economic and diplomatic advantages to nations, in the United States fewer than one in five children in elementary school has the opportunity to develop foreign language skills. The National Council of State Supervisors of Foreign Languages (NCSSFL) endorses beginning foreign language instruction in the elementary grades for all students. They recognize the use of three elementary school foreign language models: FLEX, FLES, and Immersion. FLEX (foreign language experience or exploratory) is designed to provide limited foreign language experience to presecondary students. FLES (foreign language in the elementary school) seeks to provide students sequential language learning experiences that work toward proficiency. Immersion programs deliver all or a large part of content learning through means of foreign language.

## Teaching Culture

Many advocates of foreign language instruction promote the goal of teaching culture. Lambert (1967) argues that foreign language classrooms can realize their potential for intercultural growth only if students learn languages from the beginning in a setting that provides carefully developed cultural contexts.

Herron and Hanley (1992) find that children retain information about French culture after viewing a brief video with audio in the language related to but not identical to the content of a subsequent reading. This certainly could have implications for instruction in all foreign languages. A number of video programs are available to specifically teach foreign culture. Cultural instruction also needs to help students unlearn stereotypes acquired from popular media.

## Challenges for Foreign Language Teachers

Tedick and Walker (1996) list a number of factors that make the teaching of foreign language increasingly more challenging:

- The emphasis on technology for foreign language learning and teaching requires teachers to keep informed about new technologies and their instructional uses.
- The emphasis on collaborative learning and student self-directed learning requires that teachers act as facilitators, guides, counselors, and resources—not just language experts.
- The current emphasis on exclusive use of the target language in the classroom requires that teachers have strong language skills.
- The variety of reasons students have for learning foreign languages and the different ways they approach this learning require that foreign language curricula and instruction address a range of student goals and learning styles.

## How Technology Is Integrated into Foreign Language Education

### The Internet

Internet technology has great potential as a computer-assisted language learning (CALL) tool. Web sites facilitate exchanges between students of different nations, although primarily in the English language. Most efforts to facilitate second language exchanges with students in other countries are limited in scope, but anticipated technological developments promise a bright future for synchronous (i.e., "chat type") discussions in other languages. LAN technology has shown potential to facilitate communication in foreign language instruction. As two or more students converse in real time on a network, reticent students are more likely to participate. Other uses in foreign language instruction include the following.

- Students are able to chat or exchange e-mail with native foreign language speakers (see Example Lesson 10.2 on page 250).
- Background information about different cultures and countries can be easily researched.
- Students plan a trip to a country where a foreign language is spoken. E-mail messages can be written in the native language.
- News accounts from foreign sources can be obtained. Multiple perspective can then be discussed.
- Students can study a book from another culture with a group of students that represent that culture.
- Using videoconferencing technology such as CUSeeMe, students are able to have face-to-face conversations with native speakers.

### Computer Software

CALL programs have improved considerably in the past few years. In the past, most computer software for foreign language instruction have provided grammar-based drill and practice, and some programs provided vocabulary and translation practice. However, enhanced voice recognition and multimedia capabilities of software, along with more powerful hardware, now make it possible for students to have a language immersion experience without leaving the classroom. These newer software tools promise to revolutionize the CALL strategies traditionally used in foreign language instruction (Sargent, 1999). Sargent describes the best of the software packages available for this purpose.

Some foreign language teachers also use word processing and hypermedia authoring tools in their classes. These applications are useful for engaging the students in applying what they know and help to promote automaticity (see Figure 10.4). Some other uses of these tools include:

**Figure 10.4**  *Berlitz Think and Talk Spanish* **Software**

The Learning Company - Berlitz "Think and Talk-Spanish"

Source: Copyright © 1998 The Learning Company. Berlitz *Think and Talk Spanish*. Courtesy of The Learning Company.

- Students who have limited vocabulary use graphics with word processing to help them overcome frustrations (Lewis, 1997).
- Students apply their target language knowledge by developing menus or writing their autobiographies.
- Some programs use the immersion approach and present all information in the target language.
- One program offers dozens of video clips from French national television. Students can watch the clips at their own pace; if they find the native speech too fast for them to understand, they can slow it down to a more comfortable level (Higgins, 1997).

## Video

Several videodisc programs teach foreign languages within the context of native cultures. These programs typically are divided into short (15-minute) segments tied to bar codes and student workbooks. Another use of videodisc technology in foreign language instruction tells a story of young people unwittingly involved in a dangerous mystery. Bar codes enable users to quickly repeat segments of the pro-

**Figure 10.6**  **Instructional Software with Tutorial Features and Video Presentations:** *Spanish Now!*

Source: Courtesy of RXL Pulitzer.

gram, thus making it easy to see and hear information as many times as needed.

- A videodisc version of a movie is used to demonstrate racial and cultural stereotyping. Bar codes are created that enable users to easily replay exact segments.
- Classes use a video camera to create a foreign language program that will be sent to their teammates in another country (see Figure 10.5).
- Teachers use video resources to provide foreign language instruction geared toward visual learners. These programs usually will project the dialogue on screen.
- A number a videodisc programs have a second track recorded in Spanish. This resource can be used to integrate Spanish with another subject.

Some software packages integrate tutorial and drill features of instructional software with video presentations, so that students can see and hear people speaking the language in various contexts. An example is shown in Figure 10.6.

**Figure 10.5**  **Foreign Language Students Using Videocamera**

Source: Anthony Magnacca/Merrill.

## Useful Web Sites for Foreign Language Instruction

- **American Council on the Teaching of Foreign Languages**
  (http://www.actfl.org/)

  This site is for the major organization of foreign language teachers. It includes a variety of resources for teachers.

- **Language Links—Teaching with the Web**
  (http://polyglot.lss.wisc.edu/lss/lang/teach.html)

  This site presents a compilation of ideas for using WWW resources as a language teaching tool. It also offers links to sites that have pedagogical information.

- **FL Teach**
  (http://www.cortland.edu/www_root/flteach/flteach.html)

  Foreign language teaching methods are presented, including school/college articulation, training of student teachers, classroom activities, curriculum, and syllabus design.

- **Internet Activities for Foreign Language Classes**
  (see Figure 10.7)
  (http://members.aol.com/maestro12/web/wadir.html)

  Favorite teacher URLs—use these Web sites to write your own Internet activities. There are 480 links to authentic documents on the Web. They include geography, newspapers, foods, sports, music, literature, museums, artists, leisure, history, holidays/celebrations, weather, search engines, and comics.

- **Language Learning and Technology**
  (http://polyglot.cal.msu.edu/llt/)

  This is the site for the *Language Learning and Technology* journal. Selected articles from the current issue are online.

### Figure 10.7   Internet Web Site for Foreign Language Students

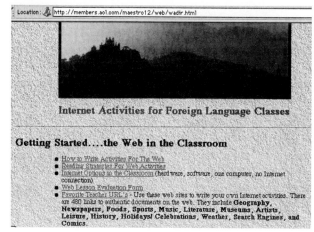

Source: Courtesy of California Foreign Language Project Web Page.frame.

- **University of Toledo—The Famous Foreign Language Bookmarks**
  (http://www.forlang.utoledo.edu/BOOKMARK/Bookmark.html)

  Classical, French/Francophone, German, Japanese, Latin American/Spanish, and Russian bookmarks are shown.

## Sample Integration Lessons for Language Education

Additional activities are available on the accompanying *Integrating Technology Across the Curriculum* CD-ROM.

---

### Example Lesson 10.1
### The First Job Interview

**Level:** Upper elementary/secondary

**Required Resources:** Computer, word processing software, printer

**Integration Strategy.** Integration to increase transfer of knowledge to problem solving

**Directions for Lesson Activities**

*Setting the Stage.* Copy the following scenario and pass it out to the class. This is an excellent activity to do in a writing lab.

   *Scenario*—You are almost done with your interview for your first job—so far, so good. The job you are applying for is at Super Burger, a fast-food chain with a reputation for treating its workers very well. It's considered by young people to be "the place" to work. Just when you thought you were done, the manager pulls out a piece of paper and hands it to you. "Before I make a final decision I would like you to complete this activity," she says.

   You read the paper and here is what it says:

*Continued*

One day while you are working, a customer comes in and orders a Super Burger Deluxe. You ask him if he wants any fries or dessert and he suddenly becomes agitated. Instead of maintaining your cool, you get offended and start behaving in a rather insolent manner. The customer then becomes further upset and goes to the manager to complain about the "rude employees" at Super Burger. He storms out, yelling that he won't ever come into the restaurant again.

The manager talks with you about the incident to help you understand what you did wrong, and she explains how this type of incident could be avoided in the future. She also asks you to write a note of apology to the irate customer, Mr. Big.

After you complete reading the activity, the manager leads you to a small office where you are asked to sit at the computer. "Please write a note of apology as though you were the employee in the incident," she says. "I'd like it done in fifteen minutes."

***Preliminary Activities.*** After students read the scenario, ask them to think about what a manager could tell about a potential employee by reading a note of apology. Lead a class discussion after the students have had time to reflect.

Students follow the directions given in the scenario. Set a timer for 15 minutes. If time permits, the teacher might want to role-play the manager and critique the note with the author.

Source: Jack Edwards.

## Example Lesson 10.2
## Raising Cultural Awareness

**Level:**  Secondary
**Required Resources:**  Computer, hypermedia authoring software, assorted tools for hypermedia development, e.g., camcorder, scanner, digital camera, sound recording equipment, Internet access.

**Integration Strategy.** Integration to foster multiple intelligences

**Directions for Lesson Activities**
***Background.*** Many schools are facing the challenge of accepting immigrants from all over the world. Quite often they are not prepared to adequately welcome students from different cultures. This project is designed to produce a tool that will provide the school with a valuable resource and, in the course of developing it, provide students with an opportunity to practice new languages and learn about the cultures of a variety of countries.

***Audience.*** The projects are intended to be used by students and faculty currently attending the school who want to find out information about the culture and language of incoming students.

***Procedures.*** Students team up with one or two other students and choose a country to research. They should choose a county representative of one of the recently arrived immigrant groups in their communities. Information should focus on language, politics, demographics, customs, religion, food, common phrases, and history. Groups plan and develop a hypermedia project geared toward helping the audience gain insight into the backgrounds of people who have recently immigrated. If possible, links to Web sites related to the target country should be included. If the resources exist, the project could be linked together and recorded on a CD-ROM disc.

***Note to Teachers.*** If this activity is to be done by foreign language classes, then much more emphasis should be placed on the language component of the project. Another option for a project similar to this would be to develop a program to be used by ESOL students. It might focus on helping the students understand the meanings of American idioms.

Source: Jack Edwards.

# Exercises

## Record and Apply What You Have Learned

**Activity 10.1: Chapter 10 Self-Test**  To review terms and concepts in this chapter, take the Chapter 10 self-test. Select Chapter 10 from the front page of the companion Web site (located at http://www.prenhall.com/roblyer), then choose the *Multiple Choice* module.

**Activity 10.2: Portfolio Activities**  The following activities will help you add to your professional portfolio. To complete these activities online and save or submit the materials electronically, select Chapter 10 from the front page of the companion Web site (http://www.prenhall.com/roblyer), then choose the *Portfolio* module.

*Integration Skills*  Select one of the integration strategies from the chapter and develop a classroom activity for a language arts content area. Be prepared to teach or demonstrate the activity to the class. If possible, use your activity with the targeted age group before you bring it to the class. The lesson and your reflections on the teaching experience should be placed in a portfolio.

*Hypermedia/Web Page Authoring*  Develop a hypermedia stack or Web page project designed to teach a specific language arts or foreign language content area of your choosing. Use the themes offered by the standards and the integration strategies offered in this text as a reference point for your project. If possible, link the project to Web sites and, within your project, offer your guidance through the individual sites. You should also include review quizzes that are to be answered when students complete working through a site or stack. Include a hard copy of the stack or Web pages in your portfolio.

**Activity 10.3: Questions for Thought and Discussion**  These questions may be used for small group or class discussion or may be subjects for individual or group activities. To take part in these discussions online, select Chapter 10 from the front page of the companion Web site (http://www.prenhall.com/roblyer), then choose the *Message Board* module.

- Many educators believe that with the growth of media and information technology media literacy should be a central focus of the K-12 language arts curriculum. How do you feel about this issue? If it is not placed under language arts, in what area of the curriculum should it be covered?

- Read the "Challenges for Foreign Language Teachers" section in this chapter. Are there ways that instructional technology could be used to ease any of the challenges? (Address all of the challenges and be specific.) Could technology help with the shortage of foreign language teachers?

**Activity 10.4: Collaborative Activities**  The following may be developed in small group work. Completed group products may be copied and shared with the entire class and/or included in each person's Personal Portfolio.

*Evaluation*  Work with a colleague and evaluate three language arts and three foreign language software products. Use the software evaluation form in Figure 4.15 in Chapter 4. Include a copy of evaluations in your portfolio.

*Evaluation*  Work with a colleague and reread the list of points stressed in the "Issues and Problems in Language Arts Education" section in this chapter. Select two of the points and locate Web sites or software products that would be effective resources for students or teachers who want to acquire the kind of skills referred to in the points. Write a brief description of the Web sites or software products and tell why the sites or products are exemplary. Include the written descriptions in your Personal Portfolios.

**Activity 10.5: Integrating Technology Across the Curriculum Activities**  Use the *Integrating Technology Across the Curriculum* CD-ROM packaged with this textbook to complete the following exercises:

a. Several of the lesson on the CD-ROM that address NCTM standards also address NCTE standards. Examine lessons that illustrate some of the ways language arts and mathematics standards can be addressed in the same activities. Go to *Find Lesson Plan* and click on *Find by Keyword.* Under the *Objective* fields, type "NCTE and NCTM," and click *Search.*

b. The Internet is becoming a more common presence in foreign language classrooms. Pose this question: What unique contributions does the Internet make to teaching and learning of foreign languages? Formulate a tentative answer to this question by reviewing some of the ways the Internet is being used to teach French or Spanish in the lessons on the CD. Go to *Find Lesson Plan* and click on *Find by Criteria.* Under the *Technologies* descriptor, select Internet, and under the *Content Area* descriptor, select Foreign Languages; click *Search.* Do these lessons support the answer you gave?

# References

Armstrong, K. & Yetter-Vassot, K. (1994). Transforming teaching through technology. *Foreign Language Annals, 27*(4), 475–486.

Beauvois, M. H. (1992). Computer-assisted classroom discussion in the foreign language classroom: Conversation in slow motion. *Foreign Language Annals, 25*(5), 455–463.

Birch, R. (1994). Every picture tells a story: The negotiation of meaning within an interactive social context at key stage 1. *English in Education, 28*(3), 17–24.

Chin, B. (1996). Standards yes: Let's use the NCTE/IRA standards in our classrooms and communities. *English Journal, 85*(5), 14, 16.

Chun, D. M. & Brandl, K. K. (1992). Beyond form-based drill and practice: Meaning enhanced CALL on the Macintosh. *Foreign Language Annals, 25*(3), 255–265.

Cohen, M. & Riel, M. (1989). The effect of distant audiences on students' writing. *American Educational Research Journal, 26*(2), 67–72.

Cunningham, P., Hall, D., & Defree, M. (1998). Nonability-grouped multilevel instruction: Eight years later. *The Reading Teacher, 51*(8), 652–664.

Flood, J. & Lapp, D. (1998). Broadening conceptualizations of literacy: The visual and communicative arts. *The Reading Teacher, 51*(4), 342–345.

Fredrickson, S. (1997). Interactive multimedia storybooks. *Learning and Leading with Technology, 25*(1), 6–10.

Glasgow, J. N. (1997). Keep up the good work: Using multimedia to build reading fluency and enjoyment. *Learning and Leading with Technology, 24*(5), 22–25.

Gottfried, J. & McFeely, M. G. (1998). Learning all over the place: Integrating laptop computers into the classroom. *Learning and Leading with Technology, 25*(4), 6–12.

Green, J. & Feyten, C. (1997). Webspinning: Language learning on the world wide web. *Learning and Leading with Technology, 24*(6), 35–37.

Hamilton, P. (1997). The morning announcements. *Learning and Leading with Technology, 24*(7), 20–21.

Heaney, L. F. (1992). Children using language: Can computers help? *Gifted Education International, 8*(3), 146–150.

Herron, C. & Handley, J. (1992). Using video to introduce children to a foreign culture. *Foreign Language Annals, 25*(5), 419–425.

Higgins, C. (1997). Update your language lab. *Electronic Learning, 16*(3), 18–22.

Holland, H. (1996). Way past word processing. *Electronic Learning, 15*(6), 22–26.

Johnson, A. (1998). The Internet pyramid. *Learning and Leading with Technology, 25*(4), 36–37.

Keller, J. (1999). A closer look: Accelerated reader. *Technology and Learning, 19*(2), 18.

King, R. & Vockell, E. (1991). *The computer in the language arts curriculum.* Watsonville, CA: Mitchell-McGraw-Hill.

Kinzer, C. & Leu, D. J. (1997). The challenge of change: Exploring literacy and learning in electronic environments. *Language Arts, 74*(2), 126–135.

Kline, C. (1998). The commission on composition (http://www.ncte.org/about/trend.html#comp).

Lambert, W. E. (1967). *Children's views of foreign people.* New York: Appleton-Century-Crofts.

Lewis, P. (1997). Using productivity software for beginning language learning. *Learning and Leading with Technology, 24*(8), 14–17.

Mandel, B. (1980). *Three language arts curriculum models: Pre-kindergarten through college.* Urbana, IL: National Council of Teachers of English.

Marcovitz, D. M. (1997). I read it on the computer, it must be true. *Learning and Leading with Technology, 25*(3), 18–21.

McMillen, L. & Shanahan, S. (1997). Materials that make the mark: Integrating technology in the classroom. *Language Arts, 74*(2), 137–149.

Milton, K. & Spradley, P. (1996). A renaissance of the renaissance—using Hyperstudio for research projects. *Learning and Leading with Technology, 23*(6), 20–22.

Nourse, K. (1994). An enterprise technology project as part of German exchange. *Language Learning Journal, 9,* 26–27.

Pitkoff, E. & Roosen, E. (1994). New technology, new attitudes provide language instruction. *NASSP Bulletin, 78*(563), 36–43.

Porter, C. (1998). *Trends and issues in English instruction, 1998 summaries of informal annual discussions of the commissions.* Urbana, IL: National Council of Teachers of English (ERIC Reproduction Service No. ED 416 489).

Purcell-Gates, V. (1995). Research for the 21st century: A diversity of perspectives among researchers. *Language Arts, 72*(1), 56–60.

Rankin, W. (1997). The cyberjournal: Developing writing, researching, and editing skills through e-mail and the world wide web. *Educational Technology, 24*(7), 29–31.

Reinking, D. (1997). Me and my hypertext: A multiple digression analysis of technology and literacy (sic). *The Reading Teacher, 50*(8), 626–643.

Reissman, R. (1997). Recording student ideas and ongoing discussions. *Learning and Leading with Technology, 24*(6), 22–23.

Rose, D. H. (1994). The role of technology in language arts instruction. *Language Arts, 71*(4), 290–294.

Salomone, A. M. (1991). Immersion teachers: What can we learn from them? *Foreign Language Annals, 24*(1), 57–63.

Sargent, M. (1999). La plume de ma tante. *Technology and Learning, 19*(5), 23–28.

Schwartz, E. & Vockell, E. (1988). The computer in the English curriculum. Santa Cruz, CA: Mitchell.

Tedick, D. J. & Walker, C. L. (1996). *Foreign languages for all: Challenges and choices.* Lincolnwood, IL, National Textbook.

U.S. Department of Labor. (1992). SCANS (The Secretary's Commission on Achieving Necessary Skills) report. Washington, DC: U.S. Government Printing Office.

Viau, E. A. (1998). Color me a writer: Teaching students to think critically. *Learning and Leading with Technology, 25*(5), 17–20.

Weisendanger, K. & Roberts, E. (1999, under review). Survey of current reading practices of elementary school teachers.

Wepner, S. B. (1993). Technology and thematic units: An elementary example on Japan. *The Reading Teacher, 46*(5), 442–445.

Wepner, S. B. (1994). Saving endangered species: Using technology to teach thematically. *The Computing Teacher, 22*(1), 34–37.

Whitley, S. M. (1993). Communicative language teaching: An incomplete revolution. *Foreign Language Annals, 26*(2), 137–149.

Wilson, T, F. & Utecht, G. (1995). The Internet at Eagan High School. *T.H.E. Journal, 22*(9), 75–79.

## Foreign Language Resources

### Videodiscs

*World Cultures and Youth Series*—Coronet/MTI

*Mexico Vivo, España Viva, A Vous la France! La Maree et Ses Secrets*—Films Incorporated, available from EISI

*Windows on Science/Windows on Math*—Optical Data Corp.

### Software

*Spanish Grammar Series*—Intellectual Software, available from EISI

*Hagar the Polyglot*—Gessler, available from EISI

*French Tutor*—Queue, available from EISI

*Berlitz Interpreter*—Microlytics/Software Holdings, available from EISI

*French Vocabulary Beginners*—Microcomputer Workshops, available from EISI

*Learn to Speak Series*—HyperGlot Software, available from EISI

*Berlitz Think and Talk*—HyperGlot Software, available from EISI

*French Micro Scrabble*—Gessler, available from EISI

*Whodunit: French, German, Spanish*—Gessler, available from EISI

*Slavic Swiss Cyrillic Fonts, 3-D Keyboard*—Exceller Software Corp., available from EISI

*National Geographic's KIDSNET*—National Geographic

*International Expanded Book Toolkit*—Voyager Inc.

*Spanish Story Tailor*—Humanities Software

## Language Arts Resources

### Word Processors for Children

*Kid Works II*—Davidson

*The Writing Center, Children's Writing and Publishing Center*—The Learning Company

### Integrated Software Packages

*Microsoft Works*—Microsoft Corp.

*ClarisWorks*—Claris Corp.

*WordPerfect Works*—Corel, Inc.

*Read-Listen-Speak Series*—Transparent Language, Inc.

### Desktop Publishing/Word Processing Programs

*WordPerfect*—WordPerfect Corp.

*Microsoft Word, Microsoft Publisher*—Microsoft Corp.

*MacWrite Pro*—Claris Corp.

*Pagemaker*—Adobe

*QuarkXpress*—Quark

*Toucan Press*— Pelican/Toucan

*Big Book Maker*—Pelican Toucan

*Super Print*—Scholastic Inc.

### Other Software

*Grammatik*—WordPerfect Corp.

*Writing to Read*—EduQuest

*Tapestry*—Jostens

*Playroom*—Brøderbund

*The Vocabulary Games*—J & S Software, available from EISI

*Crossword Magic*—Mindscape Educational Software, available from EISI

*Milliken's Comprehension Power*—Milliken & I/CT

*Speed Reader II*—Davidson

*Storybook Weaver*—MECC

*RightWriter*—RightSoft/Que Software, available from EISI

*Literature Series*—Sliwa/Queue, available from EISI

*Adult Education Reading*—BLS, Inc., available from EISI

*Thinkanalogy, Editor in Chief, Dr. DooRiddles Software*—Critical Thinking Press

### CD-ROMs

*Shakespeare—The Complete Works*—CMC Research, available from EISI

*Compton's Multimedia Encyclopedia*—Compton's New Media

*A Visit to the Smithsonian*—National Geographic

*Discus Books*—Discus

*Brøderbund's Living Books*—Brøderbund

*C. D.'s Story Time*—Houghton Mifflin Co.

### Videodiscs

*To Kill a Mockingbird*—Media Learning Systems/Image

*How the Elephant Got His Trunk*—Encyclopedia Brittanica

*About Huckleberry Finn*—Encyclopedia Brittanica

*Masterpiece Series*—Silver Burdett and Ginn

*Old Mother Witch, Literature Navigator Series*—BFA

*Illuminated Books and Manuscripts*—EduQuest

# Chapter 11

# Technology in Science and Mathematics Instruction

All of us have a stake, as individuals and as a society, in scientific literacy.

National Science Education Standards Overview

The challenge to designing a new math curriculum is to create one that is teachable. You cannot do that without technology.

Judah Schwartz, as quoted in Hill (1993)

## This chapter covers the following topics:

- Current issues and problems in science and math instruction

- How technology is integrated into science and math instruction

- Example World Wide Web site resources for science and math instruction

- Example activities for a variety of integration strategies in science and math instruction

# Objectives

1. Identify some of the current issues in science and math instruction that may impact the selection and use of technology.

2. Describe popular uses for technology in science and math curricula.

3. Identify exemplary World Wide Web sites for science and math.

4. Create instructional activities for science and math instruction that model successful integration strategies.

# Introduction

The surge of technological change is pushing the limits of humans' ability to adapt to it. At the forefront of this "knowledge age" are the disciplines of mathematics and science; they are closely intertwined with each other and with technology. Indeed, citizens of tomorrow's world will not have the option of leaving mathematics and science for those who are perceived to have special gifts in these areas. People in all walks of life will need more proficiency in these technical areas than most people have attained today. Education, of course, will be the key to preparing students for tomorrow's world. In this chapter, we will discuss the uses of technology in the mathematics/science curriculum and offer concrete suggestions on how to integrate instructional technology into these fields.

# Issues and Problems in Science Education

## Science Education Standards

In a world filled with the products of scientific inquiry, scientific literacy has become a "basic" for nearly everybody. In ever increasing numbers, people need to use scientific information to make choices that arise every day. People need to be able to engage intelligently in public discourse and debate about important issues that involve science and technology. And everyone deserves to share in the excitement and personal fulfillment that can come from understanding and learning about the natural world.

Scientific literacy also is of increasing importance in the workplace. More and more jobs require advanced skills that require that people be able to learn, reason, think creatively, make decisions, and solve problems. An understanding of science and scientific processes contributes to the mastery of these skills.

The most ambitious effort to reform science instruction is the National Science Education Standards Project sponsored by the National Research Council (NRC), an agency of the National Academy of Sciences and the National Academy of Engineering. The National Science Education Standards were released in late 1995. The standards document states the following principles at the outset:

- All students, regardless of gender, cultural or ethnic background, physical or learning disabilities, aspirations, or interest and motivation in science, should have the opportunity to attain higher levels of scientific literacy than they do currently. This is the principle of equity

- All students will learn science in the content standards.

- All students will develop science knowledge as defined in the content standards and an understanding of science that enables them to use their knowledge as it relates to scientific, personal, social, and historical perspectives.

- Learning science is an active process.

- For all students to understand more science, less emphasis must be given to some science content and more resources, such as time, personnel, and materials must be devoted to science education.

- School science must reflect the intellectual tradition that characterizes the practice of contemporary science.

- Improving science education is a part of systemic education reform.

## Inquiry Approaches

These standards clearly favor an inquiry approach. According to the standards document, inquiry "involves making observations, posing questions, examining books and other sources of information to see what is already known, planning investigations, reviewing what is already known in light of experimental evidence, proposing answers and explanations, and communicating the results" (NRC, 1995, p. 5).

The standards do not state how curriculum should be organized, leaving that task to the states. They do ask teachers to help students become inquirers, but the standards do not pass judgment on how best to teach inquiry skills. The inquiry-based approach is not popular with all teachers. Many teachers decry the standards' philosophy of depth over breadth and, instead, believe firmly that students need to know a wide variety of science terms and facts (Weiss, 1993).

## Integrating Technology

Also, the new standards do not spell out clearly the role of instructional technology. But given the ambitious nature of the goals, a broader repertoire of teacher resources seems essential if schools are going to elevate students' science competency in the ways described. Industry will certainly be marketing a variety of technology-based products geared toward helping students attain the new standards. Technology is mentioned directly in the following vein: "The use of tools and techniques ... will be guided by the questions asked and the investigations that students design. The use of computers for the collection, summary, and display of evidence is part of the standards. Students should be able to access, gather, store, retrieve, and organize data, selecting hardware and software designed for these purposes" (NRC, 1995, p. 31).

## How Technology Is Integrated into Science Education

### The Internet

The emergence of the Internet has enabled students to engage in authentic scientific experiences in a way that was previously not thought possible. By linking students to real-time data, scientists in the field, and a plethora of resources that can be found only at major university libraries; this area of educational technology truly promises to change the way science is taught. In one example, in a high school biology class, students work in small groups to prepare class presentations about an infectious disease of their choice. The presentations include information about the infectious agent and its biological classification, details of its interaction with the human body, and an explanation of how these interactions result in symptoms characteristic of the disease. Via the Internet students are able to reach government offices, universities, and professional organizations that are repositories for a wide variety of data collected from the field. In many cases these Internet resources are set up in a user-friendly format with search capabilities provided to help the student find specific information. Integrating technology in the fashion mentioned above is an example of making learning more efficient for highly motivated students. Some examples of how other teachers and students use the Internet include:

- Middle school students use the Internet to conduct research, collect clip art, graphics, and sound effects on dinosaurs. They then use the resources to develop a hypermedia presentation.

- Chemistry classes research and evaluate Web sites related to topics such as molarity, alcohol, or titration. Exemplary sites are then linked to the school's chemistry Web page as a resource for others.

- Students use a Web survey to help identify environmental problems that need to be addressed.

- Students ask scientists/mentors to help them develop outlines for their projects.

- Student teams develop and implement a science-based public service campaign via the school's Web site.

### Simulations

Science simulations can be an extremely effective tool in helping students understand and experience practical applications of scientific thinking. One program uses video to present students with an intriguing mystery. They are gradually given pieces of the puzzle and must work in small

**Figure 11.1   Internet Simulation Site**

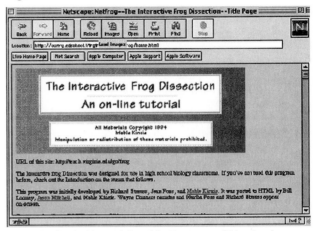

teams to solve the problem. In the process students learn to apply scientific thinking, discern between relevant and irrelevant information, filter out erroneous data, and draw conclusions based upon incomplete data. Applications like this are often extremely motivating for students. Some other ways that simulations are used include:

- Software developed at the University of Michigan enables students to develop their own simulations, or models, using data collected from the field (Soloway, 1997).

- Students use a Web application or computer software that simulates the dissection of a frog (see Figure 11.1).

- Students are assigned specific roles and must work together to solve an environmental crisis that befalls a community. In the process they must examine the problem from the scientific, economic, political, and environmental perspectives.

- Software enables students to learn more about the human anatomy by taking a simulated tour through the human body

### Hypermedia Authoring

Some teachers have their students use hypermedia authoring tools to write what are essentially electronic term papers or reports. This use is legitimate, but does not represent the best use of this powerful technology. Perhaps a better example would be what a science class in New York City did (Mihich, 1996). In this example the students collected data on the water quality of the Hudson river. The health of the water was based on tests like: dissolved oxygen, fecal coliform, pH, and temperature. Then the test results were incorporated into a hypermedia program that brought the raw data to life via the use of animation and other hypermedia components. By using hypermedia tools in this manner, the students were able to develop their creativity and "add value" to rather dry scientific data. Other examples of hypermedia integration might include:

**Figure 11.2 Teacher Using Videodisc and Bar-code Reader**

Source: Anthony Magnacca/Merrill.

- Upper elementary students use a hypermedia authoring program to simulate a highly realistic ocean ecosystem complete with dolphins.
- Students develop an anti-smoking display for their school using hypermedia software with a Level III videodisc configuration.
- High school students create a model of a physical science phenomenon using video and animation. The projects are then shared with elementary and middle school teachers.
- Teams develop a project with Internet links that is designed to guide the user through a study of whales.
- Students or teachers use software to create dynamic presentations that may include photographs, sound, or animation.

## Software/Video Resources

Virtually all categories of computer software are available for science teachers and students to use. In addition, given the visual nature of much science content, video resources also abound. For example, a high school anatomy teacher used barcoded videodiscs to create presentations that accelerate student interest in a rather dry subject (see Figure 11.2). By adding these enhanced visuals to his teaching he was able to generate a greater motivation to learn on the part of many of his students. The following examples point out some other integration strategies (Baugh, 1993; Dahl, 1994).

- Middle school students use spreadsheet, database, and word processing software while studying genetics.
- Fourth grade students use graphics programs to create Venn diagrams that compare genetic characteristics and to design totem poles that tell about themselves and members of their families.
- A teacher uses a videodisc-based curriculum program for the directed instruction component of teaching. The videodiscs are controlled by bar codes and provide a wide

variety of resources including video, slides, animation, and sounds.

- Primary students learn basic scientific concepts through stories presented on videodisc. The students use a written log that helps guide them through the story. The videodisc also has a large visual database that the teacher can access with a bar-code reader.
- Elementary and middle school students are taught science via a networked program that lets them work at their own pace. Each 20-minute lesson uses video, sounds, and animation to teach scientific content. Periodically students take a break from the computer for hands-on activities.

## Probeware

Probeware is a type of instructional software tool consisting of hardware devices (probes) and software that allows scientific data to be gathered and processed by either a computer or a calculator (see Figure 11.3). Microcomputer-based laboratories (MBLs) and the newer calculator-based laboratories (CBLs) empower students by providing them with immediate feedback and graphical displays of numeric data. MBLs are more powerful but more expensive, while CBLs are more convenient for the collection of field data but limited in data storage and manipulation capabilities. These tools enable students to perform a variety of hands-on scientific experiments that help build skills in data collection and analysis. Typically, an MBL/CBL package includes probes and software to measure, record, and graph heat, sound, velocity, pH, color

**Figure 11.3 Students Collecting Data with Probeware**

Source: Courtesy of Vernier Software.

intensity, voltage, and pulse rate. A teacher may integrate this technology by having her students use the temperature probe to test the insulation value of paper, styrofoam, and ceramic cups filled with hot coffee. The experiment then might be extended by testing different liquids or the brand of the cups. Integrating technology in this fashion helps to remove the logistical hurdles of performing the experiment and graphing the data manually. Other integration activities include the following examples.

- Students compare the breathing rate (oxygen used per gram of tissue) of earthworms and germinating peas.

- Students test the stress that various alcohols have on biological membranes. A colorimeter is used to monitor color released from damaged cells.

- Teams design and build models of a solar house. Probeware is then used to record the inside temperature of the house over a designated period of time.

- Elementary students build a model city, then simulate an earthquake by shaking the table the model is built on. Probeware motion and light sensors are used to record the intensity of the earthquakes.

## Useful Web Sites for Science Instruction

- **National Science Teachers Association**
  (http://www.nsta.org/)

  This site of the largest science teacher organization includes resources, standards, and current issues.

- **Eisenhower National Clearinghouse (ENC)**
  (http://www.enc.org/)

  Resources included are lesson plans for teachers, activities for students, and a monthly "Digital Dozen" of top Web sites.

- **FEMA for Kids Homepage**
  (http://www.fema.gov/kids/)

  Maintained by The Federal Emergency Management Agency, this site helps kids cope with and understand disasters. There are special activities for younger children, and opportunities for children to communicate with one another about what it means to experience natural disasters. In addition, this site has games, jokes, and cartoons, many dealing with how to prevent disasters.

- **Neptune's Web**
  (http://www.cnmoc.navy.mil/educate/neptune/neptune.htm)

  The U.S. Navy has created this Web resource to help teachers and students explore the mysteries of the deep. The Teacher's Realm has oceanography lesson plans that combine art, literature, math, science, and social studies. The Student's Sea of Knowledge includes a quiz, a section on careers in oceanography, and links to other ocean Web sites.

- **Classroom of the Future**
  (http://www.cotf.edu/)

  Supported by a grant from NASA, the faculty and staff of Wheeling Jesuit College provide a series of educational materials for high school students. This site provides updat-

ed information on most of NASA's educational programs, including Astronomy Village: Investigating the Universe, BioBlast, Challenger Learning Centers, and Exploring the Environment.

- **Science Education Master Home Page**
  (http://www-hpcc.astro.washington.edu/scied/science.html)

  This site provides a wide variety of resources, including dozens of links to specialists who will answer students' questions.

- **Turning Students into Inventors**
  (http://jefferson.village.virginia.edu/~meg3c/id/id_sep/id_sep.html)

  The Invention and Design (I&D) project is the result of extensive research into the mental and practical aspects involved in the development of new ideas and/or products. The goal of the project and its Web site is to facilitate a better understanding of the processes involved in invention and design through extended case studies.

## Issues and Problems in Math Education

### Standards in Math Education

The driving force behind most changes in mathematics instruction today is the Curriculum and Evaluation Standards for School Mathematics, published by the National Council of Teachers of Mathematics in 1989; the Professional Standards for Teaching Mathematics issued in 1991; and the Assessment Standards for School Mathematics, issued in 1995. The Curriculum Standards is a comprehensive document that calls for major revisions in the way schools teach mathematics in order "to ensure that all students have an opportunity to become mathematically literate … and become informed citizens capable of understanding issues in a technological society" (NCTM, 1989, p. 4). The Standards for School Mathematics document identifies five broad goals designed to prepare American students for the demands of a global economy in the information age.

**Value mathematics.** Students must appreciate and understand the value of mathematics in society. One of the math teacher's great challenges is to connect mathematics to the real world in ways that students appreciate.

**Reason mathematically.** American culture often treats mathematics as a series of skills to memorize as opposed to a way of thinking. Many believe this antitheoretical bias has its roots in the pragmatic nature of the American education system, which often stresses the product (the right answer) over the process.

**Communicate mathematically.** Learning to speak, read, and write about mathematical topics is a natural extension of mathematical reasoning ability. The writing process is an ideal vehicle to help students clarify their own understanding and provides an excellent way to address various learning styles. Allowing students to work cooperatively with access to word processing software further extends these benefits.

**Solve problems.** The ability to apply mathematical principles has gained paramount importance in an increasingly technological world. Students need to experience a variety of problems that differ in scope, difficulty, and context.

**Develop confidence.** In tomorrow's workplace, employees will need a mathematical fluency that few have developed today. The need for confidence in applying mathematics has never been greater.

The math standards were always considered a work in progress. With this in mind and in light of the clamor over our nation's poor performance on the Third International Mathematics and Science Standards (TIMSS) and the National Assessment of Educational Progress (NAEP), the NCTM began a review and revision of its landmark 1989 standards. Its Commission on the Future of the Standards and a standards writing group will develop Standards 2000, which will build on the original message of the standards but will reflect the knowledge gained over the past 10 years. Preliminary information on these new standards indicates that they will reflect more basic skills than in the past.

### Implementing Curriculum, Instruction, and Assessment Standards

Getting teachers to modify their teaching styles to adapt to the NCTM standards has not been an easy task. The requested changes in teaching methodology are not trivial. The teaching standards seek a fundamental shift in the way most teachers work (Burrill, 1997).

In many cases, texts and programs have made superficial changes and then claim to be "standards-based." This has resulted in somewhat of a backlash against the standards. Because significant progress has not been made since their introduction, the standards are sometimes blamed for the lack of improvement.

The NCTM (1997) suggests that instead of blaming the content for the lack of success, the real problem lies in the implementation process. As efforts to implement large-scale reform began, instructional issues were addressed marginally. Only short-term training was made available to teachers, and no real implementation plans were designed. It is suggested that, for the reforms to be successful, classroom teachers affected by it need to be involved in all implementation stages:

* Building awareness and a vision of the reform changes
* Designing and developing curriculum
* Implementing new curricula and instructional practice in the classroom

* Reflecting upon practice
* Refining the implementation process and continuing to learn and grow

**Providing hands-on, minds-on, and authentic learning experiences.** Hands-on, minds-on, and authentic experiences in mathematics can be defined as follows (NCTM, 1997):

*Hands-on.* This involves students in really doing mathematics, experimenting first-hand with physical objects in the environment, and having concrete experience before learning abstract mathematical concepts.

*Minds-on.* This focuses on the core concepts and critical thinking processes needed for students to create and recreate mathematical concepts and relationships in their own minds.

*Authentic.* This allows students to explore, discover, discuss, and meaningfully construct mathematical concepts and relationships in their own minds.

If teachers must rely on workbooks and textbook drills to deliver instruction and cover materials, they will not be able to move toward the types of activities mentioned above. Simulation, modeling software, and Internet access to real world resources have the potential to make hands-on, mind-on, and authentic experiences a reality.

### Opposition to Change

Arguably, the practice of teaching mathematics has been more traditional than any other curriculum area. The point of view that opposes the call for reform holds that the existing system is adequate, that change is not necessary, and that the standards movement and mathematics reform are passing fads—similar to the "new math" of the 1960s—and will eventually go away. Many community members, including parents and teachers, do not see any reason to change. They argue that the new standards are too complex and that we need only teach the majority of students the "basic skills."

There also has been an ongoing controversy about the use of calculators in mathematics classes. Many teachers and parents feel that students will never learn mathematics concepts unless they do these operations themselves, and that society is becoming too dependent on technology to do our thinking for us. These views continue to shape the way technology is—and is not—used in classrooms.

## How Technology Is Integrated into Math Education

### Software

Computer software offers a variety of valuable resources for mathematics students and teachers. Drill and practice programs have been in use for years and help students build automaticity and retain skills. But software also is available for developing higher-level skills. For example, geometric exploration programs are available for all levels and enable users to create shapes and then experiment with mathematical properties of an object. The NCTM makes it clear that this kind of "what if" interactivity is necessary for developing the ability to reason and communicate mathematically. Other uses of computer software include the following.

- Relatively quick and easy data graphing
- Help students explore transformational geometry, e.g., tessellations
- Comprehensive math tutorial and drill and practice
- Math integration programs that include graphing capabilities, calculator, word processor, algebra system, and a large collection of facts and formulas
- Equation editors that enable students to write research papers
- Deriving complex calculations via programs that let users enter formulas that can then be simplified, integrated, differentiated, approximated, plotted, or expanded

## The Internet

Most of the math-related applications on the Web are geared toward connecting students for collaborative problem solving. One sixth-grade class set up a Web page to solicit data on the probability of heads or tails when flipping coins. They received data from over 100 other schools and then shared the results with their online partners. This is a good example of how technology can be used to foster group cooperation. There are many other ways to use the Internet in the math classroom, including:

- Aligning students with professionals who use math at work
- Using government or commercial sources to collect data for statistical analysis
- Using geographical differences to collect data
- Having students set up and monitor a "problem of the week" on the Web
- Learning basic statistics through surveys and polling
- Directing students to allocate a budget for a simulated trip

## Simulations

Simulation programs enhance mathematical instruction primarily by helping to bring math to life. Video scenarios have been created to model the authentic use of math. In one videodisc program, student teams are called on to figure out the most efficient way to rescue a bald eagle that has been shot. To develop the optimum solution, the teams must sort through a variety of mathematical data and correctly apply that data to a series of variables like rate of speed, fuel consumption, distance, time, etc. In using technology in this manner, students learn to transfer prior knowledge to problem solving. Many simulations are now on the Internet (see Figure 11.4). Simulations may be used

**Figure 11.4   Math Simulation on the Internet**

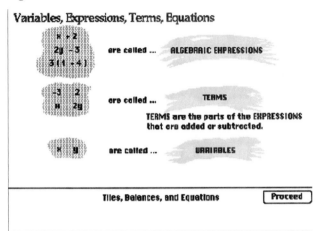

Source: ThinkQuest courtesy of Advanced Network & Services.

in a variety of applications, including mock stock market trading; immersion in occupations as doctors, engineers, detectives, and fire fighters to learn how math is used in real-life situations; manipulating the layout of buildings on a city block to develop spatial reasoning skills; and experiencing many of the financial dilemmas that may occur when operating a business.

## Spreadsheet

Spreadsheets are given their own category because it seems to be one area of computer technology that math teachers are gravitating toward. There are spreadsheet programs available for all age levels. One program for younger children even uses graphical figures in lieu of numbers. One of the most common ways to use spreadsheets involves having students allocate a budget. Some teachers have catalogs and newspaper ads available for student use. One of the more powerful aspects of spreadsheet use is the "what if?" possibilities that can be tried. Because it is so easy to change variables in a spreadsheet, students can quickly learn the dynamic aspect of budgeting. Many students who usually are not motivated by mathematics will readily participate in activities when spreadsheets are used. Spreadsheets are also used in mathematics (McLintock & Jiang, 1997; Miller & Castellanos, 1996): to search for patterns, construct algebraic expressions, simulate probabilistic situations, justify conjectures, generalize concepts, and graph and chart data.

## Graphing Calculators

Calculators with advanced capabilities can be of great assistance to learning higher-level mathematics and science. Physics and algebra rely increasingly on these devices, especially in combination with devices to "capture" data (e.g., probeware systems). Together, these resources make it possible for students to carry out various experiments and concept demonstrations (see Figure 11.5).

**Figure 11.5    Students Using a Graphing Calculator**

Source: Courtesy of Texas Instruments.

## Useful Web Sites for Math Instruction

- **National Council of Teachers of Mathematics**
  (http://www.nctm.org/index.htm)

  This site is rich in resources related to the implementation of the math standards.

- **Los Alamos National Laboratories**
  (http://www.c3.lanl.gov/mega-math/)

  This site has stories and activities for K-12 students.

- **Ask Dr. Math**
  (http://forum.swarthmore.edu/dr.math/dr-math.html)

  Students submit questions to Dr. Math by filling out Web forms or by sending e-mail. Answers are sent back by e-mail. Questions and answers are compiled in a searchable database for future references.

- **Family Math**
  (http://theory.lcs.mit.edu/~emjordan/famMath.html)

  This is a program developed by EQUALS, at the Lawrence Hall of Science, University of California, Berkeley, California. The goal of FAMILY MATH is to encourage under represented groups (especially girls and minority students) to enter careers that use mathematics.

- **Math Magic**
  (http://forum.swarthmore.edu/mathmagic/)

  MathMagic is a K-12 telecommunications project. It provides strong motivation for students to use computer technology while increasing problem-solving strategies and communications skills. MathMagic posts challenges in each of four categories (K-3, 4-6, 7-9, and 10-12) to trigger each registered team to pair up with another team and engage in a problem-solving dialog. When an agreement has been reached, one solution is posted for every pair.

- **PBS Mathline**
  (http://www.pbs.org/learn/mathline/index.html)

  Here is a professional development program for teachers. PBS Mathline uses both the Internet and video for year-long professional development seminars. Teachers become part of online communities to discuss math content, pedagogy, assessment, and the use of the Internet as a teaching tool. This Web site includes Connections—a monthly feature with teaching tips, math challenges, and ideas for assessment.

## Sample Integration Lessons for Science and Math Education

Additional activities are available on the accompanying *Integrating Technology Across the Curriculum* CD-ROM.

### Example Lesson 11.1
### Students' Action Campaign

| | |
|---|---|
| **Level:** | All |
| **Required Resources:** | Varies depending on which activity is selected |

**Integration Strategy.** Integration to develop multiple intelligences

**Directions for Lesson Activities**
*Setting the Stage.* The President's Health Care Task Force concluded that one of the key components of reforming our health care system is to convince people to adopt a wellness approach toward their personal health. The federal government has embarked on a massive educational/advertising campaign designed to affect change in peoples' attitudes from treatment to prevention. It is anticipated that in order for this program to be effective, it will take a major effort for years to come. One key element is to place emphasis on educating students in the K-12 age range.

The educational consulting firm StudentPro has contracted with the class to develop a student-generated informational/educational program on the circulatory system. The program needs to include a

*Continued*

large display component that will be shown in museums, hospitals, and malls around the country. The objective of the display is to educate children about the human circulatory system and how to properly care for it. The contract stipulates that all the information included in the display has to be scientifically and medically accurate and that no spelling or grammatical mistakes are evident.

The class members need to educate themselves on the circulatory system—the wellness approach to health.

**Preliminary Activities**

*Internet Research.* Students conduct Web searches for content necessary to complete the task. Organizations like the American Heart Association or the American Lung Association might offer good starting places. Searches on wellness and public relations will also offer valuable resources.

*Online Mentors.* The Web offers many possibilities for students to link up with experts in the field or retirees. Encourage students to be prepared with good questions and to strive to maximize the effectiveness of the mentor's time. They should treat mentors as members of their teams.

*Guest Speakers.* Invite speakers from a museum, hospital, university, health organization, etc. Also check with the American Association of Retired People to see if they have a speakers' bureau. See if speakers would be willing to serve as consultants or mentors to student groups. If classroom visits are not practical, students and mentors may be able to communicate via phone, fax, or e-mail.

*Field Trip.* The nature of the trip would depend on local resources but could include visits to museums, universities, hospitals, health clubs, or wellness centers. Student teams should videotape the trip; this may provide material for multimedia projects.

*Call for Collaborators.* Use the Web or e-mail to seek out classes in other schools that would like to collaborate on this project.

**Suggested Projects**

*Multimedia/Hypermedia Display.* Use authoring software to develop a stack that educates users about some aspect of the circulatory system and wellness approach. Teachers may want to include a "quiz" section.

*Web Page.* Develop a Web page that helps facilitate the project's objectives. Include a number of high-quality links. Require students to evaluate the links they select.

*Brochure.* Create an educational brochure that informs the reader about the causes and preventions of heart disease. Include the URLs and brief descriptions of relevant Web sites. Students use a desktop publishing program and, if possible, their own graphics.

*Bar-code Activity.* Develop a bar-code activity to access selections from a videodisc on the circulatory system.

*Poem.* Have students write a poem related to wellness. It could then be used in a brochure, Web page, newsletter, or hypermedia stack.

*TV Special.* Produce a "special" or commercial to be shown on the school TV station.

*Internet Guide Stack.* Create a hypermedia stack designed to guide users through Web pages.

*Big Book.* Develop a book resource for primary classrooms. A primary class could be involved in the creative process.

*Poster.* A computer draw or paint program could be used to develop a poster. In primary classrooms, the teacher may want to use an LCD panel to create a poster in front of the class. The students could then color the poster after it is printed out.

*Slogan/Banner.* Have student teams create a motto that helps promote the wellness theme. It could then be printed out using appropriate software.

*Continued*

*Activity for an Elementary Class.* Have students in upper grades develop activities to be used in primary classrooms, then create a booklet of activities for teachers to use. If possible, they should field test their activity.

*Wellness Newsletter.* Design and publish a newsletter for the general public with articles, research summaries, and Web site reviews.

*Script for Skit.* Write and produce a skit that educates the audience about health problems. It could then be performed at a PTO meeting and videotaped for viewing on public access channel.

*Database of Food and Fat Content.* Have students bring in food labels from home and enter data into a spreadsheet and database. Spreadsheets can be used to calculate fat as a percentage of calories and create charts. Databases can be used to analyze trends.

## Example Lesson 11.2
## Developing Scientific and Mathematical Communication Skills

**Level:** Middle/secondary
**Required Resources:** A variety of math and science software and the required hardware

**Integration Strategy.** Integration to foster information literacy, integration to facilitate self-analysis and metacognition

**Directions for Lesson Activities**

*Setting the Stage.* In an effort to improve mathematics and science achievement in your school district, the school board created the position of mathematics/science quality supervisor, and hired a recent immigrant, Dr. Illova Textbooka, to fill the position. She has an excellent background in science and math and has worked in the Russian education system for years. Dr. Textbooka can best be described as a traditionalist. She believes the teacher should be the focal point in the classroom and that educational content should be delivered primarily through textbook readings, lectures, and teacher demonstrations. A sizable minority of the teachers, parents, and school board members agree with her.

This philosophy has created a problem for many stakeholders in the school district. They are convinced of the merits of educational technology and believe that if the district doesn't move forward with implementation, then their students will be at a great disadvantage in the future. Dr. Textbooka is in the process of allocating funds for next year's budget and has agreed to have an open mind toward educational technology. In order to gain input for her decisions, she has asked schools to prepare presentations that state the case for technology use in education. Your school welcomes the opportunity to demonstrate the merits of educational technology but now needs to come up with a strategy for the presentation. The pro-technology teachers and parents at your school believe that the best way to influence Dr. Textbooka is to have students deliver the presentations.

*Background.* Each student group will deliver a presentation to Dr. Textbooka that demonstrates an effective use of educational technology in the areas of math and science. Some possible areas include the World Wide Web, videodiscs, technology-intensive curriculum packages, simulations, and science probeware. Students should try to contrast good versus inferior products. They should also point out to Dr. Textbooka that technology is a means to an end and not an end in itself.

*Suggestions for the Teacher.* Discuss the scenario in detail. At this important phase, the teacher must present the activity in a manner that motivates the students. Students may be receptive to the idea of taping their presentations for future viewing. Explain the presentation procedure to the class. It is very important that students understand that they must develop an in-depth presentation; it should be a simple "show and tell." This activity has the potential to help students learn to communicate mathematically or scientifically.

*Continued*

Lead the class through a brainstorming session for the activity. Ideas will be general since the students have not focused on a specific technology yet. This activity will get the students thinking about the project. Brainstorming or mind-mapping software may be used but it is not essential.

Discuss various roles and responsibilities and how to divide up the work. Set tentative timelines rather than leaving the planning stage open-ended. Students will need considerable guidance at this point; project planning software may be helpful.

Divide the class into groups of four or less. Each group will develop its own presentation focusing on an area of instructional technology used in math or science learning.

Groups meet to plan and develop their presentations; the teacher monitors and consults.

Student teams deliver their presentations. The class may want to play out the scenario by selecting an adult to play Dr. Textbooka. Retired math and science teachers may be recruited to form a judging panel. Administrators from the central office may be invited to view student presentations.

# Exercises

## Record and Apply What You Have Learned

**Activity 11.1: Chapter 11 Self-Test**  To review terms and concepts in this chapter, take the Chapter 11 self-test. Select Chapter 11 from the front page of the companion Web site (located at http://www.prenhall.com/roblyer), then choose the *Multiple Choice* module.

**Activity 11.2: Portfolio Activities**  The following activities will help you add to your professional portfolio. To complete these activities online and save or submit the materials electronically, select Chapter 11 from the front page of the companion Web site (http://www.prenhall.com/roblyer), then choose the *Portfolio* module.

*Integration Skills*  Select one of the integration strategies from the chapter and develop a classroom activity for a science content area. Be prepared to teach or demonstrate the activity to the class. If possible, use your activity with the targeted age group before you bring it to the class. The lesson and your reflections on the teaching experience should be placed in your portfolio.

Select one of the integration strategies from the chapter and develop a classroom activity for a mathematics content area. Be prepared to teach or demonstrate the activity to the class. If possible, use your activity with the targeted age group before you bring it to the class. The lesson and your reflections on the teaching experience should be placed in your portfolio.

*Hypermedia/Web Page Authoring*  Develop a hypermedia stack or Web page project that is designed to teach a specific science or math content area of your choosing. Use the themes offered by the standards and the integration strate-

gies offered in this text as a reference point for your project. If possible, link the project to Web sites and, within your project, offer your audience guidance through the individual sites. You should also include review quizzes for when students complete working through a site or stack. Include a hard copy of the stack or Web pages in your portfolio.

**Activity 11.3: Questions for Thought and Discussion**  These questions may be used for small group or class discussion or may be subjects for individual or group activities. To take part in these discussions online, select Chapter 11 from the front page of the companion Web site (http://www.prenhall.com/roblyer), then choose the *Message Board* module.

All of us have a stake, as individuals and as a society, in scientific literacy. An understanding of science makes it possible for everyone to share in the richness and excitement of comprehending the natural world. Scientific literacy enables people to use scientific principles in making personal decisions and to participate in discussions of scientific issues that affect society. A sound grounding in science strengthens many of the skills that people use every day, like solving problems creatively, thinking critically, working cooperatively in teams, using technology effectively, and valuing life-long learning.
—National Science Education Standards Overview

The above quote makes a strong case for developing a high degree of scientific literacy among all citizens. Is this really necessary in the age of the Internet? Won't it be possible to easily contact experts or other resources that can compensate for lack of scientific knowledge?

The national call for the reform in mathematics teaching and learning can seem overwhelming, because it requires a complete redesign of the content of school mathematics and the way it is taught. The basis for reform is the widespread belief that the United States must "restructure the mathematics curriculum—both what is taught and the way it is taught—if our children are to develop the mathematical knowledge (and the confidence to use that knowledge) that they will need to be personally and professionally competent in the twenty-first century. Simply producing new texts and retraining teachers will not be sufficient to address the major changes being recommended.

—Mathematical Sciences Education Board, 1991

The above quote offers a rather pessimistic view on reforming mathematics instruction in this country. Will technology be able to expedite the process? Can we revamp our mathematics instruction by "teacher proofing" instruction via multimedia and Internet technologies?

**Activity 11.4: Collaborative Activities** The following may be developed in small group work. Completed group products may be copied and shared with the entire class and/or included in each person's Personal Portfolio.

*Evaluation* Work with a colleague and evaluate three mathematics and three science software products. Use the software evaluation form in Chapter 4. Include a copy of evaluations in your portfolio.

*Evaluation* Work with a colleague and reread the list of the principles/goals for the science and mathematics standards offered in this chapter. Select two each of the science principles and mathematics goals and locate Web sites or software products that exemplify the "spirit" of those principles and goals. Write a brief description of the Web sites

or software products and tell why the sites or products are exemplary. Include the written descriptions in your Personal Portfolios.

**Activity 11.5: Integrating Technology Across the Curriculum Activities** Use the *Integrating Technology Across the Curriculum* CD-ROM packaged with this textbook to complete the following exercises:

a. Technology resources frequently are used to make mathematics concepts more "visual" and less abstract so that students can understand them more readily. Find 5 to 7 example lessons in the CD that use graphics to make mathematics activities more visual. Review the lessons to answer this question: Is this approach used primarily at elementary levels, or does there seem to be a need for more visually-oriented mathematics learning at higher levels as well? Go to *Find Lesson Plan* and click on *Find by Criteria.* Under the *Technologies* descriptor, select *Graphics Tools,* and under the *Content Area* descriptor, select *Mathematics;* click *Search.*

b. How can probeware support an inquiry approach to learning scientific methods? Review lessons that use probeware and develop an answer to this question. Go to *Find Lesson Plan* and click on *Find by Criteria.* Under the *Technologies* descriptor, select *Probeware/MBL,* and under the *Content Area* descriptor, select *Science;* click *Search.* Write a description of how probeware supports the inquiry approach in these lessons.

# References

Baugh, I. (1993). Hooked on genetics. *The Computing Teacher, 20*(8), 17–21.

Becker, J. P. (1993). Current trends in mathematics education in the United States, with reference to computers and calculators. *Hiroshima Journal of Mathematics Education, 1,* 37–50.

Ben-Chaim, D. (1994). Empowerment of elementary school teachers to implement science curriculum reforms. *School Science and Mathematics, 94*(7), 356–366.

Bitter, G. G. (1987). Educational technology and the future of mathematics education. *School Science and Mathematics, 87,* 454–465.

Bitter, G. G. (1989). Teaching mathematics with technology: Finding number patterns. *Arithmetic Teacher, 37*(4), 52–54.

Brown, J. M. (1996). How do you use math? *Learning and Leading with Technology, 24*(2), 24–25.

Brown, J. M. & Verhey, R. (1997). A capital idea—project based mathematics learning. *Learning and Leading with Technology, 25*(3), 31–37.

Bruder, I. (1993). Redefining science. *Electronic Learning, 12*(6), 20–29.

Burrill, G. (1997). The NCTM standards: Eight years later. *School Science and Mathematics, 97*(6), 335–339.

Bybee, R. W., Ferrini-Mundy, J., & Loucks-Horsley, S. (1997). National standards and school science and mathematics. *School Science and Mathematics, 97*(7), 325–333.

Caniglia, J. (1997). The heat is on: Using the calculator-based laboratory to integrate math, science, and technology. *Learning and Leading with Technology, 25*(1), 22–27.

Coleman, F. (1998). I sing the body electronic: Students use computer simulations to enhance their understanding of human physiology. *Learning and Leading with Technology, 25*(8), 18–21.

Dahl, B. (1994). Windows on the world: Using literature to integrate the curriculum. *The Computing Teacher, 21*(7), 27–30.

DeVitt, T. (1997). Six reasons to infuse science with technology. *Electronic Learning, 16*(5), 41–46.

Enderson, M. C. (1997). Old problems, new questions: Using technology to enhance math education. *Learning and Leading with Technology, 25*(2), 28–32.

Friedlander, A. (1998). EXCELlent bridge to algebra. *The Mathematics Teacher, 91*(5), 382–383.

Hill, M. (1993). Mathematics reform: No technology, no chance. *Electronic Learning, 12*(7), 24–32.

Hoyles, C. (1994). Learning mathematics in groups with computers: Reflections on a research study. *British Educational Research Journal, 20*(4), 465–483.

Huang, S-Y, L. & Waxman, H. C. (1996). Classroom observations of middle school students' technology use in mathematics. *School Science and Mathematics, 96*(1), 28–33.

Kaput, J. J. (1994). Technology in mathematics education research: The first 25 years. *Journal for Research in Mathematics Education, 25*(6), 667–684.

Lehman, J. R. (1994). Technology use in the teaching of mathematics and science in elementary schools. *School Science and Mathematics, 94*(4), 194–202.

Lonergan, D. (1997). Network science: Bats, birds, and trees. *Educational Leadership, 55*(3), 34–36.

Lustick, D. (1998). Combining chemistry and the Internet. *The Science Teacher, 65*(2), 27–29.

Manouchehri, A., Enderson, M. C., & Pugnucco, L. A. (1998). Exploring geometry with technology. *Mathematics Teaching in the Middle School, 3*(6), 436–442.

Masalski, W. J. (1997). Powerful new math tools. *Electronic Learning, 16*(5), 28–30.

McClintock, E. & Jiang, Z. (1997). Spreadsheet: Powerful tools for probability simulations. *The Mathematics Teacher, 90*(7), 572–574.

McKinney, W. J. (1997). The educational use of computer based science simulations: Some lessons from the philosophy of science. *Science and Education, 6*(6), 591–603.

Mihich, O. (1996). Computing the water quality index: The Hudson River project. *Learning and Leading with Technology, 24*(2), 27–31.

Miller, L. M. & Castellanos, J. (1996). Use of technology for science and mathematics collaborative learning. *School Science and Mathematics, 96*(2), 58–62.

National Council of Teachers of Mathematics. (1989). *Curriculum and evaluation standards for school mathematics.* Reston, VA: National Council of Teachers of Mathematics.

National Research Council. (1995). *National science education standards.* Washington, DC: National Academy Press.

NCTM. (1997). *National Council of Teachers of Mathematics 1997–98 Handbook: NCTM goals, leaders, and position statements.* Reston, VA: Author. (ERIC Document Reproduction No. ED 421 343).

Nelson, G. M. (1997). Internet epidemiology. *The Science Teacher, 64*(3), 30–33.

Niess, M. L. (1997). Using Geometer's Sketchpad to construct geometric knowledge. *Learning and Leading with Technology, 24*(4), 27–31.

Pittman, K. (1997). Digital dinosaur discoveries. *The Science Teacher, 64*(9), 22–25.

Rice, M. (1995). Issues surrounding the integration of technology into the K-12 classroom: Notes from the field. *Interpersonal Computing and Technology Journal, 3*(1), 67–81.

Ritz, J. M. (1995). Lunar exploration resources in technology. *Technology Teacher, 54*(7), 15–22.

Robinson, M. (1994). Using e-mail and the Internet in science teaching. *Journal of Information Technology for Teacher Education, 3*(2), 229–238.

Roerden, L. P. (1997). *Net lessons: Web-based projects for your classroom.* Sebastopol, CA: Songline Studios and O'Rielly & Assoc.

Schwartz, J. L. (1992). Of Tinkertoys, technology, and the educational encounter. *Technos, 1*(2), 15–18.

Skovsmose, O. (1994). Toward a critical mathematics education. *Educational Studies in Mathematics, 27*(1), 35–37.

Slater,T. F. & Beaudrie, B. (1998). Doing real science on the web. *Learning and Leading with Technology, 25*(4), 28–31.

Slater, T. F. & Fixen, R. L. (1998). Two models for K-12 hypermediated earth system science lessons based on Internet resources. *School Science and Mathematics, 98*(1), 35–39.

Soloway, E. (1997). ScienceWare's model-it: Technology to support authentic science inquiry. *T.H.E. Journal, 25*(3), 54–56.

Steen, L. A. (1989). Teaching mathematics for tomorrow's world. *Educational Leadership, 7*(1), 18–22.

U.S. Office of Technology Assessment. (1988). *Power on: New tools for teaching and learning.* Washington, DC: U.S. Government Printing Office.

Weiss, I. (1993). *A profile of science and mathematics education in the United States.* Chapel Hill, NC: Horizon Research.

Willis, S. (1995, Summer). Reinventing science education. *ASCD Curriculum Update, 37,* 2–7.

Wilson, T. F. & Utecht, G. (1995). The Internet at Eagan High School. *T.H.E. Journal, 22*(9), 75–79.

Zech, L. (1994). Power on! Bringing geometry into the classroom with videodisc technology. *Mathematics Teaching in the Middle School, 1*(3), 228–233.

## Resources

### Math Software

*Adventures in Flight*—Sanctuary Woods
*Counting on Frank*—Creative Wonders
*Money and Time Workshop*—Scott Foresman
*Math Keys*—MECC
*Physics and Calculus, Probability Theory*—Cross
*Hands-On Math: I, II, III*—Ventura Educational Systems
*GeoExplorer*—Scott Foresman
*Mathematics Exploration Toolkit*—Sterling Swift Software
*The Mathematics Teacher's Workstation*—Sterling Swift Software
*Math Sequences*—Milliken
*Skills Bank II-Mathematics*—Skills Bank Corp.
*MicroWorlds Math Links*—LCSI
*TesselMania! Delux*—MECC
*Graphers*—Sunburst
*Unifix Software 2.0*—Didax
*Shape Up!*—Sunburst
*Mathematica 3.0*—Wolfram Research, Inc.
*Scholar 2.01*—Future Graph, Inc.
*Study Works for Math*—MathSoft, Inc.
*MathView*—Waterloo Maple, Inc.
*Derive 4.0*—Soft Warehouse, Inc.
*Geometer's Sketchpad*—Key Curriculum Press
*Green Globs and Graphing Equations 2.2*—Sunburst
*Virtual Tiles*—William K. Bradford Publishing Co.
*Math Type 3*—Design Science, Inc.

### Math Videodiscs

*The Adventures of Jasper Woodbury*—Optical Data Corp.
*The Adventures of Fizz and Martina*—Tom Snyder, Inc.
*The Perfect Pizza Caper*—HRM Video
*Windows on Math*—Optical Data Corp.

**Science Software**

*The Multimedia World FactBook*—Quanta
*The CIA World Factbook*—Quanta
*Science Cap*—Demco
*Ecology Treks*—Magic Quest/EarthQuest
*Balance of the Planet*—Brøderbund
*SimEarth*—Maxis
*Biology Labs*—Cross
*Operation Frog*—Scholastic, Inc.
*Visifrog*—Ventura Educational Systems
*The Lab: Experiments in Biology*—Mindplay
*The Science of Living Things*—Victoria Learning Systems
*Science in Your World*—Macmillan/McGraw-Hill
*CHEMiCALC*—Chemical Concepts Corporation
*Chemistry of Achievement I: Mathematics of Chemistry*—
    Microcomputer Workshops
*Water Budget*—EME
*Physical Science Laboratory*—Focus Media
*Science Toolkit Plus*—Brøderbund

*Temperature Experiments*—Hartley
*CBE MultiMedia Sequencer*—Emerging Technology Consultants
*Science Sleuths*—Videodiscovery
*Database of Images*—Digital Imaging

**Networks**
*KIDSNET*—National Geographic

**Science Videodiscs**
*Windows on Science*—Optical Data Corp.
*Weather: Air in Action Series*—AIMS Media
*Garbage: The Movie—An Environmental Crisis*—HRM Video
*Science Sleuths*—Videodiscovery
*The Great Solar System Rescue*—Tom Snyder, Inc.
*BioSci II*—Videodiscovery
*Interactive NOVA: Animal Pathfinders, The Miracle of Life,*
    *Race to Save the Planet*—Scholastic, Inc.
*Physics of Sports*—Videodiscovery
*The Great Ocean Rescue*—Tom Snyder, Inc.

# Chapter 12

# Technology in Social Studies Instruction

The words of this song are stained with our blood,
Within them are sorrow and grief,
Yet your camp song will carry beyond these barbed wires,
To a distant place unknown to you.

From the Piesn Obozowa, *Camp Song,* written by Zbigniew Kocsanowicz at the Falkansee Concentration Camp in Poland (April, 1945). On the U.S. Holocaust Memorial Museum Web site. Used with permission of the U.S. Holocaust Memorial Museum.

## This chapter covers the following topics:

- Current issues and problems in social studies instruction

- A description of how technology is integrated into social studies instruction

- Example World Wide Web site resources for social studies instruction

- Example activities for a variety of integration strategies in social studies instruction

# Objectives

1. Identify some of the current issues in social studies instruction that may impact the selection and use of technology.

2. Describe some popular uses for technology in social studies curricula.

3. Identify exemplary World Wide Web sites for social studies.

4. Create instructional activities for social studies instruction that successfully model integration strategies.

# Introduction

Since the Industrial Revolution, science and technology have shaped the world in fundamental ways. In the past decade, computer technologies and the emergence of the Internet have served to accelerate this influence. Better, faster, worldwide communications have made the world at once smaller and more complex. Life was simpler—and less informed—when people did not know so much about themselves so quickly. Now there is much more information to learn about the world and its people and more decisions to make about how we want our world to look and function.

The National Association for the Social Studies (NCSS) has adopted the following formal definition for the social studies:

Social studies is the integrated study of the social sciences and humanities to promote civic competence. Within the school program, social studies provides coordinated, systemic study drawing upon such disciplines as anthropology, archaeology, economics, geography, history, law, philosophy, political science, psychology, religion, and sociology, as well as appropriate content from the humanities, mathematics, and the natural sciences. The primary purpose of social studies is to help young people develop the ability to make informed and reasoned decisions for the public good as citizens of a culturally diverse, democratic society in an interdependent world (NCSS, 1994, p. 3).

As an area that focuses on the interconnections of people and the earth, social studies education has been affected by the impact of technology perhaps more than any other content area. Not only is there more to learn about the world than ever before, the information is changing constantly and dramatically. Fortunately, the same technologies that created this more complex world also can help teach about it.

# Issues and Problems in Social Studies Education

## Social Studies Instruction Standards

The national social studies standards were released by the The National Association for the Social Studies (NCSS) in 1994. Because educational standards were developed in social studies as well as many of the individual disciplines that make up social studies, it is necessary to point out the distinction. Social studies standards address overall curriculum design and comprehensive student performance expectations. The individual discipline standards for civics, economics, geography, government, and history provide more specific content detail. The NCSS hopes that curriculum designers will use the social studies standards for creating the overall framework and then fill in the detail using the discipline standards. The ten themes that form the framework of the social studies standards, along with a brief description of each, are presented below (NCSS, 1994).

1. **Culture.** The study of culture prepares students to answer questions such as: What are the common characteristics of different cultures? How do belief systems, such as religion or political ideals, influence other parts of the culture? This theme typically appears in units and courses dealing with geography, history, sociology, and anthropology as well as multicultural topics across the curriculum.

2. **Time, continuity, and change.** Humans seek to understand their historical roots and to locate themselves in time. Knowing how to read and reconstruct the past allows one to develop a historical perspective and to answer questions such as: Who am I? What happened in the past? How am I connected to those in the past? How has the world changed and how might it change in the future? Why does our personal sense of relatedness to the past change? This theme typically appears in courses in history and others that draw upon historical knowledge and habits.

3. **People, places, and environments.** The study of people, places, and human-environment interactions assists as they create their spatial views and geographic perspectives of the world beyond their personal locations. Students need the knowledge, skills, and understanding to answer questions such as: Where are things located? Why are they located where they are? What do we mean by "region"? How do landforms change? What implications do these changes have for people? This theme typically appears in units and courses dealing with area studies and geography.

4. **Individual development and identity.** Personal identity is shaped by culture, groups, and institutional influences. Students should consider such questions as: How do people learn? Why do people behave as they do? What influences how people learn, perceive, and grow? How do people meet their basic needs in a variety of contexts? How do individuals develop from youth to adulthood? This theme typically appears in units and courses dealing with psychology and anthropology.

5. **Individuals, groups, and institutions.** Institutions such as schools, churches, families, government agencies, and the

courts play an integral role in our lives. It is important that students learn how institutions are formed, what controls and influences them, how they influence individuals and culture, and how they are maintained or changed. Students may address questions such as: What is the role of institutions in this or other societies? How am I influenced by institutions? How do institutions change? What is my role in institutional change? This theme typically appears in units and courses dealing with sociology, anthropology, psychology, political science, and history.

6. **Power, authority, and governance.** Understanding the historical development of power, authority, and governance and their evolving functions in contemporary U.S. society and other parts of the world is essential for developing civic competence. In exploring this theme, students confront questions such as: What is power? What forms does it take? Who holds it? How is it gained, used, and justified? What is legitimate authority? How are governments created, structured, maintained, and changed? How can individual rights be protected within the context of majority rule? This theme typically appears in units and courses dealing with government, politics, political science, history, law, and other social studies.

7. **Production, distribution, and consumption.** Because people have wants that often exceed available resources, a variety of ways have evolved to answer such questions as: What is to be produced? How is production organized? How are goods and services distributed? What is the most effective allocation of factors of production such as land, labor, capital, and management? This theme typically appears in units and courses dealing with economic concepts and issues.

8. **Science, technology, and society.** Modern life would be impossible without technology and the science that supports it. But technology raises many questions: Is new technology always better than old? What can we learn from the past about how new technologies result in broader social change, some of which is unanticipated? How can we cope with the ever-increasing pace of change? How can we preserve our fundamental values and beliefs in the midst of technological change? This theme draws upon the natural and physical sciences, social studies, and the humanities and appears in a variety of social studies courses, including history, geography, economics, civics, and government.

9. **Global connections.** The realities of global interdependence require understanding the increasingly important and diverse global connections among world societies and the frequent tension between national interests and global priorities. Students need to be able to address such international issues as health care, the environment, human rights, economic competition and interdependence, age-old ethnic enmities, and political and military alliances. This theme typically appears in units or courses dealing with geography, culture, and economics, but may also draw upon the natural and physical sciences and the humanities.

10. **Civic ideals and practices.** An understanding of civic ideals and practices of citizenship is critical to full participation in society and is a central purpose of the social studies. Students confront such questions as: What is civic participation and how can we be involved? How has the meaning of citizenship evolved? What is the balance between rights and responsibilities? What is the role of the citizen in the community and the nation and as a member of the world community? This theme typically appears in units or courses dealing with history, political science,

and cultural anthropology and fields such as global studies, law-related education, and the humanities.

## Depth versus Breadth

Depth versus breadth—and its closely related issue of teaching for understanding—are major issues in social studies instruction, particularly in the history discipline. Standardized testing and many curriculum architectures tend to emphasize broad survey coverage and mastery of facts. Those who stress depth point out that covering historical episodes in a thorough fashion breathes life into the past and is pivotal to the development of understanding. Others counter that the study of changes over a long chronological period remains central to students' understanding of historical context. This issue is complex and not likely to be resolved soon. In fact, a broad consensus may never be reached. It is more likely that individual school districts, principals, school improvement teams, and front line teachers will ultimately make the choice of how best to educate their students.

## Perils of the Information Explosion

Information related to social studies topics and issues is prolific on the Internet; this ready availability of information creates several concerns. First, some believe that Internet information has the potential to alter the traditional relationship between student and teacher since students no longer depend on the teacher as a primary source of facts or opinions. Teachers tell of students bringing printed Web pages to school that contradict what the textbook says, or even what the teacher says. In the past, most information that students learned was sifted through some sort of filter; today, those filters often are nonexistent. Students can find sites that profess Nazi and Ku Klux Klan ideology, treat rumor as fact, and promote conspiracy theories that range from UFO landings in Roswell, New Mexico, to the CIA selling drugs in American cities. Even very bright students may be drawn to some of these sites and never question their accuracy.

Many educators believe we need information or media literacy now more than ever. Some believe that rather than shying away from the hate or conspiracy sites, we should be using them as demonstration tools to teach our students how to become critical consumers of information. As Harp (1996) puts it, schools must "mobilize their curriculum leaders into quality management" (p. 38) to monitor and help students become more analytical about the information they receive.

## The "History Wars"

Harp (1996) also describes a battle over world and American history standards that has raged over the last several years—a battle that shows just how important Americans view the teaching of history. The controversy centers around whether or not U.S. history curriculum excludes or marginalizes non-European cultures and fails to represent the perspectives of minorities. As Harp notes, the call for a "more inclusive history" resulted in a major project at UCLA to "draw up a new social studies curriculum stressing more multicultural themes and encouraging critical perspectives" (p. 34). However, the history standards released in 1995 by the UCLA project were so controversial that the U.S. Senate voted to disavow the group's work. Subsequently, social studies leaders have been working to develop a more balanced approach to these standards and the views of our history they represent. In the meantime, states such as Vermont have developed their own standards as well as a CD-ROM that they feel will "help teachers begin to make better sense of the myriad influences bombarding their history and social studies classrooms" (Harp, 1996, p. 38).

## How Technology Is Integrated into Social Studies Education

Social studies instruction traditionally has been "fact driven." The nature of the subject matter, with its historic dates and geographic names, certainly has contributed to this approach. In addition to organizing and presenting such information quite effectively, technology resources for social studies instruction also support a treatment of social studies content that many educators feel results in more meaningful learning. The book by Brown, Fernlund, and White (1998) describes these technology resources in some depth. They are summarized briefly here.

### Simulations

One way to make history and other social studies topics come alive for students is through simulations. Teachers use software such as *The Oregon Trail* (MECC) to help students understand the perils faced by pioneers; packages like *SimCity* (Maxis Software) to study economic and environmental issues; and series such as *Decisions, Decisions* (Tom Snyder) to study topics ranging from the constitution to urbanization. For example, a teacher may decide to use a simulation that creates a hypothetical environmental crisis in a small city. The students work in teams, each assigned a different role as campaign advisors to the mayor. The advisors are provided with written material that provides them with background information and social studies content. The team must decide as a unit on a series of decisions the mayor must make to deal with the crisis. The computer guides the teams through the crisis and records their decisions. Like many other simulations of its kind, a program like this enables the student to learn information in a just-in-time fashion, apply it immediately to a problem-solving scenario, examine situations from multiple perspectives, and work with others on a team to make complex decisions.

**Figure 12.1  Simulation Program**

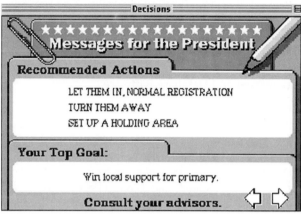

Source: Reprinted with permission from Tom Snyder Productions.

Although quite powerful today, simulations promise to become even more powerful in the future in conjunction with Internet capabilities and virtual reality (Kay, 1991). Other simulation ideas are presented here.

- A class uses Internet resources in combination with spreadsheet, database, and word processing software to plan a simulated trip to Washington, D.C. They plan all aspects of the trip including travel, itinerary, hotel accommodations, and budget.

- A class is given a scenario in which they have been commissioned to compile a "First Ladies" virtual museum. The students form committees and research the lives and accomplishment of previous First Ladies. They design and post a Web page that displays their project.

- A simulation program places students in the middle of an immigration crisis. They must work in teams to provide the President with the advice he needs to resolve the crisis (see Figure 12.1).

### Map Utilities

Through their graphics and animation capabilities, computers help students examine cartography in unique ways. One type of program lets students use a drawing tool to create a contour map and see a three-dimensional view of the terrain. Using technology in this fashion is an example of integrating to overcome logistical hurdles. Other map utility resources include programs that place the user in the role of a city planner who must lay out the design of the city while factoring in many social and geographic considerations and electronic atlases and almanacs that provide valuable resources for student research, let students plan trips, and make charts and graphs of geographic data.

### Global Positioning Systems

Another developing technology that promises to have an impact in social studies instruction is global positioning systems (GPS). These remarkable instruments are made possible by a satellite that pinpoints where the GPS signal originates, cross-references it with mapping software, and gives the exact position of the GPS location. This device may become a standard part of any geography classroom. For example, students connected together via distance learning can use GPSs to locate each other and to study their geographic locations.

### Spreadsheet and Database Software

With the rapid growth of automated systems to retrieve factual information, teachers now realize the need to teach how to synthesize and use data. Spreadsheets and databases can help address this need. Spreadsheets let students deal with numerical data, while databases help with text data. Brown, Fernlund, and White (1998) recommend spreadsheets to let students create projections and make predictions based on historical trends. For example, students can plot population growth and use this information to analyze the social, political, and economic consequences.

Database programs contribute extensively to many social studies areas such as geography, where such programs help students navigate through huge amounts of geographic data. Programs often go beyond just providing data; they also help students identify important information and guide them toward effective uses. Many database programs let students input their own data and then generate activities for them to do based on these data. Other databases make available vast collections of historical data that can help students search for trends. Such uses can help develop strong information literacy skills. Other database examples include the following.

- Primary teacher uses e-mail to solicit data on how many teeth her student's keypals have lost. This data is then entered into a database along with geographic data of the keypals. The activity encourages students to take an interest in geography (Boehm, 1997).

- Students use large databases like the CIA World Factbook to analyze demographic data and recognize trends.

### Multimedia and Hypermedia

These powerful resources serve to empower and motivate both social studies teachers and their students. For example, history becomes more visual and interesting when teachers incorporate photos, videos, and animations. Videodiscs, presentation software, and hypermedia are commonly used to introduce topics and to allow students to present the results of their research projects. Example multimedia uses include:

- Students using videodiscs to compile slide show presentations of geographical features (Etchinson, 1995),

- Classes using hypermedia authoring tools to develop political cartoons that present a variety of political points of view. The projects can then be displayed at open house or during a social studies fair.

- Students using a digital camera to take photos of local geographic or historic sites. They then put together a hypermedia presentation or a Web page that features their

**Figure 12.2** **Web Travel Expedition Site**

Source: Copyright © Classroom Connect.

photographs. Photo essays of historic field trips are another possibility.

### The Internet

The Internet arguably has more potential to enhance social studies instruction than any other curriculum area, not only because of its wealth of relevant information but because of its potential for "head, heart, and hand" learning. The Internet can help students acquire facts (head), do something with them (hand), and see better the value and impact of the information (heart). For example, it is exciting for students to follow travelers and interact daily with them as they pursue their adventures. Such activities make the study of geography more real and meaningful. There are a number of Internet projects that center on a wide variety of integrated curriculum units around the travels of individuals or small teams. Some travel by bicycle and visit Mayan ruins, some follow Amelia Earhart's last flight by airplane, some sail solo around the world. All have in common two compelling qualities: the ability to communicate with students in real time and the promise of adventure. Many of these projects are free, and all curriculum materials can be downloaded. Using technology in this fashion for social studies instruction offers an example of integrating to remove logistical hurdles (see Figure 12.2). Other uses of the Internet are described here.

- A primary teacher locates an expert on Zuni Indians. Her students use e-mail to ask questions of the expert. This activity seems to increase the students' motivation (Etchinson, 1996).

- As a part of studying different styles of architecture around the world, high school students consider five basic components of geography: location, place, human-environmental interactions, movement, and region. They then design a house that harmonizes with the components. They work with other teams around the world and offer their houses for sale. Spreadsheet, draw, and database software is used in this activity (Mollica, 1995–1996).

The sheer volume of educational technology resources available in social studies can be overwhelming. To help educators filter through the morass and select quality products, Rose and Fernlund (1997) suggest that the following questions be considered when evaluating the use of technology-based resources for social studies instruction.

1. Does the technology-based resource help promote *meaningful* social studies?

2. Does the technology-based resource help promote social studies that is *integrative?*

3. Does the technology-based resource help promote *value-based* social studies instruction?

4. Does the technology-based resource help in planning social studies instruction that is *challenging?*

5. Does the technology-based resource help in designing learning activities that *actively engage* students in significant social studies content?

## Useful Web Sites for Social Studies Instruction

- **National Council for Social Studies**
  (http://www.ncss.org/)

  This site includes archives of resources, professional development activities, student competitions, meetings, and a section devoted to guiding students through Web resources.

- **Smithsonian Institution**
  (http://www.si.edu)

  Resources found here include online publications and photographs, historical perspectives, and online tours.

- **Library of Congress**
  (http://lcweb.loc.gov/)

  This site contains a variety of excellent resources including sections on legislative information, library services, exhibitions, research tools, and exploring the Internet.

- **Edsitement**
  (http://edsitement.neh.gov/)

  Provided here are links and search capabilities for a number of sites dealing with the humanities including history. Study guides include detailed lesson plans and exercises that draw on materials from different sites.

- **Intercultural E-Mail Classroom Connections**
  (http://iecc.org)

  This is a free service designed to help teachers and classes link with partners in other countries and cultures for e-mail classroom, pen pal, and project exchanges (see Figure 12.3).

- **University of Oklahoma Law Center—Chronology of U.S. Historical Documents**
  (http://www.aw.oa.edu/ushist.html)

  This site offers full text versions of historic documents ranging from the Magna Carta to the German surrender of WWII to the most current State of the Union Address.

**Figure 12.3   Web Site for E-mail Exchange**

Source: Courtesy of Academic Computing Center, St. Olaf College.

- **The History Channel**
  (http://historychannel.com)

  This site provides many resources including audio versions of several great historical speeches, online simulations for students, and a "This Day in History" database.

- **Census Bureau Data Maps**
  (http://www.census.gov/ftp/pub/statab)

  With its links to state and county maps, this site provides a fertile area for lesson plans. Students enjoy perusing census data and seeing frequencies of various characteristics such as last names.

- **Current Events CNN Interactive**
  (http://www.cnn.com)

  A wealth of current events, news, and features, this site is updated frequently, giving students and teachers up-to-date information on worldwide events.

- **National Weather Service**
  (http://www.noaa.gov)

  This site lets students have the most up-to-date information on worldwide weather events as well as gives them links to local weather forecasting sites.

- **The White House**
  (http://www.whitehouse.gov)

  This is the Web site for the President of the United States (Teachers should be sure to have their students use the "gov" suffix here. At least one other suffix (".com") yields a Web site with objectionable content.)

## Sample Integration Lessons for Social Studies Education

Additional activities are available on the accompanying *Integrating Technology Across the Curriculum* CD-ROM.

## Example Lesson 12.1
## Students as Historians

**Level:** Secondary

**Required Resources:** Computers, hypermedia authoring programs, and additional equipment to facilitate hypermedia development and research such as scanners, Internet connection, digital cameras, video recorders, etc.

**Integration Strategy.** Integration to foster creativity

**Directions for Lesson Activities**

*Setting the Stage.* The faculty at Jane Goodall High School have recently begun to team teach across curriculum areas. Two faculty members pioneered this approach at Goodall: Ms. Sanchez, a history teacher, and Mr. Bono, an English teacher. They have taught as a team for the past two years and find that the areas of history and English are well-suited for integration. Sanchez and Bono have been busy for the past month guiding their 11th grade classes through a study of World War II. They now believe that the students have sufficient background knowledge to move on to the next level, which is the development of hypermedia projects. The teachers envision the students working in groups of three or four, and expect that the projects will take six weeks to complete.

*Present Scenario to Class.* As the country advances to a new millennium, those who lived during WWII are rapidly passing on. With them will pass their unique and personal knowledge of a world at war. In an effort to preserve some personal accounts of WWII, we would like to capture the reflections of local residents who lived through this momentous period. We would like this project to move beyond the traditional method of conducting interviews and then recording them on paper. We worry that these invaluable resources will end up collecting dust on a shelf somewhere. We would like to have the students collaborate with some of the local WWII generation citizens to develop a series of hypermedia projects that would help capture the essence of local life during the war.

*Suggestions for Teachers.* Students should select themes for their projects, for example: the homefront, women at work, women in the armed forces, race relations, rationing, when the soldiers came home, etc. Upon completion, the projects could be displayed on Veterans Day or Memorial Day in local libraries or malls. They could also be used by local schools for teaching, incorporated into a Web page, or put on a CD-ROM and sold for fund-raising purposes. If the logistics of interviewing people in person creates a problem, e-mail interviews may be substituted by posting a message to SeniorNet (http://www.seniornet.org), soliciting interviewees.

Source: Jack Edwards.

## Example Lesson 12.2
## The Big Splash: Problem Solving with Jasper Woodbury

**Level:** Intermediate/middle

**Required Resources:** The *Jasper Woodbury* videodisc "The Big Splash" (Optical Data, Inc.), videodisc player, monitor, and, depending on which follow up activities: Internet connection, integrated software package, printer

**Integration Strategy.** Integration to increase transfer of knowledge to problem solving

**Directions for Lesson Activities.** The *Jasper Woodbury* videodiscs are a series of video-based problem solving activities designed by Vanderbilt University's Cognition and Technology Group. The videos and their accompanying activities are designed to engage students in problem solving by presenting them with problem scenarios and challenging them to work together in groups to create a solution.

*Continued*

The activity described here is based on one of these scenarios: "The Big Splash." The problem students must solve is to help develop a business plan for the school principal to obtain a loan for a fund-raising project. "The Big Splash" integrates math and economics in a context that provides an introduction to business that is both relevant and engaging for the upper elementary and middle school student. The overall problem is multi-dimensional and includes the use of a statistical survey.

The program comes with extensive instructions for the teacher. The following activities are designed to be used as a follow up to the lessons learned during "The Big Splash" simulation. They are integrative but primarily focus on the area of economics.

*Loan Application.* Students request loan applications from a local bank and go through the process of filling them out. Teachers may contact local bank representatives to see if one can come to class and evaluate the applications.

*Develop Brochure or Web Page for Business.* Students work in teams of three or four and decide on a type of business they would like to start. After naming the company, they then use computer software to develop a logo and advertising brochure or Web page. Students may also create their own business cards.

*Design Layout of Offices.* Students use a drawing program to lay out the design for their executive offices.

*Allocating Resources.* Provide the students with catalogs from office supply companies and a budget for furnishing and supplying their offices. Students must then work as a team to allocate their resources. Since a process like this often is done using trial and error, a spreadsheet is very useful for experimenting with different options and keeping an eye on the bottom line.

*Examining Multiple Perspectives.* Students from one company write letters of complaint to another company. The students must then write letters of apology to the offended customers. This could also be done using e-mail.

*Expansion Plans.* Explain to the students that their companies are going to expand operations and set up facilities in new cities. Assign each company a new city and instruct them to research "quality of life" information for their employees who will be moving. Students can use the Internet to search for the information and then write a report on such factors as education, sports, cost of housing, museums, etc. A hypermedia stack could be developed in lieu of a written report; this stack should include buttons that provide links to useful sites concerning the new cities.

Source: Jack Edwards.

# Exercises

## Record and Apply What You Have Learned

**Activity 12.1: Chapter 12 Self-Test**  To review terms and concepts in this chapter, take the Chapter 12 self-test. Select Chapter 12 from the front page of the companion Web site (located at http://www.prenhall.com/roblyer), then choose the *Multiple Choice* module.

**Activity 12.2: Portfolio Activities**  The following activities will help you add to your professional portfolio. To complete these activities online and save or submit the materials electronically, select Chapter 12 from the front page of the companion Web site (http://www.prenhall.com/roblyer), then choose the *Portfolio* module.

*Scenario*  You have been teaching social studies for 10 years at both the elementary and high school levels. The emergence of the Internet and the World Wide Web has interested you, but you are very concerned about the proliferation of misinformation that has coincided with the growth of the Internet. You would like to do a presentation at the next state social studies conference to help alert your colleagues about the pressing need for information literacy in social studies instruction. Before you go through the process of applying to present, you need to search the Web for dramatic examples of erroneous or misleading information. Assume the role of the teacher in the scenario and locate some examples that could be shown at a presentation for social studies teachers. Be prepared to show and narrate your examples to the class. Include a written report of your findings in your Personal Portfolio.

*Integration Skills*  Select one of the integration strategies from the chapter and develop a classroom activity for a social studies content area. Be prepared to teach or demonstrate the activity to the class. If possible, use your activity with the targeted age group before you bring it to the class. The lesson and your reflections on the teaching experience should be placed in your Personal Portfolio.

**Activity 12.3: Questions for Thought and Discussion**  These questions may be used for small group or class discussion or may be subjects for individual or group activities. To take part in these discussions online, select Chapter 12 from the front page of the companion Web site (http://www.prenhall.com/roblyer), then choose the *Message Board* module.

- Discuss how the following description of the Internet may affect history teaching in the future. For example, what does it mean to the teacher when students come to class armed with three or four different perspectives on a historical issue? Is there any going back to the "one right answer" approach that many textbooks promote?

On the Internet alone, even the most misbegotten searches can lead to detailed information about any number of historical figures and events, from the life of Martha Washington to the christening of the *USS Arizona* to the 1942 Lee Street Riots of Alexandria, LA. Four different sources on the life of Napoleon may yield four distinctly different views of the French general (Harp, 1996, p. 33–34).

- Discuss the following description regarding gender bias in geography education. Do you think that technology plays a role in this gender gap? Is geography software part of the problem or part of the solution? How about Web sites? What would you do in your classroom to try to rectify this disparity?

The "Bee" (geography) has also shed light upon the apparent gender bias in geography education.... Of the 57 finalists sent to Washington each year, only a handful are girls; of the 60 students who have appeared in the televised finals over the past six years, two have been girls. That few girls make it to the final competition in the "Bee" then, "has nothing to do with the National Geography Bee," says one observer. "It

has to do with exposure to the geography through media." And it's the media, he maintains, that expose boys and girls to different kinds of geographic experiences (Checkly, 1996, p. 4).

**Activity 12.4: Collaborative Activities**  The following may be developed in small group work. Completed group products may be copied and shared with the entire class and/or included in each person's Personal Portfolio.

*Hypermedia Project*  Develop a hypermedia stack designed to teach a specific social studies content area of your team's choosing. Use the themes offered by the standards and the integration strategies offered in this text as a reference point for your stack. If possible, link the stack to Web sites and, within your stack, offer guidance through the individual sites. You should also include review quizzes to be answered when students complete working through a site. Include a disk copy and a hard copy of this stack in your Personal Portfolio.

*Software Review*  As a team, evaluate six software titles that relate to one of the social studies content areas. Use the questions offered by Rose and Fernlund (1997) as a guideline for judging the usefulness of the software. Write a response to each question for each software title. Include these evaluations in your Personal Portfolio.

**Activity 12.5: Integrating Technology Across the Curriculum Activities**  Use the *Integrating Technology Across the Curriculum* CD-ROM packaged with this textbook to complete the following exercises:

Young students frequently find voting and elections complex and confusing concepts. They do not understand exactly why people vote or how a U.S. president is elected. Technology resources can help clarify many of these concepts in visual and engaging ways. Go to *Find Lesson Plan* and click on *Find by Keyword*. Under the *Lesson Directions* field, type "election." Now click on *Find by Descriptor* and select the *Elementary* level under the *Grade Levels* descriptor; click *Search*. Review these lessons. Repeat these steps to locate lessons at the middle school level. Review all these lessons. Now develop a lesson of your own for elementary or middle school students that addresses an important concept related to U.S. elections.

# References

Bellan, J. M. & Scheurman, G. (1998). Actual and virtual reality: Making the most of field trips. *Social Education, 62*(1), 35–40.

Boehm, D. (1997). I lost my tooth! *Learning and Leading with Technology, 24*(7), 17–19.

Brady, R. H. (1994). An overview of computer integration into social studies. *Social Education, 58*(5), 312–314.

Brooks, D. L. (1994). Technology as basic to history—social studies: It's long overdue. *Educational Technology, 34*(7), 19–20.

Brown, J., Fernlund, P., & White, S. (1998). *Technology tools in the social studies curriculum.* Wilsonville, OR: Franklin, Beedle, & Associates.

Carroll, T. (1995). Carmen Sandiego: Crime can pay when it comes to learning. *Social Education, 59*(3), 165–169.

Checkly, K. (1996, Spring). Geography's renaissance. *ASCD Curriculum Update.*

Dyrli, E. (1995). Surfing the World Wide Web to education hot spots. *Technology and Learning, 16*(2), 44–51.

Eisner, E. W. (1991). Art, music, and literature within social studies. In J. P. Shaver (Ed.). *Handbook of Research on Social Studies Teaching and Learning.* New York: Macmillan.

Engle, S. H. (1989). Proposals for a typical issue-centered curriculum. *The Social Studies, 80*(5), 187–191.

Etchinson, C. (1996). Native knowledge: Asking questions by e-mail. *Learning and Leading with Technology, 23*(8), 70.

Evans, R. W. (1992). Introduction: What do we mean by issues-centered social studies education? *The Social Studies, 83*(2), 93–94.

Goldsworthy, R. (1997). Real world field trips. *Learning and Leading with Technology, 24*(7), 26–29.

Harp, L. (1996). The history wars. *Electronic Learning, 16*(2), 32–39.

Johnson, C. & Rector, J. (1997). The Internet ten: Using the Internet to meet social studies curriculum standards. *Social Education, 61*(3), 167–169.

Kay, A. C. (1991). Computers, networks, and education. *Scientific American, 265*(3), 138–148.

Lombard, R. (1995). Children, technology, and social studies. *Social Studies and the Young Learner, 7*(3), 19–21.

Marcovitz, D. M. (1997). I read it on the computer, it must be true. *Learning and Leading with Technology, 25*(3), 18–21.

Massialas, B. G. (1992). The "new social studies"—retrospect and prospect. *The Social Studies, 83*(3), 120–124.

Mollica, D. (1995–1996). Architects of the world. *Learning and Leading with Technology, 23*(4), 56–59.

National Council for Social Studies. (1994). *Expectations of excellence: Curriculum standards for social studies.* Washington, DC: Author.

Parker, W. C. (1991). Trends: Social studies—the newest reform proposals. *Educational Leadership, 48*(3), 85.

Parker, W. C. (1994). The standards are coming. *Educational Leadership, 51*(5), 84–85.

Peterson, G. A. (1994). Geography and technology in the classroom. *NASSP Bulletin, 78*(564), 25–29.

Rembelinsky, I. (1998). "Us" and "them" multimedia explorations of prejudice and intolerance in American history. *Learning and Leading with Technology, 25*(4), 42–47.

Risinger, F. C. (1998). Instructional strategies for the World Wide Web. *Social Education, 62*(3), 110–111.

Rose, S. A. & Fernlund, P. M. (1997). Using technology for powerful social studies learning. *Social Education, 61*(3), 160–166.

Rose, S. A. & Winterfeldt, H. F. (1998). Waking the sleeping giant: A learning community in social studies methods and technology. *Social Education, 62*(3), 151–152.

Saxe, D. (1990). A plea for rapprochement in social studies reformation. *Social Education, 54*(6), 351–352.

Semrau, P. (1995). Social studies lessons integrating technology. *Social Studies and the Young Learner, 7*(3), 1–4.

Shaver, J. P. (1992). Rationales for issues-centered social studies education. *The Social Studies, 83*(3), 95–99.

Shawhan, J. P. (1998). Civil war online, using the Internet to teach U.S. history. *Learning and Leading with Technology, 25*(8), 22–27.

Singleton, L. R. & Giese, J. R. (1998). American memory: Using library of congress online resources to enhance history teaching. *Social Education, 62*(3), 142–144.

Thomas, D. F., Creel, M. M., & Day, J. (1998). Building a useful elementary social studies website. *Social Education, 62*(3), 154–157.

U.S. Department of Labor. (1992). *(The SCANS Secretary's Commission on Achieving Necessary Skills) Report.* Washington, DC: U.S. Government Printing Office.

White, C. (1995). Two CD-ROM products for social studies classrooms. *Social Education, 59*(4), 198–202.

White, C. (1997). Technology and social studies: An introduction. *Social Education, 61*(3), 147–148.

Wilson, E. K. & Marsh, G. E. (1995). Social studies and the Internet revolution. *Social Education, 59*(4), 203–207.

## Resources

### Social Studies Software

Alpha Technologies
*American Media*
*Clip Art (2 volumes)*

Brøderbund
*Carmen Sandiego series*
*Where in the World...*
*Where in Time...*
*Where in the USA...*
*Where in Europe...*
*SimCity*
*SimEarth*
*SimTown*
*Maps & Facts*
*CIA World FactBook*—Bureau of Electronic Publishing
*Visual Symbols*—CMCD, Inc.
*Time Almanac: Reference Edition*—Compact Publishing
*Culture 1.1*—Cultural Resources
*Cyberian Base Map*—Cyberian Software

Davidson & Associates
*Headline Harry*
*Vital Links*

EarthQuest
*EarthQuest*
*Time Treks*

EduCorp
*History of Railroads*
*American History*
*CD SourceBook of American History*
*Grand Canyon*
*Indian Monsoon*
*Great Barrier Reef*
*3D Atlas*—Electronic Arts
*Australian Walkabout*—Envill Holdings
*Facts On File*—Facts on File
*The Revolutionary War*—Fife & Drum Software
*Infopedia*—Future Vision

*American Discovery*—Great Wave Software
*Grolier's New Encyclopedia*—Grolier Electronic Publishing
*Guiness Records*
*Websters 9th New Dictionary*—Highlighted Data
Intellimation
*Student Atlas Series*
*USA*
*World*
*Counties of the USA*
*Faces of the Presidents*
*Balance of Power*
Interoptica Publishers
*Great Cities Vol. 2*
*Astonishing Asia*
*Empire State Building*
*Angkor Wat*
*Egyptian Pyramids*
*The Great Wall*
*Venice*
*Inca Ruins*
*Taj Mahal*
*The Trans-Siberian Railway*
*The Panama Canal*
*Chartres Cathedral*
*From Alice to Ocean*
MECC
*Wagon Train 1848*
*Amazon Trail*
*US Geography*
*World Geography*
*Balance of Power*—Mindscape
*GTV: American History*—National Geographic Society
*The Cities Below*—Now What Software
Optical Data
*Communism & the Cold War*
*The '88 Vote*
*In the Holy Land*
*Martin Luther King*
*Powers of the President*
*Quake of '89*
Quantz Media
*Career Opportunities*
*Atlas Explorer Queue*
*Let's Visit Mexico*
*Let's Visit Spain*
*Let's Visit South America*
*Explorations*
*Magnificent Rocky*—REMedia
Scholastic
*Point of View*
*Hidden Agenda*
*History in Motion*
*Macmillan Dictionary for Children*—Simon & Schuster

Softkey
*The American Heritage*
*Talking Dictionary*
Software ToolsWorks
*Multimedia Encyclopedia*
*World Atlas*
*Capital Hill*
*US Atlas*
Tom Snyder Productions
*Mapping the World by Heart*
*Chronos*
*On the Campaign Trail*
*Saving the Earth*
*American History Pack*
*Critical Issues Pack*
*Urgent Issues Pack*
*Choices! Choices!*
*Immigration*
*Colonization*
*Building a Nation*
*Ancient Empires*
*Feudalism*
*Geography Search*
*RainForest Researchers*
Warner New Media
*Desert Storm*
*Clinton: Portrait of Victory*
*Sports Illustrated*
*Seven Days in August*
*Time Almanac*
*The View from Earth*
Wayzata
*The Washington Times*
*World FactBook*
*Who Built America*—Voyager Company
*The National Gallery of Art*
*Time Table of Science*—Xiphias

## Videodisc Programs

*ABC Interactive Series*—ABC News Interactive
*The Adventures of Jasper Woodbury*—Optical Data Corp.
AIMS Media
*The American Lifestyle Series*
*Had You Lived Then*
BFA
*Asia: An Introduction*
*South America People and Culture*
Coronet/MTI
*American Documents: The Lincoln-Douglas Debates*
*Roosevelt and the Fireside Chats*
*World Cultures and Youth*
*Eyes on the Prize: The Civil Rights Years*—Image Entertainment
*National Geographic Specials*—National Geographic

# Chapter 13

## Technology in Art and Music Instruction

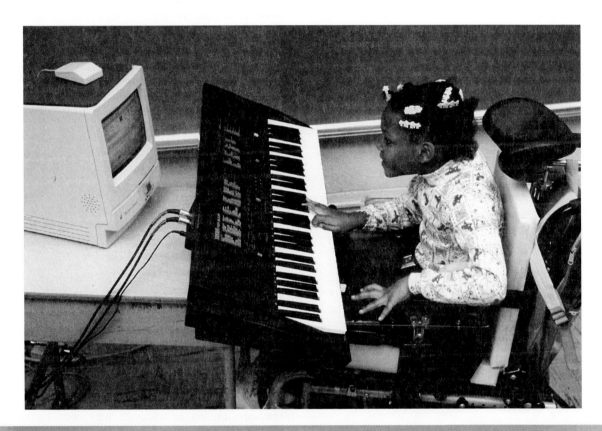

... Arts instruction provides many unique opportunities for students to hone analytical skills to critically evaluate the flood of messages that fill a technologically saturated environment. The communicative language of the new technologies—sound, animation, music, drama, video, graphics, text, and voice—is also the language of the arts.

R. Robinson and C. Roland, from *Technology in Arts Education* (1994)

### This chapter covers the following topics:

- Current issues and problems in art and music instruction

- How technology is integrated into art and music instruction

- Example World Wide Web site resources for art and music instruction

- Example activities for a variety of integration strategies in art and music

# Objectives

1.  Identify some of the current issues in art and music education that may impact the selection and use of technology.

2.  Describe some popular uses for technology in art and music curricula.

3.  Identify exemplary World Wide Web sites for art and music.

4.  Create instructional activities for art and music instruction that successfully model integration strategies.

# Introduction

Many arts educators have resisted pressure to use computers and other instructional technologies, complaining of contradiction in blending impersonal machines with traditionally humanistic endeavors. In reality, however, technology always has played a part in the arts. Over the centuries, technology has provided tools, materials, and processes that aided artists' creative expression. In more recent times, the phonograph in music and the camera in visual arts have changed people's definitions of *art*. The integration of computers and other forms of electronic technology represents the next logical step in the evolution of the arts.

# Issues and Problems Common to Art and Music Education

## Why Teach Music and the Arts?

A combination of the back-to-the-basics movement in the early 1980s and budget constraints in recent years has led many American schools to systematically dismantle arts programs (Fowler, 1989). The National Center for Educational Statistics estimates that almost half of all American schools have no full-time art teachers on staff.

The arts have been easy prey for legislators and administrators who believe they are less important than other subjects to a school's curriculum. Many assume that schools can either ignore arts instruction or cover it with the traditional classroom teacher. Many who consider art classes as educational "frills" do not comprehend tremendous social shifts. In fact, technological advances compel schools to place more weight than ever on teaching the arts. Arts instruction will help students develop the values and sensibilities that will enable them to function as healthy citizens in an increasingly artificial, high-tech environment (Robinson & Roland, 1994). A background in the

arts helps to foster uniquely human qualities like willingness to take risks and challenge convention, self-discipline, self-assessment, and a commitment to developing individual creative talents.

## Separate versus Interdisciplinary Arts Instruction

One way schools propose to keep arts education in the curriculum during a time of cutbacks is to use interdisciplinary projects to integrate arts and music instruction into other content areas. For example, an art teacher can collaborate with a mathematics teacher to have students build models of mathematical concepts, students can create illustrations and models for science projects, or history teachers can have students develop theatrical or musical performances and visual arts productions based on various historical periods. Quesada (1998) describes two examples of how this integration strategy can work.

**Arts and communications program.** One school's curriculum "interlinks art, drama, and music with English, French, history, social studies, physics, and chemistry" (p. 52). A student in this program said, "Being involved in art helped me to learn history" (p. 523). But some arts educators are dubious about the depth of knowledge art or music students can achieve this way.

**"Kids 'n Blues" CD.** Songs on this CD came from more than 650 students from schools in Memphis, Tennessee. This interdisciplinary project had students learn about the history and cultures that produced various kinds of blues "from early rural chants rooted in West African culture to rock 'n roll which mainstreamed the blues into American culture" (p. 56). The project involved reading, writing, mathematics, and the arts as teachers worked across grade levels to plan the curriculum.

## Standards in Arts Education

In 1994, the Goals 2000 initiative was expanded to include national goals and standards for the arts. The standards for the arts challenge schools to provide a broader and deeper arts education for all students. They suggest that students work toward comprehensive competence from the very beginning, preparing in the lower grades for deeper and more rigorous work each succeeding year. As a result, the joy of experiencing the arts is enriched and matured by the discipline of learning and the pride of accomplishment. Essentially, the standards recommend that students know and be able to do the following by the time they have completed secondary school. Students should:

- Be able to communicate at a basic level in the four arts disciplines—dance, music, theatre, and the visual arts. This includes knowledge and skills in the use of basic vocabularies, materials, tools, techniques, and intellectual methods of each arts discipline.

- Be able to communicate proficiently in at least one art form, including the ability to define and solve artistic problems with insight, reason, and technical proficiency.

- Be able to develop and present basic analyses of works of art from structural, historical, and cultural perspectives and from combinations of those perspectives. This includes the ability to understand and evaluate work in the various arts disciplines.

- Have an informed acquaintance with exemplary works of art from a variety of cultures and historical periods and a basic understanding of historical development in the arts disciplines, across the arts as a whole, and within cultures.

- Be able to relate various types of arts knowledge and skills within and across arts disciplines. This includes mixing and matching competencies and understandings in art-making, history and culture, and analysis in any arts-related project.

### The Arts in the Information Age

Many educators and members of the community question the need for instructional technology in the arts curriculum. Even some proponents of technology applications in other disciplines balk at investments in technology for the arts. Robinson and Roland (1994) offer four reasons to link the goals of a school arts program with rapidly developing instructional technologies.

1. By integrating new technologies into the arts curriculum, instructors expose students to new and exciting modes of artistic expression. All media have a place in the curriculum if they enable students to achieve desired instructional outcomes. New technologies warrant special attention because they constitute entirely new genres of art that may alter paradigms about art.

2. The new technological culture requires today's students to develop a whole new set of literacies that go far beyond computer literacy. Arts instruction provides many unique opportunities for students to hone analytical skills to critically evaluate the flood of messages that fill a technologically saturated environment. The communicative language of the new technologies—sound, animation, music, drama, video, graphics, text, and voice—is also the language of the arts. Thus, arts teachers are particularly well-positioned to help students develop skills as both critical producers and critical consumers of electronic media.

3. In the workplace of tomorrow, workers often will have to generate creative solutions to problems. An arts program that develops students' potentials for innovation in the areas of music, animation, graphics, multimedia, desktop publishing, and other emerging technologies will enable those students to compete in tomorrow's global business environment.

4. The arts counterbalance the massive infusion of technological change that society is experiencing. Technology can be seductive, and people need to keep in mind unique human abilities. Citizens of tomorrow's world will need coping skills that enable them to keep their aesthetic sensibilities in the face of breathtaking technological advances. Arts education will help develop and maintain these skills.

## Issues and Problems in Art Education

### Academic versus Studio

Many visual arts educators advocate redefining the field to give it a larger role in the school reform movement. They want to rethink who receives art education and how it is taught. In many school districts, students receive an hour or so of art instruction per week. The lessons often focus on producing some art products, leaving little time for curriculum that introduces students to other aspects of art, such as art history, aesthetic principles, or criticism. At the end of elementary or middle school, schools direct students with obvious talent toward elective courses that continue the focus on producing art. Critics of this approach argue that it reaches a relatively small number of students, and even then it narrowly defines art education. From a political perspective, this approach gives art educators a weak power base and subjects the discipline to the constant scrutiny of budget cutters.

But how can art instruction give all students strong art backgrounds that go beyond just producing art? Much debate recently has centered on a philosophy of art instruction called Discipline-Based Art Education (DBAE). Proponents of DBAE want to give students four kinds of broad and rich experiences with works of art.

- Making art (art production)
- Responding to and making judgments about properties and qualities in visual forms (art criticism)
- Acquiring knowledge about the contributions of artists and art to culture and society (art history)
- Understanding how people justify judgments about art objects (aesthetics)

Art production, art history, art criticism, and aesthetics are the foundation *disciplines* that make up DBAE. Critics of DBAE worry that studio training within art instruction will suffer and that students' creativity will be stifled. Some contend that proponents of DBAE are more interested in producing a population of museum patrons than in developing individual artistic expression. Others believe that DBAE's emphasis on academics will discourage students who may not perform well in the traditional classroom, but find the process of creating art fun and motivating.

DBAE seems to have influenced the development of the visual arts standards. Proponents believe that art will gain acceptance as a mainstream subject only by broadening instruction to include more than just students who draw or paint well. DBAE's supporters believe it offers just such a broad framework.

# How Technology Is Integrated into Art Education

## Hardware

The most common type of hardware resource in art instruction is image digitizing equipment. Graphic scanners are computer peripherals that transfer print materials into digital images on a computer. A scanner can transfer any image, photograph, line drawing, or text into a graphics file in a cost-effective and efficient manner. An artist can also capture an image from a video source (camcorder or VCR) using digitizing software. Finally, a digital camera records images directly to disk. This equipment provides the user with an extremely flexible system for developing digital images (see Figure 13.1). Students can then use computer software to manipulate digital images. This is a good example of using technology to foster creativity. Indeed, the ability to digitize still images and video has opened up a whole new genre of art.

## Paint and Draw Software

A wide variety of software is available to teachers and students who are interested in producing computer art. Simple paint programs are available for very young students; in fact, teachers often use these types of programs when first introducing students to the computer. Integrated software and hypermedia authoring programs always include fairly sophisticated draw or paint tools, which provide good intermediate tools for the developing computer artist. High-level programs suitable to the advanced artist would be used primarily at the high school level. One way a student might use paint or draw software would be to design the layout for a hypermedia project. By using these tools, a student who does not possess a great deal of artistic ability can produce a very attractive design. Using technology in this fashion models the strategy of integration to remedy an identified weakness.

## Animation, Graphics, and 3-D Design Software

Art educators can choose among a number of software options to let students explore graphic design. There are a range of animation programs, from simple cell-type animation to more advanced programs that offer features like "tweening." The latter enables the user to change one frame to the next by moving through as many as 64 intermediate positions in between. Other programs are specifically geared toward cartoon production and allow artists to add music and sound. Today's more powerful programs speed up the process by providing two-dimensional animation.

An art studio would not be complete without an image manipulation program like *Adobe PhotoShop,* which enables students to edit clip art or digitized photos. High-end programs provide hundreds of options and special

**Figure 13.1   Digital Camera**

Source: Anthony Magnacca/Merrill.

effects for altering images. Morphing software enables the user to transform smoothly from one shape to another. This technique offers tremendous potential for artistic expression and, by demonstrating how easily images can be altered, helps foster the development of visual literacy skills.

Finally, as Quesada (1998) described, students can use 3-D and modeling and animation software to communicate ideas visually through computer-generated models, animation, and imagery (p. 53). One such activity is in an interdisciplinary assignment called "Pocket Lint Project." Students use whatever they can pull out of their purses or pockets as the basis for developing a character. They use 3-D and animation software to create a model for their characters and use geometry to "convey a sense of emotion" (p. 54).

## Desktop Publishing with Graphics

Many schools look to their own graphics arts programs to create brochures and newsletters as part of student learning activities. Because students get such good experience creating and producing these publications, the activities can be considered a kind of internship to prepare for actual jobs as graphic artists in newspapers or other companies.

## Video

Videodiscs and videotapes have many programs that guide users through art experiences using a variety of approaches. Some study specific artists; others simulate journeys through famous museums. The high quality of videodisc images along with the technology's quick access give both students and teachers a powerful and flexible teaching and learning tool. Integrating high-quality, interactive video into instructions often enables the teacher to increase students' motivation to learn.

## The Internet

The Internet offers a number of resources that are helpful to the art student and teacher. Many museums around the world have sites that enable the user to take a virtual tour through the museum. Although clearly this is not the same as viewing the works in person, these sites do offer a way for students to easily explore and expand their knowledge base. Some sites make their server available for students to post their own creations and learn how to create using a certain medium like paper maché, batik, or origami (see Figure 13.2). Some teachers are using the Internet as a way to develop students' problem-solving abilities and to foster group cooperation skills by having students create their own Web sites. Others use these sites as the basis for multicultural "field trips" to gather examples of art and music around the world (Quesada, 1998). It is important to remember when using the Internet for arts instruction that the images are reproductions; students will need to be made aware of the idea of scale and constantly be reminded that they need to keep the limitations of digital imagery in perspective.

## Useful Web Sites for Art Education

- **National Art Education Association**
  (http://www.naea-reston.org/)

  This general arts education site contains useful information about NAEA programs and also has a long list of contacts in state education departments.

- **ArtsEdge**
  (http://artsedge.kennedy-center.org/artsedge.html)

  The Kennedy Center's national arts education dissemination network offers lesson plans, curriculum planning information, and other resources.

- **ArtsEdNet**
  (http://www.artsednet.getty.edu/)

  The Getty Center for Education in the Arts provides extensive curriculum, lesson plan, and resource collections, including a library on discipline-based arts education and a catalog of arts education materials for purchase.

- **Arts World Wide**
  (epals.home.minspring.com/ArtsWorldwide/default.htm)

  This is an EricPals course for grades 10–12 that promotes cultural literacy and creative expression through the visual arts.

- **Worlds of Art**
  (http://www.smartlink.net/~jcrane/intro/key-inqu.html)

  Worlds of Art is a curriculum resource that offers teachers ideas they can use to help students broaden their understanding of art and culture. Worlds of Art uses a discipline-based approach to art education; the lessons are interdisciplinary, thematic, and inquiry based. In addition to increasing student understanding of culture and art worlds

### Figure 13.2   Web Site for Art Instruction

Source: Courtesy of CraftsFair Online.

through its lesson plans, Worlds of Art provides professional development opportunities with a graduate credit option for teachers.

- **Berit's Best Sites for Children**
  (http://db.cochran.com/li_showElems:theoPage:theo:3531:0.db)

  This site lists and evaluates the best art sites for children and is frequently updated and covers a wide variety of art perspectives.

- **WebMuseum**
  (http://sunsite.unc.edu/wm/)

  This excellent site for students to learn about artists and art history contains over 10 million documents including many images and extensive biographical information on artists (see Figure 13.3).

### Figure 13.3   Web Museum Site

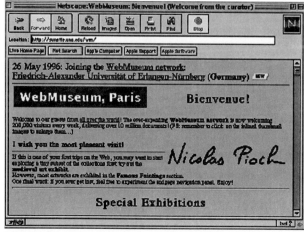

Source: Courtesy of WebMuseum, Paris, http://sunsite.unc.edu/wm/ and Nicholas Pioch.

- **The Art Teacher Connection**
(http://www.primenet.com/~arted)

This site has links to lesson plans and art resources on the Web as well as a student art connection.

## Issues and Problems in Music Education

### Theory or Performance?

The community of music educators defines a broad spectrum of opinions on how to teach music. At one end of the spectrum, some believe that music theory is a basic competence that students need to understand and appreciate music. At the other extreme, some believe that students learn by doing and should spend most of their instructional time performing music. The new national music standards offer a balanced interpretation of this issue.

A related issue in middle schools, and especially in high schools, concerns band competitions. Many music educators criticize perceived overemphasis on competitions that places a great deal of pressure on students and teachers for a perfect performance of a particular musical selection. They say students spend much time practicing a few pieces over and over instead of broadening their musical expertise and knowledge about music theory. On the other hand, supporters of band competitions note that this area of arts instruction in schools often inspires strong support in the community. Also, many music directors feel that students' involvement in competition does not rule out a good foundation in music theory and skills; both can be done if the program is handled well.

## How Technology Is Integrated into Music Education

### MIDI

The Musical Instrument Digital Interface (MIDI) standard enables computers, electronic musical instruments, and software to communicate. MIDI-compatible electronic keyboards are equipped with ports through which they connect via cables to other MIDI devices. The standard governs translation of analog musical sound into a digital format that computers can process. MIDI technology gives users a special ability to create, edit, and recreate music. It can be compared to the piano roll that allows a player piano to replay a tune. Holes punched in the roll trigger a mechanical device that plays a piano note. MIDI does what the old piano roll does but in a digital format. It assigns a number to every aspect of musical sound including pitch, length, and instrument. When the MIDI device receives these numbers from a computer, it plays the appropriate musical sound. Because MIDI is an industry standard,

**Figure 13.4   Music Editors and MIDI Synthesizers**

equipment and software from various manufacturers work together. This also has facilitated the widespread availability of MIDI files on the Internet.

### MIDI Synthesizers and Networks

Electronic musical instruments constitute the cornerstone of music technology. Piano-like keyboards replicate the sounds of both acoustic instruments, like the guitar, and original electronic sounds such as television sound effects. Synthesizers also can split tones to produce more than one sound at a time. In effect, this provides the user with his or her own orchestra. Ohler (1998) describes the many applications of this capability (see Figure 13.4).

Now it is possible to network MIDI devices in much the same manner as computers are networked. In such a network, students work at MIDI keyboards instead of computers. These keyboards are then connected to a single, teacher-controlled computer. This system lets the teacher monitor student progress and musical achievement in a very efficient manner. The student gets immediate feedback, which promotes independent development. Research has indicated that a MIDI network increases student achievement (Moore, 1992) and may also be used to remedy an identified weakness.

## Sequencers

Software in this category enables users to record, edit, and play back music. A composer can save short sequences and then easily manipulate them and paste them together to form larger works. In many ways, the sequencer brings to music composition what word processing software brought to the writing process. This use of music technology can often generate a motivation to learn on the part of the student. After saving work as a MIDI file, the user can easily transport the music and revise it virtually at will. This provides tremendous flexibility for musical composition and performance on any hardware or software configuration. In addition, programs are available that can synchronize music to film, video, multimedia presentations, or multitrack audio tape.

## Musical Notation Software

Musicians use this type of software to print scores for music they create using synthesizers and sequencers. It is a particularly helpful tool for students working on creative and composition skills. As with creative writing, seeing the results of one's effort in print seems to drive the creative process (Moore, 1992). This software also facilitates portfolio assessment. Some programs combine sequencing and music notation software, enabling users to edit any size score, lead sheet, or choral style.

## Multimedia Software

In multimedia applications, students combine music with video or animation. They can generate soundtracks with sequencers and synthesizers or record audio from other sources using microphones. Students can also alter sounds through cut-and-paste techniques. In addition, they can create special effects by playing sounds backward and changing their pitch or length characteristics.

## Instructional Software

Music teachers employ a number of types of instructional software. Some provide music students with ear training while other programs help students improve music and performance skills through guided exercises. This type of program records the student's performance and begins a new session at the previous ending point. Other types of applications teach various aspects of music like rhythm, melody, and form.

## Video

A number of Level I videodiscs provide recorded presentations of music performances. Educators like these resources for their high-quality video and audio outputs along with the capability of randomly accessing segments of music.

**Figure 13.5    Composers in Electronic Residence Web Site**

Source: Courtesy of Composers in Electronic Residence.

They include no software or teacher's guides, so successful applications depend on the teacher or students repurposing them. These programs provide recorded concert music along with analyzed scores, scholarly commentary, and slides of cultural and historical highlights. Individual students use some of these in-depth programs to facilitate self-analysis and metacognition.

## The Internet

As in many other content areas, the Web offers a tremendous resource of information. If students want to research an area of music like jazz or blues, they can find a wealth of information and listen to examples of the music. The capacity for music to be transmitted over the Internet will increase dramatically in the near future. The Internet becomes even more powerful as a resource when more sites like the Composers in Electronic Residence become available (see Figure 13.5). This site offers students the options of sending MIDI files to professional composers for their evaluations. This is an example of using technology for the purpose of optimizing scarce resources.

## Useful Web Sites for Music Education

- **American Canvas**
  (http://arts.endow.gov/NEAText/Community/AmCan/Contents.html)

  This is a landmark report on "Arts and Education" prepared by the National Endowment for the Arts.

- **Music Educators National Conference**
  (http://www.menc.org/)

  This site of the national music teachers group provides information about the organization and many links to resources on the Internet.

**Figure 13.6   Immersion in Music Web Site**

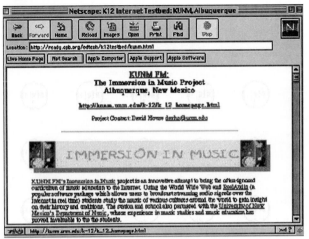

Source: Courtesy of KUNM-FM and the University of New Mexico's Department of Music.

- **Rock and Roll Hall of Fame**
  (http://www.rockhall.com/educate/lssnplan/index.html)

  This Web site has a collection of interdisciplinary lesson plans related to rock music and pop culture.

- **Technology Institute for Music Educators**
  (http://www.ti-me.org/)

  The Technology Institute for Music Educators (TIME) is a non-profit corporation registered in Pennsylvania whose mission is to promote technology as it applies to music edu-

cation. This page serves as a listing site for interesting applications of technology to music education.

- **Worldwide Internet Music Resources**
  (http://www.music.indiana.edu/music_resources/)

  This site, provided by the William and Gayle Cook Music Library at the Indiana University School of Music, includes a wealth of resources for instructors and serious music students.

- **Composers in Electronic Residence**
  (http://www.edu.yorku.ca/CIERmain.html)

  CIER is an interactive conference site designed to explore original student music in the classroom. Through a dynamic exchange of MIDI music files and comments, schools from Canada, the United States, Europe, and Japan communicate with professional composers.

- **Immersion in Music**
  (http://ready.cpb.org/edtech/k12testbed/kunm.html)

  Students study music of various cultures from around the world to gain insights on their history and traditions (see Figure 13.6).

## Sample Integration Lessons for Music and Visual Arts Education

Additional activities are available on the accompanying *Integrating Technology Across the Curriculum* CD-ROM.

---

**Example Lesson 13.1**
**Designing an Art Calendar**

**Level:**                         Elementary art
**Required Resources:**      Computers, paint and draw software, scanner, digital camera

**Integration Strategy.** Integration to foster creativity

**Directions for Lesson Activities.** Discuss with students the idea of using art they create on a computer in a calendar that will be distributed throughout the school. Explain that it will take a great deal of effort and time to complete a quality project. Each piece of art should have a title and the artist should write a brief description of the piece. The actual calendar portion of the project could be developed with a calendar-making program. Relevant school calendar dates should be included.

   This project can be done on a small scale by an individual class or, perhaps more appropriately, as a whole school project that involves the PTO and the art department.

Source: Jack Edwards.

## Example Lesson 13.2
## Creating an International Multicultural Art and Music Exhibition

**Level:**    Secondary/art and music

**Required Resources:**    Computers, Internet access, any equipment that would normally be found in an advanced art or music classroom

**Integration Strategy.** Integration to increase transfer of knowledge to problem solving

**Directions for Lesson Activities**

*Setting the Stage.* Wilson High School has acquired a great deal of technology over the past five years, but many of the faculty members are reluctant to use these resources in their curricula. The music, arts, and social studies departments have been an exception to this trend. Most of the teachers in these departments have embraced the new technologies with great enthusiasm. They have decided to put on an all-day presentation for the school and an evening program for the parents and community. They have in mind an international theme that models the integration of technology in a manner that will encourage other teachers and students to "take the technology plunge." The presentation includes the following activities.

*International Mentoring.* Students research various art forms like batik or origami. Via the Internet, they can contact students or professionals in countries where these art forms have originated or are popular: Indonesia and Japan. Students may then create a book geared toward helping elementary school students learn the art form.

*Web Page Projects.* Student art work and MIDI files may be added to the school Web page. In addition, a page can be added that gives other schools tips on how to set up their own music and art exhibitions. Any interesting cultural information that has been gathered from international sources can also be added to the site.

*MIDI Accompaniment.* Music students develop MIDI files to accompany works of art developed by art students. These can then be incorporated into a hypermedia project so that when the user clicks on a picture, the accompanying music plays. The project can then be set up kiosk-style for the exhibition.

Source: Jack Edwards.

## Example Lesson 13.3
## Compare and Contrast

**Level:**    Middle/secondary

**Required Resources:**    Computer, Internet access, projection system for computer

**Integration Strategy.** Integration to optimize scarce resources

**Directions for Lesson Activities.** Students use the Internet to visit art museums (WebMuseum, http://sunsite.unc.edu/wm/, is a good resource). They then research two different themes, for example expressionism and abstract expressionism, to compare and contrast them. The students then write a paper or develop a hypermedia stack and either conference with the teacher or deliver a report to the class.

Source: Jack Edwards.

**Example Lesson 13.4**
**Evaluation of Web Sites**

Level:                     Upper elementary to high school
Required Resources:        Computer with Internet connection

**Integration Strategies.** Integration to develop multiple intelligences; developing information literacy and technology skills

**Directions for Lesson Activities.** Ask students to examine thoroughly at least five art- or music-related Web sites. Initially, they should evaluate these sites for the quality of their art or music resources. After they have completed the initial project, discuss the various intelligences proposed by the multiple intelligence theory. Now ask the students to review the sites from the perspective of the various intelligences. Conduct a class discussion to see how perceptions of a site's quality differ when looked at from a variety of perspectives. Ask students to reflect on which intelligences they see as their strengths and which they view as a weakness.

Source: Jack Edwards.

**Example Lesson 13.5**
**Getting Started with Paint Tools**

Level:                     Primary
Required Resources:        Computer with paint software

**Integration Strategy.** Integration to promote fluency or automaticity of prerequisite skills

**Directions for Lesson Activities.** Many teachers believe that paint programs are superior to draw programs for students just beginning to learn the computer. Paint programs seem to be much more intuitive for young students. When first teaching students how to use paint programs, it is better to have a structured activity rather than just turning the students loose. For example, initially have the students draw a simple object like an orange. They can then progress to drawing leaves on the orange and then a tree on which the orange is placed. Gradually the students can begin to explore and develop their own ideas.

Source: Jack Edwards.

**Example Lesson 13.6**
**Study the Blues**

Level:                     Middle/secondary
Required Resources:        Blues music, computer

**Integration Strategy.** Integration to make learning efficient for highly motivated students

**Directions for Lesson Activities.** The teacher introduces the students to blues music by playing a variety of selections. A brief background is then presented noting the historical roots of this American music genre. Internet resources can provide a wealth of information about this subject. In addition, students can join a newsgroup and participate in dialogue concerning issues of the day in the blues community. Students then may decide on a variety of choices for projects, including presenting a self-generated MIDI program, hypermedia stack, Internet presentation, or art posters or brochures for a hypothetical blues festival.

Source: Jack Edwards.

**Example Lesson 13.7**
**Instruments of the World**

Level:                 Elementary/middle (music and social studies)
Required Resources:   Computer, *Musical Instruments* CD-ROM, Microsoft Corp., or other software resources, Internet connection if available

**Integration Strategy.** Integration to remove logistical hurdles

**Directions for Lesson Activities.** Students use Microsoft's *Musical Instruments* or other resources such as the Internet to develop a presentation for the class. Working in pairs, students select three instruments. The teams then research the development of the instruments. Upon completion of the research, they develop a presentation to be shown to their classmates. A logical extension of this is to make contact with students from the country of origin of their instruments.

Source: Jack Edwards.

# Exercises

## Record and Apply What You Have Learned

**Activity 13.1: Chapter 13 Self-Test** To review terms and concepts in this chapter, take the Chapter 13 self-test. Select Chapter 13 from the front page of the companion Web site (located at http://www.prenhall.com/roblyer), then choose the *Multiple Choice* module.

**Activity 13.2: Portfolio Activities** The following activities will help you add to your professional portfolio. To complete these activities online and save or submit the materials electronically, select Chapter 13 from the front page of the companion Web site (http://www.prenhall.com/roblyer), then choose the *Portfolio* module.

*Integration* Select one of the integration strategies from the chapter and develop a visual arts and/or music classroom activity. Be prepared to teach the activity to the class. If possible, use your activity with the targeted age group before you bring it to class. The lesson and your reflections on the teaching experience should be placed in your Personal Portfolio.

*Scenario* You have accepted a job as a coordinator for a new charter school that will center its curriculum around the study of art and music. Your budget allocation for art and music technology is $75,000. Prepare a budget proposal for the board of directors that describes how you plan to spend the funds. In the course of completing this project, you should contact teachers in the field, vendors, and col-

lege instructors. Keep a log of contacts and a summary of your conversations. You are encouraged to use the Internet as much as possible for your research. The final budget proposal should be included in your Personal Portfolio.

**Activity 13.3: Questions for Thought and Discussion** These questions may be used for small group or class discussion or may be subjects for individual or group activities. To take part in these discussions online, select Chapter 13 from the front page of the companion Web site (http://www.prenhall.com/roblyer), then choose the *Message Board* module.

*Rebuttal* Examine the quote from the introduction to the chapter. Robinson and Roland offer a compelling argument for placing a strong emphasis on teaching the arts in school. Working in teams of three, prepare a rebuttal to their argument and present it to the class. Handouts and computer-generated visuals should be a part of your presentation. Include hard copies of documents in your Personal Portfolio.

*Mechanization of Experience* Examine and discuss the following perspectives. Does Holzberg's point of view have validity or is she overly optimistic? Does viewing art electronically deprive us of the true experience?

Students who would never spend time in a regular "hands-off" museum can now examine the world's masterpieces electronically. Engaging interactive presentations make it easy, with a range of features that let them zoom in to study brush strokes, hear narrated commentary, create their own slide shows, and more. (Holzberg, 1997, p. 16)

I've been in cyberspace. My body has been sitting at the computer, but my mind has been navigating the planet. I can't help but wonder if such a disassociation of my mind from my body is healthy. Max Frisch, an acknowledged critic of technology, has said, "technology has the knack of so arranging the world that we do not experience it." (Gregory, 1996, p. 50)

**Activity 13.4: Collaborative Activities** The following may be developed in small group work. Completed group projects may be copied and shared with the entire class and/or included in each person's Personal Portfolio.

* Search the Internet for art or music-related Web sites. Select five or six that are appropriate for use in school either by students, teachers, or both. Now write an article for an educational technology magazine that reviews the sites and points out the strengths and potential uses of each. An alternative to the magazine article is to develop a newsletter to parents with some activities for the students to complete. Local resources might be featured. Include in portfolio.

* Working as a team, evaluate six software titles, three art programs, and three music programs. Use the criteria checklist for evaluating instructional software from this textbook. Include the completed checklists in your portfolio.

**Activity 13.5: Integrating Technology Across the Curriculum Activities** Use the *Integrating Technology Across the Curriculum* CD-ROM packaged with this textbook to complete the following exercises:

a. Art activities can be a natural and effective way for students to learn about and appreciate other cultures. One lesson that reflects this natural combination is "Interactive Videodiscs Help Teach Art and Culture." Review this lesson to get some ideas about how to support multicultural education through art activities. Go to *Find Lesson Plan* and click on *Find by Keyword*. Under the *Title* field, type "Interactive Videodiscs"; click *Search*. Adapt this lesson to create one of your own to show students how art is a reflection of culture.

b. MIDI synthesizers are becoming an increasingly common resource in music education classes. Moreover, they can be useful to support the integration of music into other content areas. Review a lesson that illustrates this. Go to *Find Lesson Plan* and click on *Find by Criteria*. Under the *Technologies* field, click on MIDI synthesizer, and click *Search*. Find an example of a lesson that uses MIDI synthesizers to integrate music into a content area lesson. Create one of your own that incorporates this strategy.

# References

Beckstead, D. (1996). Telecommunications and MIDI. *Teaching Music, 4*(4), 43–45.

Bell, B. & Vecchione, B. (1993). Computational musicology. *Computers and the Humanities, 27*(1), 1–5.

Berg, B. & Turner, D. (1993). MTV unleashed: Sixth graders create music videos based on works of art. *TechTrends, 38*(3), 28–31.

Bristor, V. J. & Drake, S. V. (1994). Linking the language arts and content areas through visual technology. *T.H.E. Journal, 22*(2), 74–77.

Brouch, V. (1994). Navigating the arts in an electronic sea. *NASSP Bulletin, 78*(561), 43–49.

Carlin, J. (1996). Videotape as an assessment tool. *Teaching Music, 3*(4), 38–39, 54.

Chia, J. & Duthie, B. (1993). Primary children and computer-based art work: Their strategies and context. *Art Education, 46*(6), 23–26, 35–41.

Dunn, P. C. (1996). More power: Integrated interactive technology in art education. *Art Education, 49*(9), 6–11.

Dunnigan, P. (1993). The computer in instrumental music. *Music Educators Journal, 80*(1), 32–37, 61.

Forest, J. (1995). Music technology helps students succeed. *Music Educators Journal, 81*(5), 35–38.

Fowler, C. (1989). The arts are essential to education. *Educational Leadership, 47*(3), 60–63.

Fuller, F., Jr. (1994). The arts for whose children? A challenge to educators. *NASSP Bulletin, 78*(561), 1–6.

Gouzouasis, P. (1994) . Multimedia constructions of children: An exploratory study. *Journal of Computing in Childhood Education, 5*(3–4), 273–284.

Gregory, D. C. (1996). Art education reform: Technology as savior. *Art Education, 49*(9), 50–54.

Heise, D. & Grandgenett, N. F. (1996). Perspectives on the use of Internet in art classrooms. *Art Education, 49*(9), 12–18.

Hicks, J. M. (1993). Technology and aesthetic education: A crucial synthesis. *Art Education, 46*(6), 42–47.

Johnson, M. (1997). Orientations to curriculum in computer art education. *Art Education, 50*(3), 43–47.

Julian, J. (1997). Basics for the art teacher online. *Art Education, 50*(3), 23–42.

Kersten, F. (1993). A/V alternatives for interesting homework. *Music Educators Journal, 79*(5), 33–35.

Klinger, M. (1995). The one-computer music classroom. *Teaching Music, 3*(3), 34–35.

Koos, M. & Smith-Shank, D. L. (1996). The world wide web: Alice meets cyberspace. *Art Education, 49*(9), 19–24.

Madeja, S. S. (1993). The age of the electronic image: The effect on art education. *Art Education, 46*(6), 8–14.

Matthews, J. & Jessel, J. (1993). Very young children use electronic paint: A study of the beginnings of drawing with traditional media and computer paintbox. *Visual Arts Research, 19*(1), 47–62.

McAdams, C. A. & Nelson, M. A. (1995). Beginners guide to the Internet. *Music Educators Journal, 82*(1), 17–24.

Michael, J. A. (1991). Art education: Nurture or nature: Where's the pendulum now? *Art Education, 44*(4), 16–23.

Moore, B. (1992). Music, technology, and an evolving curriculum. *NASSP Bulletin, 76*(544), 42–46.

Nolan, E. (1994). Creativity with instant feedback. *Teaching Music, 2*(3), 36–37, 55.

Norman, K. (1996). Introducing students to the world wide web. *Teaching Music, 3*(5), 34–35.

Ohler, J. (1998). The promise of MIDI technology: A reflection on musical intelligence. *Learning and Leading with Technology, 25*(6), 6–15.

Quesada, A. (1998). The arts connection. *Technology and Learning, 19*(2), 52–58.

Reimer, B. (1997). Music education in the twenty-first century. *Music Educators Journal, 84*(3), 33–38.

Robinson, R. & Roland, C. (1994). *Technology and arts education.* Tallahassee, FL: Florida Department of Education.

Roland, C. (1990). Our love affair with new technology: Is the honeymoon over? *Art Education, 43*(3), 54–60.

Silverman, M. (1997). 101 destinations: Great musical spots on the web. *American Music Teacher, 23*(4), 26–32, 83.

Tomaskiewicz, F. (1997). A ten-year perspective on visual art technology. *Art Education, 50*(5), 11–16.

Turner, D. (1994). Creating music videos with works of art. *Teaching Pre K–8, 24*(6), 55–57.

Wagner, M. J. (1988). Technology: A musical explosion. *Music Educators Journal, 75*(2), 30–33.

Wagner, M. J. & Brick, J. S. (1993). Using karaoke in the classroom. *Music Educators Journal, 79*(7), 44–46.

Webster, P. R. (1990). Creative thinking, arts, and music education. *Design for Arts in Education, 91*(5), 35–41.

Wongse-Sanit, N. (1997). Inquiry-based teaching using the world wide web. *Art Education, 50*(2), 19–24.

## Music Resources

### MIDI Interfaces
*Passport MIDI Pro Interface*—National Educational Music
*Roland MPU-IPC*—Electronic Courseware
*Sentech Mini MAC*—Electronic Courseware

### Sequencers
*Performer 4.2*—Mark of the Unicorn
*Master Tracks Pro*—National Educational Music

### Musical Notation Software
*Finale 3.1*—Coda Music
*Composer's Mosaic*—Mark of the Unicorn
*MusicTime*—Coda Music
*MusicPrinter Plus*—Temporal Acuity
*SoundMaker*—Allegiant Technologies
*Overture*—Opcode

### Instructional Software and Videodiscs
*Jam Session Bundle*—Queue
*Magic Flute*—Ztek
*Composer Quest*—Compton's New Media
*So I've Heard Vol. 1: Bach and Before*—Voyager
*Musical Instruments*—Microsoft
*Alfred Music Achievement Series*—Alfred Publishing Company
*Diatonic Chords*—Temporal Acuity
*Clip-Sounds*—Monarch Software
*FracTunes*—Quanta
*Play It by Ear*—Practica Musica

*PianoDiscovery System*—Jump! Music
*MetroGnomes' Music*—The Learning Co.
*Melodious Dictator*—Temporal Acuity
*Computer Karaoke for Kids*—Computer Karaoke Associates
*Anatomy of Music*—Tom Snyder Productions
*Kid Riffs*—IBM
*Julliard Music Adventure*—Theatrix
*Domingo Live from Miami*—Ztek
*Beethoven & Mozart*—Voyager
*Imagine the Sound*—Voyager/S.M.S. Optical
*Instruments of the Symphony Orchestra and Bachdisc*—Britannica Software
*The University of Delaware Videodisc Music Series*—Videodiscovery
*Mozart: The Dissonant Quartet*—Voyager
*A Little Kidmusic*—Arts Nova
*Making Music*—Voyager

## Art Resources

### Graphics Software
*MacPaint*—Claris
*Canvas 5*—Deneba Software
*New KidPix*—Brøderbund
*SuperPaint 3.0*—Adobe Systems
*FreeHand*—Macromedia
*Poser 2*—Fractal Design
*Painter 5*—Fractal Design
*Adobe Illustrator*—Adobe Systems
*ArtPad II*—Wacom Technology
*KidCad*—Davidson

### Animation Software
*Flip Book*—Intellimation
*FantaVision*—Wild Duck
*The Animation Studio*—Walt Disney/Buena Vista
*Cartoonin'*—Remarkable Software
*Specular Infini-D 3.0*—Specular International

### Graphics and Image Manipulation Software
*Adobe Photoshop*—Adobe Systems
*Morph 2.0*—Gryphon/ACS
*Photographer*—Brighter Paths
*Astound*—Astound
*PhotoEditor*—GST Technology
*Collage*—Specular International

### Instructional Software and Videodiscs
*Dabbler 2*—Fractal Design
*Draw to Learn*—Draw to Learn Associates
*BrushStrokes*—Claris
*Fresh Arte*—Quanta
*Graphics at Your Fingertips*—Vicki Legu
*Van Gogh Revisited*—Voyager
*Michelangelo Self-portrait*—Voyager
*The Louvre*—Voyager
*Draw and Color Funny Doodles with Uncle Fred*—Fred Lasswell, Inc.
*National Gallery of Art Tour Guide*—Laser Learning Tech
*With Open Eyes*—Voyager
*Visual Almanac*—Voyager
*Art Lesson by Tomie de Paola*—MECC
*Drawing With Charcoal*—Crystal Productions
*Early American History Through Art*—CLEARVUE

# Chapter 14

# Technology in Physical Education and Health

Schools could do more than perhaps any other single institution in society to help young people, and the adults they will become, to live healthier, longer, more satisfying, and more productive lives.

Carnegie Council on Adolescent Development

## This chapter covers the following topics:

- Current issues and problems in physical education and health instruction

- How technology is integrated into physical education and health instruction

- Example World Wide Web site resources for physical education and health instruction

- Example activities for a variety of integration strategies in physical education and health

# Objectives

1. Identify some of the current issues in physical education and health instruction that may impact the selection and use of technology.

2. Describe some popular uses for technology in physical education and health curricula.

3. Identify exemplary World Wide Web sites for physical education and health.

4. Create instructional activities for physical education and health instruction that successfully model integration strategies.

## Introduction

Many of the health challenges facing young people today are different from those of past decades. Advances in medications and vaccines have largely eradicated diseases that once were the primary threat to childrens' health. Today, the health of young people, and the adults they will become, is critically linked to the health-related behaviors they choose to adopt. The major behaviors that threaten today's youth are tobacco use, unhealthy diet, inadequate physical activity, alcohol and other drug use, sexual behaviors that result in sexually transmitted diseases and unwanted pregnancies, and behaviors that may result in intentional injuries (violence and suicide) and unintentional injuries (motor vehicle crashes). These behaviors usually are established during youth, persist into adulthood, and are interrelated; however, they can be altered through education.

Strong evidence exists that participation in health and physical education classes can help develop healthy behaviors in children. The most effective methods of instruction are student-centered approaches: hands-on activities, cooperative learning activities, and activities that include problem solving and peer instruction to help students develop skills in decision making, communications, goal setting, resistance to peer pressure, and stress management (Kane, 1993; Seffrin, 1990). Given the obvious importance of teaching students the skills necessary to maintain their well-being, it's ironic that so little emphasis is placed on these subjects in school. However, in an age when information is power, educational technology may offer physical education and health education teachers valuable resources in their efforts to inform and empower students.

## Issues and Problems in Physical Education and Health

### Lack of Student Motivation

School physical education has expanded from physical training and calisthenics to performance-related fitness and

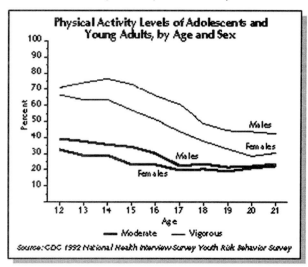

Figure 14.1 **Graph of Physical Activity Levels**

the behavioral competencies and motor skills needed for lifelong engagement in enjoyable physical activity. The Surgeon General's Report on Physical Activity and Health (1996) states that daily enrollment in physical education classes remained unchanged during the first half of the 1990s. However, daily attendance dropped from 42 percent to 25 percent among high school students between 1991 and 1995 (see 1992 graph in Figure 14.1). In addition, the percentage of high school students who were enrolled in physical education and who reported being physically active for at least 20 minutes in physical education classes declined from approximately 81 percent to 70 percent during the first half of the decade.

Participation in all types of physical activity declines strikingly as age or grade in school increases. Graham, Holt-Hale, and Parker (1998) point out that today's children are less physically active, in part because they spend more of their free time on television and computer games, rather than outside physical play. This society-wide trend affects both the motor development and health of our country's youth.

### Meeting Standards for Physical Education

The physical education standards, introduced in 1995, propose broad changes in the way physical education previously has been taught. Just how to get teachers and administrators to implement these standards is an ongoing concern. Drawing on findings from the School Health Policies and Programs Study (SHIPPS), Pate (1995) states: "Instruction practices in physical education often do not reflect the goals set by either the national health objectives or the National Physical Education Standards. Many states, districts, and schools provide students with less exposure to physical education than called for in the national health objectives and the activities most commonly included in physical education courses are more likely to be competitive team sports rather than lifetime activities (p. 312)."

The content standards in physical education (National Association for Sport and Physical Education, 1995) state that a physically educated student

1. demonstrates competency in many movement forms and proficiency in a few movement forms,

2. applies movement concepts and principles to the learning and development of motor skills,

3. exhibits a physically active lifestyle,

4. achieves and maintains a health-enhancing level of physical fitness,

5. demonstrates responsible personal and social behavior in physical activity settings,

6. demonstrates understanding and respect for differences among people in physical activity settings, and

7. understands that physical activity provides opportunities for enjoyment, challenge, self-expression, and social interaction.

## Meeting Standards for Health Education

Health educators note that the goals of schools are consistent with the goals of health promotion. Because healthy children learn better than children with health problems, schools must help address the health needs of students to achieve their educational mission. Educational technology can play a role in this crucial process. The Joint Committee for National School Health Education Standards developed the following standards to guide school health education.

1. Students will comprehend concepts related to health promotion and disease prevention.

2. Students will demonstrate the ability to access valid health information and health-promoting products and services.

3. Students will demonstrate the ability to practice health-enhancing behaviors and reduce health risks.

4. Students will analyze the influence of culture, media, technology, and other factors on health.

5. Students will demonstrate the ability to use interpersonal communication skills to enhance health.

6. Students will demonstrate the ability to use goal-setting and decision-making skills to enhance health.

7. Students will demonstrate the ability to advocate for personal, family, and community health (Sumerfield, 1995).

## Models of Health Education

One of the issues that the school health profession faces is which philosophical model to follow. Although the resources described in this chapter will be useful to promote any of these models, the materials and how they are used will depend on which of these models is selected. The most frequently used models include medical, pastoral, and community (Regis, 1998):

**Medical.** Changing behaviors to encourage people to avoid risk factors will improve their health. The teacher's job is to give pupils information that will help students make healthy choices.

**Pastoral.** Health education should try to put people in charge of their own lives: schools should develop pupils' self-esteem and self-awareness. People need to develop the skills and attitudes necessary to make healthy choices and put them into practice. Students will learn better if they are actively involved in lessons; good and varied stimulus material for group discussion is necessary. Teachers help young people develop a strong sense of personal identity and make them aware of society-wide emphasis on healthier environments.

**Community.** Health education in schools should be conducted in a community context. Health education should include and be involved with the process of implementing local environmental changes in order to promote health. It should take pupils out into the community and involve them in local research and debates.

## A Focus for Health Education

The list of issues and problems that confront today's youth is staggering. A major problem in the school health education field is what to focus on. Teachers complain of having to deal with problems ranging from suicide, AIDS, drugs, violence, and pregnancy. Teachers often ask, "Where do we place the focus?" Many health education teachers complain that they face a "topic of the year" mentality on the part of state legislatures. Some health educators believe that if the focus were placed on a "wellness" approach, then all of the other problems would, in time, be effectively addressed.

## Controversial Health Issues

Another health issue is how to deal with controversial subjects. In a time when it's difficult to reach any kind of consensus regarding priorities, many special interest groups can cause a curriculum to be watered down to the point of ineffectiveness. One area of particular concern is human sexuality. Many believe information and guidance on sexual decisions are essential, while others feel students should be taught that abstinence is the only choice and that teaching about a controversial subject tends to legitimize it in the mind of the student. Other controversial topics include date rape, suicide, drugs, violence, and character education. Technology resources such as videos and videodiscs can provide valuable insights on these topics as well as help to facilitate the logistics of instruction when only a subset of the total class is involved.

## Interdisciplinary Links with Physical Education and Health

School systems are moving away from requiring daily physical education and special courses on health. This trend has several consequences. First, it makes it less likely that students will get the physical activity and information they need to live healthier lives. Second, physical education teachers frequently must teach other subjects in addition to the content area for which they were trained. Often, they are given health classes to teach. Physical education and health are a natural "fit," but teachers lack training in methods of integrating them.

Finally, since opportunities for physical exercise and fitness concepts are becoming more limited, schools must find ways of integrating these topics across the curriculum. Mohnsen (1998) offers an example of a health-related fitness unit where health and/or physical education teachers focus on health issues related to diet and the benefits of physical training and conditioning; the science teacher explores how the digestive system works; and the mathematics teacher teaches word problems on the input and output of calories. As has been described in other chapters, technology can help with these interdisciplinary units with research support such as the Internet and presentation tools (multimedia) that let students show the results of their learning across the content areas.

## How Technology Is Integrated into Physical Education and Health

### Heart Rate Monitors

Several devices are designed to help people monitor, analyze, and improve their performances during physical activity. One such device is a heart rate monitor. Heart rate telemetry is a method of monitoring the intensity of the heart rate with the use of an automatic measuring and transmission device. Heart rate monitors come in various forms such as ear clips and watch-like devices (see Figure 14.2).

Students wear the heart watches around their wrists while an elastic band holds the transmitters around their chests. The transmitter senses the heartbeat from the heart's electrical impulses and transmits each beat to the wristwatch receiver through radio transmission. Target heart rate ranges are programmed into each watch so that the students hear a beep when their heart rates fall below their goals. Monitors can also be programmed to record data over a period of days. This feature can be helpful in integrating this technology to foster group cooperation. For example, heart rate telemetry can be used to set individual goals. Each student may strive to increase the sustained number of minutes devoted to moderate and/or vigorous activity during physical education or while at home. Other uses of heart monitors include the following.

- Heart-rate printouts are used for homework assignments. Teachers formulate questions related to intensity levels and duration of time in a training zone.

- Based on heart monitor data, the physical education instructor provides individual prescriptions to parents with

**Figure 14.2   Heart Rate Monitor**

Source: Courtesy of Polar Electro Inc.

suggestions on how to help their child reach suggested fitness levels (Strand & Reeder, 1993).

- Individual heart rate results from a previous day's lesson are used as a daily motivation for class members.

- By downloading data from monitors to computers and entering it into a database, students can maintain data over time to measure improvement in their physical activities.

### Video

Video cameras are excellent tools to help students develop physical skills (see Figure 14.3). For example, the instructor may record a student's tennis swing, then analyze the results and offer suggestions for improvement. Many newer model video recorders have 3" or 4" LCD monitors that allow for immediate feedback. In addition to higher-level skills, they can help teachers demonstrate activities that research has shown to be developmentally appropriate for each age in K-12 education (Pangrazi, 1998).

In addition, video cameras and other video resources may be used to achieve several objectives, including helping students understand what movement patterns are and how to analyze them and motivating students to improve by

**Figure 14.3   Physical Education Student Using Video Camera**

Source: Anthony Magnacca/Merrill.

showing their increases in skill over time. In addition, commercially produced videos can be used to demonstrate proper techniques, especially in cases when the instructor does not have the necessary expertise. Student-produced videos also can motivate students to learn the rules of a sport. One teacher had students work in teams to video-tape models of rule infractions. They then analyzed the rules and how to properly play the sport (Mohnsen & Johnson, 1997). Also, the special effects capabilities of VCR or videodisc technology can be used to teach students the beauty of sports.

Another way to use video in physical education is to show students videotapes of model performances or concept demonstrations. These video resources either can be created by the teacher or purchased from vendors that specialize in physical education materials. Trinity and Annesi (1996) suggest that teachers who use video cameras in physical education instruction should replay tapes immediately after a performance, use verbal feedback and provide cues while replaying the tape, use video replay frequently and repeatedly, zoom in to focus on specific aspects of a performance, vary camera angles, include perspectives of the environment, and watch a split screen or dual monitor.

Video resources also are an efficient way to remove logistical hurdles when teaching health-related issues. Resources that let students see the consequences of ill-advised choices, whether it be smoking, drugs, or poor nutrition, are extremely valuable to the teacher. Video resources also include video-based simulation programs that foster decision making and critical thinking skills on health-related topics and videotaped role-playing activities, an effective tool in conflict resolution, in which critical points can be reviewed.

### Software

**Software for physical education.** Compared to other subject areas, physical education has a limited number of software titles. This is not surprising since the focus of physical education has always been to encourage physical activity—in many ways the antithesis of sitting at a computer. One area that shows promise is software that puts students in charge of developing their own fitness goals and then provides guidance and feedback. Figure 14.4 shows an example of a software package that guides students through the five areas of health-related fitness: flexibility, muscular strength, muscular endurance, body composition, and cardiorespiratory endurance. This example demonstrates how technology can be used to make learning efficient for highly motivated individuals.

Software also is used in physical education in other ways. For example, spreadsheet applications can be used to calculate and graph individual or group fitness goals (see Figure 14. 5). In addition, commercial software is available that enables students to simulate playing a specific sport.

**Figure 14.4    Physical Fitness Software**

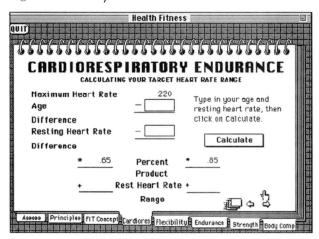

Source: Courtesy of Bonnie's Fitware.

By using software like this, students can develop game strategy and learn the rules of the sport.

**Software for health.** When attempting to get people to change their lifestyles and adopt a wellness approach toward their health, information alone is not enough. Software is available to guide students through the process of making changes. These programs help students apply their knowledge to problem solving. Record keeping, visual representation, and data analysis are all components of these programs. Software in health education is also used in the following ways.

* Simulation programs place students in situations where they have to apply their knowledge to solve medical or health mysteries.

* A number of software titles guide users through a study of the human anatomy.

* Teachers assign a report on a communicable disease; students can access up-to-date information on a variety of CD-ROMs that deal with wellness.

* A teacher assigns the class to study the side effects of commonly used medicines. CD-ROM resources enable students to quickly retrieve information.

**Figure 14.5    Spreadsheet for Class Activity**

| | A | B | C | D | E |
|---|---|---|---|---|---|
| | | NUMBER OF PUSH-UPS | | | |
| 1 | | DATE | | | |
| 2 | | | | | |
| 3 | NAME | 5/28/97 | 5/30/97 | Average | |
| 4 | Alice Thomas | 23 | 24 | 23.5 | |
| 5 | Bill Jones | 13 | 23 | 18 | |
| 6 | Charlie Angel | 24 | 34 | 29 | |
| 7 | Bill Cody | 34 | 21 | 27.5 | |
| 8 | George Fulbright | 11 | 12 | 11.5 | |
| 9 | Nelson Eddie | 12 | 10 | 11 | |
| 10 | Shelia Wilson | 10 | 22 | 16 | |
| 11 | Carrie Budde | 15 | 17 | 15 | |
| 12 | Angela Harcum | 16 | 19 | 16.5 | |
| 13 | Jo Jo Vinta | 26 | 28 | 27 | |
| 14 | Doris Dravos | 44 | 43 | 43.5 | |
| 15 | Class Average | 20.73 | 23.00 | 21.86 | |
| 16 | | | | | |

- Pangrazi (1998) recommends programs such as *Diet Analysis* to help students analyze their own nutrition and calorie intakes.

## Portable Technologies

Handheld and laptop computers offer great potential to physical education instructors. Assessment programs enable teachers to record observations of progress both effectively and efficiently. In addition, these programs also allow for a simplified way of handling class management chores such as grading and attendance taking. The data subsequently can be printed out in report format. This is an example of how technology can help teachers overcome the logistical hurdle of trying to assess and teach simultaneously. In the future, the cost of technology will continue to decrease; thus, it may be possible for older students to assume much of the responsibility for their own assessments.

Portable technology is also used to allow students to record reflections on performances; record and analyze statistical data on sporting events for various student projects, which can be especially useful for integrating mathematics and physical education; and record relevant data immediately upon completing an activity.

## Internet Resources

As in every other content area, widespread use of the Internet has made it easier for students to communicate and work together on health and physical education topics. Two ways of integrating Internet resources into these topics are described here.

**Web sites.** The World Wide Web has many good sites dealing with physical education and health education issues (Ellery, 1997). For the motivated learner, this resource offers tremendous opportunities. Figure 14.6 is an example of a health-related site targeted to young students. As students research health information on the Web, they learn to discern legitimate sites from those that simply want to sell a product or promote questionable practices. Students may use the Web to post information about the physical education or sports programs at their schools, including intramural events and results. Also, health and fitness information can be included on a school's Web page (Mills, 1997); physical education teachers can coordinate efforts with computer teachers and assign classes to do Internet research on a physical education or health education topic, and students can review Web sites to locate and learn sports rules.

**E-mail and videoconferencing.** An Internet search on "mentors" produces a large number of sites that facilitate on-line mentoring opportunities for students. When dealing with all of the complex issues in health education, a

**Figure 14.6   Web Site for Children to Learn about Health**

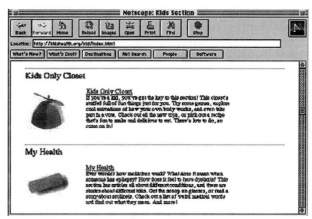

Source: Courtesy of the Nemours Foundation.

mentoring relationship offers great potential for promoting self-analysis and metacognition on the part of the older student. E-mail and videoconferencing may also be used to set up on-line projects with other classes around the world. For example, fifth-grade classes in different parts of the world collaborate on studying aerobic fitness. When they complete their research, they collaborate on developing a Web page that promotes respiratory system wellness. Students also are able to discuss the differences between various cultures with regard to subjects like drug use or government sponsored health care.

E-mail has been used to facilitate virtual competitions between physical education classes (Churchill, Pavionka, & Topp, 1995). Students who might otherwise be disinterested in running timed events will be excited about the prospect of competing against students from other cities, states, or countries. Activities that are easily quantifiable, like track and field or swimming, are particularly suitable for this type of project.

## Useful Web Sites for Physical Education and Health

- **American School Health Association (ASHA)**
  (http://www.ashaweb.org/)

  Resources for educators who wish to stay current on school health issues and information can be found here.

- **Center for Disease Control (CDC)**
  (http://cdc.gov/)

  This site offers a broad range of current information and is excellent for students and teachers to find quality information.

- **Center for Science in the Public Interest**
  (http://www.cspinet.org/)

  This site contains sections that can be used as supplements to health instruction such as nutritional quizzes, health facts, and a kid's index.

- **Go Ask Alice**

  (http://www.columbia.edu/cu/healthwise/index.html)

  This site lets the student or teacher ask questions about health and wellness issues. Visitors simply send in their questions, which are then answered by a team of experts from the Columbia University Health Question & Answer Service.

- **Kids Health**

  (http://www.kidshealth.org/)

  This site helps parents, children, and professionals find answers to commonly asked health questions. Topics include the benefits of different types of vitamins, the food pyramid, healthy children's recipes, how to read food labels, and keeping fit. Children can also submit their own questions.

- **Drug Related Street Terms/Slang Words**

  (http://www.addictions.org/slang.htm)

  This site is full of information dealing with different types of drugs. Some of the features to this site include an alphabetic listing of slang words related to drug use and abuse and their meanings, a breakdown of different categories of drugs with signs and symptoms of abuse, and characteristics and information on specific substances. This site can be very helpful for students who need to research drug abuse and illegal substances.

- **National Association for Sport and Physical Education**

  (http://aahperd.org/)

  A good resource for the teacher and interested students, this site offers links to physical education standards and other materials

- **PE Central**

  (http://www.chre.vt.edu/~/pe.central/PEC2.html)

  This site provides an abundance of resources for highschool students and instructors. Resources include lesson plans, Web links, adapted PE, and equipment information.

- **Fitness Partner Connection**

  (http://primusweb.com/fitnesspartner/)

  This site contains the Fitness Library that provides visitors with a variety of short articles about health and physical activity and tips for purchasing fitness equipment and provides a number of links to health and physical activity sites that may prove beneficial to physical education teachers. Also included is an activity calorie calculator that lets students type in weight and duration of activity and then instantly computes how many calories are burned.

- **Fitlife**

  (http://fitlife.com/)

  This site provides a wealth of information dealing with many health-related issues such as fitness, health promotion, wellness, and lifestyles.

- **The Fitness Files**

  http://sunsentinel.webpoint.com/fitness/)

  This site offers four main areas to navigate: Fitness Fundamentals, Get Active, The Injurenet, and Fuel for Fitness. Within these links, students can learn the basic principles of fitness, how to calculate their target heart rates, which activities can help them stay active, how to stretch properly, and what foods are essential for a healthy diet.

## Sample Integration Lessons for Physical Education and Health

Additional lessons are available on the accompanying *Integrating Technology Across the Curriculum* CD-ROM.

---

### Example Lesson 14.1
### Developing a Violence Prevention Newsletter

**Level:**    Middle school/high school

**Required Resources:**    Desktop publishing program, scanner, camera, printer

**Integration Strategy.** Integration to facilitate self-analysis and metacognition

**Directions for Lesson Activities**

*Rationale.* Violent behavior is a major problem in many high schools. School health teachers often are assigned the task of teaching conflict management skills. This activity offers a process approach that actively engages the school population. The process of working on a project like this involves the students in thinking about their thinking.

*Continued*

*Setting the Stage.* The student council at Southside High School has decided to launch an anti-violence program. One of the council members approaches Ms. Ramirez, the health teacher, to seek guidance. Ms. Ramirez agrees to help and the next day broaches the subject with her classes. In the course of her conversations with students, Ms. Ramirez realizes that many situations exist where conflicts are resolved without the students resorting to violence. Later, she comes up with the idea for an anti-violence newspaper that relies on students' stories of how they resolved conflicts peacefully. Ms. Ramirez discusses the idea with the technology and English teachers and they decide to work as a team on the project.

*Interviews.* Students interview classmates who have resolved conflict peacefully. The interviews are then published in a school newsletter. A variety of topics can be covered in one newsletter or a number of newsletters may be produced throughout the school year, each one focusing on a specific type of conflict. Types of conflict may include student/teacher, student/parent, athlete/coach, boyfriend/girlfriend, gang, etc.

*The Technology Connection.* Desktop publishing programs are used to create the newsletter. A scanner or digital camera is used for pictures. The project can be publicized on the school Web page along with a call for people to come forward with their stories. The Internet may also be used for research on newspaper design or to look for similar projects at other schools.

*Suggestions for Teachers.* The best place to use the newsletter is in the classroom as a way to facilitate group discussions.

Source: Jack Edwards.

## Example Lesson 14.2
## Well, Well, Well!

**Level:** Upper elementary
**Required Resources:** Computers, Web page software, integrated software package, printer, Internet connection.

**Integration Strategy.** Integration to foster creativity

**Directions for Lesson Activities**
*Setting the Stage.* The fifth-grade team at Rosa Parks Elementary School has decided to work with their classes on a "wellness unit." They plan on integrating all of the subject areas into the wellness theme. A core facet of the plan is to positively affect the exercise and dietary habits of students and their families. Internet technology will be one of the key components of the plan.

*Planning.* Teachers and students formulate a plan that will encourage their families to increase their level of wellness. The plan may include things like attitudinal surveys, pre- and posttests on health and fitness knowledge, and e-mail collections of data on fitness levels of the families. Students can use database and spreadsheet software to record, compute, and analyze data.

*Research.* Students search the Internet for Web sites geared toward helping individuals and families achieve a higher degree of wellness. They should look for interactive sites, for example, ones that allow users to ask specific questions or that provide opportunities for users to enter personal data and get feedback on fitness or nutrition levels.

*Web Site.* Students design a Web site that explains the project and provides links to helpful Internet sites.

*Wrap Up.* The unit culminates with a healthy picnic and fitness field day for families participating in the program.

Source: Jack Edwards.

## Example Lesson 14.3
## Let's Do It Right

**Required Resources:**    Video camera, playback device

**Integration Strategy.** Integration to remedy identified weaknesses

**Directions for Lesson Activities.** In the course of teaching a particular skill, for example the overhand throw, the physical education teacher notices which students are having a difficult time completing the task. While the rest of the class is working cooperatively, she uses the video camera to record the efforts of students who are struggling. She then plays back their efforts and provides them with additional instruction.

Source: Jack Edwards.

## Example Lesson 14.4
## Physical Education with a Heartbeat

**Required Resources:**    Heart rate monitor

**Integration Strategy.** Integration to make learning efficient for highly motivated students

**Directions for Lesson Activities.** Heart rate watches are used to monitor endurance workouts. At the beginning of a class period, distance and heart rate intensity are assigned. For example, the teacher may assign a one-mile distance at a heart rate intensity of 60 percent. During the workout, class members exercise in their respective groups, the leader being the student with the monitor. Subsequently, individual results from the previous day are used as a daily motivation for class members.

Source: Jack Edwards.

## Example Lesson 14.5
## Dealing with Complex Problems

**Required Resources:**    *SimHealth,* Maxis Corporation

**Integration Strategy.** Integration to increase transfer of knowledge to problem solving

**Directions for Lesson Activities.** This simulation program enables students to explore the impact of changes in government, health manpower, funding, taxation, and politics in the health of a community.

Source: Jack Edwards.

## Example Lesson 14.6
## "Just Say No: Is It That Easy?"

**Required Resources:**  *Decisions/Decisions: Substance Abuse 5.0,* Tom Snyder Productions

**Integration Strategy.** Integration to foster group cooperation

**Directions for Lesson Activities.** This simulation program has student teams confront peer pressure, responsible versus irresponsible behavior, and relationships with authority. Students set goals, look at facts, and weigh divergent points of view. Finally, they make decisions and face consequences. The computer and accompanying booklets guide students through the decision-making process.

Source: Jack Edwards.

## Example Lesson 14.7
## Are We Getting Enough Oxygen?

**Required Resources:**  *National Geographic Kids Network,* National Geographic

**Integration Strategy.** Integration to generate motivation to learn

**Directions for Lesson Activities.** Students investigate the human body's respiratory and circulatory systems and test their own vital capacities, including aerobic activity levels and recovery times. By exchanging data with teammates from around the world via telecommunications, student-scientists understand how individual behavior can affect their health.

Source: Jack Edwards.

## Example Lesson 14.8
## Long Distance Track Meet

**Required Resources:**  Computer, e-mail

**Integration Strategy.** Integration to optimize scarce resources

**Directions for Lesson Activities.** Teachers use e-mail to arrange a virtual competition between schools. Physical education students from several schools compete in track and field events at their respective sites. Spreadsheets are used to tally results. Scores are exchanged and winners are announced via e-mail. This is a great way to develop a sense of teamwork among physical education classes. By using the metric system, this can be done with classes around the world. Another option, and a way of encouraging participation by non-athletic students, would be to measure a student's improvement over a baseline score rather than measuring the fastest run or longest throw.

Source: Jack Edwards.

**Example Lesson 14.9**
**The Great Debate**

**Required Resources:**   Internet and other resources. In order to save time, the teacher may provide the students with some relevant Web site URLs.

**Integration Strategy.** Developing information literacy and technology skills

**Directions for Lesson Activities.** Select a health-related topic that can be approached from multiple perspectives. An example might be the use of illegal drugs in the United States. The students are asked to use the Internet to research at least three different perspectives on the problem. In this case, they may be decriminalization, treatment, and law and order. After the students are thoroughly familiar with each approach, ask them to choose which one they favor. Next, assign each student a position that is not his first choice and ask him to prepare to debate from that perspective.

Source: Jack Edwards.

**Example Lesson 14.10**
**Designing a Wellness Campaign**

**Required Resources:**   Computer, printer, graphics, Web site, and desktop publishing programs

**Integration Strategies.** Integration to foster visual literacy

**Directions for Lesson Activities.** Students use the Internet and other resources to develop a promotional campaign to encourage people to take personal responsibility for their health. The campaign can include many activities that offer opportunities for the student to improve visual literacy skills, including graphic design, Web site design, video production, using persuasive language, etc.

Source: Jack Edwards.

**Example Lesson 14.11**
**Developing a Knowledge Navigator**

**Required Resources:**   Hypermedia authoring program with Internet access

**Integration Strategy.** Integration to develop multiple intelligences

**Directions for Lesson Activities.** Each student selects a topic related to health or physical education. An example might be the use of tobacco "dip" by athletes and the health risk it poses. The student then creates a hypermedia stack that focuses on "adding value" to Internet information. In other words, the stack helps the "audience" filter through the information on the Internet and guides the user through a reflective look at the issue. The hypermedia authoring process provides the developer the opportunity to use a number of the intelligences.

Source: Jack Edwards.

# Exercises

## Record and Apply What You Have Learned

**Activity 14.1: Chapter 14 Self-Test**  To review terms and concepts in this chapter, take the Chapter 14 self-test. Select Chapter 14 from the front page of the companion Web site (located at http://www.prenhall.com/roblyer), then choose the *Multiple Choice* module.

**Activity 14.2: Portfolio Activities**  The following activities will help you add to your professional portfolio. To complete these activities online and save or submit the materials electronically, select Chapter 14 from the front page of the companion Web site (http://www.prenhall.com/roblyer), then choose the *Portfolio* module.

*Integration*  Create an activity in an elementary setting that encourages students to engage in exercise activities such as walking around the campus each day. Include a spreadsheet template for recording distances and charting progress and an example of computer-generated advertising. In addition, develop flyers and sign-up sheets for the activity. Place a copy of all products in your Personal Portfolio.

*Research*  Contact a health teacher who is interested in having her classes work on research projects using the Internet. Offer to do some preliminary research for the class. You then need to compile a list of quality Web sites that are useful to the students. Provide the teacher with a disk copy of the bookmarks or a simple hypermedia stack that includes buttons to the links.

**Activity 14.3: Questions for Thought and Discussion**  These questions may be used for small group or class discussion or may be subjects for individual or group activities. To take part in these discussions online, select Chapter 14 from the front page of the companion Web site (http://www.prenhall.com/roblyer), then choose the *Message Board* module.

> Support is greatly needed if physical activity is going to be increased in a society as technologically advanced as ours. Most Americans today are spared the burden of excessive physical labor. Indeed, few occupations today require significant physical activity, and most people use motorized transportation to get to work and to perform routine errands and tasks. Even leisure time is increasingly filled with sedentary behaviors, such as watching television, surfing the Internet, and playing video games. (Satcher, D. 1997, foreword)

What type of support do you think the author is talking about? Is instructional technology part of the problem, part of the solution, or neutral? Is the problem likely to get worse or better? With the help of computer technology, more and more people are now working from their homes. Will this trend lead to more or less physical activity?

> Schools could do more than perhaps any other single institution in society to help young people, and the adults they will become, to live healthier, longer, more satisfying, and more productive lives. (Carnegie Council on Adolescent Development)

To what extent do you agree or disagree with the quote above? If you agree, what would schools need to do in order for the statement to become a reality? What role would instructional technology be able to play?

**Activity 14.4: Collaborative Activities**  The following may be developed in small group work. Completed group projects may be copied and shared with the entire class and/or included in each person's Personal Portfolio.

*Scenario*  Your principal approaches you and your teaching partner and asks for your help in writing a grant. The purpose of the grant is to develop a holistic approach toward changing students' sedentary habits. Ms. Wong, the principal, is an excellent grant writer but she needs background information on the topic. She has asked for your help because you two are the most Internet savvy people at the school. Due to a pressing deadline, time is of the essence. You accept the challenge and head for your computers.

Use the Internet to find information on the topic; simply printing out pages from Web sites is not enough. Use the copy and paste feature to filter out relevant information. You will need to compile a synthesis of the information you find. Include disk copies of any charts or graphs that may be used in the grant proposal. Include hard copies of all research in your Personal Portfolio.

*Newsletter*  Work with your team to develop a computer-generated parents newsletter. The newsletter should provide parents with health tips and information on how to engage their children in quality physical fitness activities. Resources may include teachers in the field or on the Internet. Include a copy of the newsletter in your Personal Portfolios.

**Activity 14.5: Integrating Technology Across the Curriculum Activities**  Use the *Integrating Technology Across the Curriculum* CD-ROM packaged with this textbook to complete the following exercises:

a.  Because many schools are de-emphasizing physical education classes, one way to make sure these important concepts are addressed is by combining them with activities in other content areas. Go to *Find Lesson Plan* and click on *Find by Keyword.* Under the *Content Area* field, select "Physical Education" and click *Search.* Locate the lesson plan that illustrates how technology can support teaching physical education and mathematics together. What technology could support teaching physical education and English/language arts together? Physical education and science?

b.   Several lesson plans on the CD focus on nutrition concepts. However, all are for the middle school

and high school levels. Review these plans and decide how they can be modified to begin learning the same concepts at earlier levels. Go to *Find Lesson Plan* and click on *Find by Criteria.* Under the *Topics* descriptor, select "Health and nutrition"; click *Search.* Review three lessons: A Nutrition Project for Junior High Students, Nutrition Track, and Using Spreadsheets to Analyze Our Eating Habits. What technologies are used to help students learn these concepts? Create one of your own using the same technologies but at elementary levels.

# References

Anderson, A. & Weber, E. (1997). A multiple intelligence approach to healthy active living in high school. *Journal of Physical Education, Recreation, and Dance, 68*(4), 57–68.

Benham-Deal, T. & Deal, L. O. (1995). Heart-to-heart: Using heart rate telemetry to measure physical education outcomes. *Journal of Physical Education, Recreation, and Dance, 66*(3), 30–35.

Churchill, J. J., Pivonka, J. M., & Topp, N. W. (1995). An intercontinental track meet. *Journal of Physical Education, Recreation, and Dance, 66*(7), 14–15.

Collins, J. L. & Small, M. L. (1995). School health education. *Journal of School Health, 65*(8), 302–311.

Dorman, S. (1997). CD-ROM use in health instruction. *Journal of School Health, 67*(10), 444–446.

Dorman, S. (1997). Evaluating health-related web sites. *Journal of School Health, 67*(6), 232–235.

Dorman, S. (1998). 10 reasons to use technology in the health classroom. *Journal of School Health, 68*(1), 38–39.

Dorman, S. M. (1997). Video and computer games: Effect on children and implications for health education. *Journal of School Health, 67*(4), 133–137.

Ellery, P. J. (1996). Embracing computer technology in physical education instruction. *The Chronicle of Physical Education in Higher Education, 51*(7), 3–18.

Ellery, P. J. (1997). Using the world wide web in physical education. *Strategies, 10*(3), 5–8.

Fargen, T. (1996). Surfing the Internet in gym class: Physical education e-mail keypals. *Teaching and Change, 9*(3), 272–280.

Friesen, R. & Bender, P. (1997). Internet sites for physical educators. *Strategies, 11*(1), 34–36.

Graham, G., Holt-Hale, S., & Parker, M. (1998). *Children moving: A reflective approach to teaching physical education.* Mountain View, CA: Mayfield Publishing Co.

Greenockle, K. M. & Purvis, G. J. (1995). Redesigning a secondary school wellness unit using the critical thinking model. *Journal of Physical Education, Recreation, and Dance, 66*(8), 49–52.

Grosse, S. J. (1997). Send your students out to cruise. *Strategies, 11*(2), 18–20.

Hinson, C. (1994). Pulse Power: A heart physiology program for children. *Journal of Physical Education, Recreation, and Dance, 65*(1), 62–68.

Ignico, A. A. (1997). The effects of interactive videotape instruction on knowledge, performance, and assessment of sport skills. *The Physical Educator, 54*(1), 58–63.

Justice, B. (1996). Eating right? Fat chance! Teaching math and nutrition with spreadsheets. *Learning and Leading with Technology, 23*(6), 16–19.

Kane, W. M. (1993). *Step by step to comprehensive school health: The program planning guide.* Santa Cruz, CA: ETR Associates.

Kirk, M. F. (1997). Using portfolios to enhance student learning and assessment. *Journal of Physical Education, Recreation, and Dance, 68*(7), 29–33.

McLean, D. D. (1996). Use of computer based technology in health, physical education, recreation, and dance. *Eric Digest, ED 390 874.*

Mills, B. (1997). Opening the gymnasium to the world wide web. *Journal of Physical Education, Recreation, and Dance, 68*(8), 17–19.

Mitchell, D. L. & Hunt, D. (1997). Multimedia lesson plans— help for preservice teachers. *Journal of Physical Education, Recreation, and Dance, 68*(2), 17–20.

Mohnsen, B. (1998). *Concepts of physical education: What every student needs to know.* Reston, VA: National Association for Sport and Physical Education.

Mohnsen, B., Chestnut, C. B., & Burke, D. (1997). Using multimedia projects in physical education—part III. *Strategies, 11*(5), 10–13.

Mohnsen, B. & Mendon, K. (1997). Electronic portfolios in physical education—part IV. *Strategies, 11*(1), 13–16.

Mohnsen, B. & Schiemer, S. (1997). Handheld technology— practical application of the Newton messagepad. *Strategies, 11*(2), 12–14.

Mohnsen, B. & Thompson, C. (1994–1995). Physical education: Teaching biomechanics through interactive laserdiscs. *Computing Teacher, 22*(4), 30–32.

Mohnsen, B. & Thompson, C. (1997). Using video technology in physical education—part II. *Strategies, 11*(6), 8–11.

National Association for Sport and Physical Education. (1995). *Moving into the future: National Standards for Physical Education.* Reston, VA: Author.

Pangrazi, R. (1998). Dynamic physical education for elementary school children. Needham Heights, MA: Allyn and Bacon.

Pate, R. R. & Small, M. L. (1995). School physical education. *Journal of School Health, 65*(8), 312–317.

Pealer, L. N. & Dorman, S.M. (1997). Evaluating health-related web sites. *Journal of School Health, 67*(6), 232–235.

Ragon, B. M. & Bennett, J. P. (1996). Something more to consider, combining health education and physical education. *Journal of Physical Education, Recreation, and Dance, 67*(1), 14–15.

Regis, D. (1998) Models of health education. The four models of health education. www.ex.ac.uk/~dregis/teaching models.html#medical.

Satcher, D. (1997). Physical activity and health: A report of the Surgeon General. U.S. Government Printing Office, Washington.

Seffrin, J. R. (1990). The comprehensive school health curriculum. *Journal of School Health, 60*(4), 151–156.

Spalt, S. W. (1995). A letter to my principal: Why is it always health education? *Journal of School Health, 65*(2), 69–70.

Strand, B. & Mathesius, P. (1995). Physical education with a heartbeat, part 2. *Journal of Physical Education, Recreation, and Dance, 66*(9), 64–68.

Strand, B., Mauch, L., & Terbizan, D. (1997). The fitness education pyramid—integrating concepts with the technology. *Journal of Physical Education, Recreation, and Dance, 68*(6), 19–27

Strand, B. & Reeder, S. (1993). Physical education with a heartbeat: Hi-tech physical education. *Journal of Physical Education, Recreation, and Dance, 64*(3), 81–84.

Sumerfield, L. M. (1995). National standards for school health education. ERIC Clearinghouse on Teaching and Teacher Education, Digest #94-5, http://askeric.org.

Tishman, S. & Perkins, D. N. (1995). Critical thinking and physical education. *Journal of Physical Education, Recreation, and Dance, 66*(8), 24–30.

Trinity, J. & Annesi, J. J. (1996). Coaching with video. *Strategies, 10*(8), 23–25.

U.S. Department of Health and Human Services. (1996a) *Physical activity and health: A report of the Surgeon General.* Atlanta, GA: U.S. Department of Health and Human Services, Centers for Disease Control and Prevention, National Center for Chronic Disease Prevention and Health Promotion.

U.S. Department of Health and Human Services. (1996a) *Physical activity and health: Adolescents and young adults.* Atlanta, GA: U.S. Department of Health and Human Services, Centers for Disease Control and Prevention, National Center for Chronic Disease Prevention and Health Promotion.

U.S. Department of Health and Human Services. (1996a) *Physical activity and health: The link between physical activity and morbidity and mortality.* Atlanta, GA: U.S. Department of Health and Human Services, Centers for Disease Control and Prevention, National Center for Chronic Disease Prevention and Health Promotion.

Weiler, R. M. (1996). Creating a virtual materials and resource index for health education using the world wide web. *Journal of School Health, 66*(6), 205–209.

Wilkinson, C. (1997). Software: Choose a winner. *Strategies, 11*(7), 13–16.

## Resources

### Organizations

Agency for Instructional Technology
Box A
Bloomington, IN 47402-0120
(800) 457-4509
http://www.ait.net

American Alliance for Health, Physical Education,
   Recreation, and Dance
1900 Association Dr.
Reston, VA 20191
(800) 213-7193
http://www.aahperd.org/

American School Health Association
7263 State Route 43
P.O. Box 708
Kent, OH 44240
(330) 678-1601
asha@ashaweb.org
http://www.ashaweb.org/

American Academy of Kinesiology and Physical Education
c/o Human Kinetics
P.O. Box 5076
Champaign, IL 81820-2200

National Association for Physical Education in Higher Education
http://www.napehe.com

National Association for Sport and Physical Education
1900 Association Dr.
Reston, VA 20191
(703) 476-3410
(800) 213-7193

### Vendors

Bonnie's Fitware
18832 Stefani Ave.
Cerirtos, CA 90703
(562) 924-0835
http://home.earthlink.net/~bmohnsen/Fitware/fitware.html

Creative Health Products
5146 Saddle Ridge Rd.
Plymouth, MI 48170
(800) 742-4478

Futrex Inc.
6 Montgomery Village Ave., Suite 620
Gaithersburg, MD 20879
(301) 670-1106
info@futrex.com
www.futrex.com

Polar Electro Inc.
99 Seaview Blvd.
Port Washington, NY 11050
(800) 227-1314

Stretching Inc.
P.O. Box 767
Palmer Lake, CO 80133
(800) 333-1307
strech@usa.net
http://www.streching.com

## Web Sites

Physical Education Digest
http://domains.cyberbeach.net/pedigest/

California Physical Education Resources
http://www.stan-co.k12.ca.us/calpe/

Physical Activity and Health—A Report of the Surgeon General
http://www.cdc.gov/nccdphp/sgr/sgr/htm

## Videos

*PE-TV* (32 segments)—Whittle Communications
*Teaching Lifetime Fitness*—Audio Visual Designs
*Golf with Al Geiberger*—SyberVision
*Personal Fitness: Looking Good/Feeling Good*—Kendall/Hunt
   Publishing Company
*The World of Volleyball*—Human Kinetics
*The Jump Rope Primer*—Human Kinetics
*All Fit with Juggling Star*—Human Kinetics
*Slim Goodbody*—Human Kinetics
*Science and Myths of Tennis*—Human Kinetics
*Motor Learning: Secrets to Learning New Sports Skills*—
   Human Kinetics
*Seen But Not Heard Series*—Centre Communications
*Physics of Sport*—Videodiscovery

## Software

*Bodyworks*—Softkey International
*Choices, Choices*—Tom Snyder Productions
*Diet Analysis*—Parsons Technology
*Diet Detective*—Focus Media
*Decisions, Decisions/Substance Abuse*—Tom Snyder Productions
*Emergency Room*—IBM Multimedia Publishing Studios
*Effects of Drugs Bundle*—Education Associates
*Harvard Guide to Women's Health* —Pilgrim New Media
*Healthy Living Series*—Education Associates
*Health Powerpak*—Softkey International
*Health Risk Appraisal*—Queue/HRM Software
*InnerBody Works*—Tom Snyder Productions
*MacFitness Report, MacHeart Monitor, MacPortfolio
   Complete*—Bonnie's Fitware
*Mayo Clinic Family Health Book*—Interactive Ventures
*National Geographic KidsNet—What Are We Eating? Are We
   Getting Enough Oxygen?*—National Geographic Society
*PC Fitness Report, PC Health Related, PC Softball Strategy*—
   Bonnie's Fitware
*PharmAssist*—Softkey International
*Pyramid Challenge*—DINE Systems
*The Body Awareness Resource Network (BARN)*—
   Pyramid Media
*3D Body Adventure*—Knowledge Adventure
*You R What U Eat*—Teacher Made Media
*Vital Signs*—Texas Caviar
*What Is a Bellybutton?*—IVI Publishing

## Heart Monitors

*Pulse Watch, 1-2-3 Heart Rate Monitor*—Polar
*Cardiosport*—Country Technology

# Chapter 15

## Technology in Special Education

PCs are the Swiss Army knife for people with disabilities.

Member of the President's Committee on Employment for People with Disabilities, as quoted in a 1998 article by Michael Lyman and Mary Anne Mather

## This chapter covers the following topics:

- Current issues and problems in special education
- How technology is integrated into special education
- Example World Wide Web resources for special education
- Example activities for a variety of integration strategies in special education

# Objectives

1.  Identify some current issues in special education that impact the selection and use of technology.

2.  Describe some popular uses for technology in special education.

3.  Identify exemplary World Wide Web sites for special education.

4.  Create instructional activities for special education that successfully model integration strategies.

# Introduction

As Chapters 10 through 14 have shown, content areas such as science and mathematics are no longer as separate from each other as they once were. In the same way, the once distinct lines between instruction for regular and "special" students are now becoming increasingly blurred. Whitworth (1993) observes that now more than ever before, many children fall into the "gray area between regular and special education" (p. 133), as people begin to recognize the overlap in the needs of these students. Hanley (1993) observes that "For a very large number of special education students, the regular classroom is a critically important educational setting" (p. 167). Even though the curriculum applications may be different for regular and special students, Hanley assigned many of the same benefits—and limitations—to technology for all students, regardless of the groups in which school systems place them. Finally, legislation shows a definite trend toward making sure all students receive the same educational opportunities regardless of their disabilities. Whitworth (1993) identifies additional responsibility on teachers of regular students noting that "Shared responsibility (means that) ... teaching and preparing students with disabilities to enter the adult world is the responsibility of everyone, not just special educators" (p. 132).

Because the same technologies are used for regular and special students, it is not surprising that the special education literature describes many of the same technology resources and integration activities that have already been described in previous chapters for the content areas. Some technology resources such as Braille printers and word prediction software have been designed especially to meet the unique needs of students with certain disabilities. Also, schools use some types of resources and applications in ways that specifically meet the needs of special students (telecommunications and drill software). Still, schools seem to use most of the same products with students identified as having special needs as they use with regular students, and they use those products in very similar ways. This chapter describes technology applications to meet the regular and special

learning needs of children with learning disabilities, physical or intellectual disabilities, speech or language impairments, significant developmental delays, and gifted students.

# Issues and Problems in Special Education

### The Impact of Federal Legislation

Several federal laws enacted in recent years have addressed the need to provide education to special needs students. These laws have dramatically changed the requirements placed on schools to educate these students and increase technology applications for them.

**The Education for All Handicapped Children Act of 1975 (Public Law 94–142).** This landmark legislation is based on the Supreme Court's 1954 *Brown v. Topeka Board of Education* decision that separate education was not equal education under the 14th Amendment to the Constitution (Behrmann, 1998). It sought to "ensure that all disabled children have a free and appropriate public education, to ensure that the rights of disabled children and their parents are protected, and to assist state and local agencies in providing this education" (Clinton, 1992, p. 307). At the time the law was passed, nearly two million children were excluded from schools in the United States.

**The Technology-Related Assistance for Individuals with Disabilities Act of 1988 (Public Law 100–407).** This law speaks directly to the need for schools to provide handicapped students and their families with access to technology resources. It provides funds to help states obtain and deliver assistive technology service. Lewis (1993) noted that, as of 1991, approximately half of the states had been awarded such funding.

**The Individuals with Disabilities Act (IDEA) of 1990 (Public Law 99–457).** This amendment to Public Law 94–142 includes specific references to the need to provide assistive/adaptive technologies (and related services) for the disabled.

**The Americans with Disabilities Act (ADA) of 1990 (Public Law 101–336).** This law amounts to a "civil rights bill intended to eliminate discrimination against persons with disabilities" (Lewis, 1993, p. 12). Although not directed specifically toward education, it places many requirements on public schools to provide access to the same services for both students with special needs and regular students and employees.

**The Individuals with Disabilities Act (IDEA) of 1997 (Public Law 105–17).** This law reauthorizes and amends the original IDEA law. Among other changes, it requires that all children who are disabled be considered for assistive technology devices.

Together, these laws have increased the responsibility of schools to provide equal access to resources and activities for both disabled and non-handicapped students. Schools have not always agreed with parents on how to interpret legal requirements, and lawsuits have resulted. In many cases, meeting these special needs—especially technology needs—has resulted in substantial additional costs to education systems.

## Controversies Related to Mainstreaming and Inclusion

Federal laws require schools to place students with special needs in regular classrooms whenever possible. Sometimes, however, these regular classroom teachers feel unequal to the task of meeting the special needs of these students. Also, parents of non-disabled students raise objections occasionally to the amount of time spent on special students. For some time, this has been the greatest issue in the field, and it will have consequences for curriculum development and implementation methods for the foreseeable future. Schools have tried to provide equal access to educational opportunities through mainstreaming, inclusion, and collaboration.

**Mainstreaming.** This strategy, which grew out of schools' efforts to comply with PL 94–142, places students diagnosed with disabilities in regular classes whenever possible. However, it retains the classification of special education students and leaves the primary responsibility for planning for and tracking their progress to special education teachers.

**Inclusion.** The premise underlying inclusion differs slightly from that of mainstreaming. All students attend regular classes unless the school can show a compelling reason why they should not. Friend and Cook (1993) claim that this approach is increasingly common.

**Collaboration.** Sometimes special education teachers are assigned to the special duty of collaborating with regular classroom teachers to help special students adjust to the classroom and to support the regular teacher in meeting their academic needs. Sometimes this involves team-teaching or developing learning stations to manage the variations in abilities.

Mainstreaming and inclusion are both service delivery systems that may provide for a student's right to a free and appropriate public education (FAPE) in a least restricted environment (LRE). Some educators perceive technology as a double-edged sword. It can make the mainstreaming and inclusion processes more feasible but can also create extra demands on school systems to make sure that *all* technology opportunities are accessible to *all* students.

## Transition Needs

In spite of the tremendous legal push in recent years toward assisting students with special needs and the obvious dedication of educators in the field, special education programs for mildly handicapped or learning disabled students have not shown much success in graduating employable people. IDEA (PL 99–457) inspired one strategy in which students identified with disabilities had to have Transition Plans (TPs) as well as Individual Educational Plans (IEPs) to show how their educational experiences help to prepare them for the world of work. Technology resources can help with the TP/IEP requirement in at least two key ways. First, software products can assist with paperwork and record-keeping related to TPs and IEPs. Second, adaptive devices such as voice recognition systems have helped people with disabilities demonstrate marketable skills.

## Access Issues Based on ADA

Previous laws implied the need to provide equal access to resources, but PL 101–336, commonly known as ADA, gave legal teeth to this requirement. As one implication of ADA, schools must be careful not to create any barriers for any children (special education students or others) as they configure technology systems. For example, if a school purchases an Integrated Learning System, it may have to provide adaptive devices such as special switches and voice recognition software to assure that all physically handicapped students at the grade level can use the instruction.

## Costs versus Potential Benefits

Technology can certainly make life-changing differences for people with special needs, especially those with physical disabilities. Some technology systems can allow people to communicate and move around on their own for the first time, giving them a level of freedom and self-determination they would not otherwise have. Lewis (1993) and Male (1994) describe in detail the benefits of technology for educating people with special needs. However, since these technologies serve only limited markets, they sometimes are among the most expensive educational technology resources. The federal laws described earlier have allocated substantial amounts of funds for purchasing and using these technologies. As Lewis (1993) notes, however, the speed of technology changes makes it difficult and expensive for schools to keep up with new developments. Hardware/software compatibility problems seem even greater for adaptive devices and special needs software than for other products. Lewis cautions that, although technology can make many kinds of contributions to education for special needs students, "costs must be weighed against potential benefits" (p. 10). Schools that already face budget problems often must decide whether or not to purchase expensive systems that will benefit only a few students.

## Frustrations with Technology

Educators who attempt to apply technology solutions to instructional problems of physically disabled students report three kinds of problems (Clinton, 1995). First, parents and/or those who provide support often have unrealistic expectations that technology will cure handicapping conditions. "Assistive technology has been sold as 'the great equalizer' and, in some cases, has lived up to the billing. But individuals with severe physical and/or cognitive disabilities cannot be normalized by using technology tools.... [However, students] have opportunities to maximize their abilities with less stress and frustration than ... with conventional tools" (p. i). Special education teachers and students alike feel frustrated when hardware or software requires extensive initial training. Clinton cautions that assistive technology should offer plug-and-play solutions when possible so students can direct their energies to learning. Finally, despite hopes of teachers and students and some amazing recent advances in assistive technologies, Clinton notes "some handicapping conditions for which present technology offers no satisfactory solutions" (p. i). There is hope that future advancements in technology will lessen or eliminate these frustrations.

## More Resources for Parents

Thanks to the Internet and other online resources, families now have more access than ever before to information that can help them work better with school personnel (Smith, Polloway, Patton, & Dowdy, 1998). The National Rehabilitation Information Center (NARIC)—which has access to 42 databases, 700 organizations, and 100 resource directories—will do searches for families to locate products and devices, support organizations, and funding opportunities. The U.S. Department of Education's Office of Educational Research and Innovation (OERI) also provides similar support services to families. This kind of access helps parents better understand their child's special needs and gather information that will help them work with teachers to meet these needs.

## Trends and New Initiatives for Gifted Programs

In recent years, there has been a trend for program goals and definitions of giftedness to be constantly revised to reflect changes in social education reform philosophies (King, 1997). The trend over the past six years has been to eliminate separate programs for intellectually gifted children in favor of "setting high academic standards for all children." Consequently, appropriate identification of intellectually gifted students is becoming less and less of a priority for schools. Some warn that the catch-all phrase "all of our children are gifted" should be viewed as a warning that indicates a lack of understanding of the needs of gifted children (King, 1997; Winner & von Karolyi, 1998). However, in 1998, a new federal legislation initiative entitled "The Gifted and Talented Students Education Act"

was introduced into Congress. Supported by the National Association for Gifted Children (NAGC), this legislation would provide grants to states to strengthen services for gifted children (NAGC Communique, 1998). It calls for funding for distance learning and for state infrastructures to include the development of new programs and curricula. This may signal new support for meeting the unique learning needs of gifted and talented students.

## Goals of Gifted Programs

Some programs designed for high-achieving students advocate that curriculum acceleration be the primary goal of the program. Others believe in a more holistic approach designed to accommodate the needs of all gifted students. Technology often plays a vital role in addressing the goals for gifted programs (Clark, 1997).

- Provide opportunities and experiences particularly suited to the needs of gifted learners and through which they can continue developing their potentials.
- Establish an environment that values and enhances intelligence, talent, affective growth, and intuitive ability.
- Allow active and cooperative participation by gifted students and their parents.
- Provide time, space, and encouragement for gifted students to discover themselves, their powers, and their abilities, and to become all they can be.
- Provide opportunities for gifted students to interact with children and adults of various abilities (including the bright and talented) and to be challenged to know and revere humanity for its uniqueness and its connectedness.
- Encourage gifted students to find their place in human evolution by discovering their abilities and in what areas they wish to contribute.

## The Role of Technology: Two Trends

The divergent characteristics of directed-instruction and constructivist teaching strategies are reflected vividly in curriculum for special students. The special education literature reports numerous traditional applications of technology to teach basic life skills and basic academic skills such as drill and practice and tutorials. But other goals and activities clearly are constructivist: developing problem-solving skills, teaching students to work together in cooperative groups, helping them visualize concepts and gain experience with unfamiliar topics, and making them feel empowered as learners. Yet these differences seem to spark less controversy in special education than in other areas of education. Both strategies and aims are seen as necessary and appropriate, depending on students' needs and abilities (Whitworth, 1993; Cates, 1993).

Although constructivist strategies have seemed well-suited to the special needs of gifted students (Morgan, 1993), successful constructivist activities are also reported with other special education groups. For example, Hasselbring (1994) describes video-based instructional strategies to benefit hearing-impaired students, although the original work was actually done with learning disabled students. These methods are designed to help students build mental models in order to grasp abstract concepts that may be unusually difficult to understand for those who lack verbal skills.

This move toward less formal, less structured strategies for special needs students may result from the research finding that skill-by-skill instruction frequently has not resulted in levels of competency needed to make students employable after graduation. Since instruction in isolated skills has also been criticized as unmotivating and unproductive for other students, the trend may reinforce Hanley's (1993) observation that technology applications can help those categorized as "special needs students" in the same ways that they can help all students.

## How Technology Is Integrated into Special Education

Special education encompasses several different student populations that range from developmentally delayed to physically disabled (hearing impaired or visually impaired students) to gifted students. The widely varying needs of these groups demand dramatically different technology resources and applications; however, some general benefits of technology seem common to most or all types of special education students.

- **Improved motivation and self-concept.** Technology tools often have the ability to motivate special education students, get them to spend more time on instructional tasks, and generally improve their self-confidence. Several characteristics other than novelty promote this ability. First, the patience and privacy of a computer-based learning environment appeal to many non-special education students who have failed in traditional settings. For a learning disabled or physically disabled student, even the completion of a simple drill and practice assignment becomes an accomplishment and a source of pride. Second, students who have experienced little control over their bodies and their minds find powerful motivation in the ability to control their learning environments and undertake activities completely on their own. Finally, many special education students achieve new respect from their peers and their families by demonstrating proficiency with computer hardware and software. Lewis (1993) claims that computer use can improve students' feelings of self-worth and make others perceive their capabilities (see Figure 15.1).

- **Increased opportunities to use communication and interaction skills.** For students who have problems expressing themselves clearly or who are unable to communicate at all, technology can fulfill its promise as "the great equalizer." Holzberg (1994, 1995) and Lewis (1993) report some dramatic successes in which special education students used word processing software and MIDI synthesizers to express themselves in words or music. This increased ability not only improves students' self-concepts, but it also allows them to

**Figure 15.1** **Child Using *My School* Software**

Source: Courtesy of Laureate Learning Systems.

interact more equally with other students. Holzberg notes that "kids with behavioral and emotional problems rarely have a chance to experience such cooperative activities as working together to write a song or a research report" (1994, p. 20). She quotes one school principal as saying that technology helps students with disabilities uncover and release an intellectual potential that has been buried under layers of frustration and emotional conflict (p. 20).

- **More support to help teachers cope with paperwork.** Since schools and teachers are required by law to document how they provide equal access to educational opportunities for all special students, special education is an area known for its tremendous paperwork load. Teachers must document that IEPs have been developed and that they are making progress to carry out these plans. Furthermore, teachers must analyze student deficiencies and make decisions about their continued eligibility for special services. Smith, Polloway, Patton, and Dowdy (1998) say that technology resources can improve teachers' productivity strategies in ways that help them cope with this additional load. They can use lesson development software and productivity tools to plan instructional strategies and interventions; utilities and authoring systems to create special instructional materials for special education students; and IEP generation and tracking software and other computer-based tools to monitor and manage data on student performance.

### Assistive Technologies

Many students with learning disabilities, behavioral problems, and mental disabilities find that reading skills deficits represent their main obstacle to school achievement. Thus, most technology tools and applications for these students have focused on remedies for reading problems. In addition to this area of emphasis, a variety of other technology applications serves this population.

**Traditional applications (tutorials, drill and practice, games).** As Higgins and Boone (1993) observe, over the

**Figure 15.2   Screen from Talking Word Processor**

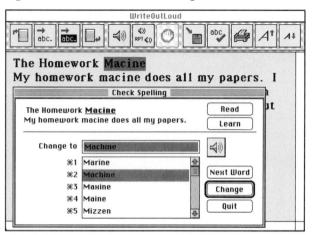

Source: Courtesy of Don Johnson, Inc.

**Figure 15.3   Screen from Word Prediction Software**

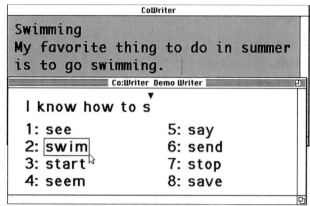

Source: Courtesy of Don Johnson, Inc.

past 10 years technology applications for children diagnosed with reading disabilities have centered on tutorial and drill and practice software to build fluency in basic skills. The greatest concentration works on decoding and vocabulary skills. But Spence and Hively (1993) criticize that students need fluency not only in reading skills, but also in other basic skill areas such as writing and arithmetic. "You can't read meaningfully when you are spending most of your energy trying to decode words.... You can't write effectively when you are worrying about how to form letters or how to spell.... In [math] exploration and problem solving ... solutions come more readily to the fluent mind" (p. 15). These authors find that computer-based drill and practice has proven the ideal means of providing needed practice for LD students. Many examples also illustrate uses of game-type software to motivate students with learning problems to stay on task longer and focus more on skills they need to acquire. Hearing impaired students also profit from several types of computer-assisted instruction (CAI) programs, for example, sign language tutorials and programs that provide visual feedback on student responses.

**Word processing.** After drill and practice, the second most common application for children with LD and behavioral problems is word processing. Holzberg (1994) reports that word processing has helped students with a variety of disabilities and emotional problems make great strides in improving their written language skills. "Children who may be incapable of writing an essay, paragraph, sentence, or even a word on paper ... find they can write with a word processor" (p. 19). Talking word processors can be very useful with these students (see Figure 15.2).

**Simulations.** Simulation programs offer students opportunities to see the consequences of their choices. They often are designed to model reality, which enables students to develop their decision-making and problem-solving skills

within the context of a safe learning environment. When well designed, these programs can provide some of the authentic learning experiences students need for success outside of school. They may provide opportunities for instruction in settings not generally available in schools. In addition, they may provide students with disabilities extensive practice in using skills learned in the classroom. Retention and transfer of such skills can be improved when students are engaged in simulation activities (Olson & Platt, 1998).

**Other technology applications.** Although drill programs and word processing applications have been the most common technology uses for this population, some indications (listed below) suggest growth in more open-ended, constructivist technology applications for exceptional children as much as for the population at large (Higgins & Boone, 1993; Whitworth, 1993; Holzberg, 1994; Lemons, 1997).

- Teachers involve mildly handicapped students in both regular and special classrooms in cooperative group activities such as writing and multimedia development.

- Graphics and drawing software are gaining wide popularity.

- Holzberg describes a videodisc-based anti-victimization training program directed at teenagers with mental disabilities as well as several multimedia applications to teach communications skills.

- Higgins and Boone (1993) review several successful projects that have used videodisc and hypermedia technology in reading programs for learning disabled students.

- Cognitive organizers often are helpful with LD students.

- Steele and Raab (1995) describe an expert system to identify appropriate teaching strategies for students with learning disabilities.

- Finally, students with learning disabilities frequently find help in word prediction software. Although originally designed to allow physically disabled students to construct sentences on a computer screen, as Figure 15.3 illustrates, these prompting systems have helped such students build their language skills.

## Recommended Resources and Applications for Physically Disabled Students

Educators who have worked with physically disabled students often praise technology eloquently and passionately as a means of freeing these students to develop their potentials. Clinton (1993) explains, "There is really no question that computers and related technologies are providing … unique possibilities for the physically disabled. There are thousands of [such students] who have spent a part of their lives trapped inside dysfunctional bodies. The quality of their lives will remain dramatically diminished until teachers provide the technical tools that give them avenues for communication and environmental control" (p. 70). In the highest-profile uses of technology for physically disabled students, adaptive devices let them communicate and/or use the computer for word processing or speech (Clinton, 1995). Lyman and Mather (1998) and Messever (1997) give excellent reviews of assistive technology devices for special needs students. Several of these are described here.

**Input devices to compensate for various disabilities.** Clinton (1992, 1993) observes that many students with physical disabilities such as cerebral palsy cannot use traditional input devices like the mouse and keyboard. Several alternative devices allow these students to use the computer: a wide range of switches (see Figure 15.4); touch screens; touch tablets; customized, alternative expanded keyboards (Figure 15.5); optical pointers; voice-controlled devices; and word prediction software systems.

**Output devices for visually impaired students.** Fitterman (1993) reviews output devices that visually impaired stu-

### Figure 15.4 Switch Used in Lieu of Keyboard

Source: Courtesy of Don Johnson, Inc.

### Figure 15.5 Child Using Alternative Keyboard

Source: Courtesy of Don Johnson, Inc.

dents can use to overcome their disabilities. Software or special hardware such as closed circuit television (CCTV) can enlarge computer images and text; speech output devices can "tell" what a program does; printers can produce large print or Braille; and tactile output devices that scan a page and translate the text into a vibrating, tactile display that a trained person can "read."

**Augmentation technologies for students with speech and language disorders.** Glennen and DeCoste (1996) describe devices that can help nonspeaking students or those with speech and language disorders. Some of these are single-purpose, dedicated devices that perform one function such as language analysis, while others are computers with software and adaptive devices. All of these systems are known as *augmentation aids*. Some are a combination of input and output devices and can serve as voices for nonspeaking students. Giordano and Stuart (1994) describe uses of these augmentation systems to enhance reading skills of nonspeaking students. Smith, Polloway, Patton, and Dowdy (1998) describe uses for such devices, including phonologic analysis and drills to develop articulation skills and biofeedback programs to let students develop greater fluency in speaking skills.

**Captioned video and other technologies for deaf learners.** Captioned video simply provides subtitles for television and other video presentations so that hearing impaired people can read what others hear. Hairston (1994) reports on a variety of projects that have used captioned video successfully in instructional programs for the deaf and hearing impaired. Hairston also notes that speech recognition systems have brought great benefits to those with hearing deficits as well as to visually impaired people.

**Figure 15.6   Special Education Web Site**

**Telecommunications applications for physically disabled students.** Telecommunications technologies offer several unique advantages for physically disabled students. Telecommunication devices for the deaf (TDD) allow many hearing impaired people to communicate over the telephone (Hairston, 1994). Although not a significant benefit to instruction, TDDs allow students and teachers to communicate over distances when necessary. Coombs (1993) describes present and potential uses of distance learning and telecommunications programs for physically challenged students. Telecommunications can equalize opportunities for students with many kinds of disabilities (especially hearing impairments), since students at the other end may not even know that a caller is disabled. Rozik-Rosen (1993) reports on technology that brings increased access to educational opportunities for homebound students. See Figure 15.6 for a sample special education Web page.

**Virtual reality.** Finally, the future holds the promise of even greater freedom for physically disabled students through new technologies. Woodward (1992) and Miller (1993) describe almost limitless capabilities that virtual reality (VR) provides for those who cannot walk or control their movements. Learning in "cyberspace" could allow complete freedom of lifelike movement in simulated, 3-D environments. Students with no mobility can simulate walking around a VR room or driving a car or piloting an airplane in a VR simulator. Other practical applications include wheelchair and mobility training.

Silverman (1997) describes some of the technologies that make these activities possible. These include input devices in "wired clothing," speech recognition devices, and head-mounted displays. But perhaps the most intriguing technology for students with limited body control is what Silverman calls "biosensors." These electrode-based devices detect electrical activity within the body and can change the display a person sees as though he or she touched or moved it.

Although these possibilities are alluring, Roblyer and Cass (1999) point out that most VR projects are in the demonstration and testing stage at this point, with few VR materials developed for actual use as instructional aids.

## Recommended Resources and Applications for Gifted Students

At the other end of the special education spectrum, special problems and challenges also confront students who are gifted and/or talented. Teachers often report that the most gifted students can be difficult to motivate with regular curriculum and the least likely to sustain interest in a topic. Morgan (1993) describes several technology applications that can help.

**Productivity tools.** Many students quickly grow impatient with mundane tasks such as writing and looking up information as part of research, problem-solving, and production work. Resources such as word processing systems, statistical and graphing packages, and searchable online and CD-ROM databases can make these tasks more interesting as well as easier to accomplish. One of the traits of many gifted students is a lack of organizational skills and a strong tendency toward right-brained, non-sequential thinking. Technology can provide considerable assistance to these students in the form of laptop computers or personal digital assistants equipped with database, calendar, and note taking software.

**The Internet.** Gifted students find motivation in open-ended resources that give them freedom to explore as well (Mann, 1994). Morgan (1993) writes that "telecommunications activities offer the opportunity to expand the learning environment beyond the confines of the classroom" and put students in touch with an unlimited number of people and information resources. The Internet is a "virtual playground" for those who like to discover new things and communicate with new people. He notes that e-mail helps teachers keep in touch with students and provides the individual attention and feedback students often need to keep on task. Mentoring is a strategy that has long been advocated in gifted education. The Internet provides a wealth of opportunities for students to foster student-mentor relationships with experts in business, medicine, higher education, etc. (Maltby, 1996).

**Simulations.** One of the strategies currently advocated in gifted education is curriculum compacting (Renzulli & Reis, 1998). Curriculum compacting is an instructional strategy used to streamline learning activities for students who demonstrate proficiency in curricular objectives prior to teaching (Reis & Westberg, 1998). It has been widely recognized and suggested by educational experts as a way of addressing the needs of high-ability and high-achieving students. Computer simulations can be a very effective tool in this compacting process. Simulations designed to compress time or to make the impossible possible are especially suited to use with the compacting model.

**Multimedia production and presentation activities.** The constructivist aspects of multimedia production and presentation projects are especially appealing to gifted students. In addition to providing motivational goals that focus their attention and abilities, these activities allow gifted students to work cooperatively with others—a skill area in which they frequently are lacking. In gifted education, students with very high abilities in the nonverbal or abstract realm are routinely identified for special services, but their true talents rarely emerge (Mann, 1994). Using technologies now available for hypermedia authoring, Web page development, image processing, and other graphic applications, these students can explore and develop exceptional talents.

**Robotics and other emerging applications.** The literature has reported a variety of uses of new and emerging technologies with gifted students. Smith (1994) describes a project with robotics that focuses on teaching creative thinking and problem solving. Mann (1994) reviews instructional activities involving expert systems. The novelty of these new resources appeals to gifted students, as does the opportunity they provide for exploration and discovery.

## Useful Web Sites for Special Education

- **Council for Exceptional Children**
  (http://www.cec.sped.org/home.htm)

  The Council for Exceptional Children (CEC) is the largest international professional organization dedicated to improving educational outcomes for individuals with exceptionalities, students with disabilities, and/or the gifted.

- **ABLEDATA**
  (http://www.abledata.com)

  This is a Web site on adaptive technologies from the National Institute on Disability and Rehabilitation Research.

- **Closing the Gap**
  (http://www.closingthegap)

  This site has a searchable database of information on technology resources for people with special needs.

- **Special Education Resources from the Curry School of Education at the University of Virginia**
  (http://curry.edschool.virginia.edu/go/cise/ose/resources/)

  Included here are such topics as general sources about disabilities, resources about assistive technology, discussions about special education, and links to regional resource centers.

- **Special Education Resources on the Internet (SERI)**
  (http://www.hood.edu/serihome.htm)

  This site provides a collection of Internet accessible information resources for those involved in the special education field.

- **pwWebSpeak Release 2**
  (http://www.prodworks.com)

  This is a browser that translates Web content to speech for sight-impaired Web users.

- **The National Information Center for Children and Youth with Disabilities (NICHCY)**
  (http://www.nichcy.org/index.html)

  NICHCY is the national information and referral center that provides information on disabilities and disability-related issues for families, educators, and other professionals with a special focus on children and youth (birth to age 22).

- **National Association for Gifted Children (NAGC)**
  (http://www.nagc.org/)

  The NAGC is an organization of parents, educators, professionals, and community leaders who address the unique needs of children and youth with demonstrated gifts and talents as well as those children who may be able to develop their talent potentials with appropriate educational experiences.

- **Gifted Resources Home Page**
  (http://www.eskimo.com/~user/kids.html)

  This page contains links to a wide variety of gifted resources: enrichment programs, talent searches, summer programs, gifted mailing lists, and early acceptance programs. This page is intended to be a convenient starting point for gifted students, their parents, and educators to access gifted resources.

## Sample Integration Lessons for Special Education

Additional activities are available on the accompanying *Integrating Technology Across the Curriculum* CD-ROM.

## Example Lesson 15.1
## The Information Sleuths

**Students:**          Gifted

**Required Resources:**  Computer with Internet connection, Web authoring software, any other electronic research resources

**Integration Strategy.** Integration to foster information and visual literacy

**Directions for Lesson Activities**

*Introduction.* Gifted students usually are very interested in supernatural occurrences such as the alleged mysterious disappearances of ships and airplanes in the Bermuda Triangle. This activity is designed to enhance students' information and visual literacy skills by asking them to research the validity of a supernatural theory. The second part of the project will ask students to develop a Web site, or other technology-based product, that presents information—both pro and con—about the various theories.

*Select a Topic.* Divide the students into groups of 2 or 3 and ask them to select a topic to research. Provide them with examples such as Bigfoot, the Loch Ness Monster, UFOs, the Lost City of Atlantis, Stonehenge, etc.

*Examine Research Options.* In this phase of the project, students examine different research choices. In a sense, they are "researching their researching" at this point. They should be encouraged to search the Internet for mentoring opportunities. They may be able to link up with experts in the field who will provide them with guidance and information.

*Gather Research.* Students use the Internet and other resources to learn as much as they can about their subjects. This will be a good time for the teacher to intervene and provide instruction on information literacy. Students should be encouraged to look for examples of bias on the part of the author as well as evidence of the critical examination of facts.

*Students Publish Results.* The final phase of the project involves having students publish the results of their findings. Depending on the resources available, they may want to develop a Web page, a hypermedia stack, or use desktop publishing software to develop a newspaper. No matter what the product, it should be attractive and provide a critical assessment of the topic.

*Suggestions for Teachers.* The success of this project will depend on the teacher's ability to keep students focused on the objectives of the activity: helping them develop their information and visual literacy skills. Many students can be very gullible and may have a tendency to "jump on the bandwagon" of a theorist. Teachers will need to be vigilant about keeping students focused on finding the truth.

Source: Jack Edwards.

## Example Lesson 15.2
## Students Teaching Grammar

**Students:**          LD

**Required Resources:**  Computer with hypermedia authoring software

**Integration Strategy.** Integration to remedy identified weaknesses and to foster creativity

*Continued*

**Directions for Lesson Activities**

*Purpose of Activity.* This activity asks students to use hypermedia authoring software to develop a simple tutorial program that helps users learn the difference between a noun and a verb.

*Getting Started.* Students need to learn the basics of hypermedia authoring, including how to create a "hot link." They are then instructed to use resources such as an English textbook to gather sample sentences. At this point, students develop a simple hypermedia program geared toward an audience of their peers. The program should include an interactive quiz that provides users with opportunities to correctly identify whether a word is a noun or a verb.

*Suggestions for Teachers.* Students seem to respond well to an activity like this because it provides them with a different approach to learning something they may have struggled with for a long time. It is important to stress to students that what they are doing has value. Encourage them to be creative and to make the program attractive for the audience. Stress the importance of accuracy and neatness. Some teachers have found that assignments like this can be highly motivational for their students. Provide students an opportunity to display their products to the class, administrators, parents, etc.

Source: Jack Edwards.

# Exercises

## Record and Apply What You Have Learned

**Activity 15.1: Chapter 15 Self-Test**  To review terms and concepts in this chapter, take the Chapter 15 self-test. Select Chapter 15 from the front page of the companion Web site (located at http://www.prenhall.com/roblyer), then choose the *Multiple Choice* module.

**Activity 15.2: Portfolio Activities**  The following activities will help you add to your professional portfolio. To complete these activities online and save or submit the materials electronically, select Chapter 15 from the front page of the companion Web site (http://www.prenhall.com/roblyer), then choose the *Portfolio* module.

*Integration Skills*  Identify a specific special education population and level. Create instructional activities that integrate technology appropriately for that population and level. Each of these activities should meet the following criteria:

- Integrate one or more types of technology described in the chapter.

- Show how to adapt this activity for large- and small-group instruction.

- Describe the required preparation for this activity.

- Describe the benefits you would hope to derive from using technology resources in the lesson.

*Develop a Hypermedia Stack*  Use a hypermedia authoring program to develop a program to be used by a specific special education population and level. It should be theme based and include a number of Web site links. A hard copy and disk copy should be included in your portfolio.

**Activity 15.3: Questions for Thought and Discussion**  These questions may be used for small group or class discussion or may be subjects for individual or group activities. To take part in these discussions online, select Chapter 15 from the front page of the companion Web site (http://www.prenhall.com/roblyer), then choose the *Message Board* module.

Many teachers stress that with technology, the student will get the right answer, faster. The obsession with getting the right answer and producing high results on quantitative tests could result in severe reduction in the willingness for the student or the teacher to be creative. Creativity calls for a willingness to make mistakes or to produce results that lie outside the estimated norms. While there is software which encourages students to use their imagination, most of it emphasizes there is only one right answer. How can teachers encourage alternative, creative ways to arrive at a solution, when the equipment the students employ will only tolerate the most direct answer? (Vertrees, Beard, & Pannell, 1997, p. 34)

What do you think about this comment? Does much of the software used today actually stunt creativity? How does this statement relate to special education populations?

> Although there are many arguments on both sides of the issue, it is apparent that new technologies can provide the tools to bring more children with disabilities into "regular" educational settings. In my opinion, assistive technology will certainly mainstream more and more children in wheelchairs, children who cannot physically speak, see, or hear, and children who need computers to write, organize, think, and function educationally (Behrmann, 1998).

This is an optimistic view on the influences that assistive technology will have on children with disabilities. What do you think those on the other side of the issue would say?

**Activity 15.4: Collaborative Activities** The following may be developed in small group work. Completed group products may be copied and shared with the entire class and/or included in each person's Personal Portfolio.

*Develop a Presentation* Use presentation software to create a presentation that explains how each of the following current special education issues and trends affect the selection and use of technology.

- Recent federal legislation related to special education and individuals with disabilities

- Trends toward mainstreaming and inclusion for all students, regardless of disabilities

- Traditional emphasis on directed-instruction models and new emphasis on constructivist instructional models for various special education students

*Software Recommendations* Review the suggestions offered by Clark under the heading "Goals for Gifted Programs" in this chapter. Choose three of the goals and locate software applications that might be capable of assisting teachers and students in reaching the goals. Create and publish a list of the software titles you have selected. The list should be presented in the form of a flyer or brochure that could be sent home to parents.

**Activity 15.5: Integrating Technology Across the Curriculum Activities** Use the *Integrating Technology Across the Curriculum* CD-ROM packaged with this textbook to complete the following exercise:

Technology resources have been used extensively in the past to support direct strategies (e.g., tutorial, drill) that help students with learning disabilities learn specific skills. However, other technology resources now are being used to support constructivist strategies to build student confidence, self-esteem, and general study skills. Review lessons on the CD that illustrate these strategies. Go to *Find Lesson Plan* and click on *Find by Criteria*. Under the *Teaching Strategies* field, click on "Constructivist." Under the *Target Students* field, click on "Learning Disabled." Review these lessons and develop a list of characteristics that seem common to the strategies used in these lessons.

# References

Alliance for Technology Access. (1994). *Computer resources for people with disabilities.* Alameda, CA: Hunter House.

Behrmann, M. (1998). Assistive technology for young children in special education. *ASCD 1998 Yearbook.* Arlington, VA: ASCD 73–93.

Bradley, K. & Dodds, M. (1991). Geotour USA. *The Florida Technology in Education Quarterly, 3*(2), 97–98.

Brett, A. (1997). Assistive and adaptive technology—supporting competence and independence in young children with disabilities. *Dimensions of Early Childhood, 25*(3), 14–15, 18–20.

Cambridge, T. & Abdulezer, S. (1998). Sharing Shakespeare: Integrating literature, technology, and American Sign Language. *NASSP Bulletin, 82*(594), 19–23.

Cates, W. (1993). Instructional technology: The design debate. *The Clearinghouse, 66*(3), 133–134.

Clark, B. (1988). *Growing up gifted.* Columbus, OH: Merrill Publishing.

Clinton, J. (1992). Technology for the disabled. In G. Bitter (Ed.). *Macmillan encyclopedia of computers.* New York: Macmillan.

Clinton, J. (1993). Why use technology to teach disabled students? Why ask why? *The Florida Technology in Education Quarterly, 5*(4), 64–79.

Clinton, J. (1995, March 2). Taming the technology. Materials distributed at the Florida Assistive Technology Impact Conference, Orlando, FL.

Coleman, M. R. (1998). Are we serious about meeting student needs? *Gifted Child Today, 32*(4), 40–41.

Coombs, N. (1993). Global empowerment of impaired learners: Data networks will transcend both physical distance and physical disabilities. *Educational Media International, 30*(1), 23–25.

Dunbar, M. (1989). Story machine. In *The Computer Learning Foundation's Special Education Lesson Plans.* Palo Alto, CA: The Computer Learning Foundation.

Ellsworth, N. & Hedley, C. (1993). What's new in technology? Integrating technology: Current directions. *Reading and Writing Quarterly, 9*(4), 377–380.

Fitterman, J. (1993, May). Present vision—future vision: Technology for visually impaired students (ERIC Document Reproduction No. ED 363 321).

Foster, K., Erickson, G., Foster, D., Brinkman, D., & Torgeson, J. (1994). Computer-administered instruction in phonological awareness: Evaluation of the DaisyQuest program. *Journal of Research and Development in Education, 27*(2), 126–137.

Friend, M. & Cook, L. (1993). Inclusion. *Instructor, 103*(4), 52–56.

Fuchs, D. & Fuchs, L. S. (1995). What's special about special education? *Phi Delta Kappan, 76*(7), 522–529.

Gatti, J. (1993). Student weather broadcast. *The Florida Technology in Education Quarterly, 5*(3), 63–64.

Giordano, G. & Stuart, S. (1994). Pictorial literacy activities for children with disabilities. *Day Care and Early Education, 21*(3), 44–46.

Glennen, S. & DeCoste, D. (1996). *Handbook of augmentative and alternative communication.* San Diego, CA: Singular Publishing Company.

Hairston, E. (1994). Educational media technology for hearing-impaired persons. *American Annals of the Deaf, Special Issue, 139*, 1–11.

Hanley, T. (1993). The future has been a disappointment: A response to Woodward and Noell's article on software development in special education. *Journal of Special Education Technology, 12*(2), 164–172.

Hasselbring, T. (1994). Using media for developing mental models and anchoring instruction. *American Annals of the Deaf, Special Issue, 139*, 36–44.

Higgins, K. & Boone, R. (1993). Technology as a tutor, tools, and agent for reading. *Journal of Special Education Technology, 12*(1), 28–37.

Holzberg, C. (1994). Technology in special education. *Technology and Learning, 14*(7), 18–21.

Holzberg, C. (1995). Technology in special education. *Technology and Learning, 15*(5), 18–23.

Keefe, C. H. & Davis, R. (1998). Inclusion means …. *NASSP Bulletin, 82*(594), 54–63.

Kenney, S. L. (1997). Effective management of instructional computer use: Elementary special education teachers share their strategies. *The Florida Technology in Education Quarterly, 9*(2), 18–25.

King, V. J. (1997). Is my child gifted? http://www.access.digex.net/king/.

Landrum, M. S., Katsiyannis, A., & DeWaard, J. (1998). A national survey of current legislative and policy trends in gifted education: Life after the national excellence report. *Journal for Education of the Gifted, 21*(3), 352–370.

Latham, A. S. (1997). Technology and LD students: What is the best practice? *Educational Leadership, 55*(3), 88.

Lemmons, R. (1997). How using technology can aid in teaching disabled learners. *The Florida Technology in Education Quarterly, 9*(2), 37–45.

Lewis, B. A. (1996). Serving others hooks gifted students on learning. *Educational Leadership, 53*(5), 70–74.

Lewis, R. (1993). *Special education technologies: Classroom applications.* Pacific Grove, CA: Brooks/Cole.

Lyman, M. & Mather, M. (1998). Equal learning opportunity: Assistive technology for students with special needs. *Technology and Learning, 19*(4), 55–60.

Male, M. (1994). *Technology for inclusion: Meeting the special needs of all students.* Boston: Allyn & Bacon.

Maltby, F. & Beattie, J. (1996). A task for telematics. *Gifted Education International, 7*(1), 149–155.

Mann, C. (1994). New technologies and gifted education. *Roeper Review, 16*(3), 172–176.

Miller, E. (1993). Special experiences for exceptional students: Integrating virtual reality into special education classrooms (ERIC Document Reproduction No. ED 363 321).

Morgan, T. (1993). Technology: An essential tool for gifted and talented education. *Journal for the Education of the Gifted, 16*(4), 358–371.

Morrissey, P. A. (1998). The individuals with disabilities education act amendments of 1997: Selected observations. *NASSP Bulletin, 82*(594), 5–11.

Olson, J. L. & Platt, J. M. (1998). *Teaching children and adolescents with special needs.* Upper Saddle River, NJ: Merrill/Prentice Hall.

Pullen, R. & Sanders, B. (1994). Thematic units: My house. Handout from a Broward County, FL workshop.

Randolph, L. & Fleming, D. (1997). Unlocking the future (with an expensive key): How communities can share the costs, and the benefits, of assistive technology. *The Florida Technology in Education Quarterly, 9*(2), 4–17.

Reis, S. M. & Westberg, K. L. (1998). Curriculum compacting and achievement test scores: What does research say? *Gifted Child Quarterly, 42*(2), 123–128.

Renzulli, J. S. & Reis, S. M. (1998). Talent development through curriculum differentiation. *NASSP Bulletin, 82*(595), 61–74.

Roblyer, M. D. & Cass, M. (1999). Virtual reality in special education: Still more promise than potential. *Learning and Leading with Technology, 26*(8), 51–53.

Rozik-Rosen, A. (1993). Special needs, special answers: The story of TLALIM at the service of sick children. *Educational Media International, 31*(1), 36–41.

Silverman, F. (1997). *Computer applications for augmenting the management of speech, language, and hearing disorders.* Needham Heights, MA: Allyn and Bacon.

Smith, R. (1994). Robotic challenges: Robots bring new life to gifted classes. *Gifted Child Today, 17*(2), 36–38.

Smith, T., Polloway, E., Patton, J., & Dowdy, C. (1998). *Teaching students with special needs in inclusive settings (2nd ed.).* Needham Heights, MA: Allyn & Bacon.

Spence, I. & Hively, W. (1993). What makes Chris practice? *Educational Technology, 33*(10), 15–20.

Steele, J. & Raab, M. (1995). FERRET: An expert system for identifying teaching strategies for students with learning disabilities. *Tech Trends, 40*(3), 13–16.

Vertrees, D. R. & Beard, L. A. (1997). Special education technology: … And then what? *The Florida Technology in Education Quarterly, 9*(2), 26–36.

Whitworth, J. (1993). What's new in special education: An overview. *The Clearinghouse, 66*(3), 132–133.

Winner, E. & von Karolyi, C. (1998). Gifted and egalitarianism in education: A zero sum? *NASSP Bulletin, 82*(595), 47–58.

Woodward, J. (1992). Virtual reality and its potential use in special education: Identifying emerging issues and trends in technology in special education (ERIC Document Reproduction No. ED 350 766).

Zaugg, L. (1991). Let's write it right! *The Florida Technology in Education Quarterly, 3*(2), 75–77.

Zorfass, J., Corley, P., & Remz, A. (1994). Helping students with disabilities become writers. *Educational Leadership, 51*(7), 62–66.

## Resources

### Hardware and Software Resources for People with Disabilities

Alternate keyboards—Don Johnson, Inc.; Exceptional Computing, Inc.; Intellitools; Sunburst; TASH, Inc.; Zygo Industries

Arm and wrist supports—ErgoFlex Systems; KLAI Enterprises

Braille displays—American Thermoform Corporation; HumanWare, Inc.; TeleSensory

Braille translators and embossers—American Thermoform Corporation; Blazie Engineering, Inc.; Enabling Technologies Co.; TeleSensory

Closed circuit TVs—HumanWare, Inc.; Seeing Technologies, Inc.; TeleSensory

Electronic pointing devices—Ability Research; Inocomp; Madenta Communications; Prentike-Romich; Words+, Inc.

Interface devices—AbleNet, Inc.; BEST; Brown & Company; Consultants for Communication Technology; Don Johnson, Inc.; TASH, Inc.; Words+, Inc.

Joysticks—KY Enterprises; McIntyre Computer Systems; Penny and Giles; Prentke Romich Co.; TASH, Inc.

Keyboard accessories (keyguards, moisture guards, alternate labels)—Don Johnson, Inc.; Intellitools; Prentke Romich Co.; TASH, Inc.; Toys for Special Children

Menu customizing programs—Apple Computer Co; Edmark Company; Microsoft Corporation; Symantec

Pointing and typing aids (sticks or wands for those who cannot hit keys with fingers)—Crestwood Co.; Extensions for Independence; Maddak; North Coast Medical

Reading comprehension programs—Advanced Ideas, Inc.; CompuTeach; Continental Press; Creative Learning, Inc.; Davidson and Associates; Don Johnson, Inc.; Great Wave Software; Hartley Courseware, Inc.; IBM Special Needs Systems; Laureate Learning Systems; The Learning Company; MECC; Milliken Publishing Co.; Optimum Resources, Inc.; Scholastic; SVE; Sunburst; Tom Snyder, Inc.

Screen enlargement software—Apple Computer, Inc.; Arctic Technologies; Berkeley Systems; HumanWare, Inc.; Microsystems Software, Inc.; TeleSensory

Screen reader software for the blind—American Printing House for the Blind, Inc.; Berkeley Systems, Inc.; Biolink Research and Development; GW Micro; IBM Special Needs Systems; OMS Development; TeleSensory

Speech synthesizers—American Printing House for the Blind, Inc.; AICOM, Inc.; Digital Equipment Corporation; Echo Speech Corporation; HumanWare, Inc.; TeleSensory

Switches (with software)—Creative Switch Industries; Don Johnson, Inc.; Luminald, Inc.; Prentke Romich Co.; TASH, Inc.; Toys for Special Children; Zygo Industries

Text telephones (TT) for the hearing impaired—AT&T Accessible Communications Products; IBM Special Needs Systems; KRI Communications; TeleSensory

Touch screens—Edmark, Inc.; Information Strategies, Inc.; Microtouch Systems

Trackballs—APT, Inc.; CoStar Corporation; Kensington Microwave Ltd.; Logitech; Mouse Systems, Inc.; Penny and Giles Computer Products Ltd.

Voice recognition systems—Apple Computer Co.; Articulate Systems; Dragon Systems; IBM Special Needs Systems; Kurzweil Applied Intelligence; Microsoft Corporation

Word prediction programs—Don Johnson, Inc.; Innovative Designs; Microsystems Software; Pointer Systems; Prentke Romich Co.; Words+, Inc.

Word processors with speech and large print—Davidson and Associates; Don Johnson, Inc.; Hartley Courseware, Inc.; IBM Special Needs Systems; Intellitools; SkiSoft Publishing Co.

Writing aids and writing skill software—Blissymbols Communications International; Creative Learning, Inc.; Davidson and Associates; Don Johnson, Inc.; Hartley Courseware, Inc.; Humanities Software; IBM Special Needs Systems; Scholastic, Inc.; Teacher Support Software; Tom Snyder, Inc.; William K. Bradford Publishers

### Organizations

Accent on Information
P.O. Box 700
Bloomington, IL 61702
(309) 378-2961 (V); (309) 378-4420 (fax)

Access Unlimited
3535 Briarpark Dr., Suite 102
Houston, TX 77042-5235
(713) 781-7441 (V); (800) 848-0311; (713) 781-3550 (fax)

ADAMLAB
33500 Van Born Rd.
Wayne, MI 48184
(313) 467-1415 (V); (313) 326-2610 (fax)

Alliance for Public Technology
901 15th Street NW, Suite 230
Washington, DC 20005
(202) 408-1403 (V)

Center for Applied Special Technology (CAST)
39 Cross St.
Peabody, MA 01960
(508) 531-8555 (V); (508) 531-0192 (fax)

Center for Computer Assistance to the Disabled (C-CAD)
1950 Stemmons Frwy., Suite 4041
Dallas, TX 75207-4041
(214) 746-4217 (V)

Closing The Gap, Inc.
P.O. Box 68
Henderson, MN 56044
(612) 248-3294 (V); (612) 248-3810 (fax)

Computer Foundation for Handicapped Children
5871 S.W. Bonita Rd.
Lake Oswego, OR 97035
(503) 624-9196 (V)

CSUN Center on Disabilities
California State University at Northridge
18111 Nordhoff St.
Northridge, CA 91330-8340
(818) 885-2869 (V); (818) 885-4929 (fax)

Direct Link for the disABLED, Inc.
P.O. Box 1036
Solvang, CA 93464
(805) 688-1603 (V); (805) 686-5285 (fax)

DRAGnet
119 N. 4th St.
Minneapolis, MN 55401
(612) 338-2535 (V)

EdLINC
P.O. Box 14325
Columbus, OH 43214
(614) 793-0021 (V); (800) 736-1405

International Society for Technology in Education
University of Oregon
1787 Agate Street
Eugene, OR 97403-9905

National Council on Disability
1331 F St., NW, Suite 1050
Washington, DC 20004-1107
(202) 272-2004 (V); (202) 272-2022 (fax)

National Rehabilitation Information Center (NARIC)
8455 Colesville Rd., Suite 935
Silver Spring, MD 20910-3319
(800) 346-2742 (V/TTY); (301) 587-1967 (fax)

ProMatura
428 N. Lamar
Oxford, MS 38655
(601) 234-0158 (V); (601) 234-0288 (fax)

RESNA
1700 N. Moore St., Suite 1540
Arlington, VA 22209-1903
(703) 524-6686 (V); (703) 524-6639 (TTY)

Technology for Language and Learning
P.O. Box 327
East Rockaway, NY 11518-0327
(516) 625-4550 (V); (516) 621-3321 (fax)

Trace Research and Development Center
University of Wisconsin
1500 Highland Ave.
Rm. S-151, Waisman Ctr.
Madison, WI 53705-2280
(608) 262-6966 (V); (608) 263-5408 (TTY)

**Internet Web Sites**

Able Informer
http://www.sasquatch.com:80/ableinfo/
Apple's Disability Solutions
http://www.apple.com/disability/welcome.html
Archimedes Project (design issues for tomorrow's technology)
http://www.cs.rulimburg.nl/~wiesman/archimedes
Breaking New Ground Resource Center
http://pasture.ecn.purdue.edu/~agenhtml/bng/
Cornucopia of Disability Information
gopher://val-dor.cc.buffalo.edu
Disability Access
http://www.pavilion.co.uk:80/CommonRoom/
DisabilitiesAccess/
disABILITY Resource on the Internet
http://www.eskimo.com/~jlubin/disabled.html
Disability Resources (Evan Kemp Associates)
http://disability.com
DREAMMS for Kids, Inc.
http://users.aol.com/dreamms/main.html
EASI, Access to Information for Persons with Disabilities
gopher://sjuvm.stjohns.edu:70/11/disabled/easi
http://www.rit.edu:80/~easi/
HandsNet
http://www.handsnet.org/handsnet/index.html
IBM Special Needs Solutions
http://www.austin.ibm.com/pspinfo/snshome.html
Job Accommodation Network
http://janweb.icdi.wvu.edu
National Center to Improve Practice (NCIP) in Special
Education through Technology, Media, and Materials
http://www.edc.org/FSC/NCIP
National Rehabilitation Information Center (NARIC)
http://www.cais.net/naric/home.html
NCSA Mosaic Disability Access Page
http://bucky.aa.uic.edu/
Project Link
http://cosmos.ot/buffalo/edu
RESNA Technical Assistance Project
http://www.resna.org/resna/hometa1.htm
Resources for Disabled Index
http://www.aip.org/aip/urls/disable.html
Speech Recognition Resources on the Web
http://146.230.32.40/homes/duncan/speech.html
Trace Research and Development Center
http://www.trace.wisc.edu
UCPA Assistive Technology Funding and Systems
Change Project
http://www.assisttech.com/atfsc.html
WebABLE
http://www.webable.com/

# Appendix

## Fundamentals of Microcomputer Systems

It's difficult for teachers to integrate technology into a classroom when the computer itself is a "mysterious box" with unknown parts and unpredictable behaviors. If teachers are to use this "classroom machine" with ease, it helps to know as much as possible about how it works—without needing to be a technician. This appendix takes some of the mystery out of computers by explaining some basics about their parts and operations. It is a primer for the novice user as well as a good summary for the skilled "cookbook user," who may have been doing a lot of things without knowing exactly why.

### What Is a Computer and How Does It Work?

A computer is not one object, but several different components that function together as a system. What is commonly called a computer is more accurately called a *computer system* and may be defined as a combination of electronic components *(hardware)* with which humans can communicate through sets of coded instructions *(software)*. Every computer system, from a handheld personal digital assistant (PDA) to a giant supercomputer, has these same basic elements: hardware and software. Actual combinations of hardware and software components vary considerably according to the power of computer systems and the purposes for which they were designed. A computer system usually is made up of hardware, software, and media to store the software.

### Hardware

All of the devices or equipment in the computer system include input devices to get user requests into the system; the central processing unit (CPU), which carries out user requests; output devices that display the results of the CPU's action; and internal memory, which stores instructions in the computer system. Every computer system must have a CPU, memory, and at least one input device and one output device. Optional hardware includes external storage devices such as hard drives, disk drives, and communications devices such as modems. All devices outside the CPU and internal memory hardware are referred to as *peripherals*.

**Input devices.** Some devices serve only as channels to let users give instructions and information to the computer system. Any device that lets users send instructions or information *into* a system is classified as an input device. Some of the most common input devices that carry out this function are shown in Figure A.1. Input devices include keyboards, mice, joysticks and game paddles, bar code readers, scanners, touch screens and light pens, voice recognition units, microphones, optical character readers, and graphics tablets.

**Processing and internal memory devices.** The CPU performs the actual work of the computer system—processing user instructions. This is the part of the system that can most accurately be called the *computer*. In today's computer systems, CPUs are a series of electronic circuits arranged and stored on silicon chips. In microcomputers, these chips are housed on a component called a *motherboard*. Although not visible to the naked eye, the CPU consists of two parts.

- **The control unit.** This part of the CPU directs the activities of the whole system. It resembles an air traffic controller or the manager of a busy courier service. The control unit directs all parts of the computer system to work together to accomplish tasks that the user gives it. The control unit completes no functions itself that are considered the actual work of

**Figure A.1   Example Input Devices**

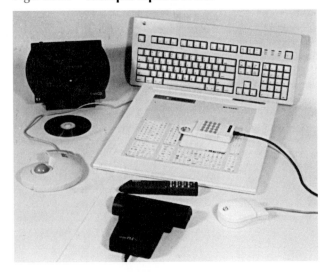

the system; its job is to direct the work of the other members of the system.

- **Arithmetic/logic unit (ALU).** All operations in a computer system are based on computations. A computer's basic arithmetic operations of adding, subtracting, multiplying, and dividing actually are all based on addition. But the computer's operations also include sorting and comparing bits of information. All of these computation operations—arithmetic, comparing, and sorting—are done by the ALU.

A computer's most complex activities really are just combinations of simple steps arranged in sequence. For any task, the CPU follows the same general sequence of functions over and over again.

**Step 1**  The controller gets an instruction from the system's internal memory (discussed in the next section) and puts it in a temporary storage location called a *register.* (These instructions got into internal memory in the first place when the controller directed an input or storage device to place them there.)

**Step 2**  The controller directs the ALU to do necessary computations. The result is stored in another register.

**Step 3**  The controller gets the result from the register and stores it once again in internal memory.

The CPU may complete hundreds of iterations of this three-step sequence to accomplish a basic task such as drawing a line on a screen and can perform millions of tasks in the blink of an eye. The speed at which it completes these operations is measured in *mips,* or, millions of instructions per second, and has much to do with how fast the task gets done.

A limited amount of space is arranged inside a computer for storing instructions. On a microcomputer, this memory is all on chips on the main circuitboard—the motherboard. The size of this space is measured in units called *bytes,* which are made up of several (usually 8) electronic circuits called bits (*bi*nary dig*its*), so called because each can hold a pulse of electricity that can represent a "1" or hold no electric pulse, which makes it a "0." The combination of these 1s and 0s can represent a number, letter, or symbol; this storage system is the basis of how we communicate with computers. The power of a microcomputer is based in part on the amount of its random access memory (RAM) in *bytes.* Each byte can store a character of information such as a letter or number. Users may describe computer memory or storage in *kilobytes* (thousands) or KB, *megabytes* (millions) or MB, *gigabytes* (billions) or GB, or *terabytes* (trillions) or TB. (Sometimes these are shortened to K, M, G, and T.) Teachers need to be familiar with two kinds of internal memory.

- **Random access memory (RAM).** This kind of memory serves as temporary storage for user requests in the form of applications program commands and the data that programs use. The control unit may place a program and data at any location, that is, randomly, in RAM. RAM is also called

**Figure A.2  Example Output devices**

*volatile memory;* it depends on electricity to hold information in the circuits. When electricity goes off, RAM is erased.

- **Read only memory (ROM).** ROM is a type of memory designed to hold instructions permanently within the computer. "Read only" indicates that the user cannot place information in ROM circuits; the manufacturer stores only systems software there when building the computer. The computer system uses this software each time it starts up; however, unlike RAM, it does not erase when the computer is turned off.

**Output devices.** Some devices display the results of what the computer does. Any device that makes it possible to determine what the computer does with user requests is classified as an output device. Some common output devices are shown in Figure A.2. The most common output devices are printers (dot matrix, inkjet, and laser), monitors (cathode ray tube or CRT, or liquid crystal displays or LCD), plotters, and speech synthesizers.

**External storage or I/O devices.** Disk drives function primarily as storage devices, but in order to use this secondary storage, they also act as input/output or I/O devices. External devices store information on disks magnetically rather than in off/on electrical circuits that combine to form bytes. Still, disk or tape storage is also measured in bytes.

**Communication devices.** An optional device called a *modem* is designed to change (*mod*ulate) the information from the digital format produced by computers into an audible format that can be sent across telephone lines. When the information reaches the receiving computer, that machine changes it back (*de*modulates it) into the digital format. Modems vary in price according to the speeds at which they send and receive information. At one time, users rated speed as *baud rates,* but they currently measure it as bits of information per second or *bps.* Modem speeds range from 2,400 bps to 56,600 bps, but this capability is increasing rapidly. Some kinds of modems can also send and receive faxed information.

## Software

Sets of instructions written in computer languages that let users give directions to the hardware are *programs* or *software.* (*Software program* actually is redundant!) The instructions in programs are translated into "machine language" or the 1's and 0's the computer "understands" at an electronic level.

**Types of software.** Hardware needs two kinds of instructions, which means it needs two kinds of software.

*Systems software.* Systems software tells the computer how to do basic operations such as storing a program in memory or sending a document to be printed. The manufacturer includes some parts of the systems software in the computer's Read Only Memory (ROM) when it is built; other parts are read into Random Access Memory (RAM) from a disk or from a ROM chip when the computer starts up. Educators need to be most concerned with a type of systems software known as the *operating system.* This software is an important choice because it acts as a visible interface between the machine and the user. It determines both what the user sees on the screen and the steps the user follows to do things like selecting options from menus. Different *platforms* (see section on platforms below) use very different operating systems. Since the CPU receives some of its instructions from the operating system each time the computer is turned on, the startup process came to be called *bootstrapping* the system (after the phrase "pulling oneself up by the bootstraps"), later shortened to *booting.* Starting up the system with a power switch is sometimes called a *cold boot,* while using keys on the keyboard to reinitiate the operating system is called a *warm boot.*

*Applications software.* Applications software is programs that do specific tasks such as word processing, electronic gradebooks, instructional simulations, or math drills. The software that teachers see is applications software.

**Types of programming languages.** Just as humans speak and understand a variety of languages, several kinds of computer languages also serve various purposes. The first kinds of languages developed were low-level languages that were designed as interfaces between humans and the "electrical language" of machines. Later, higher-level languages were designed that required less technical expertise, making them easier for nontechnical people (like teachers) to use.

*Low level languages.* Original computer languages include machine language and assembly language or assembler. Machine language is based on the 1's and 0's that represent on/off circuits in a computer's memory. It is programmed into the machine when it is built. Assembler is considered one step up from the binary digits of machine language and consists of symbolic commands such as *ADD* and *LOAD.* Each assembler command represents several steps

written in machine language. Although assembler is the lowest-level language used to program today's computers, most people find it still too technical and time-consuming to use; they prefer high-level languages.

*High-level languages.* These languages actually are programs written in machine language. High-level languages consist of commands that resemble human words such as *RUN* and *GO TO.* Among the dozens of high-level languages, the most common choices for educators are BASIC (Beginners All-purpose Symbolic Instruction Code), Pascal (named after an early pioneer in programming concepts, Blaise Pascal), and Logo. Other languages include C, FORTRAN, COBOL, and JAVA (used with Internet resources). High-level languages are sometimes classified as compiled or interpreted, depending on how they translate commands into machine language. Interpreted languages such as BASIC and Logo use programs called *interpreters* to translate commands (called *source codes*) one-by-one into machine code. If the interpreter finds an error, it stops interpreting and alerts the programmer. Compiled languages such as Pascal and FORTRAN use programs called *compilers* to do the translation. Compilers translate entire programs into machine language, which is then called *object code.* Programmers discover errors in language syntax only after an entire program is compiled. Programmers must also identify and correct any errors in logic after a program is compiled.

## Computer Media

Media are neither hardware nor software; they are a means of storing software to make it portable and easier to use. Software is like music stored on tape or CD. A tape or CD is not actually music, only a medium for storing it. The three most common types of removable disks (ones that can be inserted and taken out of disk drives) are diskettes, CD-ROMs and DVDs, and other removable mass storage media (see Figure A.3).

**Diskettes.** Disks that come in 3½" or 5¼" sizes are commonly called diskettes, "floppy" disks (even though only the 5¼" kind actually was flexible or floppy), or microdisks. The term *tapes* is a common but incorrect usage dating back to the time when cassette tape players were the microcomputer's I/O device. Removable disks come in various storage formats. Double-density (DD) microdisks can store from 720K to 800K of data, while high-density (HD) microdisks have from 1.2 to about 1.4 MB of storage capacity. The density of a disk refers to the format with which information is stored on the disk, and this determines how much information can be placed there.

**CD-ROMs, DVDs, and other removable mass storage media.** Media designed to hold optical as well as text information is spelled *discs* rather than *disks.* These thin media are designed to display optical information such as videos more quickly. The two types of optical storage are Compact

Figure A.3    **Example Disk/Disc Media**

Source: Anthony Magnacca/Merrill.

Disc Read Only Memory (CD-ROMs), which hold about 600 MB, and Digital Versatile Discs (DVDs, a type of rewritable magneto-optical disc), which hold 2.6 GB per side. Other types of removable disk storage include hard disk cartridges designed for use on Jaz and Zip drives. Currently, Zip disks hold around 100 MB of information and Jaz disks hold 1 GB.

## What Is the Desktop and Why Is It So Important?

Today, educators use two major "platforms" or types of microcomputer equipment. Platforms are defined primarily by the type of operating system that runs their hardware. Early microcomputer systems used either CP/M (Control Program for Microprocessors), Apple DOS (Apple Disk Operating System), or ProDOS. The UNIX operating system, originally designed by Bell Laboratories for use on larger computers such as the DEC VAX, was

Figure A.4    **Macintosh Desktop**

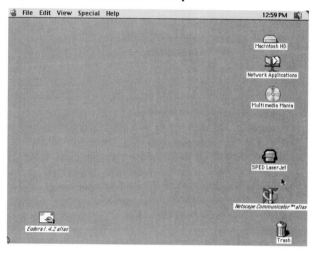

later modified for use on some microcomputer systems. Later, two other operating systems came to dominate the field: MS-DOS (Microsoft Disk Operating System) and Mac OS (Macintosh Operating System).

The ingenious concept of a desktop originated at Xerox Corporation. However, the Apple Computer Company brought it into widespread use for the first time in 1984 as part of a new system called the Macintosh, a bid to build on the success of Apple's popular Apple platform. The software that displays the desktop and lets people interact with it is called a *graphic user interface* (GUI—pronounced "gooey"). The desktop GUI makes it easier for nontechnical people to use microcomputer systems. Macintosh, MS-DOS systems with Windows 3.1, and those with Windows 95 and Windows 98 have similar looking desktops, but have many differences, especially in how they operate. Compare the two desktops in Figures A.4 and A.5. Common basic elements include icons and windows.

Figure A.5    **Windows 98 Desktop**

- **Icons.** An icon is a picture that symbolizes an object or concept. For example, a disk icon symbolizes the disk itself; the trash can icon on the Macintosh desktop symbolizes a place to discard or throw away files, folders, etc. In both systems, users move icons by dragging them around on the desktop.
- **Windows.** These rectangular boxes display information such as the contents of a disk or a folder on the screen. An open window shows a list of the items in the disk or folder along with some information about each one.

## Learning Microcomputer Operations

Every microcomputer user should know how to complete the following set of activities, regardless of the specific kind of microcomputer. The order of the list suggests an optimal sequence for learning these activities. System manuals that accompany newly purchased computers give specific information about how to complete these tasks.

### Learn General Information about Your Computer System

1. Learn about your system. How many disk drives? What size hard disk? How much RAM? What version of the operating system? What size/kind of monitor? What kind of printer? What other peripherals?

2. Locate all the ON/OFF buttons and turn on all the devices of the system. Locate the input devices (usually the keyboard and mouse), the output devices (usually the monitor and printer), and the computer cabinet itself.

3. Locate the ON/OFF switches for each of the devices. Sometimes, a switch is located on the keyboard as well as on the computer casing.

4. Find out about the capabilities of the system. How much RAM does it have? How many disk drives? Any hard disk drive? If so, what is its capacity? Is there a CD-ROM, DVD, or Zip drive? How large is the monitor? Color or monochrome? What kind of printer does the system have (dot matrix or laser)? How fast will it print? Is the printer shared among more than one computer? Is the computer connected to or part of a network? What kind of network is it? Does the system include a modem or other optional equipment such as a microphone and/or speakers?

### Learn to Operate Your Computer

1. Learn about each of the keys on your keyboard.

2. Identify the parts of the desktop: pull-down menus, icons, etc.

3. Learn how to use a mouse (point, click, double-click, drag).

4. Learn how to use the listing of disk or folder contents called *windows*. Open a window (usually by double-clicking the disk or folder icon); make a window inactive by clicking outside it and active by clicking inside it once; identify the other parts of a window; size a window (making it larger or smaller); scroll the display in a window using scroll arrows and scroll boxes; move

a window around on the screen by its handle; place two or more open windows beside each other so you can see them both at the same time; use keyboard sequences in place of menus to complete operations with windows; drag icons around within windows; and close a window.

5. Use pull-down menus.

6. Identify different icons for programs, files, and folders/subdirectories.

7. Learn how to carry out operations with folders, create and name a new folder/subdirectory; re-name a new folder/subdirectory; and place a folder inside another folder.

8. Perform operations with disks: Insert a blank disk into the drive; initialize/format it; rename a disk; prepare a label for the disk and place the label on it.

9. Learn how to move folders from the hard drive to the new disk.

10. Learn how to remove files and folders/subdirectories from a disk.

11. Learn how to copy a file or folder/subdirectory from one disk to another.

12. Learn how to copy an entire disk.

13. Learn how to remove a disk from the disk drive.

14. Learn how to use some system options such as Find file, adjusting the mouse and sound controls, and changing the background color/pattern on the desktop.

15. Shut down the computer system and turn off the devices in the system.

## Pointers on Microcomputer Use

### Using a Mouse

The mouse is a standard input device on most microcomputers. A mouse can be used to point to things on the screen and to communicate with the computer. Pointing to things on the screen with a finger cannot tell the computer what the user wants to do. The mouse controls an arrow pointer to indicate objects such as icons and menus on the screen. This procedure tells the computer to select an item or display its contents. Many people find it very difficult at first to learn the motor skills required to use a mouse. For example, many beginners have difficulty learning that they can pick up the mouse off the desk or mousepad and move it without moving the arrow on the screen; the arrow moves only if the ball of the mouse moves, usually while touching the surface of the desk or mousepad. Practice is the only answer to resolving this problem. The four operations a user does with a mouse are pointing, clicking, double-clicking, and dragging.

**Pointing.** This is the process of moving the arrow to a desired location on the screen. This usually is the first step in accomplishing clicking, double-clicking, or dragging.

**Clicking.** Depending on the software, the user may be able to select an option on the screen or complete another desired step simply by pressing the mouse button. This action is called *clicking* the mouse on an object.

**Double-clicking.** Some software calls for completing a step by clicking the mouse button twice in rapid succession. This action is called *double-clicking*. The choice between single clicking and double-clicking depends on what the software requires.

**Dragging.** Holding down a mouse button while moving the mouse on the mousepad or desk is called *dragging*. Objects on the screen can be moved around by clicking on them and dragging them. Dragging is also the way to look at options on menus.

## Starting Up and Shutting Down a Microcomputer

When a computer is turned on, electrical current begins running through the computer's circuitry and the system is said to boot up. As the system boots up, the operating system is read into the computer's RAM. When booting up is completed on Macintosh computers and on MS-DOS computer systems with Windows and with Windows 95, the screen displays the desktop. Users should remember three warnings about starting up and shutting down any computer system.

- **Don't turn off the computer until you finish using it.** Turning the system off and on is hard on its mechanical parts (switches, power supply, motors). Therefore, do not turn off the computer until you finish using it. Some beginners erroneously turn off the system automatically when they make errors. If possible, try to correct an error without turning off the system.

- **Don't turn the system off and on quickly.** Again, this action is hard on the system's devices. It won't hurt anything the first time you do it, but repeated on/off sequences will eventually break down the devices.

- **Make sure to turn on all devices in the system.** All the devices may be attached to one power switch, but sometimes a user may have to press separate power switches for devices such as the monitor.

**Using icons: Programs, files, and folders.** Icons that represent programs, files, and folders on the Macintosh desktop look very similar. Beginners may tend to think of them as essentially the same thing with different names; however, the icons serve very different functions on the desktop and within the computer system. *Program icons* represent software packages that fulfill various functions required by the system or its users. *File icons* represent places to store information created by programs or for use with those programs. For example, a word processing document created in WordPerfect becomes a file when stored on disk. Unlike programs and files, folders do not symbolize software, products of software, or data. They exist only as images on the screen and places in computer memory. *Folder icons* extend the concept of a computer screen as the top of a desk. Folder icons represent groups of pro-

grams and files the user wants to locate together, just as file folders on a real desk gather and organize papers.

## Using Disks

**Preparing disks for use.** To store programs and files on disk, users must first prepare the disk by placing a small program on it that links it to the computer's operating system. In effect, this program is part of the operating system. The process of placing this program on the disk usually is called *initializing* the disk in Macintosh systems and *formatting* in MS-DOS systems. In either system, it is done with a few simple commands from the desktop.

- **Initializing/formatting and naming.** Each disk is formatted or initialized only once, since this process begins by erasing the disk. As part of this process, the user names the disk, usually in a way that indicates the information stored on it. For example, if a teacher wants to store only letters to parents and students on a disk, the disk might be called *Letters*. A disk to store all handouts and tests for all classes in a given year might be called *Class Materials—2001*. The default name for a disk is *untitled* for a Macintosh and is unnamed for a Windows disk.

- **Labeling.** The name of a disk appears with the disk's icon on the desktop. Its label is a piece of paper stuck to the outside of the disk. A label should be typed or written first and then put on the disk. The label should contain two pieces of information: the name of the person or place to which it belongs and its purpose. If a teacher is sending a disk to another person or an organization (e.g., an article submitted to a journal for publication), the label might carry other information. For example, the label might need to specify the word processing program used to prepare the file. The recipient of the disk usually specifies the kind of information to put on the label.

**Disk treatment.** Although disks are fairly sturdy storage media, they can become damaged as a result of age, misuse, computer problems, or flaws in component materials. This risk should lead users to keep a backup disk for every data disk. Losing files when disks are lost or defective is a major problem. Keep disks from becoming defective by doing the following.

1. Treat disks gently; do not bend them, place them between books or other objects, or jam them quickly into disk drives.

2. Keep disks out of direct sunlight and at comfortable temperatures: not too cold (below 40°) or too hot (above 100°).

3. Keep away from sources of magnetism: TV sets and any machines with electric motors.

4. Do not touch any shiny surfaces beneath the plastic covering or allow dirt on these surfaces.

5. Store disks correctly. Place floppy disks in protective sleeves/envelopes and keep all disks in disk boxes or carrying cases.

6. Back up disks. Make copies of all disks with programs or files stored on them.

**Saving files on disk: Computer storage and memory concepts.** Since we are dependent on disks to store our work, it is important to understand some of the basic concepts about using them in this way.

- **Files created with applications programs are stored on a disk** *by name.* The name designates a specific physical location on the disk. The user must remember the name under which the system stored the file to retrieve it from its location on the disk. The only way to save two different versions of the same file (e.g., two copies of a word processed letter that differ only in the address) is to save the versions under two different names.

- **Files must be saved** *each time* **the user changes them.** What is on the screen when the user saves it to disk takes the place of what was there before under the same name.

- **Frequent backups of work are essential.** Anticipate problems. Always make at least two copies of everything you produce by making backup copies of programs.

# References

See the companion Web site (located at http://www.prenhall.com/roblyer) for a Microcomputer Troubleshooting Guide and other useful information on microcomputer operations.

## Resources

### I. Software

#### Virus Protection
Windows
*Dr. Solomon's Anti-Virus Deluxe*—Dr. Solomon's Group
*VirusScan*—Network Associates, Inc.
*Norton AntiVirus*—Symantec Corporation
Macintosh
*Virex*—Dr. Solomon's Group
*Norton AntiVirus*—Symantec Corporation

#### System Maintenance
Windows
*Norton Utilities*—Symantec Corporation
*PC Medic Deluxe*—McAfee Associates, Inc.
Macintosh
*Norton Utilities*—Symantec Corporation
*Conflict Catcher*—Casady & Greene, Inc.

#### Hard Drive Maintenance
Windows
*CleanSweep*—Quarterdeck Office Systems
Macintosh
*Storage Wizard Tool Kit*—FWB Software, LLC

#### Security
Windows
*Norton Yours Eyes Only*—Symantec Corporation
*Guard Dog*—Cybermedia
Macintosh
*FileGuard*—ASD Software
*Private File*—Aladdin Systems, Inc.

#### Y2K
Windows
*Check 2000 PC*—Greenwich Mean Time

*2000 Toolbox*—McAfee Associates, Inc.
*Norton 2000*—Symantec Corporation
Macintosh
None—not required

#### Utility Suites
Windows
*Norton SystemWorks*—Symantec Corporation
*Checkit 98 Diagnostic Suite*—Touchstone Software Corporation
Macintosh
*McAfee Office 2000*—Network Associates, Inc.
*Mac Super Utility Bundle*—Symantec Corporation

### II. Web Sites
Windows 95
Tips:
    http://www.geocities.com/SiliconValley/Heights/6348/
    tips.html
Windows Driver List:
    http://www.windrivers.com/
Tips and Tweaks:
    http://www.gate.net/~jsharit/windows_95/win95tips_and_
    tweaks.html
Major Help Site:
    http://help-site.com/
MAC
Doc Around the Clock:
    http://www.doctormac.net/html/docroundclock.html
Extensions Guide:
    http://www.madison-web.com/ext/
Macintosh Conflicts:
    http://www.mac-conflicts.com
Mac Links:
    http://www.omnisphere.com/~raj/macsupp/macsources.html

### III. On-Line Stores
PC/Mac Connection:
    http://www.macconnection.com
PC/Mac Warehouse:
    http://www.warehouse.com
Computer Discount Warehouse:
    http://www.cdw.com

# Glossary

**algorithm**—A step-by-step solution to a problem (e.g., a programming problem)

**anchored instruction**—Constructivist term for learning environments that focus on meaningful, real-life problems and activities

**applet**—A program that is written in the Java language and is designed to carry out a useful task on the Internet (e.g., showing a clock to tell the exact time)

**applications software**—Computer programs written to support tasks that are useful to a computer user (e.g., word processing) in contrast with *systems software*

**Archie**—A system located on the Internet and designed for finding files through lists of archived files from various locations

**artificial intelligence (AI)**—Computer programs that try to emulate the decision-making capabilities of the human mind

**ASCII (American Standard Code for Information Interchange)**—A standardized, commonly accepted format for representing data (e.g., characters and numbers) so that programs and files created with one program and stored in ASCII can be used by another program

**assembler**—A low-level programming language that uses mnemonic commands that are one step up in complexity from "machine language" (binary numbers)

**authoring system**—A program designed to help nonprogrammers write computer-based instructional programs (e.g., CAI or multimedia); can be either a high-level programming language or a series of nonprogramming prompts

**automaticity**—A level of skill that allows a person to respond immediately with the correct answer to a problem

**avatar**—A graphic representation of a real person in cyberspace; a three-dimensional image that a person can choose to represent him or her in a virtual reality environment

**backup copy**—A copy of a disk that is made to guard against loss of files if an original disk is lost or destroyed

**bar code**—A set of lines that represents a number such as a UPC (Universal Product Code)

**bar-code reader**—A device that reads and interprets bar codes

**BASIC (Beginners All-Purpose Symbolic Instruction Code)**—A high-level programming language designed for beginning programmers; popular with microcomputers

**baud rate**—The speed at which data are transmitted across communication lines between computers measured in bits per second (bps); 1 baud = 1 bps

**BBS** (See *bulletin boards.*)

**binary**—A condition of two possible states (e.g., on or off, 1 or 0). For computers, binary refers to the coding system that uses 1s and 0s

**bit**—A binary digit, either a 1 or a 0; several bits together (usually eight) make up a byte of computer storage that can hold a letter or a character

**BitNet**—A network mostly among higher education organizations; replaced by the Internet

**bookmark**—To mark an Internet location so one can remember it and return to it later; or the place so marked

**boot/boot up**—To start up a computer system; a "cold boot" is turning on the device from a power switch; a "warm boot" is restarting from the keyboard without shutting off power

**bps (bits per second)**—The speed at which data are transmitted across communication lines between computers

**browser**—A software package (e.g., *Netscape, Internet Explorer*) that allows one to look at information on the Internet in graphic, rather than just text, format

**bug**—An error in a computer program caused either by faulty logic or program language syntax (named by early programmer and systems designer Grace Hopper, who found a moth in the machinery of a broken computer)

**bulletin boards (BBS)**—A computer system set up to allow notices to be posted and viewed by anyone who has access to the network

**button**—A place on a computer screen, usually within a hypermedia program, that causes some action when the user clicks on it using a mouse; also called a *hot spot*

**byte**—A group of binary digits (bits) that represents a character or number in a computer system; designates a unit of computer storage (see also *K, M,* and *G*)

**C**—A structured programming language originally designed for use on the Unix operating system and widely used on today's microcomputers

**CAI (computer-assisted instruction)**—Software designed to help teach information and/or skills related to a topic; also known as *courseware*

**card**—One frame or screen produced in a hypermedia program such as *HyperStudio* (several cards together make a stack)

**CAT (computer-assisted testing)**—Using a computer system to administer and score assessment measures

**CAV (constant angular velocity)**—A videodisc format that makes available up to 54,000 images or 30 minutes of full-motion video per side; images can be selected and viewed randomly (see also *CLV*)

**CD-I (compact disk interactive)**—A type of CD-ROM used on special players with built-in computer and TV capabilities

**CD-ROM (compact disc-read only memory)**—Removable computer storage medium that can store images and/or up to 250,000 pages of text

**central processing unit (CPU)**—The circuitry in a computer that processes commands composed of the controller, the arithmetic/logic unit (ALU), and internal memory

**CGI (Common Gateway Interface)**—A specification on the Internet for how data will be collected at a Web site; CGI programs are written in a language such as PERL

**chat room**—A location on the Internet set up to allow people to converse in real time by typing in messages or allowing their avatars to meet and talk to each other

**chip**—A piece of silicon inside a computer on which electronic circuits have been placed by depositing small paths of a metal such as aluminum; an integrated circuit

**client**—Programs like browsers and FTP software designed to carry out various activities for people to help them use the Internet

**clip art**—One or more pieces of professionally prepared art work, stored as files and designed to be inserted into a document such as a newsletter

**clone**—A computer designed to operate like another brand of computer, but usually not made by the same company as the original

**CLV (constant linear velocity)**—A videodisc format that can hold up to 60 minutes of full-motion video; designed for playing straight through, users cannot access individual frames as CAV discs allow (see also *CAV*)

**CMI (computer-managed instruction)**—Computer software systems designed to keep track of student performance data, either as part of CAI programs or by themselves

**COBOL (COmmon Business Oriented Language)**—A high-level language designed specifically for business applications

**code**—Lines of commands or instructions to a computer written in a certain language (e.g., BASIC or C); the act of writing such instructions

**cold boot** (See *boot.*)

**command**—One instruction to a computer written in a computer language

**compiler**—A computer program that converts all statements of a source program into machine language before executing any part of the program (in contrast with *interpreter*)

**computer**—Usually equivalent to *computer system* (see below); sometimes refers to the CPU part of the system

**computer-assisted instruction** (See *CAI.*)

**computer-assisted testing** (See *CAT.*)

**computer language**—A communication syntax

**computer literacy**—Term coined by Arthur Luehrmann in the 1960s to mean a set of basic abilities everyone should have with computer systems; now has variable meanings

**computer-managed instruction** (See *CMI.*)

**computer system**—A set of devices designed to work together to accomplish input, processing, and output functions in order to accomplish tasks desired by a user

**conferencing**—Communication between people in two or more places made possible by computer systems connected by communication lines

**constructivism**—Teaching/learning model based on cognitive learning theory; holds that learners should generate their own knowledge through experience-based activities rather than being taught it by teachers (see also *directed instruction*)

**control unit (controller)**—The part of the computer system housed in the CPU that processes program instructions

**cookie**—A small piece of text transferred to a Web browser through a server for the purpose of tracking the Internet usage habits of the person using the browser

**courseware**—Instructional software; computer software used to enhance or deliver instruction

**CRT (cathode ray tube)**—A TV-like screen on which information from a computer system may be displayed; a monitor; a primary output device for a microcomputer system

**cursor**—A line, block, or underline displayed on the computer screen that shows where information may be inserted

**cut and paste**—The act of copying text from one location in a document, deleting it, and then inserting it in another location

**data**—Elements of information (e.g., numbers and words)

**database**—A collection of information systematized by computer software to allow storage and easy retrieval through keyword searching; the program designed to accomplish these tasks

**database management system (DBMS)**—Computer software designed to facilitate use and updating of a collection of information in a database

**data processing**—Organizing and manipulating data for a specific purpose (e.g., to keep track of income and expenses, to maintain student records)

**debug**—To review a computer program and remove the errors or "bugs"

**desktop**—The screen that appears first upon starting up a Macintosh computer or an MS-DOS computer with Windows; a graphic user interface (GUI) designed to make it easier for nontechnical people to use a computer

**desktop publishing**—Term coined in 1984 by the president of the Aldus Corporation to refer to the activity of using software to produce documents with elaborate control of the form and appearance of individual pages

**desktop videoconferencing**—A computer-to-computer form of live action interactive two-way video/audio; a typical desktop videoconferencing system has a video camera, microphone, and speakers at each workstation

**digitized sound**—Audible noises (e.g., music, voices) that are transferred to a computer storage medium by first coding them as numbers

**directed instruction**—A teaching and learning model based on behavioral and cognitive theories; students receive information from teachers and do teacher-directed activities (see also *constructivism*)

**disc**—A CD-ROM or videodisc; refers to video storage media as opposed to text storage

**disk**—A computer storage medium on which data and programs are placed through a magnetic process

**disk drive**—A device in a computer system used to store data on floppy disks or microdisks and retrieve data

**diskette** (See *disk.*)

**distance learning**—Using some means, electronic or otherwise, to connect people with instructors and/or resources that can help them acquire knowledge and skills

**DOS (disk operating system)**—The systems software that allows a computer to use applications programs such as word processing software; the operating system on IBM-type computers as opposed to those manufactured by Apple

**dot-matrix printer**—Output device that produces paper copy by placing patterns of dots on the paper to form letters

**download**—To bring information to a computer from a network or from a computer to a disk

**drill and practice**—An instructional software function that presents items for students to work on (usually one at a time) and gives feedback on correctness; designed to help users remember isolated facts or concepts and recall them quickly

**DVD (digital versatile disc)**—A type of CD-ROM electronic storage medium that holds a minimum of 4.7 gigabytes of information

**e-book**—A flat panel computer display that is designed to resemble a book, but offers interactive graphics and searchable text features not possible in printed books

**electronic bulletin boards** (See *bulletin boards.*)

**electronic gradebook**—Software designed to maintain and calculate student grades

**electronic mail (e-mail)**—Messages sent via telecommunications from one person to one or more other people

**emoticon**—A series of characters used together to convey emotion; for example, a sideways smiley face :-) designates a happy mood

**Ethernet**—Type of local area network (LAN) in which several data transmissions among network users can be sent at any given time (in contrast with token-passing networks, which allow only one transmission at a time)

**Events of Instruction, Gagné's**—The nine kinds of activities identified by learning theorist Robert Gagné as being involved in teaching and learning

**expert systems**—A form of artificial intelligence (AI) that attempts to computerize human expertise

**export**—To save all or part of a document in a format other than that in which the program created it (e.g., as a text file) so it can be used by another program

**external storage**—Devices outside the computer's internal circuitry that store information and/or data (in contrast with *internal memory*)

**field**—The smallest unit of information in a database

**file**—The product created by a database program; any collection of data stored on a computer medium

**file server**—In a local area network (LAN), the computer that houses the software and "serves" it to the attached workstations

**File Transfer Protocol** (See *FTP.*)

**firewall**—A system set up to prevent someone from going to certain locations on the Internet; may be done by keyword or by site name

**flame**—An e-mail or newsgroup message that usually is emotional and often derogatory in nature

**flat file database**—Database program that creates single files (in contrast with *relational database*)

**floppy disk** (See *disk.*)

**flowchart**—A planning method that combines rectangles, diamonds, and other figures joined by arrows to show the steps of a problem solution in graphic form; used by programmers to show a program's logic and operation before it is coded into a computer language

**font**—A type style used in a document (e.g., Courier, Palatino, or Helvetica)

**footer**—A line in a document that can be set to repeat automatically at the bottom of each page; usually indicates a title and/or pagination (see also *header*)

**format**—To prepare a disk to receive files on a computer; to initialize a disk; to design the appearance of a document (e.g., the font, type styles, type size)

**FORTRAN (FORmula TRANslater)**—One of the earliest high-level computer languages; designed for mathematical and science applications

**FTP (File Transfer Protocol)**—On the Internet, a way of transferring files from one computer to another using common settings and transmission procedures

**full justification** (also simply *justification*)—In word processing or desktop publishing, a type of text alignment in which text is both flush right on the right margin and flush left on the left margin (in contrast with right or left justified or centered)

**fuzzy logic**—A logic system in artificial intelligence (AI) designed to parallel the decision-making processes of humans by accounting for subjectivity and uncertainty

**G (gigabyte)**—Roughly 1 billion bytes of computer storage

**GIGO (garbage in/garbage out)**—Popular term meaning that if the data that go into a computer are faulty or badly organized, the result will also be inaccurate

**gopher**—On the Internet, a menu-based system designed to search for and retrieve files

**GPS (Global Positioning System)**—An instrument that uses a satellite to pinpoint the exact geographic location where the GPS signal originates and cross-references it with mapping software to show the location to a user

**gradebook** (See *electronic gradebook.*)

**grammar checker**—The part of the word processing software designed to check text for compliance with grammar and usage rules

**graphics tablet**—Type of input device on which pictures are hand-drawn and transferred to the computer as files

**graphic user interface (GUI, often pronounced "gooey")**—Software that displays options to the user in graphic formats consisting of menus and icons, rather than text formats (e.g., the Macintosh and Windows desktops)

**graphing calculator**—A calculator with advanced functions and a small LED display; allows users to enter equations and shows graphs that result from those equations

**hacker**—Computer user who demonstrates an unusual, obsessive interest in using the computer; a computer user who engages in unauthorized use of a computer system

**hard copy**—A paper printout of a computer file from a printer, plotter, or other output device

**hard disk (hard disk drive)**—In a computer system, a secondary storage device, usually housed inside the computer, but can be external; holds from 20 megabytes to 1 or more gigabytes of information

**hardware**—The devices or equipment in a computer system (in contrast with *software* or *computer programs*)

**header**—A line in a document that can be set to repeat automatically at the top of each page; usually indicates a title and/or pagination (see also *footer*)

**high-level language**—Computer programming language (e.g., *FORTRAN, BASIC, COBOL*) designed with syntax and vocabulary like a human language so that less technical people can use it to write programs

**hot spot** (See *button.*)

*HyperCard*—Authoring software designed for Macintosh systems to create products called *stacks* which consist of a series of frames or *cards*

**hypermedia**—Software that connects elements of a computer system (e.g., text, movies, pictures, and other graphics) through hypertext links

**hypertext**—Text elements such as keywords that can be cross-referenced with other occurrences of the same word or with related concepts

**icon**—On a computer screen, a picture that acts as a symbol for an action or item

**ILS** (See *integrated learning system.*)

**import**—To bring into a document a picture or all or part of another document that has been stored in another format (see also *export*)

**information service**—A set of communications (e.g., e-mail) and storage/retrieval options made available by a company such as America Online or Prodigy

**information superhighway**—A popular term with various meanings associated with the worldwide linkage of information; sometimes synonymous with the Internet

**initialize** (See *format.*)

**ink-jet printer**—Type of output device that produces hard copy by directing a controlled spray of ink onto a page to form characters

**input device**—Any device in a computer system (e.g., keyboard, mouse) designed to get instructions or data from the user to the processing part of the system

**instructional game**—Type of software function designed to increase motivation by adding game rules to a learning activity

**integrated circuit** (See *chip.*)

**Integrated Learning System (ILS)**—A network that combines instructional and management software and usually offers a variety of instructional resources on several topics

**integrated software packages**—Software products (e.g., *Microsoft Works* and *ClarisWorks*) that have several applications in a single package (e.g., word processing, database, spreadsheet, and drawing functions)

**intelligent CAI**—Computer-assisted instruction with software logic based on artificial intelligence (AI) principles

**interactive video**—Videodiscs that allow the user to control the order and speed at which items from the disc are displayed on a screen. (In Level I, control is through a bar code reader or remote control; in Level III, control is through a menu on a computer screen.)

**interface**—Cables, adaptors, or circuits that connect components of a computer system; the on-screen method a person employs to use a computer (see also *graphical user interface*)

**internal memory**—Integrated circuits inside a computer system designed to hold information or programs; ROM and RAM (in contrast with *external storage*)

**Internet**—A worldwide network that connects many smaller networks with a common set of procedures (protocols) for sending and receiving information

*Internet Explorer*—A popular browser software used to access the Internet

**interpreter**—A computer program that converts program code into machine language and executes one statement of a source program before converting and executing the next (in contrast with *compiler*)

**intranet**—A subset of the Internet, usually available only to the members of the organization that set it up

**I/O (input/output)**—The process of getting instructions and/or data into and out of a computer system; devices that perform both functions (e.g., disk drives)

**IP (Internet Protocol)**—A standard, agreed-upon way of coding and sending data across the Internet

**ISDN (Integrated Services Digital Network)**—A digital telecommunications system in which all types of data (e.g., video, graphics, text) may be sent over the same lines at very high speeds

**ISP (Internet Service Provider)**—A company or other organization (e.g., a university) that provides access to the Internet

**Java**—Originally called OAK, a high-level programming language developed by Sun Microsystems. An object-oriented language similar to C++, it has become popular for its ability to do interactive graphic and animation activities on Web pages

**joystick**—Input device, used primarily with games, that moves on-screen figures or a cursor

**JPEG (Joint Photographic Experts Group)**—A file format for storing and sending graphic images on a network

**justification** (See *full justification.*)

**K (kilobyte)**—A unit of computer memory or disk capacity that is roughly equivalent to 1,000 bytes

**keyboard**—Any of a variety of input devices that have keys imprinted with letters, numbers, and other symbols in order to allow a user to enter information

**keyboarding**—The act of using a computer keyboard to enter information into a computer system; sometimes used to mean efficient, ten-finger typing as opposed to hunt-and-peck typing

**LAN** (See *local area network.*)

**laptop computer**—Small, standalone, portable personal computer system

**laserdisc** (See *videodisc.*)

**laser printer**—An output device that produces hard copy by using a controlled laser beam to put characters on a page

**LCD (liquid crystal display or diode) panel**—A device consisting of light-sensitive material encased between two clear pieces of glass or plastic designed to be placed on an overhead projector; projects images from the computer screen to a large surface

**light pen**—Input device that allows a user to select items from a screen by sensing light on various points in the display

**listserv**—On the Internet, a program that stores and maintains mailing lists and allows a message to be sent to everyone on the list

**local area network (LAN)**—A series of computers connected through cabling or wireless methods to share programs through a central file server computer

**Logo**—A high-level programming language originally designed as an artificial intelligence (AI) language but later popularized by Seymour Papert as an environment to allow children to learn problem-solving behaviors and skills

*Logowriter*—A word processing program that incorporates logic and drawing capabilities of the Logo language

**low-level language**—Programming language such as assembler designed for use by technical personnel on a specific type of computer (see also *high-level language*)

**M (megabyte)**—A unit of computer memory or disk capacity that is roughly equivalent to 1 million bytes

**machine language**—A computer language consisting of commands written in 1's and 0's; designed for a specific type of computer

**mainframe**—Type of computer system that has several peripheral devices connected to a CPU housed in a separate device; has more memory and capacity than a microcomputer

**mark sense scanner**—Input device that reads data from specially coded sheets marked with pencil

**MBL (microcomputer-based laboratory)**—A type of instructional software tool consisting of hardware devices (probes) and software (probeware) to allow scientific data to be gathered and processed by a computer

**MECC** (See *Minnesota Education Computing Corporation.*)

**memory**—Circuitry inside a computer or media such as disks or CD-ROMs that allows programs or information to be stored for use by a computer

**menu**—List of on-screen options available on a specific topic or area of a program or GUI

**metropolitan area network (MAN)**—A network whose components are distributed over an area larger that a LAN but smaller than a WAN

**microcomputer**—Small, standalone computer system designed for use by one person at a time

**MIDI (musical instrument digital interface)**—A device and software that allows a computer to control music-producing devices (e.g., sequencers, synthesizers)

**minicomputer**—A type of computer system in a range between microcomputers and mainframes. (In practice, minicomputers and mainframes are becoming indistinguishable.)

**Minnesota Education Computing Corporation (MECC)**—Originally established as the Minnesota Education Computing Consortium, one of the first organizations to develop and distribute instructional software for microcomputers

**modem**—A device that changes (MOdulates) digital computer signals into analog frequencies that can be sent over a telephone line to another computer and changes back (DEModulates) incoming signals into ones the computer can use

**monitor**—An output device that produces a visual display of what the computer produces (see also *CRT*)

*Mosaic*—One of the first programs designed to allow Internet resources to be displayed graphically rather than just in text

**motherboard**—The main circuit board inside a microcomputer that holds all of the integrated circuits, chips, and connection slots for attaching additional circuit boards required to control peripheral devices (e.g., monitor, keyboard, disk drive)

**mouse**—Input device that a computer user moves around on the table beside the computer in order to control a pointer on a screen, and presses down (clicks) in order to select options from the screen

**MPEG (Motion Picture Experts Group)**—A file format for storing and sending video sequences on a network

**MS-DOS (Microsoft Disk Operating System)**—A type of systems software used on IBM and IBM-compatible computers

**multimedia**—A computer system or computer system product that incorporates text, sound, pictures/graphics, and/or video

**netiquette**—Etiquette guidelines for posting messages to online services, especially on the Internet

*Netscape Communicator*—A popular browser software used to access the Internet

**network** (See *local area network, metropolitan area network,* and *wide area network.*)

**neural network**—A type of AI program designed to work like a human brain and nervous system

**node**—One station or site on a computer network

**online**—Being connected to a computer system in operation

**operating system**—A type of software that controls system operation and allows the computer to recognize and process instructions from applications software such as word processing programs

**optical character recognition (OCR)** (See *mark sense scanner.*)

**optical disc**—Storage medium designed to be read by laser beam (e.g., CD-ROM, videodisc)

**optical mark reader** (See *mark sense scanner.*)

**optical scanner**—Input device that converts text and graphics into computer files

**output device**—Any device in a computer system (e.g., monitor, printer) that displays the products of the processing part of the system

**pagination**—Automatic page numbering done by a word processing or desktop publishing program

**password**—A word or number designed to limit access to a system to authorized users only

**PDA** (See *personal digital assistant.*)

**peripherals**—Any hardware devices outside the CPU

**personal computer (PC)** (See *microcomputer.*)

**personal digital assistant (PDA)**—A small, handheld computer that allows a user to write in freehand on a screen with a stylus and translates the writing into a computer file

**photo CD**—A compact disc format designed by the Eastman Kodak Company to store and display photographs

**piracy** (See *software piracy.*)

**pitch**—The number of characters printed per inch, usually 10-pitch or 12-pitch

**pixel**—The smallest unit of light that can be displayed on a computer screen

**PLATO (Programmed Logic for Automatic Teaching Operations)**—One of the earliest computer systems (mainframe-based) designed for instructional use; developed by the University of Illinois and Control Data Corporation

**plotter**—An output device designed to make a paper copy of a drawing or image from a computer screen

**plug-in**—A program that adds a specific feature or service to a computer system; many types of audio and video messages are played through plug-ins.

**point size**—A unit designating the height of a typeface character; 72 points = 1 inch

**presentation software**—Programs designed to allow people to display pictures and text to support their lectures or talks

**primary storage** (See *internal memory.*)

**primitive**—A simple command in the Logo programming language that does one operation (e.g., FORWARD)

**printer**—Output device that produces a paper copy of text and graphics from a computer screen

**print graphics**—Software designed to produce graphics on paper (e.g., cards, banners)

**probeware** (See *MBL.*)

**problem-solving software**—Instructional software function that either teaches specific steps for solving certain problems (e.g., math word problems) or helps the student learn general problem-solving behaviors for a class of problems

**program** (See *software.*)

**prompt**—On a computer screen, an indicator that the system is ready to accept input; can be any symbol from a C:\> to a ?

**proportional spacing**—Displaying text so that each character takes up a different amount of space depending on its width

**public domain software**—Uncopyrighted programs available for copying and use by the public at no cost

**push technologies**—A system set up to send out information whether or not anyone requests it. Some push systems are set up specifically to locate and return information with certain characteristics whenever it appears on the Internet.

*QuickTime*—Program designed by Apple Computer Company to allow short movies or video sequences to be displayed on a computer screen

**RAM (random access memory)**—Type of internal computer memory that is erased when the power is turned off

**record**—In a database file, several related fields (e.g., all the information on one person)

**relational database**—Database program that can link several different files through common keyword fields

**repurposing**—Use of a program to show videodisc images in a different sequence from the one stored on the disc and for a purpose that may be different from what the developer of the disc intended

**retrofit**—Rewiring a building such as a school to permit networked communications

**ROM (read only memory)**—Type of internal computer memory designed to hold programs permanently, even when the power is turned off

**sans serif**—Typefaces that have no small curves (serifs or "hands and feet") at the ends of the lines that make them up; usually used for short titles rather than the main text of a document

**search and replace** (also *find and replace*)—A function in a program such as a word processing package that looks for all instances of a sequence of characters and/or spaces and replaces them with another desired sequence

**search engine**—An Internet software (e.g., *Yahoo, Excite*) that helps people locate Internet sites and information related to a given topic

**secondary storage** (See *external storage.*)

**shared intelligence**—A way of looking at intellect as residing in several persons, rather than in single individuals

**shareware**—Uncopyrighted software that anyone may use, but each user is asked to pay a voluntary fee to the designer

**simulation**—Type of software that models a real or imaginary system in order to teach the principles on which the system is based

**snail mail**—Regular postal service mail, as opposed to e-mail

**software**—Programs written in a computer language (in contrast with *hardware*)

**software piracy**—Illegally copying and using a copyrighted software package without buying it

**software suite**—Software sold as one package but containing several different, unintegrated programs such as *Microsoft Office* (see also *integrated software package*)

**spamming**—Any unsolicited e-mail or other messages, usually sent in large numbers to all users of a system; the electronic equivalent of junk mail

**speech synthesizer**—An output device that produces spoken words through a computer program

**spell checker**—Part of a word processing or desktop publishing package that looks for misspelled words and offers correct spellings

**spreadsheet**—Software designed to store data (usually, but not always, numeric) by row–column positions known as *cells;* can also do calculations on the data

**sprite**—Object in some versions of the Logo programming language that the user can define by color, shape, and other characteristics and then use to do animations on the screen

**streaming video/audio**—A way of transmitting video or audio on the Internet so that it can be seen or heard as the file downloads

**structured query language (SQL)**—A type of high-level language used to locate desired information from a relational database

**supercomputer**—The largest of the mainframe computer systems with the greatest storage space, speed, and power

**switches**—Equipment to compress data in order for information to be transmitted at higher speeds (e.g., Asynchronous Transfer Mode (ATM) switches)

**synthesizer**—Any of a series of output devices designed to produce sound, music, or speech through a computer program

**SYSOP**—The SYStem OPerator in a network; a person responsible for maintaining the software and activities on the network and assisting its users

**systems software**—Programs designed to manage the basic operations of a computer system (e.g., recognizing input devices, storing applications program commands)

**telecommunications**—Communications over a distance made possible by a computer and modem or a distance learning system such as broadcast TV

**telecomputing**—Term coined by Kearsley to refer specifically to communications involving computers and modems

**teleconferencing**—People at two or more sites holding a meeting through computers and telephone lines

**test generator**—Software designed to help teachers prepare and/or administer tests

**thesaurus**—In word processing and desktop publishing, an optional feature that offers synonyms or antonyms for given words

**TICCIT (Time-shared, Interactive, Computer-Controlled Information Television)**—An early instructional computing system developed by Brigham Young University and the Mitre Corporation that combined television with computers

**touch screen**—Type of input device designed to allow users to make selections by touching the monitor

**Trojan horse**—Type of virus that gets into a computer as part of a legitimate program

**turtle**—In the Logo programming language, the triangle-shaped object that can be programmed to move and/or draw on the screen

**tutorial**—Type of instructional software that offers a complete sequence of instruction on a given topic

**URL (Uniform Resource Locator)**—A series of letters and/or symbols that act as an address for a site on the Internet

**Usenet group**—On the Internet, one of a series of news groups that offer bulletin boards of information on a specific topic

**variable**—In programming languages, a name that stands for a place in computer memory that can hold one value

*Veronica*—On the Internet, a program that searches for files across gopher servers

**videoconferencing**—An online "meeting" between two or more participants at different sites using: a computer or network with appropriate software; video cameras, microphone, and speakers; and telephone lines or other cabling to transmit audio and video signals

**videodisc** (also *laserdisc*)—Storage medium designed for storing pictures, short video sequences, and movies

**virtual office**—A space set up on a Web site to exchange documents and messages with colleagues working on the same activity

**virtual reality**—A computer-generated environment designed to provide a lifelike simulation of actual settings; usually uses a data glove and/or headgear that covers the eyes

**virus**—A program written with the purpose of doing harm or mischief to programs, data, and/or hardware components of a computer system

**visual literacy**—Skills involved in analyzing and processing information presented as images (e.g., photos, videos, multimedia)

**voice recognition**—The capability provided by a computer and program to respond predictably to speech commands

**VRML (Virtual Reality Modeling Language)**—A specification for displaying three-dimensional objects on the Internet

**warm boot** (See *boot.*)

**wearable systems**—Computer components worn on one's body or clothing; usually accessed through voice recognition or other alternative input device

**Web site**—A location on the World Wide Web identified with a Universal Resource Locator (URL); Web sites are physically located on a server connected to the Internet

**wide area network (WAN)**—An interconnected group of computers linked by modems and other technologies

**window**—A box in a graphic user interface that appears when one opens a disk or folder to display its contents

**word processing**—An applications software activity that uses the computer for typing and preparing documents

**word wraparound**—In word processing, the feature in which text automatically goes to the next line without the user pressing Return or Enter

**worksheet**—Another name besides *spreadsheet* for the product of a spreadsheet program

**World Wide Web (WWW)**—On the Internet, a system that connects sites through hypertext links

**worm**—A type of virus that eats its way through (destroys) data and programs on a computer system (see also *virus*)

# Name Index

# Subject Index

# Integrating Technology Across the Curriculum: A Database of Strategies and Lesson Plans

## A User's Guide

## Preface

### Items on the CD-ROM

- *Integrating Technology Across the Curriculum.* This database of technology integration lesson plans and strategies was prepared with the *FileMaker Pro®* database program. The database was stored as a "runtime version" so that the program itself is not needed to use it.
- *HyperStudio®* **Mini-Preview.** This abbreviated version of the *HyperStudio®* program was provided courtesy of Roger Wagner Publishing, Inc. The mini-preview allows anyone who wants to try their hand at multimedia development to develop a four-card *HyperStudio®* multimedia stack.

### Acknowledgments

Thomas Edison said that "Success is 10% inspiration and 90% perspiration." I must express my thanks to those who contributed some of the 90% on this product. At the top of the list are the fiercely competent professionals at Merrill. Debbie Stollenwerk continues to be my role model, mentor, and friend as well as my editor. Gianna Marsella is simply the best developmental editor there is—the Queen of Can-do. Pam Bennett treated all the production problems like unruly children, firmly taking them in hand and sorting them out, one by one. Thanks to Microsoft's Sue Speza and the Roger Wagner Company's Lisa Vogt for arranging their companies' contributions. Bill Castine, as usual, served as reviewer and encourager. Finally and, as always, most important, my debt is to my husband, Bill Wiencke, and my daughter, Paige. Not only couldn't I have done it without them, I never want to try.

M. D. Roblyer
State University of West Georgia
Carrollton, Georgia

## Part I: Introduction

### What Is the *Integrating Technology Across the Curriculum* Database?

*Integrating Technology Across the Curriculum* is a collection of 250 lesson plans stored in a computer program called a "database." Database programs let people put information into the computer in such a way that it is easy to get out only those items of information that meet a certain need. For example, a teacher may want lesson plans that use multimedia at elementary levels. Rather than reading each lesson to find those that meet this particular need, the teacher simply tells the database to list only those lessons that use multimedia with Grades K-5.

Classroom-tested technology integration examples have been published in many formats (e.g., articles, books, on the Web). Lessons were gleaned from several of these sources. They were summarized and placed on a database developed with *FileMaker Pro®* software.

### Why Was This Collection Developed?

This collection of lesson plans was developed to promote and support the integration of technology into teaching in content areas such as mathematics, science, and language arts. These "technology integration strategies," or descriptions of when, where, and how to use technology to help teach school topics, help schools take advantage of technology's power and potential in several ways. They help:

- **Focus teacher training on integration strategies**, rather than on how various technologies work;
- **Allow teachers to look at good, classroom-tested examples** of integration strategies in many content areas;
- **Give preservice/inservice teachers and teacher educators good models** for how to use technology resources (e.g., multimedia, spreadsheets); and
- **Help teachers find specific technology integration strategies** to meet their classroom needs.

### Who Can Use This Product?

*Integrating Technology Across the Curriculum* is useful for:

- **Classroom teachers** looking for ideas and lesson plans;
- **Teacher educators and trainers** showing examples of technology integration in various content areas; and
- **Inservice/preservice teachers** learning how to use databases.

### How Can It Be Used?

This database could supplement and enhance any teacher training course or workshop; or it could be useful to teachers in classrooms. Activities that could be done with it include the following.

- **Locating a plan to meet a certain need.** Teachers can use it to answer questions such as: "What plan could I use for teaching writing in an interdisciplinary way?" or "What are some good examples of using spreadsheets in mathematics?"
- **Illustrating technology integration strategies for various resources.** Have students ask, "How can word processing be used in areas other than language arts?"
- **Teaching database use and searches.** Show students how to locate all lessons for a given grade level, content area, and/or type (e.g., plans in science at the fifth grade level), or teach them how to add lessons of their own.

### What Do You Have to Know to Use It?

This product was designed for nontechnical teachers and students. You do not have to know much about databases to use it because this manual gives explanations and examples to help new users.

## Part II: Contents of the Database

### An Overview of the Lessons

The 250 lessons in this database are drawn from these sources:

- **The International Society for Technology in Education's (ISTE)** *Learning and Leading with Technology* **(formerly** *The Computing Teacher***).** Many articles from this popular publication are by teachers describing their own successful classroom strategies. Lesson activities selected in this database were based on the best lessons from ten years of these articles.
- *Productivity in the Classroom* **booklets** (also available as an online collection) were produced by Microsoft, Inc., in conjunction with Scholastic, Inc. Lessons in this database were based on some of these activities. Visit this site:

  **http://www.microsoft.com/education/k12/integrate.htm**
- *Problem Solving Across the Curriculum* by John Beaver (©1994 by ISTE).
- **Lesson plan issues of** *The Florida Technology in Education Quarterly.* Lessons on the database are based on those in the Spring 1991 ESE lesson plans issue, the Winter 1992 elementary lesson plans issue, and the Spring 1993 telecommunications issue (all selected by *FTEQ* Editor M. D. Roblyer).

Each lesson in the database is an edited, summarized version based on the original article or lesson plan.

### Organization of the Database

The first screen that appears shows the three main activities:

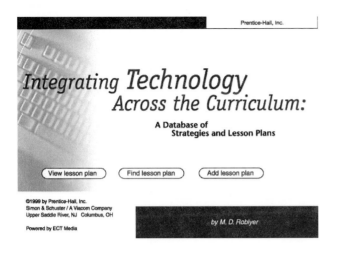

- **View lesson plan.** See a list of the 250 lesson titles. Each lesson has five main screens or "pages" (see example, beginning on this page):

  **Page 1** - Gives lesson objectives

  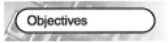

  **Page 2** - Lists the lesson descriptors

  **Page 3** - Describes lesson activities

  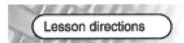

  **Page 4** - Shows images associated with the lesson

  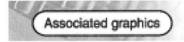

  **Page 5** - Gives reference information

  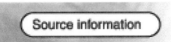

- **Find lesson plan.** Each lesson is stored with a set of "descriptors" or labels that describe the contents and let teachers locate lessons that meet their needs. For example, one descriptor is "Target Students" (the grade levels and type of students it addresses); another is "Technologies Used." (See a listing of descriptors on page 350.)

- **Add lesson plan.** This option lets teachers enter their own descriptors and lesson activities to describe a new lesson and add it to the collection.

  (Other options such as printing lessons and duplicating lessons may be selected from later screens. See pages 352–353 of this manual.)

## Anatomy of a Typical Lesson

Five screens make up the "skeleton" or structure of the database:

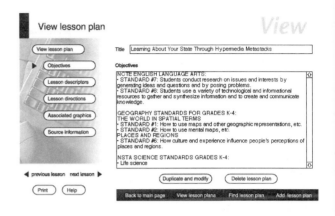

- **Page 1:** Lesson plan objectives and national content area standards the plan addresses

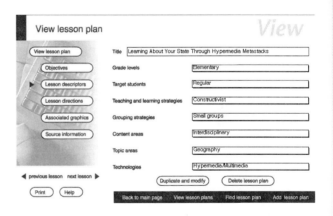

- **Page 2:** Descriptors that define the lesson plan characteristics (see a list of all descriptors in this manual, p. 350).

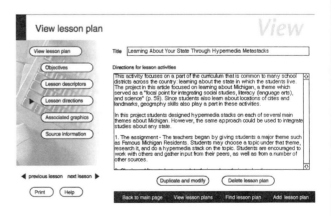

- **Page 3:** Detailed directions for the lesson. At the bottom of the lesson directions is a list of required resources a teacher needs to carry out the lesson activities.

## Lesson Plan Descriptors

• **Teaching and Learning Strategies:**
-Constructivist
-Directed
-Combination

• **Grouping strategy**
-Individual
-Large groups
-Pairs
-Small groups
-Whole class

• **Target students**
-Regular
-LD
-Gifted
-ESE
-Honors
-ESOL
-Physically challenged
-At-risk

• **Content areas**
-Interdisciplinary
-Art
-English
-Foreign languages
-Language arts
-Mathematics
-Music
-Physical education
-Science
-Social studies
-Technology
-Other

• **Topic Areas**
-Algebra
-Arithmetic
-Astronomy
-Biology
-Botany
-Business math
-Charting/graphing
-Chemistry
-Civics
-Computer applications
-Cultures
-Drawing/painting
-Economics
-Electricity
-French
-Geography
-Geology
-Geometry
-German
-Grammar
-Health and nutrition
-History
-Literature
-Math problem solving
-Math word problems
-Measurement
-Multicultural
-Musical composition
-Physical education
-Physics
-Problem solving (nonmath)
-Programming
-Reading
-Research methods
-Spanish
-Spelling
-Statistics
-Study skills
-Trigonometry
-Vocabulary
-Weather
-Writing

• **Grade levels**
-Grade-free
-Primary
-Pre-K-Elementary
-Kindergarten
-Secondary
-Grades by number (1 through 12)

• **Technologies**
-Alternative keyboards
-Animation software
-Artificial intelligence
-Atlases
-Barcode generators
-Calculators
-Charting/graphing
-Databases
-Desktop publishing
-Distance learning
-Drill & practice software
-Electronic encyclopedias
-Games
-Graphic tools
-Groupware
-Hypermedia/multimedia
-Instructional software
-Internet
-Logo
-MIDI interfaces
-Music synthesizers
-Presentation software
-Problem solving software
-Probeware/MBL
-Robotics
-Simulation software
-Spreadsheets
-Tutorial software
-Video development
-Videodisc - Level I
-Videodisc - Level III
-Word processing

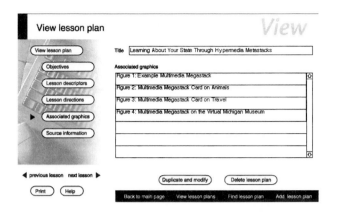

- **Page 4:** Many plans also have associated graphics, e.g., diagrams, photos, or screens of example products.

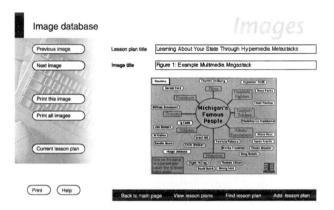

- **Page 4 continued:** Click on one of the graphics in the list, and a page with the image appears. Sometimes the size of the computer screen makes these images too small to see clearly on the screen. In these cases, it is necessary to print the image and look at the paper copy.

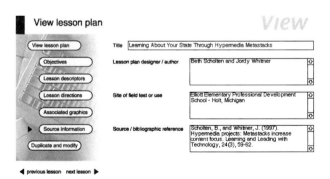

- **Page 5:** Author name(s), bibliographic source, and site of field-tests, if any.

## Part III: How to Use the Database

### How to Start the Program

The database may be opened and used directly from the CD, or it may be moved to the hard drive first and used from there.

- **To use from the CD in the Macintosh platform:**
- Insert the CD.
- Open the Macintosh folder and double-click the Lesson icon to load the database file.
- **To use from the CD in the *Windows 3.1* platform:**
- Insert the CD and select the CD drive.
- Open the Program Manager (DO NOT open the file under the File Manager); go to File Menu; select Run.
- Go to Browse and select Drives. Select the letter of the CD-ROM drive on your system.
- Go to the *Windows* folder and open it.
- Under the file names, find Lesson~1.exe and double-click on it to open it.
- Click OK to run it.
- **To use from the CD in Windows 95 or Windows 98 platforms:**
- Insert the CD.
- Double-click "My Computer."
- Select the CD drive.
- Open the Windows folder.
- Double-click the Lesson icon to load the database file.
- **To use on your hard drive:**

  If you want to modify lessons or add your own lessons, you **must** move the database to your own hard drive. (You cannot store anything on the CD-ROM.)
- Insert the CD.
- Follow your system procedures for moving the lesson and art files over to your hard drive. (Usually this means dragging the files from the CD to your hard drive window.)

### PLEASE NOTE:

**To protect the copyright on this product, we have limited the number of times you can copy it on to your hard drive.**

See Appendix B on pages 354–355 for information on how to protect the hard drive copy of your database from damage or unintentional changes.

### How to Find Lessons by Browsing through Titles

From the main screen, clicking "View" gives you a list of lesson titles through which you can scroll.

# View lesson plan

A Bottle Project for Learning About Graphs

A Bottle Project for Learning About Graphs Copy

A Capital Idea: Problem Solving with Jasper Woodbury

A Chess Club by E-mail

A Class Literary Paper

A Computer Activity for Exploring Number Patterns

A Cooperative Group World Living Project

A Database Journal for Mathematics

A Database Project with Rocks

A Dinosaur Project

A Fortune in Word Processing

A Hypertext Study of the Fall of Communism

A KidsMall Project

A Multimedia Biome Project

A Multimedia Driver's Study Guide for LD Students

A Native American Database

When you want to see more detail on a lesson, click *once* on the title to see its Objectives page. Click on one of the other tabs to see the Lesson descriptors, Lesson directions, Associated graphics, or Source information pages for that lesson.

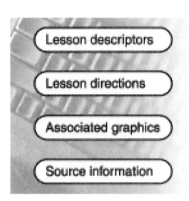

To review a lesson's descriptors, click on Lesson descriptors, then on one of the descriptor boxes; a pull-down menu will show you all the descriptors. The ones checked are those for the lesson.

| Target students | ✓ Regular |
| | Gifted |
| | Honors |
| Teaching and learning strategies | Boys |
| | Girls |
| | ESE |
| Grouping strategies | ESOL |
| | ✓ Learning disabled |
| Content areas | Physically challenged |
| | At-risk |
| Topic areas | Geography |

## How to Find Lessons by Using Descriptors

- **Click on *Find lesson plan*** from the View lesson plan screen or the main screen.
- **Click on *Find by criteria*.**
- **Select options you want** under each descriptor by clicking on a box, then clicking on the option.

  **NOTE: If you want more than one option under a descriptor (e.g., Spreadsheets AND Graphics under the Technologies descriptor), hold the Shift key down each time you select an option. Repeat this step until all desired options are checked.**

- **After you select all options, click *Start search*.** You will see a list of lessons that meet the criteria.
- **Click on a lesson title to see its contents.** When you are finished looking at a lesson, click the "Previous lesson" or "Next lesson" button to see another lesson in the group from your search.

**NOTE:** Clicking "View" at this point gives you a list of ALL 250 plans, not just the ones from your search.

## How to Find Lessons by Using Keywords

- **Click on *Find lesson plan*** from the main or the View lesson plan screen.
- **Click on *Find by keyword*.**
- **Type in words** you want to find under *each field*.
- **Click *Start search*.**

## How to Add Your Own Lessons

To add a new lesson plan, first load on to your hard drive all of the files from the CD-ROM. You cannot add lessons to the database on the CD-ROM.

- **Click on *Add lesson plan*** from the main screen.
- **Fill in information** in all descriptor boxes. Be sure to give the lesson a title so the lesson appears in the list.
- **Fill in information** for all of the related screens: Objectives, Lesson descriptors, Lesson directions, and Source information.

## How to Modify Existing Lessons

As you do for adding a new lesson plan, first load on to your hard drive all of the files from the CD-ROM.

- **Select** "Duplicate and modify" from the View screen to make a copy of an existing lesson.
- **Make changes to it** as desired. Remember to change the title; otherwise, the lesson will have the old title with the word "copy" after it. The program will save the new lesson to your hard drive automatically.

## Other Options

Additional options are at the bottom of the main pages:

- **Printing.** Print a lesson by selecting "Print." Print graphics by clicking "Associated graphics," selecting the image from the list of images, then clicking "Print this image." To print all images associated with a lesson, click the "Print all images" button.
- **Help.** Clicking Help provides you with an explanation and examples of various options and how to use them.
- **Navigation options.** You can return to the main page or choose other options to try.

## Saving to Disk

Use the following steps to save a lesson or the entire database to a disk other than the hard drive.

- **Save a single lesson plan** by selecting Import/Export, then select Export from the File menu. Then:
- **Select the location** (the disk and the folder or directory) where you want to save the lesson plan.
- **Name the file** when you see the Save As box. If you want to view the lesson plan without having *FileMaker*® on your hard drive, save in a text file or other format.
- **Save the entire database** by selecting Save a Copy as from the File Menu. (You will need a Zip or Jaz disk.)

# Part IV: Classroom Applications

This collection can be used in many ways by several kinds of people. No matter who uses it, it is best to begin by reviewing the following sequence of introductory activities.

- **Get familiar with the database structure.** You either can page through lessons one at a time, or you can search for lessons that have certain words in them or that address certain students, tools, or topics.
- **Examine the parts of an activity.** Look at the information provided with each lesson activity.
- **Peruse the lessons.** Page through several lessons to get a feel for the kinds of approaches represented.
- **Do some sample searches.** Try locating lessons that meet your needs.

## Example Applications for College Instructors

Teacher educators can use this collection of lesson plans and activities as model applications of the technology tools and teaching methods they introduce in their classrooms. Some example uses follow.

**Example Activity #1: Find a way to teach poetry.** With the whole class, do a search on lessons by using "poetry" in the "Lesson directions" field. Divide the class into small groups; have each group analyze one of the lessons in the database, discuss it, and develop a lesson based on that approach. Have each group present its lesson to the class, explaining why the technology resource they used contributed significantly to teaching poetry.

**Example Activity #2: How are videodiscs used?** With the whole class; do a criteria search on lessons using "videodisc" in the "Technologies" field. After each student reads the lessons and reviews uses of videodiscs, hold a class discussion on the ways videodiscs are being used and how they contribute to learning. Divide the class into small groups; have them develop their own lessons using videodiscs and present them to the class.

**Example Activity #3: Develop a good lesson.** Have the class form small groups and select a technology resource such as word processing or multimedia. Have them search for and review lessons that use this resource and develop a good lesson of their own to add to the database. It must specify all required descriptors and detailed directions. Have groups present their lessons to the class.

## Example Applications for Pre K-12 Teachers

Inservice teachers can use this collection as a source of ideas for how to use technology to teach various topics and content area standards. Some example uses follow.

**Example Activity #4: Collaborative projects.** An area that is seeing great emphasis in recent years is teaching students how to work cooperatively to develop products and solve problems. Teachers can locate examples of how to do this effectively by doing a search for "collaboration" or "collaborate" in the "Lesson directions" field, or for "Small Groups" in the "Grouping strategies" field.

**Example Activity #5: Addressing national standards.** Each lesson in the database lists national standards addressed for each of several content areas. Teachers can do a search on the "Objectives" field to find lessons that address desired standards, e.g., Civics, Economics, NCTE, NSTA, NCTM, History, Science.

**Example Activity #6: Interdisciplinary activities.** Teachers can locate good examples of teaching activities that address more than one content area in the same lesson. They can do a search by criteria, and select Interdisciplinary in the "Content areas" field.

### Example Applications for Teacher Education Students

As they learn how to integrate various technologies into the classroom, future teachers can see what classroom teachers consider good uses of these resources. Some example uses follow.

**Example Activity #7: Find a multicultural activity.** Many lessons model how to emphasize multiculturalism in the course of content area learning. Students can find these examples by doing a search by criteria using "Multicultural" or "Culture" in the "Topic areas" field, or by searching "Lesson directions" using the keyword "cultural."

**Example Activity #8: How is technology used in the (*insert your own*) content area?** Students can do a search for all lessons in a given content area, browse through all the lessons, and review which technology resources are used and how they are used. This activity will give them a good introduction to and overview of how technology is being integrated into their content areas.

**Example Activity #9: What are some whole-class strategies?** Many K-12 classrooms have only one computer. By searching on "Whole class" in the "Grouping strategies" field, teacher education students can see examples of how inservice teachers are making the best use of limited resources. The lessons will model how to structure goals and objectives and carry out activities that can be accomplished with one computer.

## Appendix A: *HyperStudio*® Mini-Preview Use and Copyright Information

An abbreviated version of the *HyperStudio*® multimedia development software, called the *HyperStudio Mini-Preview,* is included on the CD-ROM, courtesy of the Roger Wagner Company. Many of the lesson plans in this database refer to this software.

You can transfer this preview version to your hard drive and create a four-card multimedia product that *HyperStudio*® refers to as a "stack." This will give you a sampling of how this program works and what it can do.

## Appendix B: How to Protect the Hard Drive Copy

Once the database is on your hard drive, it is very easy to change it—even unintentionally. *For example, if you highlight one of the Descriptor fields, the one you highlight will take the place of the ones that came with the database.* However, if the copy on the hard drive becomes damaged, or you change it unintentionally and want to re-install it, you may do so only a limited number of times. That is why it is a good idea to protect the copy on your hard drive and make sure you don't make changes unintentionally by doing the following:

**Macintosh version:** Once the file is on your hard drive—and before you run the program—click once on the file name to highlight it. Then press Open-Apple-I. This box will appear.

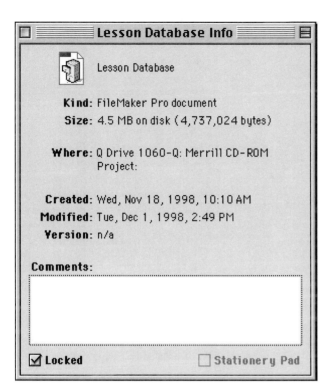

To lock the file, click on the option at the bottom left.

When you want to add or modify lesson plans, you can bring this box up again and unlock the file by clicking the same option.

**Windows versions:** Once the file is on your hard drive—and before you run the program—right-click once on the file name, and select the Properties option from the box. Under General options, select "Read only." As with Mac versions, you can unlock the file when you want to add lesson plans to the database or modify them.